Productivity Management
Text & Cases

Productivity Management Text & Cases

Gordon K. C. Chen
University of Massachusetts

Robert E. McGarrah
University of Massachusetts

The Dryden Press
*Chicago   New York   Philadelphia
San Francisco   Montreal   Toronto
London   Sydney   Tokyo   Mexico City
Rio de Janeiro   Madrid*

Acquisitions Editor:	Anne Elizabeth Smith
Managing Editor:	Jane Perkins
Copy Editor:	Lynn Perrigo
Design Director:	Alan Wendt
Production Manager:	Mary Jarvis
Design and production:	Chestnut House

Address orders to:
383 Madison Avenue
New York, New York 10017
Address editorial correspondence to:
901 North Elm Street
Hinsdale, Illinois 60521
Library of Congress Catalog Card Number:
ISBN: 0-03-048901-6
Printed in the United States of America
234-038-987654321

CBS COLLEGE PUBLISHING
The Dryden Press
Holt, Rinehart and Winston
Saunders College Publishing

Contents

Preface

During past decades the field of production/operations management attracted fewer educators or practitioners than fields of financial management, marketing management, or human resources management. As an area for commitment to teaching and research at universities or for career development through the management ranks of business or industrial organizations, production/operations management offered fewer opportunities. Responsibilities were too broad and diverse for rigorous definition. They tended to be subdivided into more specialized disciplines or bureaucratic functions. Dominating the management field were specialists in human and organizational behavior, industrial psychology or labor relations, management science, or operations research/computer information systems. Engineering specialists assumed more authority than production/operations managers in developing technologies for products and processes, which determine the structure for planning, controlling, and organizing corporate work processes and worker-machine systems. In industrial organizations, managers of production/operations were expected to respond to financial managers' concerns for growth in profitability, or marketing managers' concerns for growth in product consumption or market shares. Productivity growth was taken for granted or given much lower priority.

More recently, however, production/operations management and productivity have received more of the attention they have always deserved, because of problems of inflation, energy, shrinking shares of global markets, and stagnating growth in productivity in the United States. The attention given to productivity management in Japan and West Germany—where inflation, energy, and unemployment problems are less severe, despite far greater dependence on imports—has prompted U.S. educators and practitioners to increase their commitment to production/operations management and to productivity.

Productivity management is concerned with growth in output as measured in worker- and machine-hours devoted to procurement, production, and distribution of products, services, or information. Since every kind of institution—industrial, governmental, educational, health and welfare—is concerned with flows of information, products and services, or funds, it follows that productivity is an important measure of management's purpose and performance in every type of institution. Our aim for the book is to be useful in schools of industrial engineering and public administration, as well as business administration.

We are convinced that the production/operations manager should understand and use analytical tools for demand forecasting, work-systems design and measurement, inventory control, scheduling, and demand-resource allocation. These tools are very concisely explained in this book. But we also believe that the production/operations manager should be able to deal with concrete situations and decide *what* and *why* problems should be resolved. Such knowledge and skill may be even more important than knowing *how* to solve problems of forecasting, work-systems design, inventory control, etc., using specialized concepts and analytical techniques. Productivity management is multidisciplinary and interfunctional because it must be concerned with the integrity of commitment by managers, staff specialists, workers, union officials, and clients to productivity goals or means that may conflict with goals or means advocated by financial managers or marketing managers. We believe learning experiences afforded by the cases included in this book instill enlightened pragmatism and holistic concerns for the enterprise needed by the production/operations managers. Expressed another way, we think that elegance in the practice of production/operations or general management is quite different from elegance in the applications of science, engineering, or mathematics to areas such as forecasting, work-systems design, or inventory control.

In preparing this book we were greatly influenced by 70 professors of production/operations management and managerial economics who reported their consensus of needs:

The need is for an interdisciplinary approach covering several functional areas. . . . We can no longer confine the field to narrow interests of the firms. A greater concern for external environment is called for. The issues of social responsibilities, international implications, economic impact, minorities, environmental protection, etc., can no longer be ignored. . . .

We should extend our interest to service industries, non-profit organizations, international and multinational organizations. . . . There is need to pay much more attention to problems of implementation of the often "beautiful" solutions developed by the O.R. specialists. . .[1]

Ultimately, we believe, society judges the practice of management according to two different sets of values. One set is essentially moral, ethical, or political; the other set essentially economic, technological, or materialistic. The second set of values can be rationalized scientifically, in objective terms, but we doubt that the first can be. Moreover it may be dangerous to assume that these values are always positively correlated. History teaches us that civilization vitally depends on a dynamic equilibrium between sets of spiritual and materialistic values that society demands from all forms of institutions that it supports. Even though managers, as leaders of industry, government, or welfare institutions, are concerned ostensibly with enhancing economic or physical values, they are by no means exempted from upholding moral or ethical values. The effective manager uses knowledge borrowed from philosophers, sociologists, and historians as well as from mathematicians, scientists, and engineers.

Our book is comprised mostly of cases, because we wanted it to reflect the convictions just cited. Still, we agree with most authors that particular problems, concepts, and techniques are fundamentals of productivity management that are best explained in the text chapters. Questions posed at the end of each of the seven chapters are related to content, but it is our intention that their answers may involve the integration of ideas beyond the scope of that chapter. Our pedagogical aim is for students to synthesize the humanistic or political with the technical and economic values of productivity management. We believe a major reason for the stagnation of American productivity has been excessive compartmentalization and a lack of integration of requisite knowledge and skills of management practice.

Since the book is intended for students with divergent backgrounds enrolled in undergraduate and first year graduate courses in management of business or governmental operations, we believe its chapters and cases can be addressed effectively in a variety of sequences. Some cases should precede chapters, for example: Chicago Auto Parts Supply Company or APEX Appliance, Inc. before Chapter 4, "Inventory Management." Some chapters should precede cases, for example: Chapter 5, "Demand-Resource Allocation Decisions" should precede Chemfertils, Inc., Penn Electric Company, Mackie Paint Company, and Calnational Oil; Chapter 2, "Forecasting," should precede ABC Carbon Company, Mesa Sporting

---

1. Proceedings, POM/ME Workshop, Boston: Intercollegiate Case Clearing House, Harvard Business School, March 16–19, 1976.

Goods, and Duro, Inc. In other instances the sequential order of chapters and cases is not critical. In our instructors' manual we offer more detailed suggestions for using our book.

We wish to acknowledge our appreciation of colleagues whose names and works we have cited specifically in the text and cases. We also thank our students, who used earlier versions of our book and suggested improvements. We assume responsibility for errors readers may find and trust they will draw our attention to any need for corrections.

Amherst Massachusetts
June, 1981

Robert E. McGarrah
Gordon K. C. Chen

To Barbara and Ursula

Productivity
Management
Text

Introduction to Productivity Management

If modern managers are to conduct affairs of an enterprise successfully, be it private or public, profit or nonprofit, it is imperative that the managers be thoroughly familiar with production-distribution processes. Those processes fulfill what most people desire or need not only for themselves, but for others as well: jobs, income, housing, energy, education, health and safety, recreation, food, transportation, and clothing.

The story of how a product or service is produced and distributed is a most fascinating one, because it helps to explain how industry has made people, natural resources, and machines grow more interdependent, in terms of intensity as well as scope. For example, there are perhaps no more intensive relations than those among physicians, nurses, patients, machines, and energy sources for heart-lung resuscitation; and automotive and aircraft systems for passenger transport and energy production have expanded such interdependence to a truly global scale.

Productivity is usually defined as a ratio of output produced per unit of resource (worker-hours or machine-hours of services, quantity of materials, or energy units) consumed by the process. It is understood that products or services produced are valuable, that is, they are needed or desired by people. The organization should not produce what its customers do not need, and it should not try to market products or services it cannot produce. So productivity is a measure of performance in producing *and* distributing goods and services: value added, or sales minus purchases divided by workers employed. And when we use the term *production oper-*

ations, or just *operations,* we mean it to include practically all activities of an organization. The managers of marketing, engineering, accounting, maintenance, personnel, and finance have as much effect on the productivity of the organization as the manager of production or manufacturing. Of course, productivity has physical significance. In technical terms of efficiency it measures performance of the firm in terms of its abilities to apply concepts of science and technology—for example, units of product or service delivered divided by kilowatt hours of electrical energy consumed, or by worker-hours of effort exerted, or by units of material resources consumed. Productivity may also be defined to measure a firm's performance in terms of financial or economic significance—for example, the dollar value of a unit of product or service delivered divided by the dollar value of labor, materials, or capital utilized by the firm's work processes. With due allowances for temporary currency value fluctuations or changes in commodity or product prices there is a strong, positive correlation among time series data measuring productivity, profitability, and efficiency. All three measures indicate a rate of growth in capabilities of organizations to fulfill their missions, namely, to produce and distribute more and better products or services by managing the development and applications of technology and human resources. Growth in those capabilities also has social or political significance. For as an organization grows to provide more jobs, income, products, or services for more people its powers of influence are increased.

From 1945 to 1965 productivity in the U.S. grew at an annual rate of 3 percent. In 1945 the employment goal was jobs for 60 million Americans; by 1965 about 90 million Americans were employed. Annual sales of large firms like General Motors, Exxon, or Royal Dutch Shell exceeded the annual gross national product of nations such as Switzerland, Venezuela, or South Africa. Since 1965, annual productivity growth in the U.S. declined, until it was less than 1 percent in 1980; and there has been a commensurate decline in profits, employment, and sales. Thus, the importance of productivity management can hardly be overemphasized.

Productivity or production/operations management involves a great variety of human activity: planning, financing, acquiring, organizing, designing, allocating, and maintaining resources (or "inputs") and methods for converting the resources into products and services in quantities and at times and places where they will be needed. Productivity management also includes methods for measuring and accounting for the quality, availability, and costs of those activities.

Although production/operations managers are commonly employed in manufacturing firms, they are also indispensable officials of service organizations. Sometimes the managers' titles may not suggest explicit responsibilities for productivity management. For example, the operations manager in a retail store is often called the "store manager"; in a bank, "operating officer"; in a hospital, "hospital administrator"; and in a university, the "chancellor" or "provost." Yet all of these officers are concerned with how their organizations produce or distribute products or services.

There are also levels of operations management in an organization. The chief executive officer may also hold the title of president or chair of the board of directors. The manager at the next level is sometimes called the chief operating officer. Or, this level may include vice presidents of major regional, functional, or product divisions.

For an organization to achieve its goals and missions operations managers need the support and collaboration of other managers. It has been said that an organization stands and runs via three functions: production/operations, marketing, and finance. The production/operations function is to produce the right goods or services at the right place and time and at the right cost. The marketing function is to deliver the right goods and services at the right place, time, and cost. The financial functions are raising, allocating, conserving, and disbursing the right amounts of funds at the right place and right time and for the right purposes. The typical position of operations management in relation to other functions in the organization is depicted in Figure 1–1.

Historical Highlights

The history of formal study and practice in productivity management began in the late nineteenth century with the work of such pioneers as Frederick W. Taylor. His concern was to improve worker-machine relationships. The first hundred years of the industrial revolution had created machinery to displace manual methods of work. The practice of scientific management by Taylor, Henry Gantt, and Frank and Lillian Gilbreth focused on the human physiological aspects of work. They changed designs of machines and tools so that "no opportunity is lost to save useless motion. Americans try to arrange their machines so as to make them convenient for the workmen."[1] They developed standard tables of micromotions and time measurements using motion picture cameras and precision chronometers. The principles of motion economy developed by these early researchers are still useful in the engineering of work methods and time standards. They introduced piecework wage-incentive payments so that workers could control their earnings with their output, according to their choice of workpace or skills.

Later, scientific management of worker-machine relations gave rise to study and practice of industrial engineering and industrial psychology of workflow processes, mostly in manufacturing firms. The Hawthorne Experiments by Roethlisberger and Dickson at the Western Electric Company in Chicago were early studies of the effects of changes in working

1. *Journal of the Franklin Institute* (November 1973): p. 302.

Figure 1—1 Typical Organization Chart.

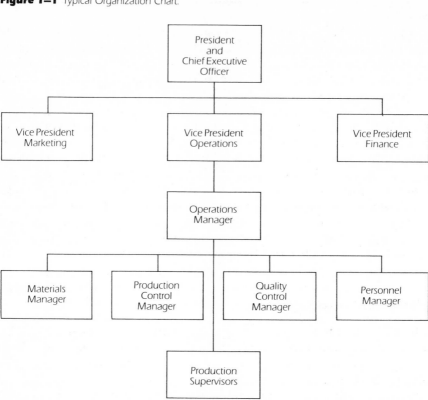

conditions on human and social behavior and productivity.[2] Along with research of work fatigue and monotony by others such as Elton Mayo, the Hawthorne Experiments were forerunners of education and practice in the industrial applications of fields known today as human and organizational behavior.

During the Great Depression of the 1930s the labor union movement transformed questions of wages, hours, and work conditions into political and legal issues. An effect of the National Labor Relations Act of 1935 and laws to regulate wages and hours was to politicize the practice of operations management. Although managers (acting on behalf of property owners) retained authority and responsibility for initiating changes in standards for industrial productivity or work methods and wage payments, unions and sometimes government officials exercised legal rights

2. Roethlisberger, F. J., and Dickson, W. J. "Management and the Workers." Cambridge: Harvard University Press, 1940, 585 pages.

to countermand those standards. Responsibilities of employee and union relations become more formalized under the authority of personnel managers or labor relations directors.

After World War II the federal government adopted full employment and industrial-economic development as explicit, national objectives. There was fear of depression caused by the decline in military equipment production. And more jobs were needed during the postwar years of booming population. Government policies were, of course, intended to reinforce business policies for increasing technical efficiency, market, and profits from industrial operations. However, full employment also meant stabilized, nonfluctuating growth of employment levels. The government raised Social Security taxes and unions negotiated supplementary unemployment benefits. These made operations more costly and less competitive for companies with frequent and large-scale hirings and layoffs of workers. Thus, in addition to the usual problems of controlling costs of operating workflow processes, the manager became responsible for minimizing costs of changes in levels of inventories and employment and in the rates of factory procurement, production, and shipments.

External, seasonal, or cyclical behavior of markets for procurement or sales caused some fluctuations beyond management's control. But management's own decisions caused operations to fluctuate, often unnecessarily, for example: shutting down operations while models of automobiles or home appliances were changed; sudden promotions of new products; changing employee vacation and factory shutdown schedules; or liquidating inventories in order to finance quarterly tax or dividend payments. By exerting efforts to reduce costs of business fluctuations, production/operations managers expanded their scope of responsibility (if not their designated authority) well beyond the confines of production operations within the factory.

Meanwhile, new methods of scientific management evolved from physicists' and mathematicians' studies of military and industrial operations. During World War II methods of statistical sampling and inference were developed for controlling the quality of manufacturing operations and for designing experiments to improve products and processes. Statistical methods for sampling and probability theories made quality predictions and control much more precise, more reliable, and far less costly. Later these theories were applied effectively in predictions of employee or customer behavior. The manufacturing progress function or corporate learning curve was applied effectively to manage worker productivity improvements and to schedule operations in airframe manufacturing. Mathematical programs were devised to maximize the utility of scarce resources for shipping war materiel. Operating-cost standards were improved as larger numbers of professional engineers were employed to develop work methods, time standards, and material usage standards. Engineered standard costs, in turn, became key elements for improving the accuracy and reliability of plans, programs, and budgets for managing industrial operations.

The post-World War II era changed two important aspects of operations management. One was that the work (planning and control activities) of operations managers themselves was subjected to scientific rationalization. Computers, telecommunications equipment, and mathematical techniques were developed to improve decision-making methods. Computerized linear programming enabled managers to balance mathematically very large aggregations of production resources with demands of customers in multinational markets. The results of linear programming are guaranteed least costly or most profitable plans for demand-resource allocations. They are a powerful alternative to results obtained by discussions and consensus of managers of national markets. Relatedly, computerized telecommunications systems were programmed with mathematical formulas for maintaining optimal inventories at many different stock locations of a company's production and distribution system. Mathematical models of waiting-line systems (for example, automobiles in lines before tollbooths at bridges, highways, or tunnels) enabled more rational and efficient decisions in scheduling staff and planning for the right amounts of facilities for operations. Thus a second effect has been a more centralized management of purchasing, manufacturing, transportation, and distribution operations. But executing the work of those remained decentralized. Also, as additional staff support for the operations manager, new professional disciplines of operations research, human and organizational behavior, and computer and management sciences were added to those of industrial engineering, personnel management, and labor relations. Operations management has become somewhat fragmented into a large variety of specialized skills required to plan and control the work of production-distribution systems.

Applications of computers, mathematics, and social sciences prompted the expansion of the production/operations manager's function in non-business organizations, which now is a key part of government organizations concerned with domestic and international affairs. The U.S. government's Marshall Plan prompted American industrial firms to expand their operations in the European Common Market. The cold war and the Soviet space vehicle, Sputnik, prompted very high levels of federal procurement contracting expenditures for research, development, and acquisitions of aerospace, electronic, and nuclear power systems. Management of operations of the government's systems-acquisition programs is a necessary counterpart to operations management of industry's production programs. Operations management of government on behalf of taxpayers' and the military's interests matches operations management on behalf of shareholders' and customers' interests in industrial goods—all as part of the same multibillion dollar programs. Each program involves the consortia of prime, associate, and subcontractors and different government agencies whose operations have to be coordinated in terms of ever-changing technical, financial, legal, and logistical requirements (schedules, inventories, shipments) of the prime contract between the federal government and industry. The programs enabled acquisitions of total, integrated systems: The government not only acquired the electronic ballistic missile early warning system (BMEWS), but also trained operating and maintenance personnel and created facilities and services for their housing, health, safety, energy, recreation, post exchange, and transportation at military bases in the U.S. and overseas.

The postwar decades were an era of military and civilian-industrial growth on an international scale. Multinational linkages between customers and producers were expanded and strengthened. Multinational interdependence upon technology, capital, nonrenewable energy, and other material resources—and most important, skills in managing those resources—became requirements for productivity, profitability, and efficiency of procurement, production, and distribution operations.

Current Perspectives

Unprecedented growth and scientific management of industrial operations have also created unprecedented challenges to the stability or integrity of relations among institutions and to moral and ethical convictions of the professional manager. Environmental pollution and waste of energy and raw materials are causing legal restrictions and quickly escalating operations costs. Populations of the poorest regions of industrialized and developing nations seem to grow faster than local industry can grow to generate more employment and income. Apparent risks of crime, terrorism, and sabotage have been rising in these nations even though per capita income and living standards are at their highest levels in history. There seem to be mounting threats to the security of essential links between the operations of industries and governments. Although those links are strong technical, economic, and political necessities for industrial growth, they are also vulnerable and fragile bonds for stability, unity, equanimity, and trust required for peaceful human and social relationships.

In light of apparent energy and other resource scarcities, abuses of technology, environmental pollution, and widening socioeconomic gaps between rich and poor people, questions are being raised about possible limits to exponential growth of industrial operations. These questions could pose serious dilemmas for operations managers, for as already noted, exponential industrial growth rates of productivity, profitability, and efficiency have been the ethic of not only managers' professional practices but of the organizations they strive to serve. Must requirements for resource conservation or pollution control conflict with needs for increased industrial efficiency, employment, and production of goods and services for more people?

Of course, sociological or ecological limits to growth pertain more to certain kinds of corporate operations.[3] For example, antipollution and energy conservation requirements are likely to have a more stringent impact on basic steel or energy-production operations than on financial or educational service operations.

Another challenge concerns the erosion of the quality of work life. Recent studies have cited evidence that growing numbers of executives, as well as office and factory workers and customers, are dissatisfied with the work of corporate operations.[4] Overzealous application of technology has too frequently dehumanized working conditions. Mechanization of factory operations and the computerization of office operations has wrought human suffering as workers were displaced. With each step toward further mechanization of work processes the tolerance for individual differences in work habits of employees is sharply reduced. Opportunities for self-expression through work have been sharply curtailed. Electronic recording and surveillance have dehumanized corporate relations. The customer, shareholder, employee, or supplier acting alone can hardly expect to be effective in an individual concern for the firm's operations. Short of organizing a political movement or publicity campaign, the only way to "count" is to express agreement with already-established rules. Statistical measures of human and social behavior are used to establish tolerance limits for behavior in relations with the operating system. Woe to individuals whose spirit or human circumstances impel them to behave outside those tolerances! Are increased technical efficiencies and profitable growth from more extensive applications of scientific management becoming a cause of corporate conformity—or even tyranny—to which even managers themselves may be subjected?

A challenge for the operations manager is to reduce bureaucratic and expand democratic methods of planning and controlling operations. Results of experiences with job enlargement and participatory management indicate that more democracy in managing operations (even operations that use scientific methods) is an effective antidote to the dehumanizing influences of more mechanization. The operations manager assumes major responsibilities for maintaining people's respect, loyalty, and trust in the role and mission of their institutions.

Problem areas

The job of the production/operations manager can be divided into four major activities: (1) determining the desired outputs, (2) determining and acquiring technologies needed to produce the outputs and the resources

---

3. Meadows, D. et al. *Limits to Growth*. New York: Universe Books, 1972.

4. Terkel, Studs. "Working." New York: Avon Books, 1975. "Work in America." Report of Special Task Force to the Secretary of Health, Education & Welfare. Washington, D.C.: U.S. Government Printing Office, 1973.

required by those technologies, (3) planning and controlling the quality, availability, and cost of work processes and their results, (4) delivering or distributing the finished products. These activities are not only themselves interrelated, but also relate directly to other functions within the organization.

Determining the desired outputs or products is a question of deciding what market the organization is to serve with specified products or services, at what quality level, in what quantities or rates, and at what price. These are questions for product planning and research by marketing staff. But they are questions to be answered also by engineers concerned with product design, development, and testing, and by other engineers concerned with process-systems design, development, and testing. Product- and process-design specifications along with market-demand specifications (quality, quantity, price) determine the necessary technologies of products, processes, and resources. They are a basis of a consensus needed for suppliers, employees, customers, shareholders, or taxpayers to make corporate operations work to achieve their purposes.

Three general types of resources are needed: human, materiel, and financial. *Human resources* are all personnel in the organization, from top to bottom, and include all technical, financial, or legal specialized talents. *Materiel resources* include such things as the purchased materials, parts, supplies, machinery, equipment, buildings, and land. Obviously, *financial resources* are the funds required to acquire the human and materiel resources.

Even though the standards of quality, availability, and cost of resources and products may have been decided, there are questions of designing and operating management information systems needed to measure and control the *actual* quality, productivity, and costs of corporate workflow processes.

Management information systems gather and process information for decisions. There may be a large number of alternative ways that available input resources can be used to produce an aggregate of different products demanded. Thus, procedures for material and staff requirements planning may involve the use of linear programming, which will be discussed in Chapter 5. The control of actual quality may require adoption of sampling and measurement procedures to ensure that "good" products are not being rejected (producer's risks) and "bad" products accepted (customer's risk) can be kept within acceptable limits. Similarly, actual expenses have to be collected, summarized, and compared with budgeted (standard) expenses. And actual quantities have to be measured and compared with scheduled quantities moving through various stages of the production-distribution system.

As materiel resources are allocated and mixed, they are combined with human and other physical resources to enter into the conversion process. Here the materials are shaped, formed, mixed, cut, and assembled to form the desired finished product. Of critical importance in the conversion process are the intricate planning, coordinating, and controlling of measurements of the quantity, quality, cost, and timing of input resources—as well as the finished outputs—during each stage of the process. These are the crux of all production/operations and occupy the bulk of operating managers' time and attention. Operating managers continuously assess methods for concerns such as process analysis and control, methods-time measurements, workflow analysis, plant layout, line balancing, production scheduling, materials handling, quality assurance, work standards, labor productivity, wage incentives, and production capacity.

The final stage of production/operations ordinarily involves the storage, delivery, and distribution of the finished product. Because of the vast geographic areas, the long distances of distribution, and the variety of modes and costs of transportation, the problems of logistics and traffic management have increasingly affected the productivity of corporate operations. Of concern to operations managers are issues such as the choice of production and warehousing facilities and locations, logistics analysis, traffic management and control, and transportation security and safety. These problems may be important to national security if the organization must manage worldwide transport of armaments, food, petroleum, uranium, or high-technology equipment and must disseminate associated operating and maintenance know-how. Some firms provide and manage their own delivery and distribution systems; others rely on special transportation service organizations such as the railroads, trucking companies, tanker carriers, courier services, and airlines to undertake the task.

If there are to be smooth and efficient operations within the organization, then the operations manager must continuously monitor and assess changes in environmental factors: market, competition, technology, consumer tastes, and supply conditions. Fiscal, monetary, labor, energy, health, and pollution-control policies of governments are likely to be changed frequently, with increasing effects on managers' operational, as well as strategic, planning decisions.

In summary, then, the problems that have to be dealt with most frequently by production/operations managers can be grouped under the following topics of chapters and cases contained in this book.

   I. Demand Analysis, Forecasting, and Feedback
      a. Product mix and markets
      b. Techniques for demand analysis and forecasting
  II. Process Analysis, Corporate Work Methods, Design, and Measurement
      a. Product-process analysis and design
      b. Methods analysis and improvements
      c. Establishing quality, productivity, cost standards
      d. Work measurement

e. Design of workflow and facilities

f. Work behavior and the quality of work life

III. Demand-Resource Allocation Decisions

a. Material and resource requirements planning

b. Methods and uses of linear programming and management

c. Resource allocation, utilization, and maintenance

IV. Inventory Management

a. Purposes of inventory

b. Criteria and mathematical models for inventory control

c. Materials handling and storage systems compatibility with information systems for inventory management

d. Managing inventories of cash, receivables, materials, fixed assets

e. Scheduling, measuring, controlling "pipeline" inventories

V. Operations Management and its Environment

a. Public policies and operations management

b. International and multinational operations

To conclude this introductory chapter let us point out that productivity management and general management have much in common. The chief concern of both is the whole institution, not just the specialized functions or professional skills required for planning and controlling operations. General managers' contributions to growth of productivity, profit, or efficiency are more effective if they understand the strength and weaknesses of specialized skills. But specialists' contributions are more effective when evaluated in terms of their impact on results of all (not just some) corporate workflow processes.

Study and discussion of cases and chapters in this book are an effective means of understanding problems and techniques of managing production-distribution systems, considered as a whole.

Questions for Discussion

Note to Student: Questions appended to this and other chapters are intended as aids to understanding corporate work processes and measurements in breadth (social or philosophical implications) and depth (technical or economic implications). Answers may be found not only in the text, but in knowledge drawn from other courses or experiences. Thus, the aim is to help develop your sense of integrity of knowledge and skills of production/operations management.

1. During the period 1945–65 productivity in the United States grew at its highest annual rate, 3.2 percent, and growth in membership and militancy of labor unions was higher than during 1965–80. Why do some authorities assert that strong labor unions are a major cause of stagnating U.S. productivity since 1965?

2. The physical and social sciences have had a greater impact on organizing and managing corporate operations in the United States than in any other nation. Yet, the productivity of U.S. organizations has not grown as rapidly as in Japanese or West German organizations during recent years. How do you explain this paradox?

3. Growth of operations of government agencies (e.g., for defense, mass transportation, education, water resource management, public health, and safety) has been necessary to support operations of business and industry. Growth in business and government has been necessary to support needs of the growing population. Do you agree or disagree? Explain why relations between business and government often seem more adversarial than cooperative.

4. Discuss possibilities that, in managing operations of institutions, surveys or tests by social scientists that assess attitudes or preferences may be used in lieu of processes of democratic discussion and debate. What are consequences of such a substitution? Might this help to explain the rise of apathy or alienation and decline in qualities of corporate work life?

5. How is the quality of corporate work life measured? How is it possible to measure loyalty, trust, or mutual commitment by all employees to goals and standards of corporate operations? Why should these matters affect productivity management?

6. Why do you agree or disagree that, in managing corporate operations, Americans tend to reward militant, no-compromise, special-interest groups, and to punish or repress individual "whistleblowers"?

7. What are the "limits to growth" of industrial production and productivity? Can those limits be avoided while growth continues at the exponential rates that are considered desirable or necessary by American managers? How?

8. Does growth in the size (i.e., number of employees) of an organization make the organization more difficult to manage, and therefore, less productive? Why or why not?

Forecasting

2

As suggested earlier, the productivity of an enterprise depends to a large extent upon its ability to deliver the right product or service at the right quality, quantity, time, and place, and at the right price. It must be able to meet the customers' demands. Few companies have exact information about their future demand. They have to rely heavily on forecasting or estimates. The purpose of this chapter is to discuss concepts and methods of demand and sales forecasting.

Importance of Forecasting

To anticipate or predict what the consumer wants, the operations manager needs to gather as much information as possible about the market and the pattern of its behavior. This is the process of forecasting.

Although forecasts provide a basis for production planning they also are important sources of information for financial, personnel, marketing, and other overall strategic decisions. Try to imagine how a financial officer could prepare cashflow or expense budgets without the information on sales forecasts! Likewise, personnel requirement planning, recruiting, and training all depend upon the volume of sales expected. At the corporate level, no strategic move, whether with respect to a new product or a new territory, can be made wisely without reliable estimate of potential sales.

Forecasts are necessary not only for private, profit-seeking businesses.

They are also essential in nonprofit public or private institutions or government agencies: The Red Cross needs to stock pints of blood in anticipation of needs of people injured over a holiday weekend, and expected demand for public transportation, parks, and recreation facilities is of constant concern to public officials. Even in the centralized, planned economy such as that of the Soviet Union, information about the future aggregate demand for a given product has to be obtained before the production quota can be assigned.

The decline in sales in the U.S. automobile industry in the early 1980s attests to the importance of forecasting changes in customer demands. In spite of the drastic decline in big-car sales following the 1973–74 Arab oil embargo, the big three automakers—especially the Chrysler Corporation—failed to take the signal seriously and continued to produce gas-guzzling, big cars. In 1979 the oil supply situation worsened, the price soared, and the big three were caught unprepared to meet the small-car demand. Thousands of big cars glutted dealers' lots. Scores of auto and auto-related plants had to be shut down, and hundreds of thousands of workers laid off. However, the imported small car sales surged to an all-time high.

Making predictions of future demands is as much an art as a science, even though mathematical, statistical, and computer techniques are powerful tools for data analysis. Statistical data measure effects or results of changes *after* changes have occurred. Forecasts are needed to predict changes *before* they occur.

Factors Affecting Demand Forecasts

Following are descriptions of some of the factors that may influence demand forecasts.

The Product

Various products and services have different patterns of demand. The demand for consumer products is certainly different from that for industrial products. Even among the consumer products, durable items are not the same as the nondurables or consumable products. In general, the more durable the product, the less stable the demand is likely to be, and vice versa. For example, the demand for breakfast cereal is far more predictable than that for washing machines.

Another product-related factor that influences the demand is the product life cycle. The evolution of demand for a successful product from its inception to its retirement can often be classified into five successive stages: product research and development, testing and introduction, increasing growth of demand, steady state demand, and phasing out. It is not easy, but it is necessary to predict those stages in order to manage profitability and productivity of operations for that product. At the initial two stages—during product development and introduction—the price tends to be high and the demand low. Once the product has established a market standing and sales volume, and the production rate and costs reach the level of the economies of scale, cost and/or competition will force the prices down; price reductions are followed by an accelerated increase in demand. As the market begins to saturate, the demand levels off. At this stage, the demand may continue at a relatively stable rate for a long time, fed by a stream of replacement orders and the flow of new customers. If the product does not receive constant improvement and marketing effort, it will eventually be replaced by a newer and better product.

As noted, it is very difficult to predict the stages and duration of a product's life cycle. For example, the growth rate of demand for microwave ovens far exceeded the manufacturers' expectations, while the market for home video recorders did not expand as fast as their manufacturers had anticipated. The demand for the traditional mechanical wristwatches was stabilized for many years, but was suddenly altered by the introduction of electronic digital watches.

The Economy and Market

Factors such as personal income, interest rate, money supply, credit policy, taxes, and general business activity all can affect demand in different industries and individual firms in different ways. Although varied from industry to industry, it is commonly true that the higher the personal income, money supply, or business activity the higher the demand for goods and services. The reverse is true for higher interest rates or taxes. Furthermore, demand is highly susceptible to the fluctuations of the business cycle; higher demand usually is accompanied by inflation, and lower demand occurs during recessions.

The nature, structure, conditions, and behavior of the market can significantly determine the demand pattern. From the point of view of the firm, the larger its market share the more accurate its predictions for demand, because it can exert more influence over its competitors in efforts to sustain or increase demand. Also, the demand pattern in the segmented market can be quite different from that of the unsegmented one. Demand for a product may be segmented by brand/price/quality distinctions or by geographical distinctions. The geographic differences between domestic and foreign markets, or northern and southern markets, require quite different approaches to their demand estimates because of cultural preferences of customers.

The Technology

Technological innovations can change demand patterns drastically and often in a short period of time. Innovations can disrupt a product life cycle and devastate a firm if it fails to adapt to such changes. The introduction of electronic watches cited earlier, for example, has almost ruined the

Swiss watch industry. The advent of pocket calculators literally wiped out the slide rule business. Technological advances are difficult to predict because they often are made in another, unrelated industry or field, and cloaked in military or proprietary secrecy until their sudden appearance on the market. Technological forecasting has special implications for long-range strategic planning and is being given increasing attention by top management.

Company's Policies and Strategies

So far the discussion has evolved around the external demand factors that are beyond the control of producers or suppliers of the product or service. There are some internal policies and strategic decisions that can also heavily influence demand. Marketing policies for pricing, advertising, channels and methods of distribution, target market, product positioning, or market segmentation all have significant impact on the demand pattern. By the same token, production and financial policies such as quality standards, production and delivery rate, design engineering, and credit policies can also have an effect on demand. Of course, since management has considerable discretion over these variables it can manipulate them to arrive at a combination to its best advantage.

How far into the future must managers predict demands? The answer depends on the duration of commitment implied by the planning decisions. To decide where and how large new factory or warehouse facilities should be, demand prediction should extend for perhaps the next 10 to 15 years. To decide what levels of aggregate production, employment, and inventories should be, or what cash inflows and outflows will be, the demand prediction should be for the next several weeks or months. Thus, the planning-horizon time period for decisions to invest in fixed assets is longer than for decisions affecting current assets or working capital.

Seasonality or climatic changes may define the planning-horizon time. The shipping season on the Great Lakes or the crop planting to harvesting cycle may define the planning-horizon time.

The procurement-production-distribution leadtime is also relevant. This is the elapsed time required by corporate work processes to respond to customers' needs. A shipbuilder or an aircraft manufacturer may take years; a consumer product firm may require only days or weeks.

Planning-horizon time periods are also defined for purposes of legal or financial needs. There are quarterly payments of taxes or dividends; reports of compliance with health, safety, or environmental regulations; reports to shareholders. The financial management information system may require that budgeted and actual cashflows be compared daily, weekly, or monthly. Accordingly, forecasted sales revenues, cash inflows, and disbursements may have to be revised daily, weekly, or monthly.

The most logical or practical planning-horizon time period for purposes of planning for production/operations management and for financial management may not be of the same duration. And although demand forecasts needed for both kinds of planning would not be the same, their equivalence would have to be clearly understood in order for management controls to be effective.

Types of Forecasts

The use of economic forecasts for strategic planning is quite widespread. Economic forecasts are available from government agencies or private firms. A wealth of information is published by the U.S. Department of Commerce, including the *Survey of Current Business* and the annual *Industrial Outlook*. Private firms such as Data Resources Incorporated offer forecasts of macroeconomic conditions to subscribers or members. Industrial and trade associations provide similar information services.

Of direct concern to production/operations and financial managers are medium- and short-range forecasts. The medium-range forecasts provide information for tactical decisions such as capacity planning, cashflow, and capital budgets. These forecasts can be divided into three stages. The first stage begins with demand forecasting, which means in this discussion the forecast of expected aggregate demand at the industry level, often measured in terms of a gross common denominator, such as dollar amount or total tonnage. Presumably, each firm in the industry estimates its proportionate share of the forecasted aggregate demand for the industry. The potential share may be a goal or an estimate—it need not necessarily represent the actual expected sales or the sales forecast upon which operating decisions are to be based.

Sales forecasting follows demand forecasting in the second stage. The two forecasts may or may not be the same. The demand forecast reflects the amount of a product or service that *could* be sold, while the sales forecast represents the amount that *is expected* to be sold. The discrepancy can be a result of a number of factors, for example: the limit of plant capacity; the required leadtime; the availability of materials, labor, or transportation facilities; and the learning curve, or status of the firm with respect to its corporate productivity (discussed in Chapter 6). As we discussed earlier, it is believed that the slump in car sales in 1979–80 was not so much a result of the drop in the aggregate demand for automobiles as a shift in demand from large to small cars, which caught the American automakers unprepared to meet that demand despite the abundance of big-car inventory.

Demand forecasting and sales forecasting differ in another sense. While the former is measured in an aggregated common denominator—usually dollars—sales forecasting is customarily broken down into specific physical units, such as departments, product lines or groups, model numbers, or geographic areas.

Figure 2–1 Types of Forecasts

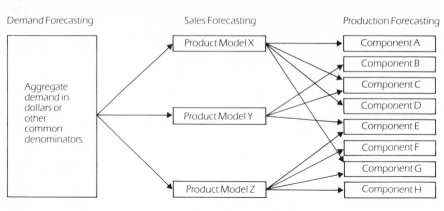

The translation from the forecasted sales to the actual planning of production takes place in the third stage, the process of production forecasting. In production forecasting, the sales orders are translated into resources and component requirements, commonly known as *material requirements planning* (to be discussed in Chapter 5), or manufacturing resource planning. The stages of demand, sales, and production forecasting are depicted in Figure 2–1.

The task of forecasting is not performed by one individual or department, but is a joint effort by managers of marketing, finance, and production at all levels. The characteristics of the various types of forecasting can be summarized in Table 2–1.

Forecasting Methods and Information Sources

Forecasting methods involve both subjective and objective sources and uses of information. Some may consist of data compilations representing judgments of top executives or of sales personnel. Top executives often forecast total sales of aggregate products or marketing regions. Sales personnel usually forecast sales of individual products or territories comprising the total aggregate. Of course, these judgments may require adjustments, especially if they are bases for future bonus incentives. Similarly, forecasts may be obtained by a "jury" of experts, known as the *Delphi method*. Experts may consist of members of the board of directors or consultant economists.

Forecasts also may be determined by extrapolating data that measure past demand rates. Thus "to forecast" is defined strictly, meaning to "throw ahead." The logical premise for such statistical forecasts via auto-

Table 2—1 Forecasts and Their Uses

Type of Forecast	Long-range	Medium-range	Short-range
Objective:	Strategic	Tactical	Operational
Time span:	2 years or more	3 months to 2 years	Hourly to quarterly
Scope:	Broad	Narrow	Specific
Level of management involved:	Top or high-level management	Middle- to high-level management	Supervisory, low- to middle-level management
Applications:	Product planning Market planning R & D programs Plant and equipment planning	Cashflow budgets Capital budgets Sales planning Capacity planning Personnel planning	Production and operations planning and control Inventory control Process control Job scheduling Employment scheduling
Information required:	Technological forecasts Environmental forecasts Economic forecasts	Demand and sales forecasting Market analysis Sales rate and trend Business indices and indicators	Production component requirement forecasts Resource requirement forecasts Production flow rate Downtime and reject rates

correlations is that the past and recent demand data serve as an accurate prologue to future demand.

Any forecaster should be concerned with the costs and benefits of forecasting. Elaborate forecasting procedures cost money. Benefits accrued from fractional increases in forecasting accuracy may be far less than the cost. This is especially true in cases where a large number of items must be estimated, such as when a product has thousands of parts and components that require fast, inexpensive estimates for operational planning and control purposes. The trade-off between the costs and benefits of forecasting methods must be balanced to arrive at a minimum. Table 2–2 summarizes most common forecasting information sources and data bases.

Tools and Techniques

A number of tools and techniques are available for data processing, reduction, and analysis. These may include statistics, econometrics, mathematics, simulations, and computers. These techniques will be grouped into six categories: estimation, interpolation, association, extrapolation, adaptation, and simulation. Techniques that are most helpful for operations managers will be given greater emphasis than those that are the domains of other disciplines and thus are beyond the scope of this book.

Table 2—2 Data Bases and Information Sources

	Information Sources	
Data Bases:	Internal	External
Subjective:		
Personal judgment	Company personnel	Dealers
Opinion polls	Field personnel	Customers, users
Survey research	Private surveys	Research institutions
Panel consensus	Company personnel	Users, consumers
Jury of experts (Delphi method)	Company experts	Outside experts
Objective:		
Historical data	Company record	Industry record
Test Market data	Company's own	Others
Product life-cycle data	Company product	Comparable product
Post audit data	Company product	Comparable product
Experimental data	Company's own	Research organizations
Leading indices	Company data	Economic indicators
Diffusion index		Economic indicators
Environmental signals		News and reports

Forecasting by Estimation

Almost all forecasts involve some estimation. Estimation can be judgmental or statistical, for a specific value, range, or distribution. Judgmental estimation can be informal, based on insight, intuition, or experience, and sometimes may even be "guesstimates." Statistical estimation usually carries a special meaning, which is the selection of a statistical estimator that approximates the value of a decision parameter or statistical population. Among the simplest and most reasonable estimators are the sample mean, $\bar{x}$, for estimating the population mean μ, and the sample proportion, p, for estimating the population proportion π. If, for example, a soft-drink company is interested in finding out the potential size of a market, it can obtain the information about the average amount of soft drinks bought or consumed per household in a given market, multiplied by the total number of households. The data can be obtained from the census or trade publications, or from sample surveys. Statistical estimators also can make use of less formal data bases, such as judgment samples or consensus.

Estimation for a specific value is known as the *point estimate*, as distinguished from the *interval estimate*, which approximates a range of values. Forecast by point estimate, for example, may be represented by a dollar amount or a number of units. Point estimates are unlikely to be the same as the actual outcome, since they are subject to errors. Interval estimates take into consideration such errors and incorporate them into the estimate. They simply add an upper or a lower limit or both as a tolerable variance. In such cases, forecasts would be a given value plus or minus a certain percentage or dollar variance. Estimation can also be made in terms of frequency distribution. For example, a seller may wish to forecast the potential sales for different age brackets.

Forecasting by Interpolation

When data are grouped or stratified, it is often necessary to interpolate them to arrive at a statistical estimate. For example, sales among various outlets of a fast-food chain vary a great deal, depending upon the location, population, seating capacity, etc. It is impractical to forecast sales or assign sales quotas to each outlet individually. The chain management often classifies the restaurants into several types. Class A restaurants, for example, are those with annual sales of $200,000 or less; Class B, between $200,001 and $400,000; Class C between $400,001 and $600,000; and Class D, $600,001 or more. To forecast sales or to set a sales goal for each class, the management can select the median, or midpoint, as the representative figure, which would be $100,000, $300,000, $500,000, and $700,000 or more, respectively. Besides using the median, the range of values can also be interpolated in term of quartiles, deciles, or percentiles.

Forecasting by Association

As stated earlier, demand and sales are sometimes heavily influenced by, or closely related to, certain factors. Statistical methods have been developed to measure the relationship. They include regression analysis (simple or multiple, linear or nonlinear) and the econometric method. Forecasting by association can be illustrated by a simple linear regression example. Assume that a home appliance manufacturer has discovered that its sales of washing machines relate closely with the number of residential housing starts. Table 2–3 shows the company annual sales in units as compared with the total housing starts for the past eight years.

In order to apply the relationship to forecasting, we need to know the nature of relationship, that is, *how* are the variables related, as well as the

Table 2–3 Sales versus Housing Starts

Year	Housing Starts (Millions of units)	Sales (Thousands of units)
1	1.5	30
2	1.3	29
3	1.7	32
4	1.4	30
5	1.8	34
6	2.0	38
7	1.9	35
8	1.6	34

Figure 2–2 Sales versus Housing Starts

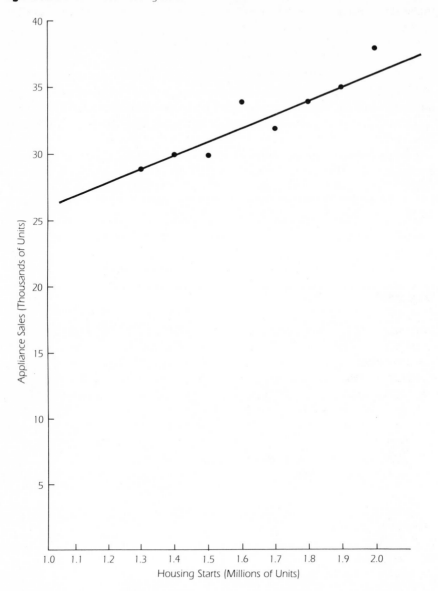

degree of relationship, or *to what extent* they are related. In regard to the nature of relationship, a cursory inspection of the above data indicates that they approximate a linear relationship, as portrayed in Figure 2–2, a scatter diagram.

The diagonal line between the dots represents a regression line of the equation $\hat{y} = a + bx$, where $\hat{y}$ is the dependent variable or the estimated unit sales, a is the intercept, b is the slope, and x is the independent variable, i.e., housing starts. The value of b and a can be obtained by solving Equation 2–1:

$$b = \frac{n\,\Sigma xy - \Sigma x \Sigma y}{n\,\Sigma x^2 - (\Sigma x)^2} ,$$ **2–1**

where
Σ = Sum of all values of the variables in this term following the symbol
n = The number of observations
$\bar{y}$ = The arithmetic mean of the dependent variable y
$\bar{x}$ = The arithmetic mean of the independent variable x.

To facilitate calculation, we prepared Table 2–4.

Table 2–4 Calculation of Regression Line

Year	Housing Starts (x)	Sales (y)	xy	x^2	y^2
1	1.5	30	45.0	2.25	900
2	1.3	29	37.7	1.69	841
3	1.7	32	54.4	2.89	1,024
4	1.4	30	42.0	1.96	900
5	1.8	34	61.2	3.24	1,156
6	2.0	38	76.0	4.00	1,444
7	1.9	35	66.5	3.61	1,225
8	1.6	34	54.4	2.56	1,156
	$\Sigma x = 13.2$	$\Sigma y = 262$	$\Sigma xy = 437.2$	$\Sigma x^2 = 22.20$	$\Sigma y^2 = 8,646$

With the above figures, we can solve the equation for b and a.

$$b = \frac{n\,\Sigma xy - \Sigma x \Sigma y}{n\,\Sigma x^2 - (\Sigma x)^2} = \frac{8(437.20) - 13.2(262)}{8(22.2) - (13.2)^2} = \frac{39.20}{3.36} = 11.67.$$

$$a = \bar{y} - b\bar{x} = \frac{262}{8} - 11.67\,\frac{13.2}{8} = 13.49.$$

Thus, the values for the regression equation are

$$\hat{y} = 13.49 + 11.67x.$$

If the housing starts for year 9 are 2.1 million units, the estimated sales would be 13.49 + 11.67(2.1) = 38 million units. But how closely are the two variables associated? To answer this we need to measure the degree of their relations by means of the correlation coefficient, r, of the sample data. Equation 2–2 is a simple formula for computing the value of r for a given sample:

$$r = \frac{n\Sigma xy - \Sigma x \Sigma y}{\sqrt{\{[n\Sigma x^2 - (\Sigma x)^2][n\Sigma y^2 - (\Sigma y)^2]\}}} . \qquad\qquad \textbf{2–2}$$

Thus the degree to which washer sales are correlated to the housing starts can be measured

$$r = \frac{8(437.2) - 13.2(262)}{\sqrt{\{[8(22.2) - (13.2)^2][8(8646) - (262)^2]\}}} = \frac{39.2}{42} = .93.$$

The correlation coefficient may vary from −1 through 0 to +1. The positive and negative signs represent the positive and negative correlations. The closer the coefficient to +1 or −1, the closer the dependent variables related to the independent variable. Therefore, a coefficient of +.93 suggests that the sales of washers are highly influenced by the housing starts.

Forecasting by associating more than one variable requires the use of advanced techniques such as multiple regression or econometric models, which are beyond the scope of this book.

Forecasting by Extrapolation

Whenever and wherever historical data are available, future demand or sales can be projected or extrapolated from that data. The most frequently used technique for projection is the time-series analysis, and recently, the Box-Jenkin method of time-series analysis. Other techniques include the Markov Chain method and the input-output analysis.

Forecasting with time series must first analyze the historical data and isolate their components in order to trace the movement and pattern of demand. The components that form the data in the series can be assumed to be interrelated as follows:

$$Y_t = T_t \times S_t \times C_t \times R_t, \qquad\qquad \textbf{2–3}$$

where
  Y_t = the data at time t
  T_t = the trend at time t
  S_t = the seasonal factor at time t
  C_t = the cyclical factor at time t
  R_t = the random elements or noise.

This equation implies that Y_t is the product of the four components. An alternative relationship is

Table 2—5 Sales Data

Year	Quarter	X_t	Y_t
1978	1	1	32
	2	2	29
	3	3	45
	4	4	58
1979	1	5	53
	2	6	46
	3	7	64
	4	8	70
Average		4.5	24.81
1980	1	9	70
	2	10	52
	3	11	59
	4	12	68
1981	1	13	65
	2	14	45
	3	15	53
	4	16	66
Average		12.5	29.88
Grand Average		8.5	27.35

$$Y_t = T_t + S_t + C_t + R_t. \qquad\qquad \textbf{2—4}$$

This implies that the magnitude of the four elements are additive, which means that each element affects Y_t, but not any other element. Since Y_t represents the composite of the four components, we need to identify the value of each component in order to project the future demand.

The usual procedure is to find the trend (T) line first. One way to proceed is to use the regression equation described in the preceding section. A simpler method is to divide the series of data into two halves and take the average of each to establish a trend line. For example, sales data for the last four years (sixteen quarters) are given in Table 2—5.

Assuming the trend time is linear, we can compute the values of b and a as follows:

$$b = \frac{\bar{Y}_2 - \bar{Y}_1}{\bar{x}_2 - \bar{x}_1} = \frac{29.88 - 24.81}{12.5 - 4.5} = \frac{5.07}{8} = .64,$$

$$a = \bar{Y} - b\bar{x} = 27.35 - .64\,(8.5) = 21.91,$$

$$\therefore \text{Trend} = 21.91 + .64\bar{x}.$$

Table 2—6 Moving Averages

Year	Quarter	Y_t	2-item moving total	2-item moving average	4-item moving total	4-item moving average
1978	1	32	61	30.5		
	2	29	74	37.0	164	41.0
	3	45	103	51.5	185	46.3
	4	58	111	55.5	202	50.5
1979	1	53	99	49.5	221	55.3
	2	46	110	55.0	233	58.3
	3	64	134	67.0	250	62.5
	4	70	140	70.0	256	64.0
1980	1	70	122	61.0	251	62.8
	2	52	111	55.5	240	60.0
	3	59	127	63.5	244	61.0
	4	68	133	66.5	237	59.3
1981	1	65	110	55.0	231	57.8
	2	45	98	49.0	229	57.3
	3	53	119	59.5		
	4	66				

It should be noted that the trend line is not always linear; if the data plotted on a scattergram show a nonlinear trend, another method should be used. Having identified the trend, we have yet to isolate the seasonal and cyclical elements, which are discussed in the next section.

Forecasting by Adaptation

The forecasting techniques discussed so far have been concerned with the projection of the direction and trend of demand. But a viable forecast must be sensitive and responsive to the movements and changes in demand. Furthermore, one of the most difficult problems in forecasting is to detect the turning point in the course of directional changes. Adaptive forecasting techniques are designed to track the movement and to respond to the turning points. Techniques that are capable of tracking demand include moving averages, exponential smoothing, and some econometric models.

Moving averages   One simple and easy-to-use technique is moving averages. These averages can be taken for any number of periods. However, the more periods being averaged, the smoother the series becomes and the less responsive the technique becomes in tracking the movements and changes. This effect is demonstrated in Table 2—6, using the same data as Table 2—5.

It can be observed from the preceding table that the 2-item moving averages are much more sensitive to the ups and downs of the actual data than the 4-item ones. How sensitive a forecast should be depends, of course, upon its purpose and intended use. If the forecast is prepared for the purpose of long-range planning, a more smoothed series provides a broad view of the movement without being obscured by the erratic, short-term movements. On the other hand, if a sensitive response is required for short-range operations planning, a shorter moving average would be more desirable.

Seasonal variations   One element in a time series that fluctuates periodically is seasonal variations. Various methods have been developed to measure such variations. One of the most widely used is the ratio-to-moving-average method. To isolate the seasonal factor with this method, we assume the moving average to be the product of trend, cyclical, and random elements. Hence, the ratio-to-moving-average can be stated as follows:

$$\frac{Y_t}{Moving\ Average} = \frac{T_t \times C_t \times S_t \times R_t}{T_t \times C_t \times R_t} = S. \qquad \textbf{2-5}$$

Using the 2-item moving averages from Table 2−6 we prepare a worksheet (see Table 2−7).

Table 2−7 Moving Averages Worksheet

Year	Quarter	Y_t	2-item moving average	Ratio to moving average
1978	1	32		
	2	29	30.5	95.1
	3	45	37.0	121.6
	4	58	51.5	112.6
1979	1	53	55.5	95.5
	2	46	49.5	92.9
	3	64	55.0	116.4
	4	70	67.0	104.5
1980	1	70	70.0	100.0
	2	52	61.0	85.2
	3	59	55.5	106.3
	4	68	63.5	107.1
1981	1	65	66.5	97.7
	2	45	55.0	81.8
	3	53	49.0	108.2
	4	66	59.5	110.9

Table 2–8 Seasonal Indexes

Year	1	2	3	4	Total
1978		95.1	121.6	112.6	
1979	95.5	92.9	116.4	104.5	
1980	100.0	85.2	106.3	107.1	
1981	97.7	81.8	108.2	110.9	
Medial Average	97.7	89.0	112.3	109	408
Seasonal Index*	95.8	87.2	110.1	106.9	400.0

*Seasonal Index = Medial Average $\times \dfrac{400}{408}$

By taking the medial average, i.e., the average without the highest and lowest values, we can compute the seasonal index (see Table 2–8).

Having isolated the seasonal and trend factors, only cyclical and random elements are left. The procedure commonly used to smooth out the season- and trend-adjusted series is to take a moving average again. The extreme values left after the smoothing are assumed to be the random element, and the rest reflects a cyclical pattern.

Exponential smoothing   Perhaps the most adaptive method of forecasting is the exponential-smoothing technique. This technique actually is another form of moving averages, but exponentially weighted to give the most recent data greater weight than those farther in the past. Furthermore, the moving average takes into account all of the previous data, not just certain items. Although this method averages all previous data, it does not have to carry a long string of data for computations. The computation procedure is relatively simple. The simplest model is single-exponential smoothing, which simply keeps a running average of the latest actual demand and the latest forecast, as represented in the following equation:

New forecast = Old forecast + α (actual demand – old forecast).

If we let F_t = New forecast made at time t for next period
$\quad\quad\quad F_{t-1}$ = Old forecast of the previous period
$\quad\quad\quad A_t$ = Actual demand during this period
$\quad\quad\quad \alpha$ = Weight or correction rate; $1 \geq \alpha \geq 0$
then, F_t = $F_{t-1} + \alpha(A_t - F_{t-1})$.   **2–6**

Note that the term $(A_t - F_{t-1})$ actually represents the forecast error. What the equation tries to do is to arrive at a new forecast by adding to the previously made forecast a correction of the error made in the old forecast.

This is, in effect, a simplified negative feedback system that can be designed to respond to errors and correct itself. By rearranging the terms, Equation 2−6 can be restated:

$$F_t = \alpha A_t + (1 - \alpha) F_{t-1}. \qquad\qquad \mathbf{2-7}$$

Based on past experience, assume at the beginning that the forecasted demand for the current month is 100 units. The actual current demand turns out to 130 units, and we realize that our forecast was off by 30 units. So in order to correct the past mistakes and adjust our forecast for the next month, we must decide to what extent we wish to make the adjustment. This decision will determine the value of α, or the correction rate. If we wish to correct the error by only 10 percent, then our new forecast will be:

$$\begin{aligned} F_t &= \alpha A_t + (1 - \alpha) F_{t-1} \\ &= .1(130) + .9(100) \\ &= 103. \end{aligned} \qquad\qquad \mathbf{2-8}$$

If, on the other hand, we wish to correct the error by 90 percent, the new forecast will be:

$$F_t = .9(130) + .1(100) - 127.$$

By comparing the two forecasts, we can easily observe that the larger the correction rate, α, the larger or faster the response. Table 2−9 shows a

Table 2−9 Comparison of Forecasts

t	A_t	$F_t(\alpha = .1)$	Absolute error	$F_t(\alpha = .9)$	Absolute error
Base		100		100	
1	130	103	30	127	30
2	95	102	8	98	32
3	80	100	22	92	18
4	115	102	15	112	22
5	105	102	3	106	7
6	75	99	27	78	31
7	110	100	11	107	32
8	90	99	10	92	27
9	120	101	21	117	28
10	85	99	16	88	32
11	105	100	16	103	17
12	90	99	91	91	13
Total	1,200	1,306	189	1,310	290

comparison of the two forecasts in the demand for a twelve-month period. To assess the relative accuracy of the two forecasts, we can compute a convenient measure known as the *mean absolute deviation* (MAD):

$$\text{MAD for } F(\alpha = .1) = \frac{189}{12} = 15.75.$$

$$\text{MAD for } F(\alpha = .9) = \frac{290}{12} = 24.17.$$

As can be seen from the above comparison, a large response rate may not be the best policy. In fact in this case it resulted in a larger error than for the smaller rate. Of course, how much the response rate should be depends upon the pattern of demand and other factors, such as the cost of over- or underestimating. By the use of simple computer programs, we can experiment with the values of α and arrive at the one that has the least error.

If the demand pattern has a consistent trend of rising or falling, the exponential smoothing will respond to that trend accordingly. However, the response will always lag farther and farther behind the trend. To alleviate this defect, the trend effect can also be corrected by exponential smoothing as in Equation 2–9:

New trend $\quad$ = Old trend + β(apparent trend)
Apparent trend = $F_t - F_{t-1}$

$$\therefore T_t = \beta(F_t - F_{t-1}) + (1 - \beta) T_{t-1}, \qquad \textbf{2-9}$$

Where
$\quad \beta$ = Correction rate for trend; $1 \geqslant \beta \geqslant 0$.

Hence, the expected demand with trend is

$$E(D) = F_t + \frac{(1 - \beta)}{\beta} T_t. \qquad \textbf{2-10}$$

Here again, the larger the β the more responsive the adjustment to the current apparent trend will be and vice versa. The quotient $(1 - \beta)/\beta$, serves to dampen the adjustment if the β is set too high, and to accentuate it if the β is set too low. T_t is added to the forecast at a parity when β is set at .5.

Similar adjustments can be made for seasonal effects. The formula for seasonal adjustment is:

New seasonal effect = $\gamma \dfrac{\text{Actual sales}}{\text{New forecasts}} + (1 - \gamma)$ old seasonal effect

or $\qquad\qquad S_t = \gamma \dfrac{(A_t)}{F_t} + (1 - \gamma) S_{t-n}, \qquad \textbf{2-11}$

where

| γ | = correction rate |
| n | = number of periods in a seasonal pattern that can be an index shown in the preceding section. |

Thus the trend- and season-adjusted forecast is:

$$F_t = (F_t + \frac{1 - \beta}{\beta} T_t) S_{t-n}. \qquad \qquad \textbf{2–12}$$

The forecast by the adaptive method can be monitored by a "tracking signal" to prevent it from straying far off the actual course. The tracking signal is a simple comparison of the running sum of the errors with the mean absolute deviation. Hence,

$$\text{Tracking signal} \quad = \quad \frac{\text{Running sum of forecast errors}}{\text{Mean absolute deviation}} \quad = \quad \frac{\Sigma(A_t - F_t)}{\text{MAD}}. \qquad \textbf{2–13}$$

Forecasting by Simulation

One relatively new forecasting technique is the use of simulation models or the so-called "what if" approach. With this approach, the forecast is based on a mathematical or computer model that simulates the behavior of the demand pattern. The model incorporates the internal (endogenous) and external (exogenous) variables that may affect the demand. The parameters of these variables can be manipulated to test their effects on the demand. And managers can select certain policy or decision variables that promise to generate the greatest potential sales. Industrial Dynamic model, for example, has been used for forecasting the demand and growth patterns for the airlines industry, urban housing, and even the world's natural resources. This rather involved and specialized technique will not be discussed in detail here.

Summary

Although many quantitative methods are available for forecasting demand, they should be used judiciously according to the objectives, cost, and benefit of the forecast. Besides, although no forecast is error free, a highly sophisticated technique may improve its accuracy. This is not always true, however. Judgment, experience, and insight of managers and staff directly involved can play an important role and should always be included in the forecasting process. After all, they are the ones who have to live with the consequence of the outcomes predicted by the forecasts.

Questions for Discussion

1. Can you think of any decisions in an organization that are not contingent upon or affected by the forecasts of demand or sales?
2. Name any factors other than the ones mentioned in the text that have an effect on the pattern or behavior of demand. In what way can they affect the demand?
3. Comment on the statement "Forecasting is as much an art as a science."
4. If you were the manager of a retail hardware store, would you need to perform any forecasting? Why or why not? If yes, what type of forecasting would you need?
5. Who is responsible for demand forecasting? Sales forecasting? Production forecasting?
6. Look up in the library some additional public and private agencies that publish their forecasts.
7. Discuss the relative merits and weaknesses of various subjective and objective data bases used for forecasting. Think of other possible sources of information that are useful for forecasting.
8. Of all the methods presented in the text, which do you think is best suited for production forecasting? Why?
9. Referring to Table 2–4, suppose Years 9 and 10 had housing starts of 2.3 and 2.5, respectively. What would the forecasted washing machine sales be for these two years if the trend as shown in Table 2–6 holds true?
10. Compute the forecast and the MAD, using $\alpha = .3$ for the data in Table 2–9.

Relevant Cases

1. ABC Carbon Co.
11. Crown Dairy Products Co.
12. Duro Inc. (A)
13. Duro Inc. (B)
15. Home Products Co.
17. Land Use Management
21. Mesa Sporting Goods
22. Metropolitan Power Co.
30. United Food Products Co. (A)
31. United Food Products Co. (B)

Workflow Design, Analysis, and Measurement

3

The importance of planning and controlling the corporate workflow of information, material and products, funds, and services is difficult to overemphasize. They are essential concerns, not only of production managers, but of all levels and types of managers. Corporate work processes are a dominant way of life for a great majority of industrialized societies because they provide most of the employment and income—as well as products and services—people want or need.

The purpose of this chapter is to explain the fundamentals of design and performance measurement of corporate work systems. Our discussions will emphasize technical-economic and social-political considerations. The manager should choose the most efficient, productive, or profitable methods for combining materials, information, energy, capital, and staff into products and services. Those processes also determine to a large extent how affairs of the organization are governed. If work processes are to function according to their design, then everyone concerned (managers, employees, suppliers, customers, unions) must agree to work performance standards and strive to convert the designs into realities.

Work Standards

Products and processes of work are measured quantitatively in three dimensions: quality, availability (i.e., time, quantity, place), and cost (or price). These define the *economic* value or utility of the product. These dimensions exist simultaneously in each unit of a product or resource. They are interdependent. Changes in one dimension tend to create conflict with the other two. For a given technology of the product or its process an increase in quality means an increase in cost and a decrease in availability; if an increase in output rate (availability) reduces the cost, it probably lowers the quality. Consequently, work methods must be designed so that products have the right combination of quality, availability, and cost (or price). The ultimate tests of this combination are customers' procurement and use of products. Product planners (market researchers and design engineers) and production planners (methods, tool, or process engineers; systems analysts; value engineers; cost analysts) work continuously to improve the value of products and work methods for their production and distribution.

Planning and controlling each attribute of value are usually separately organized functions of operations management. *Quality* is of primary concern to design engineering, quality-inspection, and control groups in manufacturing and equipment service organizations; to writers, editors, proofreaders, computer programmers, or auditors in publishing or financial service organizations; and to faculty in educational institutions. *Availability* is of primary concern to industrial engineers, logisticians, or expeditors responsible for the size or location of facilities and for the amounts of materials and products flowing through "pipelines" that link producers and users. *Cost* (or price) is of primary concern to the treasurer or comptroller, cost analysts, or accountants and auditors, because they plan and control operations in financial terms of money and time. The operations manager must coordinate and be guided by these three different groups.

Every member of an organization, from top executive to the unskilled laborer, produces units of some commodity, service, or information. The work of each individual somehow has to be planned and controlled in terms of quality, quantity per unit of time, and cost. The organization will achieve its goals of profitability, productivity, or efficiency as long as managers maintain a strong consensus and commitment of suppliers, employers, shareholders, and customers to the right combination of quality, availability, and cost of its products and resources. Let us consider how each affects work methods and measurements.

Quality Standards and Measurements

Quality standards evolve from a dialogue between those who use or maintain products and those who design and produce the products. Users specify functions they want a product to perform, the reliability of its performance, or its appearance. These specifications are translated into product designs. Then, production or process engineers specify the work methods (i.e., how staff's skills, tools and equipment, and materials are to be used). Technology and human preferences change rapidly. Accordingly, quality standards are updated by continuing discussion and ever-changing compromises of quality, availability, and cost. Alternative designs are examined in terms of how costly, quickly, and reliably peoples' needs can be fulfilled.

Representatives of the Army, Navy, and Air Force play roles in weapons development. Consumer-product firms engage in market research to solicit customers' preferences for new product designs. Consumer-research organizations and government agencies test and evaluate performance, safety, and health characteristics of products. Professional organizations of scientists, engineers, lawyers, physicians, and educators adopt quality standards and discipline their members who violate the standards. As resource scarcities, health and safety hazards, and energy and pollution problems have become more apparent, concerns about product and process quality standards have intensified and spread. They are no longer just technical-economic issues left for professional experts to resolve. They are social-political issues, sometimes of national or international significance. For the operations manager in every kind of organization (business, government, health, education, or philanthropic) there are no more important ethical responsibilities than those of its maintaining and improving the quality of products, services, and work methods.

Product Designs versus Process Quality Capabilities

Product-design specifications define a tolerance range within which actual results of work must be measured. The nominal dimension indicates a target toward which the worker should aim, or what the measured result *should* be. The maximum and minimum tolerance dimensions indicate the range of measures within which actual results *must* be. Tolerances are necessary because variations in the quality of materials, staff, or equipment are either too costly or technologically impossible to eliminate from work processes. Of course, the quality standards of products or services must be matched or exceeded by quality capabilities of production processes. The product designer argues for narrower tolerances, often in order to assure higher *product* performance reliability even under abuse by customers. But the process designer argues for wider tolerances in order to assure a higher *process* performance reliability. The operations manager plays a key role in resolving such controversies.

The quality capability or reliability of work methods can be estimated from a frequency distribution of measurements from results. Figure 3–1 illustrates a distribution of 420 measurements observed about nominal dimensions of metal parts produced on a machine. All of the 420 measurements were within ± 0.0005 inches; 399 or 95 percent were within

Figure 3–1. Frequency distribution of 420 quality measurements produced by a work process.

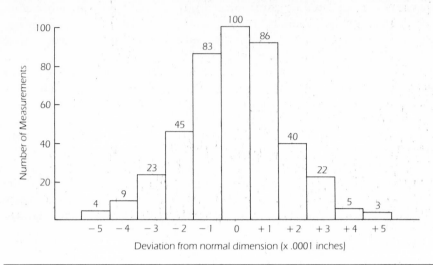

Deviation from normal dimension (x .0001 inches)

± 0.00024 inches, and 354/420 or 85 percent fell within ± 0.0002 inches. If this pattern of variation remains stable, then the reliability and quality capability of the work process are shown.

The level of quality assurance is determined by considering possibilities and consequences (costs) of accepting bad quality products as if they were good, and of rejecting good quality products as if they were bad. Inspection methods are designed to provide the level of quality assurance desired.

Suppose that a given product design tolerance was ± 0.0002 inches, and that work quality capabilities were as shown in Figure 3–1. Suppose further that management wanted to assure acceptable quality with a probability of 0.98. Figure 3–1 indicates that 66 of 420—or about 15 percent of the results—were outside and 85 percent were within the tolerance range of ± 0.0002 inches. The process-quality capability of 0.85 does not match the desired product-quality assurance level of 0.98. Inspection of all units would not give the quality assurance desired. But, if the product design tolerance had been ± 0.0005 inches, then the process quality would be satisfactory, and random-sample measurements would assure the quality level of 0.98 desired.

As long as variations in a quality measurement remain stable, the process for producing that measurement may be said to be in statistical control. For all dimensions produced, the average and the variance (i.e, sum of the squares of deviations from the average) remain constant. Such stability is the basis for using random-sampling inspection and quality control charts to assure quality. Inspecting small random samples of work is far less costly and more reliable than inspecting 100 percent of the work results.

If every quality characteristic of every unit produced had to be inspected, the time and cost of assuring quality might be prohibitive. Two kinds of quality characteristics should be examined: those most critically affecting the performance, safety and reliability, or appearance of the product; and those produced by work processes with such uncertain quality capabilities that the range of variations produced is greater than the range of product design tolerance.

Quality Control Procedures

Quality control of work involves four management decisions: (1) choosing the stage of the work process at which a quality characteristic should be inspected; (2) selecting the method of measurement and comparison required in the inspection or test; (3) prescribing the means of recording and communicating results; and (4) delegating authority and responsibility for actions to be taken when work quality is found out of control.

Choice of Process Stage for Inspection Operations

In general, a quality characteristic can be inspected at any stage after it is produced. Inspection should take place before the workpiece leaves its workstation. The sooner defects are discovered, the less costly their consequences. Many highly mechanized processing machines are equipped with inspection devices for this reason.

Should production employees be responsible for certifying that their work meets both quality and quantity per unit of time standards? Some managers argue that a separate inspector is needed to avoid bias. Others argue that workers should measure and certify that their work has met time standards and quality standards. Both arguments have merit. The issue may be resolved by comparison of expected costs or perhaps by union-management negotiations. Since a significant proportion of the time and budget of inspection may be expended merely in handling each unit inspected, whenever several quality characteristics must be assured, they should be inspected at a single workstation.

Quality characteristics must sometimes be produced in order to improve quality capability of work at a later stage. For example: Metal cleaning is required to ensure proper quality of plating and painting metal surfaces; verbal and numerical information has to be translated into binary computer machine language before processing; and patients may have to have special preparation for surgery.

Determining the Method and Number of Measurements for Inspection

When fewer measurements must be taken there is less chance of error in measurements. If the process is in control, a small random sample is all that may be required to determine that the desired quality level has been attained.

When it is sufficient to verify that actual quality is either acceptable or not acceptable, a method called *attributes inspection* is used. Inspection devices such as "go/no go" types of gauges are used to separate "good" units from "bad" units. However, like pass-fail grades in courses, inspections by "attributes" do not provide precise calibrations of *how* good or bad the actual quality may be. Inspection by variables requires more precise measurements of quality. The method may take longer, but fewer units have to be inspected to provide the same level of quality assurance. Also, measurements obtained by variables inspection give a more precise estimation of the process-quality capability.

Documenting and Communicating Quality Measurement Data   There are many special interests vested in the quality of work results, such as managers, customers, unions, government agencies, and insurance companies. Therefore, documenting and communicating quality measurements may be required by law. Whenever unacceptable quality is discovered, such documents enable specialists—product engineers and machine, tool, and gauge maintenance personnel—to trace and eradicate the cause(s). Wage-payment and cost-accounting procedures of some organizations may require that quality (i.e., accuracy of calculations) be verified before vouchers and cash disbursements are authorized.

On the other hand, the principle of management by exception may be used. Because of the high costs of paperwork, it may be preferable to record only information relating to incidents of failure to meet quality standards.

Authority and Responsibility for Actions Taken in Controlling Quality Quick action is essential in quality control. Whenever actual quality deviates too far from the standard quality, safety of personnel and equipment may be jeopardized, production and shipments may be delayed, and waste of resources may become excessive.

The common quality problems should be anticipated from results of product test and evaluation procedures. Specific personnel should be authorized and instructed to take appropriate remedial actions promptly.

Having considered essentials of planning and controlling *quality*, let us turn to matters of *productivity* of work and its results.

Work Methods and Time Standards

Four conditions are fundamental to establishing individual or corporate work methods and time standards: (1) people's need, desire, and purchasing power for products or services must create demand at a price that will cover costs; (2) proven technology (tools, information, staff skills, equipment, materials) to produce products or services must exist; (3) capital to develop or acquire that technology must be available; (4) equitable shares in responsibilities and rewards (to owners, managers, workers, suppliers, customers) from the work must be devised.

Work-methods design is a problem of assigning the right kinds and sequence of task elements for accomplishment by machine or staff so that the rate of production is responsive to the rate of demand. Since task sequence refers to the time order (or schedule) of tasks, it follows that production schedules affect choices of work methods. Thus, productivity standards are established in terms of the design of the work method or process and the production schedule. Production schedules are discussed in Chapter 6. Following is a checklist for establishing or improving the efficiency of work methods and time standards:

1. Select the job or process to be improved.
2. Analyze the job in terms of its task elements.
3. Simplify the method.
4. Synthesize and evaluate the proposed method.
5. Establish and promulgate the method and time standard.

Selecting the Job to be Improved

A job is a work system; to improve one small part of the system can be detrimental to the performance of the whole. The job need not be confined to the activities of a single operator, nor should the choice of job be limited to one machine if one person can keep two or more machines productively occupied.

The job should be chosen after considering relative needs to improve productivity of all jobs. This need can be established by isolating the "bottleneck" activities—those inhibiting the flow of work through the shop or office. Jobs that create bottlenecks include:

1. the one most frequently associated with delays in meeting production schedules, causes of which include machine or tool breakdowns, scrap and rework, clerical errors, material shortages, and inadequate capacity.
2. the one in which the highest ratio of idle worker-hours and/or machine-hours to total operating hours occurs most frequently.
3. the one showing the largest unfavorable operating expense variance from standard or budgeted costs.
4. the one associated most frequently with complaints about health and safety hazards or materials or energy wastes.
5. the ones most profitably improved by adopting new, proven technology, automation, computers, or materials.

Opportunities for improving job methods and time standards stem from almost unlimited sources. Matching those opportunities with jobs of greatest need is crucial to the success or failure of operations managers and their organizations.

Breaking the Job Down into Its Task Elements

The purpose of job analysis is to gain more precise, scientific insights on improvements and means for control of the job's results. Task elements of the work cycle controlled by a machine should be distinguished from those controlled by the worker. Strictly repetitive elements should be separated from unrepetitive elements (e.g., occasional adjustments or replenishment of supplies). Also, task elements should be no smaller in detail than the precision capability of the timing device—whether stopwatch, chronograph synchronous speed film camera and projector, or other equipment. Methods analyses can be too refined and costly if they divert management's attention from the integrity of all jobs in the organization.

Job-method analyses are greatly facilitated by using predetermined motion-time data, for example, methods-time measurement (MTM) data derived from empirical work studies. Table 3–1 is an abbreviated summary of MTM data. Note that time measurement units (TMUs) are in one-hundred-thousandths of an hour. They were obtained from many filmed observations of human task elements performed in the course of actual work. The observed workpace and skill of employees were normalized, i.e., rated by a consensus of experts that the data represent work by trained operators of average capabilities.

There are several advantages from describing work methods in terms of predetermined motion-time (PMT) data. Table 3–1 can be used as a standard glossary of terms to describe *all* manual jobs. Thus when management, employees, and unions are willing to discuss issues of a "fair day's work" in terms of the PMT data, communication and understanding usually increase and unnecessary grievances are avoided. Since each motion element has its associated time, there is no need for stopwatch-time observations of each change of the job. Use of PMT data requires that attention is focused on elements of the method, not their time. Further discussion of PMT data is offered in Case 27, Necchi SpA.

Simplifying the Method

Work simplification has been defined as the "organized application of common sense." Again, a checklist of questions might be devised to explore the job itself and then each job element. Can the element be eliminated? Can it be combined with some other element? Can all or part of the sequence of elements be changed? Methods engineers and physiologists have developed principles of motion economy or human engineering design of equipment and tools. For example: In assembly work, both hands should begin and end their activity in a cycle at the same time and

Table 3—1 Example of Predetermined Micromotion-Time Data

Simplified Methods-Time Measurement Application Data

Hand and arm motions			Body, leg, and eye motions	
Reach or move		TMU		TMU
1"		2	Simple foot motion	10
2"		4	Foot motion with pressure	20
3" to 12" 4 TMU + length of motion over 12" 3			Leg motion up to 10"	10
TMU + length of motion (For Type 2 reaches and moves use length of motion only)			Leg motion over 10"	20
			Side step case 1	20
Position			Side step case 2	40
Fit	Symmetrical	Other		
Loose	10	15	Turn body case 1	20
Close	20	25	Turn body case 2	45
Exact	50	55	Eye time	10
Turn—apply pressure			Bend, stoop, or kneel on one knee	35
Turn		6	Arise	35
Apply Pressure		20		
			Kneel on both knees	80
Grasp			Arise	90
Simple		2		
Regrasp or Transfer		6	Sit	40
Complex		10	Stand	50
Disengage			Walk per pace	17
Loose		5		
Close		10		
Exact		30	TMU = .00001 hour	
(All times on this Simplified Data Table include 15% allowance)			= .0006 minute	
			= .036 second	

Methods Engineering Council

should work simultaneously with duplicate parts in opposite and symmetrical directions; tools or gauges should be designed to minimize changes in eye fixations or directions and movement of fingers, forearm, full arm, or body.

Uninhibited, "creative thinking" or applied imagination is also helpful in job design. In challenging each task element, analysts need not confine themselves to the existing status of jobs. Employee participation via suggestion systems can be very beneficial.

Synthesizing and Evaluating the Proposed Method

After the method has been analyzed and simplified, it should be put back together again and tested. Job syntheses may require a verbal-numerical description of the method, a drawing or layout, or construction of a laboratory model or a pilot plant. Final evaluations are expressed in terms of productivity, i.e., time, cost, and quality of the method and its results. These are observed or derived from results of controlled experiments. Evaluation criteria also include factors of health and safety; the lineal distances moved; foot pounds of manual work; the number of direction changes made in the operator's movements; the number of pickups and laydowns of materials, documents, or tools; and the extent to which workpace is controlled by human or machine power.

Cost evaluations entail such matters as capital investment in additional building space or equipment; startup costs, such as motivating and training personnel to adapt to the standard methods; disruptions of other jobs in the area; and maintenance and operating costs, such as materials and supplies consumed, repairs, property taxes, insurance, power, and operators' wages.

Time Measurement

The literature on work measurement is extensive. All work-measurement techniques are based on a process of sampling a number of observations of the time it takes to do a job. These observations may be drawn by sampling job-time tickets collected by a timekeeper, by timing job-method elements with a stopwatch, by taking motion pictures of the job with a synchronous speed camera and counting the film frames, or by making recordings at randomly determined time intervals so that probability distributions can be estimated for the time devoted to various productive or to nonproductive activities (known as work sampling). A set of PMT data compiled from stopwatch or film studies of previous jobs is also useful. Each of these techniques has its advantages and disadvantages. Their time and cost of use and the precision and accuracy of their results are not equal. A general comparison of these techniques is difficult. Even within a single company it might be advisable to use different techniques to match different needs.

The stopwatch is a very common device. Time observations of six to ten work cycles are recorded and also rated as to whether the employee's workpace or skill is above or below average. The arithmetical means of the observed times are computed and summed to determine the rated or leveled time of strictly repetitive elements of the work cycle. Then, percentage allowances for nonrepetitive tasks (such as cleaning, inspections, adjustments, and replenishing materials) and for personal needs (such as rest periods and lavatory needs) are determined, sometimes by negotiation with unions, and applied as additions to rated time to compute the standard time.

Several questions remain about the validity of these measurement techniques.

One pertains to how effects of human input factors, such as skill, effort, workpace, and learning proficiency, may be measured in such a way that the standard job time truly represents that required by a normal, adequately trained operator who has average skills and who exerts normal efforts—otherwise called rating or leveling. Time-study engineers and industrial psychologists are trained professionally to assess observations of workpace and to assign rating factors accordingly. Predetermined motion-time data such as those in Table 3–1 represent a consensus of such experts. There may still be a question of whether such consensus accurately reflects climatological or cultural differences among workers of different regions or nations.

Another question pertains to methods of imputing measurements for personal time allowances for rest periods, smoking, going to the lavatory, and job-time allowances for cleaning and adjusting tools or machines and rearranging materials. Job and personal allowances are often determined by negotiations with unions.

Finally, there is the question whether all cyclical task-element times are additive. Additivity is assumed by all time-study techniques, especially those involving predetermined motion-time data. It means that the time to perform one elemental task is *not* dependent on the preceding or succeeding tasks, and therefore, the job time equals the sum of the times for its task elements, regardless of their sequential order. The validity of this assumption is questionable. But it is necessary and fundamental to scientific methods of work design and measurement. Perhaps the assumption is made tenable by adding time for job and personal allowances to establish the standard time.

Work Sampling

Time measurements of work also may be established by work sampling, that is, by observing at random instants whether the operator is idle. Workers' productivity is deduced from their output and from the percentage of the observations during which they were at work during the total observation period. Detailed motion elements of the work method are of little concern. However, it must be presumed that the workers are familiar with the work method and that variations in their rate of performance are stable, so that the mean and variance of the distribution of actual time per unit of work produced remain constant. (This is analogous to the presumption of stability of the distribution of *quality* characteristics produced by the work process, as mentioned in our discussion of quality control.) Work sampling is generally used when a large number of workers are employed for the same job.

Very simply, work sampling presumes a normal distribution of two different states of employees (or machines) working productively or idle, and that the probability of finding those states remains constant. A number of random observations must be taken to validate this presumption. The standard deviation of a binomial random distribution of percentages is:

$$s_\% = \sqrt{\frac{P(1-P)}{N}},$$

where

   $s_\%$ = standard deviation in the percentage of observations samples
   P = percentage of total number observations of worker or machine in a nonproductive or idle state
   $(1-P)$ = percentage of total number observations of working or productive state
   N = number of observations taken randomly.

A desired confidence level of 0.95 means that there is a 0.95 probability that the actual percentage of working or idleness is within $\pm\, 2s_\%$, and that $s_\% = .05/2 = .025$.

A percentage idleness, P, is presumed or estimated in advance. The number of random observations, N, is calculated from the formula for the standard deviation. The observations are then actually taken at random intervals of a chronological period of study of machines or workers. The actual values of P and $(1-P)$ are then calculated from the sample.

Consider an example. The manager of facilities maintenance decided to use work sampling to confirm with a probability of 0.95 that his maintenance crews were actually idle no more than 15 percent of the time, which was the allowance he had assumed in scheduling and estimating costs of maintenance jobs. Verification involved making a number of observations at random instants during the crews' operating shifts and calculating the actual percentages of observations of idleness. To achieve the confidence level of 0.95, the standard deviation in the percentage $(s_\%)$ of his observations had to be $\frac{.05}{4}$ or .0125. The number of observations, N, could then be determined as follows:

$$.0125 = \sqrt{\frac{0.15\,(1-0.15)}{N}}$$

$$N = \frac{0.15\,(0.85)}{(.0125)^2} = 813$$

Uses of Methods and Time Standards

Ordinarily, the planning, execution, and supervision of work are not accomplished by the same person. So work methods and time standards should be understood and approved by persons who supervise, perform, and are affected by results of work. Accordingly, work methods and time standards should be matters of carefully maintained records.

There are many purposes for documenting work standards. Such documents enable the employment office to recruit and select personnel with skills most suitable to the job specifications; they also provide a specific training objective for supervisors, training specialists, and employees learning the job. They serve as a basis for an evaluation of one job relative to all other jobs and for devising equitable schemes for wage and salary payments—in other words, as a basis for job evaluation and merit rating.

Time standards are used in estimating staffing or equipment requirements of production schedules. Thus, they are quantitative bases for hiring, transferring, and/or laying off personnel with different job skills; for determining budget or payroll and cash requirements; for estimating or quoting standard labor costs; for pricing in-process and finished-goods inventories; for determining the starting and finishing times for production jobs—in other words, job or product scheduling; and for designing systems for wage payment (group or individual piece-work incentive, or straight hourly wage).

Documents of methods and time standards are also a basic source of reference for union-management negotiations to establish fair work conditions.

Dynamics of Work Standards

Work standards are always subjected to changes. As employees gain experience, they learn to work more productively. Workers doing what accountants classify as "direct labor" and "indirect labor" (maintenance, janitorial services, technical staff planners), and supervisors learn to work more efficiently together as a team. Such corporate learning and synergism effect very significant changes in work methods and productivity, especially during the startup period of new jobs or corporate programs. But, less detectable "creeping method changes" almost always continue with older jobs. It is axiomatic that because work methods, resources, and their environment are inevitably changing, work standards and performance measures must be changed, if they are to remain valid.

Yet, the subtle changes in existing methods and resources tend to be ignored. Each change is so small its effects are not easily detected. There may be a mistaken presumption of permanence about engineered work standards. However, if the operations manager periodically compares measures of actual with standard productivity, he/she can detect a trend of wider deviation, indicating need for revision of method and time standards. The validity of work standards needs to be maintained because they serve as bases for cost estimates, incentive wage payments, job evaluations, material and staff planning, and production scheduling. Corporate morale and qualities of work life (as well as productivity and profitability) depend on the validity and reliability of work standards.

The corporate learning or experience curve (discussed in Chapter 6) is an effective tool for managing the change in productivity.

Work Cost Standards

Work cost standards are translations of work quality and method standards into monetary dimensions. Standard costs may be the average, median, or modal value of historical expenses for accomplishing work. Preferably, standard costs indicate what work expenses should be in the future, based on engineered specifications of work methods.

As job methods and quality standards are the concerns of technical specialists, job cost standards are concerns of specialists in economics, accounting, or finance.

To establish standard costs, it is useful to understand pertinent economic dichotomies of business costs: fixed versus variable, controllable versus uncontrollable, incremental versus sunk, and opportunity versus out-of-pocket.

Fixed versus variable costs. Costs are either fixed or variable as the quantity of units produced is changed. Fixed costs are the expenses that remain the same regardless of the number of units produced using facilities of a given capacity; variable costs change with the number of units produced.

Controllable versus uncontrollable costs. Since controllability refers to limits of what *people* (organizations) may or must do, controllable costs are measures of the authority, responsibility, and accountability assigned to managers for incurring expenses of operating their organizational units for a specified time period. An uncontrollable cost consists of expense(s) whose incurrence is outside the scope of authority or responsibility of managers. Thus, each expense is identified uniquely in terms of the functions or levels of management defined by the organization chart of the business.

Incremental versus sunk costs. These costs relate to the kind and extent of changes affecting costs. *Incremental costs* are incurred as a direct consequence of a decision to change work conditions. In other words, incremental costs are expenses that would be *avoided* if *no* change were made. Sunk costs are expenses incurred because of *previous* capital investment decisions. A *sunk cost* is that portion of capital investment that cannot be recovered via depreciation expenses in the event of replacement or sale of the asset representing that investment.

Opportunity versus out-of-pocket costs. Whenever an operations management decision is to be made about work conditions, there are always at least two choices. One is to maintain status quo and the other is to execute a proposed change. To make one choice would result in certain cash expenditures; another choice would result in certain other cash expenditures (or out-of-pocket costs). The difference is the opportunity cost of the choice causing the higher expenditures, or the losses from choosing one course of action with higher costs compared with another. For example, a company can always put its surplus cash in the bank instead of plowing it back into expansion of operations or facilities. The difference between the interest paid by the bank and the profit gained from investing the cash in its own business is an opportunity cost.

Uses of Cost Standards

Standard costs of work methods or products may be used in setting selling prices, evaluating inventories, or budgeting future expenses. Using standard costs obviates the necessity for computing actual (historical) costs for each job or product as it passes through the workflow process. Raw materials, work-in-process, and finished-goods inventories are costed at standard expenses for material, labor, and overhead applied to each unit. Keeping records of each change in the financial status of each inventory is simply a matter of multiplying the standard cost per unit by the physical number of units added or withdrawn from the inventory. Periodically, the variance between actual and standard costs can be apportioned among these inventories. The clerical work of keeping a perpetual record of the value of inventories is substantially reduced because inventories are priced at standard unit values. Product cost accounting is greatly simplified by using standard costs because they obviate the necessity of identifying actual expenses incurred with each unit of product or service produced.

Work standard costs also facilitate preparation of budgets for controlling expenses of organizations. Each type of expense is identified with the organizational unit responsible for its incurrence. These units are designated as cost centers. Standard costs of products or services to be produced by cost centers are summed in order to derive the expense budget for the organization.

Standard job or product costs also are used in preparing and evaluating planning decisions: price quotations in bids for contracts; pro forma (or budgeted) profit and loss statements; projections of cash outflows for purchased materials and services, payroll, etc., made in preparing cash budgets; and capital budgeting decisions.

Thus work standards are determined by the quality, productivity, or cost standards of resources and product of work.

Corporate Workflow Process Planning

Having considered work-method analysis, measurement, and design for a single job or workstation let us now consider workflow processes comprised of many interdependent jobs that are all dedicated to providing products, information, or services and funds. Planning and controlling workflow processes are essentials of operations management.

Workflow Process Charts

In order to assess their companies' operations, managers should first describe their workflow processes in terms that suggest means for their improving the processes. As the term "workflow" implies, some object (material, product, information, money, or person) flows through and is changed by the process. The following symbols are useful in order to depict concisely and rigorously the state of that object as it is processed through successive stages:

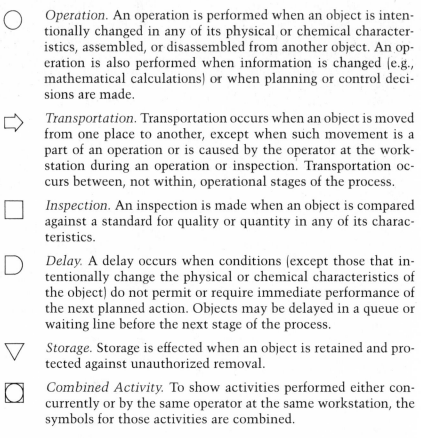

Operation. An operation is performed when an object is intentionally changed in any of its physical or chemical characteristics, assembled, or disassembled from another object. An operation is also performed when information is changed (e.g., mathematical calculations) or when planning or control decisions are made.

Transportation. Transportation occurs when an object is moved from one place to another, except when such movement is a part of an operation or is caused by the operator at the workstation during an operation or inspection. Transportation occurs between, not within, operational stages of the process.

Inspection. An inspection is made when an object is compared against a standard for quality or quantity in any of its characteristics.

Delay. A delay occurs when conditions (except those that intentionally change the physical or chemical characteristics of the object) do not permit or require immediate performance of the next planned action. Objects may be delayed in a queue or waiting line before the next stage of the process.

Storage. Storage is effected when an object is retained and protected against unauthorized removal.

Combined Activity. To show activities performed either concurrently or by the same operator at the same workstation, the symbols for those activities are combined.

Beside each workflow process symbol notation should be made to convey particular characterization of that stage of the process, for example: time, distances, physical or chemical changes; the extent to which the workpace is controlled by staff or machine; by whose authority the work activity was designed and executed; costs; and the probable occurrence (relative frequency) and effects of interruptions for preventive or remedial maintenance, delays, safety hazards, etc.

These symbols are arrayed on various forms of flow charts designed to highlight workflow processing stages with respect to their sequential relationships with references to time, distances, space, or the organizational units responsible. Consider some examples.

Figure 3–2 depicts the workflow processing of a factor sales order by various units of the National Cash Register Company to ship adding machines to dealers and distributors.

The flow chart in Figure 3–3 depicts on the factory floor plan the workflow process for testing automotive transmissions to indicate distances between successive stages. Figure 3–4 is a tabular form of the same workflow process that makes it easier to add notations for each stage and to compare the number of different elements comprising the work process. Since the value that work elements contribute to the results of the process differs (e.g., "operations" or "inspections" are more valuable than "storages" or "delays"), such a comparison may suggest possibilities for improvement by eliminating, combining, or changing the sequence of elements.

Figure 3–5 highlights the parts production and assembly operations for a simple hand drill. It indicates the technological sequence of operations. With annotations of resource requirements (materials, machines, required worker skills) this chart could facilitate planning for resource requirements. It is also useful for orientation / training of individuals interested in learning the highlights of products and manufacturing processes of their organization.

PERT Network   Figure 3–6 is a chart of work activities and events of a project to develop and promote the sale of a computer program. Often called a PERT (Project Evaluation Review Technique) network this chart reveals the technological sequence or *"paths"* of work activities and events. The project's time duration is determined by the largest sum of the times for work activities along work paths. The work path with the largest sum is called the "critical path" (note that there are two critical paths in Figure 3–6). PERT charts are widely used by managers of building construction projects or weapon systems development projects in order to plan and control costs, availability, allocation, and required resources and time to complete the project. A PERT network was used to manage activities of hundreds of contractors and government organizations who worked successfully to complete the missions of the Apollo (moon landing) Program of the National Aeronautics and Space Administration.

Organization Charts   Figure 3–7, an organization chart, depicts the workflow process for governing the relations of principal managers of all levels and functions of an organization. Such a chart facilitates assess-

Figure 3–2 Forms-distribution chart of factory ordering procedure formerly used by the Adding Machine Division of the National Cash Register Company.

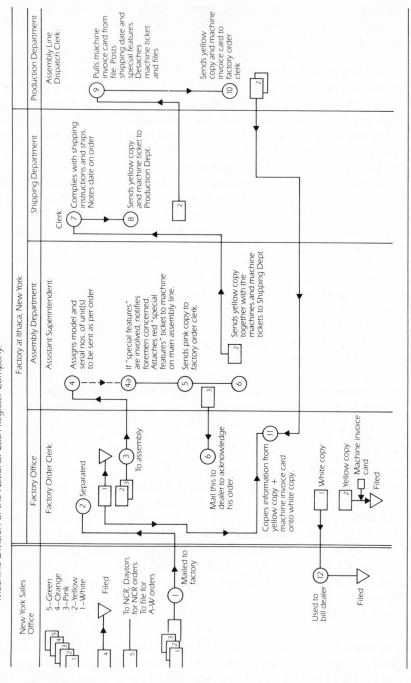

Figure 3–3 Flow diagram of process for noise testing of automotive transmissions.

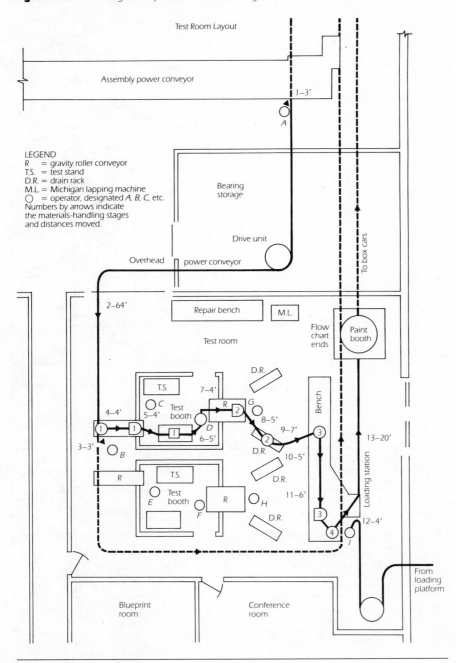

Figure 3—4 Flow process chart. Noise testing of automotive transmissions.

Part Name	Automotive Transmission		Part No.	101	Date	
Process	Audible Test		Dept.	Ind. Eng.	Analyst	REM

◯ = Operation   ⇨ = Transportation   D = Storage   ☐ = Inspection

_____ Present _____ Method

Symbol	Description	Distance Moved	P.U. & L.D.	How Moved
1⇨	Load overhead conveyor		1	Man
2⇨	On overhead conveyor	189		Power
3⇨	To roller conveyor	3'	1	Man
◯1	Fill with grease			
4⇨	On roller conveyor	4'		Gravity
D	On roller conveyor			
5⇨	To test stand	4'	1	Man
☐1	For noises			
6⇨	To roller conveyor	·5'	1	Man
7⇨	Down roller conveyor	4'		Gravity
D2	On roller conveyor			
8⇨	To drain rack	5'	1	Man
◯2	Remain drain plug; place protector tube; drain; replace plug			
9⇨	To bench	7'	1	Man
◯3	Tighten plug			
10⇨	Shove along bench	5'		Man
D3	On bench			
11⇨	Shove along bench	6'		Man
D4	On bench			
◯4	Place gearshift dust seal grease front and rear face			
12⇨	Load on overhead conveyor	4'		Man
13⇨	To paint booth	20'		Power

Summary Operations..........4   Hand....................................9
        Inspections..........1   Gravity...............................2
        Delays..............4   Power.................................2
        Transport..........12   Number of 'pickups' and 'laydowns'......7

Figure 3–5 Operations process chart. Manufacture and assembly of hand drill.

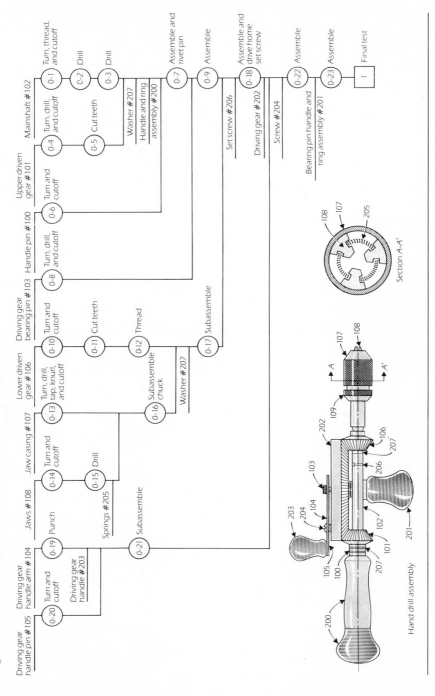

Figure 3—6 An activity network to develop and promote the sale of a computer program to be used in scheduling activity networks. The critical activities are shown with heavy lines. There are two critical paths for this project. Note: The broken line labeled "dummy" indicates a precedence relationship between events 2 and 4 and 5 and 7, but there is no job activity required to connect these events.

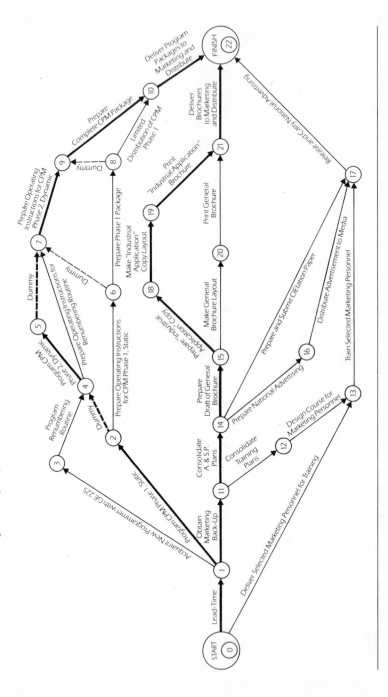

Figure 3—7 Typical organization chart.

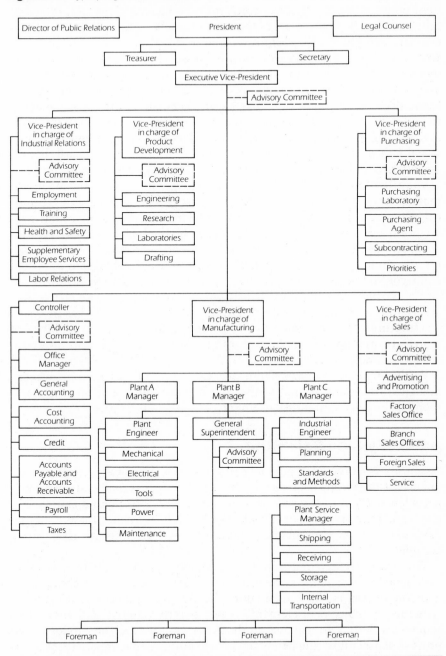

ments for improving lines of communication, organizational behavior, and development. As schematics of governance, organization charts highlight political aspects (i.e., concerns for *who* has authority and responsibility) of workflow processes of the institution. Workflow diagrams or process charts highlight the technical-economic aspects (i.e., the *what, how, when, where,* and *why*) of workflow processes and their results. Together organization and workflow charts depict roles or missions of institutions. To say whether work processes are designed primarily to fit talents and capabilities of managers, or managers with specialized talents are selected to match technological specifications of workflow processes is a difficult, perhaps impossible generalization. But effective management, organizational behavior, and development require that optimal compatibility be established and maintained among managers, employees, and their jobs.

Workflow process charts enable the manager (or operations analyst or management consultant) to describe concisely and rigorously the technical, economic, and organizational facts of corporate operations. Such a description serves important purposes: it can be the logical basis for considering alternatives for operations improvements, and it can be the means for all employees (managers, staff specialists, workers) to gain a unified and rigorous understanding of the role and mission of their organization and how they contribute to that mission. Workflow process charts also are useful for orientation training purposes; they may be used as the basis or structure for planning and controlling the quality and availability of materials, manpower, funds, and information needed for workflow processes to function.

Workflow process charts define accountability of corporations in technological or organizational terms; the balance sheet and income statement specify accountability in financial or economic terms.

Assembly-Line Balancing

Assembly is a process of putting parts together. A critical factor is the sequence. If the wrong sequence is chosen, the process may end with some parts left over, as in the case of an amateur who took apart a grandfather clock and then tried to put it back together. The sequence for assembling parts determines whether the product will perform after its assembly is complete.

Thus, the first step in assembly-line balancing is to define the assembly task sequences that *must* be followed in strict order. Assembling each component part is a task element of the assembly process. However, the sequence of many task elements is not strictly ordered, and alternative sequences define alternative methods for assembling the product. The process of assembly-line balancing is to examine and compare these alternative methods using criteria for a perfectly balanced assembly line. These criteria are: that the work cycle times for all workstations on the

Figure 3–8 Precedence graph for the assembly process of dressing. The graph is intended to show the feasible alternate sequences for assembling one's clothes. This graph can be used to highlight alternative sequences for assembling parts of a product. Note that socks must precede shoes, but that shoes and socks may be assembled at any stage of the process after "dry" and before "inspect."

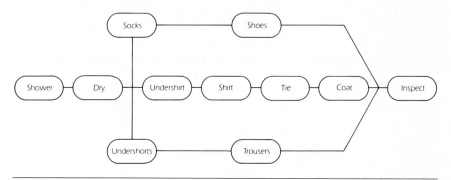

line be nearly equal as practicable; that there be a minimum of idle (non-productive) time for the assembly line; and that assembly rates are at least equal to demand rates.

Example of Assembly-Line Balancing

Consider the process of assembling one's clothes. First, the required sequences should be established: socks must precede shoes, shirt must precede necktie, etc. Figure 3–8 is a precedence graph for the assembly process of dressing. It shows the strict precedence between socks and shoes, undershorts and trousers, and so on, but it also reveals that certain other assembly tasks are not strictly ordered. For example, socks can be assembled any time before shoes, and undershorts can be assembled any time before trousers.

Table 3–2 illustrates how the assembly task elements for the job of dressing can be timed to enable us to quantify effects of feasible alternative assignments of task elements to sequential workstations for assembly. Such evaluations would depend on the validity of the assumption that the task-element time is not affected by the sequence in which it is combined with other task elements. This assumption concerns the additivity of task-element times. From the list in Table 3–2 the time for task elements 3 + 4 + 5 is 0.9 minutes. The assumption would hold that the time for task elements 5 + 3 + 4 is also 0.9. As noted earlier, this assumption is basic to the validity of all predetermined motion-time data used in work-methods design.

Suppose the clothes-assembly process involved cleaning and dressing mannequins on a continuous conveyorized assembly line containing several workstations. Imagine further that the demand for assembled mannequins required a production rate of 1.0 per minute. The assembly-line balancing problem in this case would be to assign the task elements to workstations so that there would be a minimum total amount of idle workstation time and so that the time at each workstation would not exceed 1.0 minute per mannequin.

Because the required production cycle time is 1.0 minute per mannequin and the total time for the 11 task elements is 3.7 minutes per mannequin, we conclude that there must be *at least* 3.7 / 1.0 = 3.7 (or rounded off to 4) workstations. However, we wish to investigate the possibilities of a better balance if there were more than 4.0 workstations.

Referring to the list of task-element times in Table 3–2 and the assembly precedence graph in Figure 3–8, we can try out feasible alternative assignments to those listed in Table 3–3. Table 3–4 shows the better assignment of task elements to workstations.

The example is trivial, but it illustrates salient aspects of assembly-line balancing procedures that are trial-and-error examinations of every feasible assembly task sequence and number of line workstations. Real problems contain many task elements and workstations, which make the assignment of alternative combinations of assembly task elements much more complex and tedious.

Some Generalizations about Assembly-Line Balancing

Assembly-line balancing procedures require a number of steps.

Product examination   First, a product examination is needed to identify each component explicitly and to determine the number of sequences possible for their assembly. Parts inside a product have to be assembled before ones on the outside, but there may be many different assembly sequences in working from inside to outside.

Process Limitations   Next, these sequences are modified by invoking certain process limitations. For example, if assembly calls for the use of several fasteners (nuts, bolts, screws, and rivets) it might be better to tighten all or some of the fasteners at one time to avoid providing duplicate power-driven tools and having them picked up too often. Another process characteristic affecting the assembly sequence is the position an operator must assume to assemble a part. If he / she must stoop to assemble one part, perhaps the operator ought not to be required to climb on top of the product to assemble the next. Another process restriction might be that certain parts are fed on conveyors installed at fixed points along the assembly line to be balanced. Still another factor might be that some task elements require operators who are paid more than others, and it would not be economical to assign them to low-skill tasks. Such process restrictions as these tend further to limit the number of alternative sequences

Table 3—2 Timing Assembly Task Elements for Dressing

Task Element	Description	Standard Time (Minutes)
1	Shower	0.8
2	Dry	0.4
3	Socks	0.2
4	Shoes	0.5
5	Undershirt	0.2
6	Shirt	0.4
7	Tie	0.3
8	Coat	0.1
9	Undershorts	0.2
10	Trousers	0.4
11	Inspect quality of dress	0.2
		3.7

Table 3—3 Trial 1, Five Workstations

Workstation	Task Elements Assigned	Work Time (Minutes)	Idle Time (Minutes)
1	1	0.8	0.2
2	2, 3, 5, 9	1.0	0.0
3	6, 7	0.7	0.3
4	4, 8, 10	1.0	0.0
5	11	0.2	0.8
	Total	3.7	1.3

Table 3—4 Trial 2, Four Workstations

Workstation	Task Elements Assigned	Work Time (Minutes)	Idle Time (Minutes)
1	1	0.8	0.2
2	2, 3, 5, 9	1.0	0.0
3	4, 6	0.9	0.1
4	7, 8, 10, 11	1.0	0.0
	Total	3.7	0.3

for assembling parts. The assembly line is balanced by equalizing workload of all workstations, while taking those restrictions into account.

Precedence graphs or other varieties of flow charts are useful models in planning feasible alternative sequences of task elements.

Assignment of Task-Element Times   Next, the task-element times are assigned to different numbers of workstations and comparisons are made of productive and idle times for different sets of assignments.

The required assembly cycle time is derived from the forecasted sustained rate of demand for this product. *Assembly cycle time* is the rate at which the assembly line must produce units to meet the demand rate; a balanced line is one whose workstations are productively scheduled throughout this cycle time. The minimum number of workstations is the nearest whole integer-quotient obtained by dividing the sum of the assembly task-element times by the required assembly cycle time. More than this minimum number of workstations may result in a better time balance in the sense that total idle time is shared more equitably.

The line-balancing computations are iterative and also are tedious. A computer may alleviate the tedium: Task-element time data may be coded according to feasible alternative sequences; the computer is programmed to examine different sequences in terms of scheduled workstation productive time and idle time. Since there is no known logical algorithm for "optimizing" these assembly-line balancing computations, the best balance is determined only after calculating productive and idle time for all feasible sequences task assignments and workstations.

Assembly lines have to be rebalanced each time changes occur in demand rate and product or process designs. Once a line has been balanced, it has also been scheduled. All that remains is to allocate the materials at the appropriate rate to the correct workstations and to see that operators are willing and able to perform their tasks accordingly.

Facilities Location, Equipment Layout

Our discussion of workflow-process analysis has emphasized a goal of *reducing time*—and by implication, *reducing cost* and achieving optimal productivity with acceptable quality. If workflow processes minimize *distance* traversed by materials, products, suppliers, employees, and customers, then they are even more economical. The choices of facility location and equipment layout are important determinants of travel distance and time.

Of course costs of land and building space (taxes, insurance, security protection services, etc.) and availability and quality of infrastructure services (education, cultural activities, housing, openspace land, recreation, health, safety, energy, water, waste disposal, and transportation) have important bearing on the choice of facility-location decisions. Often community, regional, or state governments or chambers of commerce compete with each other in efforts to attract business or industrial organizations to their locations. They offer public financing of land and water rights, building construction, tax abatements, etc. Their aim is to expand employment, increase income for their citizens, and spread costs of public services over larger numbers of residents or industrial firms.

Facilities location and equipment layout decisions are usually enhanced if alternative, feasible choices are assessed before a final choice is made. Since each assessment may entail many different factors or tedious computations, computer models or template models may be helpful in assessing alternative locations. Linear programming (discussed in Chapter 5) is a useful analytical model for assessing alternative locations of factory and warehouse facilities for industrial operations.

Quality of Corporate Work Life

Since most of the work of industrial societies is organized and conducted via corporate workflow processes, their influence is powerful and pervasive. They specify and control the transformation, rate of movement, and locations of materials, information, staff, or products. They regulate conditions for employment and income. They determine the quality, availability, and cost of products and services or information and funds. Consequently, they affect the attitudes and behavior of the majority of people who must relate to organizations as employees, customers, suppliers, shareholders, or citizens. Corporate workflow processes are subjects of concern to the production/operations manager. They are not confined to factories. The role and mission of every kind of organization—industrial, governmental, financial, health, philanthropic—are characterized by its workflow processes, because they are the links connecting the organization's resources with its objectives.

A traditional and universal conviction is that since practically every organization exists in a competitive environment and has scarce resources, the organization must either grow stronger or it will succumb to environmental forces. In other words, corporate operations must either grow or else they "die" (i.e., lose their identity). So, the operations manager must continuously assess and adopt opportunities for *corporate growth*. Of course, such assessments emphasize technical and economic values: profitability, efficiency, and productivity, as well as technological advancement achieved usually by increasing the consumption of some form of energy (mechanical, electrical, thermal, chemical, or nuclear).

More recently, however, operations managers have had to impute values of *corporate stability or equanimity* in their assessment of workflow processes. Government, the press, unions, and consumer or conservation groups are holding managers accountable for effects of corporate operations on moral, ethical, and ecological values. There is a growing public awareness but not yet an agreement on who should be held accountable or responsible for the impact of technological change or economic growth of corporate operations on people and their natural environment.

Work Life Quality and the Limits to Growth

Some authorities argue that corporate efforts to improve quality of work life or social or environmental health and safety are almost bound to conflict with efforts to increase corporate growth or technological change. Debates about "limits to growth" have profound implications for industrial and developing nations. These issues are far from resolved, and they affect and are affected by the production manager. However, corporate growth and technological change can be made to preserve or improve social and environmental health while they improve the economic well-being of more people.

During the post-World War II decades, 1948–68, productivity of U.S. corporate operations increased at a rate of about 3 percent each year. During the 1970s, the annual rate of productivity growth dropped to about 1 percent, causing inflation rates to increase, and a decrease in shares of domestic and foreign markets for U.S. based firms. The decline in productivity may indicate a decline in the material standard of living in the U.S.

Among the reasons cited for this decline was a deterioration in the "quality of work life" of managers as well as office or factory workers. Attitude surveys and anthropological studies revealed increasing resignation, apathy, or antagonism about work conditions, even in organizations providing high salary or wage levels, fringe benefits, and employment security. Absenteeism, unauthorized work stoppages, and sloppy workmanship increased.[1]

It is an unexplained irony that the quality of corporate work life has deteriorated. Why have three decades of unprecedented technological innovation, increasing wealth and education, and strategies for improving worker and organizational behavior resulted in less trust and dedication to corporate operations? Does the fact that employees are much more educated than they were during the 1940s mean that worker expectations about qualities of work life have become unrealistic? Or does it mean that capabilities of employees are not being fully utilized?

Changes in Organizational Behavior or Development

It is widely held that, as organizations grow larger, they become more bureaucratic and increase their levels of administrative hierarchy. Thus, their governance or management processes become more formalized, with bureaucratic or hierarchical rigidities. Informal, democratic or participative management by workers together with planners, designers, or

---

1. The case of "Lordstown Plant of General Motors" is an example. Also, "Work in America," a study by the U.S. Department of Health Education and Welfare, Washington, D.C. 1973. "The Changing World of Work," Report of the 43rd American Assembly, Columbia University, New York, 1973.

controllers of corporate work processes is not practical in large organizations. Moreover, individual employees (either management staff or worker/union member) encounter more pressures to conform with corporate procedures and fewer opportunities to express their individual preferences or identity in their work. Hence, there is a decline in loyalty, dedication, and enthusiasm for corporate goals and work processes. Employees become more apathetic, resigned, resistant. They care less about their work. Absenteeism and work defects increase. The quality of corporate work life and the quality of products and services decrease; productivity declines.

Such analysis is both erroneous and confusing. The increase in bureaucracy and management hierarchy *are* major reasons for the decline in qualities of work life, products, and services and rate of productivity of American organizations. But growth in the organization size is not a cause. Consider some observations of American dealers and a vice president of the Ford Motor Company comparing Japanese and American automobile manufacturers of comparable size:

Not only did the American makers fail to acknowledge the need for fuel-efficient, front-wheel drive cars, they let their U.S. manufacturing plants deteriorate to a point where they were incapable of delivering a quality product.

Four to six U.S. cars out of 100 must be repainted. The figure for Japanese is one per thousand.

On similar sales volume, our Datsun warranty and policy expenses are one-fifth of our American car expense.

In Ford, in a similar plant we have 11 layers of organization. Toyota has five. We've got six excessive layers of management. In engines per day per employee, in similar plants, Ford produces two; Toyota produces nine![2]

If growth in the number of employees of an organization led inevitably to more rigid bureaucracy in its management, then goals of industrial growth and concepts of economies of scale, or productivity improvements through technological innovation would not be valid or effective. But the evidence clearly indicates that they are valid and effective.

The rise of bureaucracy—and decline of democracy—in management of American organizations are due to preoccupation with special interests and neglect of common interests of all concerned in their role and mission.

As with all professions, to become a manager in the U.S. one must earn a college degree. And to be progressive or efficient organizations must adopt more scientific, hence more specialized, methods for conducting their operations. Consequently, education and practice of management have been fragmented into specialized areas of scientific concentration:

2. Harry B. Ellis. "More Lessons From Japan." *The Christian Science Monitor*, December 15, 1980, p. 1.

systems analysis, human and organizational behavior, computer science and information systems, quantitative analysis and decision-making, and operations research. Each area has its own special interest group concerned with its own scientific concepts and techniques for management education and practice.

Effects of Specialization

One must specialize in order to acquire intellectual and professional competence considered necessary for entry-level positions in management of industry or government operations. Generalists are recognized only after they have reached positions at the highest levels of the business, government, or university hierarchy.

Disciplines of science have been used to increase the consistency, objectivity, or rationality of managers'—as well as workers'—jobs. Specialized experts subdivide responsibilities into smaller, more controllable activities of machines and humans in order to process materials or information into products, services, or decisions. Goals and performance characteristics are quantified in dimensions that can be more precisely predicted and controlled. Concentration has been on resources, activities, and results that are tangible, hence objective. Subjective characteristics of human resources like loyalty, mutual trust, creativity, and dedication are intangible, not measurable. Hence, they tend to be taken for granted and neglected. Thus, it should not seem strange that bureaucratic or technocratic formalities have come to replace democratic, humanistic informalities of American organizations and management.

Within the education and practice of each specialized area of management academicians and practitioners have created scholarly or professional associations, published journals to share ideas on research and experience, and formed their own bureaucratic hierarchies within universities, industry, and government—all to advance the status of their specialized discipline. Their concepts, explained by mathematical symbols or technical jargon, tend to strengthen the public's sense of scientific rigor and uniqueness about their field of expertise. Recognition and achievement are measured primarily by one's contributions to his/her professional specialty and secondarily to one's institution.

Emphasis on Credentials   Clientele (i.e., peer-associates in management, workers, customers, or taxpayers) who lack academic or professional credentials for understanding experts' decisions nevertheless must accept them. They are scientific, and all progress must be based on science. And it is inefficient, a waste of time, indeed, impossible for laypeople to learn—or experts to explain—every kind of specialized expertise required by organizations.

Thus, communications barriers are formed between experts and clients (workers, customers, other professional managers, and taxpayers). Debate about the social, moral, or ecological implications of computerized decision models, control techniques, materials processing standards, or Skinnerian theories of behavior modification is repressed. Sometimes public relations experts or communications experts are assigned to deal with such problems, but their efforts often are directed toward avoiding controversies by creating the appearance of solutions. The sociological survey is used increasingly to convey the appearance of democratic consensus about choices.

Statistically significant, random samples are continuously made of employees', customers', shareholders', or citizens' attitudes concerning corporations' choices of goals and corporate work processes. The issues raised and alternative choices for their resolution are judgments of professionals, and each sampling process is scientific and efficient. So there are almost no grounds for debating the validity of results, and individuals affected have almost no recourse but to agree and comply with results.

But resolution or consensus by a statistical majority sampled in a survey is not the same as resolution or consensus reached after face-to-face discussion, debate, or vote by people concerned. Nor are surveys a substitute for participatory management or democratic self-governance, which by nature is unscientific and inefficient, and often subjective or irrational. However, if individuals affected by corporate operations are not given genuine opportunities to participate in controlling changes in work standards, then sooner or later, the qualities of work life, products, and services are likely to be jeopardized.

Worker Alienation   This is not to condemn the concept of specialized expertise, only the abuses of that concept by bureaucrats. It helps to explain why individuals feel ignored or deceived by professional special-interest groups; and why these groups are straining the bonds of mutual trust and comity necessary for managers to manage.

Nor is the foregoing to suggest that, if chosen more democratically and less bureaucratically, methods of planning and executing corporate operations would be less scientific or mechanical. On the contrary, given an opportunity to participate in planning and controlling their work, most people would choose to take advantage of the efficiency, added productivity, and profitability from computerized information processing or mechanized materials processing—especially if income, security, and work opportunities are shared more equitably. Japanese firms have demonstrated the advantages of worker participation in management decisions to increase quality and productivity through technological improvements and employment security.

If organized applications of science and technology are to serve people (and not vice versa) then democratic, participatory management is necessary. Morality, productivity, science, and technology require the creative abilities of individual human beings.

Efficiency may require specialized bureaucracies in government and industry. But effectiveness requires more humanized democracy.

Several decades ago, when applications of automation and computers began to intensify and spread rapidly, Samuel Miller, dean of the Harvard Divinity School, commented on ethics and morality of corporate work:

For business and industry, the ethical question with reference to things can be rephrased as the transformation of raw materials into usable commodities. . . . The quality and dependability of the product *is* the ethic at this level of man's reality. And in this particular, an aetheistic carpenter who makes a good table is a better man ethically than a pious one who botches the job. . . . In the ethic of persons, freedom is on both sides of the question—not merely on one, as with things. Persons cannot simply be used; rather, because their freedom varies so greatly, the permissible amount of use will vary. For some persons, work on an assembly line is a relatively minor abrogation of freedom, whereas for others, . . . it would be a drastic evil.[3]

Since work is what most people need and want to do for a living, work is an important, if not crucial, way of life. And, since life is a pursuit of interacting values, spiritual as well as materialistic, work methods and their results should be measured accordingly. Work may liberate or repress workers' spirits, enable them to serve or to dominate others; or work may provide for selfish fulfillment or selfless dedication. Such values are moral, ethical, or of the spirit. They are intangible, metaphysical, implicit, and never explicit, per se. They have to be sensed intuitively or inferred, perhaps statistically from empirical evidence that is presumed relevant. In our age of expanding technology, industrialized cultures, and global interdependence on economic and natural resources, perhaps deteriorating qualities of work life and declining productivity are reminders that metaphysical values are no less important than materialistic values of efficiency or profitability. The human species is of nature. Therefore work is motivated by tangible goals and guided by scientific laws. But goals of human beings transcend nature. Therefore work is also subject to cultural laws and spiritual values. These should never be taken for granted or ignored by the operations manager. Corporate operations cannot be sustained without employees' faith, trust, and dedication to corporate goals and work methods.

Questions for Discussion

1. Should individual workers be held accountable for the quality, rate of output, and cost of jobs even though workers do not plan or provide for the tools, facilities, materials, or technology of the method?

3. Samuel H. Miller. "The Tangle of Ethics," *Harvard Business Review,* (January–February, 1960), p. 61.

2. In terms of probability and statistical concepts, what does it mean to say that the quality of a work process is under control?

3. If a work process is not "in control," can random inspections provide assurances of quality? Precisely what is meant by "quality assurance" of products?

4. What are the four fundamental conditions for determining work methods and time standards cited in the section on "Work Methods and Time Standards"? Are these necessary and sufficient conditions?

5. Work-methods design problems are matters of assigning combinations and sequences of task elements accomplished by machines or staff so that the rates of production are responsive to rates of demand, and so that budgetary and quality standards are met.
   a. Does this mean that the work of product design is not affected by the work of process design, and vice versa? How are they related?
   b. Are work-methods design problems of government agencies, hospitals, or welfare organizations different from those of business or industrial organizations? Explain.
   c. Why or how do production schedules affect choices of work methods?

6. Any job method can (or should) be improved in order to meet constantly changing demands, resources, or technologies. But whether a particular job method should be improved is a question that the manager must answer, *before* assigning costly staff technicians or analysts to problems of *how* or *what* improvements are needed or desired. But if managers decide which jobs are to be improved, then the managers may anticipate or even prejudge results of efforts by staff specialists before those specialists have examined the problem. How should managers deal with such a dilemma?

7. Job-method descriptions serve many purposes: personnel recruiting, selection, and training; improving job-method standards; job classification and evaluation schemes; staff planning; union-management negotiations; and grievance procedures. There may be a separate description for each purpose.
   a. For which of these purposes should the job description be most rigorous, detailed, and complete?
   b. Why is it desirable or necessary to verify that all descriptions of the same job are, indeed, of the same job? How is this verification accomplished, if at all, in most organizations?

8. Regarding the cost dichotomies discussed in the section on "Work Cost Standards":
   a. Why is it "useful to understand these economic dichotomies of business costs"?
   b. Should the budget for an organizational unit contain only those expenses (or costs) that are "controllable" by personnel of that unit?

Should the salary of the manager or supervisor be considered part of the budget for the department or unit?

c. Is the budget for an organization the same as the standard cost of operating that organization for the budget period?

d. If "sunk costs" are not affected by a decision whether to replace the facilities for work, and if the old facilities have not been fully depreciated, then what about the loss sustained *if* the facilities are replaced (but not if they are not replaced)? Is not this loss attributed to the decision to replace?

e. Do cost accounting records contain "opportunity costs"? Why not? Should opportunity costs be assessed before work-method standards are established? Why?

f. Are costs of hazards to health and environment (e.g., lost productive time, medical welfare expenses, increased costs of air, water, and land resources) that are attributable to corporate work processes accounted for as costs of corporate operations? Should they be? Why do some critics argue that government regulations (pollution, health and safety) increase product prices unnecessarily and reduce productivity and jobs?

9. Are the terms *corporate workflow process management* and *operations management* practically synonymous? Why?

10. Why are workflow process charts of importance to operations managers?

11. *Workflow process charts* explain the technological (changes of form or substance) or logistical (changes of location, quantity, and time) flow stages of objects (materials, products, personnel, information) being processed. *Organization charts* explain the subdivisions and channels for orderly communication of authority and responsibility among levels and functions of management. The two must be compatible. Accordingly, should organizations be structured *after* the workflow process has been designed and not vice versa? Discuss.

12. Workflow process improvements are specialized responsibilities of process or system designers. Organization improvements are the responsibility of specialists in organizational behavior or development. Discuss problems of coordinating the work of these specialists, whose professional education is probably divergent. Is the deterioration of the quality of work life attributable to their lack of coordination?

13. Do you agree that to explain corporate accountability, workflow process charts are as important as financial statements? Why or why not?

14. Should all employees in an organization be knowledgeable of corporate workflow processes?

15. Is it true that to increase productivity, generally it is necessary to "dehumanize" corporate workflow processes by further specializa-

tion, mechanization, or computerization of work methods? Why or why not?

16. Regarding human and social aspects of work standards:
    a. Why should work standards represent a compromise: (1) between conflicting values of quality, availability, or cost; (2) of what the work method and time should be or must be; (3) of divergent interests (customers, lawyers, economists, accountants, behavioral scientists, union leaders, workers, and managers)? Is collective bargaining between union and management negotiators the most effective means for maintaining the agreement?
    b. Do you agree that the process for planning and controlling work methods and measurements has become more technocratic or bureaucratic than democratic? What are implications of this statement for the quality of work life and corporate development?
    c. Do you agree that human and social satisfaction with corporate work processes has decreased? What evidence can you cite?
    d. Discuss the significance of the quotation of corporate work ethics by Dean Samuel Miller. Has the freedom of persons to express themselves through their work been curtailed in recent years?
    e. What, if anything, can managers do to ensure that work enhances the moral and cultural values, as well as technical and economic values, of society?

Relevant Cases

1. ABC Carbon Co.
3. Andrews Machine Co.
5. Berkeley Savings and Loan Association
6. Calnational Oil Co. (A)
7. Calnational Oil Co. (B)
9. Chicago Auto Parts Supply Co. (A)
10. Chicago Auto Parts Supply Co. (B)
14. Foster Optical Equipment Co.
18. Lordstown Plant of General Motors (A)
19. Lordstown Plant of General Motors (B)
25. National Electronics Co.
28. Penn Electric Co.
29. Pharma Co.
32. University Book Store
33. University Physical Plant

Inventory Management

4

In its broadest perspective the challenge of inventory management is to keep the most economical amount of one kind of asset in order to facilitate an increase in the total value of all assets of the organization—staff, machines, building space, information, cash and credit, materials, and products. Demands for and supplies of inventory occur at varying rates not always predictable in precise terms. Since inventory is an asset not yet utilized (i.e., idle materials, staff, machines, or floor space), and since its value may not increase unless it is utilized, the purpose of inventory management is to avoid excessive inventory (idle assets) on the one hand, and excessive loss of opportunity to use (or sell) the inventory on the other. In this sense inventory management encompasses nothing more or less than management of assets of the total enterprise.

Managers should keep this broad, totalistic perspective in mind. While preoccupied with their responsibilities for controlling particular assets, managers tend to ignore the cooperation and interdependence necessary for the firm to keep and utilize the proper types and quantities of all assets. What is done to change the inventory of one asset probably affects the inventory of another. The more cash that is tied up in materials, the less cash there can be for more machines, building space, or accounts receivable. Consider other examples of such interdependence.

Liquidating inventories of finished products is one means to generate cash needed, say, for a dividend or tax payment. But lower inventories may increase the risk of lost sales. The cost of that increased risk may be much greater than the cost of a loan made to finance the dividend or tax payment, and such a loan would obviate reducing inventories and increasing the risk of lost sales. This example illustrates the interdependence of managing inventories of cash, finished products, accounts payable, and (prospective) accounts receivable.

Huge investments have been made in computers, systems analysis staff, and telecommunications equipment for operations management. But they may be of questionable profitability, unless the cost of those investments in data banks and techniques for information flow are more than offset by a decrease in the cost of facilities for the flow of materials and products.

Staff specialists also often ignore the interdependence among kinds and quantities of inventory in applying scientific operations research or systems management. Most computerized, analytical techniques for controlling the inventory of every item of an aggregate of materials or products require the user to discount or ignore the degrees of interdependence among the products. Most quantitative techniques applied to manage inventory are based on the assumption of mutual independence of items in the aggregate inventory to be controlled. (The validity of this assumption is a matter for the manager to judge, as will be discussed in greater detail later.) Since the size of the staff and the facility (equipment, office space, laboratory, etc.) indicates the relative importance the executive officer has assigned to the management of various classes of assets, each staff unit is tempted to expand, often without sufficient regard for needs of other sections of the staff. Bureaucratic specialization and Parkinson's law (that number of employees tends to increase, regardless of economic needs for their employment) often spoil benefits afforded by use of scientific methods.

Thus, holistic concerns for inventory management of all assets of the organization are necessary. On the other hand, analytical and specialized concerns for different kinds of assets are also necessary in order for inventory planning and control to be managed in practical terms. The treasurer is made responsible for inventories of cash, the credit manager for inventories of accounts receivable, the materials manager for inventories of supplies and finished products at the factory warehouse; the librarian for inventories of information. These managers have to be flexible and discrete to make decisions and control their inventories according to their schedules and budgets. Thus a reasonable degree of interdependence between inventories is necessary for effective organization and management.

The discussion of inventory in this chapter includes (1) purposes, (2) dual systems for management, (3) analyzing aggregates into manageable classes, (4) decision models to execute its purposes, and (5) managing levels of aggregate and item systems.

First, let us define inventory clearly. In this discussion *inventory* is considered to be a separate business facility, that is, an aggregate stock of materials or products set apart physically from the other stages of the corporate workflow process in a stockroom, warehouse, retail store, or supermarket. Or, inventory might be comprised of a file or library of information. Such inventories are kept under distinctive supervision and custody. Accumulations of materials and products on a factory floor or on shipping or receiving platforms are in the "pipeline"—we do not consider them inventory in this discussion.

Purposes of Inventory

A clear delineation of the purposes of inventory serves to sharpen inventory policies and techniques required for their execution. Five purposes of inventory are: (1) to promote sales by reducing product-delivery time; (2) to afford intermittent use of production facilities for different products; (3) to sustain material or product flow despite random differences between rates of supply and demand; (4) to execute a policy of smoothing procurement, production, and employment levels, and (5) to provide a means for gaining profits through price speculations. Now let us consider each in more detail.

Promoting Sales by Reducing Delivery Time

The fact that products are physically available at the marketplace means that customers do not have to wait for whatever they may wish to buy. Indeed, immediate availability may be the impetus for sales to customers who otherwise had no overt intention to buy at that time. Hence inventory may facilitate impulse buying. Supermarket, discount merchandising, and mass-distribution channels, which involve geographically nonexclusive dealers and distributorships, provide the structure for carrying the inventory to improve product-delivery service. Generally, the larger the number of distributors and dealers a manufacturer supplies the greater the total inventory required. Thus, to promote long-term sales, the structure of the distribution system and the purpose of carrying inventory are mutually related.

Of course, sales may be promoted not only by *eliminating* the wait for deliveries, but also by *reducing* customer waiting time from what it formerly was. There may be a significant competitive advantage for a firm able to deliver custom-made products in 30 days when other firms require 60 days. This advantage may be supported by stocks of semifinished products and/or components kept further upstream from consumers. In other words, inventory may promote sales by eliminating or reducing leadtime to some shorter time than would be possible without inventory.

Another way of describing this reason for having an inventory is to say that finished-goods inventory may reduce investment in the total "sales facility." Generally, a sales force has to promote three attributes of a product in order to "sell" to a customer: (1) price, (2) quality (aesthetic and functional), and (3) delivery service. The existence of inventory may reduce marketing efforts to make products available. The marketing manager can concentrate on promoting price and quality attributes because the delivery service has already been provided by the inventory. Therefore, conceptually at least, the expense or investment to facilitate selling efforts that would be required without inventory is reduced.

Having fixed the structure of its distribution system, a manufacturer may carry ad hoc inventory to support special sales promotions. For example, in short-term promotions the manufacturers of soaps, detergents, beverages, and cigarettes occasionally offer their products in special forms such as Christmas-gift packages or those that "tie in" one product (or package size) with another. The stock to support "two-for-one" sales and one-cent sales by manufacturers and distributors of drug products may also be classed as "special sales promotion inventory." Of course, stock-clearance sales may be intended for the short-term purpose of reducing excessive inventory.

Allowing Use of Facilities for Different Products

Most plants produce more than one product in the same, multipurpose facility. Machines, personnel, floor space, and/or raw materials are utilized to produce more than one item, but only one product (or one type of material) at a time. Hence the term *intermittent processing*. Inventory sustains the demand for one kind of material or product while a facility produces another kind. Thus, a second purpose of inventory is to reduce the total investment that would be required if the facilities were used to produce only one type of product. The term *cycle stock* is used by some firms to designate inventory carried to sustain operations while facilities are used intermittently to produce a mix of products in a more or less rigid time sequence.

Sustaining Material or Product Flow Despite Differences in Supply and Demand Rates

Rates of demand are, of course, subject to uncertainties of sales forecasts and plans. Similarly, actual rates of supply are almost certain to differ from the predicted rates. Forecasting, planning, and scheduling the actual rate of production or transportation may be subject to randomlike errors that are as significant as errors in forecasting and planning the rate at which customers actually will buy. The incidence of scrap, spoilage, equipment failures, and errors of communication and human judgment—all of these short-term disturbances affect the actual production rate just as changes in the weather and the whims of customers may affect actual rates of demand. Inventory serves to sustain the flow of materials and products in spite of these errors. Such inventory is variously called "safety stock," "buffer stock," or "cushion reserve." If carried at all, the amount will depend on the difference between actual amounts produced and consumed during the time delay in discovering and compensating for this difference. Thus the goal of planning and control is to keep this difference and time delay as small as is practical. With present-day organization and communication facilities, corrective action may be taken in a matter of hours or days. In electric-power generation and distribution systems the time delays are measured in seconds, but capacity must be sufficient for meeting demands of peak or emergency loads.

Executing a Policy of Smoothing Procurement, Production, and Employment Levels

The amount of inventory carried to enhance the stability of production and employment is probably significantly greater than that carried to sustain random differences between rates of production and consumption. The purpose of the former inventory is to avoid, say, monthly or seasonal changes in production rates and employment levels, whereas the purpose of the latter may be to sustain flows despite changes occurring hourly, daily, or weekly. For this reason procurement, production, and employment stabilization may be considered as a fourth, separate purpose of aggregate inventory. Costs of hiring and laying off trained and reliable employees have increased steadily as a result of collective bargaining with unions and rising costs of Social Security and unemployment compensation insurance employers must pay as taxes. Companies like Procter and Gamble use inventories to facilitate management's policies for guaranteed annual employment. We explore this purpose of inventory further in Case 4, Apex Appliances, Inc., and Case 15, Home Products Company.

Providing a Means for Gaining Profits through Price Speculation

Inventory may provide a means for dealing with volatile commodity prices. Some firms deliberately stock materials to profit from buying at low prices and selling at high prices. Other firms stock materials with volatile prices to help stabilize material costs of their own products, whose market prices are relatively steady. Prices of certain agricultural commodities may be classed as volatile. Thus the inventory carried by firms engaged in trading and processing farm products permits them to speculate with the prices of farm commodities. Similarly, inventories of corporate stocks in financial investment portfolios may be classed as "speculative stocks." This purpose arises from special characteristics of a business or its environment. Methods for managing speculative stock are beyond the scope of this discussion.

Some Conclusions about Purposes of Inventory

Any one or a combination of the five purposes cited may be a criterion for deciding whether a stockroom or warehouse facility should be assigned a stage in a system for procuring, processing, and distributing products. (Of course an itemized list or file of information is needed to account for each inventory of materials.) The purposes are not mutually exclusive—it is almost impossible to give a single comprehensive reason for adding an item or taking an item out of stock. However, the inventory level to accommodate all five purposes is likely to be higher than an inventory intended for fewer than the five purposes cited. Each purpose suggests a reasonable (i.e., formulated) amount of inventory to be carried to assure that the proper inventory level is achieved—as will be demonstrated in later discussion.

Dual Systems Necessary for Inventory Management

Inventory management is facilitated by two systems: one for storing and handling (packaging) materials or products, the other for storing and handling (communicating/processing) information. The two systems stimulate and respond to changes in their status: a change in the physical quantities of material flowing in or out of stock effects a change in information stored or processed, and vice versa. Since the two systems act interdependently, their capabilities should be compatible—this point seems obvious. But in practice it may be ignored. Since they are affiliated with separate staffs with different professional skills, information systems designers often fail to coordinate their efforts with designers of materials handling and storage facilities. The result may be that large investments in computerized telecommunications equipment to improve the speed and accuracy of information is uneconomical because the system for material handling and storage is not capable of responding to the computer system, or vice versa. Of course, both information and materials flow systems are affected by systems for flows of funds or financial credit.

Planning and designing the dual systems of inventory management can be analyzed in terms of the following elements.

Information-Processing Methods and Facilities

1. Choosing methods for deriving and maintaining accurate parameters of the following:
   (a) Inventory costs—carrying costs and stockout costs.
   (b) Order preparation and setup costs for replenishing stock.
   (c) Probability distributions of expected rates for the stock demand and supply.
   (d) Delivery service the stock is supposed to afford.
2. Designing decision models for formulating and solving for stock-replenishment order quantities, stock order frequencies, "safety-stock" levels, or max-min stock limits for "triggering" control decisions.
3. Determining methods of accounting and recording changes in the stock status:

(a) Periodic versus perpetual updating of stock records.

(b) Form and frequency for summarizing and communicating stock status reports to others in the organization.

(c) Reconciliations between stock records and physical quantities on hand.

4. Problems of designing and operating information systems:

(a) Evaluating and selecting equipment for information transmission and processing.

(b) Determining forms and procedures for (1) reporting pending and actual stock shortages and stock surpluses and (2) obtaining feedback information relevant to pending stock receipts and withdrawals.

5. Organizational problems:

(a) Defining and delegating clerical, technical, and supervisory responsibilities to available personnel; job performance standards.

(b) Evaluating, training, and motivating personnel.

(c) Keeping personnel informed about recent improvements in techniques and facilities for inventory planning and control.

Materials Handling Methods and Facilities

1. Determining optimal geographical location(s) and sizes(s) of stockroom(s) and warehouse(s).

2. Problems of stockroom layout:

(a) Allocation of space for (1) item storage, access to and from item storage for stock picking and stock replenishing, (2) accumulations of stock receipts and stock shipments, (3) storage and maintenance of equipment, and (4) personnel.

(b) Determining and maintaining orderly storage locations when staff conflict about the bases for arrangement, such as whether to use stock-picking frequencies; serialized catalog-item numbers; or relative weights, quantities, and/or volume of items versus relative stock-replenishment frequencies.

(c) Selection of alternative types of storage and handling equipment.

3. Problems of designing methods of stockroom operation:

(a) Methods of stock picking and stock replenishment.

(b) Allocating and scheduling materials handling jobs so that staff and equipment can be utilized and delays in handling stock withdrawals and receipts minimized; coordination of scheduled receipts and withdrawals.

(c) Making and reporting accurate and inexpensive physical counts to verify quantities in stock records and stock receipts and to control over- and under-issues from stock.

(d) Devising "housekeeping" rules and procedures for (1) protecting the inventory against pilferage and deterioration, (2) avoiding loss and damage of containers and equipment, (3) promoting safety of

personnel, (4) breaking open packages or cartons to obtain "odd lots," and (5) promoting the cleanliness of stockroom and warehouse.
4. Organization and personnel:
   (a) Establishing work standards and delegating jobs to stockroom personnel.
   (b) Personnel selection, training, and performance evaluation.
   (c) Maintenance of employee morale.

Dividing Aggregate Inventories into Manageable Classes

At most stock points (i.e., stockrooms or warehouses) in a manufacturing and distribution system there may be a variety of several hundred or even several thousand items in the inventory to be managed. How should available talent and facilities be used most effectively to manage the aggregate inventory? Very likely the stock levels of some items should be more carefully planned and controlled than others.

In sales management it is useful to know which of a large aggregate of prospective customers are most likely to produce the largest percentage of the total predicted revenue so that sales efforts can be allocated accordingly. Similarly, efforts to manage aggregate inventory may be made on the basis of predicted costs of acquiring and carrying the aggregate inventory.

Suppose we decided that there should be three different procedures (A, B, and C) for managing an aggregate inventory. Procedure A will ensure more careful inventory management, but must be used to plan and control fewer items than procedure B; procedure B will ensure more careful inventory management, but must be applied to fewer items in the aggregate than procedure C. Thus we must classify each item in the aggregate inventory for assignment to one of the three different control procedures.

To make these assignments, we need an "inventory priority index" for ranking each item in relation to all other items. One such cost index is an estimate of the relative investment in the inventory formulated in the following manner.

For each item the forecasted number of units demanded is multiplied by its standard (or estimated) cost per unit. The sum of these results would be the estimated total dollars per year invested in the particular aggregate stock being examined. The estimated cost of each item next year expressed as a percentage of estimated cost of all items would provide a means for ranking the items, from highest to lowest, according to the *relative* amount of money that would be tied up in the aggregate inventory. Figure 4–1 illustrates how perhaps 10 to 20 percent of the items in the highest ranks would then be candidates for the most stringent inventory management procedure (procedure A), the next 15 to 25 percent

Figure 4—1 Typical plot of subaggregates of a large aggregate inventory. Items are classified A, B, or C, symbolizing their identity with "most," "moderate," and "least" stringent procedure for managing the aggregate inventory.

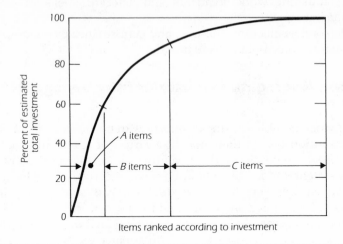

of the ranked items would be candidates for the next most stringent planning and control procedure (procedure B), and procedure C would be used for the lowest 55 to 75 percent of the items in the aggregate.

This scheme for indexing items in the aggregate implies a premium on minimizing the dollars tied up in the aggregate stock. However, dollar turnover may not be the only factor included in the cost index. Storage costs must be considered in addition to investment costs. If storage space is scarce, then stock quantities of bulky items should be carefully planned and controlled, even though the items themselves may be relatively cheap. Also, some items may require special racks, containers, and air conditioning to preserve their "shelf-life." Consideration of such storage costs may modify the results of the A, B, and C classifications that were based solely on percentages of dollars invested. Thus, the index for classifying items may be a composite of several factors.

Although this scheme offers practical advantages, there are serious disadvantages if it is abused.

First, conditions affecting classifications are always changing. A items may soon become C items, and vice versa. Obsolescence, changes in styles, or customers' preference can occur quickly, so items should be reclassified regularly.

When the A, B, and C stock classification scheme is used for retail inventories, an insidious correlation may arise between the classification assigned an item and the treatment given customers who buy it. Thus, purchasers of class A items are treated as class A customers; purchasers of C items are treated as class C customers. Such treatment may lead to illogical, undeserved discrimination against some customers. Inventory or merchandise management should aim at diffusing and improving the socioeconomic status of customers, not at making their status more distinct or rigid. Unfortunately, however, like the "ABC" stock-classification scheme, this principle of antidiscriminatory treatment of customers may be violated. Owners or financiers of real estate properties have been accused of "redlining" certain locations of homes so customers of minority races or lower socioeconomic classes are excluded as purchasers. The inventory manager should avoid such discrimination and abuse of the classification scheme.

Decision Models to Execute Purposes of Inventory

Optimal Cycle Stock and Economic-Order Quantity

Recall that the purpose of cycle stock is to assure an adequate supply of one item while its replenishment facilities are used to produce other items. This implies that the frequency of stock replenishment orders should not be so high that costs of order preparation or process equipment changes are excessive, nor so low that costs of carrying inventory are excessive.

The purpose of an economic-order quantity (EOQ) formula is to minimize the sum of two kinds of costs incurred during some extended period of time: inventory carrying costs and the costs of ordering some number of lots. A basic EOQ formula is derived from the following terms, each defined for a particular item in an aggregate inventory:

S = setup costs, including expenses for preparing order specifications; machine setup, order followup, expediting, and receiving; and costs of processing the invoice for payment. S is assumed to be a known, fixed cost per purchase order or production order.

D = demand (in units of the item) predicted for the time period (T) of the decision. D is a rate of demand presumed certain and constant throughout the time period. D is known.

c = cost in dollars per unit added to stock. If the lot is to be purchased, then c is the purchase price per unit. If the lot is to be produced, then c is the direct manufacturing cost per unit (excluding fixed, allocated, manufacturing expenses). c is assumed to be linearly related to the number of units ordered.

C_T = total cost of ordering and carrying stock

Figure 4–2 Costs considered in a basic formula for economic-order quantity.

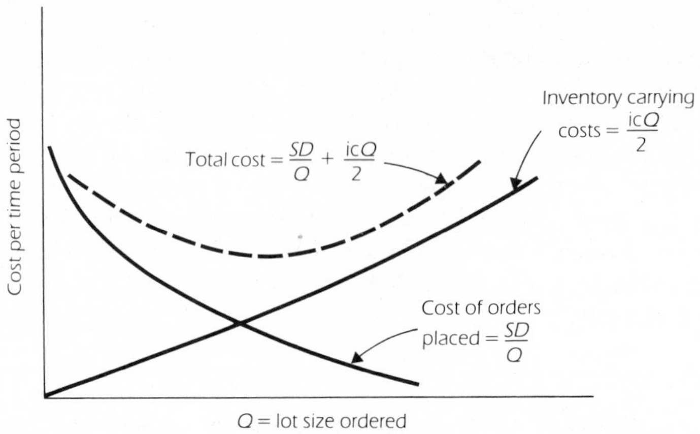

(d) = total cost with respect to the quantity ordered

i = a percentage rate of obsolescence, deterioration, and forfeited return per dollar tied up in inventory for the time period (T) of the decision. Thus ic represents the cost of carrying an item in inventory presumed linearly dependent on the average number of that item in stock during T.

Q = quantity (in units) ordered, which is the unknown decision variable. Q^* is the most economical quantity. It is assumed that there will be $Q/2$ units in stock, on the average, during the time period (T).

In addition to the assumptions given with these definitions, the time when an order will be received is assumed known with certainty, and the entire lot will be received at one delivery.

The time period (T) for the lot-size decision could be a season, a year, or even several years, but for purposes of clarity we shall discuss the problem of minimizing the setup and carrying costs in terms of one year.

Using the terms as defined, the number of orders placed will be D/Q, costing SD/Q dollars for the year. The larger Q is, the smaller the ordering costs will be for the next year.

The cost of carrying the average inventory of $Q/2$ units will be $icQ/2$ dollars for the year. The smaller Q is, the smaller the inventory carrying costs will be. Figure 4–2 shows how these costs depend on Q. The total variable cost to replenish and carry the inventory for the year, as shown in the figure, will be

$$C_T = \frac{SD}{Q} + \frac{icQ}{2}.$$ **4–1**

Differentiating C_T with respect to Q,

$$\frac{dC_T}{dQ} = (-)\frac{SD}{Q^2} + \frac{ic}{2}.$$ **4–2**

Setting this derivative equal to zero and solving for Q gives a basic formula for Q^*, the economic-order quantity:

$$Q^* = \sqrt{\frac{2SD}{ic}}.$$ **4–3**

Example: S = $48/lot ordered
   D = 12000 units per year
   i = 25%
   c = $12.00 per unit

$$Q^* = \sqrt{\frac{2(48)(12,000)}{0.25(12)}} = 620 \text{ units.}$$

Economic-Order Frequency = D/Q* 12,000/620 = 19.4 orders/year
Replenishment cycle time (interval between successive orders) = Q*/D = .052 year

According to assumptions of the EOQ formula, over time, the actual (cycle) inventory is presumed as shown in Figure 4–3. But the assump-

---

Figure 4–3 Graphic portrayal of inventory assuming constant and known rate of future demand and leadtime. The basic EOQ formula implies this inventory-time relationship.

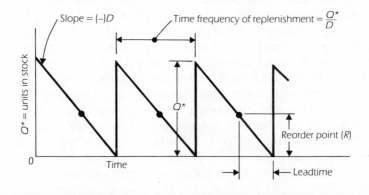

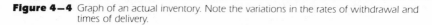

Figure 4—4 Graph of an actual inventory. Note the variations in the rates of withdrawal and times of delivery.

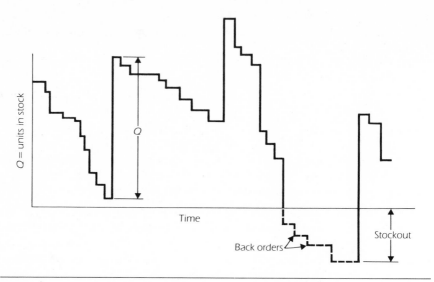

tions of constant rate of demand and certainty about the leadtime are not realistic. The actual cycle inventory is more realistically portrayed in Figure 4–4. Nevertheless, the economic-order quantity formula is useful to estimate the frequency, D/Q^*, for issuing stock replenishment orders so that ordering costs and carrying costs are controlled effectively.

Anticipating Uncertain Demand and Making One-time Only Orders

For many inventory items there may be only one opportunity to decide how much to order, because the order frequency has been predetermined by operating conditions. Examples are merchandise packaged and promoted for special, limited-time sales, items with a very limited shelf-life, or products with a quick obsolescence rate, such as fresh foods, magazines or newspapers, and high fashion clothing. Certain mobile military units (ships or aircraft squadrons) have missions that may preclude more than one opportunity to stock up on spare parts and supplies.

In such a situation, neither ordering costs nor reordering frequency is a decision criterion; ordering costs must be accepted as given by the inventory manager, and there will be no chance to reorder.

The decision criteria in this case are inventory carrying costs and stockout costs. *Stockout costs* are those losses incurred because the quantity in stock is insufficient to meet needs. Thus, in this situation, the strategy is to keep adding one more unit to the order quantity until the cost of acquiring and carrying the item equals the cost of the loss sustained if that unit is not ordered. Also, in this situation we can treat demand more realistically as a distribution of probable demands, as shown in Figure 4−5.

To formulate the economic-order quantity we need to define the following algebraic terms:

$p(D>d_i)$ = probability that demand (D) is at least d_i units. The probability that cumulative demand is *not* greater than d_i units is $[1-p(D>d_i)]$. The distribution of $p(D>d_i)$ is known.

ic = cost of carrying one unit in stock during the period of the decision. This cost and the period of the ordering decisions are presumed known.

c = cost or price of one unit to be stocked, also known.

r = net revenue per unit sold. Or, if units are used instead of sold, then r symbolizes the loss per unit avoided by having the unit stocked and used during the time period of the decision; r is presumed known.

L = loss per unit stocked but *not* sold or usable after the known time period of the decision has elapsed.

The cost of a decision to acquire and store one more unit in stock would be $c + ic + L[1-p(D>d_i)]$.

The net revenue accrued (or loss avoided) per unit available in stock and

---

Figure 4−5 Cumulative probability distribution of demands, d_i.

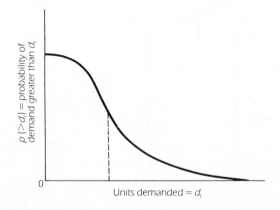

either sold or used is $r[p(D>d_i)]$. Equating marginal cost to marginal revenue,

$$c + ic + L[1-p(D>d_i)] = r[p(D>d_i)].\qquad\qquad\text{4—4}$$

Since the probability distribution is (presumed) known, Equation 4—4 may be solved for the particular probability $p(D>d_i)^*$ equating marginal cost and marginal revenue:

$$p(D>d_i)^* = \frac{c + ic + L}{L + r}.\qquad\qquad\text{4—5}$$

By referring to the graph or table of probable demands (such as shown in Figure 4—5), the number of units, d_i, corresponding to $p(D>d_i)^*$, is the economic-order and anticipation-stock quantity.

Safety-Stock and Reorder-Point Quantities

Many merchandise inventories in supermarkets or discount stores are replenished at regular time intervals determined by contracts negotiated with freight carriers, or by the economics of utilizing the firm's own trucks. The amount ordered for each delivery is determined essentially by the rationale presented here.

Figure 4—6 illustrates that, by balancing carrying costs with stockout

Figure 4—6 Inventory comprised of cycle stock and safety stock. Note the differences in the leadtime for the three orders delivered to stock.

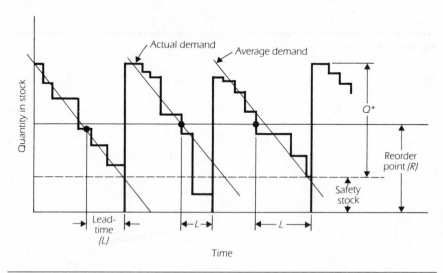

Figure 4—7 Probability density function of leadtime for orders to replenish stock.

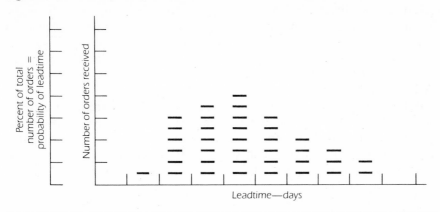

penalty costs, we can also derive the economical safety stock and reorder point and combine these with cycle stock derived by the EOQ formula.

Safety stock is an amount added to cycle inventory to reduce the effects of variations in demand, leadtime, and stockout penalties. Figure 4–6 illustrates inventory containing the components for safety stock and cycle stock. The *reorder point* (R) is that stock quantity at which a replenishment order for Q^* units is necessary. The figure shows effects of variations in demand during the leadtime, which is measured from the instant an order for a lot is placed to the instant the lot is received in stock. Stockouts occur for one or both of these reasons: unexpected, excessive delays by suppliers; unexpected, excessive demands by users (customers). Further examination of the figure indicates that a stockout is most likely to occur between the time an order is placed and the time it is delivered to stock. Thus, in the formula for determining the reorder point (R) we assume that a stockout will occur only while awaiting receipt of an order.

Estimating Probabilities of Stock Usage During Leadtime

To determine the economic-reorder point we need to know the *joint* probabilities of leadtime and stock demands. Suppose, after examining stock-order receipts, we chose a time unit of one day to measure increments of leadtime (keeping in mind that one calendar day may be different from one operating day when materials and products can be moved closer to stock). A tabulation could then be made to compile a frequency distribution of "typical" leadtimes for a series of orders received, as shown in Figure 4–7.

Data included in the sample should be somewhat selective; for example, prolonged leadtime delays caused by strikes, inclement weather, or serious accidents should be excluded. It may be that leadtime can be assumed to be a Poisson or normal random distribution. If so, the mean and variance are all that are needed to determine conveniently all probabilities of leadtimes from tables of data given in most statistics books. A chi-square (statistical) test may be used to assess the validity of assuming that leadtimes are randomly distributed. The empirical distribution may more closely fit other theoretically described distributions, e.g., log-normal, Erlangian, hyperexponential.

A similar procedure may be used to estimate the probability of demand per day. From dates and quantities on recent stock requisitions, a frequency distribution of number of days (ordinate) may be tabulated against the number of units withdrawn from stock (abscissa). Again, discretion may be necessary to question the inclusion or exclusion of unusually large withdrawals.

Having empirical estimates of variable leadtime and demand patterns, the stability of these patterns should be verified by examining distributions of samples taken from different sets of empirical data, say for distant or more recent history—in other words, to repeat the process described.

Suppose that after these studies, their leadtime and demand-rate distributions were presumed normal and Poisson, respectively, and therefore only the mean and variance parameters of each distribution were required to describe the joint probability distribution of stock usage during leadtime.* The mean and variance of this joint distribution could be estimated from the mean and variance and empirical data sampled from each. Let

$\bar{d}$ = mean stock demand in units per day or some other increment of time (T) as calculated from the sample.

σ_d^2 = variance of the stock demand distribution in units per day, presumed known from the sample of empirical data.

$\bar{L}$ = mean leadtime measured in days or another increment of time used for estimating d, as derived from sample.

σ_L^2 = variance of the leadtime distribution in days, also from sample data.

Using these terms, the mean $\bar{u}$ and variance (σ_u^2) of the joint probability distribution of usage during replenishment leadtime are:

$$\bar{u} = \bar{d}\bar{L}.$$
$$\sigma_u^2 = \bar{L}^2\sigma_d^2 + \bar{d}^2\sigma_L^2. \qquad \textbf{4-6}$$

---

* If demand rates and leadtimes are not randomly distributed, then the joint probability distribution can be derived from the sample distributions by using Monte Carlo Simulation techniques. From the sample data, random choices of demands are divided respectively by random choices of leadtimes. The frequency distribution of demand/leadtime data is thus the joint probability distribution, based on past experiences.

Figure 4—8 Cumulative probability of stock usage during varying leadtime.

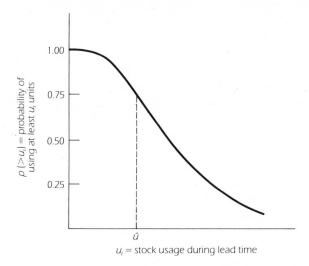

u_i = stock usage during lead time

Probabilities of usage during leadtime can be distributed as shown in Figure 4–8, which represents the cumulative pattern of variability in leadtime and stock demand each time a stock replenishment order for Q^* units is placed. This pattern is presumed stable. With this information, we can now logically determine a particular reorder point (R) or a particular leadtime (L) that will economically balance the penalty costs of having too much and not enough stock.

The problem of determining the reorder point may be stated: Given the probability distribution of usage during leadtime, what number of units should we have in stock so that, over time, when the orders for Q^* units are received, the costs of carrying this "unused" number of units will just offset the costs of stockouts? The marginal cost analysis might proceed in the following manner. Let

$P(u>u_i)$ = probability that usage during leadtime is at least u_i units. All values of $p(u>u_i)$ are presumed known and stable (see Figure 4–8); $\bar{u}$ is the mean usage during leadtime.

R = reorder-point quantity, unknown.

ic = cost of carrying one more unit in inventory for the decision period (e.g., a season or a year), known.

π = penalty cost per unit of stockout, presumed known and linearly dependent on the number of units needed but not available.

Q = units ordered to replenish stock. Q^* is the economic-order quantity, presumed known.

$\bar{D}$ = predicted demand for the decision period (e.g., a season or year). $\bar{D}$ is known.

We can calculate the costs on the basis of one order-cycle period ($Q^*/\bar{D}$), that is, from the time one order is placed until the next. The cost of carrying one unit during the order-cycle time would be $icQ^*/\bar{D}$.

We know that R depends on $p(u>u_i)$. If we decide to add one more unit to R, we may have to carry this unit for an order-cycle time. Thus, if we carry the unit and the unit is used, the cost will be $(icQ^*/\bar{D})[p(u>u_i)]$. If we carry the unit and it is not used, then the cost will be $(icQ^*/\bar{D})[1-p(u>u_i)]$.

If we decide not to carry the unit and there is need for it, then the cost will be $\pi[p(u>u_i)]$; but, if we do not carry the unit and it is not needed, then no cost is incurred.

Equating the costs of carrying the unit to the cost of *not* carrying it,

$$\frac{icQ^*}{\bar{D}}[p(u>u_i)] + \frac{icQ^*}{\bar{D}}[1-p(u>u_i)] = \pi[p(u>u_i)]. \qquad \textbf{4-7}$$

Solving this for $p(u>u_i)$ gives that probability of usage for which the costs of carrying the additional unit are equal to penalty costs of not carrying it:

$$p(u>u_i)^* = \frac{icQ^*}{\pi\bar{D}}. \qquad \textbf{4-8}$$

Referring to the known probabilities of usage during leadtime (see Figure 4-8), we can determine that u_i^* corresponding to $p(u>u_i)^*$, and u_i^* is then the economical reorder point (R).

The safety stock is the amount by which the reorder point exceeds the average usage during leadtime, that is, $R - \bar{u} > 0$.

Uses of Formulas for Cycle Stock and Safety Stock

Estimating Penalty Costs of Stockouts

For a retailer the cost of not having the merchandise a customer wants may be the profit margin per unit times the number of units out of stock. However, the customer may be nice enough to wait until the retailer receives the stock, in which case the cost of the stockout is less than the permanent loss of the profit margin. Or the customer may be irate enough to leave the store, never return, and advise friends not to patronize the retailer, in which case the penalty costs probably are substantially greater than the profit margin sacrificed, especially if the customer is influential.

For distributors, the cost of a stockout may be viewed as the costs of special handling, expediting, and/or transshipments that the distributors could have avoided if their stock had been adequate to meet customers' needs. If their customers are patient and willing to wait, perhaps these costs will not be incurred. On the other hand, if their customers are impatient, then the cost of stockout may be viewed as analogous to the retailer's stockout cost.

A manufacturer's stockout costs may include those of lost production, idle labor and machine time, extra handling and expediting to minimize delays, as well as lost profit margins on sales to customers. However, if downstream from the stock the labor and equipment can be shifted to work on some other materials during the stockout period, then these costs may not be relevant, although the cost of jeopardizing customer relations may be.

Thus, it is difficult to estimate the cost of a stockout for all occurrences during a decision period or even to suggest a practical method of making this estimate. Even if an estimate is made by one qualified expert it may be difficult to obtain a consensus from another expert.

Instead of trying to estimate or reach a consensus of informed judgments on the stockout penalty costs for each or all items, most managers have agreed to choose a stockout probability to be tolerated, or $[1-p(u>u_i)]$ for each or all items. Thus, if the stock is to be sufficient to meet usage demands with $p(u>u_i) = 0.95$ then the tolerable stockout probability is $[1-p(u>u_i)] = 0.05$.

Recall that $p(u>u_i)^* = icQ^*/\pi\bar{D}$ is that probability associated with the reorder point (inventory quantity) that balances stockout penalty costs with inventory carrying costs. If the manager arbitrarily decides that $p(u>u_i)^* = 0.95$, then, the unit stockout penalty cost can be estimated:

$$\pi = \frac{icQ^*}{\bar{D}[p(u>u_i)^*]}.$$
4—9

If such calculated estimates seem too high or too low, then different values of $p(u>u_i)^*$ can be assumed accordingly.

In practice, because of difficulties estimating and agreeing on stockout penalty costs, many managers use a single safety stock-protection probability, e.g., $[p(u>u_i)^* = 0.95]$ for *all items* of an aggregate. But, as is clear from the formula, the amount of safety stock is actually dependent on carrying costs and stockout penalty costs associated with *each* individual item, and on the frequency or interval between successive stock replenishments of each item. The effect of this practice is that safety stock tends to be higher than economically desirable for items with high frequency—and lower for items with low frequency—of stock replenishments. Therefore it might be preferable to adopt a $p(u>u_i)^* = .090$ for items with a higher frequency of stock replenishment and a $p(u>u_i)^* = 0.98$ for items with low frequency of replenishment.

Relating Q* and R

Is the replenishment leadtime for an order for 5,000 units certain to be longer than the leadtime for an order for 50 units? If so, then the economical order quantity (Q^*) and reorder point (R) are mutually dependent, and more complicated formulas are required to determine Q^* and R simultaneously. The formulas derived thus far would not give reliable results, because they presume Q^* and R are independent.

Consider three elements of leadtime (L), which is proportionately related to the reorder point (R). Leadtime consists of time to prepare the work, time to execute the work order, and time for delays associated with both preparation and execution. Preparation time and delay time are not affected by the quantity ordered. Preparation time and delay (or waiting) time may comprise 90 percent of the total leadtime, so that an order for 50 units could take longer than an order for 5,000 units. Most manufacturing and distribution operations involve intermittent processing of job-lots. The number of lots awaiting to be processed, not the number of units per lot, most critically determines the total leadtime. Products such as steel, petroleum, chemicals, and prepared foods may be processed continuously through production facilities, but intermittently through distribution facilities (trucks, ships, barges, railroads, or air freighters) as job-orders. So, in most cases it is practical and reasonable to assume that leadtime and reorder point are not affected by the quantity ordered for inventory replenishment and that Q^* and R are mutually independent.

Computer Routines

Many, if not most, inventory control systems are facilitated by computers and telecommunications equipment. Stock withdrawals are reordered (e.g., by the checkout clerk at the cash register in discount stores) and communicated to the computer, which subtracts the amount withdrawn and computes a new stock balance. The computer then compares the sum of the stock balance plus the amount previously ordered with the reorder point (R). If this sum is less than the reorder point, the computer computes the reorder quantity (Q^*) and prints a purchase or production order for inventory replenishment. Briefly, this is the routine for inventory composed of cycle stock and safety stock. If the economic-order quantity formula is not used, then the computer prints an order quantity sufficient to restore the stock to its economical reorder point (R).

Q^* and R are thus key parameters for controlling the inventory of each item. Whenever there are changes in demand, methods of supply, or costs, the programmed formulas for Q^* and R have to be changed. The work of maintaining and updating computer programs for inventory control is, therefore, significant, and should be carefully planned and controlled. For example, *A* items should be updated more carefully or frequently than *B* or *C* items.

Relatedly, a physical count of stock items should be compared periodically with the stock balance recorded in the files in order to ensure effectiveness of inventory controls. Physical counts are a most practical way to verify records or to detect and account for pilferage, damage, or other losses. The information system for inventory control must activate and respond to changes in the true, physical status of inventory. Because this statement is a truism it is often taken for granted or ignored by inventory managers. Specialists in information systems assume that specialists in materials storage and handling systems will be responsible for accurate reconciliation of the two systems (or vice versa). The operations manager must coordinate the efforts of those specialists so that the two systems remain compatible.

Computer Effects on Organization for Inventory Management   Computers and electronic data communications systems have not only automated office work but have greatly centralized the authority and responsibility structure for inventory control.

Airlines maintain a central computer file record of inventories of passenger seats on all flights. Travel agents from scores of offices operate remote terminals linked with the computer to make reservations or cancellations, thus changing the inventory status. The airline operations manager can quickly decide whether an additional aircraft should be deployed on a flight fully booked in advance of departure time.

The management of inventories at each retail outlet and central warehouse of large merchandising firms also has become centralized. The manager of each store has far less authority to plan and control merchandise inventory than before a computer was used for inventory control.

Generally, the added investment in computer and data transmission equipment has reduced not only the expenses of office and clerical personnel, but also the amount of working capital invested in inventories needed to sustain operations of the organization. For example, the Procter and Gamble Company reduced inventories of its soap and detergent division by $6 million, and at the same time improved the availability of products for customers.

But the centralization of inventory management may also result in a kind of dehumanization of business transactions, which could be costly. For instance, in responding to the customer who asks about the future availability of merchandise not in stock, the clerk or manager of a discount store can honestly say, "Don't ask me. The managers at headquarters have a computer and they, not I, control the inventory for this store." This response is true, but it is not gratifying to the customer, who is made to feel that to obtain an answer to a simple, reasonable question, he/she must talk to a computer or to managers hundreds of miles away. This is an undesirable effect on customer relations similar to the reaction of a customer who is given class C treatment, because of his/her request for an inventory item in class C.

The point is that computers and data communication equipment can so dehumanize the work of inventory management as to constrain or demoralize the customer relationships that are essential to effective business operations.

Managing Levels of Aggregate and Item Inventory

At the beginning of this discussion two points were stressed: that inventory management concerns all assets of the organization—cash, receivables (customers), facilities, materials, products, staff; and that for large aggregates to be manageable they had to be subdivided into smaller aggregates. We then considered mathematical formulas for rational determination of components of inventory managed for separable purposes: cycle stocks, special promotion stock, and safety stock.

To facilitate a policy for smoothing changes in production and employment levels requires an amount added to the *aggregate* inventory of finished products. Managers' decisions—to increase or decrease employment, to operate another shift or allow overtime, or to cut back production rates—have impact on the inventory level of *all* finished goods. Obviously if aggregate inventory is increased to facilitate a policy of smoothing seasonal fluctuations in production and employment, then the level of inventory of each item also will be increased. We know of no generalized or widely used formula for quantifying the effects on finished goods inventory of such a policy. But since costs of changing production and employment levels have been rising (e.g., because employers' expenses for unemployment compensation have been increasing) many firms are adopting policies for smoothing levels of operations. (For examples, see the cases of Home Products, Inc. and Apex Appliances, Inc.)

Still, the question of how relations between levels of aggregate and item inventory should be rationalized is profound and needs to be addressed, even though a mathematical formula is not used.

The accountant's balance sheet shows that aggregate inventory (in dollars) equals the sum of the item inventories (in dollars). But does the accountant's model of *results* mean that operations are managed that way? Operational plans are expressed in financial terms of budgets (i.e., dollars worth of aggregate inventory) *and* logistical terms of physical units of each and every kind of material or product. The question is whether the financial budget is derived strictly (mathematically) from the logistical plan, or the logistical plan is derived from the financial budget (by a mathematical allocation of budget dollars to items of finished product inventory). It is like asking whether the aggregate whole is derived by summing its given parts or whether the parts are derived by allocating portions of the given, aggregate whole. The operations manager must face and resolve this question in planning and controlling inventories. Intuition and consensus judgments remain as important as quantitative formulations are to the effective practice of inventory management.

Questions for Discussion

1. Do you agree that there is a contradiction in stressing inventory management as the holistic interdependence of all assets of the organization on the one hand, and as specialized analytical concern for each kind of asset on the other hand? Discuss.
2. Regarding the purposes served by inventory:
   a. Can you cite purposes other than the five discussed?
   b. Intuitively, rank the importance of those purposes in order of the relative amounts of finished goods inventory you would expect to be carried by a consumer durable-product manufacturer (e.g., of household appliances).
   c. Why do you think the importance of defining purposes of inventory is (or is not) of more theoretical than practical significance?
3. With reference to the discussion of "dual systems" for inventory management:
   a. Compare the educational qualifications and organizational status of specialists concerned with designing and operating inventory information systems with those of specialists concerned with designing and operating inventory storage and materials handling systems.
   b. Are authority structures and functions of inventory management usually organized so as to ensure compatibility in the design, operation, and maintenance of those dual systems? Why?
4. Discuss the strengths and weaknesses of analyzing aggregate inventory in terms of manageable classes, A, B, and C.
   a. Does the computer obviate the need for such analysis?
   b. How might these classes affect choices of stock locations for automotive spare parts?
   c. What is your assessment of possibilities that the A, B, C item classification might affect classification and treatment of customers?
5. What conditions affect the decision of whether to use the economic-order quantity (EOQ) formula for cycle stock?

Relevant Cases

2. AeroSpace Electronic Systems, Inc.
4. Apex Appliance, Inc.
9. Chicago Auto Parts Supply Co. (A)

10. Chicago Auto Parts Supply Co. (B)
11. Crown Dairy Products, Inc.
12. Duro Inc. (A)
13. Duro Inc. (B)
21. Mesa Sporting Goods
31. United Food Products Co.
32. University Book Store
33. University Physical Plant

Demand-Resource Allocation Decisions

5

There is no more important responsibility assumed by the operations manager than that of maintaining the most economical equivalence between demands to be served and resources to be utilized. That production and sales/usage rates must be equal is obvious. A firm should not produce what it cannot sell and should not sell what it cannot produce. Like many truisms, keeping the balance between changing demands and resources may be taken for granted or ignored. Production, marketing, and financial managers tend to concentrate on planning and controlling their own specialized functions. They may not coordinate their efforts voluntarily. As a result demands and resources grow out of balance. This is a most common cause of economic failure of any kind of enterprise—business, educational, governmental, health services.

Coordinating the efforts of managers or specialists is not the only difficulty in demand-resource allocations. There are problems of uncertainty in predicting demands or availability of resources. (Forecasting problems and methods are discussed in Chapter 2.) And there are problems of developing and maintaining the extensive data banks and computer programs to process the large quantities of technical and economic information needed.

Material Requirements Planning (MRP)

Demand-resource allocation decisions are based on input-output analysis. The numbers and kinds of products to be produced (outputs) are "exploded" into equivalent dimensions of specific resources (inputs). For example, if one automobile contained 1,200 pounds of sheet steel, then 100 automobiles would require 100 × 1,200 or 120,000 pounds of sheet steel. This is a process of planning and control. To the military logistician this is a matter of planning for the equivalence between military mission requirements and the kinds, numbers, and locations of weapon systems, spare parts, and staff skills needed to accomplish the mission. A municipal public works administrator analyzes roads, buildings, or sewer construction and maintenance projects in terms of necessary equivalent amounts of construction materials, hours of equipment usage and staff skills, and funds. Demand-resource allocation decisions are essential to the management of every kind or purpose of organization. However, our discussion of further details will be in terms of manufacturing operations.

According to the product and process design technologies, "fixed" information (or any technical parameter) is obtained from product and manufacturing engineering documents for each type of finished product. The product engineering documents include lists of parts and materials contained in each product. Manufacturing engineering documents consist of operation sheets, which summarize the method of manufacturing each product in terms of hours of staff skills and machine-hours by type of processing, testing, and handling equipment.

In addition, "variable" information is obtained from unit-sales forecasts or shipping schedules and latest inventory-status summaries of finished goods, work-in-process, and purchased materials inventories. We might think of these fixed and variable data in the form of lists and tables. Determining resource requirements is a matter of multiplying, adding, and subtracting the appropriate data in these lists and tables. Figure 5–1 illustrates the process for determining gross requirements in simplified, schematic terms.

To determine net (additional) resource and staff requirements for future operating periods, available quantities of subassembly and individual parts in existing inventories are subtracted from the "gross requirements."

Detailed, single parts may be stocked to supply subassembly operations, and subassemblies of parts may be stocked to supply operations to produce larger subassemblies. Thus, calculations of net requirements are needed for different levels of inventories. For example, a V-6 automobile engine might be defined at the first level of subassembly as consisting of one block, two head assemblies, two head gaskets, six pistons, six connecting rods, etc. At the next level a head assembly might be described as consisting of one machine head casting, one camshaft assembly, three intake valves, three exhaust valves, etc.

In material requirements planning, the gross requirements of like components at a given level are combined and net requirements are calculated by deducting inventory currently in stock and/or due to be received in stock before the components are needed for assembly operations.

Figure 5–1 Material and Staff Requirements Planning. A schematic illustration of a process of analyzing parts requirements in terms of expected workstation hours required to produce the parts. Measures of staff time for each required labor skill can be inferred from the data on workstation hours.

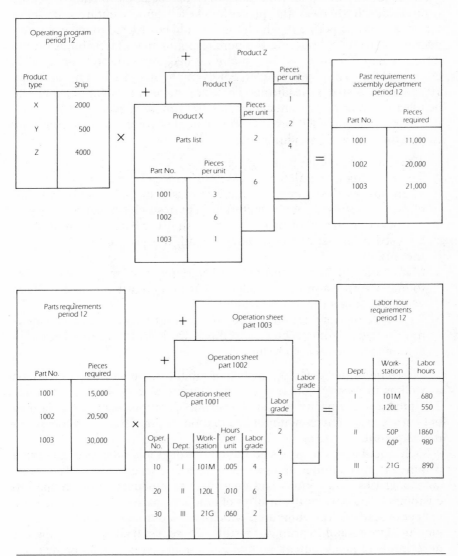

Net requirements may be adjusted to reflect economies of purchasing or manufacturing (quantity, price discounts, minimum orders, etc.) economic-order quantities (EOQ). See Chapter 4 for more details.

Net requirements (planned orders) may also be determined for specific time periods. In this way, the quantities of each component item are set in terms of the time period in which they should be ordered to meet the production plan. By subtracting the purchasing or manufacturing leadtime from the date the material is actually needed, an "order release date" is calculated for each planned order. For example, if an item is needed May 10 and it takes 90 days leadtime to produce, its procurement order should be released on or before January 8 to assure timely arrival.

Calculations for MRP become more complex when one or a combination of the following conditions exist:

1. The finished product mix is large.
2. There are many detailed parts assembled in each finished product.
3. There are various interchangeable subassemblies, or sub-subassemblies, detailed parts, or raw materials kept in stock, so that a single part is stocked in many forms for its use with other parts, which, in turn, are used interchangeably to assembly all, most, or a few products in the mix.
4. Many different "unconnected" workstations or operations are needed to manufacture a product, each requiring different hours and skills in various manufacturing departments.
5. Each type of workstation in the production or service department is multipurposed, or expected to facilitate work on a large number of operations for the mix of products.

These conditions exist in job-shop or job-lot manufacturing operations as well as in mass-production line or continuous processing operations. The productive capacity of manufacturing operations cannot be planned or controlled effectively without calculations for material or staff requirements planning.

Such calculations require a computer. Product and process engineering parameters are compiled and stored on magnetic tapes or discs. The "variable" logistics data—kinds and quantities of products to be shipped to customers, and current inventories of products, parts, and materials—are fed periodically to the computer, which is programmed to make the simple calculations and to print out results. These results define the program or schedule of procurement, production, warehousing, and shipping operations for the next time period. As changes in demands, product or process designs, or inventory control and scheduling procedures are made the computer program for material requirements planning must be changed.

If there is a *unique* set of parameters for converting outputs demanded into equivalent inputs required to produce those demands, then there is one and only one way to process a unique combination of materials into finished products. MRP converts the master schedule of products to be produced or shipped into specific materials and tasks required.

More often, however, the operations manager has a choice of numerous alternative materials, workstations, equipment, or staff skills that may be used to produce products or services with acceptable quality; or the manager has a choice of numerous products to which limited resources might be assigned. Since the time or cost of utilizing different combinations of resources may differ significantly for responding to the same set of demands, the manager should examine alternatives and choose the most economical demand-resource allocation. And there may be complex choices of many different kinds and quantities of products to be produced and shipped. Thus demand-resource allocation decisions are subjects of mathematical programming techniques, of which linear programming, to be discussed later in this chapter, is the most widely used.

In a multiechelon demand-resource allocation process whereby a finished product is made from a number of components—each of which may, in turn, be composed of several parts—the MRP system has been developed in recent years to determine the right kinds and the right quantities of components needed and to ensure that they are made available when and where needed. The concepts that comprise MRP are not new and are relatively simple. Operations managers had to deal with material requirements problems throughout the history of industrial production. As long as the product structure and manufacturing processes remained simple, planning for material requirements could be handled manually or mechanically. However, as the products and processes grew more and more complex, it became virtually impossible to keep track of the thousands of components, subcomponents, and raw materials that had to be purchased, processed, assembled, and delivered on time. Often chaos resulted and delivery was delayed. When computers became available, MRP was developed to provide material requirement information; it was an efficient control system designed to alleviate these problems.

Through the efforts of Dr. Joseph Orlicky, his colleagues, and the American Production and Inventory Control Society (APICS), MRP has received wide recognition and attention. Advocates claim that MRP, if properly designed and implemented, improves customer service, reduces inventory investment, and improves plant operating efficiency. Computer programs and software for MRP are now commercially available. However, before operations managers jump onto the bandwagon, they should be aware of the fact that the acquisition of an MRP system is by no means inexpensive or simple, nor will it guarantee success. A viable MRP system must not only be well designed, but also be carefully implemented. Effective implementation requires the full support of top management and the cooperation of the operating personnel who must be sold on the benefits of the system.

Like other production planning processes, MRP begins with the demand forecast. As we discussed in Chapter 2, "Forecasting," production forecasts are concerned with the projected requirements of components, parts, and raw materials, derived from or dependent upon the demand and sales forecasts of the finished products. Hence, the demand for the material requirements often is referred to as the *dependent demand* or *derived demand*, as opposed to the *independent demand*, which is the forecasted demand for each finished item. Since the dependent demand is based on the independent demand of the end products, the expected requirements can be calculated with relative certainty. For example, if the estimated demand for an item is 1,000 units, and each end product requires six components at a given time, then the derived demand for the component is 6,000 on or before that time.

In an MRP system, the item produced can be a finished product, a service part, or any other output item that has its own independent demand from customers, distributors, users, or other departments. Thus, the items produced in one department can be the components for another. For example, a finished automobile engine is the end product of the engine plant, but becomes one of the required components for the assembly plant. Whether an output is considered as an end product or a component part depends upon the *product structure* of the item. A product structure is the specification of what an item is made of and how it is put together. It usually involves some hierarchical order and levels. Figure 5–2 shows a tree representation of the product structure of a sample item, *E*.

In Figure 5–2, *E* represents the end product and is identified as a zero-level hierarchy, signifying that the item has been completed for shipment to the customer or the next department. Levels C1 and C2 are components, P1 through P5 are parts, and R1 and R2 are raw materials. There may be more or fewer levels in a product structure, and the components, parts, or raw materials can be either purchased or manufactured items. To plan the production of an item, the MRP system not only prescribes the amount of materials, parts, or components required, but also schedules the purchase and release of materials and parts orders and keeps track of the changes in their inventory status. A typical MRP operating system is shown in Figure 5–3.

Figure 5–3 shows that an MRP system is basically an information processing system that receives inputs from three major sources and produces a number of primary and secondary reports, orders, and schedules. It also updates inventory status and schedules.

MRP Inputs

The three key inputs that must be fed into an MRP system are:

☐ a master production schedule,
☐ a bills of material file, and
☐ an inventory status file.

Figure 5—2 A Typical Product Structure.

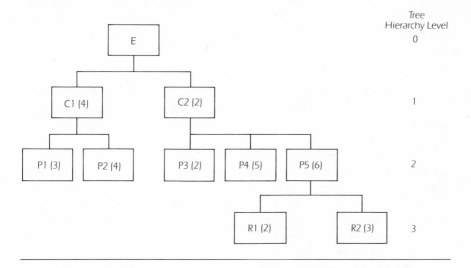

Figure 5—3 The MRP System.

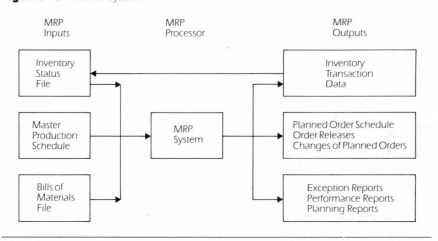

A master production schedule (MPS) is a timetable that specifies what, when, and how many of a certain item will be produced. It ordinarily contains information about:

☐ product or material identification;
☐ quantity of each product or material; and
☐ timing—due date, starting date, or processing period.

Table 5–1 A Master Production Schedule for Item E.

Week number	1	2	3	4	5	6	7	8
Requirements			50		30		40	20

The quantity of scheduled production is based on the orders received from the customer and the estimated demand forecasted. It also includes requirements for replenishing inventories for finished goods or replacement and service parts.

A feasible MPS must not violate the restrictions of the production capacity and the availability of material and other resources. The feasibility test is generally done by trial runs and by some computer subroutine checks. Once an MPS is proved feasible, it is frozen some time before the production actually begins. Although an MPS may be revised from time to time, once frozen it becomes very expensive—if not impossible—to change. A simplified MPS for end item, *E*, is shown in Table 5–1.

A bills of material, or product structure, file is a complete list of all finished products, the quantity of each material and component in each item, and the structures and relationships among them. With a complete and up-to-date bills of material file, an item in the MPS can be exploded into assemblies, subassemblies, parts, and raw materials required.

An inventory status file is a complete, perpetual inventory record of each material held in inventory. It records and updates inventory transactions about receipts, issues, scraps, planned orders, order releases, etc. It also contains such information as quantity on hand, quantity on order, lot sizes, leadtime, safety stock, and scrap rate for MRP uses.

MRP Processor

Given a feasible MPS, the MRP computer program will:

1. calculate the number of items needed for each time period, or *time bucket.*
2. add to the item count any replacement or service not previously included in the MPS.
3. explode the MPS and replacement part into gross raw materials required for each time period.
4. calculate the net requirement as follows:

$$
\begin{bmatrix} \text{net} \\ \text{requirement} \end{bmatrix} = \begin{bmatrix} \text{gross} \\ \text{requirements} \end{bmatrix} - \begin{bmatrix} \text{inventory} \\ \text{on hand} \end{bmatrix} + \begin{matrix} \text{safety} \\ \text{stock} \end{matrix} + \begin{bmatrix} \text{inventory} \\ \text{already} \\ \text{allocated} \end{bmatrix}
$$

5. order the material required, if the net requirement is greater than zero.

6. schedule the delivery due date for each material, allowing sufficient leadtime so the material will be available when needed.

MRP Outputs

The primary outputs of an MRP system are all concerned with the schedules of materials. They are:

☐ planned order schedule—a timetable for ordering materials from suppliers or other departments;

☐ order releases—authorizations to produce the materials according to the planned order; and

☐ changes of planned orders—orders to change the time or quantity previously planned.

The secondary outputs are used primarily for monitoring and control purposes. They include:

☐ exception reports that inform management about such deviations from standards as late orders, excessive scrap, etc.;

☐ performance reports that measure system performance according to certain criteria, such as inventory turnover rates, stockout rates, etc.; and

☐ planning reports that provide additional information such as value analysis, demand services analysis, etc., for future material planning.

In addition to the primary and secondary outputs, MRP also generates inventory transaction data that serve as an input for updating the inventory status file.

Example of an MRP Application

An office furniture manufacturer is planning to produce a number of Model T typewriter tables. The product structure of Model T is listed in Table 5-2.

Table 5—2 Product Structure Data.

Component	Description	Quantity per Unit Required	Leadtime Required
A	1" dia. ⅛" steel tubing	15 feet	2 weeks
B	24 × 18 × ½" pressed board	1 piece	2 weeks
C	18 × 8 × ½" pressed board	2 pieces	2 weeks
D	2" dia. plastic caster	4 pieces	1 week
E	1" dia. metal bushing	4 pieces	1 week
F	3" metal lock hinges	4 pieces	1 week
G	2½" metal screw	4 pieces	1 week

Table 5—3 Master Production Schedule.

Week number	1	2	3	4	5	6	7	8
Requirements				100			200	

Table 5—4 MRP Schedule for Model T.

Component	Week Number	1	2	3	4	5	6	7	8
A	Gross requirement				4,500				9,000
Lot size =	Available	1,500	1,500	1,500	1,500	3,000	3,000	3,000	3,000
6,000 ft.	Net requirement				3,000				6,000
	Scheduled receipts				6,000				6,000
	Planned order release		6,000				6,000		
B	Gross requirement				100				200
Lot size =	Available	50	50	50	50	150	150	150	150
200 units	Net requirement				50				50
	Scheduled receipts				200				200
	Planned order release		200				200		
C	Gross requirement				200				400
Lot size =	Available	100	100	100	100	300	300	300	300
400 units	Net requirement				100				100
	Scheduled receipts				400				400
	Planned order release		400				400		
D	Gross requirement				400				800
Lot size =	Available	300	300	300	300	400	400	400	400
500 units	Net requirement				100				400
	Scheduled receipts				500				500
	Planned order release			500				500	
E	Gross requirement				400				800
Lot size =	Available	500	500	500	500	100	100	100	100
1,000 units	Net requirement				− 100				700
	Scheduled receipts								1,000
	Planned order release							1,000	
F	Gross requirement				400				800
Lot size =	Available	400	400	400	400	0	0	0	0
1,000 units	Net requirement				0				800
	Scheduled receipts								1,000
	Planned order release							1,000	
G	Gross requirement				400				800
Lot size =	Available	2,000	2,000	2,000	2,000	1,600	1,600	1,600	1,600
3,000 units	Net requirement				−1,600				− 800
	Scheduled receipts								
	Planned order release								

Table 5—5 Planned Order Schedule.

Component Week number	1	2	3	4	5	6	7	8
A		6,000				6,000		
B		200				200		
C		400				400		
D			500				500	
E							1,000	
F							1,000	

The master production schedule for the next eight weeks is assumed to be the amount shown in Table 5–3.

With the above information, plus the inventory status data, we can proceed to prepare an MRP schedule as illustrated in Table 5–4. Note that on the MRP schedule, the lot sizes and quantities available for each component are assumed figures. In an actual situation, those would be calculated according to certain criteria or bases. Besides the MRP schedule, the MRP system also outputs a planned order schedule, as shown in Table 5–5.

In summary, MRP is a viable tool for modern production and inventory planning and control, particularly in a complex multiechelon manufacturing environment. It is expensive to install and requires use of a computer. With the rapidly declining cost of computing, its use is expected to spread. However, management must be cautioned that MRP is not a panacea. Its success hinges on the proper design, installation, and implementation of the system, and on the support of all concerned.

Introduction to Linear Programming

Linear programming is a method of allocating available resources that can be used in alternative ways to meet demands. The *simplex method* for solving linear programming problems was developed in 1947 by Dr. George B. Dantzig, a member of a research group engaged by the U.S. Air Force known as Project SCOOP (Scientific Computation of Optimum Programs). Dantzig also developed the *transportation method*, a special case of linear programming, in his attempt to maximize the utilization of ships carrying supplies to allied military forces deployed in regions of Europe and North Africa during World War II.

As the name implies, linear programming involves a series of computations to find a unique solution to a set of m simultaneous linear equations, relating resources to n demands for those resources. The unique solution sought is one that minimizes or maximimizes a linear criterion function relating unit costs or gains from demand-resource allocations.

Step-by-step trial solutions or iterations are necessary to obtain the optimal solution. Dantzig's contribution was to devise several computational rules, called algorithms, to assure efficiency in finding the solution.

Linear programming is used in many ways. Airlines use it to assign aircraft to meet traffic demands of different route schedules. Multinational integrated oil companies use it to determine the most profitable mix of crude oil inputs, tanker routes and destinations, and refinery outputs (grades, automotive gasolines, jet fuel, diesel, heating oils, etc.) demanded by different national markets in different seasons. Food service institutions use linear programming to plan nutritional menus, meet customers' tastes, and utilize available food supplies at the lowest cost. Marketing managers might use linear programming to decide the most economical assignments of salespeople to territories. In production organizations, it is a valuable tool for deciding how to minimize the cost of utilizing available materials, staff, and equipment to meet customers' demands. Corporate planners or financial managers have used linear programming in capital budgeting to ascertain the types, locations, and extent of fixed assets that should be changed in order to achieve the most profitable balance between long-term demands and fixed capital resources. These examples indicate the importance and widespread uses of linear programming. It enables operations managers to make the most efficient demand-resource allocation decisions. Since they are the *manager's* decisions, it is important for him/her, not just the staff specialist, to understand techniques for linear programming and conditions affecting the validity of their applications.

Following are descriptions of the transportation and simplex procedures for solving linear programming problems. Both procedures are simple, but tedious, so they are almost always programmed for execution by a computer. However, to be effective, the operations manager must understand applications of linear programming and control what goes into, through, and out of the computer. This is why we offer the following discussions of the transportation and simplex methods for linear programming.

Transportation Method of Linear Programming—An Example

The Jones Machine Company, a jobbing machine shop, uses general-purpose machines in a variety of work. Jobs can be run on almost any type of machine available. The information in Table 5–6 summarizes the load-capacity requirements and costs per standard machine-hour.

PROBLEM: to allocate jobs *A*, *B*, *C*, and *D* to machine groups I, II, and III so that direct machining costs may be minimized. Note that each of the machine groups can handle some or all of the machine work required by the job orders.

Assumptions.
1. Hours of machine downtime for job setups and minor preventive main-

Table 5—6 Jones Machine Company. Customers' Jobs to be Allocated to Machine Groups.

Order Hours Machine Group	A	B	C	D	Standard Machine- Hours of Running Time Available
		Cost per Standard Machine-Hour ($)			
I	10	20	30	30	50
II	10	15	25	22.50	150
III	15	10	15	10	300
Standard machine-hours required	100	50	300	50	500

tenance have been deducted from the total hours. Thus, standard machine-hours of running time are available entirely for productive purposes. In other words, for practical purposes the job orders are competing simultaneously for the machine's capacities, and the sequence in which two or more jobs might be assigned to a given machine does not affect the validity of our solution.

2. Machine costs per hour are constant and total machine costs increase at a constant, linear rate as hours of utilization are increased.
3. Duplicate sets of tools have been provided so that it is economical to set up one job on more than one machine simultaneously.

Algebraically the problem is defined as follows:

Let X_{IA} be the number of hours of order A loaded on machine group I; X_{IIB} hours of order B on machine group II, etc.

OBJECTIVE: Minimize

$$10X_{IA} + 20X_{IB} + 20X_{IC} + 30X_{ID}$$
$$+ \ 10X_{IIA} + 15X_{IIB} + 25X_{IIC} + 22.50X_{IID}$$
$$+ \ 15X_{IIIA} + 10X_{IIIB} + 15X_{IIIC} + 10X_{IIID},$$

subject to the machine capacity restrictions

$$X_{IA} + X_{IB} + X_{IC} + X_{ID} = 50$$
$$X_{IIA} + X_{IIB} + X_{IIC} + X_{IID} = 150$$
$$X_{IIIA} + X_{IIIB} + X_{IIIC} + X_{IIID} = 300,$$

and customers' requirements

$$X_{IA} + X_{IIA} + X_{IIIA} = 100$$
$$X_{IB} + X_{IIB} + X_{IIIB} = 50$$
$$X_{IC} + X_{IIC} + X_{IIIC} = 300$$
$$X_{ID} + X_{IID} + X_{IIID} = 50$$
$$X_{IA}, X_{IB}, X_{IC}, X_{ID} \geqslant 0$$
$$X_{IIA}, X_{IIB}, X_{IIC}, X_{IID} \geqslant 0$$
$$X_{IIIA}, X_{IIIB}, X_{IIIC}, X_{IIID} \geqslant 0.$$

No negative values of X will be accepted in the solution.

A Six-Step Transportation Solution Procedure *Step 1.* Set up the matrix shown in Table 5–7 for the first trial solution and assign jobs to machines.
   a. The row and column total requirements should be fulfilled.
   b. The number of assignments should be equal to one less than the sum of the rows and columns in Table 5–7. (Let the number of rows and columns in the matrix be equal to m and n, respectively. This rule then states that the number of assignments should be equal to $(m + n - 1)$. No single assignment of a job to a machine group is the *only* assignment in both a row and a column in the matrix of the first solution. These two rules are to avoid degeneracy of the computational procedure, explained later. The circled values in Table 5–7 represent the initial assignments in our demonstration problem.
   Even after following these instructions there is still a wide choice of initial job assignments to the machines—particularly in a real problem in which there are many rows and columns.
   Step 2. Transpose the costs (listed in Table 5–6) to the small box in the corresponding cells in Table 5–7. We can then compute the total direct cost of the machine load in our first solution, as shown in Table 5–8.

Table 5—7 Jones Machine Company. Initial Allocation of Customer Job Orders to Machine Groups.

Machine Group	A	B	C	D	Row Total	Row Value
I	10 (50)	0 (20)	10 (30)	5 (30)	50	0
II	25 (50) (10) (+)	15 (50)	25 (50) (100) (−)	20 (22.50)	150	15
III	15 (0) (50) (−)	5 (10)	15 (250) (200) (+)	10 (50)	300	5
Column Total	100	50	300	50	500	
Column Value	10	0	10	5		

Table 5—8 Jones Machine Company. Total Cost of Initial Allocations of Jobs to Machine Groups.

Assignment	Number of Standard Machine-Hours	Direct Cost per Standard Machine-Hour ($)	Cost Total Direct Cost
IA	50	10	$ 500
IIIA	50	15	750
IIB	50	15	750
IIC	100	25	2,500
IIIC	200	15	3,000
IIID	50	10	500
Total			$8,000

Step 3. With reference to Table 5–7, assess costs of alternative job-machine assignments.

To make this assessment, we can try shifting to other possible assignments and evaluating the cost of each shift. Examples of alternative changes in the present assignment are tabulated in Table 5–9. Note that for every hour of job *A* assigned to machine group II we save $15, relative to our solution of Trial 1.

This method is rather time consuming and cumbersome. So a faster procedure, using an algorithm, is as follows.

To evaluate the opportunities of alternate machine loads, we derive *row values* and *column values* associated with the trial solution. We assign arbitrarily a row value of 0 to row I. From this all other row and column values are determined by a rule that the *sum* of the row value plus column value must equal the real cost of the designated assignment. Thus, given the cost of $10 for the assignment in cell *IA* and the arbitrary row value of 0 for row I, the column value for column A is 10. With this value and the fact that the cost in cell III*A* is 15 we determine that the row value for row III is 5. Similarly, the column value for column *C* is determined as 10; the row value for row II is 15—thus, we derive a *unique set* of row values and column values associated with our trial solution. This trial solution may or may not be the optimum, depending upon whether an opportunity cost exists for not using alternative solutions.

To compute the *opportunity costs* of that solution we sum row and column values and note the results in cells without assignments. The values in the small boxes of the unassigned cells represent the cost (dollars per standard machine-hour) of *not* loading the machine with the job order indicated. If the cost *exceeds* the real (out-of-pocket) cost per hour of loading a job on the unassigned machine, then savings are possible. The amount of potential savings represents the opportunity cost.

Table 5—9 Jones Machine Company. Cost of the First Trial Assignment of Job Orders to Machine.

	To do this without violating total requirements, complete the following:					Results	
Alternative	Add One Hour to	Add One Hour to	Incremental Cost $/Hour	Subtract One Hour from	Cost Avoided $/Hour	Net Saving per Hour ($)	Net Loss per Hour ($)
	IIIB	IIC	25	IIB	15		
		IIIB	10	IIIC	15		
1			35		30		5
	IID	IID	22.50	IIC	25		
		IIIC	15.00	IIID	10		
2			37.50		35		2.50
	IIA	IIA	10	IIIA	15		
		IIIC	15	IIC	25		
3			25		40	15	
	IB	IB	20	IIB	15		
		IIC	25	IIIC	15		
		IIIA	15	IA	10		
4			60		40		20

To facilitate the comparisons of opportunity costs with real costs the latter are transposed from Table 5–6 to the appropriate cells in the matrix of Table 5–7, and noted in parentheses. For cell IIA the opportunity cost, $25, less the real cost, $10, indicates a savings of $15 for each hour shifted to that cell. For all other unassigned cells the opportunity cost is less than the real cost. So a shift of assignment to cell IIA is the only opportunity for cost reduction.

Step 4. Shift assignments to cell with largest opportunity for further savings, without violating the total requirements of demands and resources (indicated by row totals and column totals of Table 5–7).

Looking over the assignments in Table 5–7, we can see by inspection that a maximum of 50 machine-hours can be shifted to cell IIA. This is done by deducting 50 machine-hours from IIIA and IIC and adding 50 machine-hours to IIA and IIC. Accordingly, we can now set up the matrix for our second trial solution, Table 5–10.

Step 5. Assess opportunities from changing assignments by repeating Step 3.

(a) Establish row and column values such that their sum equals the corresponding cost value noted in the small boxes of the assigned machine loads (the circled values).

(b) Compute the opportunity costs per standard hour of *not* assigning the machine loads as programmed so far.

(c) Compare the opportunity costs with the out-of-pocket cost for each unassigned cell of the matrix. If the cost of *not using* a machine for an order is *greater* than the cost of *using* a machine for an order when a machine is not presently assigned, further improvement is possible.

Degeneracy of Computational Procedure The transportation procedure becomes degenerate when it is not possible to derive a *unique* set of row values and column values from a given set of allocations. If m equals the number of rows and n equals number of columns of the matrix, then degeneracy occurs when the number of assignments is either greater or less than $(m + n - 1)$. Degeneracy becomes apparent when it is not possible to perform Step 3.

When degeneracy occurs because of too few assignments, a value ε is assigned to the cell of the matrix to permit the computation of row and column values. The epsilon remains as if it were a real assignment until the optimal solution is reached. For example, the insertion of ε in Table 5–11 makes it possible to define the row and column values.

Table 5–10 Jones Machine Company. Second Trial Allocation of Job Orders to Machines.

Machine Group	Order A	B	C	D	Row Total	Row Value
I	10 (50)	15 (20)	25 (30)	20 (30)	50	0
II	10 (50)	15 (50)	25 (50)	20 (22.50)	150	0
III	0 (15)	5 (10)	15 (250)	10 (50)	300	−10
Column Total	100	50	300	50	500	
Column Value	10	15	25	20		

The procedure can become degenerate when the number of assignments *exceeds* $m + n - 1$, as in Table 5–12. Note that in Table 5–12 there are seven circled values instead of the required six. In this case, 10 might be subtracted from *BI* and *CII* and added to *CI* and *BII*, thereby eliminating the 10 in *BI*. Alternatively, 5 might be subtracted from *CI* and *BII* and added to *BI* and *CII*, thereby eliminating the 5 in *CI*. Degeneracy of this kind can always be overcome by this procedure.

Yet another condition for degeneracy exists when an assignment exists alone in both row and column of the table, even when the number of assignments is proper. However, this condition can be avoided by using discretion in making the initial assignment.

Our brief description of the transportation method of linear programming necessarily omits the various shortcuts in computations, for example, the "northwest corner rule" and Vogel's approximation method. But these are mere refinements of computations ordinarily accomplished by

Table 5–11 Illustration of Degeneracy Caused by Insufficient Number of Allocations.

	I	II	III	Row Total	Row Value
A		5 (40)		40	0
B	10 (10)	6 (ε)	4 (10)	20	1
C			3 (40)	40	0
D		3 (40)		40	-2
Column Value	10	80	50		
Column Total	9	5	3		

Table 5—12 Degenerate Procedure Caused by an Excessive Number of Assignments

	I	II	III	
A	(30)			
B	(10)	(25)		
C	(5)	(20)		
D		(5)	(15)	

computer, so they were excluded from this summary of the transportation method.

Now let us consider an example of the more general and powerful linear programming method of demand-resource allocation—the simplex method.

Simplex Method of Linear Programming—An Example

The XYZ Company manufactures two types of gears from round steel stock material, using automatic screw machines and gear hobbing machines. At this time the demand for these gears is so great that the company can sell all it can produce of both types. The supply of steel stock is adequate, but machine capacity is limited, as detailed in Table 5–13.

PROBLEM: To allocate the available machine capacity for the most profitable utilization.

Stated algebraically, the problem is:

Maximize $0.32G_1 + 0.40G_2$

Subject to:
ASM $3G_1 + 4G_2 \leq 5{,}760$ **5—1**
HM $5G_1 + 3G_2 \leq 6{,}480$
$G_1, G_2 \geq 0.$

Since linear programming is a method of solving simultaneous linear *equations*, we introduce two dummy products (commonly known as

Table 5–13 XYZ Company. Determination of Quantities of Gears 1 and 2 to Maximize Profits.

	Gear Type 1 (G_1)	Gear Type 2 (G_2)	Machine-Minutes Available[b]
Profit contribution[a] in $/unit	0.32	0.40	
Process specifications:			
Operation Workstation			
1 Automatic screw machine (ASM)			
in min/unit	3	4	5,760
2 Hobbing machine (HM)			
in min/unit	5	3	6,480

[a] Profit contribution = sales price − variable expenses per unit produced and sold.
[b] The machine-minutes of capacity are those remaining after the industrial engineers have deducted estimated time for setup changes and preventive maintenance during the operating period.

"slack variables"), G_3 and G_4, so that the respective capacities of the ASM and HM are fully utilized. In other words, we add G_3, which is one minute of idle time on the ASM, and G_4, which is one minute of idle time on the hobber. The profit associated with each is zero. Now the algebraic statement is:

Maximize $0.32G_1 + $0.40G_2 + 0G_3 + 0G_4$

Subject to:
$$3G_1 + $G_2 + 1G_3 = 5,760$$
$$5G_1 + 3G_2 + 1G_4 = 6,480$$
$$G_1, G_2, G_3, G_4 \geq 0.$$

5–2

Step 1. Set up the first trial solution so that resources are idle and only dummy products are produced. This is simply a matter of rearranging terms of the algebraic statement to establish the first trial solution, which is to produce 5,760 units of G_3 and 6,480 units of G_4, the dummy products, as shown in Table 5–14.

A *vertical* reading of columns has significance. For example, column G_1 means that one unit of G_1 has a profit contribution of $0.32 and is equivalent to 3 units of G_3 on the screw machine *and* 5 units of G_4 on the hobber; column G_2 means that one unit of G_2 has a profit contribution of $0.40, and is the equivalent of 4 units of G_3 and 3 units of G_4 on the screw machine and hobber, respectively. The profit contribution of G_3 and G_4 are noted as shown under column C_j.

The term *vector* refers to any row or column of the table, and the numbers in the row or column are component values of the vector. Components of the *basis vector* specify which outputs are to be produced. Components of the *requirements vector* specify the maximum quantities produced. Thus, Table 5–14 shows that a maximum of 5,760 units of G_3 and 6,480 units of G_4 are to be produced on the automatic screw machine and hobber, respectively. *Structural vectors* identify the real outputs of a program, and *slack vectors* identify the dummy outputs of the program.

Step 2. Select a new vector to be brought into the basis of the solution. To introduce either G_1 or G_2 into the current program, we must *displace all* of either G_3 or G_4 from the bases. To decide whether G_1 or G_2 would be preferable, we compare the effects on profit contribution by introducing one unit of G_1 (reading down column G_1):

we gain $0.32
but we must give up (or displace)
   3 units of G_3 on the ASM @ $0/unit, 3(0)   = 0
and
   5 units of G_4 on the HM @ $0/unit
     5(0)   = 0   0.00
Therefore, the net gain would be $0.32

By introducing 1 unit G_2 (reading down column G_2)
we gain $0.40
but we will displace
   4 units of G_3 @ $0/unit on the ASM, 4(0)   = 0
and
   3 units of G_4 @ $0/unit on the HM5 3(0)   = 0 $0.00
                                               $0.40

Comparison of the net marginal gain shows that we should bring G_2 into the solution. We designate the column headed by G_2 as the K column. This completes Step 2.

Step 3. Determine the vector to be displaced from the basis of the trial solution. The next question is, what is the maximum feasible quantity of

Table 5–14

Basis Vectors			Structural Vectors		Slack Vectors		Requirement Vectors
			G_1	G_2	G_3	G_4	
	C_i	P_i	0.32	0.40	0	0	
ASM G_3	0		3	4	1	0	5,760
HM G_4	0		5	3	0	1	6,480
	$P_j - C_i$		0.32	0.40	0	0	
				Ⓚ			

G_2 to be brought into the program? Or which basis vector—G_3 or G_4—should be *entirely* displaced from the present solution? Since we know that $1\,G_2 = 4G_3$, it follows that on the ASM a maximum of 5,760/4, or 1,440 units of G_2, could be produced. On the HM, since $1\,G_2 = 3G_4$, a maximum of 6,480/3, or 2,160 units of G_2 can be produced. We choose to displace the 5,760 units of G_3 by 1,440 units of G_2. Put another way, since G_2 must be machined on *both* the screw machine *and* the hobber, and since the ASM can produce a maximum of 1,440 G_2, we have to displace G_3 from the basis and bring in 1,440 units of G_2.

An important rule to remember in this step is that *only positive numbers* in the table may be considered. (Often the "matrix coefficients" may be negative.)

Step 4. Set up the matrix for the next trial solution. Refer again to the first trial solution, repeated here.

Basis Vectors			Structural Vectors		Slack Vectors		Requirement Vectors
			G_1	G_2	G_3	G_4	
	C	P	0.32	0.40	0	0	
'ASM G_3	0		3	4	1	0	5,760
HM G_4	0		5	3	0	1	6,480
Net marginal profit	P − C		0.32	0.40	0	0	

⒦

Because we decided to bring G_2 into the basis and displace G_3 we know that the next table should show G_2 and G_4 in the basis. So we designate the column headed by G_2 as the column K and row G_3 the row R.

For row R (i.e., the first row) of the *new* matrix, we divide values in the row R of the *old* matrix by 4, which is the index of equivalence between G_2 and G_3 and therefore $G_1 = \frac{3}{4}\,G_2$; $G_3 = \frac{1}{4}\,G_2$. Thus if the matrix coefficients in row R of the *old* matrix are designated a_{rj}, and in row R of the new matrix, a'_{rj}, then the first algorithm for the simplex method is

$$a'_{rj} = \frac{a_{rj}}{a_{rk}}.$$

5—3

The second algorithm to determine the coefficients a'_{ij} for all other rows of the new matrix is

$$a'_{ij} = a_{ij} - a_{rj}/a_{rk}\,(a_{ik}).$$

5—4

The a'_{ij} designates coefficients of the table for the new solution; a_{ij} the coefficients for the table for the old solution. The table contains m rows ($i = 1, 2, 3, \ldots m$) and n columns ($j = 1, 2, \ldots n$).

For the initial solution, HM was producing 6,480 (i.e., a_{25}) units of G_4.

Table 5–15

	C.	P	G_1	G_2	G_3	G_4	
			.32	.40	0	0	
ASM G_2	S.40		¾	1	¼	0	1,440
HM G_4	0		1¼	0	$-$ ¾	1	2,160
ⓡ	P $-$ C		S.02	0	S $-$ .10	0	
			Ⓚ				

For the next solution, $5,760/4$ (i.e., a_{rs}/a_{rk}) or 1,440 units of G_2 are to be produced on the HM. This means the hobber will produce $5,760/4$ (3) fewer units of G_4, because 3 (i.e., a_{ik}) is the index of equivalence between G_2 and G_4 on the HM. Thus, the hobber will produce the 1,440 units of G_2 and $6,480 - 5,760/4$ (3) $= 2,160$ units G_4.

All other coefficients in row 2 are determined by the algorithm of Equation 5–4.

Table 5–15 illustrates our next trial solution.

Step 5. Repeat steps 2–4 until no further gains are possible by displacing basis vectors of the matrix.

a. By bringing in 1 unit of G_1, the gross gain is $0.32.
   But we must give up

   ASM   ¾   (.40) = \$0.30
   HM   1¼ (0)   = \$0.00   .30
   _____
                    Net Gain \$0.02

   By bringing in 1 unit of other products the net gain is \$0 for G_2 and G_4 and \$ $-$ .10 for G_3.
   Therefore G_1 is vector K to bring into the basis.

b. To determine vector R to be displaced we compare the quotients:
   ASM Capacity $= 1,440/¾ = 1,920$
   HM Capacity $= 2,160/1¼ = 785$
   Since G_1 requires *both* machines we choose the smaller quotient and bring in 785 units of G_1 by displacing 2,160 units of G_4. Thus G_4 designates the row R.

c. Using the simplex algorithms, Equations 5–3 and 5–4, we establish the matrix for the next trial solution, shown in Table 5–16.

The fact that net gains are zero or negative indicates that the optimal solution is to produce 851 units of G_2 and 785 units of G_1 for a total profit contribution of \$.40(851) + \$.32(785) = \$591.60.

Simplex Method for Cost Minimization   The preceding example shows that the simplex method can be used to optimize resource allocation by

Table 5—16

	C	P	G₁ .32	G₂ .40	G₃ 0	G₄ 0	
G₂	.40		0	1	$5/11$	$-3/11$	851
G₁	.32		1	0	$-3/11$	$4/11$	785
P − C			0	0	$S - .095$	$S - .006$	

maximizing profit. Actually this is a powerful tool for a variety of applications, including production planning and scheduling, stock splitting, materials handling, plant location, and personnel evaluation. One of the most common applications among the chemical, petroleum, and food-processing industries is the "blending problem." The problem can best be illustrated by the following example.

The Nutrex Company is planning to produce a new blend of feed that will contain at least 10 percent protein and 20 percent calcium. The feed can be produced from two basic ingredients, A and B. A contains 10 percent protein and 30 percent calcium per pound, and B contains 20 percent protein and 20 percent calcium per pound. A costs $.10 and B costs $.15 per pound.

PROBLEM: How many pounds of A, B, or both A and B should the company use to minimize cost and also meet the nutritional requirements?

Let X_A be the number of pounds of A used
  X_B be the number of pounds of B used

Then: $.10X_A + .20X_B \geq .10$ Protein requirement per pound
  $.30X_A + .20X_B \geq .20$ Calcium requirement per pound
  $X_A, X_B \geq 0.$ Requirements must be positive

Simplex procedures require that the inequalities be converted into equations. To do so we need to add a dummy variable to each of the above inequations, as we did in the previous example. Since the nutritional requirements or the constraints are greater than or equal to a certain amount and must be positive, the dummy variables must assume a negative value to achieve equality. Thus,

$.10X_A + .20X_B - S_1 = .10$ **5—5**

$.30X_A + .20X_B - S_2 = .20,$

where S_1 and S_2 are slack variables. However, with a negative value of the slack variable, the final solution may also result in a negative value, which does not make sense. For instance, if both X_A and X_B in Equation

5–5 have a value of zero, then $- S_1 = .10$, or $S_1 = - .10$ in the first instance and $S_2 = - .20$ in the second, which would mean minus 10% of protein and minus 20% of calcium would be used for production. So to rectify this defect, we have to introduce an artificial variable, A, with a positive value into the equation, as follows:

$$.10X_A + .20X_B - S_1 + A_1 = .10 \qquad\qquad\textbf{5–6}$$
$$.30X_A + .20X_B - S_2 + A_2 = .20$$
$$X_A, X_B \geqslant 0.$$

Given the constraints, the objective, then, is to minimize the total cost. To do so we need to assign a cost figure to the dummy variables as well as the artificial variables. Since dummy variables imply no real materials, we shall assume their cost to be zero. Even though the artificial variables may mean the use of an artificial, nonexisting material, we should avoid using them as much as possible. Therefore, we should assign an arbitrarily high cost of, say, $1,000,000 or $M per pound to the artificial variables. Having a cost attached to each of the variables, the objective function can then be stated as follows. Minimize $\$.10X_A + \$.15X_B + \$0S_1 + \$0S_2 + \$MA_1 + \$MA_2$.

Given the preceding objective function and constraint equations, we can proceed to solve the problem with the simplex algorithm as shown in the gear company example.

Step 1. Set up a simplex table and try the first feasible solution, as shown on Table 5–17. The initial trial shows that by using a pound of A_1 and A_2, it is feasible to meet the nutritional requirement, but yields no product. So we must try a lower cost alternative.

Table 5–17

Row	Basis Vector Column		Structure Vectors		Dummy Vectors		Artificial Vectors		Requirement Vector
			1	2	3	4	5	6	7
			X_A	X_B	S_1	S_2	A_1	A_2	
	C_i	P_j	.10	.15	0	0	M	M	
1　A_1	M		.10	.20	−1	0	1	0	.10
ⓡ 2　A_2	M		.30	.20	0	−1	0	1	.20
		$P_j - C_i$	(.10−.4M) ⓚ	(.15−.4M)	(M)	(M)	(0)	(0)	

where
　P_j = unit cost of the variables in column j
　$j = 1, \ldots 7$
　C_i = unit cost of the variables brought into the solution in row i
　$i = 1 - 2$

$P_j - C_i$ = Cost of using materials in column j as compared to that of using the materials in the trial solution in row i, i.e., unit cost in column j minus the sum of the product of C_i and the exchange or matrix coefficient. Any value less than zero indicates potential savings, the one with least value or highest negative value indicates the most savings. This is just the opposite of the profit maximization problem, in which the highest positive value indicates the highest profit improvement.

Step 2. To find an alternative solution, we scan the $P_j - C_i$ row, and note that the K column 1 under X_A has the lowest value of $.10-.4M$, which suggests the most savings. Thus, X_A should be chosen to replace one of the two variables in the solution (or basis vector).

Step 3. To determine which variable to replace, we need to know which of the two variables takes less X_A to replace. From Table 5–17 we can observe that a pound of X_A yields 10 percent protein and 30 percent calcium, while a pound of A_1 also yields 10 percent protein but no calcium, and a pound of A_2 yields only 20 percent calcium and no protein. In other words one pound of X_A will replace one pound of A_1, but only ⅔ pound of X_A is needed to replace a pound of A_2 and it can yield all the calcium requirement plus ⅔ of the protein requirement. Thus, by comparison, it takes less X_A to replace A_2 than A_1, so X_A should replace A_2. We do this by (a) placing X_A on row 2 (the r row) of the basis, and (b) dividing each coefficient in row 2 by .30, as shown in Table 5–18.

Step 4. Since X_A has been used to replace A_2, it cannot replace others, so its exchange coefficient for A_1 in row 1 will have to become 0. This result can be computed by using Equation 5–4, shown in the last example.

$$a'_{ij} = a_{ij} - a_{rj}/a_{rk}(a_{ik}) = 1 - .3/.3(1) = 0.$$

The rest of the exchange coefficients can be computed in the same way. The new coefficients are shown on row 1 of Table 5–18.

Step 5. Repeat steps 2–4 until no further cost savings are possible. The optimum solution is shown on Table 5–19.

The table shows that the best solution is to use ¼ pound of B blended with ½ pound of A to produce the feed that just meets the nutritional requirement at a minimum cost that is $(¼) .15 + (½) .10 = .0875$, or 8¾ cents.

Table 5–18

Row	C_i	P_j	X_A .10	X_B .15	S_1 0	S_2 0	A_1 M	A_2 M	Req.
1	A_1	M	0	2/15	−1	1/3	1	− 1/3	1/30
2	X_A	.10	1	2/3	0	− 10/3	0	10/3	2/3
		$P_j - C_i$	(0)	(−2/15 M + 1/12)	(M)	(− 1/3 M + 1/3)	(0)	(1/3 M − 1/3)	(1/30 M + 1/15)

Table 5–19

		X_A	X_B	S_1	S_2	A_1	A_2	
.15	X_B	0	`1	-7.5	$5/3$	7.5	$-1/4$	$1/4$
.10	X_A	1	0	5	$-40/9$	-5	$1/2$	$1/2$
	$P_j - C_i$	(0)	(0)	(.625)	(7/36)	(M − .625)	(M − 7/36)	(.0875)

Summary of Simplex Algorithm. *Step 1.* Set up the simplex table and try the first feasible solution that brings into solution either the dummy variables as in the case of profit maximization problems or the artificial variables as in the case of cost minimization problems.

Step 2. Check the bottom row to see if improvements are possible. Any positive value of $P_j - C_i$ indicates a potential profit improvement, and a negative value would suggest possible cost savings.

Step 3. Replace the less profitable or more costly variable by a more profitable or less costly one.

Step 4. Recalculate the coefficients in the new matrix, and try for further improvement.

Step 5. Repeat steps 2–4 until an optimum solution is reached. When the values in the bottom row are negative or zero, the profit is maximized. When they are positive or zero, the cost is minimized.

Necessary Conditions for Linear Programming Applications

The operations manager or operations analyst should ascertain that two sets of conditions exist if linear programming is to be used effectively for demand-resource allocations. One set is essentially technical or economic; the other is managerial or organizational.

Technical/Economic Conditions *Linearity in relations between demands and resources.* The cost, gain, or amount of resource used remains the same for each unit of demand produced or served. Thus, in the real situation there must be valid linear relations between demands and resources available to meet those demands.

Units demanded or produced

When actual relationships are curvilinear instead of linear, then linear approximations may be used to satisfy the conditions of linearity. The manager should be mindful of errors in such approximations.

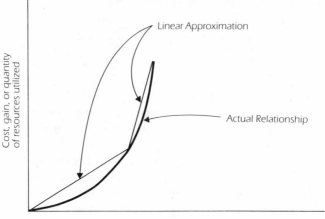

Units demanded or produced

$\Sigma Inputs = \Sigma Outputs$. The sum of resources available must be equal to the sum of the demands for each resource. In reality, there is nearly always an inequality between demands and resource availability. Thus the "real world" involves sets of linear inequations, but the linear programming model requires linear equations.

This condition is met simply by adding dummy inputs or dummy outputs as extra resources or demands, and treating each as if real, with zero cost or gain. (Recall adding dummy products G_3 and G_4 in the gear company example.)

Demands compete simultaneously for use of resources; the sequence in which one resource serves two or more demands does not affect the availability of that resource. Recall the example earlier in this chapter of the transportation method for allocating the job orders A through D to the three machine groups of the Jones Machine Company. The assumption was made that the standard machine-hours available were available entirely for productive purposes, regardless of the sequence in which a machine was used to produce two or more different jobs. Generally the validity of this assumption is questionable in every case.

Actually, the nonproductive time for changing the setups of equipment varies for different sequences of job orders: A, B, C, D, or A, D, B, C, or A, C, B, D, etc. Thus the amount of setup time and the amount of productive time *are* affected by the sequence.

Or take an example of a paint company that produces different colors of paint using the same equipment. The time to clean the equipment is greater for a change from black to white paint than for a change from white to black paint, because black pigment is dominant. Sequence does affect times for setup changes.

The question to be answered a priori by the manager is: Do different sequences for serving two or more demands *significantly* affect the availability of the resource likely to be assigned to produce several different demands? Solving several linear programs with different parameters of resource capacity may give insight to this question. If the answer is yes, then linear programming should not be used for the demand-resource allocation decision. Instead, perhaps dynamic programming (a much more complex system with less efficient algorithms) should be used. Management's judgment about this condition for linear programming is essential.

Determinism of alternative demand-resource relationships. Parameters for demand, resource availability, and for every technically feasible unit relationship between demands and resources (i.e., linear rates of usage, costs, and profitability) are known explicitly and with certainty. This condition ignores realities of uncertain variations in future demands or of resource availability. Significant variation may require that several linear programs be solved for maximum and minimum probable demands or resources available.

Parameters of all technically feasible, *alternative* methods of resource utilization should be known, a priori, in order for linear programming to be useful.

Typically, production or systems-engineering documents contain parameters for only the "one best way" (in the long run) to convert each resource into each product. Records may not contain parameters relating alternative resources to products, because those alternative methods are less efficient. However, results of linear programming are optimal and significant only if they reflect examinations of *all* technically or economically feasible, alternative uses of resources to meet demands. The parameters for those alternative demand-resource relationships must be known explicitly before linear programming can be used.

Examining the alternatives has the benefit of requiring the manager to learn and use explicitly more information than he/she hitherto considered, which engenders more prudence about how resources are used to serve customer demands.

The unit of resource (input) availability is identical with the unit of product (output) demand. This condition pertains only to the transportation method. Recall in the example of Jones Machine Company that the unit of demand by all jobs was one standard machine-hour and the unit of capacity of all machine groups was also one standard machine-hour. When such an identity between input and output units can be established, the transportation model of linear programming can be used. An advantage is that computations are more rapid than those required by the simplex method. However, with a computer to solve practical problems such an advantage is not very significant.

Managerial and Organizational Conditions   The operations manager should think of linear programming as a machine tool for producing decisions just as a new computer-controlled machine is a tool for word processing in offices or materials processing in the factory. For the tool to be effective, the operations manager should plan carefully for the organization to develop, test, evaluate, install, and maintain the linear programming model of operations. Some may argue that since a linear program (i.e., a set of linear equations) is intangible software, unlike the numerically controlled milling machine in a factory, it is too difficult to predict costs, benefits, or other effects of linear programming applications. Indeed, there are difficulties in predicting the effects of changing modes for making demand-resource allocation decisions that affect functional managers. But these should not excuse the manager from assessing technical/economic conditions or organizational and personnel changes necessary for effective application of linear programming.

Participatory Management. Staff and line management personnel responsible for demand-resource allocation planning decisions should participate in the development and application of the linear programming model for that purpose. Linear programming models are often proposed and developed by professionals (e.g., specialists in computer science or operations research) who are *not* responsible for demand-resource allocation problems that the techniques are intended to help solve. On the other hand, managers currently responsible for demand-resource allocation problems may not be familiar with linear programming. Thus many organizations contain anomalous capabilities among their own management staff: people with problems looking for solutions and people with solutions looking for problems.

Perhaps because of differences in professional groups, academic disciplines, or bureaucratic affiliations, people with problems may not understand mathematics or statistics and people with the solutions may not understand aspects of problems that may not fit their formulated models. The former may perceive linear programming as threatening to eliminate their jobs. Computer specialists may perceive "traditionalists" as impediments to scientific progress. Yet both must work together as a team, if demand-resource allocations are to be planned more effectively with linear programming.

Demand-resource planning and allocation decisions require cooperation and consensus among those responsible for managing different resources for production, distribution, transportation, marketing, finance, and accounting functions. If results of a proposed linear program are not "in the same ballpark" with results obtained from functional managers who are responsible for demand-resource allocations, then advocates of the linear program should bear the burden of reconciling the differences. After all, the survival and growth of enterprise operations planned without linear programming is *historical proof* of effective planning, which advocates of the linear program cannot claim.

That linear programming results in optimal demand-resource allocations has been proved on mathematical grounds. But these are not the only grounds for survival and growth of the organization. In summary, *advocates of linear programming should work with those in management whose jobs are likely to be affected when and if linear programming is to be applied.*

Authority for *planning* demand-resource allocation decisions usually becomes more centralized by using linear programming, even though authority for *executing* those decisions remains unchanged. If the linear programming model is developed with the participation of those who execute demand-resource allocation decisions, then changes of effective application are much greater. The case of Calnational Oil Company dramatizes this point.

A plan to develop, test, evaluate, install, and maintain the linear programming model. In developing the linear programming model, critical decisions must be made about the number and kinds of input-output parameters and relationships to be included in the model and about the means for meeting necessary conditions for linearity and simultaneity of those relationships. These judgments should be by mutual agreement between those most familiar with work processes that link demands and resources. Alternative choices should be assessed in terms of their effects on results of allocating the *entire* set of demands and resources of the system as a whole. The model should not be developed by concentrating one at a time on each isolated resource to be included in the model. The process of comparing results of the model with those of actual operations is called *sensitivity analysis*.

In testing and evaluating the linear programming model, comparisons should be made of results using linear programming with those attained by existing systems for demand-resource allocations. In general, results from the linear program should be lower (linear) costs or high (linear) profits. Existing methods may consist of intuitive, pragmatic judgments. These judgments require more time and under similar conditions they may not be as consistent as results obtained from linear programming. But greater speed and consistency are not the only virtues of decision-making processes. There should be a consensus and commitment by those who carry them out that decisions made are the "best" and "right" decisions to be executed.

In testing the model care should be taken to impute changes in parameters and to eliminate possible "bugs" in the computer program. The linear program should be operated parallel with the existing method and its results compared with those from the present system, under different conditions of demand and resource availability. The linear program should be installed only after test results are judged valid and reliable by the managers concerned. Then personnel authority and responsibilities can be changed.

In operating and maintaining the linear programming model numerous parameters need to be updated as technical and economic conditions change. Results should be examined continuously for insights to improve the model. The responsibilities for maintaining the accuracy of the model are likely to be substantially different from those for existing methods; for instance, more knowledge of mathematics and computers may be needed. These differences and job changes should be anticipated and acted on accordingly, so that morale problems during the adjustment are kept to a minimum.

Cost assessments are composed of estimates—mostly of staff and computer time required to develop, test, evaluate, operate, and maintain the linear programming model—comparing existing methods of planning demand-resource allocations with the new system. Generally, linear programming is likely to reduce management staff requirements and costs. Although such savings may be significant, linear programming cannot replace the line-management personnel required for the *execution* of those decisions.

In addition to those savings there are possible benefits afforded by linear programming in deciding the kind, location, and amount of change of fixed capital assets in order to improve overall profitability. These decisions are issues of capital budgeting. Without linear programming they are not as easily or as logically examined and resolved with explicit reference to economics of the enterprise as a whole. Such added benefits may be even more significant than those from using linear programming for routine, repetitive allocations of working capital. (The cases of Mackie Paint Company and Chemfertils, Inc. illustrate those benefits.)

Questions for Discussion

1. A new factory, a new engineering laboratory, or a new warehouse should be designed and built to suit future demands, say for the next 15 years. This raises the possibility of idle facilities and cash shortages during the early stages of the life cycle of each new facility. However, advocates have strong, special interests in expanding or improving facilities for their function.
   a. Discuss financial, technical, logistical, and organizational implications of these issues.
   b. How can they be handled by demand-resource allocation policies and procedures?

2. Discuss the interdependence of staff and functions of work-methods design and measurement and demand-resource allocation decisions.

3. The Limerock Corporation supplies limestone for steel mills from three different quarry locations as follows:

Quarry Location	Customers					Tons Provided per week
	Trucking Cost per Ton ($)					
Plymouth	6	2	5	6	6	90
Greenburg	4	5	4	4	5	53
Slippery Rock	5	8	4	6	6	60
Tons required per week	33	68	30	27	45	203

PROBLEM: Allocate quarry locations to customer demands so as to minimize total trucking costs.

4. The X-Cello Company management wishes to decide how to allocate its resources to meet its seller's market demands using this data:

	Processing Stage			
Product	#1 Stamping	#2 Milling	#3 Assembly	Profit Contribution per 100 Units ($)
	Hours per 100 Units Completed			
J	.05	.15	.40	6
K	.04	.12	.50	8
L	.06	.18	.30	7
	Productive Hours Available			
	150	400	500	

PROBLEM: Decide how to allocate the resources to meet market demands in the most profitable manner.

5. Regarding the necessary and sufficient conditions for linear programming applications:
   a. What is the meaning of the phrase, "necessary and sufficient"?
   b. Of those conditions categorized as "technical/economic," which are most likely to require analysis and judgment by operations analysts or managers?
   c. Why are those categorized as "organizational/managerial" as important as those characterized as "technical/economic"?

6. Do you agree or disagree that linear programming applications have the effect of centralizing the planning, but not the execution, of demand-resource allocation decisions? Why or why not? If this statement is true, then how does linear programming relate to the concept of participatory (democratic) management of corporate operations?

Relevant Cases

6. Calnational Oil Co. (A)
7. Calnational Oil Co. (B)
14. Foster Optical Equipment Co.
20. Mackie Paint Co.
26. NATO Hawk Program
28. Penn Electric Co.

Scheduling, Measuring, and Controlling Operations

Scheduling decisions establish the sequential order and time when products, information, or people move through processes. These decisions control the time when work resources are used to accommodate different demands. They are the essential decisions for managing work-in-process inventory. They affect the productivity of operations because they determine the quantity, timing, rate of workflow, and utilization of work facilities and methods. Scheduling decisions are interdependent with three other kinds of decisions that operations managers make: (1) to plan and control inventories (as discussed in Chapter 4), (2) to establish work methods and time standards (as discussed in Chapter 3), and (3) to allocate resources to be used for the demands to be served (as discussed in Chapter 5).

In mass-production operations (e.g., those for automobiles or home appliances) assembly-line balancing decisions take the place of scheduling decisions. In continuous processing operations (e.g., those for petrochemicals or foods) scheduling decisions are practically subsumed by demand-resource allocation decisions. Methods and resources are specialized and physically linked according to the technology of particular products of more limited variety, so that operations are scheduled at the time equipment feeds and speeds are adjusted.

Resources and facilities for most corporate operations, however, are organized and arranged physically according to their functions, so that they can be used in workflow processes to serve many different purposes or needs of customers. Thus orders are identified as jobs, job lots, or projects and separately accounted for at each processing stage. Scheduling or dispatching decisions are necessary to manage the productivity of what are often called "job-shop" operations or "job-lot" processes.

Scheduling decisions should be made so as to minimize three kinds of expenses: (1) costs of starting or completing a customer's order too early (work-in-process or finished-inventory carrying costs) or too late (e.g., contract delivery penalties, risks of loss of future orders from customers); (2) costs of nonproductive resources (idle equipment, idle staff; unnecessarily frequent or drastic changes in uses of equipment and staff), and the low employee morale resulting therefrom; and (3) costs of operating and maintaining the management information system needed to make the scheduling decisions.

Following are descriptions of useful concepts and methods of scheduling.

Master Scheduling Decisions

Master schedules establish the total aggregate production rate during a future operating period. The following equation defines the master schedule:

$$\sum_{i=1}^{N} P_t = \sum_{i=1}^{N} \left[S_t - I_t + I_{t+1} \right],$$

6–1

where

P_t = aggregate production of N products, i = 1, 2, . . . N during period t
S_t = aggregate shipments of N products during period t
I_t = aggregate finished inventory of beginning period t
I_{t+1} = aggregate inventory desired at end of period t (or beginning of period t + 1)

Master schedules also determine the frame of reference for detailed schedules of customers' orders and specific work activities.

A logical objective of master scheduling for successive time periods is to minimize the sum of costs of changing production or employment levels and costs of inventories. In other words, a logical policy for managing finished-inventory levels is to carry enough inventory to absorb interim fluctuations in shipping demands so as to reduce the frequency or amplitude of production and employment changes and thus minimize the costs associated with those changes.

During recent decades the costs of changing production rates and unstable employment have increased, for example: selecting and training new employees or transferring old employees to different jobs, payments of unemployment compensation insurance and supplementary unemployment benefits to employees who are laid off, revising contracts with suppliers of materials and services, expediting or slowing down rates of shipments, increased spoilage of materials, and problems in union/employee relations because of disruptions or changes in jobs. Unions and all levels of government have increased pressures for *stabilized* growth in employment and income because of rising costs caused by fluctuations in levels of corporate operations. Management's response has been to reduce fluctuations in employment and production levels. Levels of finished inventories are planned more carefully to sustain—but not grossly exceed—customers' demands and worker levels during periods of staff vacations, production-model changeovers, and off-season demands.

The cases of Apex Appliances, Inc. and Home Products Company describe examples of policies that smooth production and employment levels for master scheduling.

Delivery Promises

Delivery promises made to customers and reliability in keeping those promises may be as important as reliability in meeting cost quotations or product-quality/performance specifications. Measures of workflow process and cycle times indicate how much time the producer needs to add values and the amount of time the customer should expect to wait before receiving the product. Sales personnel are usually responsible for analyzing prospective customers' required delivery times and advising production personnel accordingly. Production personnel should be responsible for analyzing workflow process times and advising sales personnel accordingly. The operations manager should see to it that such two-way communications are effective so that delivery-time quotations to customers are met.

Delivery-time performance measures are likely to vary most in job-shop operations that are devoted to custom-designed products or services. One way to analyze delivery-time performance is to maintain a record of the percentage of delivery promises kept. A "kept promise" denotes a customer's order has been completed and shipped on or before a promised shipping date. The percentage of promises kept indicates the measure of reliability in meeting delivery-time requirements.

Complementing this, another record might contain the actual elapsed time taken to fulfill orders. This record would indicate workflow process leadtimes. Data might be summarized in the form of a cumulative probability distribution such as shown in Figure 6–1.

Scheduling Productivity Improvements

The corporate learning curve or manufacturing progress function illustrated in Figure 6–2 is a useful, analytical means for planning and controlling changes in productivity. It is applicable to capital-intensive and labor-intensive operations. It is based on the premise that productivity is

Figure 6–1 Cumulative probability distribution of actual job-completion times for orders issued to job-shop manufacturing activities. Elapsed times depicted in this manner might present insights for setting realistic completion dates for job orders issued by the operations manager.

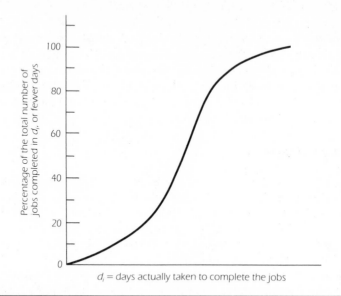

d_i = days actually taken to complete the jobs

Figure 6–2 Corporate Learning Curve. Note that productivity increases (or labor input decreases) exponentially with the organization's experience in producing and distributing a product.

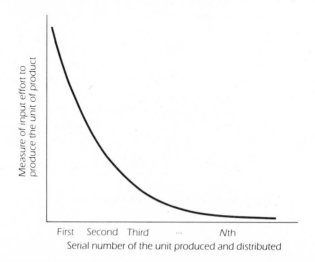

Serial number of the unit produced and distributed

improved through management-worker cooperation in upgrading worker-machine systems for corporate work processes.

For many years, psychologists have measured learning rates of individuals and groups. The learning curve measuring the corporate rate of increase in productivity was first reported by Dr. T. P. Wright in 1936.[1] Because it traces simply and quantitatively the dynamic trend of changes in productivity—while making good common sense—the corporate learning curve is an effective tool for operations planning and control.

The curve in Figure 6–2 quantifies the rate of decrease in input effort required to produce each successive unit. Analytically, the manufacturing progress function is specified by the equation for an exponential curve:

$$Y_i = y_1 i^{-b},$$
6–2

where

y = input parameter for effort required to produce the unit i of a series of products being produced without significant interruptions

  = the cumulative count of units produced. i = 1, 2, . . . , N; i measures the experience in producing the product

− b = the rate at which effort and time decrease as work experience increases.

The amount of input effort continues to reduce logarithmically, depending on the value of $-b$. The corporate learning curve is identified by the percentage rate of progress as the production count is doubled; for example, an 80 percent progress rate, a 70 percent progress rate, or a 72 percent progress rate. The progress function is usually characterized by the relative amount of reduction in input effort when the cumulative number of units completed has doubled, in other words, when $i_2 / i_1 = 2$. Thus, for an 80 percent progress curve, $b = 0.322$ because $2^{-0.322} = 0.80$. An 80 percent progress curve means that labor costs (or hours) for the fourth unit are 80 percent of the labor hours for the second unit; the labor costs for the eighth unit are only 80 percent of that for the fourth unit, and so on.

For convenience, the curve is transformed into a straight line by plotting it on log-log graph paper and by rewriting Equation 6–2 in terms of logarithms:

$$(\log y_i) = (\log y_1) - b(\log i).$$
6–3

The greater the absolute value of b (and the smaller the nominal percentage progress rate), the steeper the curve slopes downward. Knowing (or presuming) the coordinates of one point (y_i, i) and the progress rate (or slope) enables a plot of the increase in productivity.

Each succeeding unit of output produced and its total direct labor hours expended may be plotted more conveniently as a straight line on log-log

1. T. P. Wright, "Factors Affecting Costs of Airplanes," *Journal of Aeronautical Sciences*, Vol. 3, No. 4 (February 1936), pp. 122–28.

graph paper. Or the cumulative average direct labor hours (or cost) may be plotted.

Studies of empirical data (production count and direct expenditures of labor hours or costs) have revealed corporate learning curve patterns in the manufacture of aircraft, radar equipment, ships, and cameras. Corporate learning curves are especially useful in planning and controlling productivity changes during the startup phase of new production programs. During this debugging period, opportunities for improving work methods are usually most numerous and significant. The corporate learning curve is useful as a planned progress path for managing improvements in work standards.

The corporate learning curve is useful in many ways: as a basis for specifying price and delivery terms of production contracts for complex systems (it is widely used in procurement-production planning for military and civil aircraft), for scheduling the employment and training of staff, or in the buildup of material delivery rates or product completion dates. (During World War II when workers were in short supply, the corporate learning curve was used by the federal government to assure equitable assignments of staff among airframe manufacturers.) It is also used to decide corporate strategy in competing with other firms' "corporate experience" with productivity growth and shares of markets. The case of "Foster Optical Equipment Company" contains a detailed account of how one company used the corporate learning curve.

Priority Rules for Real-Time Scheduling or Dispatching Decisions

Scheduling decisions are made in "real time," that is, whenever necessary to answer the question: Which one of several job orders should be assigned next to a workstation? Such a pragmatic approach to scheduling is preferable because the cost of trying to predict far into the future which orders will be assigned to particular workstations is too great and the validity or reliability is too low. Following are typical priority rules for choosing from among several jobs awaiting dispatch to a given workstation:

☐ First come, first served. The first job to arrive at the dispatcher's desk is given the highest priority; priorities of other jobs are ranked according to their order of arrival.

☐ Earliest due date. The job with the earliest completion date for shipment to customer is assigned the highest priority. This rule emphasizes the importance of fulfilling delivery quotations to customers.

☐ Largest number of operations remaining. The higher the number of remaining operations, the higher the priority assigned the job.

☐ Shortest setup change time for preparing the workstation. This rule emphasizes need for minimizing nonproductive "downtime" for changing workstations from one job to the next.

□ Discretion of the employee in charge of the workstation. The worker selects the next job according to his/her attitudes about job difficulty, job pay rates, etc.

Note that in order to be expeditious and simple, each rule emphasizes one of several criteria pertinent to scheduling or dispatching decisions. The choice of rules is an issue for operations managers to decide for their own situations. Although such rules have been tested using computerized simulation models, there is no general conclusion from comparison of results. It is generally agreed that consistent use of one rule is preferable, however.

Of course, there are occasions when a rule has to be violated, perhaps because of unusual pressures for expediting job orders. However, priority scheduling or dispatching rules have proved their effectiveness.

Measurement and Control of Operations

In Chapter 3 we emphasized that value added by production operations are measured in three kinds of dimensions: quality, availability, and costs. Accordingly, the manager must constantly measure operations, compare actual results with planned results, and take necessary actions to control their divergence. This is an essential challenge of operations management. For in the process of measurement and control the manager is likely to encounter conflicts of both technical-economic and sociopolitical significance to the organization and his/her career.

There is a question of different requirements and capabilities of management information systems (MIS) for measuring and controlling operations. For a given workflow process the most desirable choices of speed, accuracy, or process stages are not the same for taking and recording measurements of quality, availability, or cost. These latter aspects of production are organized and managed separately. The financial controller coordinates systems for budgets and actual expenditures; the materials or logistical manager is concerned with schedules and inventories; the director of quality control and safety needs to weigh these factors in measuring operations of the same workflow process. Their procedures for taking measurements, for comparisons of results with plans or standards, and for actions based on those comparisons may disrupt workflow, seriously and sometimes needlessly.

Consider two examples. If deviations from product or process quality standards raise hazards of consumer or employee safety, then the manager needs to know and act much more quickly about the quality than about the cost or availability of the operation's results. Therefore, the MIS for quality management may require higher capabilities of speed, sensitivity, and accuracy than the MIS for measuring performance with respect to costs or schedule.

An effective MIS for financial control must collect and convert data on consumption of materials, energy, and services into dimensions of money and time; it must also summarize and compare those actual expense data with budgetary standards. This takes more time than needed by an MIS for measuring and controlling performance with respect to standards of quality or schedule. Thus, although three different systems may be needed for measurement and controlling operations, the systems are generating redundant quantities of information about the same resources, stages, or results of the manager's workflow processes. If the manager is not prudent about choosing computers, systems analysts, etc., costs of the MIS may exceed costs of the workflow processes to be controlled.

There is often a conflict about the significance of quality, availability, or financial measurements, as illustrated by our second example.

A production/operations manager concluded that her department would have to work overtime so that orders being processed would not fall behind schedule. But overtime operations would mean a 50 percent increase in hourly labor costs. Thus she faced a conflict in managing operations: Is operating on schedule more or less important than operating within budgeted expenses? If her supervisor informed her of customers' penalties for late deliveries, she might compare these with excessive expenses from overtime operations and choose the lesser penalty. But even under such conditions, there is uncertainty about probable loss of future business even if late delivery penalty is paid in order not to exceed the budget. Her dilemma may be even more complicated if she were led to believe her performance as a manager (hence her eligibility for promotion, bonus, etc.) would be judged more on the basis of the financial budget than the schedule issued for operations.

In an immediate situation or for a particular customer, supplier, or employee, the quality of resources or products may be far more important than their availability or costs. But in the long run, all are of equal importance to the growth in efficiency, productivity, or profitability of corporate operations. Moreover, there has to be a consensus among the growing numbers of customers, suppliers, and employees about the *combination* of quality, productivity, and cost standards to be upheld. Yet, because profits seem to be the bottomline concerns of top management, there may be pressures to overemphasize financial measurements and control. These pressures can be so great as to impede efforts to measure and control the quality or availability of resources or products.

For example, some companies liquidate portions of work-in-process inventories in order to raise cash for quarterly payments of dividends or income taxes and to avoid financial (interest) costs of borrowing the necessary cash. But the costs of disruptions in material and product flow to customers and consequent loss of employee morale and productivity—all caused by the decision to liquidate work-in-process inventories—may be much greater than the interest costs of bank loans of the cash for dividend and tax payments.

Such obsession with finances and neglect of quality and delivery capabilities or results of corporate operations are not trivial matters. Responsible critics have alleged that they are important reasons why productivity, market shares, and employment of American manufacturers declined steadily during the 1970s.[2] The production/operations manager can exert a crucial role in efforts to sustain a balance of efforts to plan and control the quality, productivity, and cost of corporate operations. Case 2, Aero-Space Electronic Systems, Inc., illustrates this point.

Questions for Discussion

1. Discuss the significance of the following statements:
   a. Scheduling and controlling corporate operations significantly affect policies and procedures for managing inventories of purchased materials and finished products, and vice versa.
   b. Scheduling decisions can assure that products or services are delivered on time only if resource capabilities (staff, materials, machine-hours available) have been maintained at a level equal to or greater than their demands.
2. With specific reference to productivity management, why are operations scheduling decisions as important as work-methods design decisions?
3. In light of the fact that scheduling decisions are interdependent with material requirements planning decisions and work-methods design decisions, discuss problems of assigning responsibility for controlling costs affected by scheduling decisions.
4. Why have costs of changing levels of procurement, production, and employment been increasing steadily for American firms? Would you expect those costs to be as high in some U.S. firms and most Japanese firms that guarantee employment and income security?
5. In scheduling operations and controlling inventories the workflow process cycle-time period is important. In financial planning and control a calendar-time period (period between successive comparisons of budgeted and actual expenses, P&L statements, etc.) is important. If these two cycle-time periods are of different duration or are nonconcurrent, what are the likely effects on managing corporate operations?
6. Do you agree that the corporate learning curve reflects the effectiveness of participatory corporate operations management? Discuss.

---

2. For example, see *Business Week Magazine*, special issue on the "Reindustrialization of America," June 30, 1980.

7. Why is it preferable for a manager to use one, consistent rule for dispatching jobs to workstations?

8. What is indicated from a comparison that indicates costs of acquiring, operating, and maintaining the MIS exceed the costs of acquiring, operating, and maintaining the workflow process? Is such a comparison likely to be realistic? Why or why not?

9. Why do financial management decisions often take precedence over operations management decisions in planning and controlling the work of organizations?

Relevant Cases

2. AeroSpace Electronic Systems Inc.
4. Apex Appliance, Inc.
11. Crown Dairy Products Co.
12. Duro, Inc. (A)
13. Duro, Inc. (B)
15. Home Products, Inc.
20. Mackie Paint Co.
26. NATO Hawk Program
32. University Book Store
33. University Physical Plant

Governmental, Industrial, and Multinational Operations

Operations managers, like all professionals, need a holistic perspective on the evolution and environment of their practice. Growth of productivity, profitability, or efficiency of operations of their organizations affect operations of government. The security of government depends on policies for stabilized growth in employment and income opportunities for growing populations. And growth of governmental operations affects operations of private-sector organizations. Procurement, production, and distribution of products and services have expanded the scope and intensified pressures for interdependence to a global scale. Actions of governments of the oil producing and exporting countries (OPEC) have dramatized the impact of *multinational* governmental-industrial operations because they affect the energy needed by developing, as well as industrial, nations.

In previous chapters we have tried to balance our discussions of problems with discussions of concepts or methods the manager can choose to resolve or control those problems. Our aim in this concluding chapter is to suggest problems or issues not entirely controllable by the operations manager, and which are as yet far from resolved. We raise such issues because we are convinced that the production/operations manager can make an important contribution to the means for their control; and that those issues are of growing significance to the practice of operations management.

Planning and controlling procurement-production-distribution operations are subject to a combination of political-legal forces of government and socioeconomic forces of the marketplace. Thus, operations managers practice their profession at a confluence of important issues affecting relations of government and industry: development and application of science and technology; exploitation and conservation of nonrenewable natural and human resources; hazards of products and processes to human and environmental health; and processes for the production and distribution not only of products, but also of shares of political and economic wealth, as well as military power, derived from those processes.

There is no conflict about the need for growth in efficiency, productivity, or profitability of operations. But there are growing conflicts between ideologies of socialism and capitalism or between alleged evils and virtues of growth in the power of industry or government. Whether they manage functions of research and development, procurement, production, or distribution, the operations of government and industrial firms are interdependent. Relations may be mutually cooperative or competitive, stimulative or responsive, friendly or antagonistic. Government may restrict or enhance the growth of industry, and vice versa. There are so many examples of such interdependence only a few can be highlighted here.

Governmental-Industrial Programs

There is the agribusiness complex consisting of government, industry, and universities, to research, develop, produce, and distribute foods and fibers more efficiently and effectively throughout America than ever before. Its growth in productivity caused a demographic transformation of America from a rural to urban society in less than 100 years. Results are profound. Today 5 percent produce and distribute more agricultural products than were produced by 40 percent of Americans in 1900. American farmers used to be considered stereotypes of provincial national isolationism and economic conservatism; they are now among the strongest advocates of expanding multinational operations of government and industry and more liberal terms for trade with communist or developing nations. Central cities of the U.S. are heavily populated by displaced farm workers of minority races who encounter difficulties with employment, housing, health, education.

In the areas of transportation the interdependence in growth of governmental and industrial operations has also been strong. The construction and maintenance of highways, airports, and waterways by government have matched the development, production, and uses of automotive and aircraft equipment. These, too, have had profound effects, especially on energy consumption. The U.S., with about 6 percent of the world's population, consumes about 30 percent of the total petroleum resources used. Middle- and upper-income families have abandoned cities for the sprawling suburbs. The decline in facilities and use of rail transportation may be attributed to complementary policies of industry and government that encouraged automotive transportation. Because of increasing energy costs, we now see mass (rail) transportation systems being improved.

The U.S. military-industrial establishment has developed scientific specialties and technology and expanded the international operations of government, industry, and higher education. Its products and services have not only helped to ensure the defense security of Western democracies but, via technological "spinoffs," created the era of aerospace travel, computers, satellite communications, and nuclear energy. Since President Eisenhower warned in 1959 of the consequences from too much power vested in the military-industrial complex, its role has been controversial. Of necessity, its operations have been cloaked in secrecy, which has inhibited assessment and open debate about the "good" and "bad" results of those operations. There have been cost overruns, late deliveries, and faulty performance of equipment. Market, economic, and competitive forces have to be ignored because our armed forces cannot risk a loss of supply source when contractors fail to compete. Yet, defense contracts have helped industrial development and employment. Arms exports are important avenues of sales and profits of U.S. contractors and play a big role in foreign affairs of our government. Experiences in weapon systems acquisition programs for military security set precedents that are very useful in planning, organizing, and controlling operations of government-industry-educational programs against national and global hazards. Outgrowths have affected health, environmental pollution, shortages of energy and other materials, and the development and exploitation of resources of the seas.

Multinational Operations

Prior to World War II few American operations managers thought in terms of international operations and interdependence. They were preoccupied mostly with growth of operations to serve the vast North American market. Unlike their European or Japanese counterparts, they did not have to rely as much on foreign countries for supplies of energy or industrial materials or for sales revenues from foreign customers. Most European firms conducted multinational operations, even though they were of modest size compared with counterpart U.S. firms.

However, events after World War II prompted a large number of American companies to make irrevocable commitments to multinational markets.

When the Bretton Woods Agreement of 1945 established the U.S. dollar as the standard reserve currency for trading nations, Americans expanded their involvement in international financing. A few years later, the Marshall Plan and the establishment of NATO were the impetus for large exports of U.S. equipment and American technical and managerial know-how to help rebuild European and Japanese industries that had been destroyed in the war. The European Common Market made it desirable for U.S. companies to establish manufacturing operations in Europe so they could take advantage of the rapid, coordinated economic growth within the West European community. NATO prompted American defense contractors to expand their export sales and service operations. After European industrial capabilities were restored, U.S. and European defense contractors and governments conducted cooperative NATO defense systems acquisition and production programs. See Case 26 for details.

Typically, multinational operations of a company grow in stages. The first stage is to export products and to depend on indigenous importers to manage distribution operations in foreign countries. When sales have grown sufficiently, the company takes over the management of marketing activities, often by acquiring the importing firm initially engaged. Growth in marketing means growth in product maintenance services for customers; such growth leads eventually to the establishment of manufacturing facilities in foreign countries.

However, multinational operations do not evolve solely and smoothly on terms established unilaterally by managers of the firm. As suggested earlier, governments have become more active—even aggressive—in executing policies for industrial growth and full employment. Accordingly, governments provide incentives (e.g., tax abatement, financing for land and factory buildings, staff recruitment and training services) to encourage foreign manufacturers to operate factories in their countries. Or they may penalize (i.e., revoke import licenses or invoke import fees, quotas, or tariffs) companies who decline to establish and operate factories in their country. Initially, manufacturing is confined to final assembly operations. But government influence and market or economic conditions may require more fully integrated operations, including procurement and processing of materials into component parts.

Thus, national governments often exert great influence on American operations managers' decisions affecting changes in the timing, size, location, and growth of plant facilities and staff to serve international markets. In some instances it seems as if national governments compete with each other to attract investment and growth of industry, employment, and income from international trade. This is, of course, similar to measures taken by different communities and states within the U.S.—but within the U.S., industrial firms are held accountable in accordance with a uniform set of laws or regulations.

Impact of National Governments and Customs on Operations Management

Meanwhile, operations managers abroad contend with significant differences in governments' policies, laws, or regulations affecting taxes, tariffs, export or import licenses, wages, employment and working conditions, union-management relations, financial accountability, liability for safety and health hazards of products or processes, and environmental pollution control. Cultural differences are also significant, for example: public support for education and development of professional skills, mobility of employees and families, roles of women in commercial/industrial affairs, language, and customs regarding fees or bribery payments. In Italy, instead of working for an eight-hour shift without interruption, employees take a midday siesta of several hours. The German government prohibited transport of explosives by railroad, while the Italian government prohibited transport by truck; this caused some difficulty in operations of the NATO Hawk missile system production program. In Germany, companies with more than specified sales or number of employees are required by law to place labor union members on their boards of directors.

Because of such differences, multinational operations managers' decisions to change facilities or sources of supply or to adjust levels of inventories, employment, and products often provoke strong criticisms. For example, complaints include exporting jobs to other countries with lower pay scales; tax payment avoidance; and exportation of capital badly needed in one country to another country because of unfair transfer prices charged by one operating division to another operating division (e.g., by a production unit to a refining or marketing unit of a multinational integrated oil company). Critics have alleged that the U.S. government was forced to devalue the dollar in terms of the price of gold and other major currencies, because of pressures created when U.S. multinational companies transferred billions of their Eurodollars into Swiss francs or German marks. Occasionally there have been suspicions or even antagonistic feelings between multinational industrial operations managers and officials of national governments.

A major difficulty stems from the fact that national governments are sovereign powers. There is no higher authority than the authority each government exercises under its own laws, which reflect political and cultural customs and values of each nation. At the same time, however, multinational companies possess powers to develop and distribute capital; increase technology; and plan and control production and distribution of products, services, jobs, and income across national boundaries. The rate of growth of multinational companies far exceeds the growth rate of gross national product (GNP) of many industrial nations. Annual sales of single companies (e.g., General Motors or Royal Dutch Shell) exceed the GNP of Switzerland or Venezuela. International powers of multinational companies and national powers of governments sometimes conflict.

One American office equipment manufacturer accepted a government offer of liberal financing to build a factory in France. The company moved production equipment into the government-financed building and hired and trained 1,500 employees. Within a year, the company decided to close the factory. Together with its plants in Scotland, Germany, and the U.S. the French factory was producing more office equipment than could be sold. In response to the company's decision, the French government not only harassed the manufacturer's efforts to find other jobs for employees laid off, but it refused for years to purchase office equipment and products of other divisions operated by that manufacturer.[1]

Consonance between political-economic operations of government and production-distribution operations of multinational companies is not easily maintained. Governments may take advantage of differences in management of different companies, and multinational companies take advantage of differences in policies of different governments. A result is that on some occasions governments compete with each other to gain the favor of multinational firms; on other occasions, multinational firms compete with each other for favorable decisions of governments. And there have been many complaints that government regulations interfere with growth in profitability or productivity of industrial operations.

On the other hand, harmony and cooperation between industry and government have increased substantially. Governments provide strong support to the expansion of multinational corporate operations. By way of foreign policy and diplomatic actions, or by extending tax privileges or export subsidies, financial credit guarantees the Japanese, West German, and French governments supported expansion of marketing and production operations of industries for shipbuilding, steel, automotive and electronic equipment, and nuclear power equipment. They are formidable competitors of U.S. firms operating in those markets with, perhaps, less support from the U.S. government. The Food for Peace program, Export-Import Bank, and Overseas Private Investors Corporation of the U.S. government provide support for exports by U.S. firms. The British and French governments financed the development and operations of the Concorde supersonic transport aircraft. (After spending several billions of dollars the U.S. government gave up its support of the American supersonic transport program.) The U.S., British, and French governments promote export sales of about $15 billion annually for arms to nonaligned governments in Asia, Latin America, Africa, and the Persian Gulf. Purposes have been to strengthen the military security of recipient governments and to spread the soaring development and production costs of tanks, fighter aircraft, or missile systems among a larger number of governments.

Events during the 1970s have indicated that governments of industrialized nations need to be more cooperative if the growth of multinational industrial operations is to continue.

The OPEC cartel placed an embargo on oil shipments, and within five years increased their oil prices 500 percent, making it clear that Western

---

1. R. E. McGarrah, "Logistics for the International Manufacturer," *Harvard Business Review* (March–April 1966), p. 154+.

governments of oil-consuming countries need to unite in stronger policies affecting energy consumption, conservation, development of alternative sources, and environmental pollution. There has been a vast increase in flow of Western currencies to OPEC nations and more uncertainty about how OPEC governments will use those currencies needed for Western industrial operations.

Threats of radiation hazards and of proliferation of materials for nuclear weapons have increased pressures for more stringent controls of technology and equipment for nuclear power.

Governments of Third World nations are acting together to demand a "new international economic order" to help close gaps between "rich nations and poor nations." Outward migrations of skilled people, scarce capital, and the inflationary cost of Western products have seriously hampered development. Yet industries in developed countries need materials such as copper, tin, aluminum, uranium, and chromium from those nations. And Third World nations need capital and professional know-how from the industrialized countries.

The increasing migrations of workers from Asia, Latin America, Europe, and North America and the increasing investments by European, Japanese, and American firms to build more factories in Latin American and Asian countries may be transforming the nature of operations management in developing and industrialized countries. Americans, Japanese, and Europeans are likely to become more involved with producing and distributing information and services (i.e., research, development, and maintenance or regulation of high-technology systems) while Latin Americans (especially Brazilians or Mexicans) or Asians (Koreans, Taiwanese, Philippinos) become more involved in manufacturing steel, aluminum, copper, automobiles, textiles, electronic products, etc. Lower labor and energy costs in countries like Mexico, Venezuela, or Indonesia and higher costs and educational levels of labor in the U.S., Japan, and Western Europe are an impetus for this transformation.

Costs of research, development, and maintenance of high-technology systems needed for *all civil and military* improvements have escalated beyond the resources of single nations—think of aerospace satellite communication systems, surface mass-transportation systems; weather and pollution detection systems; control of fusion processes for energy; and weapon systems for military security.[2] To develop and produce the next generations of transport aircraft that will operate during the 1980s and beyond, American companies are cooperating with government-controlled counterpart companies of the United Kingdom, France, and Japan. The U.S., Norwegian, Danish, Belgian, and Dutch governments formed a cooperative program to fund, produce, and export F-16 tactical fighter air-

2. R. E. McGarrah, "Let's Internationalize Defense Marketing," *Harvard Business Review* (May–June 1969), pp. 146–55; "An Assessment of A Policy for U.S.–Allied Military Industrialized Cooperation," *Defense Management Journal* (September 1978), pp. 36–41.

craft, thereby creating employment in each member country and a multinational market estimated at $15 billion during the period 1975–85.

Under the auspices of the United Nations, all member governments have been cooperating to reach common agreement on a "law of the seas." Such a law will provide a uniform, consistent set of rules for managing the exploitation, conservation, processing, and distribution of minerals, food, and petroleum resources for the benefit of *all* nations. These laws will affect the deep-sea mining of globules containing rich concentrations of manganese, copper, and nickel; food; and other resources of international waters.

These are only brief citations of many reasons why the operations manager should be aware of governmental-industrial-multinational interdependence.

The growth of international business and industrial operations feeds and is fed by a kind of peoples' international revolution of rising expectations from science, technology, and management of economic and natural resources. Since this revolution transcends limits of ideological, cultural, or geographical boundaries, industrial growth is likely to continue. But whether growth will be steady and peaceful is the question. Obviously, managers of industrial and governmental operations exert key roles. Future industrial growth requires more prudent use of limited global resources and more equitable distribution of wealth produced by industrial processes so there can be more peaceful interdependence among all societies.

Questions for Discussion

1. Why is it practical and desirable (if not necessary) for the operations manager to maintain a perspective and awareness of the interdependence of governmental, industrial, and multinational operations?
2. Discuss implications of the industrial revolution and the ethics of growth.
   a. Must operations of an organization grow if the organization is to retain its identity in relation to others? Is "do or die" competition effective or necessary?
   b. What have been the effects on gaps and relations between rich and poor *within* industrial societies and between industrial and developing nations?
3. Cite concrete examples of relations between industrial and governmental operations that are essentially:
   a. adversarial, competitive, antagonistic.
   b. complementary, mutually reinforcing.
4. How do results of growth of military-industrial operations affect the growth of civil-industrial operations? Do they tend more to conflict

than reinforce each other? Compare the U.S. with Japan and West Germany in this respect.

5. Why should operations managers be aware of possible effects of their decisions on conflicts of political, economic, moral, or ecological values?

Relevant Cases

4. Apex Appliance, Inc.
5. Berkeley Savings and Loan Association
17. Land Use Management
18. Lordstown Plant of General Motors (A)
19. Lordstown Plant of General Motors (B)
26. NATO Hawk Program
30. United Food Products Co. (A)
31. United Food Products Co. (B)

Productivity
Management
Cases

Preface
to Cases

Although organization or company names have been disguised, most cases in this book describe actual situations affecting productivity management. Problems to be defined and resolved are more apparent in some cases than others. But in every case there is a challenge for the student to define and resolve issues in terms of their effects on corporate operations as a whole.

In almost every situation it is easy to conclude that there is insufficient information in the narrative or exhibits to decide what actions the company's management should take. But this is true for almost every real situation; no manager has all the information he/she would like to have about past, present, or future conditions. Often there is neither time nor available resources to obtain the information. So the operations manager must interpolate, extrapolate, or make assumptions using information drawn from relevant experiences and from facts given in the case. It may be helpful to project yourself emotionally as well as intellectually into the role of a key manager before deciding what actions the firm should take. A decision grounded on technical, economic, or legal principles pertinent to a case might conflict with a decision based on moral or ethical principles equally pertinent to that case. Thus, there may be no single best solution. The best decision and the consequences that one manager must live with (e.g., to defend or to convince peers, superiors, or subordinates to support its execution) may not be the best decision for another manager. Nor is the best decision determined by that course of action preferred by a majority of those discussing the case.

The test of the manager's understanding of textbook concepts or techniques occurs in efforts to apply them. Unlike problems appended to textbook chapters, cases describe real situations, in which neither problems nor relevant techniques may be obvious. Moreover, effects of definitions or problems and the means for their resolution are much more likely to be controversial.

Inevitably, assumptions have to be made about perceptions, attitudes, or behavior of people as well as about the relevance of facts or principles raised in the case—and their effects on the future growth in productivity, profitability, or efficiency of corporate operations.

The controversy and compromise from discussions of the case serve to sharpen one's abilities to select facts and define and resolve problems from concrete situations. To be analytical and decisive and to hold strong convictions are essential qualities of effective managers. But to be persuasive, to listen, and to be willing to let the wisdom of others' analyses and convictions persuade you—are also necessary qualities. Thus we believe that study, analyses, and discussion of cases substantially comprise the *practice* of management. Such practice is a most effective way to gain knowledge, skills, and proper attitudes for managing productivity of corporate operations.

ABC Carbon Company

1

The ABC Carbon Company, located near Albany, New York, manufactured one-time carbon to be used in business forms. In 1980 it had sales of around $2.225 million annually. Fifty percent of this output went to company accounts, most of which were close to the Albany Plant. Some branch plants of these accounts, however, were located in the Midwest and Southeast. ABC Carbon also supplied customers located in New England, New York, Pennsylvania, and in the Southeastern United States.

In the spring of 1981, ABC Carbon was considering the possibility of locating a branch in the Southeastern United States to supply its customers there. This consideration had arisen as a result of several factors.

First of all, the Albany plant was presently operating at full capacity and still was unable to meet the needs of their customers. The plant contained four coaters, each of which was capable of producing about $550,000 worth of carbon annually.

The second factor was the high expense of shipping carbon from Albany to Southern customers and the inability of ABC to provide service to the customers, particularly the branch plants of its accounts, which ABC was eager to retain. ABC's two largest competitors in Atlanta were able to

This case was prepared by Ernest A Elliot and Thomas L. Parkinson under the supervision of Professors Gordon K. C. Chen, Harold E. Hardy, Edward A. Zane at the School of Business Administration, University of Massachusetts, Amherst, Massachusetts. Cases are not designed to present illustrations of either effective or ineffective handling of administrative problems.

offer three-to-four-day service to accounts in the South, while ABC usually needed one to two weeks to deliver.

Shipping from Albany was done by truckload as much as possible, but it was often necessary to ship some of the sales LTL at a great increase in cost. ABC knew that they were just breaking even on their Southern operations and, therefore, had not actively solicited additional business. They had one salesman in Atlanta who was then selling about $170,000 annually to various accounts. Sales to the branch plants of the direct company accounts were $68,850 in the Atlanta area and $42,000 in North Carolina. These customers were supplied directly from Albany. It was estimated that an additional $63,000 worth of current sales were being lost due to an inability to deliver.

These outside accounts had been retained with the expectation of expanding operations into the Southeast at some future time. For several reasons the management of ABC felt that now might be the time to consider this expansion. First, the business forms industry was expanding at a rate of 10% nationally due to the over-all expansion of business and increased use of business forms by computers. Second, the Southeastern United States seemed to have large potential sales and showed great promise of growth in the future. Three new business forms manufacturers had commenced operations in the past six months in North Carolina alone.[1]

In order to make an intelligent selection of a plant location it was decided to make a more specific estimate of market potential for business forms in the Southeast. Since it would be unprofitable to locate more than one plant in the area, ABC wanted to pick a location that would effectively serve its customers at that time and in the future.

Obtaining information on market potential was somewhat difficult, because most companies manufacturing business forms were privately owned and data about sales or the percentage of sales which were composed of business forms were not readily available. It was also necessary to know something about expected growth rates, since business in this area seemed to be growing faster than the rest of the country.

In order to obtain this needed information a questionnaire (Exhibit 1–1) was designed and sent to more than 70 printing companies in the Southeast.[2] The first question was added to get some idea about the desirability of different areas for the location of a plant; results are shown in Exhibit 1–2. The company considered the 50% return of the questionnaires as giving a fairly complete picture of the market. Estimates were made of business forms sales for those companies which did not reply so as to

[1] Reported by these firms on the questionnaire.
[2] List compiled from Dun and Bradstreet Reports, Jobber's list of customers, and ABC Carbon Company's customers.

Exhibit 1—1 Survey Questionnaire

Please check or fill in the appropriate answer.

1. How would you rate your area in terms of business climate?

	Excellent	Good	Fair	Poor
Taxes	____	____	____	____
Community Services	____	____	____	____
Industrial Services	____	____	____	____
Transportation	____	____	____	____
Real Estate Cost	____	____	____	____
Labor	____	____	____	____
Labor Relations	____	____	____	____
Cost of Living	____	____	____	____
Others (please specify)	____	____	____	____

2. At what rate do you expect gross sales to expand in your area in the next five (5) years?

(__less than 5%) (__5–10%) (__10–15%) (__15–20%) (__more than 20%)

3. At what rate do you expect sales to expand in your firm in the next five years?

(__less than 5%) (__5–10%) (__10–15%) (__15–20%) (__more than 20%)

4. Do you feel that the growth of your firm varies directly with and at the same rate as general business conditions?

__yes   __no

If no, what relationship do you feel exists, if any? _____

_____

5. Do you foresee any reason for a sudden variance in your predicted growth rate?

__yes   __no

If yes, for what reason? _____

_____

6. Approximate gross sales (1964) of your company. _____

7. What are your major products?   % of gross sales

1. _____   _____%

2. _____   _____%

3. _____   _____%

Thank you very much for your cooperation.
Please do not sign this or in any way identify yourself.

Exhibit 1—2 Business Climates

Atlanta (5)

	Excellent	Good	Fair	Poor
Taxes		5		
Community Services	5			
Industrial Services	4	1		
Transportation	2	2	1	
Real Estate Cost		5		
Labor	1	4		
Labor Relations		5		
Cost of Living		5		
Others (please specify)				

Georgia, Excluding Atlanta (4)

	Excellent	Good	Fair	Poor
Taxes	1		2	1
Community Services	2	1	1	
Industrial Services	2	1		1
Transportation	2	1	1	
Real Estate Cost	1	1	2	
Labor		2	2	
Labor Relations	2	2		
Cost of Living		2	2	
Others (please specify)				

North Carolina (8)

	Excellent	Good	Fair	Poor
Taxes		6	2	
Community Services	3	5		
Industrial Services	4	3	1	
Transportation	4	4		
Real Estate Cost	3	4	1	
Labor	2	3	3	
Labor Relations	5	3		
Cost of Living	1	6	1	
Others (please specify)				

Exhibit 1—3 Questionnaire Statistics

	Sent	Returned	% Returned
Atlanta	11	5	45.5
Georgia, except Atlanta	7	5	71.4
Tennessee	11	5	45.4
North Carolina	19	10	52.6
Alabama	8	2	25.0
Mississippi	3	2	66.7
Florida	8	5	62.5
South Carolina	3	2	66.7
Washington D.C. & Virginia	3	2	66.7
TOTAL	73	38	52.1

Exhibit 1—4 Projected Current Carbon Paper Potential

	Business Form Sales	Carbon Sales
Georgia (other than Atlanta)	$ 888,500	$ 133,275
Atlanta	5,956,000	893,400
North Carolina	5,677,000	851,550
Florida	2,250,000	337,500
Tennessee	5,300,000	795,000
Alabama	596,000	89,400
TOTAL	$20,667,500	$3,100,125

make the study as complete as possible. Exhibit 1–3 shows the number of questionnaires sent out to each area along with the number returned.

Answers to the third question revealed what had been expected about growth rates. In North Carolina and Georgia the majority of expectations of growth ranged from 15% to 20%, while the other areas reported about 10%.

The study yielded the results shown in Exhibit 1–4 and the total projected current demand for carbon paper was computed to be $3.1 million, on the assumption that 15% of total business form sales represented the amount of carbon paper used.[3]

There was some question as to what part of this potential carbon sales ABC could reasonably expect to capture now and in the next five years. It was believed that ABC's penetration was 30% of its current accounts and

[3] The 15% was based on past experience.

Exhibit 1–5 Potential Sales Under Different Degrees of Penetration (Current)

	10%	15%	20%	30%
Georgia	$127,605	$127,919	$128,235	$128,865
Florida	89,100	92,138	95,175	101,250
North Carolina	143,231	163,815	184,398	225,566
Tennessee	79,500	119,250	159,000	238,500
Alabama	11,820	15,570	19,320	26,820
Atlanta	86,918	87,234	87,548	87,870
TOTAL	$497,484	$565,241	$632,989	$767,876

For all degrees of penetration where ABC is currently servicing an account the degree of penetration was held at 30%.

Exhibit 1–6 Potential Sales Under Different Degrees of Penetration (5 years)

	Degrees of Penetration[1]			
	10%	15%	20%	30%
Georgia[2]	$171,500	$172,115	$172,728	$173,956
Florida[3]	136,324	143,671	145,618	154,914
North Carolina[2]	279,299	319,438	359,577	439,853
Tennessee[3]	121,635	182,453	243,271	361,905
Alabama[3]	18,085	23,823	29,560	41,035
Atlanta[2]	262,880	290,721	319,376	376,690
TOTAL	$989,723	$1,132,221	$1,270,130	$1,548,353

[1] For all degrees of penetration where ABC is currently servicing an account the degree of penetration was held at 30%.
[2] An expansion rate of 13% a year for four years, and 5% for one year was assumed.
[3] An expansion rate of 10% a year for four years, and 5% for one year assumed.

it was felt they could reasonably expect to maintain an average of 30% of current customers' accounts. In dealing with new customers, it was felt that ABC would probably be able to sell half of the accounts which had not yet been contacted. Since this left the problem of actual penetration to be expected somewhat unclear, Exhibits 1–5 and 1–6 were prepared to show expected potential sales under the assumption of different degrees of penetration for both 1981 sales and projected sales five years later.

Possible Methods of Servicing Accounts

Several possible methods of servicing these accounts were considered. The first method considered was the establishment of a manufacturing

Exhibit 1—7 Investments Associated with Proposals

TOTAL INVESTMENT REQUIRED FOR SOUTHERN PLANT

Machinery:

Coater	$27,000	
Slitting	17,000	
Core Cutter	1,000	
2 Dope Kettles	3,000	
Hot Water Piping	3,000	
Install Piping	7,000	
Incinerator	500	
Misc. Equipment	3,000	
		$61,500

Working Capital:

30 Days Receivables	40,000	
Cash in Bank	6,000	

Inventory:

Paper	20,000	
Ink & Misc. Supplies	10,000	
Packaging, etc.		
Finished goods		$137,500
Misc. Expenses and Moving		15,000
		$152,500

Investment required if new coater kept in Albany

Machinery:

New Coater	27,000	
New Slitter	17,000	

Working Capital:

30 Days receivables on increased volume	40,000	

Inventory:

Probable increase in raw materials due to increased volume	15,000	$99,000

Exhibit 1—8 Relevant Costs of Operations

With x = total sales, costs of manufacturing related to sales are:

Tissue	.454x
Other Materials	.11x
Freight in	.02x
Factory supplies	.02x
Sales commissions 15,000+	.01x
Shipping supplies	.02x
Administrative Expense	.02x
Labor	Foreman $8,200 + 4 men a shift for each coater. (One coater will produce $550,000 worth of annual sales.)

Gross Margin excluding sales and administrative expense is 26%.

Net Profit excluding shipping from Albany is 11%.

Labor

Charlotte	$96 / week
Georgia	$106 / week
Massachusetts	$110 / week

Rent

Charlotte	60¢ / sq. ft. / year
Atlanta	75¢ / sq. ft. / year
Athens	50¢ / sq. ft. / year
Albany	60¢ / sq. ft. / year

Exhibit 1—9 Freight Costs

	Current 10%	Current 15%	5 Years 15%	5 Years 20%	5 Years 30%
Albany to Points in South	$60,832	$69,069	Not Relevant		
Albany to Atlanta TL	28,960	32,905	$65,912	$73,939	$90,136
Albany to Charlotte TL	29,138	33,107	66,316	74,393	90,689
Charlotte to Points in South	34,791	39,520	67,121	74,922	90,409
Atlanta to Points in South	28,594	32,950	56,625	64,483	80,075
Athens to Points in South	33,403	38,382	67,643	76,244	93,224

---

plant in the South. Since the bulk of the business was in North Carolina and Georgia it was felt that one of these two states would be best. Two locations which looked promising were Charlotte, North Carolina and the outskirts of Atlanta.

Another alternative was to establish a warehouse in the South. All of the carbon would be manufactured in Albany and shipped to the warehouse by truckloads. This would require additional space of at least 10,000 square feet with additional machinery in Albany. The Southern warehouse would occupy about 5,000 square feet and could be operated by one man. Charlotte and Atlanta were thought to be the best possible locations for a warehouse since they were located in central shipping points.

Information pertinent to a solution is contained in Exhibits 1–5, 1–6, 1–7, 1–8, and 1–9.

What action would you take as manager of ABC Carbon Company?

AeroSpace Electronic Systems, Inc.

2

Professor R. B. Talbot of the Department of Production Management, UCLA was not sure he'd been wise when he had accepted the consulting assignment by Mr. G. A. Kindig, General Manager, AeroSpace Electronic Systems, Inc. of Los Angeles, California. As Professor Talbot put it, "After over a month of talking with virtually all the key management people in AeroSpace Electronics, I felt I was still dealing more with symptoms than with the essential cause of the company's problem." (Professor Talbot was discussing his consulting assignment with the case writer, using disguised terms to protect the interests of his client.)

Mr. Kindig had shown Professor Talbot a chart of daily shipments, in terms of dollars (Exhibit 2–1). This chart showed that from 50 to 70 percent of the shipments each fiscal month were made during the last week of the month. Mr. Kindig said he had never been able to understand why there should be such a consistent pattern of surges in daily shipments occurring the last week of each month. He had asked Professor Talbot if he would be willing to investigate the situation and make recommendations for smoothing out the end-of-month peaks in the shipping pattern. Professor Talbot thought about this request a few days and telephoned Mr. Kindig to accept the assignment. Mr. Kindig had said he was pleased with

Revised version of an earlier case written by Professor R. E. McGarrah. Copyrighted © by the President and Fellows of Harvard College.

Exhibit 2—1 AeroSpace Electronic Systems, Inc. Typical Histogram of Daily Shipments

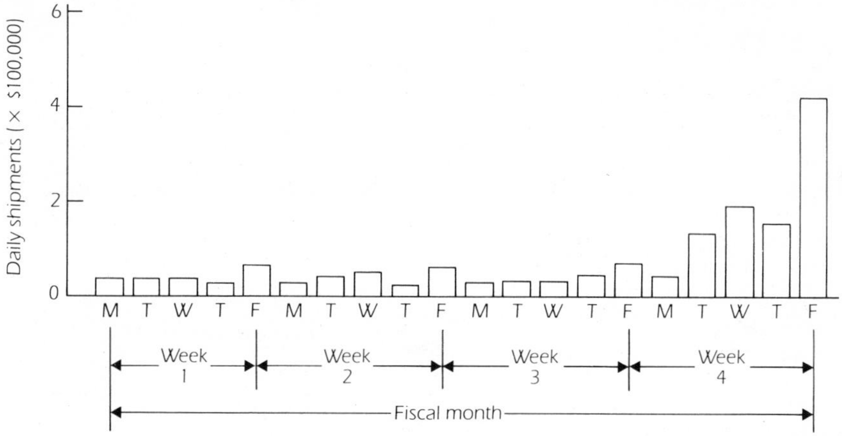

NOTE: With minor relative variations, the pattern illustrated was applicable to each of the three product assembly departments as well as to the company as a whole. This pattern had prevailed for the past three years.

SOURCE: Files of Mr. G. A. Kindig, General Manager.

Professor Talbot's acceptance, and that he would request all his functional managers to give Professor Talbot all the information he needed. (See the company's organization chart, Exhibit 2–2.)

Company Background

AeroSpace Electronics Systems, Inc. (ASES) designed and manufactured a wide variety of electronic control equipment for use principally on aircraft, missiles, and space vehicles, although a small number of these devices were installed on the ground or on board ships. ASES's engineering and manufacturing organizations operated as both a prime contractor and a second source of supply for the Air Force and Navy. Some contracts provided for ASES to design and manufacture an electronic system; others specified that ASES assume design responsibility, but not manufacturing responsibility; and still others required ASES to manufacture and install systems that had been designed by competing firms like General Electric's and Westinghouse's military electronic divisions, Sperry Division of Sperry-Rand and Raytheon.

ASES employed roughly 3,500 people, of whom 2,600 were in manufacturing, 700 in engineering, 80 in marketing and the remainder were assigned to finance, personnel and Mr. Kindig's office. Sales during the pre-

Exhibit 2—2 AeroSpace Electronic Systems, Inc. Company Organization

```
                              General Manager
                                G. A. Kindig

   Manager—         Manager—        Manager—         Manager—         Manager—
   Finance          Personnel       Manufacturing    Engineering      Marketing
   R. A. Mack       A. L. Peters     E. A. Ripley     L. R. Olson      G. A. Becker

 Manager—Budgets    Manager—       Superintendent—    Manager—         Manager—
 and Measurements   Engineering    Fire Control      Advanced Systems  Field Project
                    Personnel Services  Assembly      Development       Services—Navy
 Manager—General
 Accounting         Manager—Factory  Superintendent—   Manager—Fire     Manager—
                    and Office      Radar Countermeasures  Control Projects  Field Project
 Manager—Cost       Personnel Services  Assembly                          Services—Air Force
 Accounting
                                    Superintendent—   Manager—Radar     Manager—
                                    Missile Guidance   Countermeasures   Contract
                                    Assembly           Projects          Administration
                                                                         Services
                                    Superintendent—   Manager—Missile
                                    Parts Fabrication  Guidance Projects

                                    Manager—Purchasing  Manager—
                                                        Engineering
                                    Manager—            Laboratory
                                    Manufacturing
                                    Engineering        Manager—Drafting
                                                       and Technical
                                    Manager—           Services
                                    Quality Testing
```

SOURCE: Files of Mr. G. A. Kindig, General Manager.

vious year were about $80 million. The current backlog of unfilled orders amounted to about $115 million.

Prices of equipment produced and shipped by ASES ranged from $1,000 to $100,000 per unit, depending upon the complexity and number of "black boxes" in the system. Navy and Air Force contracts called for shipments of from one or two prototype units to 300 units at specified times, coordinated with the production schedules of aircraft and missile builders. According to historical cost records, the average manufacturing cost per unit shipped was analyzed relatively as follows: 55 percent for purchased components, 15 percent for direct labor, and 30 percent for manufacturing overhead. This cost did not include engineering and tooling expenses, which were billed separately.

Manufacturing activities consisted of three assembly departments for various types of fire control, radar countermeasure, and missile guidance equipment, and a parts machining and fabrication department. Each superintendent in charge of a department had his own staff personnel responsible for establishing methods and time standards, production schedules, and inspection and test procedures. Mr. E. A. Ripley, Manager of

Manufacturing, was responsible for coordinating the work of the four superintendents. Also, the managers of purchasing, manufacturing, engineering, and quality control reported to Mr. Ripley. The manager of purchasing was responsible for negotiations and follow-up of contracts between ASES and suppliers of tools and component parts, as well as for operating the receiving and intraplant materials handling services. The manager of manufacturing engineering was responsible for planning new types of production equipment, plant layout and maintenance services, and for advanced assembly methods, work measurement, and job classification procedures. The manager of quality control was responsible for planning production inspection and test procedures and selecting equipment, according to specifications prepared by ASES engineers and authorized by Navy and Air Force inspectors.

It took a time varying between 1–20 months for the manufacturing departments to procure and fabricate the necessary component parts, assemble, and test a typical electronic system. The first few units of a contract always required a longer time than the last few units, because of debugging problems. Mr. Ripley, whose earlier experiences had been mainly with a company manufacturing consumer radios, said,

During these debugging periods, it seems as if we're literally doing engineering and development work on the production floor. Engineers are constantly revising design and test specifications. Often, this means we have to tear down devices we've already assembled. We're plagued with material shortages because engineering changes affect our suppliers as well as us. And, debugging may mean that the Navy and Air Force inspectors will hold up final test approvals, pending instructions from their procurement commands. We try to phase production of the various contracts so no more than two projects are being debugged at any one time throughout the manufacturing organization. This helps us keep our idle labor time down. But we're not always successful. We've had from four to eight different contracts in some stage of progress on our factory floor during the past two years. With the ups and downs we have here at ASES, this is a far cry from making consumer radios. There's a lot of satisfaction in getting the bugs ironed out, but just when we begin to push units through, we have to switch to a new contract.

The Problem of End-of-Month Surges in Shipments

Mr. Kindig detailed his views of the problem to Professor Talbot.

Most of my experiences in business have been in financial management. Five years ago, when I took this job with ASES, one of the first things I did was to strengthen the budgeting procedures. We project our budget for a year by quarters, with the current quarter broken done by months. I have a monthly comparison of budgeted and actual operating statements delivered to me within a week after the end of each fiscal month. At the same time, each functional manager gets a copy of this comparison together with detailed summaries of their appropriate expense variances. I give the managers two days to analyze last month's results and to prepare their ideas of what next month's over-all performance will be. Then I have a monthly meeting of my functional managers to review last month's performance and to set the goals to be achieved by the end of the current month. This is my only routine meeting with the managers concerned with all contract activities. (Occasionally I'll call a meeting to discuss one or two current or pending contracts.) I believe these meetings have helped to maintain a good attitude toward over-all planning and control in the organization, because the emphasis is on monthly operating profit, which after all, is the only true measure of over-all performance. On the whole, our performance has been pretty satisfactory, I'd say.

About the only follow up record I keep during the month is this graph of daily shipments (Exhibit 2–1). I've kept this chart for the last three years, and these end-of-the-month surges have persisted all this time. At first, I thought this was due to the nature of this business. We're always running into technical problems, such that when they are solved, we can ship equipment in "slugs"; but then I asked myself, "why do these surges occur so persistently at the end of each fiscal month?" And I haven't come up with a satisfactory answer. We've kicked this problem around at our budget meetings, but nobody seems to have a satisfactory answer. My thought in asking you to look at this was to get a responsible outsider's opinion.

Before accepting Mr. Kindig's request, Professor Talbot had asked himself why finding the cause(s) of these end-of-the-month surges in shipments was so important to Mr. Kindig. To clarify the gravity of the problem, Professor Talbot decided to describe some costs which might conceivably be avoided if daily shipments flowed more smoothly from ASES's back door:

Labor costs

1. Unnecessary overtime premiums paid to manufacturing, test, packing, and shipping personnel, when products were rushed through during the last of the month.
2. Risks of poor employee morale. Although on wage incentives, too often, assembly personnel were probably pulled off one job and assigned to others to expedite production for the month. This meant training and retraining costs that were probably excessive.

Quality costs

1. "Crash" production and shipments at the end of each month might have implied that the severity of quality testing procedures was not uniform throughout the month. This in turn might have resulted in

field engineering service costs, and jeopardized relations with Navy and Air Force customers.

Materials control costs

1. Surges in shipments might have indicated instances of excessive vendor expediting costs, like authorizing vendors to work overtime, special handling and air freight shipments to ASES's plant, extra telephoning and paperwork expenses associated with "crash expediting."
2. Erratic shipments might have strained customer relations. If ASES's true delivery performance was indicated by the daily shipment data shown by Mr. Kindig, then who knows what negative effects this might have on customers' attitude in awarding new contracts to ASES?

The implications of these costs, more than any other factor, were what persuaded Professor Talbot to accept Mr. Kindig's request. Professor Talbot agreed to report his findings, conclusions, and recommendations within six weeks, during which he spent approximately twelve hours per week on the ASES consulting assignment.

Investigations to Solve the Problem

One of the first steps Professor Talbot took was to check the veracity of the daily shipment data reported to Mr. Kindig. He found that these data were based upon a document used to notify shipment destinations of their pending receipts. These documents could not be filled out in the traffic supervisor's office until authority had been received from one of the resident Air Force or Naval inspectors, who checked the final tests of the various electronic systems. A copy of the shipping notice was sent to the accounting office where units were priced and extended, according to price terms set forth in the particular contract involved in the shipment.

Manufacturing

Mr. Ripley, Manager of Manufacturing, said he was sure that, between Purchasing and final testing, Manufacturing departments were responsible for some of the causes for the end-of-month peaks in shipments, but not the essential causes. He pointed out that these surges were evidence of production delays but that causes of these delays lay with Marketing and Engineering as much as they did with Manufacturing.

After all, when an engineer holds up our units in some test or inspection station, we can't do a thing until he gives us the go ahead. Manufacturing has the last chunk of contracted time for delivering units to customers. But if Engineering and Marketing Personnel use too much time, trying to agree on design changes, and if the promised shipping dates in the contract are not changed, then Manufacturing is bound to look (that is, on the records) like the main source of causes for these delays.

Professor Talbot could find no documentary records enabling him to measure the extent of material shortages—and delays. Observing the procedures for issuing materials to the assembly departments, however, he found that the discovery of such shortages was delayed until the time when materials and parts were being physically accumulated for issue to the assembly floor. He made a note to suggest closer follow-up by the production control supervisors of orders they placed with purchasing and fabrication department personnel. He also thought there might be need for a closer follow-up of progress within the various assembly departments, so that delays could be discovered earlier and expediting actions could be taken appropriately to minimize delays. He observed that production control personnel apparently had no routine feed back information about technical or quality problems that caused delays. Accordingly, he made a note to recommend that production control supervisors be made responsible for following up on the quality status of units held up by inspection and test failures, and for expediting these delays at least to the extent of advising the manager of quality control about these delays.

Professor Talbot said he was surprised to learn that no effort had been made to correlate the assembly direct labor hour inputs per week for each assembly department with the dollar shipments per week. These data are shown on Exhibit 2–3. The ASES cost accounting tabulating personnel could conveniently furnish data for only six weeks, while Professor Talbot was making his study.

While examining ASES's organization chart, it occurred to Professor Talbot that the Purchasing and Parts Fabrication Departments might be bottle-necks in the flow of materials because each supported all three assembly departments.

While talking with the Manager of Purchasing, he learned that in issuing purchase requisitions, the four supervisors of production control in the parts fabrication and machining and assembly departments acted independently of each other. Consequently, purchasing personnel had to figure out for themselves which purchase requisitions had the highest priorities. In expediting receipts of quotations and shipments from suppliers, buyers and purchase expeditors often apparently concentrated on the "wrong" items of material, depending upon the viewpoint of one of the four production control supervisors.

Similarly, the superintendent of the parts fabrication and machining department said that too often assembly foremen from two different assembly departments tried, at about the same time, to persuade one of his foremen to give their orders top priority in machining. He said that his production control supervisor had tried without success to get the three assembly production control supervisors to agree on a permanent "priority rule" for deciding whose jobs should be machined first. It often happened that two or more machining jobs had the same due-dates when needed in the three assembly departments.

Exhibit 2–3 AeroSpace Electronic Systems, Inc. Assembly Direct Labor Hours per Week and Shipments per Week

Week Ending	8/26	9/2	9/9*	9/16	9/23	9/30
Fire Control Assembly						
Labor Hours	6,199	5,953	4,957	5,556	6,380	6,351
Products Shipped (× $1,000)	350	250	500	225	300	200
Radar Countermeasure Assembly						
Labor Hours	4,370	3,526	1,553	1,976	1,919	2,025
Products Shipped (× $1,000)	50	25	375	50	30	20
Missile Guidance Assembly						
Labor Hours	1,199	1,138	885	1,137	1,180	1,292
Products Shipped (× $1,000)	0	0	50	25	0	25
All Assembly Departments						
Labor Hours	11,768	10,617	7,395	8,669	9,479	9,668
Products Shipped (× $1,000)	400	275	925	300	330	245

*Includes Labor Day, September 4.

NOTE: Labor hours of personnel assigned to final testing, packing, and shipping activities are not included in these data.

SOURCE: ASES cost accounting and tabulating personnel.

(Assembly labor hours applied were recorded on IBM punch cards used by timekeepers. These cards were destroyed after they were processed for purposes of payroll and labor expense summaries. This was an important reason why it was not convenient for accounting personnel to furnish data for more than the current six weeks.)

The assembly superintendents said they couldn't very well agree on "permanent priorities." Whenever technical problems held up their work, they said they wanted to have materials available to keep their people from being idle, and that this was why they had to "heckle" purchasing and parts fabrication and machining personnel to change procurement and production schedules.

Engineering

Before becoming Manager of Engineering at ASES three years ago, Mr. L. R. Olson had been an engineering project manager at the Hughes Aircraft Company. Mr. Olson had also participated in several of UCLA's engineering education programs, because, as he said, "If we're going to keep the pace in this electronic race, then we've got to get closer to the schools of engineering and management." Before taking his ASES assignment, Professor Talbot had a nodding acquaintance with Mr. Olson.

After amenities, Professor Talbot explained his purpose for interviewing Mr. Olson, by saying he wanted to get a better understanding of the problems of engineering delays. Mr. Olson responded.

Look, you know what a tough job it is to recruit and keep good engineers in this business. The pirating of personnel between competitors is terrific and so is the turnover. No wonder my engineering departments are in a constant state of flux. And this doesn't help us expedite our systems development problems, I'll tell you! But, personnel turnover is not all.

The Navy and Air Force are much more rigid than they used to be about the system performance specifications they issue to the companies they invite to bid on their contracts. There's good reason for this. They have to be more exact about such matters as space, weight, and temperature conditions affecting the performance of their missiles. Mind you, though, they write these 'specs' without knowing that such a system or missile can be built. In developing the system, we occasionally have to ask the Air Force or Navy to loosen up perhaps, on a space-limiting 'spec' or a weight limiting 'spec.' This might be because we need bigger components in our electronic guidance system to get better reliability of the system's performance. We have to relay such requests for changes to our marketing people, who then take the problem to the Air Force. You can see that this can get to be a vicious circle of buck-passing. If we ask the Air Force for more weight, then the Air Force might have to consider asking, say, Convair or Douglas to build less weight in their missile vehicle or, Rocketdyne to provide more thrust in their rocket engine. Sometimes the Air Force or Navy comes to us with a specification change that might have originated with a development problem at Douglas or Rocketdyne. All these change-requests cause delays in shipments—ours and maybe other companies' too.

Marketing

Mr. G. A. Becker, Manager of Marketing, was a retired Air Force Colonel whose military experiences had been mainly with the Air Material Command and Development Center, at Wright-Patterson Air Force Base in Dayton, Ohio. Professor Talbot said he had only a short interview with Mr. Becker, whose travel commitments kept him away from Los Angeles most of the time.

Mr. Becker offered the opinion that engineering changes initiated by customers as well as contractors had to be expected by companies in the defense products businesses. Delays and log-jams had to be expected. He admitted that ASES's delivery performance was erratic and had occasionally held up certain Navy and Air Force Operations. However, he said he didn't think ASES's delivery performance was any worse than competitors, and he stressed the growth of ASES's sales from $5 million to $80 million in the last 8 years.

Mr. Becker also said he had complete confidence in Mr. V. B. Jamison, Manager of Contract Administration Services. Mr. Jamison's job was to expedite matters of agreement between the Air Force and Navy and ASES's operating departments. These included clarifications of customers' performance specifications, channeling engineering change requests, and acting as a general liaison between customers and ASES on interpretations of contracts currently in force.

Some Alternative Conclusions

Reviewing the notes and observations he had made, Professor Talbot had some uneasy feelings about the report he had to make to Mr. Kindig. He said:

I'm convinced that ASES's shipments are moving consistently in slugs at the end of each month and that there would be significant gains if these shipments could be smoothed out. There's naturally a bias in the views expressed by the people I've talked with, too. They all talk about delays caused by some other organization as much or more than their own. No doubt, delays are caused by customers and suppliers as well as ASES's engineers, marketing, and manufacturing personnel. But why should these delays occur and then be overcome so that daily shipments surge the last week of each fiscal month?

The idea of closer follow-up to discover material shortages sooner might help reduce delays. And, maybe a contract priority scheme could be worked out so that all engineering, manufacturing, and marketing personnel have a common basis for allocating their efforts to solve technical problems and logistics problems, one at a time, concentrating on "first things first."

I suppose I could recommend that Mr. Kindig promulgate a company-wide procedure to document the occurrence and classify the nature and disposition of all delays. I found it impossible to draw relevant inferences from inspection and test reports, production schedules and receiving reports, engineering change memoranda, and so on. I could also recommend getting more time-series data correlating dollar shipments with man hours of input. The six weeks' survey I have (Exhibit 2–3) doesn't seem to be enough to reveal much of significance. But would all these fact-finding efforts lead to the root of the problem?

Reflecting further, Professor Talbot continued:

I wonder what Mr. Kindig would do if I told him his monthly budget performance meetings were the cause of his shipping pattern. It's possible that he has made ASES's fiscal record so important that everybody in his organization exerts a crash effort the last half of the month and then catch their breath during the first half. I've seen lots of companies drain the pipelines just to make the financial statements look good at the end of a fiscal period. Something like this might be what's happening to ASES. If Mr. Kindig personally were to control operations in terms of a fiscal week instead of a fiscal month maybe the over-all operations at ASES would be tighter and the daily shipping patterns would get smoother. But can I logically blame Mr. Kindig for ASES's problem?

Andrews Machine Company

3

The Andrews Machine Company stockholders were dissatisfied with the return on investment in their company. A new management was retained and the president requested an analysis of the profit-making possibilities of the company.

Three basic product lines were produced and sold. Cost records for the preceding year and forecasted sales for the next year are summarized in Exhibit 3–1. Costs of purchased materials and labor costs expected for the coming year are as indicated.

A consolidated profit-and-loss statement for the preceding year, the most recent record of the former management, is shown in Exhibit 3–2.

The statement of net worth of the company as of the time new management took over is given in Exhibit 3–3.

Andrews profit goal was 8 percent of net worth. The new management was told that stockholders would be satisfied with a 3.5 percent return on their preferred stock equities and a 6 percent return on their common-stock equities. The rest was to be retained profit.

For purposes of simplicity, the new managers assumed that the Federal income tax rate would be 50 percent of the net profits before taxes. Accordingly, they projected a budgeted profit-and-loss statement (Exhibit 3–4) based on the data forecasted by the previous management (all × $1000). To determine how far away this budgeted operating statement was from the minimum profit goal specified by the board of directors, the new management calculated the following:

Exhibit 3—1 Andrews Machine Company Financial Operating Data

| | Product Type | | | |
	A	B	C	Total
Unit sales price ($/unit)	10.00	20.00	30.00	
Forecasted unit sales (forecast made by previous management)	200,000	135,000	10,000	
Direct costs ($/unit):				
Material	1.00	4.00	7.00	
Labor	2.00	6.00	7.00	
Overhead	1.60	4.80	5.60	
Sales and distribution	1.00	2.00	3.00	
Administrative	.50	1.00	1.50	
Fixed costs ($/year):				
Indirect manufacturing expenses				350,000
Indirect selling and distribution				200,000
Indirect administrative (general)				150,000
Interest on long term loans				100,000

Exhibit 3—2 Andrews Machine Company Operating Statement Last Year, Previous Management

Net sales	$4,000,000
Cost of sales	2,900,000
Gross profit	1,100,000
Less operating expenses	1,000,000
Operating profit	100,000
Less interest expense	100,000
Net profit before taxes	0

Exhibit 3—3 Andrews Machine Company Statement of Net Worth

Preferred stock	$1,000,000
Common stock	4,000,000
Surplus	200,000
Total	$5,200,000

Exhibit 3—4 Andrews Machine Company Budgeted Profit-and-Loss Statement Prepared by New Management

	Product A	Product B	Product C		Total
Net Sales	$2000	$2700	$300		$5000
Deduct:					
Material	200	540	70	810	
Labor	400	810	70	1280	
Overhead					
Variable	320	648	56	1024	
Fixed				350	3464
Gross profit					1536
Deduct:					
Sales expenses					
Variable	200	270	30	500	
Fixed				200	
Administration expenses					
Variable	100	135	15	250	
Fixed				150	1100
Net operating profit					436
Deduct interest expenses					100
Net profit (before income taxes)					336
Deduct income tax (or 50 percent)					168
Net profit (after taxes)					$ 168

Exhibit 3—5 Andrews Machine Company Financial Break-Even Chart

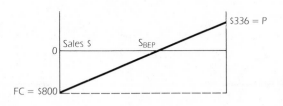

Desired profit after taxes—8 percent on total net worth, or 0.08 × $5,200,000 = $416,000.

Therefore net profit before taxes would have to be $416,000/(1 − 0.50) = $832,000.

They also charted the profit-and-loss statement budgeted by the old management in graphical form. (See Exhibit 3—5.)

Since the production and distribution facilities were used interchangeably for all three basic types of products, the break-even chart made a convenient tool for profit planning by the new management.

Geometry of the Break-Even Chart

A fundamental equation describing the operations of any business is

$ sales = $ fixed expenses + $ variable expenses + $ profit

The information in Exhibit 3–5 shows that the income from sales must be used first to pay for the fixed expenses (both book costs and out-of-pocket costs of operations) before any profit is to be accrued. Marginal income equals income from sales less the variable operating costs. Thus the rate at which profits are accrued is shown by the slope of the line connecting fixed expenses and profit. This "Profitability rate" (or profit-volume ratio P/V) is also defined by the following equations:

$$\frac{P}{V} = \frac{\text{fixed expenses} + \text{profit}}{\text{sales}} = \frac{\text{sales} - \text{variable expenses}}{\text{sales}}$$

Inserting the data budgeted by the former Andrews management:

$$\frac{P}{V} = \frac{\$800 + 336}{5000} = \frac{5000 - 3864}{5000} = 0.227, \text{ or } 22.7 \text{ percent}$$

The break-even point is reached when the total marginal income equals the total fixed expenses. The break-even point (BEP) may be defined as a dimensionless ratio expressed as a percentage of sales. The relationships derived from the data developed by the former Andrews management are shown in Exhibit 3–6.

By similar triangles,

$$\frac{FC}{S_{BEP}} = \frac{FC + P}{S_{BUD}}$$

Therefore

$$\frac{S_{BEP}}{S_{BUD}} = \frac{800}{800 + 336}$$

$$= 0.704, \text{ or } 70.4 \text{ percent of budget sales}$$

Dollar sales at the BEP are obtained simply by dividing the fixed expenses by the P/V ratio, or $800,000/0.227 = $3,520,000.

The "margin of safety" is the difference between budgeted sales and the sales at the BEP. Expressed as a percentage of budgeted sales, the "margin

Exhibit 3–6 Andrews Machine Company. Profit-Volume Graph, Showing Operating Conditions Budgeted by the Former Management

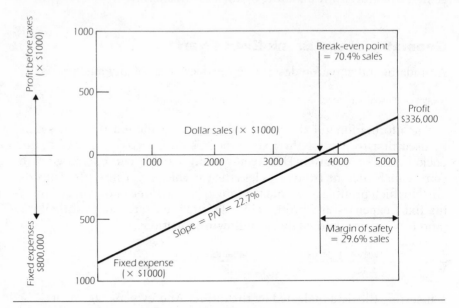

of safety" is simply 1 − BEP. Again, from the data given, margin of safety (× $1000) equals $5000 − $3520 = $1480 and is expressed as a percentage of budgeted sales $1480/5000 = 0.296, or 29.6 percent. Alternatively, the percentage margin of safety equals 1 − BEP, or 1 − 0.704 = 0.296.

The new management desired estimates of alternative ways of improving the profit picture at the Andrews Machine Company.

In general, profits can be increased by the following:

1. Decreasing expenses: (a) fixed; (b) variable.
2. Increasing sales prices.
3. Increasing sales volume of all products or of that product with the highest P/V ratio.
4. Any combination of the above means.

Questions

1. As the new controller of the Andrews Machine Company, suppose you were asked to estimate how much fixed and variable expenses would have to be reduced to achieve the profit goal with a break-even point at 50 percent of the budgeted $5 million sales.
2. (a) Which of the three products, A, B, or C is the most profitable? (b) How much would sales of this product have to exceed the sales bud-

geted by the former Andrews management to attain the $832,000-profit goal?

3. (a) To attain this goal, how much would total fixed expenses have to be reduced? (b) How much would variable expenses have to be reduced?

4. What possible actions of production/operations management are implied by your answers to questions 1–3?

5. This case illustrates uses of *profitability* as the goal for planning improvements in corporate work flow processes. Discuss differences or similarities in methods or results of such planning if *productivity* is used as a goal.

Apex
Appliances, Inc.

In November Mr. A. C. Frank, Plant Manager of the Vacuum Cleaner Division of Apex Appliances, Inc., was about to propose the production schedule. "Next year," he said, "We've got to program factory operations so we can stabilize employment and still meet the demands of marketing."

Mr. Frank had been promoted to his position early in February. Previously, he had been a manager of production control for the heavy equipment division of another company and more recently Senior Industrial Engineer on the Corporate Staff of Apex Appliances, Inc. From these professional experiences and his education in mechanical engineering and business administration, Mr. Frank had developed some definite concepts about programming manufacturing operations. In a talk given at an industrial management meeting in September, he had made the following remarks.

Every manufacturing business has a production scheduling problem at the heart of which lies a series of unknowns. The primary unknown is the sales forecast, with other unknowns being the various costs such as the cost of carrying inventory, the cost of changing schedules, and the cost of lost sales due to running out of inventory or failure to meet promised delivery dates. Manufacturing people have been wrestling with these

Revised version of an earlier case written by Professor R. E. McGarrah. Copyrighted © by the President and Fellows of Harvard College.

problems for years with the tendency to blame all their troubles on insufficient or inaccurate forecasting. I think that putting the blame on something beyond your control is an easy way to avoid taking action to solve your own problem. We in the Vacuum Cleaner Division of Apex Appliances raised particular hell with our marketing people for poor forecasting which had caused the factory to jump around haphazardly like a marionette attached to a perpetual motion machine. We screamed about the high cost involved in rapid and radical changes in schedule, the need for production leveling to keep the union out of our hair, and the general inability of people to predict next month's sales with any reasonable degree of accuracy. It is the conflict of three basic but divergent interests which results in these problems, and these lie in the areas of Marketing, Finance, and Manufacturing. Marketing is concerned only with having goods available at all times and in the proper mix to prevent any possibility of a lost sale from inability to deliver. Thus their interest in sales forecasting for production scheduling is normally selfish, that is, forecasting need only be done to provide ample finished goods inventory. Finance, on the other hand, wants accurate forecasts to prepare budgets and profit estimates, and wants zero or minimum finished goods inventory, to keep carrying costs low and return on investment up. Manufacturing, however, is interested primarily in keeping one schedule and model mix running as long as possible.

Marketing Considerations

Apex Appliances produced and sold three models of canister-type vacuum cleaners, a deluxe model, a medium-priced model, and an economy model. Recommended list prices were $89.95, $59.95 and $44.95 respectively. Over 25,000 independent retail dealers, including department stores, appliance stores, discount houses, and even some supermarkets stocked and sold Apex cleaners. Each cleaner sold had an Apex warranty card attached which advised the consumer of the conditions of the Apex Company's guarantee of performance. Consumers were to note their names, the name of the retail dealers from whom they purchased the cleaner, the date of purchase, and to mail the warranty card to the Sales Office of Apex Appliances. The purpose of the warranty card was more to enable Apex to have an accurate record of consumer sales by retail dealers, than to make a formal contract with the consumer, because Apex responded to all customers' complaints whether or not warranty cards had been filed. This was standard practice among appliance manufacturers. Over the years, Apex marketing personnel had tested the validity of warranty cards as indicators of retail sales volume, and had found that 50% of all retail customers had returned warranty cards usually within two weeks after they had bought the cleaners. Total monthly retail sales data, shown in Exhibit 4–1, are based upon warranty card returns received each month.

Exhibit 4–1 Apex Appliances, Inc. Historical Sales and Inventory Data*

(All figures in thousands of vacuum cleaners, all models)

	Jan.	Feb.	March	Apr.	May	June	July	Aug.	Sept.	Oct.	Nov.	Dec.	Estimated Total Sales or Shipments
Retail Dealers' Sales this year**	86	50	80	53	51	48	36	35	42	36	36(E)	100(E)	653
Retail Dealers' Inventory end-of-month	225	215	197	198	182	198	188	195	236	234	245(E)	215(E)	–
Inventory/Sales, Retailers	2.6	4.3	2.5	3.8	3.6	4.1	5.2	5.6	5.6	6.5	6.8(E)	2.1(E)	–
Distributors' Sales, to Retailers	51	36	54	38	32	50	27	36	72	29	45(E)	60(E)	530
Distributors' Inventory, end-of-month	116	104	116	105	96	90	141	149	140	150	117(E)	111(E)	–
Inventory/Sales, Distributors	2.3	2.9	2.1	2.8	3.1	1.8	5.2	4.1	1.9	5.3	2.6(E)	1.8(E)	–
Factory Warehouse Inventory, end-of-month	56	65	98	144	165	150	108	68	38	42	68(E)	60(E)	–
Factory Shipments to Dealers & Distributors	72	38	63	44	26	54	80	48	74	44	18(E)	62(E)	623
Production Output at Factory	39	47	96	75	50	39	38	8	44	48	44(E)	54(E)	582

*These data, rounded to the nearest 1,000 units, were obtained from Marketing and Production department records. There were certain time lags in reporting and compiling the data. Shipments of units in transit may not have been included always in the three inventories. For these reasons monthly changes in dealers' and distributors' inventory data do not agree exactly with the differences between input and output flow each month, when these differences are calculated from sales and shipments shown above.

**Based on numbers of warranty cards returned by customers.

(E) = Estimated as of November 1

Retail dealers purchased Apex Cleaners from distributors. Approximately 70 percent of the distributors were independently owned, 30 percent were owned and operated by Apex Appliances. Month end levels of inventory carried by retailers were estimated by subtracting retail sales data (based on warranty card returns) from quantities shipped by distributors to retail dealers. Retail inventory data are summarized in Exhibit 4–1. Retailers' margins averaged approximately 32 percent of Apex's suggested list price, and distributors' margins averaged about 12 percent of the suggested list price. Actual margins varied widely due to various sales promotional practices by both dealers and distributors, but Apex had a firm policy of holding stable factory prices on each model. Monthly data on distributors' stocks and shipments by distributors to retail dealers also are summarized in Exhibit 4–1. Orders received at the factory from distributors were filled by shipments from factory warehouse stocks, for which monthly data are summarized in Exhibit 4–1. Orders received at the factory from distributors were filled by shipments from factory warehouse stocks, for which monthly data are summarized in Exhibit 4–1.

Thus finished goods inventories existed at three levels in the distribution pipeline: at retailers, at distributors, and at the factory warehouse.

Market forecasts were prepared and distributed to key functional managers about 8 to 10 times each year. In preparing these forecasts, the manager of market research considered such general business indices as the Federal Reserve Board Durable Goods Index, Disposable Income, adult population and marriages, residential home construction. In addition, factors pertinent to the vacuum cleaner industry—new model designs introduced by Apex and its competitors, new merchandising techniques, average age of old cleaners traded in by customers for new cleaners—were considered. Exhibit 4–2 summarizes forecasts received by Mr. Frank. Generally Mr. Frank received the first forecast for a calendar year late in the third, or early in the fourth quarter of the preceding year. This preliminary forecast was revised several times and the one prepared in late October or early November was the forecast adopted for financial budgeting purposes.

Manufacturing Considerations

The Apex vacuum cleaner plant was located in Memphis, Tennessee. Engineering and manufacturing management personnel were in Memphis while marketing and general administrative officers of the vacuum cleaner division and the corporation were in New York City.

Most of the shop employees at the vacuum cleaner plant were members of International Union of Electrical Workers (IUE). The International Association of Machinists (IAM) represented employees in the tool room and maintenance shops. Basically, labor contract negotiations were carried out in New York on a company wide basis, but detailed matters concerning local wages, seniority, and specific grievance procedures were bargained at each plant. Apex had signed a five-year contract with the IUE

Exhibit 4–2 Apex Appliances, Inc. Summary of Retail Sales Forecasts as Received by the Plant Manager

(All figures in thousands of vacuum cleaners, all models)

	Jan.	Feb.	Mar.	Apr.	May	June	July	Aug.	Sept.	Oct.	Nov.	Dec.	Total
Sales This Year													
Forecasted Jan. 10	57	50	84	81	62	62	47	62	89	101	68	98	861
Forecasted Apr. 28	86(A)	50(A)	80(A)	51	48	45	41	41	54	51	62	95	704
Forecasted June 26	86(A)	50(A)	80(A)	53(A)	51(A)	47	41	41	68	54	48	95	712
Forecasted July 29	86(A)	50(A)	80(A)	53(A)	51(A)	48(A)	35	36	68	54	48	95	702
Forecasted Sept. 15	86(A)	50(A)	80(A)	53(A)	51(A)	48(A)	36(A)	35(A)	45	42	42	100	667
Sales Next Year													
Forecasted Sept. 15 this year	63	57	75	77	62	45	51	63	78	63	48	83	765
Forecasted Oct. 30 this year	68	62	81	81	68	48	54	68	81	68	54	99	832

(A) = Actual Retail Sales

which provided for a reopening of negotiations at local levels solely on the issue of supplementary unemployment benefits. The IUE had not been as successful as the United Auto Workers had been in obtaining supplementary unemployment benefits and had agreed to defer bargaining this matter until September of next year.[1] Mr. Frank was particularly anxious to establish a good record of employment stability at the Vacuum Cleaner Plant, so that when facing the IUE in September on the issue of supplementary unemployment benefits, he would be in a strong bargaining position with the local agent of the IUE.

The Vacuum Cleaner Plant was closed for a three-week vacation period each year during the last two weeks in July and the first week in August.

Manufacturing at the Apex Vacuum Cleaner Plant consisted of parts fabrication and assembly. Parts fabrication operations included metal stamping, piercing, and forming which were done in job lots on punch presses, plastic moulding machines, and welding machines and metal cutting operations done on lathes, drill presses, milling machines, boring mills, grinders, and other general purpose machines. Apex made its own vacuum cleaner motors, starting with coil steel stock, punching the rotor and stator laminations, then winding its own coils, machining and fabricating motor shells, and assembling the parts. Mr. Frank had continued to foster strong efforts to reduce costs by mechanizing the operations. Many progressive dies had been made to combine stamping operations at a single, large capacity punch press; spot and seam welding operations were done automatically. Apex made its own sealed bearings for the motors, its own vacuum cleaner brushes and had recently begun to mould many of the plastic parts used on the cleaners. Assembly operations were conveyorized with the lines carefully balanced using micromotion standards. More and more assembly and inspection jobs were being mechanized as cost reduction opportunities became evident. Mr. Frank had said his plant now had a maximum capacity of about 26,000 vacuum cleaners per week.

Costs of Changing Production Schedules

About six months ago, Mr. Frank had directed a major study of historical data be made to determine quantitative estimates of the costs of changing production schedules in his plant. He and key cost accounting personnel worked very closely with the manufacturing engineers assigned to make this study. Cost curves summarizing the results of this study are shown in Exhibits 4–3 and 4–4. These curves were extracted from the report by this study group.

---

[1] The UAW had been successful in negotiating a contract which provided that automobile companies contribute five cents per hour per UAW employee to build up a fund from which unemployment benefits were to be drawn when eligible employees were laid off. The contract stipulated that the companies continue to make this supplementary unemployment benefit (SUB) contribution as long as the cumulative balance in the SUB fund was at or below a stipulated amount.

Exhibit 4—3 Apex Appliances, Inc. Total Cost of Changing Production Rates—Changes Executed in a Two Weeks' "Crash" Program

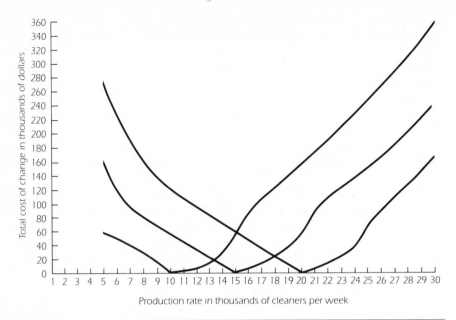

Production rate in thousands of cleaners per week

Exhibit 4—4 Apex Appliances, Inc., Total Cost of Changing Production Rates—Changes Executed in an Eight Weeks' "Normal" Program

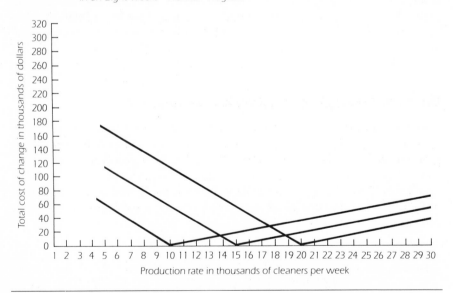

Production rate in thousands of cleaners per week

To serve as a framework for pursuing objectives of this study, three premises had been adopted by Mr. Frank and the study group to guide them in examining various records of production, cost, employment and purchasing information available.

First, they had decided that for purposes of this study there could be two *rates* at which production schedules could be changed, (1) in a minimum time of two weeks, which the group labeled a "Crash" program, and (2) in a "Normal" program of eight weeks. The determining factors for the "Crash" program period were the times required to determine new labor load requirements and to plan the new assignments of hourly paid personnel who, by union contract agreement, required a minimum of one week's notice before they could be transferred to different jobs. The key factor determining the "normal" program of eight weeks to execute a schedule change at minimum cost was the period of notice required by suppliers for Apex to avoid purchase cancellation charges or premium charges on materials such as those incurred by buying steel from mill supply firms instead of buying directly from the steel mills.

The second premise was that the costs of changing schedules would depend in part upon the current rate at which the plant was producing cleaners. The group had anticipated, for example, that the cost of increasing production by 5,000 units per week would be higher if the increase were from 20,000 units to 25,000 units per week, than it would be if production had been boosted from 15,000 to 20,000 units per week. The study group had reasoned that the means of executing a change from 15,000 to 20,000 cleaners per week were different from the means employed to change from 20,000 to 25,000 per week. The group had agreed that this premise would also hold true for the costs of decreasing the production rate from different levels. During the study, costs of changing from production levels of 10,000, 15,000 and 20,000 cleaners per week were determined. The costs of changes from other levels could be interpolated or extrapolated from cost curves plotted for these three levels.

The third premise underlying the study of costs of changing schedules was that the larger the change made in production schedules, the greater would be the cost of making these changes.

The study was completed early in October.[2]

One of the most significant findings of this study was that the total cost of decreasing production schedules was determined principally by unem-

---

[2] Illustrations of How to Use Cost Curves in Exhibits 4–3 and 4–4:

To determine the cost of changing the production rate from 10,000 per week to 15,000 per week in a "normal" program of eight weeks.

Using Exhibit 4–4:

1. Select the curve intersecting the horizontal axis at 10.
2. Following this curve out to 15,000 per week, read that the cost on the vertical axis is $20,000.

To determine the cost of decreasing the production rate from 20,000 per week to 13,000 per week in a "normal" program of eight weeks.

Using Exhibit 4–4:

1. Select the curve which intersects the horizontal axis at 20.
2. Following along this curve, upward and to the left, read that the cost of such a decrease is $80,000.

ployment compensation insurance rates. By federal law the maximum employers' contributions to state unemployment compensation insurance funds had been 3.4% of each employee's gross earnings up to the first $6,000 earned in a year. Required employers' contributions were adjusted downward if employment levels were stabilized and layoffs minimized. After working with Apex corporate staff accountants and with State of Tennessee officials, the study group learned that up to 90% of the cost of these premiums could have been avoided in past years if their plant had shown a stabilized growth in employment level, with no layoffs.

Approximately three weeks were required for a new employee to develop the proficiency required by the job rate. During the first four weeks on their jobs, the operators were assumed to average 80% of standard rates for these jobs. Consequently, to obtain an increase production on a "Crash" program basis, it was necessary to plan for an additional 20% of overtime or for extra manpower.

Labor expense variances were increased when production rates were increased or decreased. Such variances as those caused by training expense, rate makeup pay, and idle time were increased because workers were reassigned according to seniority provisions in the union contract whenever output rates were changed.

Small schedule changes of 4,000 cleaners per week or less caused very little increase in scrap, spoilage, and rework. Spoilage and rework costs attributable to schedule changes amounted to approximately 6% of the total cost of the change.

Normally, the model mix produced consisted of one deluxe cleaner, three medium-priced cleaners, and two economy cleaners. Variations in the mix of models scheduled had no appreciable effect on the costs of changing schedules according to the findings by the study group. The standard direct labor content of the deluxe cleaner was 130% of the content of the medium-priced cleaner; the standard direct labor content of the economy model was 60% of the content of the direct labor content of the medium-priced cleaner. If mix changes occurred, assembly lines were rebalanced in a matter of hours by manufacturing engineers. Direct labor operators were transferred among the three production lines with no appreciable loss of proficiency because about half the assembly personnel had been employed for at least four years, and they had developed a versatility in working on the different models. Many parts were interchangeable among the models. Parts fabrication jobs were run in job lots, so that model mix changes did not affect labor loads in the parts machining and processing departments.

Extra costs of vendor materials such as air freight transportation, contract cancellation charges, mill supply premium prices, were not incurred unless production rates were changed on a "Crash" program basis. If the

change amounted to 2/3 of the *existing* production rate, then these penalties in materials cost rose to a "staggering 50% of the total cost of changing the production schedule."

Costs of Carrying Inventories

Mr. Frank had many impressions about inventory carrying costs which he
had received from various sources. From professional journals and textbooks he had read that inventory carrying costs consisted of (1) the cost of
the risk and forfeited opportunity involved in investing cash funds in inventory and (2) the out-of-pocket expenses involved in providing physical
storage facilities for the inventory. The risk was comprised of such factors
as obsolescence, spoilage, and deterioration, and the opportunity was
comprised of the money forfeited because funds were tied up in inventory.
Both risk and opportunity were expressed as percentages of the out-of-
pocket cost of each unit added to and stored in inventory for a period of
time. The total of these percentages ranged anywhere between 6% and
30% of the out-of-pocket cost of each unit added to and stored in inventory for one year, for commercial products.

Apex accountants had advised that it cost $0.10 for one cleaner to be
put into the factory warehouse, stored one month, and taken out again.
After the first month, it cost $0.04 per cleaner per month to keep it in this
warehouse. The accountants had said that these costs were out-of-pocket
costs of handling and storing each cleaner in the factory warehouse. The
accountants told Mr. Frank that these figures covered expenses for property taxes, casualty insurance, and space rental but that they did not cover
the intangible costs of money tied up in inventory. Factory warehouse
stocks were stored in company owned and leased warehouse space.

The standard *direct* manufacturing cost per unit for each of the three
models of cleaners was:

Deluxe Model	$42.50
Medium-priced Model	33.80
Economy Model	29.40

These included standard direct materials, standard direct labor, and standard variable overhead expenses, according to cost accounting records in
September 1958. They did not include fixed manufacturing expenses, engineering expenses, or selling and administrative expenses.

Mr. Frank had never been able to pin down the marketing manager
whenever he had asked how much it cost to run out of finished stock.
"After all," the marketing manager had said, "I can't speak for independent retailers and distributors. Our company-owned distributor outlets
try to carry enough inventory to avoid stockouts 95% of the time. As far
as I'm concerned, it's good to have a stockout at the factory warehouse

once in a while because it lets our independent distributors know we are paying them to keep their own inventory. Our factory prices to independent distributors are low, compared to those charged by other vacuum cleaner manufacturers." Consequently, Mr. Frank and his study group had to determine a reasonable basis for establishing costs of carrying more than or less than "optimal" aggregate inventory quantities. The Apex Vacuum Cleaner plant employed 750 direct and indirect labor employees and produced cleaners at the rate of 12,000 cleaners per week.

Berkeley Savings and Loan Association

5

On September 1, 1971, The Berkeley Savings and Loan Association, in compliance with the New Jersey Savings and Loan Act of 1963, filed an application with the Commissioner of Banking of the State of New Jersey requesting permission to relocate its Chancellor Avenue, Newark branch office to the Five Point Shopping Center in Union, New Jersey. Pursuant to the provisions of the Act, the New Jersey Department of Banking, which administers the law, held hearings on the relocation application and opposing arguments. On September 12, 1972, the Hearing Officer, Mr. Clifford F. Blaze, submitted a report to the Acting Commissioner of Banking, Mr. Richard F. Schaub, recommending approval of the application. Upon review of the case, however, Commissioner Schaub found that such a relocation would adversely affect the economic climate of Newark and therefore would not be in the public interest. Consequently, the application was denied on January 24, 1973.

Since the case involved the issues of private versus public interests, business social responsibility, freedom of choice and movement in a free enterprise system, and the regulatory process and its attendant standards,

This case was prepared by Professors Gordon Chen and Arthur Elkins of the University of Massachusetts as a basis for class discussion rather than to illustrate either effective or ineffective handling of an administrative situation. Presented at the Case Workshop of the Intercollegiate Case Clearing House, 1973.

Copyright © 1973 by School of Business Administration, University of Mass.

Distributed by the Intercollegiate Case Clearing House, Soldiers Field, Boston, Mass. 02163. All rights reserved to the contributors. Printed in the U.S.A.

it is fruitful to review the background and developments of the events leading to the Commissioner's decision.

Company Background

Berkeley Savings and Loan Association was a mutual savings institution (that is, it served the interests of depositors only) chartered and regulated by the State of New Jersey. The Association maintained its principal office at 421 Millburn Avenue, Township of Millburn, County of Essex, and operated two branch offices in Newark—one at 88 Lyons Avenue and another at 434 Chancellor Avenue, the one for which the Association applied for relocation. Berkeley also had another branch office in East Hanover Township.

Berkeley's main office was originally located in Newark and had been relocated to Millburn shortly before the relocation issue arose. All of Berkeley's facilities were located within the "first savings and loan district" of New Jersey as defined by statute.

Berkeley was established in 1941 with assets of over $1 million and a reserve of a little over $61,000. The Association enjoyed a rapid growth and expansion during post World War II years. By June 30, 1973, the end of the fiscal year, its total assets amounted to more than $125 million with reserves and deferred income totaling over $8.6 million. The Bank offered a complete thrift and home financing service, having some 19,300 savings accounts and about 6300 mortgage accounts in 1971. The Association had 42 officers and employees in 1971. Berkeley's Chancellor Avenue Branch was opened for business in November, 1954. Because of the convenient location for its customers and the lack of competing institutions in the vicinity, the branch's deposits grew from a modest beginning of $.4 million in the first two months to $19.2 million in 1963.

Following the period of rapid growth, however, an increasing number of the branch's customers, starting in the early 1960s, were moving from the area into the suburbs of Essex and Union Counties. By 1971, 87% of its new savings customers had come from the suburban communities.

Concurrently, a number of large thrift and banking institutions moved into the vicinity during the latter part of the 1960s. This combination of increased competition plus the emigration of its older customers caused the branch beginning in 1968 to experience a decline in deposits. In 1970, the branch suffered its highest annual savings loss of more than $2 million, while aggregate savings in New Jersey rose by $600 million in that year. Similar declines were felt in other types of thrift accounts such as the Christmas Club.

Berkeley attributed the decline in business to a number of significant factors:

1. The suburban exodus of the residents.
2. The substantial increase in the number of competitive institutions.
3. The Newark riots in the summer of 1967.
4. The sharp increase in crimes of violence, particularly muggings.
5. The destruction of property for Route I78 displacing 1900 families and 7000 people.
6. The overcrowding of schools and the deterioration of the educational system.
7. The closing of most of the religious institutions, mostly of the Jewish faith as their members left the area.
8. The disappearance of most social and civic organizations.
9. Fear of safety.
10. Exodus of almost all of the Chancellor Avenue merchants.
11. Immigration of low income, financially burdened families into the Chancellor Avenue area.[1]

The Application

In view of the decline in business and the fear of further deterioration of its neighborhood, the condition of which was characterized as a "day-to-day state of siege,"[2] the management of Berkeley decided it was time to move the branch from the area. On September 1, 1971 Berkeley filed an application with the New Jersey Commissioner of Banking requesting permission to move the Chancellor Avenue office to a new site located in the Five Point Shopping Center, Union, New Jersey.

The 27 page application provided background information of Berkeley's history and operations, as well as analyses and reasonings for the proposed relocation. It also included attachments giving detailed facts and figures and exhibits in support of the application.

The proposed new branch site was located within the boundary of the so-called "second savings and loan district of New Jersey." Under the provisions of the New Jersey Savings and Loan Act (N.J.S.A. 17: 12B-26), three savings and loan districts were established. The first district consisted of Bergen, Essex, Hudson, Morris, Passaic, Sussex and Warren Counties of Northern New Jersey. The second district included Hunterdon, Mercer, Middlesex, Monmouth, Somerset and Union Counties in the central part of New Jersey. The third district consisted of the remaining eight counties in the Southern part of the state.

The New Jersey Savings and Loan Act required that a state chartered Savings and Loan Association may establish a "de novo" branch only in

---

[1] Berkeley Savings and Loan Association, *Brochure of supporting documents for application.* August 1971, p. 16.
[2] *New York Times*, p. c 39, January 1, 1973.

the same savings and loan district of its principal office, but made no mention about the relocation of any branches.

In compliance with Section 17:12B-27.1(2) of the New Jersey State Acts, which required that: "if the proposed new location is in another municipality, the state association shall comply with the notice requirements set forth in subsection 2 of section 26 of the Act," Berkeley served notice of its application to other associations having offices located in Union Township or within two miles of the proposed site. The New Jersey Department of Banking also notified the New Jersey Savings League, the New Jersey Bankers Association, and the Savings Banks' Association of New Jersey of the pending application. In September 1971, a notice of the application was published in the bulletins of the aforementioned associations.

The Hearings and the Reactions

Following the announcement and notifications of Berkeley's intention to relocate its Chancellor Avenue branch, objections to the application and requests for hearings began to pour into the office of the Department of Banking. Among the objectors were the Colonial Savings and Loan Association, the First New Jersey Bank, the Investors Savings and Loan Association, the Union Central National Bank, and the Stonewall Savings and Loan Association of Linden. The Greater Newark Chamber of Commerce also objected to the move and requested a hearing, but subsequently withdrew the request.

Upon receipt of the requests, the Department held a series of hearings conducted by Hearing Officer, Mr. Clifford F. Blaze, on February 14, March 6, March 17, and March 20, 1972. The Department, in accordance with its usual procedures, placed all relevant materials into evidence as exhibits. Included in the exhibits were the brochures prepared by Berkeley in support of its application, and some feasibility studies prepared by Berkeley's consultants. Some objectors also submitted documents and exhibits as evidence. Several people testified on behalf of the applicant and some on behalf of the objectors. Among those who testified against the application was Mr. William Cohen, Liaison Officer of the Office of Economic Development of the City of Newark, who appeared as a representative of Deputy Mayor Frisina.

At the conclusion of the hearings, the parties involved filed written summations and legal briefs in support of their respective positions. At about the same time, the Department of Banking received a letter dated June 5, 1972 from Mayor Kenneth A. Gibson of Newark. Gibson stated in part that:

I do not believe that the proposed move of Berkeley Savings and Loan Association Chancellor Avenue Office to Union is in the public interest of the citizens of Newark. I would, therefore, strongly recommend that your Department refuse to grant this application.[3]

The Hearing Officer's Findings

Subsequent to the hearings and upon review of the arguments and legal briefs submitted by both sides, Hearing Officer Blaze prepared and submitted a 26 page report and recommendations to Acting Commissioner of Banking, Richard F. Schaub. The Hearing Officer recommended approval of the application.

Blaze based his conclusions and recommendations primarily on the statutory criteria provided in N.J.S.A. 17:12B-27(2) which read:

If the proposed new location is in another municipality than that in which the existing branch is located, the State Association shall comply with the notice requirement set forth in subsection 2 of section 26 of this act, and the Commissioner, before approving the application, shall determine (1) that the establishment and operation of such proposed branch office is in the public interest, (2) will be of benefit to the area served by such branch office, and (3) that such branch office may be established without undue injury to any other association in the area in which it is proposed to locate such branch office, and (4) that the conditions in the area to be served, afford a reasonable promise of successful operation.[4]

In interpreting these provisions, the Hearing Officer found that the applicant had satisfied each and every procedural requirement set forth in Subsection 2 of N.J.S.A. 17:12B-26. The critical issue that the Hearing Officer addressed himself to with greater deliberation was the question of the relocation of a branch office across district lines, as was contemplated by the applicant. On this issue, the Hearing Officer noted that the major positions given in the objectors' arguments centered on the following points:

1. It was the intent of the Legislature in enacting the legislation pertaining to the three savings and loan districts to make the Savings and Loan Act consistent with the Banking Act, but that in the instance at bar, banks would not be allowed to relocate branch offices across district lines, so the savings and loan associations should also be prohibited.
2. The applicable rules of statutory construction require that the savings and loan districts set forth in Section 26 of the Act be "read into" the provisions of 27.1 of the Act.
3. The applicant is attempting to accomplish by indirection what it

[3] *Hearing Officer's Report and Recommendation,* Division of Savings and Loan Associations, Department of Banking, State of New Jersey, September 12, 1972, p. 54.
[4] *Ibid.,* p. 5.

cannot do by direction, i.e. to establish a "de novo" branch in a "foreign" district.

4. If the statute is read and interpreted as it has been by the applicant, results inconsistent with the purpose of the Savings and Loan Act would be reached.

5. The Savings and Loan Act, read as a whole, sets forth a consistent pattern of regulation and control, the obvious intent of which is to keep financial institutions from exercising state-wide or semistate-wide influence.[5]

It was the Hearing Officer's finding after a careful search for legislative evidence, "that the recent legislative history with respect to the provision in question does not give us a specific indication of the Legislature's intent with respect to district and/or county lines when considering branch office relocations for savings and loan associations."[6]

In his view, "as the statute in question presently stands, there is absolutely no direct reference to any district limitations."[7] He flatly rejected "the notion that the Legislature of the State of New Jersey intended that each and every branch office relocation of a savings and loan association must be constrained by district lines"[8] and concluded "that there is not, and should not be any complete prohibition contained within the wording and/or intent of N.J.S.A. 17:12B-27.1 which would prohibit the relocation, in all instances, of a branch office from one district to another."[9]

Concerning the objectors' charge that the applicant attempted to accomplish—i.e. to establish a "de novo" branch in a "foreign" district—by indirection what it cannot do by direction, the Hearing Officer found no legislative restrictions in recent cases involving the movement of certain New Jersey Banks and bank holding companies. The fact that there had been a general liberalization of New Jersey Banking Legislation since 1948 was indicative of the desire of the state to achieve and maintain some degree of competitive parity between the state chartered and the federally chartered financial institutions, according to the Examiner. He cited some recent cases in which the federal savings and loan authorities gave permission to several savings and loan associations to establish "de novo" branches across district lines. "If my reasoning and conclusions are sustained," he argued, "substantial parity between state and federal associations will exist. If my reasoning and conclusions are rejected, state associations would be left in a severely debilitated competitive position."[10]

Turning to the question of whether the relocation offered a reasonable

---

[5] *Ibid.*, p. 8.
[6] *Ibid.*, p. 9.
[7] *Ibid.*, p. 10.
[8] *Ibid.*, p. 11.
[9] *Ibid.*, p. 13.
[10] *Ibid.*, p. 16.

promise of successful operation for the applicant, one of the statutory criteria to be met before approval of an application, the Hearing Officer heard and examined testimony and presentations of expert witnesses on behalf of the applicant and the objectors. The testimony centered on the issues of trade areas and projected clientele and sales of the proposed branch. It was the Hearing Officer's opinion that the estimates and projections made by the experts in terms of relative influence of competing financial institutions within and between the trade areas, the rate of penetration, and the potential dollar deposits of the new branch in the first few years could not be credited with any great degree of precision and are likely subject to errors. However, even giving allowance to those errors and reducing the experts' estimates by a wide margin, he concurred with the applicant that the branch could operate on a profitable basis with average deposits of $6.5 million or less. Thus, he concluded that he had reason to believe that conditions in the area to be served offered a reasonable promise of successful operation.

In deliberating the possibility of the proposed branch causing "undue injury" to other associations in the area, the Hearing Officer found that there were no mutual thrift institutions located at or near the shopping center, or within the trade area. In fact, there were no savings and loan associations located within a half mile of the extremes of the trade area. Therefore, it was difficult for him to conceive that the establishment of the branch would inflict undue injury to others in a statutory sense.

On the issue of whether the proposed branch was in the public interest, Mr. Blaze found that inasmuch as the Five Points Shopping Center and its surrounding trade areas lacked any mutual thrift institution to serve their large numbers of local residents, the establishment and operation of the branch office was in the public interest and would be of benefit to the area residents. Whether or not the relocation was in the public interest of the Newark area seemed to be an irrelevant question. Mr. Blaze found that the New Jersey Savings and Loan Law provided no reference or guideline other than the requirements that notice of the application be made to the associations located within two miles of the proposed site or within the community in which the relocated office was to be placed, and that the *proposed branch* be in the public interest. It was his interpretation that the Legislature had not delegated the judgment of the public interest beyond that which pertains to the proposed branch. For this reason he felt he was not in a position to discuss this matter in a statutory sense even though he might personally have thought it a pertinent or relevant consideration.

However, in order to provide background information on this issue for the commission to reach a final decision, he summarized the arguments from both sides. The opponents' arguments were generally represented by those submitted by Mr. Manahan, on behalf of Investors Savings and Loan Association.

1. That a savings and loan association is quasi public and therefore apparently owes a duty (undefined) to the persons residing in the area it serves.

2. That the "public interest" considers the public and not an advantage or benefit to a financial institution.

3. That the applicant's two expert witnesses ignored the issue.

4. That the Lyons Avenue office of the applicant could be the "next to go."

5. That an unhealthy precedent would be established.

6. That the situation in the Chancellor Avenue branch's area is not as bad as represented by the applicant.

7. That the old site has a better potential for the applicant than the new site.

8. That the denial of the application would help solve the problems in Newark to which the applicant has referred.[11]

Countering the preceding arguments, Mr. Blaze observed that

the record demonstrates that for social, demographic and physical reasons the applicant's Chancellor Avenue office has experienced a decline in deposits and influence in the community in recent years. It might well be concluded that the residents of Newark left the Berkeley before the Berkeley decided to leave Chancellor Avenue. Furthermore, the record demonstrates that after the removal, there will remain in the Chancellor Avenue area, offices of savings and loan associations and mutual savings banks which are more than adequately located and equipped to handle the savings needs of the residents therein.

No unhealthy precedent will be established here. The decision must of necessity rest on the facts of the case. No consideration can be given to a *possible* relocation application of the Lyons Avenue branch. Finally even if the Newark site had a better potential than the Union site, such a fact could not be used to deny the application. As Mr. Manahan stated in his brief, . . . the "advantage to any banking institution be it an *applicant* or an established objector" is not dispositive of the public interest.[12]

The Commissioner's Decision and Order

Having concluded his hearings and deliberations, Mr. Blaze submitted his report and recommendation to Acting Commissioner Richard F. Schaub for final decision. Upon careful review of the complete file of the case including all records and reports of the hearings and comments, the Commissioner made an independent evaluation and arrived at the following findings and conclusions.

The Commissioner agreed with the Hearing Officer that the applicant had satisfied the procedural requirements set forth by statute. He also

---

11 *Ibid.*, p. 24.
12 *Ibid.*, p. 25.

concurred with Mr. Blaze that the trade area as delineated by the applicant was reasonable. On the issues of a promise of successful operation, of
the potential of causing undue injury to other financial institutions, and
of the likelihood of benefiting the area to be served by the branch, the
Commissioner was again in agreement with the Hearing Officer.

However, on the concept of the public interest, the Commissioner de-
parted from the Hearing Examiner's findings and opinions. It was his
opinion "that in the applicable statute, N.J.S.A. 17 : 12B-27.1(2), a specific
distinction is made between the Commissioner's determining first, 'that
the establishment and operation of such proposed branch is in the public
interest,' and second, 'will be of benefit to the area served by such
branch.'" He asserted: "If the fact that a branch would benefit a particular
area does not in itself guarantee a serving of the public interest, then I am
obliged to examine other criteria in considering this latter issue."[13] He
cited a 1959 New Jersey court ruling in which the concept of "public
interest" was broadly interpreted to mean the legislative objectives of
achieving "(1) a sound banking structure, (2) healthily competitive, and (3)
fully adequate for the needs of the community."[14] He believed, therefore,
that his decision should be based on his evaluation of the alternatives—to
relocate the subject branch or to retain it at the present site—and to select
that alternative that best meets the objectives of the public interest.

On the question of healthy competition, he noted that although the
relocation might tend to introduce more competition in the proposed
location, it also, in the meantime, would diminish to a similar extent
competition in the existing trade area. Considering the issue of providing
adequate service for the needs of the community by weighing the relative
merit of improving service outside a central city against that of decreasing
service within it, the Commissioner was of the opinion that "the continued presence of the applicant's branch office at the Chancellor Avenue
location would convey both an actual and symbolic measure of economic
stability (in the city)."[15] Although he recognized the physical and economic deterioration over the years in central city communities which
lacked the means to reverse the trend of decline, he nonetheless felt "it is
an acknowledged role of government at all levels to attempt to arrest such
trends."[16] Thus in his judgment ". . . the detriment to the public interest
which would result from the closing of the Chancellor Avenue office
more than outweighs the favorable aspects relating to its relocation at the
proposed site and . . . the subject application should therefore be denied."[17] This decision, he believed, would also contribute to the sound-

[13] *Commissioner's Decision and Order*, Department of Banking, State of New Jersey, January 24, 1973, p. 7.

[14] *Ibid.*, p. 7.

[15] *Ibid.*, p. 8.

[16] *Ibid.*, p. 8.

[17] *Ibid.*, p. 8.

ness of the New Jersey banking structure, also meeting the objective of public interest.

Having denied the application, the Commissioner conceded that while finding it in the public interest to maintain this facility, it was beyond his power "to require an association to remain within an area where its employees and customers face a real threat of physical harm."[18] And he warned that "officials of the City of Newark who deem it important to retain the Berkeley at its present site have a responsibility to ensure the safety of its customers and the residents of the neighborhood."[19] Finally having decided to deny the application based on the criterion of public interest, the Commissioner found it unnecessary to address the question of relocation across district lines.

[18] *Ibid.*, p. 10.
[19] *Ibid.*, p. 10.

Calnational Oil Company (A)

Mr. Bill Hoad, a young engineer engaged in economic analysis work at the Hinckley Beach refinery of the Calnational Oil Company, proposed that he be authorized to develop a linear programming model of the refinery's operations.

Mr. Robert Cramer, the general manager, faced the alternative of approving the plan and budget for constructing the model or of rejecting the proposal.

Company Background

The Calnational Oil Company was one of the largest fully integrated oil companies in the western part of the United States. Corporate offices were in San Francisco, California, and the company's producing wells were in oil fields in the western United States, the Gulf Coast area, and overseas. The company maintained extensive oil exploration activities, and Calnational's top management considered production of oil at the well as the key to the company's profitability.

At each of the fields in which Calnational had wells, the company operated gathering and pipeline systems to carry the crude petroleum to dockside or directly to the company's refineries. All but one of the company's

Revised version of an earlier case written under direction of Professor Philip Thurston and copyrighted by the President and Fellows of Harvard College. Revised and published with expressed permission.

refineries were located either on the Gulf of Mexico or on the Pacific seaboard of the United States and each refinery had docking facilities. The smallest refinery had a capacity capable of processing 40,000 barrels of crude petroleum per day; the largest refinery had a maximum capacity of 60,000 barrels per day.

Accessibility to water transport was important both for shipping finished products from the refinery and for receipt of crude petroleum from abroad. The purchase price of foreign oil from Calnational's own foreign operation or other sources was approximately $1 per barrel more than domestic crude. Since the margin from refinery operations was considered to be about 75 cents per barrel, potential additional earnings from domestic crude purchases were very attractive to Calnational. Domestic supplies and foreign crude prices changed rapidly to affect the profitability of refinery operations.

Calnational marketed its petroleum products in the western United States, primarily in states touching the Pacific Ocean. The company's largest dollar sales were from motor gasoline, which was sold by Calnational wholesaling outlets and through the company's leased retail stations. Partially because of warm temperatures in the company's marketing area, sales of petroleum products used for heating were proportionally lower than was true for companies in the eastern and northern United States. Calnational used a complex system of internal transfer pricing to indicate profitability within the producing, transporting, refining, and marketing segments of the business.

Motor gasoline sales were from three grades of gasoline: Super, Special, and Standard.[1] The company also marketed other products obtained from the crude petroleum in the refining process. These products included one which was lighter than gasoline. Others, kerosene, some jet fuels, heating oils, and diesel fuels were called "middle" distillates. These were heavier than gasoline. Still heavier products were fuel oils and asphalts. All of these products could be manufactured in varying proportions from the many grades of crude available to the company. Grade was determined by the proportion of the various products existing in the crude in its natural state.

The corporation's president and the vice presidents were located in the San Francisco headquarters, with the exception of the three marketing vice presidents whose offices were in the geographic regions for which they were responsible. Each refinery had a general manager who reported to the Vice President for Refining in San Francisco. Pricing and product mix policy decisions were made formally through joint approval of the marketing and refining vice presidents. Working within these policies, the sales and refinery personnel in a particular area and the producing de-

---

[1] The three grades which were sold to the public varied in formulation as determined by seasonal factors and raw material cost considerations.

partments who supplied crude to the refinery had frequent informal communication. When he felt it necessary, a refinery general manager might ask the support of the refining vice president in these negotiations.

The Hinckley Beach Refinery

One of Calnational's oldest refineries was at Hinckley Beach, north of San Diego on the California coast. Robert Cramer, the refinery general manager, had worked at this refinery for 21 years. Approximately half of the 400 men employed at the refinery had worked there more than 10 years. During those 10 years the refinery's maximum capacity had been at about 60,000 barrels of crude petroleum per day.

The refinery general manager had five men reporting directly to him: one operations manager and four managers of supporting staff departments. These five met with the general manager at least one morning a week and sometimes more often for a three- to four-hour review and planning discussion. Exhibit 6-1 portrays the formal management structure. Mr. Cramer, the general manager, spent much of his time in a typical

Exhibit 6-1 Calnational Oil Company Management Organization at the Hinckley Beach Refinery

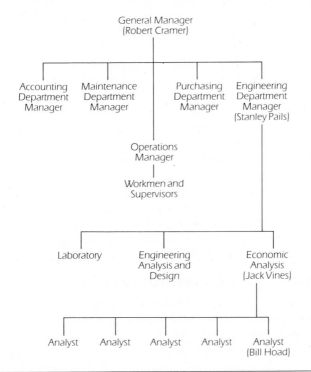

week working on problems with the operations manager and the manager of the maintenance department. The operations manager had an office directly adjoining Mr. Cramer's, and during a day they had many informal discussions about refinery problems. Before becoming general manager, Mr. Cramer had been operations manager at Hinckley Beach for eight years.

The total work force at Hinckley Beach was maintained at about 400 workers throughout the year. Since the refinery was operated 24 hours per day seven days a week, the men working in operations and in the maintenance department were assigned to four shifts. Normal operation of the refining equipment required little hand labor. Most of the work involved monitoring the refinery instrumentation. Large operating and maintenance crews were maintained, however, to insure adequate manpower to correct quickly any upsets in the several refinery processes or physical breakdown of the equipment, and to handle the extra work associated with substantial changes in volumes of products.

The 180 men supervised by the operations manager were further subdivided into four groups. Twenty-five were designated as storage and transfer men, twenty men were assigned to treating and blending, and ten men were assigned to refinery utilities. The remainder of the men were supervised by four shift foremen who reported to Mr. Cramer.

Of the 140 men in the maintenance department, most were either riggers, mechanics, pipe fitters, or electricians. A major part of the maintenance department's responsibility was preventive maintenance on refinery instrumentation. Most of the automatic control devices in the refinery were installed in parallel with hand controls, so that operations could be continued when automatic instrumentation failed.

As was generally true in oil refineries, the layout and equipment at Hinckley Beach were custom designed. All of the units in the refinery were so large that they were not enclosed in buildings. The only closed buildings were those which housed the refinery offices and the controls for the refinery units. There were five control houses in the refinery. Each control house was air conditioned and contained all the instrumentation and controls for one or several units of equipment in the refinery. Operations personnel in these control houses made all settings and adjustments to equipment operations. One control house was concerned only with the catalytic cracker which was as high as a 10-story building. The refinery, including its storage and docking facilities, covered an area of 100 acres.

The Oil Refining Process at Hinckley Beach

The following is a greatly simplified description of the refining operation at Hinckley, shown schematically in Exhibit 6–2.

Crude petroleum is composed primarily of hydrocarbons: molecules composed principally of hydrogen and carbon, but with sulfur and several other undesirable elements present in small amounts. These hydrocar-

Exhibit 6—2 Calnational Oil Company Simplified Process Flow Diagram for Hinckley Beach

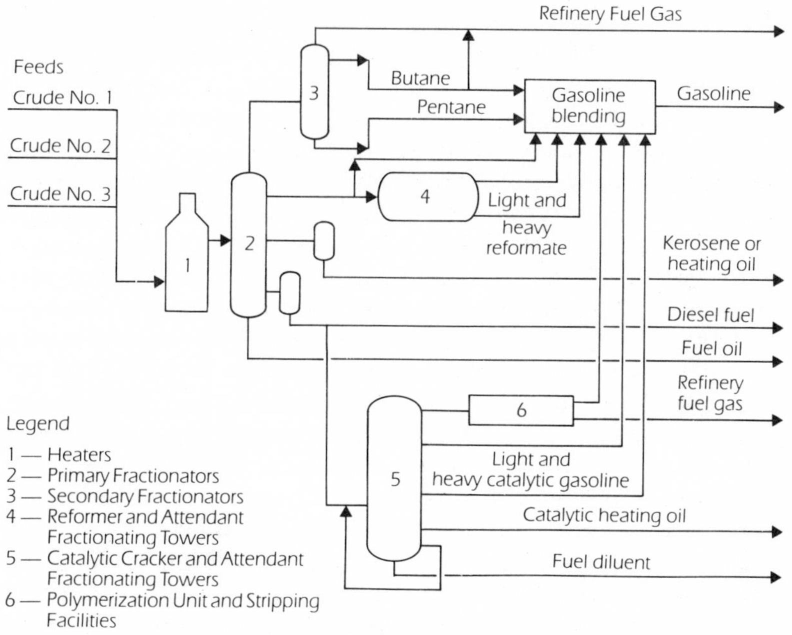

Legend
1 — Heaters
2 — Primary Fractionators
3 — Secondary Fractionators
4 — Reformer and Attendant
    Fractionating Towers
5 — Catalytic Cracker and Attendant
    Fractionating Towers
6 — Polymerization Unit and Stripping
    Facilities

bons occur as an extremely large number of different compounds, each hydrocarbon compound being differentiated by either the number of carbon or hydrogen atoms in the molecule or the way in which they are arranged. Each hydrocarbon boils at a specific temperature. Most hydrocarbons in typical crude petroleum boil between 65°F and 1100°F. The differences in boiling point are the basis for separating out the variety of products obtained from crude petroleum in the refining process.

The crudes received at Hinckley Beach contained from 8% to 12% natural motor gasoline. That is, about 8% to 12% of the hydrocarbons in the crude were of the molecular structure found most suitable for motor gasoline. Some of the remainder of the crude was further processed to make motor gasoline and some was processed into other products.

Distillation was the basic separation process in refining. First stage distillation of the crude petroleum took place in several pieces of equipment which were collectively called the "pipe stills." The crude petroleum was sent from storage through a desalting device and a series of heaters to the fractionating towers. Part of the heat was supplied by the heat of in-process products. The crude was raised to a temperature between 600°F and 700°F in the heaters, at which temperature it would have partially vaporized except for the fact it was kept under pressure. Upon introduction to the lower pressure fractionating towers the crude partially flashed to vapor. In the fractionating towers were a series of shallow "bubble trays" located one above the other. Small chimneys in each tray allowed the vapor to rise from tray to tray. The construction of each tray was such as to maintain a shallow pool of oil upon it. The crude vapor had to bubble through this oil to rise to the next tray. Each tray in the fractionating tower was slightly cooler than the one below. As the vapor bubbled through the oil on a given tray the heavier components of the vapor condensed and became part of the pool of oil on that tray. The heavier part of the crude condensed on the lower trays of the tower while the lighter constituents reached the upper, cooler trays before condensing. Each tray had a drain (called a "down-comer") which allowed the pool of oil as it was supplemented by the condensed vapor to spill over to the next lower tray. Because the tray below was slightly warmer some of the "spill" was vaporized again. In this way, the crude was continuously redistilled and separated by boiling range. Certain trays could be connected to outlets which allowed taking away from the tower the constituents of the crude which fell in relatively narrow limits of boiling range and volatility. The temperatures at which these outlet trays were maintained were to some extent variable. The petroleum fraction taken from a given tray was, in part, a function of this variable temperature. Because the petroleum fraction taken was a complex mixture of hydrocarbon compounds it boiled, in a simple laboratory distillation, over a temperature interval. The breadth of this temperature interval was a function of the mechanical design of the tower and the amount of "reflux" used in the operation. Reflux was obtained by reintroducing into the tower either the condensed and cooled vapors taken out of the top of the tower or part of the "sidestreams" taken from the outlet trays.

Only from 8% to 12% of the crude was taken from the fractionating tower in the range of hydrocarbons suitable for motor gasoline. This motor gasoline fraction consisted almost entirely of hydrocarbons with from 5 to 12 carbon atoms in each hydrocarbon molecule. Hydrocarbons with more than 12 carbon atoms had a lower volatility and so were taken from points lower on the fractionating tower than was the motor gasoline. Hydrocarbons with fewer than 5 carbon atoms were taken off the top of the tower. The heavier hydrocarbons could be run through another process which broke the molecules up so that some of the fragments would fall into the 5 to 12 carbon atom range and so be suitable for motor gasoline. This breaking-up process was called "cracking." The product of the cracking process was run through other fractionating towers. Cracking also raised the octane level of the motor gasoline fraction by causing changes in the structure and in the ratio of hydrogen to carbon in the hydrocarbon molecule.

Hinckley Beach had one cracking unit, called a catalytic cracking reactor. The central part of this unit was the "reactor," a closed chamber where the vapors were introduced at high temperature and pressure with a chemical catalyst in the form of a powder. Cracked vapors were removed from the reactor and sent to a fractionating tower. Some of the catalyst was carried off with the cracked vapors, but most of this catalyst was recovered from the bottom of the fractionating tower and reused by introducing it back into the feed to the cracker. That portion of the cracking unit which fed and regenerated the catalyst after use was a larger part of the unit than was the reactor. The cracking unit required an annual shutdown for maintenance, clean-out, inspection, and repair.

Another unit in the refinery was a "catalytic reformer." This unit converted gasoline obtained from the primary distillation towers into higher octane gasoline. The Calnational Oil Company leased the right to use a particular reforming process at a fixed cost per barrel run through the reformer. The primary operating control on the reformer was the "severity level," which in simple terms, was the octane level of the products. High severity levels gave higher octane levels but also gave a lower yield of motor gasoline because a higher proportion of unusable gas vapors was produced. The selection of severity levels for the reformer, therefore, required economic balancing of desired octane levels with the process yield.

The octane levels of the gasolines produced on the catalytic cracker and the catalytic reformer could be improved during the final blending of the three "finished" grades of gasoline by the addition of small amounts of a relatively expensive chemical compound, tetra-ethyl lead.

As noted above, products with fewer than five carbon atoms fell outside the range of motor gasoline and were taken from the top of the fractionating towers. Processes were available to convert some of these lighter products to motor gasoline. At the Hinckley Beach refinery only the light products from the cracking operation were so converted, in a process called "polymerization."

The polymerization unit contained a reactor, where the lighter vapors were put under high pressure and temperature over a bed of phosphoric acid type catalyst. In the presence of this catalyst, some of the lighter vapors—butylenes and propylene—reacted to form high octane fuel, called polymer. This product was then passed through another fractionating tower where it was again distilled to remove from the gasoline fraction the light products which did not react in the polymerization process.

There were numerous storage points in the refining process at Hinckley Beach. Crude petroleum was stored in tanks having individual capacities of approximately 150,000 barrels. This storage was divided according to the types of crude received. There was considerable tankage also within the refinery for in-process and finished product storage. The primary reason for this storage was the high cost of down time. In normal operations, much of the in-process storage was not required but could be used as finished product storage. When maintenance or repair was required on a

---

Exhibit 6—3 Calnational Oil Company Finished Products at Hinckley Beach

Propane
Aviation Gasoline
Super, Special, and Standard Grades of Motor Gasoline
Jet Fuel
Kerosene
Heating Oil
Diesel
Two Grades of Residual Fuel
Four Grades of Asphalt

---

unit the extra tankage could be used to schedule around the unit for short periods. In one sense, the in-process storage capacity was balanced against the size of the maintenance force. Without this storage ability, a far larger maintenance force would have been required to shorten the down time. Another way to avoid the need of the larger maintenance force would have been to contract out major maintenance to firms specializing in that work.

Finished product tankage was large enough to handle uneven demand. Motor gasoline demand reached a peak during the summer months. During colder weather, demand for fuel oil in the company's northern markets hit a peak. The Hinckley Beach refinery was built to produce the average expected demand over the years with the storage tankage intended to anticipate the peak demand.

Motor gasoline was blended, as were the other products, before final storage. While motor gasoline contained mainly hydrocarbons in the 5 to 12 carbon atom range, its actual composition was varied somewhat to produce the desired end-use characteristics during final blending. The variations were accomplished by changing the proportions of the gasoline fractions used to make the final blend and, to some extent, by the introduction of small amounts of the lighter hydrocarbons with three and four carbon atoms. Exhibit 6–3 lists the refinery's final products. Not all were manufactured or sold continuously.

The Engineering Department

The manager of the engineering department, Mr. Stanley Pails, was directly responsible to Mr. Cramer. Although the department was charged with preparing engineering and economic studies of refinery operations, Mr. Pails had no formal authority to implement recommendations made by his department. Reports and recommendations prepared by the engineering department were sent always to the office of the operations manager with a copy to the general manager in those cases where the study had been requested by the operations manager or his subordinates. A typical request was for a study of the catalytic cracking reactor to determine the desirability of purchasing a pump capable of a faster feed rate to the unit. When the general manager personally requested a study, copies of the report went to him only.

The engineering department was divided into an Engineering Analysis and Design branch, an Economic Analysis branch, and a laboratory. Eight men worked for the head of the Engineering Analysis and Design branch and five worked for Mr. Jack Vines, the chief of the Economic Analysis branch. Five of the eight men working in Engineering Analysis and Design were graduate engineers. Four of the five analysts in the Economic Analysis branch were also graduate engineers. Mr. Vines was not a graduate engineer, but he had worked in the refinery for 20 years and was intimately familiar with day-to-day operations.

Mr. Bill Hoad, one of the analysts in the Economic Analysis branch, was the youngest of the analysts in the section. He had received bachelors and masters degrees in chemical engineering before joining the Calnational Oil Company. In his early assignments to study the economics of operating refinery units he showed considerable skill in developing mathematical expressions for the relationships between the physical operating characteristics of the units and their costs. Mr. Hoad's skills and interest led him to apply linear programming techniques in one of his work assignments.

Hoad first introduced linear programming at the Hinckley Beach refinery to determine the amounts to be produced of the 11 constituents needed for blending the company's three grades of motor gasoline. The constituents are listed in Exhibit 6–4.

Exhibit 6—4 Calnational Oil Company Constituents of Motor Gasoline

Constituent	Alternate Dispositions Other Than Motor Gasoline
Light Virgin Naptha	
Light Reformate	
Heavy Reformate	
Light Catalytic Naptha	
Heavy Catalytic Naptha	Heating Oil
Polymer	
Aviation Alkylate	Aviation Gas
C_4 – Butane	Poly plant (if unsaturated)
C_5 – Pentane	
Light and Heavy Reformer feed	Heating Oil, Jet Fuel, Kerosene
Tetra-Ethyl Lead	

For each of the three grades of motor gasoline there were nine specifications. These specifications affected antiknock characteristics, vapor lock characteristics, and other performance characteristics. The company changed specifications for the three grades of gasoline seasonally and as on going research and development improved specifications. Specifications for each gasoline grade could change as frequently as once a month.

For each such change, Mr. Hoad had to determine the amount of each of the 11 constituents to be produced, purchased, or taken from inventory in order to blend the amount of gasoline in each grade required by demand forecasts. The nine specifications for each grade could be satisfied by a variety of blends of the 11 available constituents. Hoad's objective was to find the blends which both met the specifications and cost the least.

Hoad considered the only relevant costs in the blending problem to be those which were directly proportional to the volume of the constituent used. These costs were not constant over long periods of time. For example, one of the crudes used might yield a catalytic cracking feed requiring far more recycling than another to produce the same amount of constituents. Thus, different proportions of the crudes available at the refinery resulted in different costs of blending operations.

Mr. Hoad first attacked the blending problem by trial and error calculation. He began by assuming that the refinery's present operating program was fixed. That is, the volume of the constituents being produced would not be changed. Under this assumption Hoad still had many alternative ways of meeting specifications and demands in the three grades of motor gasoline. For instance, he might achieve octane levels in one of the blends either by using reformate from the refinery or using purchased tetra-ethyl lead as an additive. Hoad would find a feasible blend to meet specifications and demand volumes, and then calculate the variable cost of the blend. Reflected in this cost would be the value of any products which would be produced as a by-product of motor gasoline production and which would be burned as fuel to provide heat in the refining process.

Mr. Hoad usually repeated this process several times, in each case varying the blend in the hope of finding a feasible solution with a lower cost. The first calculation generally took about three hours if most of the specifications had been changed for each grade and several prices had varied from previous calculations. Subsequent trials to find a lower cost solution usually took about one hour.

Mr. Hoad had been making the blending studies for motor gasoline for six months. As he gained experience with the problem, he became more proficient in guessing low-cost solutions on the first trial and he had found several ways to speed up his calculations on the desk calculator. Despite these improvements, Mr. Hoad found the method tedious. Further, he was bothered by the fact that his best solution for any given blending problem might be far from the optimum solution possible when considering the total complex of blends to be calculated over a given period of time.

While taking evening courses in applied mathematics at a nearby university, Mr. Hoad recognized that his blending problem at the refinery was a type of linear programming problem which could be solved by the simplex method.

His other work slackened enough to allow him extra time with the blending problem. He read several articles in the published literature and then discussed his specific problem with the Representative of an IBM sales office. From IBM, Hoad obtained a standard computer program for solving linear programming problems by the simplex method.

The Hinckley Beach refinery had an IBM computer which was available both to the refinery staff and to the marketing division personnel whose regional office was close by. One man from the Engineering Analysis and Design branch was responsible for alloting time on the computer.

When he was next assigned a blending problem, Hoad prepared it for solution by linear programming. First, he wrote linear equations describing the constraints. He then wrote a profit equation which was to be the objective function. All of these equations were represented in a tabular form, similar to the greatly simplified illustration given in Exhibit 6–5.[2] Hoad's array or matrix contained the input information for the computer program. The column headings in Exhibit 6–5 identify the variables of the problem; each row represents a constraint. He used 41 rows and 74 columns. From this matrix and the linear program instructions, Hoad fed data to the computer, which then solved the blending problem.

Hoad compared his best trial and error solution with the maximum profit solution found by the computer program. The optimal solution indicated a potential profit $200 per day greater than his trial and error solution.

Hoad took both the results of the linear program and his trial and error calculations to Mr. Vines. Vines was impressed by the potential saving and commended Hoad. Later that day, Mr. Vines mentioned Hoad's use of the computer program to Mr. Pails. Pails commented: "I don't see how you'd ever know whether that added profit materialized. Perhaps the fact

---

[2] At the request of the case writer Bill Hoad prepared Exhibit 6–5 and submitted also this comment:

Professor:

It's almost impossible to describe the gasoline matrix without developing all of it in detail and this requires extensive background in engineering and petroleum economics. The matrix shown (Exhibit 6–5) is merely a starter in the most elementary sense. Any model is limited only by the ingenuity of the constructor—the linear model can approach reality to any degree desired. I would like to point out that not anybody can build or understand models even with the required academic background. Applications to real situations are even more difficult because the abstract nature is "second order."

Please note that if you yourself have difficulty constructing a similar but different in detail model, your students will probably find it close to impossible to comprehend.

I guess what I'm saying is that optimizing models are difficult and require more than the broad brush approach to comprehend.

/s/ Bill Hoad

Exhibit 6—5 Calnational Oil Company A Greatly Simplified Illustration of the Matrix Formulation for Blending Problem

	PREMIUM SPEC. S	C₄ TO PREMIUM	REFORMATE TO PREM	CAT TO PREM	REGULAR SPEC. S	C₄ TO REGULAR	REFORMATE TO REG	CAT TO REG	
PROFIT	−5.0 (Price)	+.02 (Finishing Costs, etc.)	.03	.025	−4.0	+.02	+.03	+.025	
C₄ MATERIAL BALANCE		1				1			= 0
REFORMATE MAT. BALANCE			1				1		= 0
CAT GASOLINE BALANCE				1				1	= 0
SPECIAL GRADE GASOLINE CONSTRAINTS — VAPOR PRESSURE MAX CONSTRAINT	−10.0	80.0	5.0	1.0					= 0
VOLATILITY MIN CONSTRAINT	50.0	−100.0	−35.0	−40.0					= 0
OCTANE MIN. CONSTRAINT	100.0	−105.0	−100.0	−95.0					= 0
PREMIUM VOLUME LIMIT	1								< 6.0
STANDARD GRADE GASOLINE CONSTRAINTS — VAPOR PRESSURE					−10.0	80.0	5.0	6.0	= 0
VOLATILITY					40.0	−100.0	−35.0	−40.0	= 0
OCTANE					95.0	−100.0	−100.0	−95.0	= 0
REGULAR MATERIAL BAL					1	−1	−1	−1	= 0
REGULAR VOLUME LIMIT					1				< 12.0

that using linear programming and the computer gives quicker solutions is more important than the dollar savings."

Hoad continued to submit recommendations for blending with no mention of linear programming.

Hoad continued his study of linear programming. He realized that the way in which he had formulated the blending problem for the linear programming solution neglected many related operating decisions in the refinery. He realized that, although the computer program gave a maximum profit solution for the variables included in the equations for blending operations, it was not necessarily an optimal or highest profit solution for operating the refinery as a whole.

Hoad studied the large number of economic studies on file in the Economic Analysis office files. He found more than 1,000 of these studies, prepared over the previous 10 years. Most of the studies were of one unit or part of a unit in the refinery, often as part of preparation for capital or expense budgets or expense item outlays. The reports of the studies generally contained an equation or group of equations relating physical operating characteristics of the units with costs. Included in each report was a recommendation of how the unit should be run in certain circumstances to minimize costs. Hoad noted that in most cases the study recommended settings or equipment modifications without a detailed investigation of how the recommendation might affect the economics of *other* units.

A number of the most lengthy studies in the files were of total refinery operations. These studies were prepared at least quarterly as a basis for recommending operating programs to the refinery management. Hoad himself had prepared two of these recommended total refinery operating programs. When preparing these programs, the analysts used the smaller studies of refinery units including Hoad's blending problem solutions. The analysts used the same method Hoad had used for blending: find one feasible solution and then try as many others as time permitted in an effort to increase the expected profit.

Hoad then considered the possibility of constructing a linear programming model of the total refinery operation. He reasoned that the same potential profits might be realized as he had found in applying linear programming to the blending problem. He realized that the objective function and the constraints of the problem would have to be approximated by linear equations. Hoad knew that many of the equations describing unit operations involved exponentials of some of the variables. For instance, the effect of tetra-ethyl lead on octane in blending motor gasoline was a nonlinear function of both the amount of tetra-ethyl lead already in the blend and the octane of the gasoline. Hoad thought this difficulty could be overcome by approximating these more complicated functions with linear equations.

Hoad discussed the possibility of preparing a refinery model with Mr.

Vines. Vines agreed with Hoad that some substantial savings might be possible with such a model, but he felt incapable of estimating either the amount of the savings or the difficulty Hoad might encounter in developing a working model. To help him evaluate the project, Vines asked Hoad to write a proposal. He told Hoad to include in the proposal an itemized estimate of the expected costs, the expected time to complete the model, and a description of the main problems and how he proposed to solve them.

After about a week, Hoad gave Vines his proposal. In the proposal, he estimated the project would require six months of his full time. In addition, he would require the intermittent help of other analysts as well as professional consulting help. He also included the cost of renting time on an IBM computer, at $350 per hour.

Hoad estimated in his proposal that the total costs for the project, including salaries as well as out-of-pocket costs to the company, would be $25,000.

In the proposal, Hoad asserted that the project would "produce a useful result," with a probability of 0.8, and that it would be impossible either to give a better cost or probability of success estimate before the fourth month of the project. He did not include a detailed description of the problems expected or his methods for handling them. Rather, he asked Mr. Vines that he be allowed to do this orally to any group who might pass judgment on the proposal. Hoad said that he thought the presentation would be much more effective if he were able to tailor it to his audience and respond to their questions.

Mr. Vines accepted the written part of Mr. Hoad's proposal. He discussed the proposal with Mr. Pails, admitting that he did not understand the details but suggesting that Mr. Hoad would be available for discussion. Mr. Vines recommended to Mr. Pails that Hoad be authorized to go ahead with the project. Pails described the proposal to Mr. Cramer, the general manager, and expressed confidence in Hoad's ability. Mr. Cramer directed that the proposal be heard and discussed at the next Friday morning meeting of the refinery management.

The operations manager and the department managers had received Hoad's cost estimates the day before the meeting. Hoad began his presentation by giving the group a simplified refining problem specified by cost and capacity data shown in Exhibit 6−6. After giving the men five minutes to study the data, Hoad asked each manager to decide what amount of each of the available crudes to be run. Hoad wrote down their answers on a large easel pad.

Hoad then gave a brief description of the rudiments of linear programming and distributed the equations and the matrix necessary to formulate the simple refining problem as a linear programming problem. The development of the equations and the matrix are shown in Exhibits 6−7 and 6−8. Using the matrix in Exhibit 6−8 Hoad demonstrated the first step in

Exhibit 6—6 Calnational Oil Company Data for Simplified Refining Problem

Processing Units	Capacity (MB/D)
Pipestill (PS)	10
Cat. Plant (CP)	20

Crude Availability	MB/D
Crude 1 (CR1)	6
Crude 2 (CR2)	6
Crude 3 (CR3)	6

Crude Yields (Bbls/BBL of Crude Run)	Crude 1	Crude 2	Crude 3
Virgin Naphtha (VNT)	.20	.15	
Virgin Heating Oil (VHT)	.25	.30	.25
Gas Oil (VCG)	.40	.30	.25
Pitch (PTH)	.05	.15	.40

Cat. Plant Yields (Bbls/BBL of Feed)	Virgin H.O.	Gas Oil
Pitch (PTH)	.10	.15
Cat. Naphtha (CNT)	.20	.50
Cat. Heating Oil (CHT)	.80	.50
Total Feed (BBL/BBL of Fresh Feed) 2.0	5.0	

Product Demand	MB/D Max.
Gasoline (GS)	4
Heating Oil (HT)	4
Fuel	*

Product Specifications and Blending Qualities

Gasoline—Octane Specification	80	
Component	Octane	From Spec.
Virgin Naphtha	59	21−
Cat. Naphtha	98	18+
Fuel—Ratio Blend		
Pitch—90%		
Cat. Heating Oil—10%		

Cost Data		Sales Realization	
Expenses		Gasoline	25.00 $/Bbl
Crude 1 23.75 $/Bbl		Heating Oil	24.00 $/Bbl
Crude 2 23.35 $/Bbl			
Crude 3 22.95 $/Bbl		Fuel	22.00 $/Bbl
Pipestill .05 $/Bbl Run (Incremental)			
Cat. Plant .10 $/Bbl Fresh Feed (Incremental)			

*All fuel can be sold.

Exhibit 6—7 Calnational Oil Company Development of Equations (Total 14 Equations + Profit)

Processing Restrictions: (2 Equations — Pipestill and Cat. Plant)
  Example: Pipestill
    $ICR_1 + ICR_2 + ICR_3 \leq 10$ (Max. Pipestill Capacity)
where CR_1, CR_2, CR_3 are volumes of crude run/day

Crude Restrictions: (3 Equations)
  ICR_1 ≤ 6 (Max. Crude Available)
      ICR_2 ≤ 6 (Max. Crude Available)
          ICR_3 ≤ 6 (Max. Crude Available)

Intermediate Products: (6 Equations — VNT, VHT, VCG, PTH, CNT, CHT)
                    Product used $\leq$ Product made
                            or
                  Product used — Product made ≤ 0
  Example: Virgin naphtha (VNT)
    — (Product Made)   + (Product Used) ≤ 0
  $- .20\, CR_1 - .15\, CR_2 + 1\, VNTGS + 1\, VNTFL \leq 0$

Product Volumes: (2 Equations — Gasoline and Heating Oil)
  Example: Gasoline (GS)
    $1\, VNTGS + 1\, CNTGS \leq 4$

Specification: (1 Equation — Gasoline Octane)
  Product quality must be equal to or greater than spec.
    VNTGS Below Spec. 21 Units
    CNTGS Above Spec. 18 Units
      $- 18\, CNTGS + 21\, VNTGS \leq 0$

Profit (Maximize Profit)
  Profit = +2.00 FUEL   +2.00 VNTFL   +2.00 VHTFL
           +4.00 CHT   +4.00 CNTHT
           +5.00 VNTGS   +5.00 CNTGS
           −3.80 CR_1 −3.40 CR_2 −3.00 CR_3
           −.1 TVHT   −.1 TVCG

---

the simplex method on the easel pad. He next showed the optimal solution as found by computer calculation. None of the manager's decisions approached the solution which Hoad presented as optimal.

He told the managers that while the problem at hand was not nearly so difficult as the real problem in the refinery, the solution by linear programming illustrated two things: first, that the method was systematic and could therefore be programmed for a computer, and second, the solution was not only guaranteed to be feasible but that it was also the highest profit solution possible. In response to a question he admitted that the

Exhibit 6–8 Calnational Oil Company Linear Programming Matrix 13 Activities

			CRUDE			CAT PLANT		FUEL	FUEL			HEATING OIL			GASOLINE	
	rhs	CR$_1$	CR$_2$	CR$_3$	TVHT	TVCG	FUEL	VNTFL	CHTFL	VHTHT	CHTHT	CNTHT	VNTGS	CNTGS
PROFIT		−23.80	−23.40	−23.00	−.1	−.1	22.00	22.00	22.00	24.00	24.00	24.00	25.00	25.00
CRUDE														
CR$_1$ MAX	≤6	1												
CR$_2$ MAX	≤6		1											
CR$_3$ MAX	≤6			1										
PS. CAP.	≤10	1	1	1										
INT PRODUCTS														
VNT	≤0	−.2	−.15					1					1	
VHT	≤0	−.25	−.30	−.25	1					1				
VCG	≤0	−.4	−.30	−.25		1								
PTH	≤0	−.05	−.15	−.40	−.1	−.15	.9							
CNT	≤0				−.2	−.5						1		1
CHT	≤0				−.8	−.5	.1		1		1			
CAT CAP	≤20				2	5								
PRODUCTS														
HT. VOL.	≤4									1	1	1		
GS. VOL.	≤4												1	
GS. SPEC.	≤0												+21	−18

optimal solution depended on the accuracy of the equations, but he pointed out that these same equations were used in the manual method. Hoad then briefly outlined the problems he expected to encounter. He said that he could not guarantee their solution, but he reiterated his judgment that the probability of his producing a useful result was about 0.8.

The management group discussed the proposal. Hoad was asked by the operations manager what equations he intended to use in describing the catalytic cracker. Hoad replied that he could not know before-hand which equations developed in the case studies would be used. He said that it would depend on what equations would be required to relate the various segments of the model.

Most of the men in the meeting were intrigued by the possibilities of a linear programming model for the refinery. Two of the department heads were skeptical about whether the model would ever be used even if it could be developed. The manager of the accounting department expressed concern over Hoad's inability to predict cost savings from the use of the model.

Calnational
Oil Company (B)

Mr. Bill Hoad, an economic analyst at the Hinckley refinery, proposed to a management meeting that he be permitted to attempt development of a linear programming model of the refinery. After Hoad presented his proposal, the management group discussed their doubts that the project would justify the cost. Mr. Cramer, the refinery manager, finally ended the discussion by saying: "Whatever the possible pay-offs may be, they look large to me compared with the $25,000 cost of development. I accept Hoad's estimate of 0.8 probability of success and the six months he asks for seem reasonable. I'll send a memo today authorizing the project to start immediately."

Development of the Model

Hoad began full-time work on the model. His regular assignments on blending problems and special studies were given to Mr. Carl Rosewall, another analyst. Mr. Rosewall was given the assignment with the assurance that Mr. Hoad would be available to help with any difficulties.

At the end of two weeks' work, Mr. Hoad issued his first progress report. This was a one-page document which Hoad sent to Mr. Vines, Mr. Pails, and Mr. Cramer. Mr. Vines received a copy because ostensibly he

Revised version of an earlier case written under the direction of Professor Phillip Thurston and copyrighted by the President and Fellows of Harvard College. Revised and published with expressed permission.

was supervising Mr. Hoad in his work. In fact Hoad worked independently. Hoad excluded operating people from the distribution of his reports. About this, he commented:

If I gave a detailed report of my work to the operating people, they'd become unduly excited by the approximations I made in the model. Some variables have to be left out to make the model manageable and some nonlinear functions have to be approximated. Once I have the total model working. I can show that it is not sensitive to the deleted and modified variables.

In the report issued at the end of the first two weeks, Hoad reported that he had successfully run a simulation of the refinery on the computer using a linear programming model with 80 equations and 150 variables. He acknowledged surprise and pleasure at this early success. Hoad's strategy had been to pay little attention at first to getting accurate models for each unit, but to get a small and rough total refinery model working early. As an alternative approach, Hoad said that he might have worked on the model for each unit, adding detail to get more exact representations. The material from earlier studies had turned out to be more useful than he had expected. He also had been able to find a way of approximating the nonlinear equations with linear equations.

The method Hoad used is shown graphically in Exhibit 7–1. His first step was to determine the part of the curved function in which the variable could be expected to assume values in the real situation. Then, he connected the two ends of this segment with a straight line. The equation of this straight line might be used to approximate the curve. Hoad could determine the amount of error by measuring the distance from the line to the part of the curve furthest away. If this error were unacceptably large, Hoad then used two straight lines, as shown in Exhibit 7–1, to approximate the curve. The error was substantially reduced by using two lines to approximate the curve.

The equations of these two straight lines could be used in the linear programming matrix. Hoad continued to expand and refine his model. His progress reports described his expenses incurred and brief descriptions of the state of his model. He used two mathematical consultants during the project, and obtained help from clerical workers for nontechnical jobs. At no time did he find it necessary to ask for substantial time of the other analysts.

After five months, Hoad had a working model with 140 linear equations and 270 unknowns. He had spent slightly less than the $25,000 estimate. The major subdivisions of the model formulation were listed in the final report to management as follows:

1. Primary distillation
2. Light ends processing and disposition

Exhibit 7—1 Calnational Oil Company Example of Linear Approximations of Nonlinear Relationships

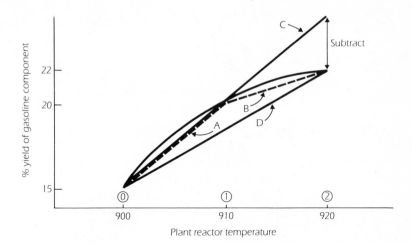

Plant reactor temperature

An inspection of the drawing given above should make apparent that the straight lines A and B yield a better approximation of the curve than does either the single line C or D. (The straight lines are the graphical representation of linear equations; the curved line represents a nonlinear equation.)

In addition the straight lines illustrate how a computer may be used to yield linear equations approximating nonlinear relationships as follows:

Let 10 increments = 1 unit

Let the equation for line A approximate the curved line for the range 0 to 1.

Let this same equation approximate the curved line for the range 1 to 2 provided a correction proportional to the abcissa is subtracted.

	RT1 (Reactor Temp. Group 900–910)	RT2 (Reactor Temp. Corrects RT1 in Range 910–920)	RHB
Profit (objective)	− .02	+ .003	
Cat gasoline compo. fraction yield material balance	− .05	+ .03	= 0
Limit RT1 to 910° without correction	1	− 1	≤ 1
Limit total range to 920°		1	≤ 1

This works because RT1 and RT2 are convex in profit space. RT1 must enter basis first, cannot enter at level higher than 1 without "pulling" in correction RT2.

RT2 is stopped from exceeding 1 ∴ original curve is approximated by two secants shown on graph.

The same procedure can be used to break a curve into any number of pieces provided functions are convex.

Exhibit 7–2 Calnational Oil Company Examples of Row Identification in Matrix Formulation (Constraints)

Row Number	Description
001	Manufacturing Cost
002	Short-range Profit
003	Long-range Profit
.	.
.	
.	
.	
.	
.	.
018	Max. Pipe Still Capacity
019	Total Crude Volume Limit
.	.
.	
.	
.	
.	
.	.
070	Catalyst Qualify-Minimum
071	Min. Recycle Temperature
072	First Cat Reactor Temperature Break
073	Second Temperature Maximum
.	.
.	
.	.
.	
.	.

3. Reformer
4. Cat cracker
5. Intermediate product transfers and imports
6. Blending
7. By-products and residuals
8. Product requirements, raw material availabilities
9. Economic information (prices, costs, etc.)

Exhibit 7–2 identifies some of the rows or constraint equations in the model. Exhibit 7–3 gives examples of column or variable identifications. Hoad stated that his selection of equations and variables to give detail to the model was done by judging the effect of the detail on the model's accuracy. In his judgment, the detail was sufficient for the precision required.

The equations required numerical values for the coefficients. Hoad described these data input requirements in his final report. The values for the coefficients were subject to change under differing operating conditions. One important part of the input data was a description of the availability and cost crudes. This description had to include, for each crude, the proportions of various products in the yield after initial distillation. Hoad stated that he required one minute of computer time and one "nontechnical man-hour" to calculate these values for a new crude. Once this was done, the data for that particular crude could be kept in a crude "library."

The cat cracker section of the formulation had nine controllable variables. Hoad's final report stated that past economic studies had shown that the Hinckley Beach cat cracker operated within a narrow range of processing conditions. For this reason, Hoad assumed he could represent the cracker with marginal changes to the nine variables. He reported that computer runs assured him the error in this procedure was less than $50 per operating day in the refinery. He foresaw no need to modify this section of the model unless the physical plant was changed or the mix of products manufactured was changed radically.

The only other section of the model which Hoad singled out as particularly sensitive to error was pricing. An equation for profit was the objective function for the model. Hoad's report commented: "The model opti-

Exhibit 7—3 Calnational Oil Company Examples of Column Identification in the Matrix Formulation (Unknowns or Variables)

Column Identification	Description	Units
Pipe Stills		
P1C1 S1R1	Pipe still 1 running crude 1	MB/D* Feed
P1C2 S1R2	Pipe still 1 running crude 2	MB/D* Feed
P2C1 S2R1	Pipe still 2 running crude 1	MB/D* Feed
P3C1 S3R1	Pipe still 3 running crude 1	MB/D* Feed
P3C2 S3R2	Pipe still 3 running crude 2	
.	.	
.		
.		
Cat Plant		
TVCG	Vacuum Gas Oil Fresh Feed	MB/D Feed
TRT1	Reactor Temperature	MB/D Feed
TCPF	Catalyst Quality	MB/D Feed
.		
.		

*Thousand barrels per day.

Exhibit 7–4 Calnational Oil Company

Total Iters	No. Etas	TP2 Recs	PHS TYP	Row No.	Current Value	Soln Feas	RHS No.
082	107	000	11	4	21.78144	Yes	01

	J	BETA		I	B		PI
		.70616737		1	.		.
		2.48157804		2	.		.
		24.25509661		3	.		.
		21.80216842		4	.		.9000000
	S1R1	7.6500000		5	7.6500000		.0192642
P1C2	S1R2	7.6500000		6	7.6500000		.0897836
UP007		.		7	.		.
UP008		.		8	.		.
UP009		.450000		9	15.750000		.
P2C1		14.400000		10	14.400000		.0720468
UP011		.		11	.		.
UP012		.		12	.		.
UP013		9.225000		13	23.6250000		.

mizes with regard to economics. It is therefore extremely important that consistent sets of prices be specified for all raw materials and products. . . . In general there are a number of prices and requirements that should be closely examined for consistency prior to running the model."

In his report, Hoad also pointed out that the solution from a computer run with the model produced an operating program for the refinery whose profit could not be increased without violating one of the model restrictions. The output of the computer was printed on long sheets of paper in the form shown in Exhibit 7–4. This example is the output of a proposed operating plan for the refinery. Exhibit 7–5 is an example of the report which Hoad prepared for management from Exhibit 7–4. Hoad had developed his own method for interpreting the computer output and transforming it into the report for management. This interpretation was done by hand. Hoad intended to write a computer program to make this transformation, but did not find time. It took Hoad approximately two hours to transform the data for one report. He had trained one of the secretaries in his office to make the same transformation in about two hours.

The output of the model also gave the marginal value to the refinery of the last small increment of crude from each of the company's crude supplies. It also gave the value at the refinery of the last small increment of output for each product both in process at most points in the refinery and as a finished product. These marginal values are shown in Exhibit 7–6 as they appeared in Hoad's report to management. The incremental values shown in the exhibit were correct for only small variations from the base values used in the model during the computer run in which the marginal values were generated. These marginal values could have been determined in the conventional hand calculation of operating programs, but were not because of the time required. By examining these marginal values, Hoad could determine the marginal value of "releasing" restricting equations as well as identify bottlenecks in the production process.

One of Hoad's objectives for the model, as described in his final report, was to provide better analyses of proposed capital improvements in the

Exhibit 7—5 Calnational Oil Company Hinckley Beach Refinery Operating Program Output Summary

	Summer	Winter	Year Average
LPG	1,593	1,394	1,518
Mixed C4 to Los A	2,340	1,728	2,098
Total Gaseous Product	3,833	3,122	3,616
Motor Gasoline			
Porterfield Super	854	680	698
Porterfield Special	6,322	4,898	5,740
Porterfield Regular	8,432	6,340	7,908
Other	—	—	—
Total Gasoline	15,608	11,918	14,446
Distillates			
Heating Oil			
Kerosene			
Other Trade Gas Oils			

Exhibit 7—6 Calnational Oil Company Marginal Values Long-Range Price Structure

	Summer	Winter	Units
Crudes Values			
Central California	.046	.027	$/BBL
Nevada	.122	.101	$/BBL
Lower California	.207	.188	$/BBL
Raw Stock Transfer Values			
Gas	1.176	1.092	$/BBL
Propylene	3.220	3.311	$/BBL
Butylenes	3.172	3.240	$/BBL
Hvy Cat Naphtha	3.709	3.492	$/BBL

refinery. This was to be done by modifying the model to represent the operating characteristics of the proposed new equipment or proposed improvements to relieve bottlenecks. By comparing the expected profit determined by a computer run simulating a modified refinery with the expected profit from the model representing the refinery as it was, Hoad hoped to be able to determine the desirability of proposed changes. This had been done previously by hand.

Hoad pointed out in his last development report that the Hinckley Beach model could be considered as one segment of a model encompassing all of the Calnational Oil Company's operations. No model for the entire company had been attempted. Hoad observed that to optimize such a total company model would require considering the effects of all price changes on the marginal costs for all refineries. It would require also introducing transportation costs from oil fields to refineries, between refineries, and from refineries to sales distribution points. Hoad made no estimate of the difficulty of preparing such a total company model.

Throughout the development, Hoad had used people within the refinery and consultants as sources of information for particular phases of the model. When he questioned the representativeness of the equations describing one of the refinery units, he would discuss with the operating man most familiar with the unit some of the assumptions which underlay the equation. In his difficulties with the mathematics in the model he sought help from the outside consultants. Frequently he found that he could get better answers more rapidly by relying on his own ability to redo studies within the refinery and to resolve the mathematical difficulties. He found that it took considerable time to bring other people up to date with his thinking so that they could comment usefully on his questions.

Operating Experiences with the Refinery Model

The refinery model was first used as a basis for a management report in late January. At that time, the general manager and the operations manager disagreed over the operating plan for the refinery then in effect for the winter period. Each felt profitability would be higher with a different proportion of the premium grades of motor gasoline to the regular, in light of recent price changes. This was the type of problem Hoad had solved previously as a blending problem. When Vines received a request for a study of the problem, he asked Rosewall to make the study using Hoad's original linear programming technique for the blending problem. Rosewall encountered difficulties with the problem and requested help from Hoad. Hoad volunteered to take over the problem from Rosewall. Rosewall consented, with Vines' approval.

Hoad attacked the problem by running simulations of the total refinery under several different demand and price structures, and using the two different proportions of high test to regular advocated by the general manager and the operations manager. On the basis of the results from these simulations, Hoad wrote a short report to management recommending a specific proportion of motor gasoline volumes by grade. In the report, he included marginal costs for conversion products within the refinery as related to each of the price structures. The report differed from earlier reports only by the added statement that because linear programming had been used the solutions were known to be optimal. Hoad did not mention in the report that he had encountered considerable difficulty in getting the computer program to work. During his first runs he had found several errors in the program which had not come to light during the development runs. This was not an unusual circumstance with large computer programs. "De-bugging" was the name used to describe this process of correcting errors in the program deck. Hoad had required help in the de-bugging from the outside consultants as well as several discussions with personnel at IBM.

During the second week in February, Mr. Vines assigned Hoad the task of preparing a five-year forecast for the refinery starting in the spring. Using demand forecasts supplied from the corporate market forecasting group, Hoad ran a simulation of refinery operations. The computer runs and time required to translate the outputs into recommendations to management occupied three weeks of Hoad's time. During this period, Hoad used two man-weeks of clerical help and two hours of time on the computer. Hoad again pointed out in his report to management that the recommendations were known to be optimal while this could not be assured in conventionally prepared long range plans.

Four smaller studies were prepared by Hoad during the period from late January to the middle of March. One considered an investment proposal to replace an outlet from the catalytic cracker, and another dealt with a proposal to expand the cracker pre-heat furnace. In both cases Hoad recommended approval on the basis of analysis with the refinery model and in both cases the recommendations were approved without further discussion with Hoad. In his recommendations Hoad gave the increased refinery profits to be expected from the modifications and compared them with the proposed investment cost. He noted in the reports that the expected profits had been calculated from marginal values obtained in earlier runs of the model.

In January, Hoad began training Mr. Rosewall in the use of the model. Mr. Vines arranged Rosewall's workload to allow his spending about five hours a week with Hoad. In addition to his engineering degree Rosewall had an M.B.A. and 10 years' experience at Hinckley Beach as an economic analyst. Hoad commented to Mr. Vines about Rosewall's competence with the model:

Rosewall understands the refinery equipment and the economics of the individual units. He also has enough mathematical ability. What he lacks is an understanding which comes with experience of how the mathematical models of the units are combined into the linear program models. He also doesn't have a grasp of total refinery and company economics. Rosewall's a capable guy, and with six months' training he could become proficient with the model.

On several occasions Hoad discussed with Mr. Vines the skills he thought use of the model required. He said:

The model produces results with a high degree of computational accuracy and assured optima. However, even the reports translated from linear programming output must be analyzed and interpreted by competent personnel to be meaningful.

Another important thing is that you never use the model the same way twice. There is always some difference in the problem which requires a modification in the way you arrange the input data. And any change in the equations required by changes in the refinery equipment must be made with an understanding of how the equations are related. The analyst who uses the model should have considerable background in mathematics and engineering and have time to understand co-relating the sections of the model and applications of microeconomics.

During the first two weeks of March Hoad sent memoranda to Mr. Vines outlining the development work which he felt should be undertaken to increase the usefulness of the refinery model. Following are the plans as Hoad outlined them:

1. A computer program to expedite answer analysis and report generation is definitely needed for maximum effectiveness of the model. Integration of operating program reports with the existing management information system should be studied before writing the report generator.
2. We are presently suboptimizing the Hinckley Beach refinery in terms of the Porterfield operations in total. The probable effects of this inadequacy should be studied.
3. Computer runs to date have already indicated the sensitivity of Hinckley Beach to certain correlations, particularly in the catalytic cracker section. A project should be initiated to develop more accurate equations in this area of the model. This should probably be done after the turnaround of the cracker in April.

On March 16, Mr. Vines and Bill Hoad learned that Hoad's request for transfer to the San Francisco home office of Calnational Oil Company had been approved. Hoad had wanted this transfer for many months. He had felt that the position of an engineering analyst at a plant would be a slow path, at best, to the managerial responsibility to which he aspired. Hoad's request for the move had been through "proper channels" and had been approved with some reluctance by Mr. Vines and Mr. Pails. Hoad felt that his request for transfer had been aided by informal discussions of his work with members of the engineering analysis group in San Francisco. This was the group to which Hoad would transfer. His efforts to prepare Rosewall as an understudy had been in anticipation of the change.

Mr. Pails spoke of Hoad's impending departure at the refinery management group meeting on March 17. Upon questioning by Mr. Cramer, Pails assured the general manager that Hoad had trained a replacement who would carry on with the work Hoad was doing with the refinery model. Mr. Cramer asked Pails to keep close contact with the work of the replacement, since the Vice President for Refining had expressed interest in Hinckley Beach's work with linear programming. The vice president had mentioned to Mr. Cramer that plans for developing models at other refineries were being considered, as well as developing a model for the company including all the transportation and marketing decisions.

Chemfertils, Inc.

8

Dr. W. A. Nelson, president of Chemfertils, Inc.[1] developed and patented a process for manufacturing two improved varieties of fertilizers. Tests of these fertilizers, known as "XLO" and "XKO," indicated that output per acre of vegetable crops was significantly increased when they were added to soils. "XLO" increased the average yield per acre of beets, carrots, or potatoes by at least 15% above yields attained by using existing fertilizers. "XKO," used for fertilizing peas, beans, and tomatoes, effected an average increase of 18%.

Dr. Nelson established Chemfertils, Inc. in Knoxville, Tennessee and his company had difficulty keeping up with the demands for "XLO" and "XKO." Describing the situation Dr. Nelson said:

I never expected "XLO" and "XKO" to catch on this fast. We've had orders for more than we can ship for the past six months. We are arranging new financing to build additional plant capacity, but this takes time. Business financing is new to me and I want to learn a little about it before we plunge too fast and too deep into an expansion program. Our competitors[2] have improved the performance of their products. Their prices are lower than ours, so I don't think we should raise our prices at this time. As I see

---

[1] Names and data pertaining to this company are disguised.

[2] Including American Cyanimid Company and International Minerals and Chemical Company.

Revised version of an earlier case written by Professor R. E. McGarrah and copyrighted by the President and Fellows of Harvard College.

Exhibit 8—1 Chemfertils, Inc. Summary of Productivity Data and Operating-Time Restrictions for February.

	"XLO"	"XKO"	Productive Hours Regular Shift	Available* Overtime
Processing Dept.—Hrs/100 lbs.	.01	.03	850	0
Packaging Dept.—Hrs/100 lbs.				
New Machine	.02	.05	700	100
Old Machine	.03	.08	900	0
Contribution to overhead & profit—$/100 lbs.				
Pkgd. on new machine— regular shift	.40	.72		
Pkgd. on new machine— overtime	.28	.64		
Pkgd. on old machine	.32	.60		

*Notes regarding productive hours available:

a. Productive hours were defined as the net operating hours for the department indicated, after deductions of estimated nonproductive hours for equipment setup changeovers, normal equipment maintenance and repairs.

b. The processing equipment was currently shut down, undergoing its annual major overhaul preparatory to the peak season production drive beginning about mid-February. For this reason, the nonproductive hours during the 10-week period beginning February 1 were estimated to be twice their average for other 10-week periods during the year. Because of shortages of technical and supervisory skills, the processing department was not operated overtime on Saturdays and Sundays except in unusual instances.

c. In addition to downtime for cycled changeovers for packaging "XLO" and then "XKO," the packaging machines had to be "taken off stream" while they were adjusted alternatively to fill the 50 and 100 bags of "XLO" and "XKO." Package size changeovers were scheduled more frequently than product changeovers. The old packaging machine was not used for overtime operations, mainly because of its higher operating cost. It frequently went out of adjustment and required especially skilled personnel in attendance. These personnel were also assigned to adjust and operate the new machine.

SOURCE: Office of Dr. W. A. Nelson, President.

it, our immediate problem is to make sure we're utilizing the present plant capacity in the most profitable manner.

Both "XLO" and "XKO" were made on the same equipment. Essentially, the process consisted of two stages: (1) grinding, mixing, heating, and hydrating; (2) packaging in 50 and 100 pound bags. Equipment for both stages had to be cleaned, adjusted; and process-feed and temperature-control devices had to be changed to adapt the equipment for the two products. Between the two stages were large storage hoppers so that either the packaging or processing equipment could be stopped for as long as 36 hours while the other continued to run. As a rule, the processing department was operated on a three-shift basis, 24 hours per day, five days per week. The packaging department was run two shifts per day. Two different packaging machines were used for both "XLO" and "XKO." One machine had been purchased secondhand and was slower and more expensive to operate than the other.

Exhibit 8–1 is a detailed summary of productivity data and operating-time restrictions for a ten-week planning period.

Required:

1. Set up and solve the linear program for the eight-week planning period beginning February 1.

   a. State the assumptions affecting the validity of this program.

2. Suppose a minimum of 8,000 100-pound bags of "XKO" *had* to be produced. From the results of the linear program above, what would be the most economical revision to make in this program?

3. Which production facility is the bottleneck and how valuable would an additional hour of productive capacity be in this facility? How many *additional* hours of productive capacity could be added before the bottleneck would shift to another production facility?

Chicago Auto Parts Supply Company (A)

9

Mr. C. J. Johnson, president and general manager of the Chicago Auto Parts Supply Company, was trying to decide whether or not to approve a proposal to build a completely new central office and warehouse facility. According to the proposition, an estimated capital expenditure of $2,000,000 would be involved. Mr. Johnson was not at all certain that the right kinds of improvements had been incorporated in the proposal.

Background

The Chicago Auto Parts Supply Company had been established for 30 years to distribute automotive parts sold by independent jobbers and distributors to automobile repair businesses. These parts consisted of engine valves, guides, springs, pistons—in general, all engine and body-support parts subject to frictional wear. (A complete list of the types of parts is shown in Exhibit 9–1.) Chicago Auto Parts Supply Company packaged its parts under the brand name of "CHAPSCO." CHAPSCO's competitors in the replacement parts business included Ford, Chrysler, General Motors, McQuay-Norris, Federal Mogul, and Thompson Products, each distributing its own line of branded replacement parts. The same manufacturer

Revised version of an earlier case written by Professor R. E. McGarrah and copyrighted by the President and Fellows of Harvard College.

Exhibit 9—1 Chicago Auto Parts Supply Company Types of Automobile Parts Stocked and Distributed by CHAPSCO

Commodity Code No.	Description	Commodity Code No.	Description
1	Valves	101	Bearings—main
2	Guides	102	Bearings—connecting rod
3	Seats	103	Bearings—cam shaft
4	Springs	104	Connecting rods
5	Retainers	201	Automatic transmission parts
6	Roto caps	250	Water pumps
7	Hydraulic tappets	300	Coil springs
51	Alloy pistons	400	Tie rods and ends
52	Cast iron pistons	450	Bushings
53	Piston pins	470	Spring shackles
54	Dry sleeves	500	Shock absorbers
56	Wet sleeves		
57	Piston pins		

NOTES: a. CHAPSCO's policy was to stock all automobile chassis and engine parts subjected to normal frictional and shock-wear.

b. The number of different parts stocked and distributed had increased at the average rate of 2,500 parts per year, from 1948–1958.

c. Part-items were declared obsolescent and obsolete as volume-demand decreased, and as the age of auto manufacturers' designs increased beyond certain periods.

d. To facilitate organization and procedures for inventory control, the aggregate of parts were classified into the following 24 basic "commodities." Eight "commodity stock controllers" were responsible for the stock levels at branch warehouses and at the central warehouse.

SOURCE: Mr. C. G. Paxton, Manager of Inventory Control

often produced parts for all the major replacement parts distributors. Although the automobile manufacturers sold most of their replacement parts to replenish service department stocks carried by their authorized car dealers, CHAPSCO, Thompson, and other "independents" competed for this business too, in effect by carrying some of the new car dealers' parts in inventory. However, most of CHAPSCO's parts were used by "independent" auto-repair garages.

Chicago Auto Parts Supply Company owned and operated one central warehouse in Chicago, Illinois to which all parts were delivered from the parts' manufacturers, who were located generally in the north-central states. Parts were received in bulk containers at the central warehouse, then packaged in CHAPSCO branded cartons, and stored until they were shipped to the branch warehouses. CHAPSCO operated 30 branch warehouses located all over the USA and parts of Canada. Customers of CHAPSCO's branch warehouses consisted of independent automotive parts distributors and jobbers, whose individual purchases ranged from $3,000 to as much as $250,000 worth of parts per year. CHAPSCO's sales had grown from $500,000 to $25 million in 20 years. Forecasts projected an average growth of $2 million per year.

CHAPSCO serviced its jobber-customers in the Chicago area from its central warehouse.

The Present Central Warehouse Facility

CHAPSCO's general offices and central warehouse were located in old factory buildings in the industrial section of Chicago. General office functions included engineering, finance, sales administration, supply administration and personnel (Exhibit 9–2). Facilities had been expanded by a succession of purchases of adjacent factory buildings, many of which had been vacated by their former factory-owners because of inadequacies for manufacturing activities.

Not all floors of these buildings had been vacated; by mutual agreement, the floors of some buildings were still used for manufacturing purposes by their former owners. CHAPSCO's central warehouse and offices occupied 18 buildings, most of which were immediately adjacent and interconnected by bridges and tunnels. All buildings were multistoried, each building having either four or five floors; the floor levels were not the same for all the buildings, so it was impossible to walk through all 18 buildings on any one floor level. To emphasize the inadequacy of the existing building facility, a statement in the "New Warehouse Proposal" report to Mr. Johnson pointed out that there was a total of 36 different floor levels among the 18 buildings. Warehousing activities occupied 24 floors. The estimated average age of these buildings was 55 years; the largest building was 30 years old. Maximum ceiling height in half the storage area was 11 feet. Floor loading capacities ranged from 60 to 200 pounds per square foot. Floor supporting columns were spaced from 16 to 30 feet apart. Floors were interconnected by elevators and stair wells.

The report entitled "New Warehouse Proposal" which Mr. Johnson was evaluating listed the following as inadequacies of the present building facility:

Present parking facilities for 450 employees are extremely inadequate. We have 95 protected parking spaces and approximately 50 more that are unprotected.

Column spacing does not lend itself to economic layout.

Included in our 18 buildings are 25 separate rest room facilities to service and maintain.

The most serious aspect of our present layout is the critical space limitation. This is felt primarily in the packaged stock or order filling area where we have an immediate need for an additional 30,000 square feet with greater stacking heights throughout. Other limitations are attributed to the extremely cut-up nature of the present space.

Exhibit 9—2 Chicago Auto Parts Supply Company Organization Charts

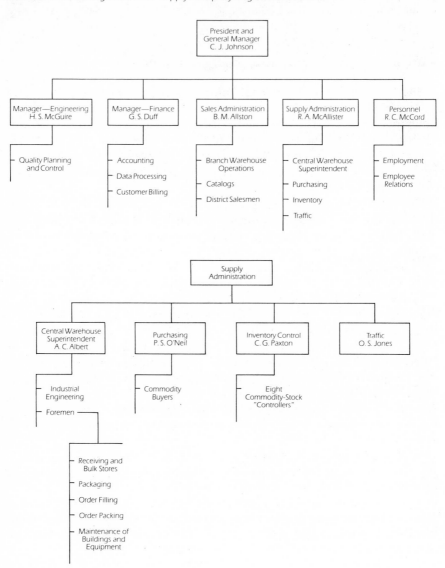

SOURCE: Office of Mr. R. C. McCord, Personnel Manager

We were warehousing 10,000 different items 10 years ago. Today we have to provide space for 35,000 items, and there is every indication that this number will increase even more rapidly because new designs are being introduced more rapidly by car and truck and engine manufacturers.

Existing Central Warehousing Operations

Central warehousing activities consisted of: (1) parts receiving, (2) receiving inspection, (3) storing parts in bulk form, (4) packaging parts in branded cartons, (5) storing the parts in branded parts stores, (6) stock-picking for branch warehouse shipments, (7) packing cartons into corrugated shipping containers for weekly shipments made to each branch warehouse. Exhibit 9–3 is a diagram showing the lines of flow and the relative locations of these activities. The workload for the various warehousing activities was not uniform at all times, so personnel were frequently transferred among the various crews who manned these seven activities.

Parts Receiving

Approximately 90% of the total aggregate of parts were received in "bulk" corrugated shipping containers ranging in sizes from 20" × 20" to 40" × 40" × 24", and weighing from 500 to 1,800 lbs. each; 10% were packaged by parts manufacturers in CHAPSCO branded cartons. All receivals arrived by truck, mostly in full truckloads. High volume-demand items were received at regular intervals (for example, semimonthly, monthly and so on); low volume-demand were received less frequently, depending upon the quantities purchased. The receiving dock could accommodate 3 trucks being unloaded simultaneously. Truck arrival traffic was heaviest during the first five working days of the month, after which, one dock-spot was all that was required. Hand trucks and electric powered, "walkie-type" trucks were used to unload the containers from the over-the-road trucks. Deliveries were deposited on pallets on the dock by the unloading crew and then moved to a temporary storage area to await receiving inspection. There were 3 men in the receiving crew who unloaded and checked the receivals by comparing bills of lading, shipping container labels and purchase order specifications (a copy of each purchase order was sent to the receiving office for this purpose).

Receiving Inspection

Quantities were further verified by weighing or by physically counting the units received. Pursuant to instructions from the quality control group in the engineering office, certain quality characteristics were measured, using various gauges such as micrometers, dial indicators, surface roughness measuring devices, plug and ring gauges, and so on. Other

Exhibit 9—3 Chicago Auto Parts Supply Company "Typical" Flow Diagram—Present Warehouse Activities

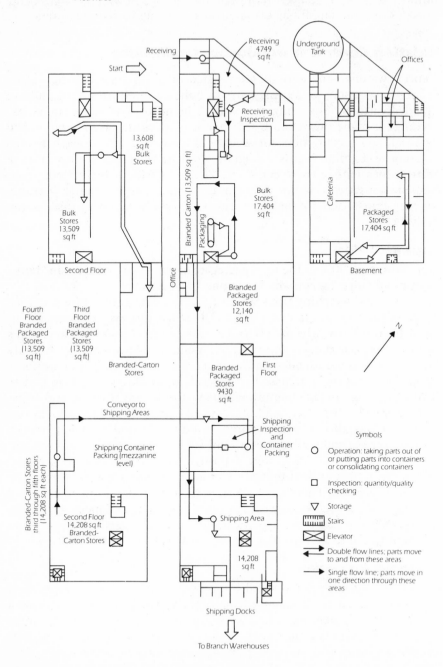

NOTE: Not all storage locations and second floors are shown on this diagram

SOURCE: Extracted from "New Warehouse Proposal," report prepared under the direction of Mr. A. C. Albert, Warehouse Superintendent.

quality characteristics were visually inspected for cracks or flaws on the surface of the parts. Generally, a random sample was inspected from each lot received; occasionally 100% inspection was required for parts received from new suppliers. Inspections were made at bench work-places, with the parts in their containers stacked on the floor nearby. CHAPSCO's policy was to assure quality at least as good, if not better than the quality of the original parts installed by the automotive engine and body manufacturer. Inspectors were trained to be versatile in the wide variety of inspection methods used. There were from 5 to 8 employees in the receiving inspection area, depending upon the workload.

After inspection, the containers were again stacked on pallets, to be taken to a bulk or packaged storage area.

Bulk Storing

After an incoming lot of parts was inspected, the parts were moved by "walkie-type" electric lift truck and elevator to the bulk stores areas, located on the first and second floors. From 3 to 5 men were assigned to jobs of putting the parts in bulk stores. Bulk stores consisted of parts stored in the containers in which they had been received. These containers were stacked on pallets and the pallets were stacked on steel shelves. Approximately half the inventory in the central warehouse consisted of parts stored in the bulk form. Bulk stores were necessary mainly for two reasons: First, the quantities received were often too large for the storage space afforded in the branded carton storage locations, and second, the branded carton packaging lines were run for the purpose of replenishing the depleted stocks of branded carton stores, instead of for the purpose of keeping the receiving inspection area clear. Packaging line schedules were determined by orders to replenish branded carton stocks in the general warehouse. Another crew of from 4 to 6 men took the parts from bulk stores to the branded carton packaging areas, using hand trucks and walkie-type electric lift trucks.

Branded Carton Packaging

Parts were packaged by individual item (for example: one piston, one gear), by individual assemblies of several different items (for example: shock absorber assemblies, steering linkages), and/or by sets of the same item or sets of assemblies (for example: 6 or 8 exhaust valves, 6 or 8 intake valves, pistons and piston pins). Sets were often determined by such factors as the number of cylinders in an engine or pairs of wheels on the car.

Packing operations consisted of unfolding or forming the carton (branded cartons were supplied to the operator in a folded-flat condition, creased for ease in forming), taking the parts out of the bulk containers and putting them into the carton, then putting the carton into a sealing machine. This machine automatically: dabbed glue on the tabs, folded the tabs, thus closing the carton at both ends, and printed the part name and number on the ends of the carton. The branded cartons were then stacked with the part name and number exposed in the corrugated cardboard containers of standard sizes to fit the shelf space assigned that part in the branded carton storage locations. When only one part was to be packed, one operator performed all the tasks. When more than one type of part was to be packed a commensurate number of operators manned a belt conveyor line, and each operator inserted a different part into the carton; the last operator on the line operated the sealing and printing machine, and stacked the branded cartons into the storage containers.

The sealing machines were set up for various sizes of branded cartons by adjusting the width of a "track" used to guide the cartons being fed to the machine, by changing the platten which stamped part name and number, and by adjusting linkages which controlled the mechanisms for gluing and folding the ends of the carton. There were six package sealing machines, four used on lines, and two at single bench work-stations.

Packaging line setup changes were frequent and rapid. For instance during a five-hour survey last March, there were 88 line setup changes among the four different packaging lines.

Packaging activities required from 30 to 35 operators, plus a foreman and two machine setters.

Storing Branded Cartons

The locations of branded carton stores were determined essentially by part-code numbers. In some instances space and floor loading restrictions made it necessary to depart from a strict part-number basis for locations. Space was a continuous problem because of the rapid expansion in the variety of any one type of part carried in stock. Some parts had to be stored in more than one location because of this problem. The cartons in the storage containers were loaded on four wheel hand trucks and taken to their appropriate locations and put away in open-shelf type steel storage racks. These racks were from six to eleven feet high and from 18 to 30 inches deep. Cartons were left in the shelf containers, which were placed on shelves with the part name and number clearly visible to the stock-pickers. Eleven or twelve men were assigned jobs of taking packaged parts to the various branded carton storage locations.

Stockpicking for Branch Warehouse Shipments

Branch warehouse replenishment orders represented a weekly accumulation of parts that had actually been removed from each branch warehouse. In other words, weekly shipments were to replace items that had been sold to customers of each branch warehouse. The branch warehouse stock levels were controlled by the Inventory Control group that was located in Chicago. The eight "commodity stock-controllers" (see Exhibit 9–2) made periodic adjustments to branch shipments depending upon customer-demand changes in the branch districts. Each weekly branch warehouse order averaged between 1,000 and 1,200 different items.

Each stockpicker was given a four wheel hand truck with shelves and a list of different parts and quantities required in the branch order for which the information was in the form of a list printed by an IBM tabulator.

The branch orders were sent to the Warehouse Superintendent's office the day before stockpicking was to begin. In this office, time standards clerks would use this list and tables of stockpicking standard time data to determine the items to be picked to fill a shelf truck in such a manner that no shelf truck would be occupied in the stockpicking location for more than 45 minutes. (This procedure had been adopted when the stockpicking foreman had requested that 50 additional shelf trucks be obtained, because they thought there was a shortage of these trucks. The industrial engineers had investigated this request and determined that 50 additional trucks were not justified by space and funds currently available, and that by limiting the time a truck was tied up by a stockpicker, the existing number of shelf trucks would be adequate when used in this manner.) The stockpicker would move his truck down an aisle, stopping to walk between stock bins to pick the parts required by the branch order, hand-carrying the parts back to his cart left on the aisle, and continuing until he had filled the truck or he had used the truck for approximately 45 minutes. He then attached a card to the truck, identifying the shelf truckload with the particular branch warehouse order, and hooked the truck to an overhead trolley, which towed the truck to the shipping area. Here, the cartons of parts were taken from the shelf truck and accumulated to be packed in shipping containers. The empty cart was then hooked to the trolley and towed back to the packaged stock area, to be used again in stockpicking. In this manner, order picking for a single branch order was carried on simultaneously, by more than one stockpicker, at several branded carton-storage locations. If the stocks were inadequate to fill an order, he would mark the branch order with the amount of the shortage, and this shortage would be made up either by expediting at reserve stock locations, or back at the receiving, bulk stores, and packaging areas, or (as was most often the case) by deferring the makeup of the shortage until a succeeding week's branch warehouse shipment.

Difficulties encountered by the stockpickers were attributed to: the complex part number designations which carried prefix and suffix numbers; the fact that occasionally, cartons had to be broken open and parts separately packed and tagged because branch order quantities were less than the quantities packed in a single carton; the fact that storage shelf locations of packaged parts had to be changed because of changes in varieties and quantities of parts that had to be stored in the limited storage space available at the stockpicking locations.

An average of between 20 and 22 employees were involved in stockpicking activities.

Exhibit 9–4 Chicago Auto Parts Supply Company Block Plan Layout of Central Warehouse and General Office Building

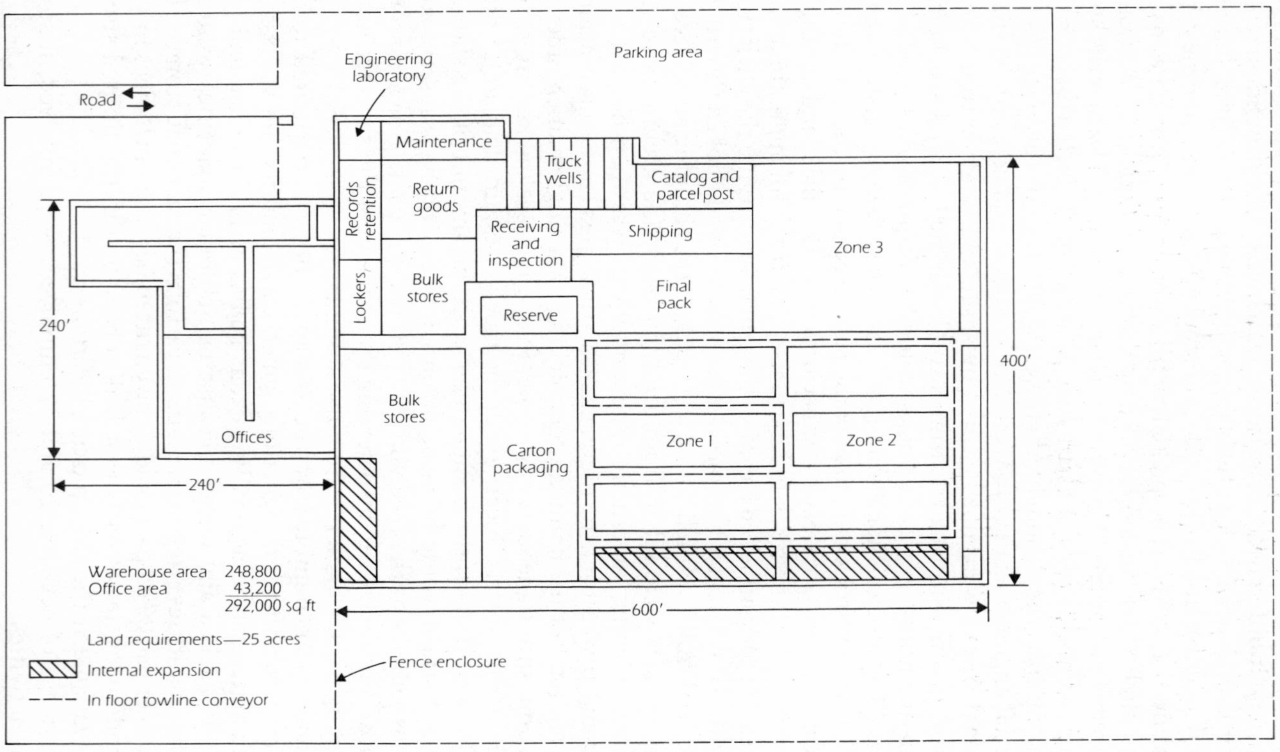

Road

Parking area

Engineering laboratory

Maintenance

Records retention

Return goods

Lockers

Bulk stores

Bulk stores

Truck wells

Receiving and inspection

Reserve

Catalog and parcel post

Shipping

Final pack

Zone 3

Zone 1

Zone 2

Carton packaging

Offices

400'

600'

240'

240'

Warehouse area 248,800
Office area   43,200
                 292,000 sq ft

Land requirements—25 acres

Fence enclosure

▨ Internal expansion

--- In floor towline conveyor

SOURCE: Extracted from report. "New Warehouse Proposal," prepared March 1959, under the direction of Mr. A. C. Albert, Warehouse Superintendent.

Shipping Container Packing

Cartons destined for a branch warehouse were assembled together and packed into corrugated shipping containers, which were then counted, weighed, sealed, and labeled with the appropriate branch warehouse address. The traffic department furnished the shipper's bill-of-lading information specifying the name of the truck-carrier, the truck-route, and whether or not a particular branch shipment was to be consolidated with other shipments to be made the same day to branches located along the same truck-route (to take advantage of possible savings in full truckload freight-rates versus partial truckload rates). To this bill-of-lading information the scale operator added the weight and number of shipping containers. Then she attached the bill-of-lading to one of the containers (which were grouped together), and sent the shipment down a conveyor to the shipping platform.

At the shipping platform the containers were cleared away from the conveyor and either temporarily stored with other shipments consigned to the same carrier or loaded immediately on a truck trailer which had been spotted at the shipping dock.

From 6 to 8 employees were involved in the final packing and shipping activities. Branch warehouse shipments were scheduled weekly, and this schedule was strictly adhered to. This meant that orders for 6 of the 30 different branches were filled on each of the five-day work week.

All the activities comprising these seven stages of warehousing were on measured daywork labor time standards which had been set by stopwatch time-studies.[1] One industrial engineer spent all his time setting time standards and refining work measurement data used. These standards were useful for planning the manpower required in the various warehouse crews manning the seven warehousing activities. Employees were frequently transferred among various activities to keep the flow of materials moving on schedule, and to keep idle man time at practical minima. Seasonal swings in demand meant that employment was at its highest during August through October, and lowest during February through April.

The cycle time, from stockpicking to shipment of a branch warehouse order, ranged from one to three working days, with an average of two days. Deliveries to branch warehouses took between one-half day and four days, depending upon the branch warehouse location and the stopovers en route.

The New Warehouse Proposal

Exhibit 9–4 is a block-plan of the proposed new warehouse. The New Warehouse Proposal Report had been prepared by the industrial engineer-

---

[1] The term *measured day work* meant that employees were paid on the basis of straight hourly pay rates, but the amount of work they were expected to accomplish was determined by these time standards.

ing group, under the direction of Mr. A. C. Albert, the Central Warehouse Superintendent. Following are essential highlights of this proposal.

Receiving and Inspection.

. . . Gravity floor conveyors will permit receivals literally to flow through a combination inspection-checking team. Present inspection equipment will be set up between parallel lines so that it may be used on either or both lines. Scales will be mounted in both lines to facilitate (quantity) checking.

Packaging on Receipt.

All parts, except those sold in bulk, will be packaged upon receipt, virtually eliminating bulk storage. Packaging equipment will be set up in a parallel arrangement. While one job is being run, the next job will be set up on an adjacent line, thereby reducing downtime delays. Immediate packaging will increase the availability of our stocks for shipments to branches. Packaged parts will be moved to their storage locations on rider-type, high speed, narrow aisle stackers, instead of the present walkies.

Packaged Carton Storage.

Instead of storage by part numbers, packaged carton parts will be stored according to the rate of movement; high-volume items will be located in Zone 1 (Exhibit 9–4), nearest the output end of the packaging area, to minimize travel distance in replenishing these stocks. High volume items packaged by vendors will be located nearest to the shipping platform. Approximately 1,000 part numbers accounting for over 70% of piece-sales will be assigned to Zone 1; the remaining 34,000 items will be stored in Zones 2 and 3. Reserve stocks for the high-volume items will be stacked on pallets and on shelves to utilize the "air-rights," beginning approximately eight feet above the floor level. Within each storage zone, parts will be located by part numbers. A continuous audit of stock-item activity will be made on the present IBM computing equipment, and inter and intra-zone storage locations of parts will be changed accordingly.

Stockpicking for Branch Warehouse Orders.

For high volume parts stored in Zone 1, parts will be picked for each order. However, different branch orders for parts stored in Zones 2 and 3 will be combined into one "batch" and picked in one tour of these zones rather than on a one tour per order basis. Orders from jobber-customers in the Chicago area, for parts stored in Zone 1 will also be combined, instead of being processed (that is, instead of having their parts picked) individually as at present. By batching customers' orders for Zone 1 parts and branch warehouse orders for parts stored in Zones 2 and 3, the ratios of the number of line items on the branch replenishment orders to the num-

---

Exhibit 9—5 Chicago Auto Parts Supply Company Expenses Involved in New Warehouse Proposal

"Last year's operations were bases on which the following expenses and savings were estimated. Sales are presumed constant to highlight the effects on profit and return."

A. Building Expense—first year of occupancy.

$78,000   Building Depreciation—First year's depreciation, using sum of years' digits, based on 40 year life on a total cost of $1,610,000.

$ 8,500   Equipment Depreciation—First year's depreciation on a total cost of $60,600, including:

Tow line conveyor	15 year period	$30,000
Truck dock lifts	10 year period	13,600
Landscaping	10 year period	8,000
Fire protection & Burglar Alarm System	20 year period	9,000

$17,000   Building Maintenance—Estimated from present building maintenance expenses, excluding elevators.

$25,000   Heat—This estimate was made by the local gas company's heating engineer.

$11,000   Warehouse Protection

$142,000   Other Building Expenses—Janitorial supplies, property taxes, insurance, but excluding labor.

Total $282,000

B. Warehouse Personnel—Annual Savings. (New Warehouse.)

1. Receiving & Receiving Inspection Labor Savings:

$5,345   One hand trucker—presently acting as an elevator operator.

5,470   One dock checker—quality and quantity inspection facilities will eliminate this man.

32,035   Six stock put-away men—improved handling and storage locations will enable elimination.

2. Packaging Line & Bulk Stores Labor Savings:

$5,400   One bulk stock put-away man.

5,500   One tow-motor truck operator—proposed rider-type narrow aisle stackers will permit this saving.

5,500   One bulk stockpicker—better handling equipment and stock locations will speed up this operation.

10,180   Two conveyor packers.

3. Carton Stockpicking Branch and Customers' Orders-Savings.

$5,345   One hand trucker—presently acting as an elevator operator.

16,720   Three order pickers—better stock location.

4,500   One salaried clerk—stock location file presently requires two clerks; improved stock location and space in proposed warehouse should reduce this to a one-man job.

11,500   Two expeditors—reserve carton stocks will be reduced. Remaining three expediters will use electric scooters.

Exhibit 9–5 (continued)

    4. Maintenance and Building Service Labor Savings.

        $12,300   Two people—new building, significant reduction in floors, windows.

        26,000   One matron and four sweepers—power sweeping equipment, fewer floors and rest rooms.

C. Additional Machinery and Equipment Depreciation, involved in New Warehouse Operation during first year.

        $ 640   In floor conveyor to be used in receiving-inspection department.

        9,100   First year's depreciation on pallet racks costing $50,000, depreciated over 10 years.

        9,000   First year's depreciation on:

4 Hydra Fork Trucks	@	$7,200
2 Hy-Rider Trucks	@	4,500
1 Personnel Carrier	@	865
3 Personnel Carriers	@	635
1 Power Sweeper	@	3,000
2 - 24 Volt Battery Charger	@	700

D. Nonrecurring Expenses.

        $200,000   Moving present warehouse to new location.

        10,000   One thousand special storage baskets for water pumps. Needed whether or not new warehouse proposal is adopted.

        7,500   Three thousand new pallets, half of which are needed for immediate replacement of existing pallets.

        18,300   Two hundred and fifty shelf trucks and 25 flat trucks. Present trucks for stockpickers are not adaptable to tow line conveying.

E. Capital Investment Data.

        $125,000   Twenty-five acre land acquisition.

        280,000   Land improvement; road access, fence protection, landscaping, utilities.

        1,610,000   New warehouse and office building to be depreciated over 40 years.

        60,600   New equipment (see A above).

        $175,000   Realtors' estimates of net proceeds available from sale of existing properties.
        − $250,000

SOURCE: Extracted from the report, "New Warehouse Proposal," prepared by the Warehouse Superintendent.

---

ber of stock locations involved in order picking increase substantially, thus enabling us to increase stockpickers' productivity.

An in-the-floor, tow-line conveyor system will be installed (dashed line, Exhibit 9–4) to reduce the man-attended transportation involved in packaged stock replenishment and completed order handling.

Space provided in the proposed warehouse (Exhibit 9–5) was estimated to be adequate for a 30% increase in the volume of parts sold, and for a 20% increase in the aggregate total (or variety of) parts stocked.

Exhibit 9–5 summarizes the estimated expense comparison of the present and proposed facilities and operations of CHAPSCO's central warehouse. The details of this proposal had been discussed with the appropriate foremen who in certain instances made suggestions which were incorporated in the proposal.

Chicago Auto Parts Supply Company (B)

10

Mr. C. G. Paxton, Manager of Inventory Control at the Chicago Auto Parts Supply Company (CHAPSCO), was preparing a statement of objectives, problems, and plans to be distributed to company executives before their next business-review meeting. Pursuant to plans for constructing a new central warehouse and general office building, CHAPSCO executives had been holding a series of weekly meetings for which each functional manager of a Supply Administration activity (see Exhibit 10–1) was to present a statement of his problems, objectives, and plans for improvement. Mr. C. J. Johnson, President and General Manager, had requested Mr. R. A. McAllister, Manager of Supply Administration, to coordinate these meetings because he wanted some integrated planning reflected in the specific proposal for the new central warehouse facility when it was submitted to CHAPSCO's board of directors. CHAPSCO's investment in total inventory amounted to 75 percent of the value of the total assets listed on the balance sheet. As manager of Inventory control in a business such as CHAPSCO's, Mr. Paxton realized that his statement could provoke some rather probing comments from the other managers about the physical work-flow facilities and procedures in the new warehouse and he therefore felt he would be "on-the-spot" at the business-review meeting.

Revised version of an earlier case written by Professor R. E. McGarrah and copyrighted by the President and Fellows of Harvard College.

Exhibit 10–1 Chicago Auto Parts Supply Company Organization Charts

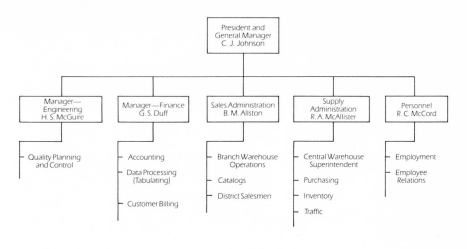

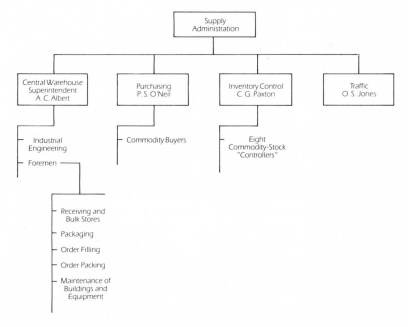

SOURCE: Office of Mr. R. C. McCord, Personnel Manager, July 1959.

Exhibit 10—2 Chicago Auto Parts Supply Company Types of Automobile parts stocked and distributed by CHAPSCO

Commodity Code No.	Description	Commodity Case No.	Description
1	Valves	101	Bearings, main
2	Guides	102	Bearings, connecting rod
3	Seats	103	Bearings, cam shaft
4	Springs	104	Connecting rods
5	Retainers	201	Automatic transmission parts
6	Roto caps	250	Water pumps
7	Hydraulic tappets		
51	Alloy pistons	300	Coil springs
52	Cast-iron pistons		
53	Piston pins	400	Tie rods and ends
54	Dry sleeves	450	Bushings
56	Wet sleeves	470	Spring shackles
57	Piston pins		
		500	Shock absorbers

NOTES: a. CHAPSCO's policy was to stock all automobile chassis and engine parts subjected to normal frictional and shock-wear.

b. The number of different parts stocked and distributed had increased at the average rate of 2500 parts per year for the past ten years.

c. Part items were declared obsolescent and obsolete as volume-demand decreased and as the age and number of automotive vehicles requiring these parts diminished.

d. To facilitate organization and procedures for inventory control, the aggregate of parts was classified into 24 basic "commodities." Eight "commodity-stock controllers" were responsible for the stock levels at branch warehouses and at the central warehouse.

SOURCE: Mr. C. G. Paxton, Manager of Inventory Control.

Background

Chicago Auto Parts Supply Company had been established to distribute automotive parts sold by independent jobbers and distributors to automobile repair businesses. These parts consisted of engine valves, guides, springs, and pistons—in general, all engine and body-support parts subject to frictional wear (see Exhibit 10–2). Chicago Auto Parts Supply Company packaged its parts under the brand name "CHAPSCO." Its competitors in the replacement-parts business were Ford, Chrysler, General Motors, McQuay-Norris, Federal Mogul, and Thompson Products, each distributing its own line of branded replacement parts. The same manufacturer often produced parts for all the major replacement-parts distributors. Although the automobile manufacturers sold most of their replacement parts to replenish service department stocks carried by their authorized car dealers, CHAPSCO, Thompson, and other "independents" also competed for this business, in effect, by carrying some of the new-car dealers' parts inventory. However, most of CHAPSCO's parts were used by "independent" auto-repair garages.

CHAPSCO owned and operated one central warehouse in Chicago, Illinois, to which all parts were delivered from parts manufacturers who were located generally in the north-central states. The Chicago facilities consisted of 18 old, multistory factory buildings interconnected by bridges and tunnels. Parts were received and stored in bulk containers at the central warehouse, then packaged in CHAPSCO-branded cartons, and stored until they were shipped to the branch warehouses. CHAPSCO operated 30 branch warehouses located all over the United States and in parts of Canada. Customers of CHAPSCO's branch warehouses consisted of independent automotive-parts distributors and jobbers, whose individual purchases ranged from $3000 to as much as $250,000 worth of parts per year. CHAPSCO's sales had grown to their current level of $25 million. Forecasts projected an average growth of $2 million per year during the next decade. Ten years ago 10,000 different parts were warehoused and distributed; currently 35,000 different items were handled and predictions were that this number would continue to increase with the increase in imported cars.

CHAPSCO serviced its jobber-customers in the Chicago area from its central warehouse.

Mr. Paxton's inventory-control group was responsible for procedures for the over-all control of commodity stocks and for procedures to control the inventory at three stages of CHAPSCO's business: (1) the branch-warehouse stocks located at each of the 30 branch warehouses, (2) the packaged-carton stocks located at the central warehouse in Chicago, and (3) the "bulk stocks" of parts stored after they were received in Chicago from suppliers. Bulk stocks were considered necessary mainly because of the insufficient space in the present Chicago warehouse to store all the parts in packaged cartons.

Over-all Control of Commodity Stocks

The aggregate of 35,000 different parts was classified into the 24 different commodities listed in Exhibit 10–2. Each commodity (or type of part) was assigned to one of eight commodity-stock controllers who determined the proper levels of stocks to be carried at the central warehouse in Chicago and at each of the 30 branch warehouses. The commodity controllers were supported by 16 inventory record clerks and by information regularly furnished by the computer, purchasing, and sales departments.

In addition to the commodity classification, each of the 35,000 different parts was assigned a classification I, II, III, or IV, according to the volume to be sold. Class I parts were the most popular; Class II the next most popular, and so on. The demand-volume classification was subject to change as the indices of age and number of each type and model of automotive vehicle requiring the part changed each year. A major portion of the commodity controllers' time was spent in reviewing and changing the volume classifications of commodities. The popularity of demand for a part differed among the 30 branch warehouses because of different proportions of total sales that had been made by the automotive-vehicle manufacturers in different geographical areas.

Every three months a sales forecast and inventory budget were made. The sales department furnished Mr. Paxton's group with forecasts of total dollar sales projected during the next twelve months for each commodity. Then the commodity controllers analyzed these forecasts in terms of physical numbers of pieces of each part to be sold.

In converting the forecasted commodity sales in dollars into forecasted unit sales in pieces of each part, the commodity controller employed the inventory-history information at his own discretion. Sometimes he would extrapolate the latest three-to-six-month trend in actual pieces sold and use it as the unit-sales forecast. In other instances the percentage change from last year's actual dollar commodity sales and the unit price of the part would be used to calculate the estimate of next year's unit-volume sales for each part. Data reflecting changes in auto-vehicle age and estimated number in use were also considered. Mr. Paxton felt that it was best for each commodity controller to exercise his own judgment in adapting the available information to forecast the unit sales per month for each part.

After the forecast of unit sales was made, the parts-procurement schedule (budget) for each part was determined for the next twelve months. To do this, the clerks used a working rule, which was to maintain a three months' supply in the system at all times, two months' supply en route and at the 30 branch warehouses, and a one month's supply at the central warehouse in Chicago. Subtracting the forecasted unit sales for next month from the actual total stock currently on hand and then comparing this remainder with the unit-sales forecast for the following three months were two steps toward a preliminary indication of the quantity and the month in which future purchases were to be made from CHAPSCO's suppliers. These suppliers required procurement lead-times of sixty to 120 calendar days. The inventory and procurement budgets were based on an average of ninety days. The purchasing department regularly furnished Mr. Paxton's group with memoranda regarding changes in lead-time requirements by each vendor. In addition to this lead-time information, the purchasing department also advised Mr. Paxton's group of the most economical purchase quantities of each part to be ordered from suppliers. Most of CHAPSCO's suppliers offered significant price-quantity discount schedules. The most economical quantities to purchase were determined by estimating and comparing the additional inventory carrying costs that would be incurred by purchasing a lot quantity larger than needed with the savings accrued by taking advantage of the lower unit price. If, for the annual forecasted demand, the estimated savings allowed by purchasing larger lots at discount prices exceeded the estimated costs of carrying the additional inventory, then the larger purchase lot quantity was recommended by Purchasing. The projected budgeted inventory and purchases of each part (in pieces per month) were then recorded.

Each lot purchased was contracted by separate purchase-order negotiations made by CHAPSCO's commodity buyers with suppliers whose product quality was approved by CHAPSCO's engineering department.

Approximately 2000 different parts (mostly Class I) accounted for 90 percent of the total annual unit sales of all parts. The inventory history cards and budgets for these parts were examined monthly. Those for the remaining 33,000 parts were examined quarterly and/or whenever a stock shortage occurred.

As a measure of over-all effectiveness, Mr. Paxton reported that for all parts the ratio of units sold to stock carried at Chicago and the 30 branch warehouses (i.e., total stock turnover) had recently averaged 1.5. For some parts the turnover had been as low as 0.1 and for others as high as 6.0.

Branch-Warehouse Stock Control

Control of stock levels at each of the 30 branch warehouses was exercised from Chicago by Mr. Paxton's inventory-control personnel who kept records of the stock balance of each part at each branch warehouse. The activities at each branch warehouse consisted essentially of materials handling: putting parts received each week from the central (Chicago) warehouse on shelves in the branch warehouse and removing parts from these shelves as ordered for delivery to the jobber-customers. Deliveries to jobbers were generally made by the jobbers' trucks or local haulers after receipt of customers' orders. Frequently customers' rush orders were serviced literally on an "over-the-counter" basis.

Each time a customer's order was taken from a branch-warehouse stock, a packing list was filled out; this list contained the customer's name and address, the date, the name, number, and quantity of each part ordered for delivery by the customer, and the quantity of each part actually delivered to the customer. (Occasionally branch stocks were inadequate to fill a customer's order.) Daily, copies of the packing lists were airmailed (requiring between 1.5 and 2.5 calendar days) to the central warehouse office, where they were used as bases for posting accounts receivable, customer billing, and inventory records and for determining the next week's replenishment order to be shipped to the branch warehouse.

At the central warehouse each part item listed on the packing list was then transcribed to computer tapes duly coded by the branch-warehouse number, part number and name, quantity ordered, the date and the quantity removed from the branch stock, and the customer code number. This transcription and verification required two working days.

First, the tapes were used to update customers' accounts. Then they were run a second time with other tapes containing the stock balance in the packaged-carton stores at the central (Chicago) warehouse. The latest branch-stock withdrawal quantities for each part were (with exceptions to be described later) exactly equal to the quantities to be shipped from the central warehouse packaged stock. This second run subtracted the quantities to be shipped and computed a new (lower) stock balance at Chicago, before the parts were physically withdrawn from the packaged stocks. The computer runs for customer billing and for computing new packaged-stock balances at Chicago required two working days.

The branch stock-withdrawal data were accumulated for four working days in a "branch withholding file." Then they were run a third time to print the branch-warehouse replenishment order. This print out listed the part number and quantities to be shipped to the branch warehouse during the week. One copy of this order was sent to the inventory-control office to be used to update branch-stock records in Mr. Paxton's office. Quantities in transit were posted as additions to branch-warehouse stocks at the time they were shipped from Chicago each week. The data representing quantities withdrawn from branch-warehouse stocks were five to eight days old by the time they were posted to the branch-warehouse stock-record cards in Chicago.

Shipments to each branch warehouse were scheduled for regular weekly departures from the Chicago warehouse, and these schedules were strictly maintained. Three days before the date of each weekly shipment the computer run was made to determine and print the branch-warehouse replenishment order. Before making this run, the data were re-sorted in the order of central (Chicago) warehouse stockpicking locations to enable stockpickers to read down the order list as they worked. The original of the order was then sent to the Warehouse Superintendent's office. Stockpicking, to fill weekly shipments to each branch warehouse, was carried on simultaneously at four different packaged-stock locations in the 18 buildings used by CHAPSCO in Chicago. (These buildings had become inadequate to accommodate the physical volume of parts handled by CHAPSCO, and this was why a new building facility was being planned as described in the CHAPSCO (A) case.) Depending on the variety and quantities of parts in a branch-warehouse shipment, it took 1.5 to 2.5 working days (at one shift per day) to pick the central warehouse packaged stocks, assemble and pack the shipment into corrugated shipping containers, and load them aboard a common-carrier truck bound for the branch warehouse. A branch shipment contained between 1000 and 1200 different parts, on the average. Shipments to several branch warehouses located along the same truck route were scheduled for departure on the same day of the week, to obtain savings on full truckload shipping rates.

The quantity of each part shipped each week to a branch warehouse was equal to the quantity that had been withdrawn from the branch-warehouse stock, as reported by the packing list and computer information-feedback procedure, unless one of Mr. Paxton's "commodity-stock controllers" changed the shipping-order quantity because of a change in the "branch normal" stock level for that warehouse. Exhibit 10–3 is a schematic flow diagram which summarizes the details of the branch-warehouse stock-replenishment system.

Branch Normal Stock Levels

Mr. Paxton's commodity control personnel established branch normal stock levels as the "best" stock level to carry of each part of each branch. Branch normal stock was "that quantity of parts that should be available at the beginning of the nominal stock-replenishment cycle (the lead-time to replenish the stock at the branch), to ensure that branch stocks would not become depleted." In algebraic terms,

branch normal stock = $ND + F \sqrt{ND}$

where

ND = normal or average forecasted demand during the nominal replenishment-cycle period. This was obtained by averaging the demand during the latest available branch stock-withdrawal data for three replenishment-cycle time periods and then adjusting this average up or down by known seasonal and local factors.

F = a multiple of the standard deviation of a normal statistical distribution with a mean of zero and variance of one. The multiple used was $F = 1.65$ to provide assurance against a stockout 95 percent of the time. The case appendix gives more details.

The replenishment-cycle time period for each branch was nominally four or five weeks, depending on the mileage between the branch and the central warehouse.

To illustrate how this formula was applied, suppose that at CHAPSCO's New York branch it took an average of two weeks from the day parts were sold to a jobber until a replenishment supply of those parts was received in New York from Chicago. Because of delays, holidays, and possible clerical errors, an additional two weeks was added, making New York's *nominal* replenishment cycle four weeks. Suppose, further, for a certain shock-absorber assembly that data on the *three* latest *four-week stock* demands information at Mr. Paxton's office had been 12, 18, and 24, or a total of 54 shock-absorber assemblies sold during the twelve weeks. The average (or normal) demand during these three replenishment cycle time periods was then determined as $54/3 = 18$ shock-absorber assemblies. If no future seasonal or local adjustment factor had to be accounted for, then the New York branch normal stock would be $18 + 1.65 \sqrt{18} = 25$ shock absorber assemblies.

Local factors affecting the normal demand included such matters as state automobile-inspection regulations in force and distributor's sales promotions; examples of seasonal factors included changes from water to anti-freeze coolants, which affected future demands for water-pump parts.

Branch normal stock levels were reviewed and readjusted—monthly for

Exhibit 10—3 Chicago Auto Parts Supply Company Branch-Warehouse Stock-Replenishment Control System Diagram

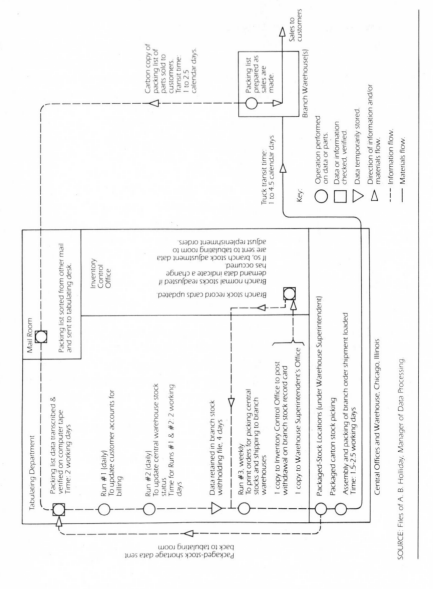

Tabulating Department

Packing list data transcribed & verified on computer tape
Time: 2 working days

Run #1 (daily)
To update customer accounts for billing

Run #2 (daily)
To update central warehouse stock status
Time for Runs #1 & #2: 2 working days

Data retained in branch stock withholding file. 4 days

Run #3. weekly
To print orders for picking central stocks and shipping to branch warehouses

1 copy to Inventory Control Office to post withdrawal on branch stock record card

1 copy to Warehouse Superintendent's Office

Packaged-Stock Locations (under Warehouse Superintendent)

Packaged carton stock picking

Assembly and packing of branch order shipment loaded
Time: 1.5–2.5 working days

Central Offices and Warehouse. Chicago, Illinois

Packaged-stock shortage data sent back to tabulating room

Mail Room

Packing list sorted from other mail and sent to tabulating desk.

Inventory Control Office

Branch stock record cards updated.

Branch normal stocks readjusted if demand data indicate a change has occurred.
If so, branch stock adjustment data are sent to tabulating room to adjust replenishment orders.

Carbon copy of packing list of parts sold to customers.
Transit time: 1 to 2.5 calendar days.

Packing list prepared as sales are made.

Branch Warehouse(s)

Sales to customers

Truck transit time: 1 to 4.5 calendar days

Key:

◯ Operation performed on data or parts.

☐ Data or information checked, verified.

▽ Data temporarily stored.

△ Direction of information and/or materials flow.

- - - Information flow.

—— Materials flow.

SOURCE: Files of A. B. Holliday. Manager of Data Processing

the most popular items, yearly for the least popular items, and whenever quantities at the branch-warehouse stocks were not adequate to fill a customer's order. The stock-record clerks used a circular "slide rule," especially calibrated according to the formula, to facilitate computing branch normal stock quantities. Whenever an adjustment to branch normal stock was required, the appropriate information was sent to the tabulating department, and the weekly branch shipment quantities were adjusted up or down accordingly. Branch normal stock quantities did not physically exist at branch warehouses; these quantities were considered "optimal" levels at which branch working-stock levels were to be maintained.

Control of Central Warehouse Stocks

As stated, CHAPSCO's Chicago warehouse contained parts stored in two forms: packaged stocks and bulk stocks. Packaged stocks consisted of branded cartons, each containing an individual part of an assembly of different parts (such as a shock-absorber assembly) or a set of the same part (such as a set of six or eight exhaust valves). Bulk stocks were parts stored in large corrugated shipping containers weighing 500 to 1800 pounds. Approximately 90 percent of the 35,000 different parts stored in the Chicago warehouse were received in bulk form; 10 percent were packaged by the manufacturers and received in CHAPSCO's branded cartons. About 5 percent of CHAPSCO's jobber-customers purchased parts in bulk form directly from Chicago, and these bulk sales represented approximately 12 percent of CHAPSCO's total annual unit sales.

Storage space at the central warehouse in Chicago had been limited throughout most of CHAPSCO's history. The storage space required per part stocked in branded-packaged form was substantially greater than that required per part stocked in bulk form. As a compromise between the necessity to limit the space for branded-carton stores and the necessity to keep a stock of packaged parts sufficient to replenish the branch warehouse, it was agreed by Mr. Paxton and Mr. Albert, Warehouse Superintendent, that an average of one half should be stocked in bulk form and one half in packaged-stock locations. Actually, for a particular part, there were considerable variations during a year from this "50-50 split" between the proportions of bulk and packaged quantities in the Chicago warehouse.

Control of Packaged Stock Quantities

Reductions in the packaged-stock balance for each part were computed daily. These latest stock-balances were compared with the reorder-point quantity (a one week's supply of packaged stock) and the replenishment-order quantity (a two weeks' supply of packaged stock) for each part. The computer was programmed to compare the actual stock quantity with the reorder-point quantity and to print the actual stock quantity and the replenishment-order quantity on a list, if the actual stock quantity was *less* than the reorder-point quantity. Mr. Paxton's group was responsible for revisions to packaged-stock reorder-point quantities and replenishment-order quantities.

The packaged-stock replenishment-order list was sent daily to the warehouse superintendent's office. Here a clerk used this list and standard work-measurement data to determine manpower requirements and schedules for packaging operations. When more than one part was to be inserted in a carton, the packaging job was done on a belt conveyor line with one operator to insert each different part and one operator for the carton-sealing machine. CHAPSCO had six carton-sealing machines which also printed the part name and number on each carton after sealing. The clerk also estimated the manpower required to pick the bulk stocks and to deliver the packaged cartons to the packaged-stock locations where they were put away.

After the packaged stocks were physically replenished, the completed order lists were sent back from the warehouse superintendent's office to update the packaged-stock balance on computer tapes.

Control of Bulk-Stock Quantities

The computer information denoting additions to packaged-stock balances was used to decrease the bulk-stock balances. As parts were inspected after being physically received from suppliers, copies of receiving-inspection reports were sent daily to the computer department, which recorded additions to bulk-stock balance.

Printed lists of bulk- and packaged-stock balances were furnished weekly to the inventory-control department. Inventory-record clerks reviewed these lists to determine the need for purchase requisitions and changes in inventory control quantities.

Problems Considered by Mr. Paxton

Mr. Paxton anticipated strong criticism from Mr. Allston, Manager of Sales Administration, at the forthcoming business-review meeting, because the number of stock shortages at the branch warehouses had increased by 15 percent over what they had been during the previous year. Also the number of shortages in weekly shipments to branch warehouses had increased by 20 percent during the same period.

Mr. Duff, Manager of Finance, would probably comment adversely regarding inventory turnover, which had not been increased fast enough in spite of the fact that sales during this year promised to be 12 percent higher than the $25 million CHAPSCO had realized last year. Mr. Duff had often contended that CHAPSCO's inventory turnover was much too low.

Within his own organization Mr. Paxton had experienced what he considered to be an abnormally high turnover among his eight commodity-stock controllers and clerks, especially the former. He and Mr. McAllister had both agreed that the success of inventory control was substantially determined by the cumulative effects of the detailed decisions made by the commodity-stock controllers. Accordingly, Mr. Paxton had hired college graduates for these jobs. But the salary levels paid them were apparently not high enough to hold these competent personnel for more than two years.

Appendix: Explanation of Method for Determining "Branch Normal" Stock Levels

Definition

The branch normal stock level was that quantity of stock that should be available for sale by the branch, at the time an order was placed to replenish the branch stock, sufficient to fulfill all customers' future demands for stock withdrawals with a probability of 0.95. (In other words, branch normal stock levels were presumed enough for 95 percent of the branch demands; stock depletions would occur not more than 5 percent of the time if branch normal stocks were properly set.) Algebraically,

$$\text{branch normal} = ND + F\sqrt{ND}$$

ND = forecasted quantity of customers' demand for the part, during the replenishment time period

F = a protection factor to assure against a branch stockout 95 percent of the time

Derivation

Assumptions

1. The distributions of probable demands for each item during its stock-replenishment period were *random*. In other words, reasons for one customer's order for a given stock item were completely independent of the reasons for another customer's order for the same item during a given period. Similarly, during the stock-replenishment period, the quantity ordered by a customer at one time was assumed completely independent of the quantity ordered by another customer or by the same customer at another time.

2. The distribution of probable weekly demand "filled" a Poisson-type of random-cause phenomena.

Test of These Assumptions

1. For a certain part the demand data in units withdrawn per week for 100 weeks from a branch warehouse were recorded in the form of the cross-hatched histogram illustrated in Exhibit 10–4. In making this 100 week survey of historical demand for this part, (i) there were just as many weeks taken from the months of high seasonal demand as from months of

Exhibit 10—4 Illustrative histograms (frequency distributions of actual and theoretical demand).

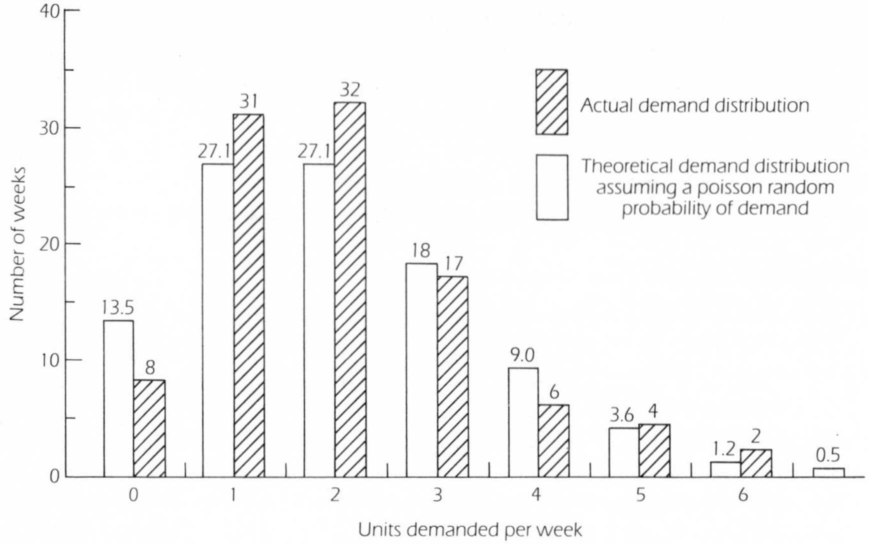

This graphical or visual similarity between the historical weekly demand data and theoretical demand data obtained from the Poisson probability formula was further substantiated by the "chi-square test," which is a statistical test to determine the probability that empirical data could have resulted from random-cause phenomena. For various tests, the chi-square test probability ranged between 0.6 and 0.9.

low seasonal demand; (ii) there were two customers who bought this part in quantities of 50 or more units each time they placed an order at this branch. These customers' demands were *excluded* from this survey because their orders were filled mostly by "back ordering" from the central warehouse instead of depleting the supply at the branch. Thus they were given "special treatment" and were therefore excluded from the normal or usual demands this branch stock was intended to supply.

2. This type of survey of historical demand was repeated for (i) the same part covering different historical periods; (ii) different parts and different branch warehouses.

For *all* histograms plotted it was noted that the shapes were essentially similar to the one illustrated. All histograms were skewed to the right (in a positive direction), and the historical average demands, although different, tended to be relatively low. In other words, although the average weekly demands were different, the shapes of all the histograms plotted were strikingly similar. This similarity indicated a persistent stability of the pattern of branch normal stock demands.

3. The mutual similarities in the patterns of historical data prompted

the question of whether these empirical histograms fit the histograms derived from Poisson's mathematical (theoretical) description of random-cause phenomena, which also have a similar pattern. If they were similar, then the probability of any demand being served by a branch warehouse stock could conveniently be estimated from published data on the Poisson type of random distribution. For the Poisson distribution the probability (i.e., the percentage "chance") of a demand of n units per week, when the average demand per week is m units, is determined by the following formula: $P(n,m) = e^{-m}m^n/n!$

$P(n,m)$ is "shorthand" for the "probability of any number such as n units demanded, given that the average demand is m units.

e is the base of natural logarithms having the value 2.7183.

n! is shorthand for n factorial; for example, $5! = 5 \times 4 \times 3 \times 2 \times 1 = 120$. (Values of $P(n,m)$ are tabulated in many statistics books, so it is not necessary to use the formula directly.)

The histogram *not cross hatched* in Exhibit 10–4 is a plot of the tabulated Poisson formula for an average demand of two units per week (the actual average of the data illustrated by the cross-hatched histogram).

Comparison of the two histograms shows a rather striking similarity, which was observed for many other studies of historical branch-warehouse weekly withdrawal data. It was concluded that actual weekly demand data "fitted" the Poisson type of random distribution. This fit was considered close enough to take advantage of the convenience in using the Poisson distribution of probable demands.

Degree of Protection against Occurrences of Stockouts Desired

Stockouts were presumed to occur only because the actual weekly demand exceeded the forecasted weekly demand.

As an index for controlling branch stock, it was decided that a stockout at a branch warehouse should be tolerated, on the average, 5 percent of the time. To carry more stock, thus to ensure protection against a stockout less than 5 percent of the time, would require inventory carrying costs which CHAPSCO's management considered excessive. An occurrence of a stockout *more than* 5 percent of the time was deemed too risky because of the financial consequences of lost sales.

Having determined the "index" for controlling branch stocks, a routine procedure had to be devised so the stock-record-card clerks accordingly could calculate branch normal stock level.

The area under the cross-hatched histogram illustrated in Exhibit 10–4 represents the sum of all probable demands for a part supplied to customers of a branch warehouse. The probability of a demand of 0 units per week was 0.08, because eight out of 100 weeks, or 8 percent of the time, 0 units were demanded; similarly, the probability of five units being demanded was 0.06 because 6/100 of the time five units were demanded. In a *cumulative* sense the probability of a demand of *five or fewer* units per week was 0.98, which is the sum of the probabilities for demands of 0, 1, 2, 3, 4, and 5 units per week. This meant that if the *average* demand was two units per week, and if five units were actually in stock at the beginning of the replenishment week, then the probability of a stockout was 0.02, which was the probability of a demand *greater than* five units per week.

Statistical tables of areas under a random-distribution curve show that 1.65 standard deviations *above* the mean of the distribution cover 95 percent of the area under the curve. This is how the "protection factor" $F = 1.65$ was determined. For the Poisson type of random distribution the standard deviation equals the square root of the average (or mean) of the distribution. Thus, if a branch had a quantity of parts available for sales equal to the average of next period's sales *plus* 1.65 times the standard deviation of the probable distribution of next period's unit sales, then the available quantity was presumed adequate to service up to 95 percent of all probable sales during the next period.

Crown Dairy Products Company

11

Mr. B. C. Fields, Executive Vice-President for Operations of Crown Dairy Products Company, Chicago, Illinois, was cooperating with a group of five students who were preparing a term report for their course in operations planning and control.

You fellows have certainly forced us to quantify our production-scheduling problems. I learned a lot from the questions you've asked to get the pertinent cost data. They've given me a new insight about how much our operating costs are dependent upon how we schedule production. But now that we have determined what you call the "parameters of our scheduling problem," you're going to have to tell me how to use them in scheduling production.

The Crown Dairy Products Company marketed nationally a complete line of cheeses, mayonnaise, and sandwich spreads. These three products were produced on the same processing facilities in each of three plants located in Chicago, Portland, and Baltimore. As an alumnus of Northwestern University's business school, Mr. Fields had worked with groups of students assigned field projects by their instructors. The field assignment for the course in operations planning and control required students to analyze and propose solutions to practical operating problems. Mr. Fields' custom was to follow closely the work students did at Crown Dairy Products.

Their fresh look at our problems is often better than we can get from expensive consulting firms. And working with students gives me opportunity to invite some excellent new men to join our organization.

Because of its proximity, the students chose to investigate production scheduling problems at the Chicago plant. The processing methods were almost the same for all three plants, so that with minor changes the students' proposed scheduling procedure could be adapted for all.

Briefly, cheese spreads, mayonnaise, and sandwich spreads were made on the same processing equipment. First, appropriate ingredients were fed continuously at controlled rates into an agitating tank, in which they were thoroughly mixed and blended. As a spread was pumped from the agitating tank, its flavor and viscosity were sampled and tested. If not satisfactory, the spread was pumped back into the blending tank. If satisfactory, the spread flowed to the packaging equipment. This equipment automatically filled jars of various sizes, screwed or clamped on the tops, and glued labels on the jars. As the filled jars continued on a conveyor passing over an automatic weight-inspection device, they were visually inspected by operators. Different jar sizes were filled for each of the three products. Finally, the jars were fed by machines into shipping cartons, which were automatically sealed. The cartons were stacked and stored in the factory warehouse.

Between the batch blending and the packaging equipment were two large tanks used to store the blended products temporarily. These tanks sustained normal differences between the output rate from the mixing and blending equipment and the output rate from the packaging equipment. The plants were designed for two-shift operation, but they were operated for three shifts during March to October, the peak months of demand. Currently the Chicago plant was manned to operate 80 hours per week.

To use the same equipment for cheese spreads, mayonnaise, and sandwich spreads meant that the jobs of setup changeover had to be planned and scheduled. First, the equipment had to be thoroughly cleaned. In addition, in the blending operations different control devices for feeding various ingredients and different agitators had to be installed and the speeds of pump-drive and agitator-drive mechanisms had to be adjusted properly. Similarly, the various mechanical and electrical drive and feed mechanisms on the packaging equipment had to be changed to suit the various jars to be filled, labeled, and packed in cartons. Setup times for the blending and packaging operations are summarized in Exhibit 11–1.

As already noted, the output rates for the blending and packaging operations were different for each of the three products. Data are given in Exhibit 11–1. The two storage tanks between these two production stages were large enough to sustain blending with or without packaging for not more than one shift (eight hours); consequently, the setup and running

Exhibit 11—1 Crown Dairy Products Company Quantitative Data for Weekly Scheduling Decisions

1. Hours Required for Setup Changeover

Mixing and Blending Equipment (First Stage)

From:	To: Cheese spreads	Mayonnaise	Sandwich spread
Cheese spreads	X	10	2
Mayonnaise	4	X	12
Sandwich spreads	3	8	X

Packaging Equipment (Second Stage)

From:	To: Cheese spreads	Mayonnaise	Sandwich spread
Cheese spreads	X	3	1
Mayonnaise	7	X	9
Sandwich spreads	8	5	X

NOTES: a. Hourly data include average of times to clean storage tanks between these two steps.

b. Time to change packaging equipment to fill different sizes of jars during runs of one kind of product are assumed negligible.

c. The plant is currently set up to process and package mayonnaise.

2. Finished Stock Availability at Beginning of Week No. 10*

Product	Number of Cases
Cheese spread	5000
Mayonnaise	4200
Sandwich spread	3000

3. Forecast of Shipments from Stock

	Number of Cases		
Product	Week 10	Week 11	Week 12
Cheese spread	6,400	6,000	6,200
Mayonnaise	24,000	23,000	20,000
Sandwich spread	8,000	7,500	7,600

4. Production Output Rates (cases per hour)

Product	Mixing and Blending	Packaging
Cheese spread	500	450
Mayonnaise	800	750
Sandwich spread	300	350

SOURCE: Students' field research data obtained from the Chicago Plant offices and the Central Planning Office.

*The company's fiscal year was coincident with the calendar year.

times for both packaging and blending operations had to be scheduled as nearly simultaneously as practicable.

After being packed into cases, the spreads were stored in a factory warehouse, pending shipment to district warehouses operated by supermarket chains and a few grocery distributors.

Once each week Mr. Fields' central planning group issued to each factory the estimated number of case-units to be shipped to customers for each of the next three weeks. Determining the quantity and sequence of runs of each product and the number of plant operating hours per week were decisions delegated to each plant manager. Actual weekly shipments did not vary from expected weekly shipments for the earliest of the three weeks' shipping forecast by more than ±2 percent. Errors for the second and third weeks' forecasted shipments were between ±10 percent and ±25 percent of actual shipment, respectively. Forecast data are shown in Exhibit 11–1.

By means of intensive questioning and examination of cost-accounting records, the students established cost data which they thought would be useful criteria for production-scheduling decisions at the Chicago plant.

Setup crews were the most highly paid operating personnel in the plants. In addition to setting up the equipment, these personnel were responsible for preventive maintenance activities. About $50,000 was spent each year for maintenance services subcontracted with outside firms. Maintenance work was interrupted whenever a different product had to be run on the blending and packaging equipment. The operators assisted in unskilled portions of the job of process changeover. The students asked the plant manager whether less maintenance work would be farmed out to subcontractors if fewer process setup changeovers were scheduled. He replied that about a third of the subcontracted maintenance work could be done by the maintenance and setup crews in the plant if more time and/or skilled manpower were available. The students then examined the plant accountant's record of setup and maintenance expenses and proposed that for each set of equipment, blending and packaging, $40 per hour would be a reasonable estimate of the cost of materials and labor used in setup changeovers. The plant manager agreed with this proposal.

There was considerable discussion about whether nonproductive equipment-time should be "charged" as part of setup changeover costs. Some students argued that while the equipment was down for cleaning and setup Crown Dairy Products lost dollars of contribution to overhead plus profit—in other words, an opportunity cost was incurred. Other students argued that such a cost was incurred only if demand was high enough to sell the products that would be produced during the downtime for setup change. To resolve this issue, the students asked the Chicago plant manager and Mr. Fields the following question: "How would you evaluate the cost of nonproductive time during setup changeovers?" The plant manager answered that this lost time should be costed at $200 per hour, which for the three products was the average hourly contribution to overhead and profit produced by the equipment. Mr. Fields comment was:

I think your question relates to our inventory control policy. We try to budget inventory levels at plant warehouses so that plant managers have one run of each product each week and so that inventory is built up and cut back before seasonal ups and downs occur. I'd say we lost some profit contribution due to lost production during setup changes. The amount we lost would depend on two things: first the frequency and extent of errors in our weekly shipping forecasts and errors in the timing of process changeovers which are decisions our plant managers make. I think it would be best for me to give you a cost figure reflecting these factors. I'd say about $80 per hour.

The plant manager had a choice of operating overtime or "undertime" (more than or less than 40, 80, or 120 hours per week) to produce the exact quantities estimated by the Central Planning Office each week; or he could schedule production of more than or fewer than the quantities estimated by the Central Planning Office. Overtime operations cost $25 per plant operating hour; undertime cost $20 per hour because operators were paid even though they were idle.

Regarding costs associated with factory-warehouse inventory, the students inferred that stockouts costs were proportional to the number of units and to the duration of stockouts. Similarly, inventory carrying costs were proportional to the number of units carried and to how long they were carried. After discussing these costs with the Chicago plant accountant and the corporate controller, the students found little agreement about quantifying these costs. The plant manager said it was impossible to put a valid figure on them. The students, on the other hand, contended that production-scheduling decisions could not be evaluated quantitatively without having cost data for stockouts and carrying inventory. Accordingly, the students proposed that a reasonable estimate of stockout cost would be $10 per unit of 100 cases. A reasonable estimate of inventory carrying cost would be $1 per unit of 100 cases. But they could not decide how *time* should be related to these costs.

During their last field visit with Mr. Fields, the students reviewed their efforts to get all the data pertaining to production scheduling decisions at Crown Dairy Products. Mr. Fields told them:

Your data all seem reasonable to me. I'd say the most tenuous are your cost data for inventory stockouts and for carrying inventory. But we can refine these data later. You fellows seem to think you can reduce our scheduling problem to some kind of formulated procedure that we can use each week to minimize costs of our scheduling decisions. This would take a lot of guesswork out of our decisions if the formula were not too complicated for us to use.

Duro, Inc. (A)

12

Duro Incorporated was one of the largest manufacturers of household paints in the United States. It had manufacturing and distribution facilities throughout the United States and Canada. One of its largest facilities, the Eastern Division, was located in the metropolitan New York-New Jersey area.

Because of the seasonal and cyclical nature of the paint business and the severe price competition in the industry, Duro constantly was faced with the problems of meeting fluctuating demand and holding down operating costs. At a recent staff meeting, Frank Simmons, Plant Manager of Duro's Eastern Division, observed:

We are always caught in a helluva bind between two evils. Every month the Marketing Department sends us a demand forecast which varies month from month. If our production schedule is supposed to keep up with the demand, it will go up and down like a roller coaster. We'll end up either paying overtime out of our ears if we want to keep the same number of crews, or hire and lay off people left and right every time we make a change in production. You can bet the union is going to raise hell about that. On the other hand, if we don't go along with the demand and keep our production steady, we'll need to build up a large amount of inventory

Exhibit 12—1 Duro Inc., Eastern Division Monthly Sales Forecast (Thousand Gallons)

Jan.	730	Jan.	380	Jan.	640
Feb.	470	Feb.	370	Feb.	495
Mar.	570	Mar.	528	Mar.	585
Apr.	560	Apr.	720	Apr.	720
May	460	May	420	May	865
June	590	June	800	June	482
July	580	July	565	July	655
Aug.	440	Aug.	430	Aug.	850
Sept.	450	Sept.	360	Sept.	621
Oct.	750	Oct.	750	Oct.	450
Nov.	450	Nov.	683	Nov.	540
Dec.	630	Dec.	546	Dec.	710

before the demand steps up. That's going to cause us a lot of troubles, too. Every day the extra inventory we keep in stock is costing us money, not only for the warehouse but also for handling, bookkeeping, and damage, etc. Besides, it's going to tie up a lot of money which the finance boys are not going to like one bit. Pretty soon those fellows at the headquarters will get on your back. Can't win, no matter what you do. It's a "heads you win, tails I lose" situation.

As if to prove his point, Simmons pulled out a memo containing the figures of the latest sales forecast for the next thirty six months (Exhibit 12–1) which he had just received from Marketing this morning. "Look at these figures" Simmons went on waving the memo, "and you will see what I mean. Marketing is again telling us we should expect sales to swing up and down from 440 thousand to 750 thousand gallons within the next twelve months. I will sure hate like hell to have to figure out a production schedule again for the next year that will make us look good, cost wise. Have you guys got any good ideas?"

Duro, Inc. (B)

13

As Frank Simmons concluded his remarks concerning his dilemma about his production schedule for the next twelve months (detailed in Part A), a member of Duro's operations staff, Mr. Irving M. Smart, a recent MBA from an eastern university volunteered: "Frank, if you would give me a clear objective of what you want to accomplish and a set of cost figures, I think I can come up with a program that will alleviate the problem."

The young Smart recalled that in his operations management course he had worked on a case dealing with a similar problem. In this case, the MBA students were given a set of cost and sales forecast figures and were required to make a series of decisions on how many units to produce and how many men to use each month aimed at achieving the lowest possible total cumulative cost at the end of the year.

"Great, Irv," Simmons declared. "I really hope you can work out something and get us out of this bind. I think Accounting has most of the figures you want. All I am concerned about is the bottom line at the end of the year, if you will come up with something that will make us look good in the over-all cost, the rest I'll not be too worried about." "But what

This case was prepared by Professor Gordon K. C. Chen of the School of Business Administration, University of Massachusetts, as a basis for class discussion and is not designed to present illustrations of either effective or ineffective handling of administrative problems. Adapted from *Planning Production, Inventories and Work Force*, by C. C. Holt, F. Modigliani, J. F. Muth, and H. A. Simon, Prentice-Hall, Inc., 1960.

Exhibit 13-1 Overtime Cost Schedule

Prod. Rate (thousand gallons)	No. of Men	60	70	80	90	100	110	120
100								
200								
300								
350		$ 1079						
400		4335	$ 812					
450		8591	3934	$ 563				
500		13847	8056	3551	$ 331			
550		20103	13178	7539	3185	$ 118		
600		27359	19300	12527	7039	2838		
650		35615	26422	18515	11893	6558	$ 2508	
700		44871	34544	25503	17747	11278	6094	$ 2197
750		55127	43666	33491	24601	16998	10680	5649
800		66383	53788	42479	32455	23718	16266	10101
850		78639	64910	52467	41309	31438	22852	15553
900		91895	77032	63455	51163	40158	30438	22005
950		106151	90154	75443	62017	49878	39024	29457
1000		121407	104276	88431	73871	60598	48610	37909

about the union if we figured it pays to lay off or rehire people some-times?" Smart followed up. "Well, we pay a price for doing that anyway, I won't worry too much about it," answered Simmons. "O.K., in that case, I'll just look into the cost figures and nothing else," Irv commented as the meeting broke up, and he headed directly toward the Accounting Department.

Mr. Smart spent the next few days digging up some cost figures relevant to the production scheduling. He found that there are four sets of costs which must be considered: regular payroll, overtime costs, hiring and layoff costs, and inventory holding costs. Although overhead and material costs were present, the production department decisions were not con-cerned with them in an over-all sense. Exhibit 13-1 shows the overtime cost schedule and Exhibit 13-2 gives the cost figures for regular payroll, hiring-layoff costs, and inventory holding costs.

Regular Payroll Cost

Exhibit 13-2 shows that on the average each man has a payroll cost of $340 per month. This does not include overtime.

Exhibit 13—2 Costs of Payroll, Hiring or Layoff, and Inventory

Regular Payroll Costs		Hiring or Layoff Costs		Inventory Costs	
Total Work Force (# of Men)	Regular Payroll Cost Per Month	Hired or Laid Off Per Month (# of Men)	Hiring or Layoff Costs	Net Inventory (Actual inventory less back orders) in thousands of gallons	Net Cost Per Month
10	$ 3400	1	$ 64	− 200	$22308
				− 150	18224
20	6800	2	257	− 100	14553
				− 50	11294
30	10200	3	579	0	8448
				+ 50	6014
40	13600	4	1029	100	3993
				150	2384
50	17000	5	1608	200	1188
				250	404
60	20400	6	2315	300	33
				350	74
70	23800	7	3151	400	528
				450	1394
80	27200	8	4115	500	2673
				550	4364
90	30600	9	5208	600	6468
				650	8984
100	34000	10	6430	700	11913
				750	15254
110	37400	15	14468	800	19008
120	40800	20	25720		

Hiring and Layoff Costs

The cost of hiring or laying off includes such things as reorganization costs, training or separation costs, etc., and on the average, the cost is the same whether for hiring or for layoff. The costs indicate that hiring or laying off should be done gradually over a period of several months for it becomes quite expensive to hire more than three or four men in any one month.

Overtime Costs

From Exhibit 13–1 it is seen that, for example, a work force of 90 men could make up to 459,000 gallons without overtime, although if they make much less than that, there would be idle times. Each man can on the average produce about 5,000 gallons per month without overtime. A work force of 90 men would require overtime costing $331 to produce 500,000 gallons.

Inventory Costs

Exhibit 13–2 shows relative holding costs for inventory which increases as the number of gallons in inventory increases over 320,000, out-of-stock conditions begin to take place with an increase in back orders, so an estimation of the cost of tolerating back orders accounts for the increasing inventory cost at low values of inventory. Negative inventory means all back orders. The optimum level of inventory is 320,000 gallons as far as inventory costs are concerned.

Mr. Smart also noted that on January 1, there were 75 men on the payroll and at the close of business on last December 31, there were 280 thousand gallons of paint of inventory on hand. Having gathered all the information, Mr. Smart proceeded to prepare a production schedule.

Foster Optical Equipment Company

14

On May 25th, Mr. William Thomas, a manager of manufacturing of the Foster Optical Equipment Company was holding a meeting to discuss and evaluate plans for the assembly activities for the KD 780 photo-reconnaissance Air Force Camera contract. These plans (Exhibit 14–1) had been developed during April and May by Mr. Robert Phillips, a superintendent of the assembly of noncommercial products of the Foster factory at Cleveland, Ohio. Mr. Thomas and others at this meeting were not at all certain that Mr. Phillips' plans were feasible. The KD 780 camera job was Foster's first defense-product contract since World War II, and Mr. Thomas was anxious for the manufacturing division to look good on this job to enhance prospects for more business with the Air Force.

The Foster Optical Equipment Company of Cleveland, Ohio, designed, manufactured, and sold optical equipment used in laboratories, factories, and medical facilities. Two years earlier, the company purchased a factory building and some machine tools, which had been declared surplus property by the U.S. Department of Defense. These new facilities provided about 25 percent more space and machining capacity than was to be required by optical equipment manufacturing, according to a ten year forecast of sales. However, the price and especially the location of this former government property were so attractive and Foster's former plant space

Revision of an earlier case written by R. E. McGarrah and copyright © by the President and Fellows of Harvard College.

Exhibit 14—1 Foster Optical Equipment Company Assembly Schedule

	Assembly Operators Added	Total Operators Available	Effective Man-Hours Available	Cameras Assembled During Month	Cumulative Total Cameras Assembled
June & July	4	4	1,280	2	2
August	20	24	2,880	10	12
September	20	44	6,080	60	72
October	0	44	7,040	124	196
November	0	44	7,040	184	380
December	0	44	7,040	210	590
January	0	44	7,040	250	840

SOURCE: Mr. Robert Phillips' KD 780 Camera Assembly Project File.

had been so inadequate that the added investment in the surplus plant and machine was easily justified. The move to the new plant had been completed and operations were running smoothly.

The previous September Mr. J. F. Pickering, president of the company, had decided to solicit government contracts to manufacture and assemble defense products in order to utilize the extra available plant space and machine tools more fully. No commitments were to be made for Foster to design or develop new products because Foster's engineers were fully occupied with optical equipment design work. Accordingly, a sales engineer and a production engineer had made a series of calls at various military equipment procurement offices. In December Foster was awarded a prime contract to manufacture 840 model KD 780 night-photo reconnaissance cameras for the Air Force. Foster had been chosen among competitive bidders as the alternate prime source of supply of these cameras, which had previously been designed and produced by the Sedgewick Instrument Company.

While discussing the KD 780 job at lunch one day in March Mr. Phillips heard the sales engineer, who had "landed" this contract, briefly describe "The Manufacturing Progress Function" (otherwise called the corporate "learning curve"), which Air Force procurement officers frequently used as a guide in negotiating price and delivery terms of contracts with manufacturers. Mr. Phillips investigated the literature[1] on this subject and as a result, decided to adapt the manufacturing progress function as a means for solving his problem of programming and controlling the KD 780 as-

[1] R. W. Conway and A. Schultz, Jr., "The Manufacturing Progress Function," *Journal of Industrial Engineering*, Jan.–Feb. 1959.

sembly activities. Briefly, the chief premise of the manufacturing progress function was that, just as the effort exerted by a single worker decreased as he acquired experience and skill in doing a set of tasks, so the labor hours or labor cost per unit of product produced by a group of workers would decrease as experience could be measured quantitatively; Mr. Phillips decided to use this concept as the basis for his assembly operations plans.

As his first step in adapting the manufacturing progress function to his assembly activities, Mr. Phillips listed pertinent conditions that would affect his assembly program.

1. After lengthy discussion with his methods engineer and technicians, Mr. Phillips decided that 90 KD 780 cameras would have been assembled by the time the assembly personnel had developed sufficient skill and experience to meet an initial standard rate of 85 total man hours per unit. This standard was determined by using predetermined micro motion time data. Efforts to improve productivity standards would continue throughout the project.

2. Starting with the nucleus crew of four assembly technicians, it was decided that additional assembly personnel could be selected, hired, and effectively trained at the *maximum* rate of 20 new employees per month. To attempt to train more than 20 new operators would overtax training facilities and personnel. The personnel manager, Mr. P. D. Kenworthy, had advised that all additional assembly personnel required for the KD 780 job would have to be recruited from the Cleveland area and would require Foster company orientation training as well as job methods training. During their first month in the KD 780 job, new employees were presumed to be 70% efficient (100% efficient meant that an operator completed the job in exactly the standard labor hours set for the assembly tasks assigned for him to complete). After the first month, all operators were presumed to be at least 100% efficient, with respect to work standards for their jobs.

3. For purposes of developing these plans, Mr. Phillips assumed that there would be 160 assembly operating hours in any calendar month. Since a calendar month contained 4⅓ weeks, this meant that every third month, a "margin of safety" of one week was available as a reserve for contingencies such as material shortages, quality problems, and other delays interfering with the flow of assembly work.

4. The KD 780 camera contained over 800 parts. Plans for the process specified assembly work to be done at 22 different work stations on four major subassemblies and 28 work stations in the final assembly area. Standard times at these work stations were not uniform, and to insure reasonable continuity of flow of work, buffer stocks were to be provided and certain operators were to be shifted among several work

stations. From these plans, Mr. Phillips estimated that the cycle time for assembling a camera would be four weeks, two weeks for final assembly and test, and two weeks for subassembly work.

5. The initial production-lot quantity planned was two cameras—just enough for the methods engineer and the four assembly technicians to check on the assembly methods, tools and work place arrangements in the assembly area. The Air Force desired to make thorough acceptance tests of the performance of the first two units produced by Foster.

6. To use the manufacturing progress function, Mr. Phillips had to make an assumption of the measured rate of progress he could expect the growing labor force to achieve while assembling the 840 KD 780 cameras. He had noted in the literature that an 80 percent learning curve was rather widely used in the aircraft industry. An 80 percent learning rate meant that each time the cumulative number of units produced doubled, the labor hours per unit dropped to 80 percent of its original value. For example, the direct labor cost or time for assembling the 20th unit was 80 percent of the average direct labor time for assembling the 10th unit completed; and the direct labor hours for assembling the 40th unit was 80% of the direct labor hours for assembling the 20th unit completed; and so on.

Mr. Phillips had realized that to choose a progress rate parameter of 80 percent, 70 percent, or whatever, he would have to use good judgment in extrapolating from past experiences. He therefore examined blueprints, methods specifications, and labor time tickets for several optical equipment products assembled by Foster employees in the past. Each past experience had some degree of similarity with the KD 780 job with respect to such factors as: the number of different parts to be assembled; the clearances between parts; the fragility of the parts; the numbers of different assembly operations required; and the total assembly hours required per units. By plotting learning curves for several such similar assembly activities in the past, Mr. Phillips had determined that the assembly progress-rate parameters for these past jobs ranged from 70 percent to 75 percent.

From this, Mr. Phillips had chosen 72 percent as the expected rate of progress that would be achieved on the KD 780 Air Force camera assembly job.

From these six presumed conditions, Mr. Phillips had developed his assembly production schedule and his manpower build-up schedule, shown in Exhibit 14–1. The detailed, step-by-step procedure Mr. Phillips followed to determine these schedules is summarized in Appendix A. Mr. Phillips had completed the work in determining these schedules on May 20th.

During a regular KD 780 camera job-progress meeting of manufacturing management personnel held on May 25th, Mr. Phillips presented his assembly schedules, and had briefly described how he had derived them.

Mr. J. D. Jorgenson, KD 780 Camera Project Cost Supervisor:

Bob, using your data on labor hours and total units assembled and some cost figures I have, I estimate that we won't make any money on the KD job until after we have shipped about 600 units. In fact, I don't think we will have absorbed our start-up costs directly incurred on this job until after we've shipped the 400th unit. We're committed to a fixed price on this job you know; we could not get the Air Force to go along with a cost-plus-fixed-fee price. Of course, there is a price renegotiation clause in the contract, but this is a long legal and costly process.

Mr. Phillip D. Kenworthy, Manager of Personnel and Relations:

The union has been after me about wage-incentive procedures for this KD 780 camera assembly job. As you know, we put a newly hired man on a straight piecework incentive wage after he has been on the job for one month. As I see this learning curve idea, we have an inevitable "looseness" built into our time standards. I know we regularly use predetermined (synthetic) motion and time standard data as well as stop watch time studies for the factory floor, to set piece rates. But if we put these KD 780 assembly personnel on an incentive pay basis too soon, their wage will get out of line with other personnel in the same labor class. If we don't put operators on incentives soon enough, the union will gripe. We don't build the same model of optical equipment in quantities compared to the 840 KD 780 cameras, so there isn't the extensive and uninterrupted opportunity for learning on comparable optical equipment assembly jobs. If all your people are put on incentive wage rates by October, Bob, and if they progress the way you say they will along your 72 percent progress curve, they will be turning out the 840th camera in less than 30 hours. But if they start pegging rates, say, after the 150th camera (when standard hours are $85/66 = 128\%$ of actual hours), won't this give you some trouble, Bob?

Mr. Phillips:

There is a possible wage inequity problem, Phil, and all I can say is that we'll have to take a good look at our whole wage payment policy and procedure, in light of this, before our next union contract negotiation. Meanwhile, I'm going to keep my methods engineer alert to keep his methods standards and time standards up to date and take more initiative in revising methods and time standards. There is nothing in the contract to prevent us from tightening the rates of jobs when we engineer job-methods changes. I'm also going to tell my foreman to encourage our people to exploit this learning opportunity and to assure our people that there will be no tightening of standards when an operator makes methods changes that enable him to beat the rates we have set.

Mr. William Thomas, Manager of Manufacturing:

Bob, this is quite a program you've planned. I had told Mr. Pickering I thought we wouldn't wind up this KD 780 job until May of next year. Now you show us shipping the last unit in January, or February. If you're wrong, and we land another Air Force contract to work on in February, we'll really be in a bind. Are you sure you can make this schedule? Another thing, if you've planned that the standard will be 85 labor hours per unit, and the contract states that we have to ship 120 units per month, then I figure we should have a capacity of $85 \times 120 = 10,200$ standard man hours per month. This is $10,200/160 = 64$ operators. Yet you say you can do the whole job with 44 operators. (If this is true with assembly work, I wonder how this idea would go with our parts machining work.)

Mr. Phillips:

Bill, I'm convinced we can do this. I'm telling my foreman exactly how I got the 72% progress curve, and that I am going to plot their actual progress each week to see how close they come to the curve. All I'll have to do is take the count of cameras coming off the packaging operation, and divide this into the total weekly direct labor hours tallied by the time-keeper. If their actual progress data plot above the curve for direct labor hours per unit, I'll know something is wrong and find out what it is. I'd like to try to carry out these plans, and I hope you will approve them and give me the support I know I'll need.

Appendix A: Using the Manufacturing Progress Function to Schedule Assembly Build-Up on KD 780

General Technical Specifications of the Manufacturing Progress Function   When empirical data on direct-labor hours per unit are plotted against the production count of units of product produced, the resulting curve appears for example, as shown in Exhibit 14–2 for the KD 780 camera assembly operations:

The curve depicts a phenomenon which makes strong intuitive sense, that is, a job requires less effort as more experience is gained and as more methods improvements are made. As production accumulates progress continues but at a decreasing rate, because further opportunities to improve the job become less and less obvious. This curve is just one of an almost infinite variety of such curves having the same "family-resemblance" that is the direct labor hours per unit decrease more or less sharply, but always steadily, as the number of units produced increases.

Exhibit 14—2 Foster Optical Equipment Company Assembly Progress Curve for the KD 780 Air Force Night-Photo Reconnaissance Camera

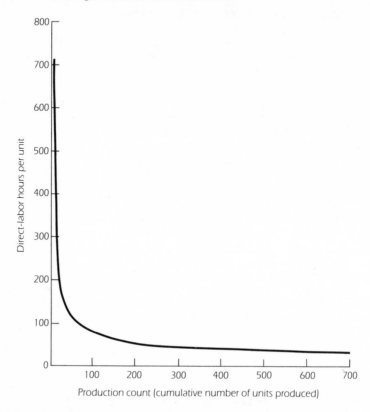

SOURCE: Mr. R. Phillips' Files.

The algebraic statement of this progress phenomenon is

$$Y_i = Y_1 i^{-b}$$

where: Y_i is the direct labor hours required to produce the ith unit of product,
i is the production count, beginning with the first unit,
Y_1 is the labor hours required for the first unit,
b is the measure of the rate at which the direct labor hours per unit are reduced as the production count increases.

When the labor hours/unit and production count data are plotted on logarithmic coordinate graph paper, or when the logarithms of these data are plotted on convential arithmetic coordinate graph paper, the curve becomes a straight line. Algebraically this fact is stated by taking the logarithmic transformation of the foregoing equation

$(\log Y_i) = (\log Y_1) - b (\log i)$.

The rate of progress is nominally described by stating the complement of the percentage reduction in labor hours per unit when the production quantity is doubled. This means that if i_2 and i_1 are any two different production counts and if i_2/i_1, always equals 2, then for an 80% progress curve, $b = -0.322$ because $2^{-0.322} = 0.80$; for a 72% progress curve, $b = -0.474$ because $2^{-0.474} = 0.72$.

Method adapting the manufacturing progress function to plans for assembling the KD 780 camera   Assumptions made:

1. The 90th camera would require 85 direct labor hours to assemble.
2. The rate of progress in assembly methods improvements, and in development of skill by assembly personnel would conform to a 72% progress function.

$Y_i = Y_1 i^{-0.474}$

The assembly progress curve (direct labor hours per unit). Using log-log graph paper, starting at the point where direct labor hours per unit equals 85 and where the production count equals 90, a straight line with a slope of -0.474 was drawn through this point. See Exhibit 14–3. This line intersects the vertical axis at 716 direct labor hours, which is the estimated time required to assemble the first KD 780 camera, according to the 72% progress function adopted.

Assembly progress curve (cumulative average direct labor hours per unit): To make the calculations easier for the assembly output build-up schedule, and for the manpower build-up schedule, this curve is drawn by using the data read from the Direct Labor Hours per Unit Curve.

The Cumulative Average Hours per Unit data in Exhibit 14–4 were also plotted as shown on the log-log graph paper. These two curves become asymptotically parallel after the 10th unit has been completed. The assembly manpower build-up schedule required that subtotals of the cumulative assembly direct labor hours be related to cumulative production. These subtotals were easily calculated by multiplying the cumulative average direct labor hours per unit by the cumulative number of units assembled. Data on cumulative average direct-labor hours per unit were simply read from the curve. (Without having this curve, calculations for the manpower and output build-up schedules would have been more tedious.) From this curve, Exhibit 14–5 was determined.

Exhibit 14–3 Foster Optical Equipment Company Graph of the 72 Percent Assembly Progress Curve

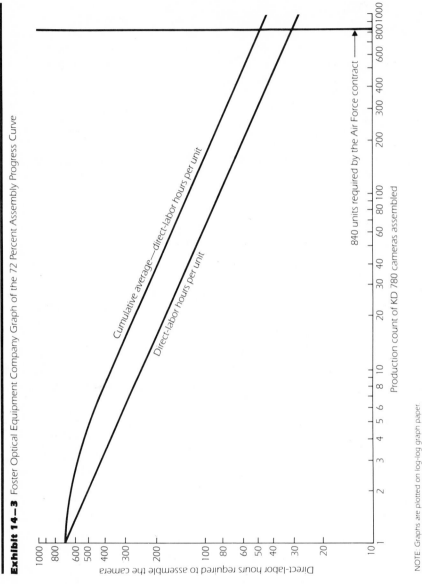

NOTE: Graphs are plotted on log-log graph paper.
SOURCE: Mr. Robert Phillips' KD 780 Camera Assembly Project Files.

Exhibit 14—4 Foster Optical Equipment Company Cumulative and Cumulative Average Employee Hours Per Unit

Production Count	Hours/Unit	Cumulative Hours/Unit	Cumulative Average Hours/Unit (Column 3 ÷ Column 1)
1	716	716	716
2	517	1,233	617
3	425	1,658	553
4	372	2,030	506
5	334	2,364	473
6	307	2,671	445
7	285	2,956	422
8	268	3,224	403
9	252	3,476	387
10	238	3,716	372

Exhibit 14—5 Foster Optical Equipment Company Table of Cumulative Production and Labor Hour Data (Derived from the Cumulative Average Hours per Unit Curve)

Cumulative Production	Cumulative Average Hours Per Unit	Cumulative Total Hours Column 1 × Column 2
2	617	1,234
10	372	3,720
12	345	4,140
15	300	4,500
20	265	5,300
40	190	7,800
60	155	9,300
75	140	10,500
100	125	12,500
150	105	15,750
200	88	17,600
250	78	19,500
300	74	22,200
400	64	25,600
500	57	28,500
600	53	31,800
700	48	33,600
800	45	36,000
840	44	36,960

Sample Calculations for Assembly Output and Manpower Schedules

June and July
    Manpower required for the first two units is approximately 1,240 man hours.
    Manpower available: 4 at 160 hours/month × 2 months = 1,280 man hours.

August
    Manpower: Add 20 new employees whose efficiency is 70%

20 × 160 × 0.70 =	2,240	
Already available: 4 × 160	640	2,880 man hours
Cumulative total man hours through August		4,160

    Output: Comparison of 4,160 with data in column 3 of
                      Exhibit 14−5 shows that the 12th unit would have
                      been produced by the end of August. During August
                      12 − 2 = 10 units would have been completed.

September
    Manpower:

Add 20 new employees—efficiency 70%	2,250	man hours
Already available as of September 1: 24 × 160 =	3,840	
Total man hours expended in September	6,080	
Cumulative total man hours through August	4,160	
Cumulative total man hours through September	10,240	

    Output: In Exhibit 14−5 comparison of 10,240 with data in
                      column 3 shows that about 72 units would have
                      been produced by the end of September. During
                      September 72 − 12 = 60 units would have been
                      completed.

October
    Manpower:

Available as of October 1: 44 × 160 =	7,040	man hours
Cumulative total expended through September	10,240	
Cumulative total man hours expended through October	17,280	

    Output: In Exhibit 14−5, comparison of 17,280 with data in
                      column 3 shows that approximately 196 units would
                      have been produced after expending 17,280 man
                      hours of assembly labor. During the month of
                      October 196 − 72 = 124 cameras would have been
                      assembled.

From October through January the output schedule was based on the 7,040 man hours available each month, and the data in Exhibit 14−5.

SOURCE: Mr. Robert Phillips' KD 780 Camera Assembly Project File.

Home Products
Company

15

The Industrial Engineering Division had spent an equivalent of six engineering man-years developing its technique called "Inventory Controlled Scheduling" (ICS). Mr. R. A. Foreman, Director of Industrial Engineering, was trying to decide what the next step should be, relative to ICS. On the one hand there were probably more refinements that his staff-group could make to strengthen ICS techniques, before he submitted a recommendation to authorize its adoption at several soap and detergent factories, at least on a trial basis. On the other hand, Mr. Foreman thought that further time and expense in refining ICS before trying it out might be far less valuable than the experience in putting the ICS techniques to a practical test. ICS has been conceived and developed as a tool to be adopted ultimately by four consumer product divisions of Home Products: soap products, food products, paper products, and toilet goods. As Director of the Industrial Engineering Division, Mr. Foreman was responsible for evaluating the technical as well as administrative feasibility of proposals developed by his four staff departments: Methods Development, Incentives and Standards, Management Control Systems, and Mathematics and Statistics (a service department for the first three departments). The ICS project was the first major proposal developed by the Management Control Systems department. The intention was to have ICS adopted to control production at all domestic and foreign factories of Home Products.

Revision of an earlier case written by Professor R. E. McGarrah. Copyright © by the President and Fellows of Harvard College.

Background to the Development of ICS

Since 1920, Home Products had operated its own HP Distributing Company, operating sales offices in major cities and responsible for moving products from factory warehouses directly to retail grocers' shelves. A major objective in shifting to direct sales was to level out production and assure steady work for employees. Direct selling eliminated shipment fluctuations caused by independent wholesale grocers' inventory policies. Thus production could be leveled at the factory. Since 1923, Home Products had guaranteed 48 weeks of employment to hourly employees with two or more years of service.

Prior to World War II, Home Products sold a variety of brands of soap produced in bar, flake, and granulated forms. In 1934 the company introduced Swift, a light-duty granular detergent made from a batch-type process originated by Germans during World War I. In 1937 Home Products converted this to a continuous process. During World War II, Swift production was halted to divert fatty alcohol production to government uses, but with some continued research in detergent chemistry, a low-cost, heavy-duty detergent was perfected that was competitive with soap products. Immediately after World War II, the company made a major move to market detergents in granular form. Swift was reintroduced and Blitz, Wave and Clean were added as additional brands. At the factories, all detergents were processed and packaged in varieties of brand sizes on equipment entirely separate from soap-making facilities. Existing factory warehousing and shipping facilities had to be modified and expanded to handle both soaps and detergents. The Industrial Engineering Division was requested to design new materials handling equipment and warehouse layouts to increase the capacity and efficiency of the warehousing and shipping activities. Commenting on this work in materials handling and warehousing, Mr. G. D. Montague, presently supervisor of the Management Control Systems Department, said:

We had redesigned the lift truck equipment to eliminate palletized handling of cases and we had also developed procedures for getting more effective utilization of warehouse space. We became convinced that any further efforts in materials handling and layout work would yield nickel and dime savings compared to the mega bucks we thought would be saved by better information systems to control finished warehouse inventories. So essentially, this is how the IE Division began its work in production scheduling and inventory control.

Two studies were started to determine ways of reducing and controlling soap and detergent inventories. One study was by the A. D. Little Company at the Baltimore, Maryland and Staten Island, New York plants. The other study was by a group headed by Mr. Montague of HP's Industrial Engineering Division; this study focused on inventory control at the Chicago and Boston plants. After about twelve months, results of these studies were so strikingly parallel that A. D. Little consultants were released. Both studies concluded that average aggregate total inventory of soaps and detergents could be reduced by approximately $3 million per year, if brand and package-size inventories could be balanced to sustain future shipping requirements.

A technique called "continuous scheduling" was adopted for trial at soap products factories and warehouses. Continuous scheduling involved the notions of "cycle inventory," "safety inventory," and "anticipation inventory" (all to be explained later). After approximately a year's experience with continuous scheduling, Mr. Foreman decided that a better technique had to be developed, because, for several reasons, average inventory levels had increased and the number of short and/or late shipments had not decreased. Commenting on experiences with continuous scheduling, Mr. Montague said:

First of all, the forecasts of average weekly case-shipments data were furnished by the Soap Products Division Sales office in terms of brands, not in terms of brand-package sizes. In order to schedule packaging line changeovers, factory personnel had to make their own estimates of projected shipments of specific brand-sizes and these were often in error. Second, the authorized quantity of brands produced each quarter was controlled rather strictly by the Soap Products Division Sales Office in New York, and each factory had to produce its quarterly production quota of each brand. I think this quota may have caused too much rigidity for continuous scheduling techniques to work as they were intended. Finally, I think we in the IE Division may have made the mistake of failing to provide thorough enough training for factory personnel who had to use the continuous scheduling technique. Also we didn't follow up on actual practices at the factories as carefully as we might have. For these reasons our Management Control Systems group invested another six man years to develop the technique we now call Inventory Controlled Scheduling (ICS). There was a lot of expensive computer time invested in ICS, too.

Description of ICS

In a paper entitled "Warehouse Inventory Studies" presented at a meeting of a professional society, Mr. Foreman described three distinctive functions of inventory:

Cycle inventories—required because more than one kind of product is made on the same equipment, and each kind of product must be available for shipment while others are being manufactured.

Safety inventories—held because the rate at which orders are received is not the same as the rate at which goods are manufactured.

Anticipation inventories—which are inventories built up in anticipation such as a special pack or a July (plant vacation) shutdown.

It costs money to handle and carry inventories, so the objective is to keep total costs at a minimum without sacrificing these other objectives: prompt shipments and steady employment.

ICS involved formulated procedures for establishing "optimal" cycle, safety, and anticipation components of total inventory of a particular brand-size, by means of cost-balancing equations and statistical analysis. To guide plant management in planning changes in the total aggregate production rate of a department, an optimal aggregated total inventory range was computed to avoid too frequent and costly changes in aggregate total production levels. Thus, for the total production in a granular detergent processing department, an "optimal range" of aggregate total inventory level was also determined by ICS procedures. This optimal total inventory range was computed by balancing the cost of carrying different inventory ranges against the costs of making different production rate changes at different frequencies in the department.

Further description of ICS procedures is probably clearer if expressed in terms of a particular brand-group, for example, Blitz, Clean, Wave, and Swift.

This "brand-group" was processed, one brand-run at a time, on the same chemical processing equipment. To meet the company's quality standards for uniformity, chemical formula, color, etc., this equipment had to be thoroughly cleaned and adjusted between runs. For instance, three or more blue Wave granules found in a package of white granule Blitz meant unacceptable quality, probably due to improper cleaning of the drying tower, the last stage of the process in which the granules were formed. From the drying tower, the granules were blown into large hoppers capable of storing approximately eight hours' production of a particular brand. From the hoppers the detergent granules were fed to the high-speed automatic packaging equipment. This equipment was adjustable to package the detergent in the desired variety of sizes, for example, "economy," "giant," "large," "medium," and "small." These packages were then inserted into corrugated shipping cases, which were sent via conveyors to the factory warehouse for storage and shipment. The number of operators on a packaging line depended mainly upon the brand-size being packed in the production run. Thus, packaging lines could be changed by adjusting the feed mechanisms on the equipment, changing carton and case sizes, and changing the number of operators manning the line.

Briefly, the ICS plan consisted in checking the weekly status of: (1) brand-size inventories in order to schedule production for the packaging line; (2) brand inventory (the aggregate different sizes of each brand) to schedule the chemical processing equipment; and (3) the brand group inventory (the aggregate of all brands) in order to schedule changes in the aggregate total production rate of the combined processing-packaging system. The level of each inventory was planned and maintained by analytical techniques for determining cycle stock, upper and lower signal limits

Exhibit 15—1 Home Products Company Production Planning and Control

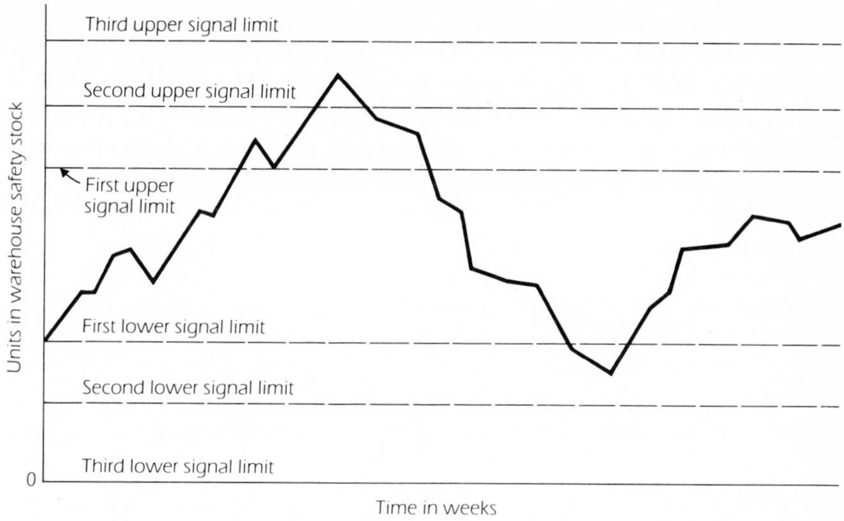

for safety stocks, and anticipation stocks. Exhibit 15–1 is a sketch illustrating some of the significant features of ICS for controlling the level of brand group production.

Exhibit 15–1 illustrates Brand Group Safety Inventory Level as affected by random and planned variations in weekly shipments (cases per week) and by planned changes in the brand group production rate. The changes were "signaled" by the limits.

As long as brand group inventory level remained between the first upper and lower signal limits, total production rates remained the same. If inventory rose or fell to or beyond the first signal limits, then the total production rate was increased or decreased by a certain planned amount. If inventory continued to rise or fall to second signal limits, a second planned change in production rate was made.

Optimum Cycle Inventory and Production Schedule

A first step in the ICS planning procedure was to determine the optimum "Semifixed Production Cycle" in which Blitz, Clean, Wave, and Swift were produced *at least* once during the cycle. The total process change-over costs per cycle depended upon the sequence (or order) of brands.

Mathematically there were 24 different sequences in which each brand was run once, but economically, fewer such sequences were feasible. For example, changeovers were less costly for Wave (a blue granule) to follow Swift (a pink granule) than vice versa; and if Blitz (an all-white granule) followed Swift, experience showed that probable color contamination was too high, and therefore, Blitz had to precede Swift. Blitz-Clean-Swift-Wave was one economical changeover sequence. If the proportions of demand for all brands in the brand group were uniform (or nearly so), then it was most economical to schedule one run of each brand in the production cycle. However, demands for Blitz and Wave from some plants were more than three times the demands for Swift and Clean. For these plants to produce Blitz and Wave once during a production cycle would have resulted in a higher brand cycle inventory than if Blitz and Wave were produced more than once during the production cycle. For these plants, Blitz-Clean-Swift-Wave-Blitz-Wave (BCSWBW) was a more economical sequence than the BCSW sequence. Thus, the first approach to determining the optimum production cycle involved computing trial sums of inventory carrying costs for an arbitrarily fixed time period, such as a month, and process changeover costs for different feasible brand sequences in a cycle, and choosing that sequence which resulted in the lowest sum of these costs.[1] This was largely a matter of "cut and try," using empirical cost data for different brand sequences, to obtain the most economical sequence (or order) of brands to run through the chemical processing equipment.

The next step was to determine the optimum number of cycles per year, or, inversely, the optimum time period for a production cycle. For any fixed cycle-time period and constant production and shipping rates, the total cycle inventory was constant. The greater the cycle inventory, the longer the cycle-time period and the fewer cycles per year. These relationships are illustrated by the simple charts shown in Exhibit 15–2. One way to determine optimum cycle-time period and cycle inventory was to assume practical cycle times. For the given forecasted annual demand and for each assumed cycle time, the sum of the annual cycle inventory carrying costs plus annual process changeover costs was computed and the lowest cost was chosen. Another way was by a mathematical formulation described in Exhibit 15–3.

This "optimum semifixed production cycle time" was calculated in terms of plant operating days, which were then rounded off to the nearest five-day work week. Thus, the total number of days and the sequence of brand-run changeovers in the production-cycle were fixed, so that a new processing cycle was started, say every Monday, or every other Monday.

---

[1] Annual inventory carrying costs per case included annual property taxes, insurance, and interest (expressed as a percent of the weighted average case value of all brands in the brand group) multiplied by this weighted average case value. Also included was the out-of-pocket expense for handling an average case unit.

Process changeover costs per cycle included out-of-pocket expenses for labor, steam, and other supplies used in cleaning and adjusting the equipment to produce the sequence of brands in the cycle, plus an estimated average value of production time lost during the cycle.

Exhibit 15—2 Home Products Company Production Planning and Control
Production Cycle Time and Cycle Stock Quantity

Illustration of the relations between production cycle times and cycle inventory level for a simple two-brand cycle. (The top sketch shows a longer cycle time period than the bottom sketch.)

Brands A and B are assumed to have constant and same production rates and constant but different shipping rates. Thus in the top and bottom sketches, the solid line and dotted line triangles are respectively similar.

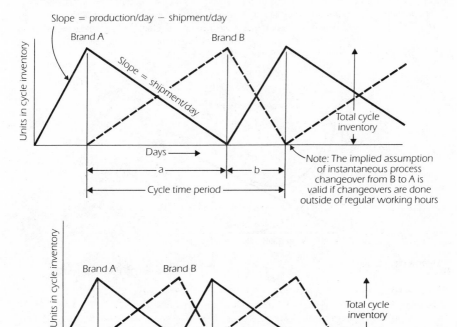

Note that the longer the cycle time period, the larger the cycle inventory, and vice versa. From the geometry indicated in the sketch,

1. The shipment rate of Brand A $= \dfrac{\text{Cycle Inventory}}{a}$; $S_A = \dfrac{I_A}{a}$.

2. The shipment rate of Brand B $= \dfrac{\text{Cycle Inventory}}{b}$; $S_B = \dfrac{I_B}{b}$.

3. Under assumptions stated, the aggregate cycle Inventory $= I_A + I_B =$ constant for a fixed cycle period.

4. Cycle Time $= a + b = \dfrac{I_A}{S_A} + \dfrac{I_B}{S_B} =$ constant.

Exhibit 15—3 Home Products Company Production Planning and Control
Determining Economical Aggregate Cycle Stock and Cycle Time

The "optimum" fixed brand-sequence in a cycle (for example, Blitz-Clean-Swift-Wave-Blitz-Wave)
was determined by iterative calculations of costs (of setup changes and carrying inventory) for
assumed cycle-time periods, for different feasible brand-sequences, and for constant production and
shipping rates. In other words, assuming constant production and demand, a "cut and try"
approach was used to answer questions such as: (1) What is the best order for brand changeovers?
(2) Should some brands be run more than once during a cycle of, say, one month or two months?

This exhibit illustrates the effect on aggregate cycle inventory of changing cycle-time periods. In
terms of costs per year, the more often a cycle is repeated the higher setup changeover costs would
be and the lower cycle inventory carrying costs would be.

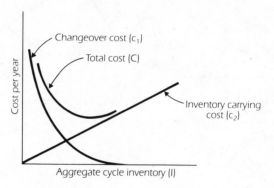

For convenience, let:

C = total cost per year.
c_1 = changeover cost per cycle of a fixed sequence of brand-runs.
c_2 = cycle inventory carrying cost per unit per year.
I = aggregate cycle inventory in units (cases).
S = brand group (aggregate) shipping rate units (cases) per week.
T = number of weeks per year.

$$C = \frac{c_1 TS}{I} + c_2 I.$$

Differentiating C with respect to I and setting the result equal to zero:

$$\frac{dC}{dI} = \frac{c_1 TS}{I^2} + c_2 = 0.$$

Solving for I gives the most economical aggregate cycle inventory, I^*

$$I^* = \sqrt{\frac{c_1 TS}{c_2}}.$$

The most economical cycle-time period (in weeks) is $\frac{I^*}{S}$.

Exhibit 15—3 (continued)

NOTES

1. Approximately every $\frac{I*}{S}$ weeks the fixed sequence of brand-runs was repeated. (The cycle time was fixed at the nearest integer number of weeks.)

2. Although the brand sequence and cycle period remained fixed, the proportionate allocations of production cycle time to individual brands during the cycle were changed, to respond to "brand-mix" changes in demand.

3. The aggregate cycle stock and the production cycle-time period remained fixed as long as the brand-group (aggregate) shipping rate remained constant.

4. A similar approach was used to determine economical brand-size cycle stocks and brand-size cycle periods. (These, of course, were made compatible with brand-group cycle stocks and brand run-cycle periods.)

However, *during* a cycle, the processing time could be shifted from one brand to others in the sequences, and this was the reason for the term, "semifixed."

Calculations analogous to those described for brand-run sequences and brand-cycle inventory were also used to determine the optimum sequence for brand-sizes and optimum brand-size cycle inventory produced by the mechanical packaging equipment. Brand-size changeovers involved handling packaging materials, adjusting container and detergent feed mechanisms, and reassigning personnel to different jobs. Thus, there was a fixed sequence of brand-sizes to be packaged in semifixed quantities, while a single brand was being processed on the chemical equipment, in such a way as to maintain optimum brand-size cycle inventory. "Basic Packing Schedules" were the result of translating optimum brand cycles into calendar schedules for brands and then breaking brand schedules down into calendar schedules for the individual brand-sizes.

The optimum cycle inventory of brands and brand-sizes was thus determined as a "fixed" amount necessary to meet *basic* shipping needs (in average shipments per week) during the year. Cycle stocks were assigned to the "prime area" of the warehouse to effect handling and shipping efficiency. Under ICS the plan was to consider optimum cycle inventory as a "constant" amount, which each week was deducted from *total* actual inventory; the remainder was the actual "safety" inventory. Actual safety inventory was then to be compared with the desired range of safety inventory. From this comparison, schedules could be set so as to restore actual safety inventory to within the desired safety range.

Safety Inventory

Optimum cycle inventory and optimum semifixed packaging cycles depended upon the assumption of a constant weekly rate of shipments throughout the year. However, actual weekly shipments varied widely about the average rate, and therefore a safety component had to be added to cycle inventory to plan against varying surges in actual rates of shipments.

In describing the manner in which safety stock was established, Mr. Montague said:

While kicking around the idea of safety stock, we came to realize we needed two kinds of safety limits. Obviously there was the needed protection against brand-size stockouts and short shipments to customers, caused by the fact the actual shipments exceeded average shipments. If a brand-size stock dropped in one week below its safety stock level, we could build it back up by scheduling a longer packaging run for that brand-size and a shorter packaging run for some other size of that brand, in the semifixed packaging cycle for that brand. If the *average* weekly shipments had not increased, chances are the stock would be satisfactory as the result of such a shift in packaging cycles. But, suppose the *actual average* weekly shipments had shifted significantly from the predicted average on which cycle stocks had been calculated. Then the only thing for us to do would be to shift the total level of production for the brand-group. So we also needed inventory signal limits, something like the limits on a statistical quality control chart to indicate that *brand-group average* shipping rates had increased or decreased to an extent that the total production level should be changed. These upper and lower inventory signal limits would form a "safety band," which had to be both wide enough to prevent us from changing the total production level too often, and narrow enough to enable us to respond to changes without too much delay. In other words, we needed to measure the possible fluctuations in brand-group shipments which we would allow to occur before we went to the expense of changing the total production level. For a constant amount of protection from stockouts of each brand size, the wider the safety bandwidth for controlling brand-group inventory, the larger the brand-group inventory carrying cost and smaller the cost of making production level changes and vice versa. So again, our approach was to balance the cost of production level changes against the cost of carrying extra inventory to avoid making these production level changes.

Variability of Brand-size and Brand-group Shipping Rates (in cases per week)

Demand-variation was measured by calculating the variance[2] of shipment data that were available in terms of the number of cases of each brand-size actually shipped per week for the past 52 weeks. The distribution of these data was presumed normal (random), so that calculations of the mean and variance of demand were all that were required to use conveniently tabulated data measuring all the probabilities of demand. Commenting on this assumption, Mr. Montague said: "Of course, these data

---

[2] The variance equals the sum of the squares of the deviations about the average of the distribution of the data. The standard deviation equals the square root of the variance.

were not 'purely-random,' but after checking,[3] we decided they were close enough to being random for our purposes."

The effect of "special-pack shipments" upon the rate of standard-pack shipments had to be isolated, because these effects were nonrandom and the ICS plan made separate provisions for special packs, via "anticipation stocks" (to be discussed later). Special packs were packages containing coupons or premiums and/or offers of temporary price reductions, all designed to entice the housewife to buy that particular brand-size. These special promotions caused the *average* standard pack shipment rate to vary through time, and therefore standard pack safety inventory calculations had to isolate effects of these special pack promotions. Mr. Montague and his associates studied historical weekly shipment data measuring standard and special packs, and derived empirically the following equations used to isolate the effects of special pack promotions:

$$V_{mean} = (P_s - 2 P_s^{3/2} + P_s^2) \quad (AWS \text{ of standard pack} + \text{special pack})^2.$$

$$S_{random} = \sqrt{V_{random}} = \sqrt{(V_{total} - V_{mean})}$$

1. V_{mean} = The component of V_{total} induced by special pack promotions causing the average standard pack shipment rate to vary through time.
2. P_s = The proportion of special packs to standard packs shipped during the past 52 weeks.
3. AWS = Average weekly shipments in cases per week, calculated for the past 52 weeks.
4. S_{random} = Standard deviation of the weekly standard brand-size shipments.
5. V_{random} = The component of total variance (V_{total}) attributed to random effects.
6. V_{total} = Variance in the weekly standard pack shipments for the past 52 weeks.

The assumption was made that V_{mean} and V_{random} were independent; thus random variations in shipments were considered independent of the mean shipment rate for a particular brand-size.

Having these procedures for calculating the variability of demand for a particular standard brand-size, the variability of a *brand-group* was simply equal to the sum of variances for each brand-size, that is:

$$V_{\substack{standard\ packs \\ for\ brand\ group}} = \Sigma V_{\substack{random \\ Standard\ packs \\ for\ all\ brand \\ sizes}}$$

A study of empirical data for all sizes in the brand-group indicated that the ratio of the variance of special pack production to the variance of standard pack shipments was approximately equal to the ratio of the proportion of special pack business to the proportion of the standard pack business in the brand-group. In other words, if P_{sb} symbolized the proportion

---

[3] The chi-square (statistical) test was applied to several empirical distributions of brand-size shipment data.

of all special packs in the brand-group shipments, and V symbolized the variance of the brand-group, then the formula for this was:

$$\frac{V_{\substack{\text{special packs} \\ \text{in brand-group}}}}{V_{\substack{\text{standard packs} \\ \text{in brand-group}}}} = \frac{P_{sb}}{1 - P_{sb}}$$

From this relationship the formula for the standard deviation of the weekly shipment data for the brand-group was:

$$S_{\text{Brand group}} = \sqrt{\left(\frac{1}{1 - P_{sb}}\right)} \; \sum V_{\substack{\text{random} \\ \text{Std packs} \\ \text{for all} \\ \text{brand sizes}}}$$

Variability of Demand During Production Change Time

Having formulated the standard deviations measuring the variability of weekly demands for standard brand-sizes and the brand-group, the next step was to adjust these standard deviations, to relate them to the time periods for making the necessary production changes to restore inventories with the "optimum safety range." The only time a stockout could occur was the period when a brand-size was *not* being packaged on the packaging line. The period was called the brand-size change time.

The brand-size change time was the sum of the average delay-time in "discovering" the need to replenish stock, plus the average lead time that would elapse before that brand-size would be run on the packaging equipment. Average delay-time was one-half a calendar week for each brand-size, because brand-size inventory status was measured at weekly intervals. The average lead time was determined to be one-half of the time measured from the instant a packaging run was completed to the instant the next run for that brand-size actually began, according to the optimum packaging cycle for a particular brand.[4] Multiplying the square root of the average brand-size change time by the standard deviation of standard pack shipments per week gave the standard deviation of standard pack shipments during the average brand-size change time. In symbolic terms:

$$S_{\text{random during brand-size change time}} = \left(S_{\text{random}}\right) \sqrt{\begin{array}{c}\text{Brand-size} \\ \text{change time} \\ \text{in weeks}\end{array}}$$

[4] The optimum packaging cycle was established by the procedure described in the section entitled "Optimum Cycle Inventory and Production Schedule."

This equation assumed that shipments during one time period were independent of shipments during other time periods. Similar calculations were used to adjust the standard deviations of weekly brand shipments to relate variability of brand demand to brand change time, and to adjust the standard deviations of weekly brand-group shipments relative to the time required to increase or decrease the total brand-group production level.

Optimum Safety Inventory Computations

The procedure for determining a set of three upper and lower brand-group inventory signal limits began by computing the cost of changing the total brand-group production rate by some planned, initial amount, generally between 20 percent and 40 percent of the standard deviation of the brand-group weekly shipments.[5] The cost of such a change was estimated by taking the average of two costs: first, the cost of an initial increase from the basic production rate then a decrease back to the basic rate; second, the cost of an initial decrease from the basic production rate and then an increase back to the basic rate. This average cost was then compared to the annual cost of holding in inventory an amount equal to one standard deviation of brand-group weekly shipments. The higher the ratio of average production rate change cost to the cost of carrying in inventory one standard deviation of brand-group weekly shipments, the more economical it was to carry more brand-group safety inventory, and vice versa.

From computer analyses of empirical data, Mr. Montague's group had derived and tabulated relationships between values of this cost ratio and "optimum band-width factors," which were multiples of the standard deviation of brand-group weekly shipments. In the table, the cost ratios ranged in increments from 0.10 to 1.0 and "band-width factors" from 1.3 to 5.5 standard deviations of brand-group weekly shipments, respectively. This table was predicated on a minimum expected frequency of production-rate changes, and a "fixed" policy of providing enough safety stock to assure against stockouts 95 percent of the time.[6] Thus, after computing the ratio of the cost of a production-rate change to the annual cost of carrying a unit of safety inventory, the table was used to choose the optimum "band-width factor."

Having selected the optimum band-width factor, the "lower signal limit" for each *brand-size* inventory was determined by multiplying band-width factor by the standard deviation of standard-pack shipments

---

[5] This amounted to about 8% of basic (or normal) production rate for the brand group expressed in terms of cases produced per week. The basic production rate was set equal to the average weekly brand group shipment rate.

[6] The "95 percent level of assurance" was determined by judgment, since true stockout penalty costs were virtually impossible to determine. Among the factors considered in setting the 95 percent level of safety stock was the fact that to provide a 98 percent level would have required two–three days of extra safety stock amounting to approximately $1 million added to inventory investment. Also, close observation of several supermarkets revealed that brand-size stockouts occurred an average of five percent of the time.

during the brand-size change time. (See the discussion of variability during production change-time.)

The brand-*group* inventory "First Lower Signal Limit" was then the sum of the "lower signal limits" for each brand-size inventory. The brand-group "First Upper Signal Limit" was equal to the First Lower Signal Limit plus the band-width factor multiplied by the standard deviation of brand-group shipments during production change time.

The *brand-size* "Upper Signal Limit" was set equal to its Lower Signal Limit plus the allocated portion of the brand group band-width (the difference between the Upper and Lower Signal Limit for a brand group inventory). Thus, the ratio of Upper to Lower Signal Limit for a brand-size was equal to the ratio of Upper to Lower Signal Limit for a brand-group.

By similar calculations, the second and third pairs of upper and lower signal limits were determined for the brand-group inventory only. There were no second and third upper and lower signal limits determined for brand-size inventories. The costs of second and third incremental changes in brand-group production levels were, of course, different from costs of the first incremental changes above "basic production." This was because methods were different for affecting these second-step changes in the brand-group production rates. For example, overtime and/or additional crews might have to be added to affect second-step or third-step increases, while a few intraplant employee transfers might be all that were needed for first-step changes in brand group production level.

The third lower signal limit was set at zero brand-group inventory.

Anticipation Inventory for Special Packs and Factory Shutdowns

Special pack promotions were conceived and authorized by the sales and advertising departments to stimulate customers' demand. Home Products had long and successful experience in using special packs, and these had a significant effect upon production at the factory. Special packs consisted of brand-size cartons containing "price off" offers, "premium offers" made on order blanks inserted in the carton, premiums inserted in the carton (for example, a spoon or dish inserted in a carton of Clean), and a "bundle" of two or more standard brand-size cartons. From the marketing point of view, special packs effectively enticed consumers to switch from competitors' to Home Product brands, encouraged retailers to give Home Products' special packs a high traffic display in the supermarket, and encouraged the consumer to stock-up and use more than normal amount of purchase. The importance of special packs was indicated by the fact that there were between two and four special promotions per year for each brand-size. National and local advertising efforts were keyed to these special promotions.

From the production point of view, special packs meant changes in packing materials, packaging manpower and methods, and a multiplying of the variety of brand-sizes to produce and stock in support of these sales promotions. Special packs had to be produced and stocked in "anticipation inventory" which was designed to become depleted in "not more than two shopping weekends."

In general, the scheduled build-up of special packs at the retail end of the pipeline was such that of the planned quantity to be sold:

25% had to be available one to two weeks before start of selling;

50% had to be available on the day selling started;

75% available five days after start of selling;

100% available ten days after start of selling.

To permit the factory enough time to produce anticipation stocks, the sales department gave 12–16 weeks advance notice of the data and estimated quantity involved in each special pack promotion. This gave Production personnel enough time to procure special cartons, plan packaging methods, and to incorporate the special packs in production schedules and planned inventory levels.

Anticipation inventory functioned also to supply shipping demands during factory vacations and holidays.

Mr. Montague and his associates analyzed large amounts of empirical data reflecting effects of special promotions and factory holidays. One of the greatest difficulties was in their attempts to isolate these effects from data on total brand-size shipments per week, the only data available. Obviously, special pack promotions affected demands for standard packs. Mr. Montague knew that the more precisely these effects could be isolated, the better the chances would be to cut total inventory without increasing risks of shortages. In terms of variability, the effects of special-pack promotions upon safety stocks of standard packs were derived in terms of the equations already stated in the section on "Variability of Brand-size and Brand-group Shipping Rates." These equations eliminated anticipation stock from safety stock. Under the ICS plan, effects of special packs upon production schedules and cycle stocks were imputed by a three step procedure: (1) the special pack production was scheduled to meet the Sales Department's requirements; (2) the "Basic Packing Schedule" was adjusted for the affected standard brand-sizes; (3) these two schedules are reconciled in terms of brand-size runs and total production capacity available.

In somewhat more detail, Mr. Montague's engineers found that on the average, a special pack promotion affected average weekly shipments of a brand-size during a twelve-week period, four weeks before the promotion, four weeks during the promotion, and four weeks after the promotion. The average proportions of total shipments that were standard and special packs during these four-week periods were computed from empirical data and the proportions of standard packs were designated as "Basic Production Modification Factors" ("B.P.M.F.'s"). One set of B.P.M.F.'s was 0.8 for the four weeks prior to promotion, 0.25 during the promotion period, and 0.6 for the four weeks after the promotion period and these were multiplied by the appropriate brand-size quantity in the Basic Packing Schedule (which was derived from optimum brand-size production cycle calculations). This gave the tentative quantity of standard packs to be produced during the twelve-week period. This tentative quantity was then adjusted up or down if the actual safety inventory was respectively near its lower or upper signal limit. In this manner, the required special pack production was "fitted" into the packing schedule.

Anticipation stocks also had to be produced to meet shipments during plant shutdowns. Under ICS, the brand-group production level was raised proportionately during the twelve weeks preceding the two-week vacation period.

Other Considerations of ICS

Mr. Foreman's Industrial Engineering Division (IED) was part of the Corporate Staff organization of Home Products. The IED had two functions: (1) to develop and recommend the adoption of new concepts and techniques and (2) to assist manufacturing management in problems arising in the various operating divisions. Commenting on the question of whether to request that ICS be put on trial at several soap division plants, Mr. Foreman said:

George Montague and his boys have made computer simulation runs which show that ICS would reduce average inventory and short shipments too. But, the simulation model wasn't the real-live production and warehouse shipping system. So I'm not sure about the true significance of these results. I know we'd have a better idea of what ICS could do if we tried it out at two of our factories in the soap products division. I think trials at two factories would be better than at one, because then we'd see how different factory personnel would use ICS. But, is ICS developed to the point where I should request Mr. Euhler (Vice President, Manufacturing Staff Organization) and Mr. Chidsey (Vice President, Soap Products Division) to give ICS a trial?

As conceived, the ICS plan would require calculations for safety stock signal limits to be repeated every three months; the production plan to produce anticipation stocks was to be determined every month; and the modified packaging schedule to maintain safety stock and build up anticipation stocks was to be determined weekly, based on weekly reports of the status of safety stock levels. Mr. Montague had recommended that a manual be prepared to give step-by-step instructions to production planning personnel responsible for making these calculations. "But," said Mr.

Montague, "I certainly don't think we should publish the manual until after we've had a year's trial experience with ICS. In my opinion, the question is whether ICS is technically sound enough to proceed with a real trial. Personally, I think it is, even though I know we'll find some bugs in some of our assumptions. But, I think these bugs will be discovered sooner and more accurately by a real trial at two factories than by continuing with more statistical analysis and simulation runs by our engineers here in the New York Technical Center. In developing ICS techniques, we've had to use production, shipments, and inventory data that were obtained from present planning techniques being used by our soap factories. To improve ICS techniques further, we need better data than these and I think we can get better data by installing ICS at our factories."

Another factor is the change in authority for scheduling factory operations. ICS would authorize factory managers to schedule their own operations; the Soap Product Division Sales Office would no longer schedule factory operations.

Kaldor
Company

16

The Kaldor Company designed and manufactured a variety of mixing, agitating, grinding, and pulverizing equipment used in the chemicals and food-processing industries.

As a result of field reports from Kaldor's salesmen and customers, Kaldor engineers had redesigned a mechanism to replace one originally installed on Kaldor Model C-43 mixers. This eccentric and rocker arm assembly (Exhibit 16–1) was designed to give greater flexibility and control in mixing and dispersing such materials as paint pigments, batches of dough for bakery products, peanut butter, and mayonnaise. The assembly was to be used on 15 new Model C-43 mixers on order, and an initial lot of 200 was to be produced and sold to replace old assemblies in use in the field. Projected demand for new and replacement assemblies was estimated at 800 units in the next two years. The engineering department released the design to the production department in November.

Process and Inspection Planning Procedure for New Products

Mr. A. C. Karlson, Production Manager, had on his staff Mr. K. W. Brink, Production and Tool Engineer, Mr. B. H. Canton, Director of Quality Con-

Revised version of an earlier case written by Professor R. E. McGarrah. Copyright © by the President and Fellows of Harvard College.

trol, and Mr. B. H. Bowen, Supervisor of Production Control. Each received a set of drawings from the engineering department.

As a general procedure, Mr. Brink and Mr. Bowen reviewed the drawings and selected the parts to be purchased from outside suppliers. Mr. Brink often marked Mr. Bowen's drawings to assist him in specifying and buying proper weights of castings and bar stock, making allowances for material removed in machining. Mr. Canton made estimates of spoilage allowances. In preparing operation sheets, one for each part, Mr. Brink specified the machines and tool setups to be used for machining the parts, and Mr. Canton specified the number and kinds of inspection operations required. Messrs. Brink and Canton often conferred with the design engineers to clarify certain specifications on the drawings. Mr. Karlson said he thought that most production managers' problems were traceable to operations plans, and so he checked and authorized all operation sheets by initialing them after Messrs. Brink and Bowen had initialed the master stencils.

To clarify areas of responsibility and authority for quality control, Mr. Karlson, after conferring with Mr. Canton, issued a standing instruction from which excerpts are quoted:

. . . The director of quality control is responsible for taking necessary steps to ensure that at least 95 percent of all products shipped to customers are of good quality. He shall have final authority on questions relating to the manufacture of products to design specifications, and accordingly he may delegate this authority to his inspectors, as required. He may direct any process to be stopped whenever, in his opinion, the 95 percent outgoing quality level would be jeopardized by continuing its operation.

. . . Machine and bench operators are responsible for setting up and running jobs to meet quality specifications. When recommended by the director of quality control, parts and subassemblies are to be inspected or tested by operators while performing their assigned jobs, and accordingly a time allowance for such inspection will be included in the time standard.

Discussing the background of these instructions, Mr. Canton said,

One thing I've learned in this business of quality control is that although you guarantee the quality of performance of 100 percent of the products shipped to customers you have to face up to the fact that a small percentage will have faulty quality. The actual quality produced by different combinations of men, materials, and machines is naturally going to vary from one unit to the next. The 95 percent quality level was chosen because this is the level that we think we can meet economically. With our design and manufacturing know-how, we think the 95 percent quality level will minimize expected costs of production and inspection and costs of repairing probable failures of our machines being used by our customers. To shoot for a 100 percent quality level would mean we'd have to

Exhibit 16-1 Kaldor Company Eccentric and Rocker Assembly

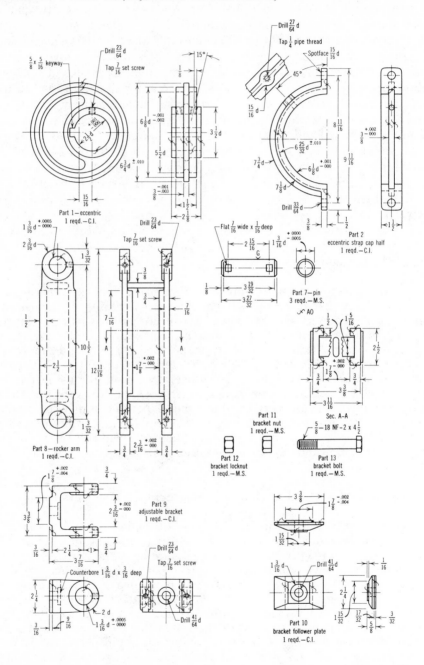

Exhibit 16—1 (continued)

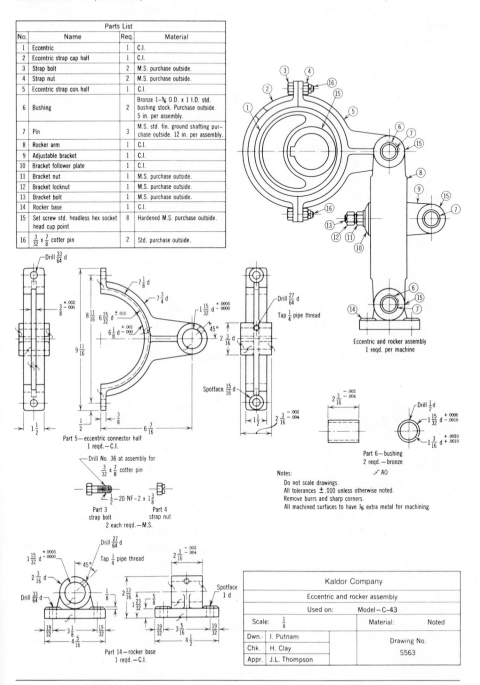

No.	Name	Req.	Material
	Parts List		
1	Eccentric	1	C.I.
2	Eccentric strap cap half	1	C.I.
3	Strap bolt	2	M.S. purchase outside.
4	Strap nut	2	M.S. purchase outside.
5	Eccentric strap con. half	1	C.I.
6	Bushing	2	Bronze 1-⅜ O.D. x 1 I.D. std. bushing stock. Purchase outside. 5 in. per assembly.
7	Pin	3	M.S. std. fin. ground shafting purchase outside. 12 in. per assembly.
8	Rocker arm	1	C.I.
9	Adjustable bracket	1	C.I.
10	Bracket follower plate	1	C.I.
11	Bracket nut	1	M.S. purchase outside.
12	Bracket locknut	1	M.S. purchase outside.
13	Bracket bolt	1	M.S. purchase outside.
14	Rocker base	1	C.I.
15	Set screw std. headless hex socket head cup point	8	Hardened M.S. purchase outside.
16	$\frac{3}{32}$ x $\frac{7}{8}$ cotter pin	2	Std. purchase outside.

Eccentric and rocker assembly
1 reqd. per machine

Part 5 — eccentric connector half
1 reqd.—C.I.

Part 6 — bushing
2 reqd.—bronze

Part 3
strap bolt
Part 4
strap nut
2 each reqd.—M.S.

Notes:
Do not scale drawings.
All tolerances ± .010 unless otherwise noted.
Remove burrs and sharp corners.
All machined surfaces to have ⅟₁₆ extra metal for machining.

Part 14 — rocker base
1 reqd.—C.I.

Kaldor Company			
Eccentric and rocker assembly			
Used on:		Model—C—43	
Scale: $\frac{1}{4}$		Material:	Noted
Dwn. I. Putnam		Drawing No. S563	
Chk. H. Clay			
Appr. J.L. Thompson			

price ourselves out of the market, and we'd probably not be able to meet delivery times demanded by our customers.

In other words, this 95 percent quality level represents the degree to which we can afford to be quality conscious and still be aware of the price and delivery obligations we have to make to our customers.

Kaldor's machine shop was operating on two shifts and employing 45 machine operators per shift. According to Mr. Bowen, too many jobs in the machining department were behind schedule, and the assembly shortage list was getting longer. The average incentive wage in the machining department was $7.35 per standard hour; the overhead expense rate was $7.15 per direct-labor standard hour. Inspectors' wages averaged $7.25 per hour, nonincentive.

Kaldor's union was a local of the International Association of Machinists (IAM). Machine operators' average output was 165 percent of standard and ranged from 125 to 190 percent among different jobs. The contract with the local union was to expire December 31, and the business agent said that the average incentive pay per hour for Kaldor's machine operators was at least 20 cents per hour lower than wages for comparable jobs in the area.

Current prices for grey iron castings ranged between 35 and 40 cents per pound. From 3 to 5 percent of the castings received contained sandholes and cracks which were not readily detected until after they were machined and thoroughly cleaned.

For the eccentric and rocker-arm assembly (Exhibit 16–1) one of the most critical dimensions was the clearance on the 6⅕-inch nominal diameters for the eccentric (Part 1), the eccentric strap (Part 2), and the eccentric connector (Part 5). Mr. Canton had inquired about the necessity for this small clearance. The design engineers replied that this clearance had to be large enough to maintain a film of lubricating oil and small enough to avoid a wobble and oil leakage between the eccentric and the two eccentric caps. When the mixer was operating, lubricating oil was pumped at a pressure of 3 pounds per square inch to lubricate and cool the three parts. Accordingly, they specified a maximum clearance of 0.003 inch and a minimum of 0.001 inch to insure a good performance of the mechanism. They stated that this clearance could not be made larger without a serious risk of oil leakage which would spoil the materials being mixed. Kaldor's chief sales engineer announced that customers had complained about oil leakage and eccentric wear on the old model eccentric assemblies which had been designed with a 0.005-inch clearance.

Mr. Canton was satisfied that the design clearance had to remain as specified by the engineering department.

To specify how these three parts were to be machined, Mr. Brink drafted the operation sheets shown as Exhibits 16–2, 16–3, and 16–4. He did not estimate setup and operating hours because he preferred to have

Exhibit 16—2 Kaldor Company Operation Sheet

Part No.   S 563-1   Material   Cast Iron 15 lbs./pc (approx.)
Part Name   Eccentric
Orig. _____   Changes _____
Checked _____
Approved _____

No.	Operation / Description	Machine	Setup Description	Hr.	Operate Hr./Unit
5	Rough and fin. turn and face: 6¾" D 6⅛" D, one side reverse piece, rechuck and repeat for other side	16" Monarch engine lathe (Kender #122)	Univ. four jaw-chuck on 6⅛" casting diameter		
10	Rough and fin. turn, face 3½" D eccentric boss, one side reverse piece, repeat other side. Rough and fin. bore 2½" D hole; ream 2½" D hole	16" Monarch engine lathe (Kender #138)	Four-jaw chuck		
15	Broach ⅝" × ⁵⁄₁₆" keyway	LaPointe broach (Kender #310)	Gang six castings in fixture		
20	Drill ²³⁄₆₄" and tap ⁷⁄₁₆" set screw holes	L. G. multispindle drill press (Kender #110)			

Exhibit 16—3 Kaldor Company Operation Sheet

Part No.   S563-2   Material   Cast Iron 9 lb./pc (approx.)
Part Name   Eccentric Strap Cap Half   Changes _____
Orig. _____
Checked _____
Approved _____

No.	Operation / Description	Machine	Setup Description	Hr.	Operate Hr./Unit
5	Rough and fin. mill 2 mating surfaces	Cincinnati mill (Kender #136)	Gang six castings in fixture		
10	Spotface and drill two holes ³³⁄₆₄" D. Drill ²⁷⁄₆₄ D pipe hole; tap ¼ pipe thread	Multispindle drill press	Piece on table piece in 45" drill jig		
15	Rough and fin. bore 6⅛" D. Bore 6²⁵⁄₃₂" diameter × ⅜" wide groove	Bullard vertical boring mill (Kender #335)	Clamp to eccentric connector half (Part S563-5), then mount both parts in four-jaw chuck		

Exhibit 16—4 Kaldor Company Operation Sheet

Part No. S563-5

Material   Cast Iron 12 lb./pc (approx.)

Part Name   Eccentric Connector Half

Changes _____

Orig. _____

Checked _____

Approved _____

	Operation	Machine	Setup		Operate
No.	Description		Description	Hr.	Hr./Unit
5	Rough and fin. mill 2 mating surfaces	Cincinnati mill (Kender #136)	Gang six castings in fixture		
10	Rough and fin. bore 6⅛" D. Bore 6²⁵⁄₃₂" diameter × ⅜" wide groove	Bullard vertical boring mill (Kender #335)	Clamp to eccentric strap cap. half (Part S563-2), then mount both parts in four-jaw chuck		
15	Mill 2¹³⁄₁₆" diameter boss, both sides	Cincinnati mill			
20	Drill and ream 1¹⁵⁄₃₂" D hole. Drill 2³³⁄₆₄" D hole	L. G. Multispindle drill press			
	Drill 2⁷⁄₆₄" D hole; tap ¼ pipe thread		Part in 45° drill jig		

Mr. Canton's comments about the quality level that would be attained. Mr. Brink said,

When drafting operation sheets for certain critical parts, I usually prefer to get Canton's comments about the quality assurance level of parts machined by my proposed methods before I estimate the setup and operating hours required. I think it's better to concentrate on quality first, because after all, if there's little or no assurance of machining to engineers' specifications, then you have no product. Estimates of time and cost are really academic until you're reasonably sure a method will meet engineering specs.

Mr. Brink put his proposed operation sheets for all S563 parts on Mr. Canton's desk with the following note attached:

11/19

Bart:

Re—S563 job for Model C-43 mixers

Please give me your reactions to the operation sheets for S563-1, 2 and 5, by 11/21. Castings are due in by 11/23 and we have to get this job started as soon as possible. I think operation sheets for the other parts need just a routine consideration.

Ken

Mr. Canton agreed with Mr. Brink that holding tolerances and clearances on the 6¼-inch diameters would be one of the toughest problems as far as quality control was concerned.

Describing his views on quality, Mr. Canton said,

I've worked in a toolroom making tools and gauges; I've also had some courses in quality control. If you ask me, this job of planning inspection operations is like trying to decide what kinds of insurance policies to buy. You've got to provide inspection operations and buy the kinds of insurance policies that'll give the greatest protection against all the risks, for the lowest cost. Inspection operations don't improve the quality; they just help to reduce the costs of being caught with bad quality.

As a practice, which he started in September, Mr. Canton had his clerk keep a record of the quality performance of the machine tools in Kender's machining department in order to assist him in planning for quality-control procedures. Exhibit 16−5 is the quality-performance record kept for the Bullard vertical boring mill on which Mr. Brink had proposed to machine the 6⅛-inch diameter on parts S563-2 and S563-5. Mr. Canton had his clerk post this record every Friday, using data available from blue-

Exhibit 16−5 Kaldor Company. Quality Performance Record* Bullard Vertical Boring Mill. Total Number of Parts Passing Inspection

Week Ending	Under nominal size [(−) 0.0001 inch] 6 and under	5	4	3	2	1	On Spec. 0.0	Over nominal size [(+) 0.0001 inch] 1	2	3	4	5	6 and over	Total
9/5	3	27	45	54	61	78	80	76	58	51	40	30	4	607
9/12		3	5	8	10	16	26	18	13	12	3	3		117
9/19	6	3	18	33	40	53	50	58	45	37	22	4		369
9/26	9	14	23	29	41	46	42	40	38	30	26	15	4	357
10/3		5	6	18	21	28	35	30	22	14	6	6	4	195
10/17	6	22	38	48	55	63	76	74	68	50	36	25	10	571
10/24	4	8	15	32	49	51	62	58	41	40	26	15	6	407
10/23	5	13	22	36	46	50	56	53	57	32	21	17	4	402
11/7	10	17	21	19	39	53	62	60	49	35	21	10	5	401

NOTES: a. Nominal dimensions are those specified on blueprints. Presumably the boring mill is set up to produce pieces at nominal size, except when design tolerances are not symmetrical with nominal dimension. In this case the boring mill is set up to produce a size at the middle of the tolerance. For example, if a blueprint calls for a 4.125" D + 0.005 − 0.000, then the boring mill set up to produce 4.1275" D is called "nominal" for purposes of this record.

b. Numbers in column headings are deviations from nominal dimensions in ten thousandths of an inch (0.0001"). "Over nominal size" means that the actual dimension is larger than called for on the blueprint; "under nominal size" means that the actual dimension is smaller than specified on the blueprint.

c. Parts with dimensions machined outside acceptable (blueprint) tolerance range are excluded from this record. When parts were machined outside blueprint tolerance specifications, the machining process was defined as being out of control; that is, the extreme variations outside total blueprint tolerance range were due to assignable causes (faulty tools, materials, operator error, etc.).

SOURCE: Mr. Canton's files.

Exhibit 16—6 Kaldor Company. Representative Machine Tool List*

Machine	Kaldor Property No.	No. of Measurements Recorded	Quality Capability† 95 Percent of Measurements Were Within a Total Tolerance Range of
16" Monarch engine lathe	122	1836	0.0007 inch
16" Monarch engine lathe	56	312	0.0012
No. 2 W & S turret lathe	58	714	0.0010
48" Reed-Prentice engine lathe	45	75	0.0018
14" Bullard vertical boring mill	335		
6" Landis horizontal external cylindrical grinder	422	866	0.0005
14" Cincinnati horizontal external cylindrical grinder	423	694	0.0005
18 × 36" Cincinnati horizontal mill	136	1240	0.0010
14 × 36" Bridgeport vertical mill	148	968	0.0008
20 × 48" LaPointe horizontal broach	526	612	0.0005
36" Cincinnati Bickbord radical drill	102	86	0.0012
18" Leland Gifford six-spindle drill	110	369	0.0015 (with jigs)

* This list does not describe every machine tool owned by Kaldor.

† Data in these columns were derived and summarized from available quality performance records. These records were begun in September.

prints and inspection measurements recorded in the machine shop. Most machining jobs with tolerances of 0.0015 inch or less were inspected by using calibrated gauges such as micrometers and dial indicators. These measurements were recorded on inspection sheets. Exceptions were in cases of lots of more than 10 parts, when "go/no-go" types of gauges were often used. Mr. Canton considered these records to reflect the over-all pattern of precision capabilities of these machines, although he admitted that the data may have been affected by differences among skills of different operators and inspectors, machinability of different workpiece materials, machine and setups, and conditions of gauges and tools.

In considering Mr. Brink's request, Mr. Canton reviewed the status of the various machine tools available and their precision capabilities. Exhibits 16—5 and 16—6 summarize this information. Discussing these considerations, Mr. Canton commented,

I think another method is to cut the 6⅛-inch internal diameters on parts S563-2 and S563-5 on a vertical milling machine, using a special 6⅛-inch diameter milling cutter that would cost about $750. This would probably be less than half as fast as Brink's method; I'm not so sure we can get desired concentricity by machining one cap at a time, even though the milling machine probably can hold closer tolerances than the boring mill. Also, we don't have milling cutters this big, and it'll probably take at least two weeks to get one. Using Brink's method, I'd estimate operating time would be about five minutes for the two pieces to be machined simultaneously, but how many castings would be spoiled? . . . Actually, it's Brink's job to plan machining operations and my job to plan for inspection operations, so maybe I shouldn't worry about suggesting alternative machining methods.

In discussing alternative methods for inspecting the eccentric assembly, Mr. Canton continued,

I could consider using micrometers, measuring and recording the dimension of every piece of a lot or measuring a sample of each lot of 200 parts. I estimate it would take about 0.80 minute per piece by this method. For about $185 per gauge, I could have a set of "go/no-go" gauges made for inspecting the parts, instead of having them measured. Inspecting time using this method would probably be 0.20 minute per piece. Maybe we don't have to inspect the 6⅛-inch outside diameter on the eccentric (Part S563-1) at all. Perhaps I ought to consider some way to check the clearance on the 6⅛-inch diameter after the three parts are assembled. We might keep a Model C-13 mixer in the assembly area and check these assemblies for oil leakage and wear by operating the mixer under simulated load conditions. But this would tie up a $8500 piece of equipment that could otherwise be sold to customers.

Land Use Management at Amherst, Massachusetts

17

Mr. Charles Dillon, Town Manager, Amherst, Massachusetts was in a quandary about an assignment he had agreed to perform. In order to prepare their recommendations, his employers, the Town Board of Selectmen[1] and the Town Finance Committee had requested his managerial and financial assessments of the unprecedented question on land management to be voted next month by members of Town Meeting:[2] Should the Town of Amherst spend $85,000 to purchase land development rights in order to assure that 58 acres of the Walton farmland would not be developed for residential or commercial purposes?

For private reasons the Walton family had decided to sell their 58 acres which they had farmed for several generations. The farm was located within a mile of the Town Hall in the center of Amherst. Mr. Walton had said that if the Town would pay him $85,000, then he would sell his farm and legally bind all future owners to preserve the open landspace. His land would be used only for purposes of farming or natural conservation, or recreation, never for housing, commercial or industrial development.

The house, barn and other buildings on 3.3 acres were not included in

---

[1] Comparable to a Town or City Council in community government.

[2] Amherst Town Meeting met semi-annually as the legislative body of town government. It consisted of 258 residents elected by town voters.

This case was prepared by Professors Robert E. McGarrah and Gordon K. C. Chen, School of Business Administration, University of Massachusetts. Names of principals and their roles were changed to protect their privacy and to strengthen educational purposes of the case. The case was prepared as a basis for class discussion. It was not designed to illustrate either correct or incorrect handling of management problems. Copyright © 1977 by R. E. McGarrah and G. K. C. Chen.

the proposed sale. They would produce tax receipts estimated at $2,066 per year. Tax receipts for the entire 61.3 acre Walton farm were $2,352 per year. Thus the purchase of development rights would result in a loss of annual tax receipts of $286 to the Amherst town government.

At the request of the Board of Selectmen, real estate appraiser Mr. Daniel Royster of Worcester, after considering zoning regulations and consulting with the Town Engineer and Planner, estimated that 50 buildings with 70 housing units could be placed on the property if it were allowed to be developed.

To finance such a purchase from the Waltons would add to the Town's expense budget—already strained. Amherst property owners were complaining louder than ever about higher property taxes. Costs of public services were rising faster than incomes for a large number of Amherst families. Town government and school employees were pressing for increases in their salaries to offset inflating costs of living. Yet, virtually all town residents agreed that open spaces for farmland and college and university campuses were special attractions to life in Amherst. Six months earlier, the Town Meeting approved the principle but did not appropriate funds to purchase land development rights from owners of Amherst farmland. Mr. Dillon had to assess the consequences from a proposal to limit growth of population and land use within the 28 square mile area of the Town of Amherst.

During the past decades, 1955–75, the town population had grown from 12,300 to 32,000. The State had transformed Massachusetts Agricultural College with an enrollment of 3,524 students and 290 faculty and staff into a university with 23,000 students, 1,200 faculty and 1,960 staff. About 13,000 were Amherst residents. Along with Amherst and Hampshire Colleges the University of Massachusetts made educational and cultural affairs the town's predominant economic activity. Because of a drop in birthrates and financial difficulties in state government, very little further growth was expected in Amherst's higher educational institutions. But, the town was an increasingly attractive place of residence for retired persons, writers and artists, or for businessmen, physicians, and lawyers, whose offices were in the nearby cities of Springfield or Northampton.

Rapid growth had strained capabilities of the town's infrastructure systems for schools, water and sewer, police and fire protection, and road maintenance. Property tax rates had risen from about $18 in the 1950s to $42 per $1,000 of assessed valuation in the 1970s. By state law, assessed values of property were kept at market values. Property of the colleges and university was not taxable. They contributed voluntary funds and services in lieu of taxes, however. Depending on its location or geological features, the assessed value of an acre of farmland ranged anywhere between 5 and 50 percent of value of an acre used for business or residential purposes. Land areas in Amherst were zoned as shown in Exhibit 17–1. During the two decades (1955–1975) of rapid growth at the university the

Exhibit 17—1 Land Use Management of Amherst, Massachusetts' Zoned Land Areas

		Acres	Percent of Total Land Area
Colleges and University		1,497	8.4
Residential			
Single family	2,710		
Two family	246		
Three family	81		
Condominiums	175		
Fraternity/sorority	123		
Small apartments	985		
Large apartments	25	4,345	37.5
Town of Amherst			
Buildings, parking, roadways, parks		1,957	11.0
Farms		3,949	9.2
Commercial/industrial		511	2.9
Vacant land		5,500	31.0
		17,759	100.0

SOURCE: Office of Town Assessor.

number of acres of Amherst farmland had decreased from 7,100 to 4,000, and the number of farms from 75 to 55.

Residents in favor of purchasing the Walton land-use option and preserving open-space land argued that further growth would make the town a more costly, less attractive place to live. They pointed to the seal of the town (Exhibit 17–2) and asked, "What would our seal symbolize if there is no more farmland to plow? Why should we abuse our land and suffer from the same experiences of growth and decay in other urban and suburban communities?" They argued further that people of Massachusetts produced only 15 percent of their needs for agricultural products on family-owned and operated farms; 85 percent was imported mainly from regions in the South and far West in the United States. Overpopulation and industrialization in those regions were causing long-term water shortages and pollution problems. Huge corporate farms of the agri-business complex had created problems of health, welfare, unemployment and crime among migratory farm workers and their families. In forms of higher Federal taxes and food prices the costs of those environmental and social problems in the South and Far West were certain to be increased and passed on to people in the industrial Northeast and Mid West. Proponents cited a letter to the Editor published in The New York Times (Exhibit

17–3), and argued, "By acting now to preserve our remaining family farmland we can keep our food and environmental costs down from what they will certainly be in the future, if we fail to vote yes on this question. The costs of living in metropolitan areas are already too high. By investing now to preserve the Walton and other Amherst farmland our future savings will far exceed the tax dollars we invest." Other arguments are discussed in Exhibit 17–4.

Other residents were against using more taxpayers' funds for restricting future land use in Amherst.

There were those who objected to the increase in tax burden from paying interest on bonds to finance such purchases. Salaries of active employees and pensions of retired employees of the university (the town's largest employer, by far) had been frozen for more than three years. Even though the $85,000 to purchase the Walton farmland would mean a very little if any immediate increase in property taxes, they worried about the precedence for future land transactions. If the town paid $85,000 for the development rights, would it have to pay even more to owners of remain-

---

Exhibit 17–2 Land Use Management at Amherst, Massachusetts
Great Seal of the Town of Amherst

Adopted by vote of Town Meeting members, April 1960, after period of Amherst's most rapid population growth (at the University of Massachusetts) had already begun.
SOURCE: Town Clerk's Office.

Exhibit 17—3 Land Use Management, Town of Amherst, Massachusetts.
Arguments by proponents of purchasing land development rights by the Amherst town government.

Suburbs: 'We're Running Out of Prime Land . . .'

To the Editor:

Time and again The Times has reported the "death" of the cities of the Northeast concurrently with a story on the exclusion from the suburbs of the low- and moderate-income family. Yet to be seen is an analysis of these social phenomena that relates them to the reduction of our energy resources and agricultural potential.

Reality is defined by the media and its usage. The "suburbs" were the farms, and the Eastern suburbs were the source of the cities' food—seldom subject, these Eastern one-family farms, to drought, or their produce to unconscionable transportation costs.

And the cities were the land of opportunity and the location of efficient systems of industrial production. The major cities were also the home of culture and innovation, which they exported to the rest of the nation.

Now, through fulminating suburbanization, the cities are killing themselves and the farmland on which they've depended. City and country are fated to survive together or die together. Out here in the disappearing farmlands there are small but tenacious groups that are neither "exclusionary" nor allied with the developers who promise homes for all economic strata, but build—preferably on flat, well-drained farmland—only for the middle and upper classes.

Until recently, we sat by and watched it all happen: Well-meaning Federal legislation on "urban renewal" that has driven the middle class from the cities; equally well-intentioned housing policies that have promoted urban sprawl; collusion between development interests and local government—perhaps the most important unwritten story of the last 30 years. Can anyone hear our witness?

Now we're scared. In our minds, these are survival questions. We're running out of prime land, out of water, and out of money to pay the costs of development. Can anyone hear?   Paul Silver
Vice President
Bucks County Land Use Task Force
Furlong, Pa., Aug. 5, 1977

SOURCE: New York Times, August 18, 1977.

---

ing farmland? Should the Amherst taxpayers risk becoming victims of real estate speculators in future land values?

Other opponents asked,

How much open space land must we have to preserve the charms of Amherst land usage? We have about 5,800 acres for natural conservation, parks and recreation and farmland. We know that statistical comparisons of different communities' per capita uses of land, wealth, tax rates, etc. can influence industry, government or lobbying organizations. But, compared with other towns, Amherst had already preserved numerous sizable plots of open land space, and has restricted commercial land development. Adjacent towns and villages are all rural and provide all the open land space Amherst residents could ever wish. Hadley, to the west, has two large shopping centers which depend heavily on patronage by Am-

---

Exhibit 17—4 Land Use Management at Amherst
Arguments by proponents of purchasing land development rights by the Amherst
Town Government.

Farmland: A Vanishing Species in Bay State

Foods grown out-of-state cost nearly $3 billion yearly

By Emilie T. Livezey, Staff writer of The Christian Science Monitor

Danvers, Mass.   Eat a Massachusetts-grown meal? As recently as a century ago Bay Staters did it three times a day.

Now farmland in the commonwealth has become an endangered species. The average resident spends $600 a year on food. Only $30 of it goes to local growers.

In the last generation Massachusetts has lost 85 percent of its farms. Farmland has shrunk from more than 2 million acres in 1945 to a current all-time low of 700,000.

With only 14 percent of its land in agriculture, Massachusetts imports 85 percent of its food—40 percent from California alone.

The impact of this trend on the state's economy is tremendous. Of more than $3 billion a year invested in food by Massachusetts consumers, $2.8 billion leaves the state.

If nothing is done to turn the tide, the commonwealth can expect to continue losing 20,000 acres of farmland and several hundred jobs every year. And the story is similar in other New England states.

Reviewing the Statistics   All these grim statistics were aired here in Danvers August 25 under striped tents pitched on the lush green lawn of Essex Agricultural and Technical Institute.

Barbecued chicken for 600 invited guests—local, state, and federal officials, farm experts, and farm families—was a highlight of Massachusetts Agricultural Week sponsored by the State Department of Food and Agriculture.

Steaming corn on the cob, buckets of butter, luscious trellis-grown tomatoes, crisp "cukes," cole slaw, homemade ice cream and man-size brownies—it was a typical evening meal at this peak harvest season.

As the climax of an afternoon tour of four Essex County farms, it was proof, too, of the many foods that are still coaxed from Massachusetts soil.

Between a brilliant sunset and a pale moonrise, with the twilight air growing nippier by the minute, speakers addressed the problem on everyone's mind. They pointed out that rising transportation and energy costs, the uncertainties of water supplies, weather conditions, and the growing worldwide demand for food all underscore the soundness of a strong policy to save Bay State farmland.

Yet almost every aspect of modern life conspires to destroy the farmer's incentive to keep on farming, Douglas M. Costle, administrator of the U.S. Environmental Protection Agency, told the crowd.

Farming costs have risen. Farm labor is hard to come by. Taxes have skyrocketed. And high prices for farm products have not kept pace. The farmer, he explained, is caught between trying to make ends meet and the temptation to sell out to developers who are offering top prices for his acreage.

And on the sidelines, Mr. Costle added, are often neighbors and local representatives who would like to see a farmer's land become a source of increased tax revenue through development.

"Unless we find a practical means of making it pay to maintain the agricultural values and uses of land, it is going to slip away from us acre by acre," he said. Nationally America is losing croplands at a rate of about 1.25 million acres a year.

As Massachusetts Food and Agriculture Commissioner Frederic Winthrop, Jr. sees it, "the most promising prospect to preserve the state's dwindling farmland is Senate Bill 888. It would provide a pilot program for the public purchase of agricultural preservation restrictions, or so-called development rights on our prime farmland." The measure proposes a 115 million bond issue to finance the project.

Exhibit 17—4 (continued)

Under such a program a farmer could voluntarily give up his rights to develop his land in any way which would destroy its agricultural potential. He would be paid the difference between the open-market and farm-use value of his land while still retaining all other rights of ownership, including privacy and the right to sell or pass his property or leave it to his heirs.

Now before the House Ways and Means Committee, the bill has enthusiastic backing from both Gov. Michael S. Dukakis and Lt. Gov. Thomas P. O'Neill III.

U.S. Sen. Edward W. Brooke was on hand here to say he believes "this kind of simple and direct intervention . . . offers the most useful tool for guiding growth away from the lands we need to save for future food production."

Senator Brooke is co-sponsoring a bill for a National Agricultural Policy Act, which would provide federal funds to support such preservation programs throughout the nation.

He reported, however, that the legislation is "in trouble" in the Senate Agriculture Committee because President Carter has opposed providing federal money for this purpose. The President contends that investment in development rights is properly a state function.

Senator Brooke called this "an irrational position." He said that "even if we get the full $5 million proposed in the state legislation, the Commonwealth could barely begin to acquire the rights to hundreds of thousands of prime acres eligible for such support."

"We must recognize," he said, "that there is virtually no time left. The moment is certainly upon us for concentrated and organized political action. . . ."

Public purchase of farmland development rights is already in operation in New Jersey and in Suffolk County, Long Island, N.Y. And a measure similar to the Massachusetts proposal is before the Connecticut Legislature.

herst residents. We need the added tax revenues more residents or business firms would generate for our town government. And more land development is required to attract more business firms and residents to Amherst.

Still others were opposed to the Walton land use proposal on ideological grounds. Some farmers felt that government action to restrict future use of the Walton property to farming would be a precedent for Amherst government to infringe on their property rights to future profitable transactions with real estate developers. Some tenants felt that existing owners of land zoned for future residential and commercial use would gain unfair, windfall profits. By limiting land available for additional residents or business firms, the value of land already zoned for those purposes would go up; owners would gain at the expense of those who could not afford to own such land. Taxes or rentals would be increased to finance the purchase of farmland rights, and paid by *all* Amherst residents or land owners. But the increased capital gains would accrue only for those owners of land already zoned for future residents or businesses. "Why should we vote and finance more windfall profits for the few wealthy landholders?" they asked.

Mr. Dillon knew that shares of costs and revenues were likely to be revised among state, local and Federal government. The issues of sales, property and income tax reforms, welfare reform, criminal code reforms were being actively debated in state legislatures and Congress. Important court decisions that had recently been made were likely to affect changes in future financing of public schools. Traditionally, schools were financed almost completely from local property taxes; Amherst schools used about two-thirds of Amherst's property tax revenues. Commenting to the case writer on those changes, Mr. Dillon said,

They all affect the future cost and effectiveness of local government in Amherst and elsewhere. In light of those possibilities an assessment of consequences of our vote on whether to preserve Amherst farmland is bound to be so speculative that its value is certain to be controversial and its use to the Town Selectmen or Finance Committee members questionable. As Town Manager, my job is to execute policies decided by members of Town Meeting and the Board of Selectmen. This land use question is surely a policy question, so their assessment is more crucial than mine. Still, they are part-time citizen volunteers while I am a full-time professional in Amherst government. I have already acceded to their request for my assessment. And the outcome of the vote by Town Meeting members will surely affect the future management of Amherst's government. If I set forth the long- and short-term implications to both sides of the question, then this may help to clarify my own and voters' positions on the question.

Lordstown Plant of General Motors (A)

18

Introduction

In December 1971, the management of the Lordstown Plant was very much concerned with an unusually high rate of defective Vegas coming off the assembly line. For the previous several weeks, the lot with a capacity of 2,000 cars had been filled with Vegas which were waiting for rework before they could be shipped out to the dealers around the country.

The management was particularly disturbed by the fact that many of the defects were not the kinds of quality deficiency normally expected in an assembly production of automobiles.[1] There was a countless number of Vegas with their windshields broken, upholstery slashed, ignition keys broken, signal levers bent, rear-view mirrors broken, or carburetors clogged with washers. There were cases in which, as the Plant Manager put it, "the whole engine blocks passed by 40 men without any work done on them."

Since then, the incident in the Lordstown Plant has been much publicized in news media, drawing public interest. It has also been frequently

---

[1] The normal defect rate requiring rework was fluctuating between 1–2% at the time.

By Professor Hak-Chong Lee, School of Business, State University of New York at Albany. Copyright © 1974 by the School of Business. Reprinted with permission.

This case was developed for instructional purposes from published sources and interviews with the General Motors Assembly Division officials in Warren, Michigan and Lordstown, Ohio. The case was read and minor corrections were made by the Public Relations Office of the GMAD. However, the author is solely responsible for the content of the case. The author appreciates the cooperation of General Motors. He also appreciates Professor Anthony Athos of Harvard and Mr. John Grix of General Motors for their suggestions which improved this case.

discussed in the classroom and in the academic circles. While some people viewed the event as "young worker revolt," other reacted to it as a simple "labor problem." Some viewed it as "worker sabotage," and others
called it "industrial Woodstock."

This case describes some background and important incidents leading
to this much publicized and discussed industrial event.

The General Motors Corporation is the nation's largest manufacturer.
The Company was a leading example among many industrial organizations which have achieved organizational growth and success through decentralization. The philosophy of decentralization has been one of the
most valued traditions in the General Motors from the days of Alfred
Sloan in the 1930s through Charles Wilson and Harlow Curtice in the
1950s and up to recent years.

Under decentralized management, each of the company's car divisions,
Cadillac, Buick, Oldsmobile, Pontiac, and Chevrolet, was given a maximum autonomy in the management of its manufacturing and marketing
operations. The assembly operations were no exception, each division
managing its own assembly work. The car bodies built by Fisher Body
were assembled in various locations under maximum control and coordination between the Fisher Body and each car division.

In the mid-1960s, however, the decentralization in divisional assembly
operations was subject to a critical review. At the divisional level, the
company was experiencing serious problems of worker absenteeism and
increasing cost with declines in quality and productivity. They were reflected in the overall profit margins which were declining from 10% to
7% in the late 1960s. The autonomy in the divided management in body
manufacturing and assembly operations, in separate locations in many
cases, became questionable under the declining profit situation.

In light of these developments, General Motors began to consolidate in
some instances the divided management of body and chassis assembly
operations into a single management under the already existing General
Motors Assembly Division (GMAD) in order to better coordinate the two
operations. The GMAD was given an overall responsibility to integrate
the two operations in these instances and see that the numerous parts and
components going into car assembly get to the right places in the right
amounts at the right times.[2]

The General Motors Assembly Division (GMAD)

The GMAD was originally established in the mid 1930s, when the company needed an additional assembly plant to meet the increasing de-

---

[2] A typical assembly plant has five major assembly lines—hard trim, soft trim, body, paint, and final—supported by sub-
assembly lines which feed to the main lines such components as engines, transmissions, wheels and tires, radiators, gas
tanks, front and sheet metal, and scores of other items. The average vehicle on assembly lines has more than 5,500 items
with quality checks numbering 5 million in a typical GMAD assembly plant in a 16-hour a day operation.

mands for Buick, Oldsmobile, and Pontiac automobiles. The demands for these cars were growing so much beyond the available capacity at the time that the company began, for the first time, to build an assembly plant on the west coast which could turn out all three lines of cars rather than an individual line. As this novel approach became successful, similar plants turning out a multiple line of cars were built in seven other locations in the east, south and midwest. In the 1960s the demand for Chevrolet production also increased, and some Buick-Oldsmobile-Pontiac plants began to assemble Chevrolet products. Accordingly, the name of the division was changed to GMAD in 1965.

In order to improve the quality and productivity, the GMAD increased its control over the operations of body manufacturing and assembly. It reorganized jobs, launched programs to improve efficiency, and reduced the causes of defects which required repairs and rework. With many positive results attained under the GMAD management, the company extended the single management concept to six more assembly locations in 1968 which had been run by the Fisher Body and Chevrolet Divisions. In 1971, the GM further extended the concept to four additional Chevrolet-Fisher Body assembly facilities, consolidating the separate management under which the body and chassis assembly had been operating. One of these plants was the Lordstown Plant.

The series of consolidation brought to eighteen the number of assembly plants operated by the GMAD. In terms of total production, they were producing about 75% of all cars and 67% of trucks built by the GM. Also in 1971, one of the plants under the GMAD administration began building certain Cadillac models, thus involving GMAD in production of automobiles for each of the GM's five domestic car divisions as well as trucks for both Chevrolet and GMC Truck and Coach Division.

The Lordstown Complex

The Lordstown complex is located in Trumbull County in Ohio, about 15 miles west of Youngstown and 30 miles east of Akron. It consisted of the Vega assembly plant, the van truck assembly plant, and Fisher Body metal fabricating plant, occupying about 1,000 acres of land. GMAD which operated the Vega and van truck assembly plants is also located in the Lordstown complex. The three plants were in the heart of the heavy industrial triangle of Youngstown, Akron and Cleveland. With Youngstown as a center of steel production, Akron the home of rubber industries, and Cleveland as a major center for heavy manufacturing, the Lordstown complex commanded a good strategic and logistic location for automobile assembly.

The original assembly plant was built in 1964–1966 to assemble Impalas. But in 1970 it was converted into Vega assembly with extensive rearrangements. The van truck assembly plant was constructed in 1969, and the Fisher Body metal fabricating plant was further added in 1970 to carry out stamping operations to produce sheet metal components used in Vega and van assemblies. In October 1971, the Chevrolet Vega and van assembly plants and Fisher Body Vega assembly plants which had been operating under separate management were merged into a single jurisdiction of the GMAD.

Work Force at the Lordstown Plant

There are over 11,400 employees working in the Lordstown Plant (as of 1973). Approximately 6,000 people of whom 5,500 are on hourly payroll work in the Vega assembly plant. About 2,600 workers, 2,100 of them paid hourly, work in van truck assembly. As members of the United Auto Workers Union, Local 1112, the workers command good wages and benefits. They start out on the line at about $5.00 an hour, get a 10¢ an hour increase within 30 days, and another 10¢ after 90 days. Benefits come to $2.50 an hour.[3] The supplemental unemployment benefits virtually guarantee the worker's wage throughout the year. If the worker is laid off, he gets more than 90% of his wage for 52 weeks. He is also eligible for up to six weeks for holidays, excused absence or bereavement, and up to four weeks vacation.

The work force at the plant is almost entirely made up of local people with 92% coming from the immediate area of a 20 mile radius. Lordstown itself is a small rural town of about 500 residents. A sizable city closest to the plant is Warren, 5 miles away, which together with Youngstown supplies about two-thirds of the work force. The majority of the workers (57.5%) are married, 7.6% are home owners, and 20.2% are buying their homes. Of those who do not own their own homes (72%), over one-half are still living with their parents. The rest live in rented houses or apartments.

The workers in the plant are generally young. Although various news media reported the average worker age as 24 years old, and in some parts of the plant as 22 years, the company records show that the overall average worker age was somewhat above 29 years as of 1971–72. The national average is 42. The work force at Lordstown is the second youngest among GM's 25 assembly plants around the country. The fact that the Lordstown plant is the GM's newest assembly plant may partly explain the relatively young work force.

The educational profile of the Lordstown workers indicates that only 22.2% have less than a high school education. Nearly two-thirds or 62% are high school graduates, and 16% are either college graduates or have attended college. Another 26% have attended trade school. The average education of 13.2 years makes the Lordstown workers among the best educated in GM's assembly plants.

---

[3] In G.M., the average worker on the line earns $12,500 a year with fringe benefits of $3,000.

The Vega Assembly Line

Conceived as a major competitive product against the increasing influx of foreign cars which were being produced at as low as one-fourth the labor rate in this country, the Vega was specifically designed with a maximum production efficiency and economy in mind. From the initial stages of planning, the Vega was designed by a special task team with most sophisticated techniques, using computers in designing the outer skin of the car and making tapes that form the dies. Computers were also used to match up parts, measure the stack tolerances, measure safety performance under head-on collision, and make all necessary corrections before the first 1971 model car was ever built. The 2300 cubic centimeter all-aluminum, 4 cylinder engine, was designed to give gas economy comparable to the foreign imports.

The Vega was also designed with the plant and the people in mind. As the GM's newest plant, the Vega assembly plant was known as the "super plant" with the most modern and sophisticated designs to maximize efficiency. It featured the newest engineering techniques and a variety of new power tools and automatic devices to eliminate much of the heavy lifting and physical labor. The line gave the workers an easier access to the car body, reducing the amount of bending and crawling in and out, as in other plants around the country. The unitized body in large components like pre-fab housing made the assembly easier and lighter with greater body integrity. Most difficult and tedious tasks were eliminated or simplified, on-line variations of the job were minimized, and the most modern tooling and mechanization was used to the highest possible degree of reliability.

It was also the fastest moving assembly line in the industry. The average time per assembly job was 36 seconds with a maximum of 100 cars rolling off the assembly line per hour for a daily production of 1,600 cars from two shift operations. The time cycle per job in other assembly plants averaged about 55 seconds. Although the high speed of the line did not necessarily imply greater work load or job requirement, it was a part of the GM's attempt to maximize economy in Vega assembly. The fact that the Vega was designed to have 43% fewer parts than a full-size car also helped the high-speed line and economy. Exhibit 18–1 shows a simplified flow chart of major assembly operations.

Impact of GMAD and Reorganization in the Lordstown Plant

As stated previously, the assembly operations at Lordstown had originally been run by Fisher Body and Chevrolet as two plants. There were two organizations, two plant managers, two unions, and two service organizations. The consolidation of the two organizations into a single operating

Exhibit 18—1 Flowchart of Major Assembly Operations

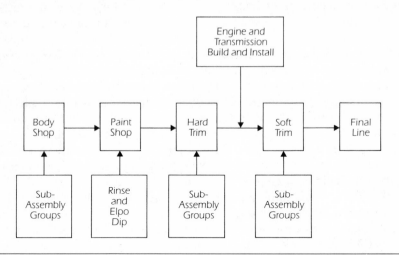

system under the GMAD in October 1971 required a difficult task of reorganization and dealing with the consequences of manpower reduction such as work slowdown, worker discipline, grievances, etc.

As duplicating units such as production, maintenance, inspection, and personnel were consolidated, there was a problem of selecting the personnel to manage the new organization. There were chief inspectors, personnel directors and production superintendents as well as production and service workers to be displaced or reassigned. Unions which had been representing their respective plants also had to go through reorganization. Union elections were held to merge the separate union committees at Fisher Body and Chevrolet into a single union bargaining committee. This eliminated one full local union shop committee.

At the same time, GMAD launched an effort to improve production efficiency more in line with that in other assembly plants. It included increasing job efficiency through reorganization and better coordination between the body and chassis assembly, and improving controls over product quality and worker absenteeism. This effort coincided with the plant's early operational stage at the time which required adjustments in line balance and work methods. Like other assembly plants, the Vega assembly plant was going through an initial period of diseconomy caused by suboptimal operations, imbalance in the assembly line, and somewhat redundant work force. According to management, line adjustments and work changes were a normal process in accelerating the assembly operation to the peak performance the plant had been designed for after the initial break-in and startup period.

As for job efficiency, the GMAD initiated changes in those work sequences and work methods which were not well coordinated under the divided managements of body and chassis assembly. For example, previous to the GMAD, Fisher Body had been delivering the car body complete with interior trim to the final assembly line, where often times the workers soiled the front seats as they did further assembly operations. GMAD changed this practice so that the seats were installed as one of the last operations in building the car. Fisher Body also had been delivering the car body with complete panel instrument frame which made it extremely difficult for the assembly workers to reach behind the frame in installing the instrument panels. The GMAD improved the job method so that the box containing the entire instrument panels were installed on the assembly line. Such improvements in job sequences and job methods resulted in savings in time and the number of workers required. Consequently, there were some jobs where the assembly time was cut down and/or the number of workers was reduced.

GMAD also put more strict control over worker absenteeism and the causes for defect work; the reduction in absenteeism was expected to require fewer relief men, and the improvement in quality and less repair work were to require fewer repairmen. In implementing these changes, the GMAD instituted a strong policy of dealing with worker slowdowns via strict disciplinary measures, including dismissal. It was rumored that the inspectors and foremen passing defective cars would be fired on the spot.

Many workers were laid off as a result of the reorganization and job changes. The union was claiming that as many as 700 workers were laid off. Management, on the other hand, put the layoff figure at 375 to which the union later conceded.[4] Although management claimed that the changes in job sequence and method in some assembly work did not bring a substantial change in the overall speed or pace of the assembly line, the workers perceived the job change as "tightening" the assembly line. The union charged that the GMAD brought a return of an old-fashioned line speedup and a "sweatshop style" of management reminiscent of the 1930s, making the men do more work at the same pay. The workers were blaming the "tightened" assembly line for the drastic increase in quality defects. As one worker commented, "That's the fastest line in the world. We have about 40 seconds to do our job. The company adds one more thing and it can kill us. We can't get the stuff done on time and a car goes by. The company then blames us for sabotage and shoddy work."

The number of worker grievances also increased drastically. Before GMAD took over, there were about 100 grievances in the plant. Since then, grievances increased to 5,000, 1,000 of which were related to the

---

[4] All of the workers who had been laid off were later reinstated as the plant needed additional workers to perform assembly jobs for optional features to Vega, i.e., vinyl top, etc., which were later introduced. In addition, some workers were put to work at the van assembly plant.

charge that too much work had been added to the job. The worker resentment was particularly great in "towveyor" assembly and seat sub-assembly areas. The "towveyor" is the area where engines and transmissions are assembled. Like seat sub-assembly there is a great concentration of workers working together in close proximity. Also, these jobs are typically for beginning assemblers who tend to make the work crew in these areas younger and better educated.

The workers in the plant were particularly resentful of the company's strict policy in implementing the changes. They stated that the tougher the company became, the more they would stiffen their resistance even though other jobs were scarce in the market. One worker said, "In some of the other plants where the GMAD did the same thing, the workers were older and they took this. But, I've got 25 years ahead of me in this plant." Another worker commented, "I saw a woman running to keep pace with the fast line. I'm not going to run for anybody. There ain't anyone in that plant that is going to tell me to run." One foreman said, "The problem with the workers here is not so much that they don't want to work, but that they just don't want to take orders. They don't believe in any kind of authority."

While the workers were resisting management orders, there were some indications that the first line supervisors had not been adequately trained to perform satisfactory supervisory roles. The average supervisor at the time had less than 3 years of experience, and 20% of the supervisors had less than 1 year's experience. Typically, they were young, somewhat lacking in knowledge of the provisions of the union contract and other supervisory duties, and less than adequately trained to handle the workers in the threatening and hostile environment which was developing.

Another significant fact was that the strong reactions of the workers were not entirely from the organizational and job changes brought about by the GMAD alone. Management noted that there was a significant amount of worker reactions in the areas where the company hadn't changed anything at all. Management felt that the intense resentment was particularly due to the nature of the work force in Lordstown. The plant was not only made up of young people, but also the work force reflected the characteristics of "tough labor" in steel, coal and rubber industries in the surrounding communities. Many of the workers in fact came from families who made their living working in these industries. Management also noted that the worker resistance had been much greater in the Lordstown Plant than in other plants where similar changes had been made.

A good part of the young workers' resentment also seemed to be related to the unskilled and repetitive nature of the assembly work. One management official admitted that the company was facing a difficult task in getting workers to "take pride" in the product they were assemblying. Many of them were benefiting from the company's tuition assistance plan which was supporting their college education in the evening. With this educated background, obviously assembly work was not fulfilling their high work expectations. Also, the job market was tight at the time, and they could neither find any meaningful jobs elsewhere nor, even if found, could they afford to give up the good money and fringe benefits they were earning on their assembly line jobs. This made them frustrated, according to company officials.

Many industrial engineers were questioning whether the direction of management toward assembly line work could continue. As the jobs became easier, simpler, and repetitive, requiring less physical effort, they required less skill but became more monotonous. The worker unrest indicated that they not only wanted to go back to the work pace prior to the "speedup" (pre-October pace), but also wanted the company to do something about the boring and meaningless assembly work. One worker commented, "The company has got to do something to change the job so that a guy can take an interest in the job. A guy can't do the same thing 8 hours a day year after year. And it's got to be more than the company just saying to a guy, 'Okay, instead of 6 spots on the weld, you'll do 5 spots.'"

As the worker resentment mounted, the UAW Local 1112 decided in early January 1972 to consider possible authorization for a strike against the Lordstown Plant in a fight against the job changes. In the meantime, the union and management bargaining teams worked hard on worker grievances; they reduced the number of grievances from 15,000 to a few hundred; management even indicated that it would restore some of the eliminated jobs. However, the bargaining failed to produce accord on the issues of seniority rights and shift preference, which were related to the wider issues of job changes and layoff.

A vote was held in early February 1972. Nearly 90% of the workers came out to vote, which was the heaviest turnout in the history of the Local. With 97% of the votes supporting, the workers went out on strike in early March.

In March 1972, with the strike in effect, the management of the Lordstown Plant was assessing the impact of the GMAD and the resultant strike in the Plant. It was estimated that the work disruption because of the worker resentment and slowdown had already cost the company 12,000 Vegas and 4,000 trucks, amounting to $45 million. There had been repeated closedowns of assembly lines since December 1971, because of the worker slowdowns and the cars passing down the line without all necessary operations performed on them. The car lot was full with 2,000 cars waiting for repair work.

There had also been an amazing number of complaints from Chevrolet dealers, 6,000 complaints in November alone, about the quality of the Vegas shipped to them. This was more than the combined complaints from the other assembly plants.

The strike in the Lordstown Plant was expected to affect other plants.

The plants at Tonawands, New York and Buffalo, New York were supplying parts for Vega. Despite the costly impact of the worker resistance and the strike, the management felt that the job changes and cost reductions were essential if the Vega were to return a profit to the company. The plant had to be operating at about 90% capacity to break even. Not only had the plant with highly automated features cost twice as much as estimated, but also the Vega itself ended up weighing 10% more than had been planned.

While the company had to do something to increase the production efficiency in the Lordstown Plant, the management was wondering whether it couldn't have planned and implemented the organizational and job changes differently in view of the costly disruption of the operations and the organizational stress the Plant had been experiencing.

Lordstown Plant of General Motors (B)

19

The labor unrest at the Lordstown Plant finally came to an end in late March 1972. The UAW Local 1112 and GM Assembly Division reached an agreement to end the strike, which had lasted for three weeks. The labor-management agreement provided for the following settlements:

Recognition of seniority and transfer rights under GMAD merger. The merging of Chevrolet and Fisher Body into a single management of GMAD had brought many changes in job assignments and operations. It had also brought changes in the union structure, combining two previously separate bargaining units into one. Involved in these changes were the problems concerning worker rights on job assignments, shifts, transfers and job progression. It was finally resolved that seniority be used to handle the worker's job assignment.

Rehiring of laid off workers. There were 375 workers who had been laid off from the GMAD's job improvement program. They were all rehired and assigned to van truck plant operations which were expanding at the time.

Settlement of grievances. With the agreement on seniority right and re-hiring of the laid off workers, the union withdrew many unresolved grievances. Discipline cases were resolved through compromises. While many employees were reinstated with varying amounts of back-pay, some em-

By John J. Crix, General Motors, and Hak-Chong Lee, State University of New York at Albany.

ployees, in extreme cases, were discharged. The latter were mostly clear disciplinary cases involving the acts of sabotage and other serious infractions of plant rules.

Interestingly, while discipline, production standards, and contract language were the big issues, job boredom and worker alienation were never an issue. The media dwelled on the one subject not discussed by the parties.

Diagnosis of Worker Problems

During the months following the strike settlement, the General Motors Assembly Division management at Lordstown initiated an intensive program of restoring normal working conditions. There was still a great deal of tension and mood for agitation among the workers after they returned to work. With the help of the corporate headquarters office, management at the Lordstown Plant attempted first to diagnose the problems and then to formulate appropriate programs of action. Management conducted attitude surveys on workers, held a series of meetings with all levels of supervisors, and solicited opinions from union officials. These produced the following conclusions:

1. There was a widespread worker distrust and antagonism toward management; the workers felt that management didn't care about their needs, feelings and problems.
2. The workers were insecure on the job; they felt that management was changing their work schedules, adding and deleting overtimes, and deciding on their "time offs" without prior warning or consultation; there was also a general feeling that the workers did not know where they stood with the company.
3. The workers felt that management was not interested in their ideas in improving work methods and plant operations.
4. Some workers showed considerable resentment over boredom in the routine and repetitive tasks in the assembly job.
5. Many workers did not understand the company objectives and programs; what management was attempting to do, the reasons why, and related problems.
6. The first-line supervisors felt that they were not given adequate information about the overall management objectives and programs to relate them to their day-to-day supervision over the workers.

Alternative Considerations

Management was aware of the root causes for these problems. While it was imperative for management to initiate the job improvement and reorganization programs to attain the production efficiency the plant was designed for, the actual implementation of the program was such to arouse an intense worker opposition. A solution had to be found to the problem.

In considering possible alternatives, management recognized some definite constraints at least from a short-run point of view. Although the repetitive nature of work tasks was a factor affecting the worker sentiment on the job, management felt that the economic and competitive reality and the existing assembly technology made the enrichment of the assembly line jobs untenable at that time. Management had some doubts about the immediate applicability of new assembly technology, developed and experimented by Swedish auto manufacturers, to the American auto assembly, considering the volume of production the American auto manufacturers had to turn out at certain desired prices. Exhibit 19–1 summarizes the main considerations underlying the complex problem of job enrichment in the auto-assembly line. The union essentially concurred with the management position on this issue. Exhibit 19–2 presents the views stated by a union spokesman.

Limiting realistic alternatives within the existing assembly technology and based on the analysis of the responses from the workers, union officials and supervisory personnel, management diagnosed the primary source of the worker problem as a lack of *communication* between management and the workers. Accordingly, management proceeded with developing ways to improve communication and the general organizational climate through better understanding between the workers and management.

Communication Programs

Beginning in October, 1972, a year after the worker unrest started, the following programs to improve communication were introduced:

1. *Daily Plant Radio Announcement.* Each day for 5 minutes, management broadcasted over the plant public address system the news items related to automobile industry, the company and the plant in general. The information announced largely dealt with the status on sales, inventory and production schedule which gave the workers an overall picture of the conditions in the industry, the company and the plant. The text was also posted on the bulletin boards around the plant (Exhibit 19–3).
3. *Information Bulletin.* As a means of direct communication between the Plant Manager and the workers, all important information pertaining to the plant operation was channeled directly to the workers and put on the bulletin boards throughout the plant. The information included any changes in products, shifts, production schedules, weekly production and incoming orders, etc. in the Lordstown Plant as well as other plants. The Plant Manager also disseminated any problems exist-

Exhibit 19—1 GMAD's Position on Job Enrichment

The following is an evaluation of Volvo's Job Enrichment Program prepared by the GMAD's Personnel Communications and Organizational Development Staff:

Volvo's experiment in team assembly has been the subject of recent public interest and has received fairly wide publicity. The following may be helpful in discussing this issue.

In early 1974, Volvo opened its new plant in Kalmar, Sweden: the first automobile plant operating without an assembly line. Its unique design consists of four adjoining hexagonal buildings with work space along the windowed outer walls and storerooms in the middle of each hexagon. Car bodies are carried on battery-powered dollies which tilt to 90° for underside installations.

The Kalmar Plant employs 600 workers and is expected to produce 30,000 cars a year, or 14 cars an hour, as compared to conventional methods which produce 40 to 100 cars an hour.

The key components of team assembly, as it applies to this plant, are:

- Each of the 25 teams of 15–25 workers is responsible for its own section of the car—i.e., the electrical system, steering controls, or brakes and wheels.
- Teams set their own work schedule, and inspect and repair their own units.
- Each team member learns to perform an average of 68 times the number of operations as a conventional assembly line worker.
- Manhours per car will be the same as in a conventional plant, according to Volvo's production chief.
- Operating costs at full production are expected by Volvo to be consistent with conventional assembly line costs; although some savings may be achieved through reduced defects, scrap material and down-time.

The Kalmer Plant cost $20 million to build, which Volvo estimates is 10% higher than a conventional plant would have cost. A $100 million Volvo car assembly plant is scheduled to be built in Chesapeake, Virginia, in 1976. This plant will product 100,000 cars a year (25 cars per hour) and is expected to use the team assembly method.

Volvo's new Skovde Engine Plant is arranged in an E shape with team work-stations in the "fingers." Like the car assembly plant, the engine is carried to teams at work-stations along the outer walls for each successive stage of assembly. At the work-station the engine can be moved or stopped at the worker's control. Buffer stocks between work-stations allow for variations in assembly times. This plant is scheduled to produce 250,000 engines per year and employ 600 workers.

Both of these plants are new, small, and experimental. Their success in terms of worker satisfaction will not be known until they have been in operation for several years.

Many job restructuring and enrichment techniques have been introduced into Volvo's older, conventional assembly line plants. These include team management, job rotation and enlargement, leadership training, and active communications programs. Participation in such programs is voluntary at Volvo. In one plant which employs approximately 7,000 people and has had such programs in operation for several years, about one fourth of the work force is participating.

Volvo has taken this step toward people-oriented assembly because it is faced with a severe labor shortage which is predicted to reach crisis level within 20 years. Specifically:

- Full Employment—Unemployment in Sweden ranges between 1%–.003%.
- Unskilled Labor Base—Foreign labor makes up to 50%–60% of Sweden's unskilled work force. Trade laws, passed in 1972, restrict further imported labor.
- Education—Presently 67% of Sweden's population has completed high school. This number is expected to reach 90% by 1980. Approximately 40% of the current U.S. work force has completed high school.
- Turnover Rates—Volvo's employee turnover rate is around 30% annually. GM's annual turnover rate for hourly workers in the U.S. was 10.1% in 1973.

Exhibit 19—1 (continued)

- Absenteeism—Volvo keeps about one-seventh (14.3%) of its entire work force in reserve to cope with absenteeism. GM's estimated absenteeism rate for 1974 is 5.3% for U.S. hourly employees. Another relevant comparison is that Volvo sold 250,000 cars in 1973 as compared to GM's 8.7 million cars sold that year.

  General Motors is experimenting with team assembly in low production situations. Other people-programs have been implemented in most of GM's manufacturing plants. These activities are directed toward employee involvement and motivation, communications and training, the structure of the organization, and teamwork on all levels.

Exhibit 19—2 The Union's Position on Job Enrichment

The following is a synopsis of the keynote address delivered by D. A. Fraser, UAW Vice President, at SAE Convention in 1974.

1. The UAW supports experiments in the area of job enrichment. In an effort to reduce worker dissatisfaction, 10 years ago the union bargained for more relief time. Now, the union is looking to get the workers out of the plant sooner, quicker and longer (earlier retirement, holidays and voluntary overtime).
2. "Life Ethic" rather than "Work Ethic": The root cause of worker alienation is that the worker today has a lower tolerance level for frustrations, rules and regulations, and systems that seek to institute conformity; moreover, he is just not that concerned about losing his job. The work ethic is being rivaled by a growing "life ethic." People are beginning to say that they have a work life and a personal life, and a balance between these must be maintained. Absenteeism on Saturdays, earlier retirement and voluntary overtime are emerging as important issues.
3. The Volvo Experiment: The work Volvo is doing is interesting and exciting, but it is questionable if it can be applied to the U.S. auto industry considering the high volume, interdependence and cost considerations in the auto production. The union's goals are to see the workplace safer, cleaner, and to gain better retirement plans and more holidays. The union would also like to see some basic restructuring in terms of management roles and how the tasks are performed so that the worker can attain a sense of achievement, accomplishment and satisfaction. But, there again is a doubt on how much can really be done with jobs on the assembly line itself.
4. Job Rotation: Job rotation changes the job and worker's satisfaction very little. It is fine to involve the worker in planning and scheduling, but the ability to do so is limited by the production requirements dictated by the customer's needs. However, there is a need for experiments to give workers more decisions to make and see what the real long-run effects are.
5. Supervision: The first-line supervisor is the toughest job in the auto industry. The first-line supervisor must be a leader. The old "boss" style of supervisor no longer works. There is a need for experiments on how workers are given more decisions to make and how they could supervise themselves.

Exhibit 19—3 Text of Radio Broadcast July 11, 1975

Good morning, ladies and gentlemen,

The first six months of 1975 show that all but one GM car division has produced more cars than in the first six months of 1974. Chevrolet is the only division that has seen production fall. Buick is up 28.6%; Cadillac is up 26.9%; Oldsmobile is up 11.6%; Pontiac is up 5.8%; and Chevrolet is down 25%. Chevrolet still accounts for 46.7% of all passenger car production in GM but in most years this one division accounts for over half of our car production. For the corporation, the five most produced cars year to date are the Oldsmobile Cutlass, standard Chevrolet, Chevrolet Monte Carlo, Chevy Nova, and the standard-size Buick. In spite of the drift towards small cars, the only compacts or sub-compacts in the first seven GM cars is the Nova.

According to the Bureau of Census, 34% of the households in this country have two or more cars in the family: 82% owned one or more cars and 18% owned one or more trucks or recreational vehicles. With the scrap rate being as low as it is presently, you can begin to see why some of the industry analysts are predicting some good years ahead for our industry, but at the same time the consumer will be more demanding of quality and expect more in the way of warranty protection; and the companies or divisions that can produce that quality will reap the harvest. Numerous surveys have shown that the single most important factor in buyer consideration of cars with similar gas mileage and pricing, is quality. The engineers have given us two cars with more than competitive gas mileage performance and our cars are priced competitively with our competition and the only factor we have any control over is quality, and this, quite frankly, is the one that could very well affect our pocketbooks.

Our past performances, when compared to both internal and external competition, have not been what they should or could be. I refuse to believe that the employees at Lordstown don't have what it takes to build the best products in the world. Until we each make a personal commitment to a quality job on our own personal jobs, and stop blaming the engineers, suppliers and each other, we can't accomplish the task. We are going to be facing stiff internal competition from the new sub-compact to be built at Wilmington and our competitors in the sub-compact business at the other corporations are out to cut our percentage of this market even further. In the first six months of this year we have seen our percentage of the sub-compact market dwindle to the point that Ford's sub-compact, Mustang II, is outselling our Vega.

Today is Elaine Magazzine's birthday; Elaine is one of our plant telephone operators. Ron Saunders of Maintenance and Bill Kovachik of Van Chassis are celebrating a birthday tomorrow and on Sunday, Al Gontero of Maintenance, Joanne Maushan of Financial, John Heston and John Sorvillo also of Financial, Tom Crkvenac of Reliability, and Ray Dickey of Van Body Shop celebrate another year. Happy Birthday to all of you.

These two items just cleared the wire: GM Board Chairman Tom Murphy confirmed that GM's new sub-compact to be built at Wilmington will be called the Chevette and will be marketed by Chevrolet. The car is also called Chevette in other countries in which it is being built. It is considered GM's "World Car." Cadillac also announced that the second quarter of 1975 was the best quarter in the division's history.

Thank you for your attention and have a nice weekend.

---

ing in the plant and solicited worker's ideas to solve them (Exhibit 19–4).

3. *Supervisory Training.* To reinforce supervisors in their person-to-person communication role on the job, all supervisors, from the Plant Manager down to the first-level supervisors, and staff personnel were given human relations and communication training. The program was

---

Exhibit 19—4 Information Bulletin From Plant Manager July 17, 1975

INFORMATION BULLETIN

There is a possibility that the Fisher Fabricating Plant will go on strike tomorrow, Friday, July 18, 1975, at 10:00 a.m. GMAD is planning to continue operations as scheduled in both the Vega and Van plants. In the event of a strike at the Fabricating Plant, GMAD employees should continue at work as scheduled until otherwise notified by their supervisors.

It is important that addresses and telephone numbers are accurate, and that all employees be aware that the local news media will be utilized as required for subsequent notification purposes in the event a stoppage occurs.

A separate bulletin will be reposted listing the radio stations normally utilized for notification purposes.

Changes in addresses and telephone numbers must be done through the personnel office.

Last night at approximately 4:00 P.M. lightning struck a power pole near the Van Plant causing an electrical pulse that activated the fire horns. (This was not a tornado warning signal.) When the fire horns are activated in this manner they have to be shut down manually, one at a time. This was accomplished by 6:00 p.m. The misunderstanding and confusion caused by the lightning strike was unusual, however, we were in the midst of a severe thunderstorm alert.

(signed)

C. Abernethy

---

aimed at heightening the supervisor's awareness of their roles in organizational liaison and communication to their subordinates. The Public Relations Coordinator and Quality Control Director, who had had a long experience in the line organization, designed and conducted the training programs.

Management appointed the Public Relations Coordinator to Coordinator of Plant Communication, to be responsible for both external and internal programs. In addition, management also developed a job rotation program, in which the workers interested in rotating their jobs were given necessary training and help to enlarge the range of their task abilities within the same group of assembly jobs which included about 30 different but essentially the same skill-level jobs.

In October, 1973, Charles Abernethy took over the Lordstown operation as the new plant manager. The new plant manager was considered as one of the most capable managers in the GMAD organization. Prior to the new assignment to head the GM's largest assembly operations at Lordstown, Abernethy had come up the rank through the Plant Manager at Van Nuys, California, where he was credited for bringing the plant up as one of GM's most efficient assembly plants. The communication programs received an enthusiastic endorsement and continued support from the new Plant Manager. He went through the training program himself and participated in all supervisory training sessions personally.

It took some time before management was able to see the effect from the communication programs. Not only that the plant had returned to normal conditions by 1974, but also in mid-1975 there were encouraging signs that the Lordstown Plant was heading toward becoming one of the more efficient assembly plants. The absenteeism had been steadily declining; grievances were down to one-third the rate of 1971–72. The production efficiency, as measured by the division, had also improved markedly. The warranty cost indicating the quality of assembly workmanship also improved (Exhibit 19–5). On the other hand, the job rotation program had attracted very little interest from the workers.

There was some thinking that the improved organizational climate and worker attitude in 1975 was related to the economic recession and high unemployment in the auto industry. However, management at Lordstown was confident that its concerted effort to improve the management-worker relations had been the primary factor in the positive result. As the Plant Manager put it,

. . . Our ultimate objective is to achieve the kind of organizational climate in which we, managers and workers, have a common feeling that we all work together here; forget about the formal barriers and freely communicate to one another. We have too much dichotomy here now, an artificial three-way separation between management, workers and union. I see no reason why we can't strengthen the relationship between the management and the worker through direct communication.

. . . . There are many limitations in the auto assembly business to

---

Exhibit 19–5 Selected Organizational Indexes

	1971	1973	1975
Absenteeism	7.4%	7.6%	5.5%
Grievance Rate[a]	15,000	8,500	4,000
Production Efficiency Rating[b]	Lowest 10%	Lower 35%	Upper 40%
Warranty Cost[c] Rating[b]	Lowest 10%	Lower 30%	Upper 50%

[a] Approximate annual rate.

[b] The ranking among General Motors' 25 assembly plants.

[c] The number and amount of dealer charge-backs to General Motors for the rework the dealers did on defect automobiles.

make the worker feel a part of the organization. We've got to work with the technology we have here to produce a certain volume in order to stay in business. A large majority of the workers understand the problem if we explain it properly. They might not like it but they certainly understand it and want to cooperate with us. There are only a small minority who don't understand the problem. We have to work at them extra hard, and most of the time we succeed. Of course, there are still some people whom the assembly work is not meant for.

. . . . I believe in job enrichment and O.D. programs. But, we have to recognize the technological limitations in the assembly plant and the situational factors unique in this plant. Here in Lordstown, we have a work force, young and well educated. They want to know everything that's going on and they don't want to be left out on anything. But, surprisingly, they accept what you tell them if you communicate to them sincerely. They want to know, and know from you first-hand, not through the second-hand grapevine. We have to design programs based on this local environment, and here in Lordstown, we believe communication is the thing which ties the daily operations together.

A New Communication Program

It was with this philosophy that the management of the Lordstown Plant was considering in summer 1975, a new communication program in addition to the ones already existing. The management was pleased with the progress made by the existing programs, but they felt that they could achieve their aims in communication even further if there were some formal attempt to tie the programs together into the person-to-person communication among the workers and the supervisory personnel. Recognizing that the first-line supervisors were too busy to pay sufficient attention to interpersonal communication, especially to their subordinates, the management developed a program to facilitate and reinforce the communication roles of the first-level as well as other supervisory personnel. The proposed program contained the following features:

1. New positions called *Communicator-Trainers* would be created with the primary purpose of integrating the work of supervisors, workers and staff personnel. A Communicator-Trainer would be assigned to each of 11 production departments, and would report directly to the Plant Manager. The Communicator-Trainer would play the role of "people problem solver."
2. The role of Communicator-Trainer would be that of a "catalyst," "integrator," or "facilitator" to the line workers, thus strengthening the communication links between the workers and their supervisors and between the line employees and the staff personnel.
3. Spending most of his time in the plant, the Communicator-Trainer could make sure that proper communication existed between the workers and the first-line supervisors and among the upper super-

visory people. He would also play the "middle role" when necessary to facilitate the line-staff communication and to see that line's needs were met by prompt staff services.

4. Communicator-Trainers would meet with the Plant Manager and Communication Coordinator each day to review and discuss the "people problems" existing in the plant.

It was thought that the selection and training of the Communicator-Trainers would be crucial to the success of the new program. The general thinking was that Communicator-Trainers should have had a considerable line experience, having served through general foremanship and demonstrated organizational and human relations skills on the job.

As the Plant Manager and Communication Coordinator were preparing a budget to propose the new communication program to the GMAD headquarters office, they were wondering what the impact of the new program would be on the organization. The Lordstown Plant was the first assembly plant to use Communicator-Trainers; no other plants had tried out anything similar to the proposal. The preliminary feedback from a few supervisors and staff people whom the Plant Manager and the Communication Coordinator had talked to was generally favorable. But, certainly, the new program and the functions of the new Communicator-Trainer

Exhibit 19—6 Communication Relationship

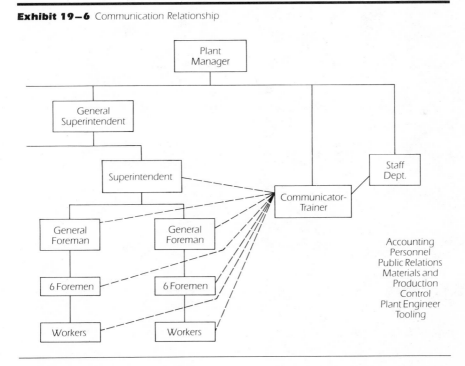

were going to affect the jobs and the work relations of the Foreman, General Foreman, Superintendent, and the staff personnel (Exhibit 19–6). The union's relation with the workers might also be changed.

It was estimated that the new communication program with 11 new Communicator-Trainers would cost the Lordstown Plant over $400,000 a year including fringe benefits. As the Plant Manager and the Communication Coordinator were completing the proposal, they were wondering what the reaction would be from the workers, union, supervisors and staff people.

Mackie Paint Company

20

The Mackie Paint Company operated four factories and five warehouses located in the New England, Middle Atlantic, and Mid-Western states. Eighty-five percent of Mackie's paint was for interior and exterior household use. Except for fifteen company-owned stores in the greater New York City area, distribution at the retail level was through 600 independent, franchised dealers.

In recent years, the company's share of the market had dropped six percentage points. Fifteen of Mackie's best retail accounts had shifted to competitors' paints. Store operators said their margin had grown too slim. Mr. B. A. Vernon, sales manager, made an intensive study of the situation and had this to say in his report:

Quality-wise and delivery-wise our performance has been as good or better than most of our competitors. It's price where we've been losing out. Our list prices are the highest in three of the four largest selling types of paint. I'm convinced that to boost our share of the market, we'll have to cut our list price across the board by a minimum of five percent, and preferably seven percent. I also recommend that we open up more of our own retail stores in all territories. This will help to offset effects of price cuts on our margin, while boosting our total volume to where it should be.

Revised version of an earlier case written by Professor R. E. McGarrah. Copyright © by the President and Fellows of Harvard College.

After discussing Mr. Vernon's report with his brother, H. B. Mackie, president and treasurer, Mr. T. A. Mackie, executive vice-president, said: "You're probably right about pushing cost reduction instead, Hank. Our margin is slim enough already. You're closer to the financial market than I am. But if you say we can't raise capital on reasonable terms to expand our retail chain beyond New York, then we'll have to try to offset a price cut by cutting costs."

Each of the four plants was equipped to manufacture all types of paints sold by Mackie. For a variety of reasons, average direct unit costs were not uniform at all plants. Pigment dispersing mills and blending equipment were twenty years old in one plant and only three, five and six years old in the other three plants; hence, hourly productivity and labor costs of operating and maintaining the older equipment were higher in the oldest plants. The f.o.b. plant costs of purchased materials (pigments, chemicals, and blending vehicles) varied because freight distances and costs were different for each plant. There were also slight differences in wages among the plants.

Briefly, the manufacture of paint in Mackie's plants involved a three-stage process. First, pigments were thoroughly dispersed in paste-like form by running them between two large, rotating steel cylinders until they reached the desired color, uniformity, and consistency. Next, the dispersed pigments were blended with selected "vehicles" (usually oils or lacquers) in large tanks equipped with mechanical agitators. Finally, the paint was packaged in a variety of standard sized cans. After being dispersed, pigments had to be moved promptly to the blending stage; however, after being blended, the paint could be temporarily stored in tanks, before being packaged. Economic batch-sizes were set by estimating the minimum sum of inventory carrying and equipment changeover costs for a year.

Freight costs of shipments from plants to warehouses varied significantly with distances from plants to warehouse. Accordingly, Mackie's "distribution policy" was to keep shipping costs at a minimum. Management had divided the multiplant-warehouse system into geographical units in such a way that each plant supplied the nearest warehouse(s). (Of course, there were minor, temporary exceptions to this policy, when inventory levels were out-of-balance.)

Mr. T. A. Mackie discussed ways he approached his cost reduction problem:

One of my first considerations was to cut costs by replacing the old equipment in our Philadelphia and Springfield (Mass.) plants. But this would have meant major capital expenditures we couldn't afford. Another alternative would have been to have our purchasing agent shop around for better prices on materials we buy. There are probably big savings opportunities here because materials are 58% of our unit cost. But I don't think this would have been a way to realize the savings quickly enough. Besides, we might have jeopardized our quality and delivery performance by changing suppliers. What we needed was a way to cut the costs of utilizing the resources we already have. This led me to reconsider our method of assigning plants to meet our warehouse requirements. We've decided to try linear programming, which, as I understand it, is a technique that guarantees to minimize the total variable costs of producing and shipping products.

The present method of programming Mackie's manufacturing and warehouse operations involved regular meetings of the four plant managers and warehouse managers. Discussions led to a consensus agreement on which factories would serve which warehouses during future operating periods. These meetings served also to formulate and assess policies and plan market promotion programs.

For the proposed linear program, Mr. Mackie requested the controller and traffic manager to obtain the shipping cost data shown in Exhibit 20–1. To obtain data measuring plant capacity available, he telephoned

Exhibit 20–1 Mackie Paint Company Cost Data: Production and Shipments from Factories to Warehouses

			From Factory			Warehouse Requirements (Gallon Per day × 100)
		I	II	III	IV	
To Warehouse		Shipping Cost,		$ per 100 gallons		
	A	4	9	3	6	30
	B	8	3	1	5	60
	C	3	6	7	9	40
	D	2	4	5	8	20
	E	6	5	2	5	10
						160
Factory capacity (Gallons per day × 100)						Total
Normal		34	54	23	80	191
Overtime		10	18	12	20	60
Manufacturing cost ($1 per 100 gallons)						
Normal		22	21	24.	25	
Overtime		26	24	28	27	
Fixed, out-of-pocket Cost, $ per day*		420	700	850	300	

*(for personnel engaged in office, maintenance, test, receiving and shipping activities; also for plant protection, including local taxes)

each of the five plant managers to explain what he wanted, and then sent a memorandum to confirm his request:

> . . . For us to use the transportation model of linear programming, we need a single measure of plant capacity in gallons per day. I realize that actual output rates vary for different types of paints made on the same equipment, and also that total output per day depends on the downtime for cleaning and adjusting the equipment between runs. However, the capacity figure I need will be accurate enough if you will compute it in the following manner:
>
> 1. Consider your (pigment) dispersing mills to be the key determinants of factory capacity, and calculate the average gallons per hour of equivalent blended paint the mills can produce. This average should be weighted by the forecasted product-mix as follows: 40 percent for series 1,000 paints (flat-coat outside paints); 35 percent for series 3,000 paints (semigloss, inside paint); 25 percent for series 5,000 paints (inside, glossy enamel paint).
> 2. Estimate the average amount of time (in hours) you shut down a mill for run changeover work, including cleaning out the materials setting and adjusting the rolls, and putting in the first load of new materials to be dispersed in the next run. Also, estimate the average number of such changeovers by the number of mills in your plant, and then multiply this result by your above estimate of average changeover time per mill. This figure should be the average hours per day for mill-run changeover time for your plant. Subtracting this from eight hours leaves the average productive time available for your mills.
> 3. Plant capacity in gallons per day is then (1) × (2) . . .

Requesting the manufacturing cost data Mr. Mackie said to Mr. R. A. Fetter, controller,

Bob, the cost data we need for each plant have to represent the average of the variable expenses per 100 gallons produced at that plant. I'd like your data to reflect whatever differences we have to pay for freight on purchased materials. Use your own judgment about the mix of materials you include in the input-output unit of equivalent standard 100 gallons; I told the plant managers to assume a 40–35–25 percentage breakdown of our three basic types of paints. You'll probably want to analyze the mix further, but I leave that to you. As far as labor and overhead costs are concerned, you know better than I that less than half our factory payroll is a strictly variable expense. I would like to have two sets of cost data, though; the cost per 100 gallons produced at each plant on straight time and the other cost on the basis of overtime.

Mr. Fetter's cost data are summarized in Exhibit 20–1. Mr. Mackie used the latest monthly shipping forecasts furnished by Mr. Vernon's assistant sales manager. These data are also summarized on Exhibit 20–1.

Problems:

1. Set up and solve Mr. Mackie's linear programming problem.
2. Discuss the validity and assumptions relevant to the application of linear programming in this case.
3. Outline the specific actions indicated by the solution to the problem and state arguments supporting these actions.
4. Based on the results of the linear program what are the effects on total costs of closing Factory III?
5. Discuss possible adverse effects on morale if Mr. Mackie replaces the operations planning meetings of factory and warehouse managers with his linear programming technique. How might these morale problems be avoided?

Mesa Sporting Goods

Introduction and History

The Mesa Sporting Goods Company was a distributor of over 12,000 items of sporting equipment to small retailers. The company started operations in 1946 from a small warehouse but as the business prospered, it outgrew its facilities and a 50,000 square foot warehouse was constructed in 1970 near the original facilities. These new facilities were well conceived with ample shelves and a rectangular conveyor system to transport picked orders to the packing and shipping areas. Orders requiring pricing labels attached to the items, a service provided for several select customers, were shunted off to a marking table and then returned to the packing benches.

In 1972 the company purchased a minicomputer system for order entry and to assist in tracking sales and inventory. Until this time, no perpetual inventory records were kept. The buyers, with general forecasts from the sales manager, bought what they believed would sell. Quarterly physicals were taken to monitor inventory investment and for the preparation of financial statements. Thus, there was essentially no sales history maintained nor any stockout data on what could have been sold.

This case was prepared by J. G. Carlson of the University of Southern California for classroom discussion and is not intended to illustrate either effective or ineffective administrative practice. Reprinted with permission.

The initial perpetual inventory system set-up on the computer kept year-to-date sales and balance-on-hand data. Reorder points and reorder quantities provided by the buyers were loaded into the initial data base. Because these parameters were guestimates with no means of updating them, the inventory reports, with special notation of items having reached their reorder point, lacked credibility and were ignored by the buyers.

Early Problems

The initial inventory computer program developed by an outside software house had several errors. For example, it took some months and several spot physicals to discover why some of the inventory balances were incorrect. The error was traced to the programmer's assumption that negative balances "were impossible" and therefore these balances were automatically reset to zero. However, issue transactions might often be processed before receipt transactions thus causing a temporary negative book inventory. If these negative quantities are set to zero, further issues would not be recorded and any subsequent receipt would yield an erroneous balance.

The credibility gap between the computer reports and data kept by the buyers continued for several years. Dan, the senior buyer, continued to keep his own log on what he bought from each vendor for each product for each buying cycle. He and the two assistant buyers appeared to delight in attempting to prove the computer report wrong. An item might show a zero balance on the report but perhaps twenty would be on the shelf. The data entry personnel would try to track down the discrepancy only to discover that the computer had processed the sales order but the physical "pick" had not as yet occurred. Data Processing, defensive at first, tired of these special audit requests and developed a validating system based on periodic cycle counting of each vendor's items.

During the implementation of the system, Mesa discovered that there were dozens of procedural changes that had to be documented and communicated in order to make a computer-based system work even in the simpler distribution environment. Management had failed to foresee the "extra" computer processing required and the necessity for everyone in the system—sales, data entry and warehouse personnel—to be aware of the sensitivity of the system and the responsibility for its success. For example, Mesa found that order picking time was reduced to one half if the pick lists were in location sequence. Thus, it was necessary to include the bin location for each item in the Item Master. Items, however, would sometimes be moved from one bin to another without informing the computer. On one occasion, the Sales Department pulled a group of fishing reels and rods into packages and put them in a separate location without notifying the computer. The individual item balances became invalid plus the special packages were essentially "lost."

Turnover vs. Stockouts

Until 1975 management had concentrated on trying to increase the number of inventory turns rather than reducing stockouts. Because demand data were not being accumulated by the minicomputer system, Mesa was not aware that 23 to 27% of total sales were lost due to stockouts ("zeros"). Mr. Kern, the controller and systems designer, believed the stockout problem was much more important than increasing inventory turnover. To assist in analyzing the inventory to prevent stockouts, a consulting firm offered to classify the inventory into A, B and C and perform a comprehensive inventory analysis on which to base reorder points and reorder quantities. For their proposal, the consultants accumulated some data and performed a sample analysis to show the potential value of developing an inventory profile and computing reorder points and economic reorder quantities from historical data. However, Mr. Kern believed that not only could he perform the complete analysis, but he could write the routines that would maintain a continuous inventory analysis and perform sales and cost analyses as well. The money that would have been spent on the one-time analysis was then committed to upgrading the computer system and adding significant programs to maintain seasonal indexes necessary in managing sporting goods purchases, inventories and sales.

System Design

The computer system to be installed during 1976 was designed such that as the sales orders were received by phone or mail each day they could be entered directly into the computer via CRT's. As each line entry was made, the inventory level was to be checked by the system. Only the amount available was to be printed on the generated pick list. If there was insufficient stock to fill the order, the amount available was to be shipped and the stock out data stored as a "lost sale," printed out on a daily "zeros" report and included as part of a weekly action report and a monthly sales and inventory analysis.

Forecasting was done in a very aggregate manner by management judgment as to whether the dollar sales of a product group would increase, decrease, or remain the same. The need for a technique that offered more visibility and understanding of probable future demand was apparent. A comprehensive way of viewing individual items as well as item groups for purchasing decisions was needed. Mr. Kern had read a little about MRP (Material Requirements Planning) and believed that the logic would be appropriate to distribution as well as manufacturing.

However, he was somewhat unsure as to how to gather the necessary data for a complete purchasing, order-entry and sales information system redesign. The direct involvement of the buyers in the design and how the buyers should be educated in the concepts of Time Phased Order Planning (TPOP) was a major question. A TPOP system (MRP applied to distribution systems), involves lead time analysis, safety stock decisions, lot sizing, combined purchases, vendor policy interpretation, seasonal indexes, forecasts, demand vs. shipment data, stockouts, carrying costs, provision for deletions, additions, item classification techniques and many more factors. The buyers should be able to have a projection of their decisions over a 12-month planning horizon. However, this should be in the form of a monthly report or in an inquiry mode on a terminal. With an interactive terminal, the buyers could compose their purchase orders as well.

The Procurement Function

In the past, each of the three buyers was assigned several categories of items and their respective vendors. Because sporting goods is a highly seasonal industry and very volatile in several specific product lines, buying was much more complex than just placing replenishment orders or processing purchase requisitions submitted by others. Fishing tackle is especially variable merchandise at the individual item level. The popularity of a particular lure can change overnight depending on word-of-mouth fishing stories, articles in sports periodicals and newspapers, etc. Sport guns and ammunition are also a difficult category to manage as their demand is a function of hunting seasons, game availability, skeet shooting popularity and policies of the suppliers.

Categorizing 12,000 items into useful subgroups for analysis is difficult. At present, two groupings are made whereby each item is assigned into one of 77 categories and which can then be summarized into 12 major groups. These groupings do not permit sufficient sensitivity for identifying changes in market demand among items. This is where the years of experience from both selling and buying sporting goods helps Dan. It was his opinion, no computer analysis or report could ever replace human experience in making optimum buying decisions.

In this type of business, no back-orders are permitted and substitutions are rare and made only with customer approval. The old monthly summary sales report is shown in Exhibit 21–1.

The "dated stock" and "early bird" options offered by several vendors was a case in point. It could not be practical to "transfer" all he knew to the computer for critical judgment buying decisions. "Dated stock" plans are those whereby if the distributor orders early and accepts pre-season delivery, the manufacturer not only post-dates the invoice by several months but also allows a discount of 5%, 10% or more. "Early Bird" plans are similar to dated stock plans except the invoices are not post-dated. The questions which then arise are: how much to order to take advantage of these plans, whether there is sufficient storage space, what will be the total sales and what will be the sales pattern.

Exhibit 21–1 Year to Date Sales, Cogs & Inventory for 77 Categories

		SALES A	COGS B	INVENTORY C	% B/A	
	MONTH 11 1975					
TACKLE	110 01	4,847	2,721	44	.56	
	111 01	101,665	80,641	36,135	.79	
	112 01	68,364	45,276	45,371	.66	
	113 01	470,670	362,718	183,711	.77	ROD
	114 01	51,745	29,326	78,059	.57	
	115 01	815,157	701,720	121,284	.86	REEL
	118 02	42,928	28,228	61,459	.66	
	119 02	479,431	393,001	66,312	.82	
	120 02	7,321	5,462	4,732	.75	
	121 02	236,931	187,789	41,580	.79	LURE
	122 02	77,138	61,107	29,404	.79	
	123 02	154,587	129,745	36,421	.84	
	124 03	66,032	44,811	9,347	.68	
	125 03	135,745	102,023	35,144	.75	
	126 03	155,389	103,833	52,362	.67	
	127 03	224,118	169,200	37,816	.75	LEADER
	129 03	126,247	102,545	19,194	.81	
	131 03	36,673	26,784	8,019	.73	
	132 03	58,460	32,915	10,091	.56	
	133 03	148,867	105,218	25,753	.71	
	135 03	26,001	16,721	19,257	.64	
CAMPING	201 11	93,747	67,675	25,823	.72	
	203 11	67,374	50,701	10,326	.75	JUG
	205 11	44,800	33,134	4,043	.74	
	207 11	18,279	13,045	6,513	.71	
	209 11	28,256	21,762	8,289	.77	
	211 11	76,796	54,121	16,872	.70	
	213 11	17,336	13,324	3,790	.77	
	215 11	44,351	33,405	6,719	.75	
	217 11	74,106	55,895	20,032	.75	
	219 11	7,024	5,324	3,503	.76	
	301 12	32,020	26,897	16,166	.84	
	303 12	11,181	8,134	1,394	.73	
	305 12	38,903	27,123	8,471	.70	VEST
	307 12	57,276	41,207	12,367	.72	
ATHLETIC	401 10	35,585	26,312	15,470	.74	
	403 10	49,076	36,044	7,007	.73	BASKETBALL
	405 10	49,908	36,910	8,626	.74	
	407 10	156,709	107,879	47,006	.69	
	409 10	86,505	64,665	27,372	.75	
	411 10	20,376	14,103	7,519	.69	
	413 10	261,640	193,922	43,605	.74	
	415 10	214,859	157,555	24,786	.73	
	417 10	237,509	191,418	31,238	.81	

Dan offered the following challenge to the computer: a vendor has announced that next year, whatever Mesa ordered during January would be delivered sometime before April. Payment need not be made until October 1 and a discount of 10% would be allowed on a dated order. For example, footballs cost $10.00 each and total annual sales are about 10,000 units. Though there is sufficient storage space to accommodate this "dated stock," should Mesa take advantage of this offer? "This can't be solved until you give the computer more data," said the controller. But Dan muttered that he didn't have any more data than this yet he had to make these types of decisions and make them promptly—he couldn't wait for a computer analysis.

An irritating problem arose occasionally with respect to the handling of "freebies" and other promotional and incentive schemes devised by manufacturers. Average costing methods were used which can easily be distorted by large variations in the costs of items purchased. For example, one vendor offered a dozen fishing rods gratis if 24 dozen were ordered. The 24 dozen arrived, were stocked and paid for. A month later, another dozen arrived with no purchase order documentation and no invoice. An accounting clerk suggested several alternatives: (1) enter them as an inventory adjustment rather than a receipt, (2) sent them back for credit, (3) give them to employees or salesmen as a bonus, or (4) pass them on to deserving retailers and have them cope with the accounting headaches.

Some Conversion Problems

The younger buyers seemed more flexible and adaptive to having a computer system help them. It was their understanding that a computer system could tell them when to buy an item by scientifically computing a reorder point which, when reached, could signal a reorder. The computer could certainly compute the most economic quantities to reorder. To reduce ordering and shipping costs, the computer, with its on-line display units, should be able to show other items from a vendor which were approaching reorder points so that consolidated purchase orders could be written. When it was explained that the data for these computerized decisions had to be provided by them, they were very disappointed. Someone, somehow must generate the seasonal indexes for 12,000 items and quantify the complexities of the variety of vendor policies. The computer, it was explained, could only provide signals and guidelines and should never be trusted to make decisions automatically. It appeared as though they would have to continue operating approximately in the same manner which even they perceived as being capricious, unmethodical, uninspiring, and unscientific. They had assumed that the new computer would make many of the decisions they presently must make.

With more computer capacity, the buyers could have much more complete descriptions on the reports of the items which they were buying.

Exhibit 21–2 Seasonal Indices by Group

GROUP	1	2	3	4	5	MONTH 6	7	8	9	10	11	12
109	147	154	155	158	138	165	85	102	69	54	16	18
110	59	72	93	116	101	156	152	135	116	88	66	37
111	77	68	118	125	110	165	146	115	129	55	31	35
112	190	129	128	128	115	119	118	71	58	31	47	64
113	100	56	111	125	75	106	112	146	95	103	80	85
114	77	64	88	146	114	170	154	108	58	65	43	112
115	79	73	116	121	118	143	128	109	78	74	82	75
116	65	42	42	106	80	94	71	122	58	165	174	177

However, the buyer who was revising the nomenclature on his own time, abandoned the project because it now appeared as if the computer would not be of much help in identifying what to buy, how much to buy and when to buy.

For computer-based purchase planning to be performed each of the 12,000 items needed its own seasonal index table. Seasonal indices could be developed from history but the data for each month was kept on a separate magnetic tape. To get a perspective of the seasonal indices, a computer routine was written which computed the indices from manually prepared data taken from twelve monthly reports of each of the 77 categories. A partial list of these indices appears in Exhibit 21–2.

Based on this output, the controller had to make a decision with respect to generating the individual item indices. Either the individual item could be represented initially by the index of its category *or* a routine would have to be written to analyze the individual items from the magnetic tapes. Each tape represented one month and the data was in year-to-date format so subtractions would be required and the data accumulated on a temporary file. The history tapes also had items that were added or deleted during the year which would present a serious programming and reconciliation problem. The tapes had only sales data and no stock out data. The existing computer record for each item was also completely full so that any additional item data would have to be stored separately. This separate item data could later be merged with other item master data when the new system was installed, but this appeared to be a very risky procedure. It was also questionable whether the minicomputer had the capacity to process all the data in a reasonable amount of time. Thus, the controller elected to use the category indexes for the initial loading of the data base.

After the indexes for the 77 categories were loaded onto the new system as indices for the appropriate individual items, an exponential smoothing routine would be needed which would update these initial indexes as each month was closed. The update procedure for each of the 12,000 items would be as follows:

D(T) = Actual demand for Period T
I(T) = Current Seasonal Index (Initially from its category Index)
C(T) = Current Smoothed Deseasonalized Demand
J(T) = Actual Index or Actual Demand / Average Demand = D(T)/C(T)
A   = Index Smoothing Factor
The computer statement could be:
I(T) Revised = I(T) + A3[J(T)−I(T)] = I(T) + A3[D(T)/C(T) − I(T)].[1]

While the controller was trying to get better insight into the buyer's problems and desires, the computer routines from the smaller system were being converted to the new computer system. Although the original routines were written in BASIC computer language, the BASIC of the new computer was slightly different and much more comprehensive. Simultaneously, new routines were being written to make use of an expanded data base which would include each item's seasonal index, its demand in addition to its sales and other useful statistics.

TPOP Education

To appreciate the ability of the proposed system to help monitor what was happening, the controller developed a TPOP (Time Phased Order Planning) exercise. Two years of sales data for a picnic jug were collected and seasonal indexes computed and averaged. Using the index, an exponential smoothing factor of .2, and an expected average demand of 100 units, the demand in successive months could be iteratively forecasted.

Index Generation For A Picnic Jug

Month	1	2	3	4	5	6	7	8	9	10	11	12	Units/Mo.
1973	0.9	0.9	0.6	0.6	1.1	1.9	2.0	1.5	0.9	0.5	0.5	0.5	75
1974	0.9	0.7	0.5	0.6	1.2	2.1	1.9	1.5	1.1	0.5	0.4	0.6	100
Average	0.9	0.8	0.5	0.6	1.2	2.0	1.9	1.5	1.0	0.5	0.4	0.7	1.0

With the above data, twelve months of experience could be simulated by operating the TPOP system as if the experimenter was both decision

---

[1] If T = 3, (March) A = .3, D(3) = 72, C(3) = 100 and the current index I(3) for March for an item was .6, then the updated index for March of next year for the individual item would be: I(3) = .6 + .3(.72 − .60) = .64.

maker and computer. With the actual data for 1975[2] what would be the successive TPOP displays as each month's actuals are revealed one month at a time? The computer routine generated the displays for each month but the buyers used a score sheet shown in Exhibit 21–3.

TPOP Display—Month 1

ITEM		NAME		COST	PRICE	VEND		SAFETY	ROQ	LEAD
3008		JUG, PICNIC		5.00	8.50	1234		25	108	3
Index		0.90	0.80	0.50	0.60	1.20	2.00	1.90	1.50	1.00
Period	0	1	2	3	4	5	6	7	8	9
FCST.DMD		90	80	50	60	120	200	190	150	100
SCHED.RCTS		108	108	0	0	0	0	0	0	0
AVAIL	61	79	107	57	-3	-123	-323	-513	-663	-763
PLND ORDS		108	108	216	108	216	108	0	108	0

This display suggests that the buyer place an order now (Planned Order for Month 1, January) for 108 units for delivery in April. If the Scheduled Receipt of 108 was received and the actual demand for the month of January is simulated as 96 units, the TPOP as of February 1 then would be computed and displayed and the buyer decides how many units to reorder for delivery during May.

TPOP Display—Month 2   REC'D = 108   January Demand = 96

ITEM		NAME		COST	PRICE	VEND		SAFETY	ROQ	LEAD
3008		JUG, PICNIC		5.00	8.50	1234		25	108	3
Index		0.80	0.50	0.60	1.20	2.00	1.90	1.50	1.00	0.50
Period	1	2	3	4	5	6	7	8	9	10
FCST.DMD		81	51	61	122	203	193	152	101	51
SCHED.RCTS		108	0	108	0	0	0	0	0	0
AVAIL	73	100	49	96	-25	-228	-420	-572	-674	-724
PLND ORDS		108	216	216	108	108	0	108	0	108

This is repeated for a number of months with the separate score sheet tallying the costs of inventory carried, the stockouts incurred, number of

[2]

		1	2	3	4	ACTUAL 1975 DEMAND 5	6	7	8	9	10	11	12
1975		96	97	25	27	84	163	90	68	52	31	22	44

Exhibit 21–3 Simulation Worksheet

Cost=$5.00 LT=3 Fcst=1200 *W(T)=Exp. Smoothed Avg., $F(T+1)=\{W(T)+.2(\frac{D(T)}{I(T)}-W(T)\}I(T+1)$

Orig. Fcst. W(1)=100	90	80	50	60	120	200	190	150	100	50	40	70
Rev. Fcst. W(T)*I(T+1)	90	81										
Period/Index T I(T)	1 0.90	2 0.80	3 0.50	4 0.60	5 1.20	6 2.00	7 1.90	8 1.50	9 1.00	10 0.50	11 0.40	12 0.70
Beg'g OnHand	61											
Receipts (Sched)	108	108		108								
Sub-Total	169											
Demand	96											
End'g OnHand	73											
Qty. Ord'd (for T+3)	108											
Holding Cost (2%/Mo)	7											
Ordering Cost ($20/Ord.)	20											
Stockout Cost (50%/Lost Cost)												
Cumulative Costs	27											

orders placed, and the total operating cost (see Exhibit 21–3). (The reader is invited to complete the exercise by entering decisions and the actuals month-by-month. No cheating.) This "compressed-time" exercise was supposed to help the buyers with their day-to-day decision making.

Present Situation

The simulation was enlightening for the buyers, but they still wanted the computer to tell them the specific quantity to reorder, and when to reorder. Safety stock was still quite arbitrarily determined by such guidelines as one month's supply, one half of the usage during lead time or by the sales manager's best guess. An ongoing measurement of variability of demand from forecast, or forecast error, was not to be performed. A mean absolute deviation (MAD) statistic could assist in predicting the service level achievable from the safety stock investment but top management was not interested in sophisticated statistics—they wanted results in the form of fewer lost sales and less inventory.

The decision of what to stock, when to reorder and how much to reorder is very difficult when dealing with 12,000 items. The new computer reports were to keep management generally appraised of stockouts, shipments and inventory investments. Stockouts, however, still averaged about 24% of sales during 1976 and the inventory was still growing as sales increased. The president upon discovering this issued an ultimatum that unless inventory was reduced by 10% and stockouts did not exceed 16% by May 1977, there would be some changes in personnel.

The buyers, Mr. Kern noted:

. . . must get more involved in the system design to communicate and maintain the special categories of information needed. Otherwise the data, reports and signals will never be valid; nor what the buyers need to help themselves. They are still very reluctant and won't take the time to sit down and discuss their needs and learn about the capabilities of a computerized system. They still view the computer as a threat because it appears to be monitoring more and more of their daily decisions and performance. Computer messages such as STOCKOUT and NOTHING ON ORDER may not help their ego but they should help the buyers reach our mutual objectives.

Questions:

1. What does a buyer at Mesa really need in the way of a daily, weekly and monthly report in order to do a better job?
2. Besides avoiding unnecessary inventory checks for the buyers, what does cycle counting do for a company?
3. If Mesa does not have to pay until October for jugs (in the exercise) which they order before April, how many should they order in January, February and March?
4. How would the controller determine the trade-off between stockouts and overstocking?

Metropolitan Power Company

22

The Company

Metropolitan Power Company was a medium size electric utility company serving a metropolitan midwest city and the surrounding communities. The following statistics indicate the scale of the company's operation in the previous year.

General

Area Served	800 square miles
Population	1,700,000
Communities	150
Total Operating Revenue	$108,100,000
Total Payroll	$ 33,000,000
Fuel Costs	$ 17,000,000
Taxes Paid	$ 19,000,000

Stockholders of common stock	52,000 +
Shares of common stock outstanding	13,200,000
Earnings per share of common stock	$1.58
Dividends per share of common stock	$1.18
Number of employees—December 31	4461

This case was prepared by Professor Gordon K. C. Chen of the School of Business Administration, University of Massachusetts, as a basis for classroom discussion and is not designed to present either correct or incorrect handling of administrative problems.

Investment in utility plant	$547,205,271
Investment per employee	$122,664
Construction	$17,800,000

Electric Operations

Generating Stations capacity:	Kilowatts	
Central	518,800	
North	388,000	
South	196,300	
East	275,700	
West	60,000	
Substation	5,100	
Generating Capacity—December 31, 1964	1,444,400	
Tie-line capacity	120,000	kilowatts
Peak load—December 13, 1964	1,225,300	kilowatts

Sales of electricity:	KWH
Residential	1,353,000,000
Commercial	1,779,000,000
Industrial	3,095,000,000
Others	144,000,000
	6,371,000,000

Customers:	
Residential	435,267
Commercial	44,155
Industrial	1,440
Others	1,539
	482,401

Residential services:	
Average use per customer	3,111 KWH
Average revenue per KWH	2.736¢
Electrically heated homes and apartments	201

Steam Operations

Total sales	1,860,832,000 lbs.
Number of Customers	446

The Characteristics of Demand

Like most of the service-conscious utility companies, Metropolitan's management constantly strived to provide instantaneous service to meet the customer's demand and to plan in advance the capacity needed for long-term growth. Because of the unique characteristics, such as the perishability of the product, the importance of the real time response, the long production lead time, which was common in this industry, Metropolitan management was extremely conscious of the importance of producing the right amount of electric energy at the right time.

To achieve the above mentioned production goal, metropolitan tried to estimate its customers' demand as accurately and as quickly as possible. However, the demand for electric energy varied a great deal from time to time and from area to area. The extent to which the demand fluctuated depended largely upon the type of customers and community it served and upon such factors as weather conditions, business activities, community customs, seasonal and secular changes. Although the demand changed widely throughout the day, the week, and the year, utility companies were more concerned with their respective peak loads than the off peak ones. This primarily was due to the fact that once the peak demand was met, the off-peak usage could also be satisfied without additional production planning. It is a common practice among the electric utilities that the generators which have been started for peak loads are not shut down completely during the day time inter-peak periods but are kept running as "spinning reserves" which are to serve as a stand-by capacity for contingencies on the one hand and which, in effect, save the costly restart-up expenses on the other in the event that the demand rises during the inter-peak periods when the generator is shut down.

Purpose and Types of Forecasting

Metropolitan was interested in forecasting its demand for a variety of reasons. For long-range capacity planning and capital budgeting, the company needed to project the probable maximum loads five to ten years in advance. For this purpose, a long-run demand forecast was important.

Demand forecasting was also useful for scheduling major equipment maintenance at the Metropolitan's several power plants. The periodic maintenance of a steam generator could take weeks and could involve the loss of thousands of kilowatts in production capacity. By scheduling its maintenance at a low peak season, Metropolitan was able to balance production without undue excess or under capacity.

From the operating management's point of view, the forecast for the daily peak demand was of vital importance. The information not only aided in planning production such as equipment scheduling, manpower assignments and raw material requirements planning, etc., but also served as a sensitive barometer for the short-run revenue planning and cash flow budgeting. In fact, the daily demand pattern often was used as the basic indicator for making other long and medium range forecasts.

Metropolitan was interested in forecasting demand not only on a day-to-day basis, but also on a minute-to-minute basis. Such a close production control was done for technical as well as economic reasons. Close scrutiny of the load pattern in each generator was a technical necessity, for it had a direct effect on the quality of the energy output, and, in the meantime, it provided the information for the overage or underage of capacity which could be sold or bought through the interconnected systems.

The Forecasting Method

Metropolitan's forecasting system was primarily one of a rule of thumb. Its method took into consideration several elements which the forecaster believed were the contributing factors for the load changes, although the precise effect of each was not certain. Experience had indicated that the day-to-day load seemed to have been influenced by the following factors:

1. The day-of-the-week effect. Experience showed that weekday loads were quite different from those of the weekends, and Saturdays from those of Sundays.
2. The holiday effect. Different load patterns prevailed during various holidays from those of the weekdays and weekends.
3. The business-activity factor. Store hours and the number of shifts operated in the factories and mines all had an effect on the loads.
4. The steel-production factor. Steel mills were the largest consumers of Metropolitan's electric energy. When operating at a normal rate of production, they accounted for about 20 to 22 percent of the total load.
5. Weather forecast. Weather conditions, measured by the indices of temperature, humidity, and cloud cover, had a direct effect on the loads.
6. Special-event factor. Special events other than the regularly scheduled holidays affected the loads considerably from time to time. For example, the load jumped to an unusually high peak when the United States sent the first astronaut into space. Other special events, such as the presidential elections, showed a similar effect.

Since so many factors affected the demand for electricity, how, then, could the company plan their day-to-day production with any degree of accuracy? Through years of experience, MPC's systems engineers had used a simple rule of the thumb to forecast their daily peaks loads. Briefly, it may be summarized as follows:

1. Base loads, i.e., basic loads under normal conditions, were established for weekdays, Saturdays and Sundays. They were estimated at 1,000,000, 800,000 and 600,000 kilowatts, respectively.
2. The loads for holidays and special event days were estimated individually on a current basis.
3. The base loads were adjusted upward or downward depending upon the temperature forecast for the next period. Temperatures between 50° and 65° Fahrenheit were considered normal, no adjustment was needed. When the forecast was equal to or below 50°, or equal to or above 65°,

an increment of 1000 kilowatts was added to the base estimate for each marginal degree.

4. A fair day was regarded as a norm; no adjustment was made to the base load. An increment of 10,000 kws. for partly cloudy, 20,000 kws. for cloudy and 30,000 kws. for rainy or snowy days was added to the base load.

5. Two methods were used for estimating the loads of the steel mills. The major mills usually served an advanced notice on the number of turns (shifts) they expected to operate the following day. In addition, special load meters were installed in the MPC's central dispatching room to register the actual usage at the mills at all times. The steel loads under normal operating conditions were accounted for in the base load. No adjustment was made unless some major changes, such as the steel or auto plant strikes, had taken place, in which case estimates were made separately. No formal records were kept for the metered steel loads.

6. The company had experienced three peaks a day during the recent years. They took place in the morning, afternoon and evening. The forecasts for these peaks were made one day in advance in order to allow ample time to start the boilers. For this reason, the forecast for the first peak was most important, as the actual conditions in the next day might be different from what was expected. If the margin of error in the morning peak estimate appeared too large, adjustments were usually made in the subsequent peaks accordingly.

Up to this year, the forecasting system just described had worked fairly well. The forecast errors between the actual and the estimate ran on the average of about 3 to 4 percent. While the error margin was considered satisfactory as compared to other companies in the industry, Mr. H. A. Ward, the Fuel and Results Engineer of MPC, was interested in seeking further improvements of the forecasts, possibly with the aid of a statistical or computer method. Exhibit 22–1 is the Load Estimate Error Record for the first 232 days in the previous year.

Exhibit 22–1 Load Estimates

January

Day	Date	Load			Weather			Note
		Estimate	Actual	% Error	Cloud Cover	Temperature	Humid.	
M	1	·600[2]	677	− 13	PC[3]	26	72	Holiday
T	2	1100	1172	− 6	S	32	81	—
W	3	1150	1138	+ 1	C	33	75	—
T	4	1110	1071	+ 4	F	46	59	—
F	5	680	1058	+ 2	F	46	60	—
S	6	840	828	+ 1	R	44	93	—
S	7	610	623	− 2	C	31	85	—
M	8	1190	1149	+ 3	C	28	85	—
T	9	1160	1180	− 2	F	12	58	—
W	10	1180	1153	+ 2	F	2	40	—
T	11	1160	1168	− 1	F	6	50	—
F	12	1152	1147	0	F	13	48	—
S	13	860	902	− 5	C	25	48	—
S	14	620	609	+ 2	F	45	34	—
M	15	1125	1176	− 4	R	40	36	—
T	16	1190	1143	+ 4	C	27	63	—
W	17	1145	1145	0	F	22	46	—
T	18	1185	1166	+ 1	F	17	62	—
F	19	1175	1151	+ 2	C	18	57	—
S	20	880	851	+ 3	C	21	74	—
S	21	620	649	− 4	C	33	83	—
M	22	1170	1166	0	R	48	89	—
T	23	1180	1150	− 3	F	21	59	—
W	24	1160	1130	+ 3	C	33	58	—
T	25	1160	1115	+ 4	F	37	70	—
F	26	1125	1162	− 3	R	35	91	—
S	27	860	834	+ 3	PC	32	66	—
S	28	650	627	+ 4	C	24	55	—
M	29	1135	1181	0	S	21	86	—
T	30	1125	1184	0	S	24	81	—
W	31	1145	1106	+ 3	F	10	59	—

NOTE:

1. These estimates are made for the morning—9 a.m. to noon—peaks only

2. Indicates kilowatt hours

3. Codes for cloud covers: F = Fair, PC = Partly Cloudy, C = Cloudy, R = Rain, S = Snow, ST = Storm.

Exhibit 22–1 (continued)

February

Day	Date	Load			Weather			Note
		Estimate	Actual	% Error	Cloud Cover	Temperature	Humid.	
T	1	1180	1170	+ 1	S	17	84	—
F	2	1185	1114	+ 6	C	21	79	—
S	3	875	818	+ 6	F	37	79	—
S	4	600	545	+ 5	PC	52	72	—
M	5	1170	1150	+ 2	R	49	88	—
T	6	1180	1179	0	PC	16	66	—
W	7	1180	1138	+ 4	PC	9	58	—
T	8	1180	1124	+ 5	PC	32	41	—
F	9	1160	1131	+ 3	S	30	89	—
S	10	850	847	0	F	14	67	—
S	11	625	632	− 1	C	15	49	—
M	12	1190	1165	+ 2	C	23	77	—
T	13	1175	1121	+ 4	C	25	69	—
W	14	1130	1135	0	C	31	76	—
T	15	1140	1120	+ 2	C	25	67	—
F	16	1130	1128	0	S	30	92	—
S	17	850	852	0	C	31	61	—
S	18	645	606	+ 3	C	31	51	—
M	19	1170	1126	+ 4	F	50	83	—
T	20	1160	1194	− 3	S	26	72	Astro. Day
W	21	1160	1137	+ 2	S	28	89	—
T	22	1150	1088	+ 5	PC	47	74	—
F	23	1125	1110	+ 1	C	27	78	—
S	24	845	852	− 1	F	24	85	—
S	25	625	616	+ 1	F	36	64	—
M	26	1130	1172	− 4	R	50	87	—
T	27	1140	1149	− 1	C	33	89	—
W	28	1150	1120	+ 3	C	35	94	—

Exhibit 22—1 (continued)

March

| | | Load | | | Weather | | | |
Day	Date	Estimate	Actual	% Error	Cloud Cover	Temperature	Humid.	Note
T	1	1140	1158	− 1	F	20	55	—
F	2	1155	1131	+ 2	F	18	48	—
S	3	850	819	+ 4	F	30	33	—
S	4	625	575	+ 8	F	33	17	—
M	5	1165	1156	+ 1	S	30	85	—
T	6	1165	1140	+ 2	S	32	82	—
W	7	1140	1090	+ 4	F	30	69	—
T	8	1135	1121	+ 1	C	33	49	—
F	9	1130	1124	+ 1	S	30	87	—
S	10	850	839	+ 1	C	36	74	—
S	11	625	560	+10	F	42	66	—
M	12	1150	1083	+ 6	F	49	77	—
T	13	1140	1146	− 1	C	38	77	—
W	14	1120	1123	0	C	35	83	—
T	15	1130	1128	0	C	32	69	—
F	16	1110	1119	− 1	S	32	61	—
S	17	850	831	+ 2	F	39	64	—
S	18	600	623	− 4	F	42	43	—
M	19	1140	1169	− 3	C	38	63	—
T	20	1140	1106	+ 3	C	44	76	—
W	21	1140	1112	+ 2	R	42	86	—
T	22	1130	1101	+ 3	C	43	82	—
F	23	1100	1086	+ 1	C	42	97	—
S	24	830	812	+ 2	F	45	45	—
S	25	610	595	+ 2	F	51	32	—
M	26	1120	1103	+ 2	PC	51	29	—
T	27	1120	1086	+ 3	F	47	27	—
W	28	1100	1094	+ 1	F	55	34	—
T	29	1100	1047	+ 5	F	69	26	—
F	30	1090	1105	− 1	R	56	77	—
S	31	830	881	− 6	R	37	88	—

Exhibit 22–1 (continued)

April

Day	Date	Load			Weather			Note
		Estimate	Actual	% Error	Cloud Cover	Temperature	Humid.	
S	1	620	648	− 5	S	32	88	—
M	2	1150	1136	+ 1	F	38	50	—
T	3	1110	1127	− 1	PC	38	51	—
W	4	1110	1086	+ 2	F	45	40	—
T	5	1120	1090	+ 3	F	58	35	—
F	6	1090	1077	+ 1	R	50	87	—
S	7	860	819	+ 8	R	54	90	—
S	8	625	617	+ 1	C	52	45	—
M	9	1115	1134	− 2	PC	48	77	—
T	10	1125	1137	− 1	F	55	40	—
W	11	1115	1087	+ 3	C	48	71	—
T	12	1110	1125	− 1	R	42	88	—
F	13	1110	1090	+ 2	R	42	82	—
S	14	840	805	+ 4	F	42	48	—
S	15	650	566	+13	S	32	86	—
M	16	1100	1122	− 1	S	37	48	—
T	17	1120	1104	+ 1	F	43	47	—
W	18	1110	1144	− 3	R	35	89	—
T	19	1115	1058	+ 5	C	53	50	—
F	20	980	858	+12	C	51	43	—
S	21	800	730	+ 8	F	60	33	—
S	22	520	494	+ 5	F	77	34	Easter
M	23	1100	1071	+ 3	C	53	55	—
T	24	1100	1081	+ 2	F	53	33	—
W	25	1085	1047	+ 4	F	73	26	—
T	26	1070	1053	+ 2	F	82	23	—
F	27	1050	1056	− 1	F	77	34	—
S	28	820	791	+ 3	F	82	42	—
S	29	610	549	+11	C	73	51	—
M	30	1080	1095	− 1	F	74	54	—

Exhibit 22-1 (continued)

May

Day	Date	Load Estimate	Load Actual	% Error	Weather Cloud Cover	Weather Temperature	Humid.	Note
T	1	1090	1078	+ 1	C	68	79	—
W	2	1080	1120	− 4	R	62	87	—
T	3	1090	1060	+ 3	F	60	53	—
F	4	1065	1011	+ 5	F	67	37	—
S	5	800	762	+ 5	F	74	33	—
S	6	550	558	− 1	C	62	75	—
M	7	1100	1032	+ 6	F	52	57	—
T	8	1060	1088	− 3	R	48	91	—
W	9	1060	1033	− 2	F	49	61	—
T	10	1050	1011	− 2	C	51	35	—
F	11	1060	1030	+ 3	F	58	53	—
S	12	750	720	+ 4	PC	65	55	—
S	13	550	526	+ 4	F	68	68	—
M	14	1090	1123	− 3	F	77	62	—
T	15	1100	1141	− 4	F	84	53	—
W	16	1160	1165	0	F	85	48	—
T	17	1170	1154	+ 2	F	82	49	—
F	18	1150	1113	+ 3	F	83	46	—
S	19	760	820	− 8	ST	75	60	—
S	20	560	552	+ 1	F	85	51	—
M	21	1140	1140	0	F	73	62	—
T	22	1160	1072	+ 7	F	70	55	—
W	23	1070	1107	− 3	F	79	54	—
T	24	1100	1129	− 2	F	75	49	Space Flight
F	25	1110	1061	+ 4	F	68	47	—
S	26	750	785	− 4	C	67	72	—
S	27	540	524	+ 3	C	65	70	—
M	28	1120	1098	+ 2	R	59	90	—
T	29	1100	1045	+ 5	F	71	64	—
W	30	600	630	− 5	F	78	62	Memorial D.
T	31	1080	1094	− 1	R	66	94	—

Exhibit 22—1 (continued)

June

| Day | Date | Load | | % Error | Weather | | | Note |
		Estimate	Actual		Cloud Cover	Temperature	Humid.	
F	1	1080	1083	0	PC	76	70	—
S	2	780	752	+ 4	C	65	68	—
S	3	540	534	+ 1	F	69	59	—
M	4	1100	1121	− 2	C	70	75	—
T	5	1120	1160	− 3	R	65	90	—
W	6	1135	1082	+ 4	C	68	76	—
T	7	1100	1067	+ 3	F	69	52	—
F	8	1050	1068	− 1	C	73	55	—
S	9	770	792	− 3	PC	79	52	—
S	10	540	534	+ 1	C	70	78	—
M	11	1110	1126	− 2	PC	77	72	—
T	12	1130	1095	+ 3	C	70	78	—
W	13	1100	1072	+ 3	R	59	90	—
T	14	1075	1070	0	C	63	75	—
F	15	1060	1016	+ 4	C	55	83	—
S	16	790	745	+ 6	F	75	55	—
S	17	535	524	+ 2	F	78	57	—
M	18	1140	1121	+ 2	F	80	54	—
T	19	1150	1148	0	PC	76	69	—
W	20	1130	1075	+ 5	PC	66	78	—
T	21	1100	1053	+ 4	PC	65	68	—
F	22	1035	1034	0	F	77	45	—
S	23	760	807	− 7	C	77	61	—
S	24	550	537	+ 2	C	76	74	—
M	25	1125	1097	+ 2	F	78	48	—
T	26	1125	1109	+ 1	PC	73	66	—
W	27	1110	1074	+ 3	F	76	48	—
T	28	1085	1092	− 1	F	81	56	—
F	29	1080	1074	0	F	85	36	—
S	30	605	767	+ 4	PC	86	44	—

Exhibit 22–1 (continued)

July

| Day | Date | Load | | | Weather | | | Note |
		Estimate	Actual	% Error	Cloud Cover	Temperature	Humid.	
S	1	535	546	− 2	PC	78	52	—
M	2	1040	998	+ 4	F	72	42	—
T	3	1020	1032	− 1	R	61	96	—
W	4	520	489	+ 6	C	72	71	Holiday
T	5	1025	953	+ 7	F	76	56	—
F	6	950	964	− 1	F	80	58	—
S	7	720	799	−11	PC	83	65	—
S	8	560	560	0	PC	85	63	—
M	9	1050	1100	− 5	C	73	59	—
T	10	1100	1048	+ 5	F	67	63	—
W	11	1070	1042	− 2	F	77	50	—
T	12	1090	1100	− 1	PC	72	83	—
F	13	1070	1047	+ 2	F	77	40	—
S	14	815	765	+ 6	R	64	87	—
S	15	580	523	+ 9	PC	67	81	—
M	16	1090	1091	0	PC	71	68	—
T	17	1110	1076	+ 3	F	73	68	—
W	18	1080	1093	− 1	F	74	61	—
T	19	1080	1053	+ 3	F	75	47	—
F	20	1050	1059	− 1	F	79	49	—
S	21	780	770	+ 1	PC	78	62	—
S	22	540	529	+ 2	PC	75	58	—
M	23	1115	1103	+ 1	PC	65	93	—
T	24	1120	1051	+ 7	C	65	63	—
W	25	1090	1071	+ 2	C	73	71	—
T	26	1080	1067	+ 1	C	64	70	—
F	27	1070	995	+ 7	F	68	42	—
S	28	770	696	+ 7	PC	75	39	—
S	29	540	534	+ 1	C	72	76	—
M	30	1100	1074	+ 3	C	77	76	—
T	31	1090	1080	+ 1	C	77	60	—

Exhibit 22—1 (continued)

		Load			August Weather			
Day	Date	Estimate	Actual	% Error	Cloud Cover	Temperature	Humid.	Note
W	1	1030	1037	+ 4	F	71	49	—
T	2	1080	1038	+ 4	F	73	37	—
F	3	1040	1032	+ 1	F	79	46	—
S	4	730	772	− 6	C	82	61	—
S	5	560	577	− 3	F	85	59	—
M	6	1080	1114	− 3	F	86	55	—
T	7	1130	1103	+ 2	C	74	74	—
W	8	1075	1068	+ 1	PC	75	66	—
T	9	1080	1044	+ 3	C	69	71	—
F	10	1020	982	+ 4	C	64	58	—
S	11	775	717	+ 6	F	72	47	—
S	12	580	508	+ 1	F	76	56	—
M	13	1110	1114	0	C	71	98	—
T	14	1130	1069	+ 6	C	65	78	—
W	15	1090	1002	+ 9	F	66	61	—
T	16	1050	1079	− 3	F	77	50	—
F	17	1050	1047	0	C	68	81	—
S	18	750	690	+ 8	F	72	41	—
S	19	530	526	+ 1	PC	78	40	—
M	20	1090	1166	-- 6	C	83	55	—
T	21	1170	1123	+ 4	PC	71	87	—

Mr. Clean & Company

23

The Company

Mr. Clean & Company was a small dry cleaning and shirt laundering company serving the Metropolitan New York area. It did its own shirt washing and pressing on the premises, but sent out dry cleaning to other operators. Mr. Clean, by zoning regulations, was limited to the employment of no more than five persons. Shirt finishing was done on both wholesale and retail bases. A competitor with dry cleaning facilities did the cleaning for Mr. Clean, who in turn did the shirt washing and finishing for other cleaners. Mr. Clean charged its wholesale customers 39¢ per shirt and its retail customers 54¢ per shirt. Its retail service on request was 24 hours.

The Shirt Pressing Operations

To perform the shirt pressing task Mr. Clean bought a three-unit Ajax shirt finishing unit five years before for $22,000.00. Life expectancy of the unit was seven to ten years. As part of the mechanical equipment an American Laundry Machine Company (since bought out by Ajax) shirt folder was used. A manufacturer's representative serviced the equipment for $20.00 per month, plus parts, which were infrequently needed.

This case was prepared by Professor Gordon K. C. Chen with the assistance of A. Reppaport for class discussion only. All rights reserved to the author.

To operate the four units two operators were used. Each was paid $3.75 per hour for an eight-hour day. Mr. Clean paid on an hourly wage rate since its experience had shown that piece rate workers pushed too hard for numbers but produced unsatisfactory results. The workers had not unionized.

Based on a revenue job 39¢ per shirt, and a desired production rate of 75 shirts per hour, this yielded a potential revenue of $234.00 per day on a eight-hour day at the wholesale rate. Expenses amounted to $60.00 a day for labor for pressing alone and an equal figure for washing and service. There were monthly rent charges of $360.00, electricity of $220,00, oil $160.00, water $40.00, detergents $80.00, plus an unspecified amount for wrappings. Management felt that 600 shirts or more per day were required to yield a fair return. Securing orders for this many shirts did not present a problem.

On the day under study only 526 shirts were finished. Revenue was down $29.00 from the expected full production of 600.

The problem then was how production could be increased to the desired minimum output of 600 per day. The manufacturer's tests claimed that, with proper handling, well over 600 a day could be achieved. Mr. Clean was willing to settle for 600 and produce a more satisfactory job. As will be shown, machine operation could be timed. However, manufacturer's recommended times had not produced the desired quality finished product.

Operating Procedures

The layout and the positions of men and machines listed below are shown on Exhibit 23–1.

Machine number 1—Sleeve Presser

Machine number 2—Collar and Cuff Presser

Machine number 3—Bosom Presser

Machine number 4—Folder

Operator A worked on machine 1 and 4 and the second operator (operator B) on 2 and 3. Operator A began his operations by mounting the shirt sleeves on a sleeve form of machine no. 1. Cuffs were tacked at top of form. By pressing a button the operator activated the presser to draw the shirt sleeves between metal plates which, by compressed air, closed over sleeves for pressing. Recommended pressing time was 16–18 seconds. Machine was timed to automatically release.

When finished, Operator A removed shirt and placed it on Rest 1. From this point Operator B took shirt and placed it on cuff and collar presser (Machine #2). After smoothing shirt on ironing head, Operator B pressed a button to activate press which closed down (power compressed air) on

Exhibit 23—1 Workspace Layout

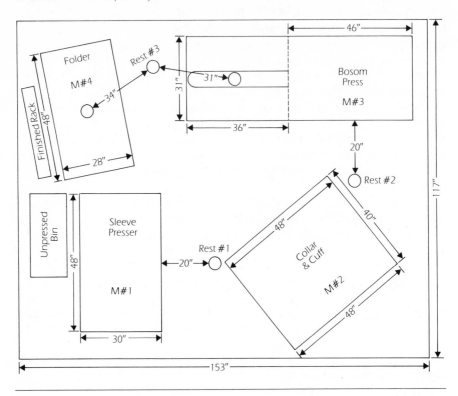

shirt. Recommended pressing time was 20 to 22 seconds. Shirt then was placed on Rest 2 to await bosom presser.

While operator B waited for cuff presser to work she was supposed to be arranging the previous shirt on bosom presser. This pressed remaining part of the shirt. Eighteen seconds between the heated plates of the bosom presser was recommended. An almost identical amount of time was necessary on the average to arrange the shirt on the bosom presser. For the 18 seconds the shirt was in the bosom presser the operator was supposed to be arranging another shirt on cuff press. When the head of the press came forward to press cuffs and collar, the operator was to be arranging shirt on bosom presser or on Rest 3 (see Exhibit 23—1). On the shirt at Rest 3 a pin was put in collar to facilitate folding.

As previously mentioned, Operator A operated the sleeve presser and the folder. While the sleeve presser was actually ironing, the operator was supposed to be at the folding machine. During operation the folding machine needed someone in attendance. While Operator A was at the folder her back was to the sleeve presser. When the presser was released a sound of steam escaping was heard and the operator was supposed to turn around, remove the finished shirt and mount a new one. If Operator B waited for the next shirt in line and Machine 1 was unattended with a finished shirt Operator B removed the shirt and proceeded to place it in position on Machine 2.

Man-Machine Operating Line   A time study was conducted and the results are shown in Exhibits 23–2 and 23–3. Exhibit 23–2, Section A gives the time needed to set the shirt on the sleeve presser, the time spent pressing and idle time. Idle time means that either an operator was not arranging for pressing or the machine was not pressing.

Section B gives the same information for Machine 2.

Section C contains an extra time column. Column three is the time spent by the operator placing the shirt on Rest number 3. If the operator was busy at Rest 3 she could not also be at Machine 2 or 3. To get the total idle time one should add the time spent at Rest 3 plus the idle time cited in Column 4 of Section C.

Exhibit 23–3 shows the actual operating time of the folder and idle time. A third column in this exhibit shows waiting time. There were no shirts waiting at Rest #3. As indicated above Machine 4 needed an operator working on it. Therefore, it had to be idle when Operator A was arranging the shirt on Machine 1.

Exhibit 23–4 shows the "pressing history" of 12 specific shirts. A dash indicates that as soon as one machine completed its function an operator was waiting. She would then remove the shirt and place it on the next unit. If shirt was resting on a machine it was due to the operator being busy at her other unit or not working. There is very little rest on machines.

Exhibit 23–5, Section A shows work and idle time of Operator A. All Operator A's idle time was due to waiting for Operator B to place a shirt on Rest 3 of diagram.

Section B shows work and idle time of Operator B. This section contains a third column because idle time of Operator B was caused by having to wait for either machine 1 or 2. Column heads cite the time waiting for each machine.

Exhibit 23—2 Sample Processing Time for Pressers (in seconds)

Machine 1			Machine 2			Machine 3			
ARRANGE	PRESS	IDLE	ARRANGE	PRESS	IDLE	ARRANGE	PRESS	REST	IDLE
10	35	4	11	27	7	–	20	4	
11	30	4	11	27		18	18	2	
17	31	2	7	27		18	18	3	
7	30	5	14	27	2	17	19	3	
8	34		13	27		20	17	12	
7	33	4	16	26		23	17	5	
10	31	3½	11	27	4	22	18	4	
11	34	4	7	27	4	20	18	4	
11	35	3	15	27	3	18	18	3	
13	34		13	27	6	19	18	6	9
7	33	3	14	27		22	18	6	
10	35		12	27	3	21	18	6	
9	31	3	13	26		19	17	4	
7	33		14	27		19	19	8	4
12	40		12	26		15	21	6	10
10	35		13	30	3	17	21	6	6
14	32		7	28		13	16	4	8
9	31		11	27		18	19	5	
11	37		13	26		14	18	11	13
7	33		13	26	6	14	17	7	
11	36		–	30		19	14	7	5
7	38		7	29		16	17	–	–
6	34		17	26	4	15	17	7	
8	36		–	28		–	20	7	
7	31		–	27		–	21	–	

Exhibit 23—3 Sample Processing Time for Folder (in seconds) Machine 4

Fold	Idle	Wait	Fold	Idle	Wait
26		1	32		1
	20	0		12	0
31		1	34		1
	30	0		8	0
28		1	33		1
	20	0		12	0
29		1	27		1
	4	0		26	0
28		1	27		1
	27	0		22	0
31		1	32		1
	16	0		7	0
34		1	34		1
	5	0		21	0
32		1	37		1
	23	0		0	0
28		1	25		1
	18	0		21	0
38		1	31		1
	4	0		18	0
26		1	27		1
	6	0		18	0
28		1	35		1
	21	0		12	0
33		1			
	10	0			

Exhibit 23—4 Pressing History for 12 Sample Shirts (in seconds)

	A	B	C	D	E	F	G	H	I	J	K	L
Arrange Machine 1	11	–	10	6	8	7	14	11	9	–	11	12
Press Machine 1	30	30	27	26	22	23	23	26	35	8	38	31
Rest On Machine 1	–	–	–	2	–	7	25	–	–	32	–	–
Rest On Rest 1	–	10	27	33	26	32	–	7	11	–	–	–
Arrange Machine 2	5	11	12	11	11	9	14	11	7	9	15	11
Press Machine 2	27	25	25	24	23	26	23	24	24	12	26	23
Rest On Machine 2	7	–	17	–	2	–	–	–	–	23	–	2
Rest On Rest 2	28	21	26	26	29	26	20	25	21	–	30	27
Arrange On Machine 3	8	11	13	21	16	16	12	14	27	23	13	16
Press On Machine 3	17	17	17	18	16	17	17	17	24	11	16	16
Rest On Rest 3	9	12	16	17	17	4	17	8	3	14	16	3
Fold	25	27	22	17	17	16	24	27	29	–	22	21

Exhibit 23-5

Work and Idle Time of Operator A (in seconds)				Work and Idle Time of Operator B (in seconds)					
IDLE	WORK	IDLE	WORK	IDLE #1	IDLE #2	WORK	IDLE #1	IDLE #2	WORK
10						30	7		
	40		46		3				180
6		4				18	5		
	40		42		3				5
4		11				25	5		
	41		85		8				30
17		3				54	–	–	
	43		15		8				125
6		8				60		4	
	42		38	3					20
8		8				70	4		
	45		15	4					35
3		–				30	4		
	255		15	4					40
4		9				65	5		
	3		35	8					60
4		8				16	7		
	95		43	3					30
35		5				48	4		
	135		90	3					35
8		12				40	6		
	44		190	3					30
8		4				34	9		
	45		45	10					40
2		4				90	–	–	–

Nashua River Quality Improvement Program

Professor R. E. White and his team of university students had just presented a briefing-report of their three month reconnaissance study of financing, organization and management of a program to clean up the Nashua River. About 65 attended the briefing session: officials of community, state and Federal governments, executives of manufacturing firms and leaders of organizations concerned with pollution control, conservation, land use and recreation.

In addition to reporting results of his group's study Professor White had formally requested a grant of Federal funds enabling his university to develop a role during the next five years as fact finder and evaluator of plans and operations of the program. He said to the casewriter:

I'm convinced there is a practical (not an academic) role for our university to serve in management of regional development or environmental improvement programs. But there are two key questions: Have we convinced leaders of government, business and community organizations? And if we do obtain the funds needed will our faculty and students from fields of environmental sciences, engineering, public health, business administration, government work effectively together?

Case prepared by Professor R. E. McGarrah for use in schools of business or public management. Based on actual experience.

Excerpt from Report of the New England River Basin Commission

The achievement of water quality goals both in the nation and in New England has been hampered by the diffusion and fragmentation of water quality control efforts. This program seeks to demonstrate that by focusing and directing a concentrated, intergovernmental effort in one river basin and by using maximum available management tools, water quality standards and reclamation of desired uses can be achieved. . . . The Nashua River has been selected for four reasons. First, the Nashua is an interstate tributary, traversing both Massachusetts and New Hampshire. The program involves a typical but manageable range of jurisdictional problems in the course of execution. The Nashua River Basin includes parts of 23 towns in Massachusetts and 4 in New Hampshire. The cities of Fitchburg, Leominster, Gardner are dominant. . . . Once busy and vital industrial centers, these cities are far below the rest of Massachusetts and the nation in terms of growth and many of their mills have closed down. Central cities are neglected and dilapidated and in need of renewal. The industrial decline has led to out-migration from the area and a low socio-economic level.

Second, the Nashua is one of the most polluted streams in New England. The combination of industrial waste from paper and plastic industries and inadequate sewage treatment has made the river virtually useless for recreation, irrigation, fish and wild life. It is aesthetically displeasing in appearance, odor, and in its corrosive effects on paint and foliage near the river. These effects are accentuated because the river flows through the middle of Fitchburg, East Pepperell Massachusetts and Nashua, New Hampshire. The condition became so unbearable that a Nashua River Clean Up Committee was formed by local citizens to press for assistance in pollution control.

Third, the Nashua River basin is sufficiently small to permit a relatively economical and short-term demonstration of a regional, river-basin approach to programs for water quality improvements. A preliminary estimate indicated that $35,850,000 would be needed for water pollution control facilities in eight towns and cities; and about $3 million would be needed during the first five years for planning and management and training of personnel needed to maintain and operate the facilities acquired.

Fourth, the communities and industries of the Nashua Basin have recognized and expressed the need for coordinated action to solve their problem. The coordinated nature of the program will allow for flexibility of choice among economic, institutional, technical and political elements.

The program was launched about a year before Professor White obtained a modest amount for funds enabling his three month reconnaissance study. He engaged two candidates for the MBA degree and the administrative assistant to the Director of the Water Resources Research Center of his university. Professor White served as a project leader. He also served as Director of the Center for Business and Economic Research and professor of management at his university. Commenting on his objectives in undertaking the study, Professor White said:

I want this study to demonstrate that our university group can serve as an "honest broker" or "activating catalyst" needed by organizations involved in this program (and others too).

It's one thing to assert that industries and communities of the Nashua River Basin have recognized and expressed need for coordinated actions to clean up their river. But it's quite another thing for all the special-interest bureaucracies of government (Federal, state, local—and remember there are 27 towns and cities), business organizations, conservation, recreation and other civic groups—to reach a consensus and act productively together in a coordinated manner. At the Federal level there are the Environmental Protection Agency, the Department of Interior, the Department of Commerce (Economic Development Administration) and the Small Business Administration, and not least, the Army Corps of Engineers—each with a vested special interest in the program. And there are counterpart organizations within the Massachusetts and New Hampshire State governments; and more or less within each of the 27 local governments. Within the private business sector there are the large paper and plastic firms (e.g. Weyerhaeuser Paper, St. Regis Paper, Fitchburg Paper owned by Litton Industries, Mead, Foster Grant, American Hoechst, Plastics Division) with plants that discharge industrial waste. And there are the business firms that depend on the travel, recreation, tourist markets that would be improved, if the Nashua were cleaned up; also the real estate developing firms that could make huge profits from investments in land adjacent to the river, which is bound to increase in value after the river is cleaned up. There are bound to be hassles over fair shares of costs of new facilities borne by taxpayers (local, state and Federal) and by private interests (customers or shareholders of companies forced to invest in waste water treatment facilities).

As I perceived it, the management of a regional improvement program like the Nashua River cleanup program had to be democratic. There simply was no single agency with total authority or funds or know-how needed for effective (let alone efficient) planning and control of overall operations. For democratic management to be effective participants need complete, unbiased information. Our university faculty and students possess the technical, economic, political or managerial know-how to gather, assess and disseminate facts needed in planning and controlling operations of the program. Furthermore our university has no vested or biased interests in operations of the program; but, we do have the intellectual and professional respect of all organizations which are or will be participating in the program. So, if we develop the role of primary fact finders and evaluators or mediators of the many issues certain to arise—while retaining the confidence and respect of all parties involved—then I think our university can serve as the "honest broker" or "activating catalyst" needed for participative or democratic management to be effective.

However, our challenge is not just off campus, but on campus as well. For our university group to be effective we've got to get our act together. There are at least a dozen different academic department or administrative offices that are separately engaged in some way with some special aspect of urban or environmental research. They are not coordinated. Instead each focuses on its own specialized interests in the scientific, engineering, sociological, political, managerial or economic aspects of problems of urban and environmental improvements. Our Nashua River project team has to have faculty and students willing to work together as a truly interdisciplinary enterprise. We'll have to collect and analyze facts in economic, scientific, political as well as practical terms. And we'll have to demonstrate our abilities to present comprehensive and well-integrated assessments of operating problems encountered in the Nashua Program. However, I'm confident that we can do this, even though our past record of interdisciplinary cooperation and enterprise is not good. Members of our project-team will realize that to serve our clientele and earn the reputation and grant-renewals all desire, they will have to cooperate and work together as a team as never before.

For their reconnaissance study Professor White and his team visited with officials of town and city government, state government, industry and conservation organizations. Their focus was mainly on financing, organization and management, less on the scientific or technical aspects of the program. The group budgeted funds to pay for a luncheon for those officials at the conference center of their university. Professor White said he thought those officials might be more willing to speak candidly about the program if they came to the "neutral grounds and forum" of the university to discuss the findings by his project team.

The briefing-report focused on three "key issues": reconciling purposes of conservation with those of business and economic development; relations between local industry and government; and regional cooperation by communities. The report also emphasized the importance of unbiased fact-finding and evaluations needed for effective decision making by the leaders of the many and diverse groups involved in the program. In his introductory remarks Professor White said:

Our only purpose is to gather, analyze and evaluate facts of the program. We have no vested interests in the program. In the process of asking questions and offering comments we were struck by the apparent lack of information various officials had about each other's plans to improve the program. So we hope to demonstrate a useful role our university could play by providing reliable information needed for officials to make participatory management work effectively.

He then turned the briefing to Paul Page, who had just completed his MBA while serving as a member of the project team. Paul described efforts of the Nashua River Watershed Association as soon as possible to acquire land or rights to land use for a proposed Greenway. This would be a strip of land 50–100 yards wide along both banks of the river preserved permanently for open-space recreation and conservation. Paul said:

Although traditionally business and conservation groups have opposed each other on questions of land acquisition and use, we find that in the long run their interests are the same, namely the increase in value of land and its uses. By providing public access to the waterway we believe that land values and economic activity in areas immediately adjacent to the greenway will be increased by amounts far greater than if the greenway were not provided. By avoiding the development of honky tonk atmosphere and the concentration of riverbank ownership in the hands of few landowners, the benefits from the Nashua River cleanup program will be increased. Our university group is planning to research trends in land values and economic activity in areas immediately adjacent to land preserved for conservation and open-spacer recreation—as compared with areas not so preserved.

Next, David Peretti, another MBA candidate discussed findings on community relationships. David said:

In Town A we found industry and local government work very closely together. Industry initiated an offer to help finance the preliminary engineering study, and later offered land at no cost for the site of the waste treatment plant. The local government benefited by taking advantage of the skills industrial firms contributed pursuant to designing, staffing and operating the technical facilities needed for cleanup of the river. Industrial firms gained by pooling their funds with public funds and entering into a long term contract for further improvements.

In Town B managers of industrial firms and municipal agencies discussed plans and designs for new waste water treatment equipment. But industry had acquired and installed its own equipment.

In two other towns local industries and government have chosen to be almost completely independent. In fact we noted rather strong antagonisms between business and government officials. In these towns progress has seriously lagged behind that observed in Towns A and B. And indications are that the costs of cleanup for these two towns will greatly exceed costs incurred by private and public concerns for cleanup in Towns A and B.

Arnold Schneider, the administrative assistant to the Director of the University's Water Resources Research Center gave the third major point of the report, advantages of regionalized approaches:

Let me stress that we do not advocate a centralized organization or a single regional approach to all problems. We know of a town whose school expenses jumped by 65 percent when it joined a regional school system. Economies of scale are not automatic. But we believe there are significant advantages when two or more towns decide to pool their efforts to acquire land, facilities, funds, and organized skills needed.

There are tasks of selecting, training and organizing personnel. It might be more economical and efficient to have a single, highly skilled maintenance and repair crew and a single stock of supplies or spare parts needed for operating waste water treatment plants. There are technical, financial and legal tasks involved in contracting for engineering and cost studies; specifying and evaluating contractors' bids, negotiating contract terms, auditing contractors' expenses. Each town neither needs nor can afford full-time engineers, cost accountants, lawyers or managers for its waste treatment facilities acquisition program. There are benefits from establishing a general information center for advisory or referral services on technical, cost or legal matters. And we believe our university group could be expanded so that faculty and qualified students in environmental science, engineering government, law as well as finance and management could work in the field to provide management information services needed by organizations participating in the program.

Professor White ended the briefing-presentation by thanking officials for cooperating with his project-group.

In his proposal for the U.S. Department of Interior to fund his university's involvement during the next five years in the Nashua River cleanup program Professor White made the following points:

We have obtained agreement by important officials to serve on an Advisory Committee to our University Project: a Senior Staff Associate of the New England River Basins Commission; Staff member of the New England Regional Commission; the Executive Secretary of the New England Interstate Water Pollution Control Commission; and the President of the Nashua River Watershed Association. We have also made arrangements for collaboration with the University of New Hampshire—its Resources Development Center and its Water Resources Research Centers, and Institute of Natural and Environmental Resources and its School of Business and Economics. We would perform surveys of socio-economic facts or opinions affecting various aspects of issues raised by the program. We would conduct tests of the reliability of water quality measurement procedures; design training programs for operating and maintenance personnel; provide information gathering and analytical services; and conduct informal conferences, seminars or colloquia to inform officials and citizens about plans and progress in operations of the program.

The proposal cited credentials of principal university faculty members who had agreed to serve as the executive committee for the project. These included the Director Water Resources Research Center, an Associate Professor of Government who had served as consultant to many Massachusetts community governments; a Professor of Environmental Engineering; Professor of Environmental Science and Public Health; a professor of business who had been a consultant to industrial firms and the state government of Illinois; and a Professor of Contract Law.

The proposed budget for the University project totaled $260,000 for a period of five years: $145,000 for Staff compensation, $18,000 for travel by staff; $20,000 for office and computer services and supplies; and $77,000 for indirect expenses of facilities, utility services, etc.

National
Electronics
Company

25

The Problem

National Electronics Company (NEC) was a small contract manufacturer specializing in military electronic equipment. The firm employed approximately 60 employees housed in two adjoining buildings.

In the months of March and April, 1978, NEC was producing a run of just under 50,000 intercommunication (intercom) stations in fulfillment of a military contract. Basically, the intercom station consisted of a small loudspeaker plus other electronic components in a diecast, weather-proof metal housing. Production and assembly of the intercom took place on a single floor in a "process flow" arrangement with work performed on several long tables. The assembly was performed, for the most part, by women who used a few tools and relatively simple machines.

The primary part of the product was the loudspeaker. Since this was a special unit which had to be rugged and capable of being exposed to the elements, it was made on the premises; its fabrication took place at the beginning of the intercom assembly line. The location of the first few operations in the loudspeaker manufacture and the general layout of the intercom assembly operation are shown in Exhibit 25–1.

After roughly the first hundred units were produced and required times for several early operations computed, it became obvious that times were

This case was prepared by Professor Gordon Chen with the assistance of Michael M. Meyers for class discussion only. All rights reserved to the author.

Exhibit 25—1 Work Flow

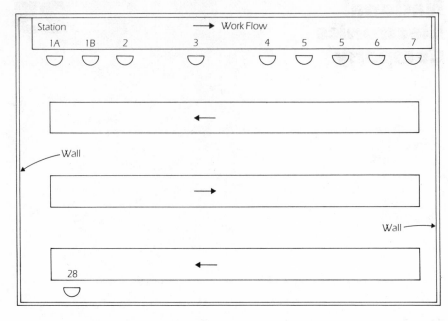

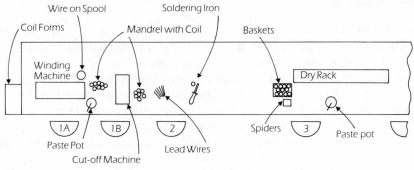

excessive and were probably restricting the production rate at subsequent operations. In particular, the first three "stations" in the production line, in which the loudspeaker fabrication was begun, had excessive per-unit times.

Synopsis of Operations

At the first station, the coil of the loudspeaker was wound. At the second, two wire leads were added to the coil. The third station involved cement-

Exhibit 25−2 Structure of military loudspeaker for intercom unit (no scale).

Air columns drilled
for acoustical quality

Back of Speaker

Magnet

Coil
Lead

Spider or
support

Lead
block

Face of Speaker

Cone

Voice Coil

ing a flexible supporting member (or "spider") to the loudspeaker frame ("basket"), then cementing the coil ("voice coil") to the center of the spider. A centering fixture was used to center the voice coil properly in the basket. Finally, the assembly was put on a rack while the cement set. An almost-completed loudspeaker is shown in Exhibit 25−2.

A quotation for one of the vital parts of the loudspeaker, the voice coil, was obtained from an outside source. For the desired quantity the price was $0.47 each but this excluded the cutoff operation (to be described later). The delicateness of the part made maintenance of quality vital; hence management hesitated to trust the voice coil to another manufacturer.

Details of Assembly

The voice coil, two leads, supporting spider, and basket were the significant pieces of the assembly—those for which unit times were felt to be unsatisfactory.

The centering fixture was used only to center the voice coil on the spider while the cement was wet; when it had dried, the fixture was withdrawn and reused to center another coil. The centering fixture somewhat resembled the magnet structure shown in the illustration (Exhibit 25−2), but the fixture had a smaller circular air gap, assuring that the coil would be centered exactly (without rubbing as it moved in and out) in the actual and slightly wider magnet gap.

Operations performed at each of the first three stations are described in detail below.

FIRST STATION:
1. Form for loudspeaker voice coil was obtained from box, wrapped around mandrel glossy side out, secured with rubber band at end opposite U-cuts in form.
2. Mandrel was placed on coil winding machine.
3. Mandrel was turned by hand and coil form coated with cement except for seam of form.
4. Copper magnet wire from dispenser was started on mandrel after three turns were wrapped about aligning pin; winder was turned ON and two layers wound on coil.
5. Winder was turned OFF; free wire-end was wrapped around second aligning pin; wire-end was cut; second coating of cement applied to coil.
6. Mandrel was removed from winder; allowed to dry for about five minutes.
7. Rubber band securing coil form was removed; area covered by rubber band was cut off (may be done on coil winder or on special machine).
8. Wire ends were untwisted from aligning pins; coil was slipped off mandrel and placed on tray; cement residue was cleaned from mandrel.

SECOND STATION:
9. Two heavier pre-stripped insulated wires were twisted on magnet wire ends and soldered; excess wire at soldered connection was cut off.
10. Insulated wires were each positioned in one of two U-cuts in coil form and twisted to "roll up" slack in end of magnet wire.
11. Voice coil was put on tray.

THIRD STATION:
12. Voice coil was selected; centering fixture from previously finished loudspeaker assembly was selected and voice coil placed over center piece; voice-coil end with U-cuts was outward.
13. Spider was selected from box, center was coated with cement, spider was placed on top of centering fixture and adhered to voice coil.
14. Loudspeaker basket was selected from box; rim which is to support edge of spider was coated with cement.
15. Centering fixture (with voice coil and spider) was up-ended and placed in basket, adhering edge of spider to basket rim.
16. Entire assembly was placed in vertical rack to dry.

General Cost Data

Direct labor cost of these operations was $4.25/hr. Overhead (including indirect labor) was 500 percent of direct labor cost of $21.25/hr. It was estimated that there were 450 minutes of working time in a shift. Materials handlers were available for movement of work. Excluding Stations 1

Exhibit 25—3 Winding of voice coil for loudspeaker (no scale).
At left, coil form is being placed on mandrel with ends meeting in butt joint. At right, completed voice coil is on mandrel (shown before cutoff is performed as shown by broken line). Magnet-wire ends are wrapped around aligning pins but for clarity, this is not shown in illustration at the right.

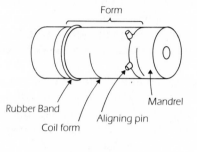

Form

Rubber Band

Coil form

Aligning pin

Mandrel

Mandrel with form
secured by rubber band.
Ready for coil to be wound.

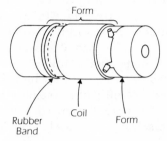

Form

Rubber
Band

Coil

Form

Mandrel after coil is
wound around form.

through 3, it was believed that final production rate of Stations 4 through 28 (which used 31 workers) would approximate 1.10 pieces/min (finished intercom units).

Time and Cost Data, Station 1   At this station, Operations 1 through 8, described in detail earlier, were performed. The winding was done on a $1,500.00 coil winder, using a mandrel as illustrated in Exhibit 25—3. Entire cost of the winder was charged to this contract for intercoms. Mandrels were made in the NEC machine shop and were estimated to cost $20.00 each with eleven required (drying time of the cement required that a mandrel with newly-wound coil be set aside to dry while the next voice coil was started on another mandrel). In addition, it was necessary to cut off one end of the form on which each voice coil was wound; this was the end opposite the U-cuts and was covered by the rubber band that held the form on the mandrel until the cement dried. The cutoff operation was performed on the coil-winder by a single-edged razor blade and was the operation just before removal of the coil from the mandrel. Then the voice coil was put aside and finally, excess cement was cleaned from the mandrel by wiping with a solvent-impregnated cloth. Time for this station was 2.06 minutes/piece, or 0.486 pieces/min, which included personal allowances, as do all times given.

Station 1 procedure was altered slightly and times taken again. The winding operation was broken into two portions, performed first at Station 1A and second at 1B; two operators were used. The first worker performed Operations 1 through 6 and the second, Operations 7 and 8. Cutoff was performed on a separate machine consisting of a slow-speed gear motor for rotating the mandrel with coil and a lever-operated, pre-set arrangement to bring the razor blade against the rotating coil (on its mandrel) at the proper point. Machine cost was $150.00. Time per coil with this altered procedure was reduced to 1.16 min/piece (0.963 pieces/min) but the operator of the cutoff machine appeared to be working at only 75 percent of normal. Due to the greater rate of production, there was insufficient drying time allowed. It was felt that ten extra mandrels would allow formation of a "bank" between Stations 1A and 1B and drying time would be adequate once again.

There was a question whether use of a second coil winder would be economical. One point considered was that there would not be sufficient room for more than two operators at this station. Hence, if a second winding machine were used, the winder operators would once again need to perform the cutoff on their winders as there would be no room for one or more cutoff machines and their operators. Delivery time for the second winder would be over a month.

Time and Cost Data, Station 2   Operations 9 through 11 were performed at Station 2 by a worker whose rate of production averaged 1.92 min/piece or 0.520 pieces/min. A soldering iron and solder were the "tools" used. The material used was pre-stripped lead wire of short lengths. There was sufficient room at the station to permit addition of a second operator.

Time and Cost Data, Station 3   Operations 12 through 16 were performed at Station 3, where there was sufficient room for two, and perhaps three, operators. Times averaged 3.12 min/piece or 0.320 pieces/min for an operator.

Centering fixtures were necessary for locating the voice coil properly so that it moved freely in and out of the air gap of the finished loudspeaker. Each worker at the station needed 40 centering fixtures which were stored in a rack within arm's reach. Each fixture cost $15.00. As at Station 1, the number of fixtures was determined by the drying time of the cement. With 40 fixtures the "bank" would be large enough so that as a worker places assembly No. 40 (consisting of fixture, voice coil, spider and basket) in the rack, No. 1 would have dried sufficiently so that the fixture could be reused (in centering assembly No. 41) and the partially completed speaker assembly passed on to the next work station.

NATO Hawk Program

26

Prologue

In 1956 the U.S. offered technical assistance to European NATO governments desiring to equip their forces with complex weapon systems of U.S.
design. As a result, seven NATO Programs were organized to produce U.S.
designed weapons. After inspecting a variety of U.S. weapons and examining their needs, in 1958, the governments of five countries—Belgium,
France, West Germany, Holland, and Italy—decided to finance the production of the Hawk ground-to-air missile system in Europe. The Hawk
system was originally designed and produced by the Raytheon Company
for the U.S. Army. Their purposes were to strengthen NATO's aircraft defenses and to develop a "European know-how" to produce, operate, and
maintain a complex yet standardized weapon system. Each government
agreed to equip a number of batallions with Hawk batteries. Each nominated an industrial firm as its national prime contractor (NPC) for the
production of Hawk equipment. The firms were: Ateliers de Construc-
tions Electriques de Charleroi (ACEC) in Belgium, Compagnie Francaise
Thomson Houston (CFTH) in France, Telefunken in Germany, Philips in
Holland, and Finmeccanica in Italy. Representatives of these firms formed
a European company in Paris known as SETEL (Société Européenne Tele-

Revision of a case study by Professor R. E. McGarrah as consultant for the Logistics Management Institute, Washington,
D.C., while conducting research as Professor, IMEDC, Management Development Institute, Lausanne, Switzerland. Used
with expressed permission.

Exhibit 26–1 NATO Hawk Program

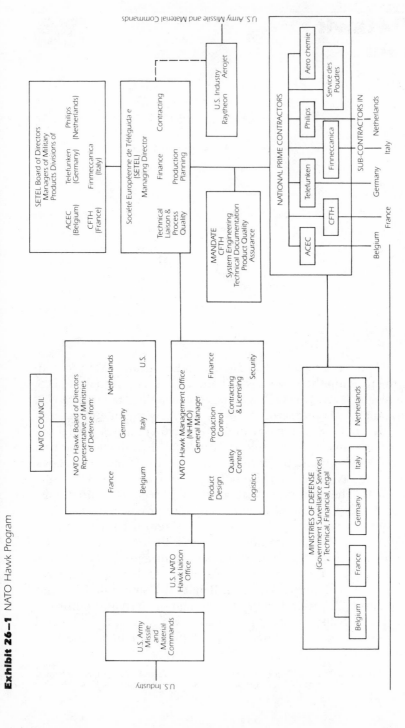

SOURCE: Records of the U.S. NATO Hawk Liaison Office.

Solid lines indicate main, official channels for communication. Dashed lines indicate unofficial, the main advisory channels for communication.

The hierarchies of government procurement agencies and industrial production organizations are depicted to show collateral levels of functional responsibility.

Each Ministry of Defense was to approve technical, financial and legal aspects of contracting and production activities of his NPC, on behalf of NHMO.

guidage), chartered under French law. SETEL was the European prime production contractor. Under auspices of the NATO Council, the five European states organized a procurement and financial management organization, known as the NATO Hawk Management Office (NHMO), in Paris. In the U.S., the Raytheon Company and the U.S. Army Missile Command were engaged to assist in technical and procurement problems. This assistance was financed by "Grant-Aid" funds appropriated under Public Law 85–477, U.S. Congress. Additional, "reimbursable assistance" was provided by the U.S. Government as credits against U.S. purchase of Hawk batteries from the NATO Hawk Consortium. Although the U.S. did not claim voting privileges on the Board of Directors of the NHMO for production matters, it participated in discussions and retained veto privileges on all matters of military security and changes in technical performance of the Hawk system. In 1963, the five European Governments decided to act in consort on problems of logistical support, after Hawk batteries had been produced. At this time, the U.S. attained voting privileges on logistical matters, and the organization became known as the NATO Hawk Production and Logistics Organization. Exhibit 26–1 is an organization chart of the NATO Hawk Program.

European manufacturers were to produce Hawk equipment so it would be interchangeable with equipment produced in the U.S. Accordingly, Raytheon and the U.S. Army Missile Command sent thousands of specifications, blue prints, test data, etc. to SETEL, whose technical, financial, and administrative functions were staffed by personnel from each of the five firms.

The five members of SETEL were known as National Prime Contractors (NPC's). The NATO-Hawk Working Group (of the NATO Council) divided production efforts among the five countries and the NPC's decided which firms would produce which equipment, according to the following criteria.

☐ Each NPC would contract to produce a dollar amount of business equivalent to the number of Hawk batteries being procured by his government.
☐ There would be a minimum of duplication of organization and production facilities in order to assure economy and efficiency.
☐ Insofar as practicable, European raw materials would be used, and minimum reliance would be placed on U.S. parts manufacturers.
☐ There was an urgent need to strengthen NATO's air defense capabilities by producing Hawk Systems as quickly as possible.

Nearly 500 European and 200 American firms were involved in the NATO Hawk Production Program, which cost over $1 billion by 1975. Delivery of European-produced batteries began after four years and many technical, financial, and political problems. Flight-tests have proved that the performance of NATO Hawk systems is as accurate and reliable as the performance of U.S. produced systems.

What is the significance of this accomplishment?

The NATO Hawk Program is one of the first experiences of multinational governments and industrial firms in operation on such a large scale. These organizations have resolved complex, technical problems and have gained much "technical know-how." But even more important, they have overcome social, political, and economic barriers that traditionally have kept nations divided and weak. The sovereignty of individual governments and the profit position of individual firms have been strengthened. The production of NATO Hawk Batteries in Europe was a large and complex task that was accomplished by practical men of governments, business, and labor organizations. Operations continued smoothly in the Hawk Program even during President de Gaulle's withdrawal of French forces from NATO command, and while his demand that NATO Headquarters be moved from Paris threatened the future existence of NATO.

Experiences of the NATO Hawk Program may contain important precedents for multinational governmental and industrial cooperation needed in managing global resources for energy, food, minerals and technology; or for controlling industrial pollution of the environment, and processes for industrial and economic development. Thus, the NATO Hawk Program might be assessed as a model for strengthening relations among members of the United Nations or for building a new international economic order between industrialized societies north and developing societies south of the equator. NATO Hawk operations may also exemplify the mode for cooperation Western societies need most in order to harmonize public interests of democratic governments with private interests of multinational business organizations. The energy, monetary, and food "crises" of the early 1970s dramatized needs for Western business and government to cooperate more effectively in community and international affairs of industrial nations. Thus, the case of the NATO Hawk Program offers valuable insights and precedents for managers of industry and government responsible for security and economic wellbeing of global societies.

The Hawk System

Exhibit 26–2 illustrates the major equipment containing more than 100,000 component parts comprising the Hawk System, and lists major European contractors responsible for their manufacture.

The Hawk System may be divided into four groups, each of which performs a specific function that enables the system to perform its mission:

Acquisition and Fire Control Group—The acquisition data required for target detection, identification and evaluation is provided by a volume

Exhibit 26—2 Study of the NATO Hawk Program. The Hawk System & its European Producers

The Hawk Battery

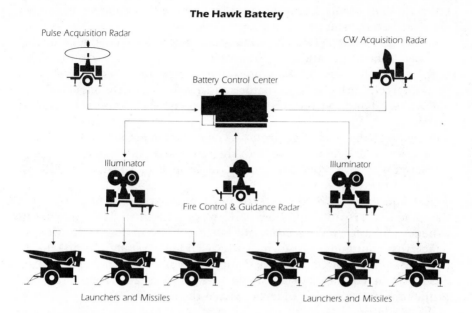

Major Item	Abbreviation	Contractor
Continuous Wave Acquisition Radar (AN/MPQ-34)	CWAR	Ateliers de Constructions Electriques de Charleroi (ACEC) Belgium
Pulse Acquisition Radar (AN/MPQ-35)	PAR	Selenia, Italy
Range Only Radar (AN/MPQ-37)	ROR	Ateliers de Constructions Electriques de Charleroi (ACEC) Belgium
High Power Illuminator Radar (AN/MPQ-39)	HPI	Telefunken, Germany Hollandse Signal Apparaten, Netherlands (HSA)
Battery Control Central (AN/TSW-2)	BCC	N.V. Philips Gloeilampen Fabrieken, Netherlands
Assault Fire Command Console (AN/TSW-4)	AFCC	Atlas-Werke, Germany
Organizational Maintenance Set/Missile (AN/TSM-43)(not shown)	OMS/M	Fabricca Italiana Apparecchi Radio (F.I.A.R.), Italy
Organizational Maintenance Set/Ground (AN/TSM-44)(not shown)	OMS/G	N.V. Philips Gloeilampen Fabrieken, Netherlands
Launcher (X7-78E3)		Fabrique Nationale d'Armes de Guerre, Belgium
		Atelier de Construction de Tarbes France
Loader (XM-501-EZ)		Henschel Werke, Germany

coverage Pulse Acquisition Radar and a horizon-searching continuous wave (CW) Acquisition Radar. The tactical control of the battery and the control of each firing section is performed from the Battery Control Central. The Range-Only-Radar provides target range information in certain electronic countermeasures environments.

Guidance Group—The CW Illuminator Radar aquires, tracks and illuminates the target and furnishes a reference signal to the semi-active homing missile. The Missile homes to intercept on the energy reflected by the target. Both the Illuminator and Missile detect the Doppler shift due to target motion and discriminate against clutter on the basis of speed.

Launching and Handling Group—The Launcher activiates the missile, aims it into a collision course with the target and launches it. A tracked Loader provides for rapid reloading of the Launcher. A Pallet provides for storage of ready missiles.

Test Equipment Group (not shown)—Organization Maintenance Test Equipment is provided to allow battery personnel to adjust equipment, conduct go/no-go tests and isolate failed subassemblies. Field Maintenance Test Equipment is used by Military Ordnance staff in its direct support mission to isolate defective components and repair sub-assemblies.

Supporting equipment such as diesel generators, interconnecting and prime movers are also provided as part of the tactical battery.

When a target is detected and evaluated as a threat, it is assigned to one of the two independent firing sections. The Illuminator in that section is designated to the target. It then acquires and tracks. A Missile is launched on command from the Battery Control Central and homes to intercept. After the intercept has been evaluated, another target may be engaged and the engagement sequence repeated as often as the situation requires. When Launchers are depleted of missiles, they are rapidly reloaded by the tracked Loader in order to sustain the high fire rate.

The Evolution of the NATO Hawk Organization

Complexities of design and performance of the Hawk System led to complex organization and management problems in the NATO Hawk Program. Details of these problems are clearer by first considering the nature of modern weapon system programs and underlying principles of the NATO Hawk Organization.

The Nature of Modern Weapon System Programs

Weapon systems are developed (i.e., their performance capabilities improved), *while* they are being produced by industry and operated by the military. This is how the rates of technological change and increase in military power are accelerated. Customers (i.e., the Defense Ministries) and producers (manufacturers) are continuously engaged in maintaining and improving a weapon system as long as it remains in the "operational inventory" of armed forces.

Consequently, the customer and producer work closely together, from "concept" of a new weapon system to operational hardware. In one sense, they are mutual protagonists for "bigger slices" from the government's total economic budget. In another sense, they are mutual antagonists about the question of whether the customer or producer knows more about military, technical, financial, and legal problems that inevitably arise, because new technologies are being applied for the first time. From this latter sense come controversies and compromises between industry's production managers and government's procurement managers about the importance of quality, delivery, and cost at every stage of the work flow process. The customer and producer have to agree on changes affecting the quality, delivery-rates, and cost of the weapon system and all its components.

When the five European states decided to equip their armed forces with Hawk Batteries, they were still being developed and improved by the U.S. Army Missile Command and the Raytheon Company. In fact, the Hawk System had not yet been declared "operational" by the U.S. Army.

Objectives of the NATO Hawk Program

On December 14, 1956 Secretary of Defense Wilson announced a U.S. policy of providing technical assistance to NATO Governments. Its purpose was "to develop a coordinated production base in Europe for modern weapon systems." The basic objectives of the NATO Hawk Program were:

1. To develop a European potential for research and development as well as coordinated production base for modern weapon systems.
2. To increase the missile production capacity of NATO states.
3. To strengthen ground-to-air defenses of NATO by deploying Hawk batteries in Europe.
4. To accelerate progress toward a common family of weapon systems in NATO.
5. To reduce duplications of weapons development costs.

Most of these objectives stress "technical know-how" for modern weapon systems development and production in European countries. If Hawk Batteries had been urgently needed, they probably would have been purchased from the U.S., whose program was already organized.

Underlying Principles of NATO Hawk Organization

The organization for the NATO Hawk Program has evolved from essentially three basic principles:

1. Proportionate share of financial participation by the government and

industry according to number of Hawk batteries each European state procured for its military forces.

2. Maximum use of *existing* European organizations in governments and industry.
3. A sense of military urgency to strengthen defenses of Western Europe as quickly as possible.

Proportionate Share of Financial Participation   In late 1958, when the NATO Hawk Program was being organized, there was no accurate basis for anticipating what the cost of a Hawk Battery would be, when produced in Europe. U.S. cost data (indicating roughly $20 million per battery) were available, but these were very tentative and were not considered accurate indicators of what costs would be under European conditions. As in the U.S., Europe Hawk production was to be financed on a "cost-plus-fixed-fee basis." In other words, a fixed percentage fee plus all contractors' expenses agreed as "reimbursable" would be paid by the governments to the industrial firms participating in the Program. Consequently, instead of cost data, in 1958, financial participation by each European state was estimated on the basis of the number of Hawk Batteries each government had agreed to purchase. The U.S. agreed to provide additional funds in accordance with its Military Grant-in-Aid Policy implemented by Public Law 85–477.

When other NATO weapon system production programs (e.g., NATO Starfighter, Sidewinder, Mauler) were launched, the financial share of one European government was greater than the sum of the shares of all other European states participating in the program. In the NATO Hawk Program, these shares were much more uniformly distributed. This greater, equality among partners distinguished the NATO Hawk Organization from organizations for other NATO weapon production programs.

Maximum Use of Existing European Organizations   For both economic and political reasons, each participating government desired that its existing technical, financial and procurement-contracting agencies be utilized to the fullest extent possible in the NATO Hawk Program. No European government wanted a large supranational organization to be created because such an organization might tend to dominate its own ministries of defense and financial affairs. If an international organization became necessary to manage the governments' procurement functions, its size and authority were to be kept as small as possible. Similarly, European industrialists were tacitly advised to avoid unnecessary duplications in the consortium's organization and facilities they chose to manufacture, assemble, and test of the Hawk Batteries to be produced.

Military Urgency   The armament race created a sense of "military urgency" about accomplishing the purpose of a weapon system program as quickly as possible, after a group of countries agreed to finance the program. Since the founding of NATO, winds of conflict between East and West had shifted from warm to cool, but still, the military protection of the West remained a vital requirement of NATO.

How the NATO Hawk Program Was Organized

The NATO Hawk Working Group

The NATO governments individually considered the U.S. offer of 1956, to decide whether or not they wished to accept it. For various reasons Belgium, France, Germany, Holland and Italy were the five European NATO members that expressed a desire to pursue the offer further. (Great Britain declined because it was already committed to its own Bloodhound ground-to-air missile program.)

These five governments, acting through the NATO Council, formed a Working Group. This group organized two committees. One committee consisted of military and technical specialists to recommend a particular U.S. designed missile system to be produced in Europe. After visiting various missile facilities in the U.S., this committee proposed that the Hawk system be produced in Europe. A key reason for choosing the Hawk instead of others was that Hawk contained the most advanced U.S. air defense capabilities. As one European member of the committee told the case writer, "We visited the U.S. Army missile test center at White Sands, New Mexico. When I saw a Hawk missile fly into a mountain instead of the target zone, I knew we were choosing the latest, not an obsolescent American missile defense system." (U.S. Hawk batteries were initially developed in 1957–1958 and continued to be improved during the next decade. They were still operational in 1981.) After approving this proposal, the five governments became known as the NATO Hawk Working Group. Later, members of this group were appointed to the Board of Directors of the NATO Hawk Management Office (NHMO).

The Hawk Working Group was the nucleus and manager of the development of the overall organization of the Program. Very early the Group adopted a rule of unanimity in all its decisions.

It was agreed that the relative importance of each member's role would be keyed to the number of Hawk batteries each government purchased for its military forces. Of course, as a former twice-defeated enemy of all other members, Germany's role tacitly was deferential. However, many if not most NATO Hawk batteries would be deployed in West Germany near the "Iron Curtain." And West German industry and markets for civilian (consumer-industrial) products were the largest in Europe.

At the meeting at which formal commitments were to be made to procure NATO Hawk batteries the French representative requested and was granted the right to speak *after* all other governments. This was an exception to agreed protocol order, which was alphabetical according to English names of member nations. Thus, after West Germany announced its commitment, France announced its intention to procure Hawk's batteries for one more Hawk battalion than West Germany. This assured a primal role for the French. (The exact number of batteries were classified. The total number exceeded 100 considered necessary to make it worthwhile for European industries to tool up for producing Hawk systems.) In percentages of this total the shares of participation were as follows:

Belgium	10.7 percent
France	35.7 percent
Germany	32.1 percent
Holland	7.2 percent
Italy	14.3 percent

With exceptions noted later, the relative contributions and benefits for partner nations (government and industry) participating in the NATO Hawk Program were planned and organized according to these percentages.

The Committee of European Industrialists

To expedite industrial participation in Europe, the NATO Hawk Working Group also nominated a Committee of five European Industrialists and asked them to propose the best way to organize industrial efforts for overall program management and for sub-system management for the NATO Hawk Program, in accordance with the principles discussed above. Members of this committee were the general managers of the military products divisions of ACEC (Belgium), CFTH (France), Telefunken (Germany), Philips (Holland) and Finmeccanica (Italy).

Organizations for Program Management of Industrial Efforts

In meetings held during December 1958–May 1959, the Committee of Industrialists considered and rejected several alternatives for organizing and managing the industrial efforts. Officials of participating governments presented their views to guide the industrialists.

1. A multinational company chartered under international laws. This would have required a treaty among the participating states, but negotiations for a suitable treaty would have taken too long to satisfy the criterion of speed in producing NATO Hawk Batteries. Hence this was rejected.
2. To choose one of the five companies to act as the European Prime Contractor. But this alternative was rejected because the burdens of technical, juridical and financial responsibilities could hardly be borne by one of the existing firms, in relation to *all* the governments.

3. To establish an "association in fact" of the firms comprising the national industrial committee. This was rejected because, at the beginning of the program, responsibilities of each industrial participant in the NATO Hawk Program could not be rigorously defined. Moreover, the "large measure of integration required of participants involved in the Hawk Program with regard to juridical and fiscal peculiarities of such an association would make its application difficult."[1]

The Committee decided that the best compromise of the aforementioned principles of proportionality of financial support, maximum use of existing organizations and facilities, and military urgency would be to organize a multinational European Company chartered under the laws of *one* of the European states. This company would function exclusively to produce Hawk Equipment; it would be owned solely by the five companies represented on the Committee of European Industrialists, which would serve as its Board of Directors; ownership would be shared in proportion to the financial shares of the respective governments; it would be legally responsible in identical terms to each of the governments financing and purchasing Hawk Batteries.

The NATO Hawk Working Group agreed to establish a single agency to coordinate their procurement and financing activities and to deal with the single European Prime Contracting firm. On June 11, 1959, the NATO Council approved these proposals and thus SETEL, and the Board of Directors of the NATO Hawk Management Office and its staff, were founded.

The questions of (1) which state would charter the Hawk European Prime Contracting Company under its laws and (2) which national manufacturer would staff which key positions in this company—were decided in favor of the French, mainly because the French government had said it would purchase the largest number of Hawk Batteries.[2] Accordingly, SETEL was chartered under French law, with offices in Paris. CFTH (the French member of the Industrial Committee) was granted the right to choose the Managing Director of SETEL. Naturally, the Managing Director of SETEL was French, a lawyer employed by CFTH. SETEL's first managers of production planning, financial planning, contract administration, and quality control were Dutch, Belgian, French, and Italian, respectively. Exhibits 26–3 through 26–7 contain more details of SETEL's organization.

By recommendation of the Hawk Working Group and decision of the NATO Council, the NATO Hawk Management Office was established at

---

[1] Report on the Committee of European Industrialists, October 1959. This report is known as "HK-42."

[2] According to remarks by several officials of the NATO Hawk Organization. Among the five countries, France and Germany had the widest and about equal diversification of industrial skills. But, in addition to being the largest participant, France was an older member of NATO than Germany.

Exhibit 26—3 Study of the NATO Hawk Program Organization Chart Société Européenne de Téléguidage SETEL

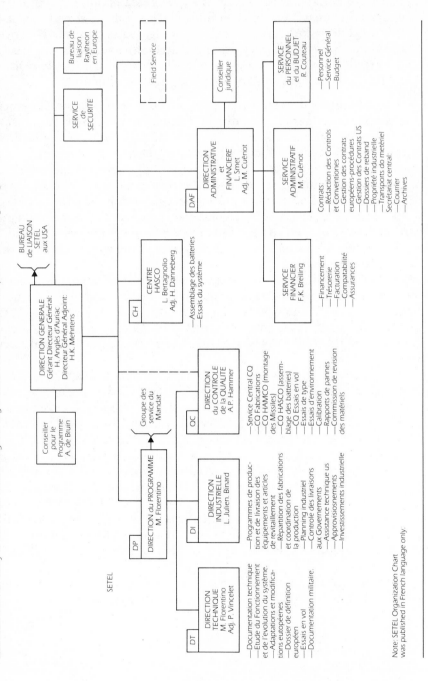

SETEL

DIRECTION GENERALE
Gérant Directeur Général:
H. Anglès d'Auriac
Directeur Général Adjoint:
H.K. Mehrtens

BUREAU
de LIAISON
SETEL
aux USA

Conseiller
pour le
Programme
A. de Brun

SERVICE
de
SECURITE

Bureau de
liaison
Raytheon
en Europe

Field Service

Conseiller
juridique

**DIRECTION
ADMINISTRATIVE
et
FINANCIERE**
L. Smet
Adj. M. Cuénot

DAF

**SERVICE
du PERSONNEL
et du BUDJET**
R. Couteau

—Personnel
—Service Général
—Budget

**SERVICE
ADMINISTRATIF**
M. Cuénot

Contrats:
—Rédaction des Controls
et Conventions
—Gestion des contrats
européens-procédures
—Gestion des Contrats US
—Dossiers de reband
—Propriété industrielle
—Transports do matériel
Secrétariat central:
—Courrier
—Archives

**CENTRE
HASCO**
L. Bertagnolio
Adj. H. Danneberg

CH

—Assemblage des batteries
—Essais du système

**SERVICE
FINANCIER**
F.K. Breiling

—Financement
—Trésorerie
—Facturation
—Compatabilité
—Assurances

Groupe des
service du
Mandat

**DIRECTION
du CONTROLE
de la QUALITE**
A.P. Hammer

QC

—Service Central CQ
—CQ Fabrications
—CQ HAMCO (montage
des Missiles)
—CQ HASCO (assem-
blage des batteries)
—CQ Essais en vol
—Essais de type
—Essais d'environnement
—Calibration
—Rapports de pannes
—Commission de revision
des matériels

DIRECTION du PROGRAMME
M. Fiorentino

DP

**DIRECTION
INDUSTRIELLE**
L. Julien. Binard

DI

—Programmes de produc-
tion et de livraison des
équipements et articles
de revitaillement
—Répartition des fabrications
et coordination de
la production
—Planning industriel
—Controle des livraisons
aux Governements
—Assistance technique us
—Approvisiosnements
—Investissements industrielle

**DIRECTION
TECHNIQUE**
M. Fiorentino
Adj. P. Vincelet

DT

—Documentation technique
—Etude du Fonctionnement
et de l'evolution du système.
—Adaptations et modifica-
tions eutopéenes
—Dossier de définition
européen
—Essais en vol
—Documentation militaire.

Note: SETEL Organization Chart
was published in French language only.

Exhibit 26—4 Study of the NATO Hawk Program SETEL Staff Statistics

Number of Personnel by Nationalities (July 1964)

Belgium	16
France	61
Germany	16
Holland	8
Italy	16
U.S.A.	1
United Kingdom	5
Canada	1
	124

Summary by functional levels

Professional personnel	58
Technicians, clerks, service personnel	66
	124

Exhibit 26—5 Study of the NATO Hawk Program Growth of SETEL Staff

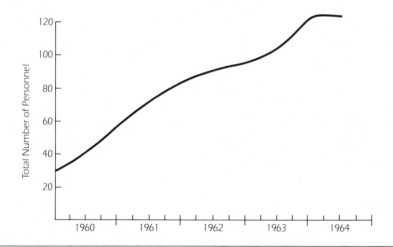

Rueil-Malmaison, just outside of Paris. It was organized to coordinate technical, legal, and financial activities of procurement and to deal with SETEL. The General Manager of NHMO was a Lieutenant General (retired) of the Royal Dutch Air Force and a former member of the Hawk Working Group. The managers of production planning, financial control, were Italian, Dutch, Italian, and German, respectively, all military of-

Exhibit 26—6 Study of the NATO Hawk Program SETEL Financial Statistics—1964 Budget

	New Francs		U.S. $ (5NF/U.S. $)
Personnel			
Engineers, Officers,			
Clerks & Technicians	4,867,800		973,560
Other	1,153,200		230,640
Operating Costs	556,800		111,360
Financial Expenses	726,500		145,300
Depreciation	135,200		27,040
Official Travel	300,000		60,000
	7,739,500	NF	$1,547,900

Exhibit 26—7 Study of the NATO Hawk Program Cumulative Expenses SETEL

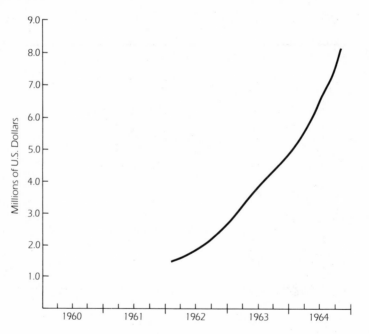

SOURCE: Financial Division, NHMO.

Exhibit 26—8 Study of the NATO Hawk Program NATO Hawk Management Office Organization Chart

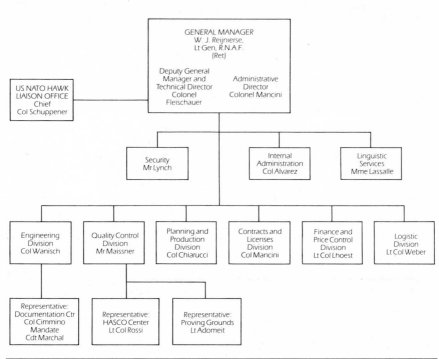

ficers. Exhibits 26–8 through 26–12 contain more details of the NHMO organization.

These two multinational organizations, NHMO and SETEL, are key characteristics that distinguish the NATO Hawk Program from other NATO Programs for weapon system production in Europe. In all other programs (i.e., those organized to produce the NATO Starfighter, the Mauler, the Sidewinder, etc.) *one* government and *one* manufacturer manage the procurement and production of the weapon system.

The System Engineering Organization (The Mandate)

Another key question of the Hawk industrial organization was one of providing technical staff and system engineering capability for SETEL. On this issue (as related by one member of SETEL's Board of Directors), the French member (an executive of CFTH) proposed staffing the technical function with French personnel. At this time (1959) CFTH (Compagnie Francaise Thomson Houston) had a "surplus" of technical personnel,

Exhibit 26—9 Study of the NATO Hawk Program NHMO Staff Statistics

Number of Personnel (by Nationalities) 15 July 1964		Summary by Functions (Nov. 1963)	
Belgium	16	Management	7
France	56	Engineering Division	11
Germany	16	Quality Control Division	7
Holland	8	Production Planning Division	14
Italy	16	Financial & Price Control Division	13
U.S.A.	1	Contracts & Licenses Division	3
England	5	Logistics Division	18
	120	HASCO (Hawk System Check Out)	3
		Services: Administration	23
		Linguistics	6
		Security	2
		International Staff	3
		TOTAL	110

Exhibit 26—10 Study of the NATO Hawk Program Growth of NHMO Staff

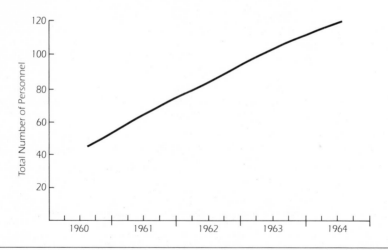

compared to the four other firms represented on the Committee of Industrialists. Thus, the French proposed that SETEL would contract with CFTH for the job of "Central Technical Management and the Coordination of Production" by all industrial firms that would participate in the program. The other members of SETEL's board agreed to this proposal. Accordingly, the French were given the authority and responsibility for

Exhibit 26—11 Study of the NATO Hawk Program NHMO Financial Statistics Budget—1964

	New Francs	U.S. $ (5NF/U.S. $)
Personnel	3,149,000	629,800
Operating Expenses	609,000	127,800
Capital Expenses	24,000	4,800
TOTAL	NF 3,782,000	$756,400

Exhibit 26—12 Study of the NATO Hawk Program Cumulative Expenses NHMO

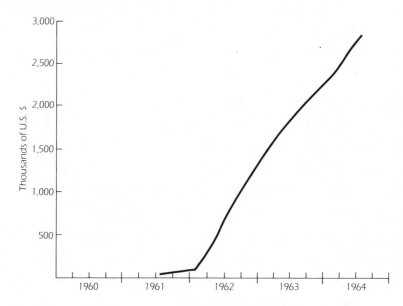

SOURCE: Finance Division, NHMO.

technical administration of the NATO Hawk Program. The organization was known as the Mandate and was staffed by CFTH personnel who render technical services exclusively for SETEL. See Exhibits 26–13 through 26–16 for more details.

Contract Repartitioning

The second major task of the Committee of Industrialists was to recommend a plan for subdividing the production of Hawk System among industries in the five European states. This involved analysis of the Hawk

Exhibit 26-13 Study of the NATO Hawk Program—The Mandate Organization

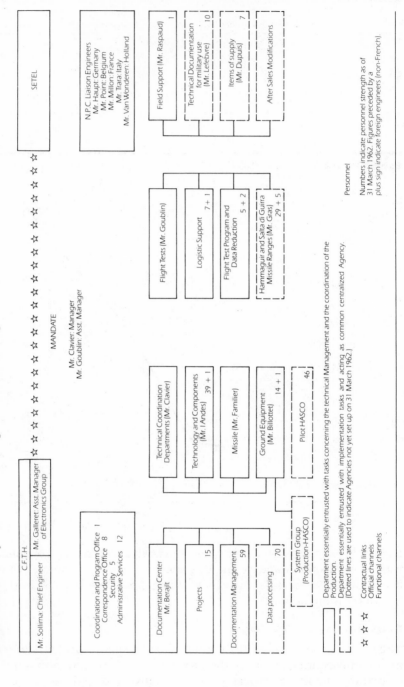

Exhibit 26–14 Study of the NATO Hawk Program—The Mandate Staff

Number of Personnel (by Nationalities) March 1952		Number of Personnel By Functions March 1964	
Belgium	1	Documentation	200
France	335	Technical Coordination	140
Germany	1	Flight Tests	70
Holland	2	Field Support	100
Italy	11	TOTAL	510
TOTAL	350		

Exhibit 26–15 Study of the NATO Hawk Program—The Mandate—Growth of Staff

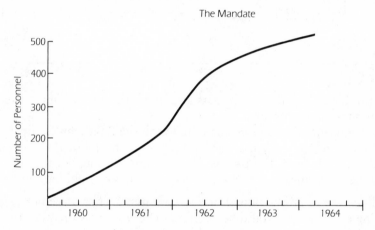

The Mandate

SOURCE: Records of the Mandate.

System and deciding which contractor would manage the production of which Hawk equipment. Again, this was a problem of compromising the three principles cited earlier.

The production of some major elements of the Hawk System was politically, technically, or economically more attractive to all participants than the production of others. This challenged the Committee's ability to avoid duplications of facilities to produce the same major elements of the Hawk System. For instance, production of missiles had to be continued as long as Hawk Systems were to be used, long after the initial quantity had

Exhibit 26—16 Study of the NATO Hawk Program—The Mandate—Financial Statistics

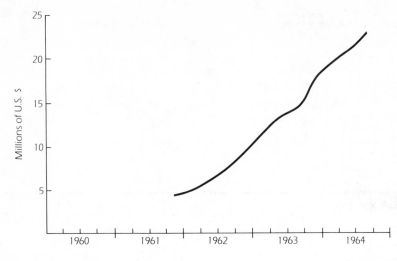

SOURCE: Financial Division, NHMO.

been produced. So all governments and industrial firms wanted the business of producing missiles.

The Industrial Committee consulted with the Raytheon Company, and representatives of the participating governments. From these consultations and their own discussions, the Committee adopted the following guidelines in planning for allocations of the Hawk production in Europe:

1. Allocation of production of non-special items, such as vehicles, generating sets, cables, would be deferred. These items were not critical in the technical sense, and would be used to adjust financial inequities resulting from the allocations of "Hawk Peculiar" items of the system.
2. The manufacture of propulsive powders and explosives was considered special, and referred to a committee of experts, which recommended the following allocations:

Explosives—Belgium	50%
Holland	50%
	100%

Propulsive powder manufacture and missile assembly—

France	48%
Germany	39%
Italy	18%
	100%

Thus, there were two sources for explosives for the warhead and three sources for propulsive powders and missile assembly in Europe.

3. The remaining hardware elements of the system and their manufacturing processes were analyzed and classified as follows:

Electronics and electrical servo mechanisms	65%
Mechanical and aeronautical	35%

Using U.S.-derived cost data as indices of financial importance (in admittedly non-precise terms), each European state would produce its financial share, and each share would consist of 65% electronics and electrical, and 35% mechanical parts of manufacturing.

4. Each country should have access to *all* new techniques for design and manufacture involved in the Hawk Program.

5. Component parts manufacture requiring significant financial or technical investment would be assigned to a single source.

6. Sub-assembly and final assembly of equipment involving relatively small investments in tools and test equipment could be accomplished at more than one source.

Preliminary cost[3] data were obtained from the U.S. and used to summarize the proposed repartitioning plan in financial terms (millions of dollars). Exhibits 26–17 through 26–22 give this plan in detail, but in brief, it was as follows:

Equipment Group	Belgium and Holland	France	Germany	Italy	Total
	Millions of U.S. Dollars				
Acquisition and Fire Control	21.5			13.7	35.2
Guidance	9.3	86.7	68.9	19.7	184.6
Launching and Handling	25.4	24.3	31.0	10.0	90.7
Test Equipment	5.7	11.4	10.2	5.7	33.0
	61.9	122.4	110.1	49.1	343.5

From December, 1958 through October 1959, the Committee of Industrialists continued to meet and hear the views of participating governments and other industrialists (especially the Raytheon Company) before submitting its final report in October 1959 to the NATO Council. This report, known as "HK-42," summarized the proposals for two multinational organizations (SETEL and the NATO Hawk Management Office)

---

[3] In the U.S., Hawk Systems were still being produced and modified by Raytheon on a cost-plus-fixed fee contract. Consequently, the unit cost data were subject to errors and were not too firm. Moreover, they did not reflect certain indirect costs of tooling and manufacturing equipment used to produce Hawk equipment.

and for the contract repartitioning plan, described above. In addition, the Committee's report stated:

1. That SETEL would serve the purposes of: "Centralizing contacts with U.S. industry and coordinating matters of patents and licenses." "Assuming Central Technical Management and coordination of production in order to insure quality and efficiency. . . ." "Centralizing the general planning for carrying out the program." "Coordinating economic and financial matters."
2. That the Mandate would: "Assume central technical management and coordination of production." "Coordinate the technical liaison with U.S. industry." "Coordinate the documentation."
3. That each NPC would have clearly allotted to it, the technical responsibility for turning out items that meet the same conditions as U.S. produced equipment and missiles.

On recommendation by the NATO Hawk Working Group, the NATO Council approved the proposals made by the Committee of Industrialists. As of this time (fall of 1959), there was a tacit understanding of the

Exhibit 26—17 Study of the NATO Hawk Program Financial Plans for Production Allocation October 1959 (millions of dollars)

Equipment	Belgium & Holland	France	Germany	Italy	Total
Battery Control					
Central (BCC)	10.1				10.1
Pulse Acquisition					
Radar (PAR)				13.7	13.7
Continuous Wave					
Acquisition Radar (CWAR)	11.4				11.4
Continuous Wave					
Illuminator (CWI)	3.3	12.1	10.8		26.2
Launcher					
Electronics	8.1				8.1
Mechanics	17.3	24.3	10.8		52.4
Loader			20.2	10.0	30.2
Maintenance Equipment					
Missile				5.7	5.7
Ground Equipment	5.7	11.4	10.2		27.3
Missiles	6.0	74.6	58.1	19.7	158.5
Total per country	61.9	122.4	110.1	49.1	343.5

SOURCE: Final Report of the Hawk Industrial Conference, HK 42, English translation, dated 20 October 1959.

Exhibit 26—18 Study of the NATO Hawk Program Financial Plans for Production Allocation November 1961 (millions of U.S. dollars)

Equipment	Belgium	France	Germany	Holland	Italy	Total
BCC				10.93		10.93
PAR					11.16	11.16
CWAR	7.37			.87		8.24
HPI		7.15	11.14	18.28		36.57
Launcher	13.20					13.20
Maintenance Ground Equipment				3.43		3.43
Maintenance— Missile					5.76	5.76
AFCC		1.13				1.13
ROR	5.00				3.29	8.29
Ramp Set			.23			.23
Loader			5.63		3.81	9.44
Pallets			.84			.84
Trailer			1.14	2.47		3.61
Shelter	2.26			1.27		3.53
FME Shops	5.52	4.13	2.60		2.44	14.69
Missiles	11.22	57.86	101.52	8.93	38.70	218.23
	44.57	69.14	124.23	46.18	65.16	349.28

SOURCE: NHMO records. This revision was proposed by SETEL on 13 June 1961 and approved by the NHMO 20 June 1961.

following conditions between the Committee of Industrialists and the NATO Hawk Working Group of the NATO Council:

1. Authority for implementing all decisions taken by the governments would remain with the governments, who would act through the Board of Directors of the NHMO. Each government would have a single vote and all such decisions would be taken unanimously. The staff of NHMO was *not* authorized to act as the procurement agency to commit governments either individually or collectively. Similarly, in industry, authority for policy decisions was to remain with each of the five National Prime Contractors (NPC's) who directed SETEL. Thus SETEL and NHMO were intended to be agencies for coordination, *not* for authority in taking and implementing the decisions to direct the overall program.

2. Organizations for overall program management in government and industry (i.e., the NHMO, SETEL, and the Mandate) would be kept as small as possible. Their size of staff and their financial budgets would be controlled by the Board of Directors of the NATO Hawk Manage-

Exhibit.26—19 Study of the NATO Hawk Program Cumulative Disbursements to Contractors (millions of U.S. Dollars)

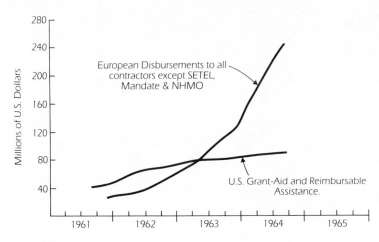

SOURCE: Finance Division, NHMO.

NOTES: Under terms agreed in the contract between SETEL and each European government, payments to contractors were made according to the following procedure.

Each NPC would present evidence to the GSS in his country of having expended efforts on Hawk Production. The GSS would endorse this evidence, which was then forwarded via SETEL to the Finance and Pricing Division of the NHMO. A special auditing committee would then examine and approve the request for payment. The NHMO would then request the appropriate government to deposit in the national bank of the NPC. The amount deposited was limited to a maximum of 95 percent of the amount requested and approved for payment.

Each NPC made periodic requests for payments. Different contractors were more or less prompt in rendering bills, so that payments were made from 3 to 12 weeks after the expenses were incurred. Moreover, since NHMO would authorize payment of a maximum of 95 percent of amounts requested and approved, the expenditure data graphed are not precisely indicative of true expenditures for the periods indicated. However, they were then as precise as could be made available.

Exhibit 26—20 Study of the NATO Hawk Program Cumulative Disbursements to Major Contractors (millions of U.S. Dollars)

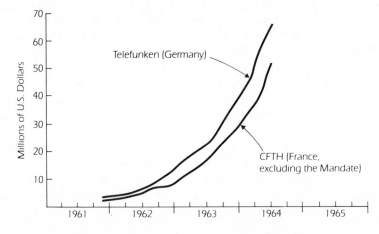

SOURCE: Finance Division, NHMO.

Exhibit 26—21 Study of the NATO Hawk Program Cumulative Disbursements to Major Contractors (millions of U.S. Dollars)

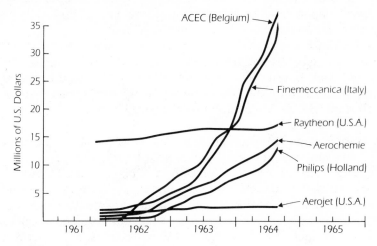

SOURCE: Finance Division, NHMO.

Exhibit 26—22 Study of the NATO Hawk Program Cumulative Expenditures for Program Management (millions of U.S. Dollars)

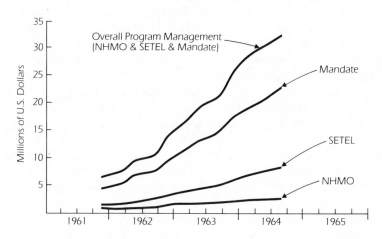

SOURCE: Finance Division, NHMO.

ment Office, which consisted of officials of the participating European governments.[4]

3. As European Prime Production Contractor, SETEL would depend substantially upon existing organizations for technical, financial, contract administration functions in each of the NPC's.

4. As the European agency for coordinating procurement, the NHMO would depend substantially on existing organizations for technical, financial, and contract administration functions of procurement already being performed by the government (chiefly, the Defense Ministry) in each state. Collectively, these functions were termed Government Surveillance Services (GSS).

5. Inasmuch as the European-produced Hawk was to be a "Chinese Copy" (i.e., an exact copy) of the U.S. produced Hawk, and technical responsibilities were "clearly allotted to the five NPC's," the Mandate would be essentially a technical services organization. In essence, its functions would be to coordinate technical liaison activities between firms in Europe and the U.S., particularly regarding technical documents (parts lists, technical drawings, test specifications, manufacturing and tool specifications, etc.).

In the fall of 1959, the Mandate set up its technical documentation center at Bagneux, near Paris. The provisional contracts between SETEL and each government were signed; and key personnel on the staffs of SETEL, the Mandate, and NHMO were sent to a Hawk Program indoctrination course taught by Raytheon Personnel at Andover, Massachusetts.

During the winter of 1959–60, the first technical documents from Raytheon were received by the Mandate; to represent the interests of the U.S. Government, the U.S. Army Missile Command staffed the U.S. NATO Hawk Liaison Office adjacent to the NHMO in Reuil-Malmaison, outside of Paris; a preliminary production schedule was drawn up indicating completion of all deliveries by early 1964; the Military Committee of the NATO Council laid plans to train European military personnel to operate and maintain Hawk Batteries when they would be put into service in Europe; drafts were made of the contracts between SETEL and Raytheon, providing for technical assistance to European manufacturers, and licensing them to use Raytheon-held patents. All these and other commitments were made even before the Program became a legal entity. As of March 31, 1960, the Hawk Production Program Agreement between the U.S. and the five European governments had *not* been signed.

The provisional contract[5] between SETEL and the five European gov-

---

[4] Although the U.S. would participate in discussions at all meetings of the Board, it would not vote in its decisions. All decisions would be taken unanimously by the Board. However, the U.S. reserved the right to veto decisions affecting military security or performance capabilities of the Hawk System.

[5] Equivalent to what is termed a preliminary "letter-contract" in the U.S.

ernments was signed on October 30, 1959. Payments to European industry were arranged on the basis of reimbursements for expenses plus percentage fees, as follows:

SETEL: Actual reimbursable expenses plus three percent of its total
           capitalization, with a maximum annual fee of 500,000 N.F.
           (approximately $100,000).

Mandate: Actual reimbursable expenses plus nine percent.

NPC's and Sub-Contractors:

           Actual reimbursable expenses (material, labor, plus over-
           head) plus nine percent if the contractor used his own facili-
           ties to produce or assemble Hawk Components; or reimburs-
           able expenses plus four percent if the contractor purchased
           the components from other sub-contractors.

All major sub-contracts were to be approved by the government and
NPC for each country, and by SETEL and the NHMO for all countries.

By the spring of 1960, planning had proceeded to the point where total
program costs during its first year (ending June 30, 1961) were estimated
to be $58 million.

Plans for Production Runs

Production of batteries were planned in terms of a series of five runs, designated A, B, C, thru E. Successive runs would involve a greater amount of
manufacturing in Europe and less manufacturing work in the U.S. Thus,
for the first six batteries in the A run, European manufacturers of major
equipment would assemble large components that were produced in the
U.S. For the next ten batteries, more European-produced (and fewer U.S.-
produced) components would be assembled into the major equipment.
Major equipment for the next fifty batteries of the C run were to be
assembled from still more European-produced parts (and fewer U.S.-
produced parts). And so on.

The idea behind these planned runs was, on the one hand, to start European manufacturing work as soon as possible, and, on the other hand, to
give time for the NPC's to develop and tool up as many sources of Hawk
production know-how of Europe as technical and economic conditions
would permit. Thus, the series of production runs (called "technical
slices") were in keeping with the principle of military urgency and the desire to utilize existing industrial capabilities in Europe.

To implement these plans, SETEL had to coordinate the contracting activities of the five NPC's consistently with the procurement lead-times
for the components to be produced in the U.S. for each assembly run
in Europe. Procurements of U.S.-produced items were to be channelled
through the NHMO and the U.S. Army contracting agencies.

NATO Hawk Program Problems

Changes in Partners and Financial Commitments

The Hawk Working Group had instructed the Committee of European Industrialists to use the following indices for organizing and allocating contrators' shares in the program:

Belgium	10.7 percent
France	35.7 percent
Germany	32.1 percent
Holland	7.2 percent
Italy	14.3 percent
	100.0 percent

Accordingly, the Industrialists proposed: (1) the establishment of SETEL as the European Prime Contracting organization chartered under French law (see Exhibits 26–3 through 26–7); (2) the establishment by the French NPC (CFTH) of the Mandate as the technical coordinating agency for European industry (see Exhibits 26–13 through 26–16); (3) the repartitioning of contracting efforts as described in Exhibit 26–17. The Industrialists reached these decisions at its meetings held during December 1958 and May 1959, and they were tacitly endorsed by the Hawk Working Group of the NATO Council.

In May, six months after General de Gaulle was elected President of France, the French representative announced that his government had to withdraw completely from participation in the NATO Hawk Program. The French had been weakened by military conflicts in Indochina and Algeria. Their industry seriously lagged behind other European industries and was not operating up to capacity. The de Gaulle government had to cut expenditures and therefore decided to withdraw from the NATO Hawk Program.

French withdrawal would have meant the collapse of the program. The number of Hawk batteries would have been too small to make it economically feasible for production by European industry.

To keep the program alive the U.S. Government decided to buy NATO Hawk batteries and persuaded the Dutch to increase their procurement and the French to reduce and not renounce its commitment to procure NATO Hawk batteries.

France reduced her share by 67 percent. As a concession to France, the German government agreed to give French industry about 22 percent of its shares of industrial participation and to have German industry produce 22 percent less than its share of European production.

Holland increased her share by 50 percent, which meant that she would procure the same number of batteries as Belgium and France.

The U.S. decided to procure Hawk batteries from European manufacturers. Originally, the U.S. had agreed to grant an estimated $30 million as technical and financial aid needed to get the program started. The decision to become a customer of European industry meant that in addition, the U.S. would finance 15.4 percent of the total costs of production, and receive 15.4 percent of the total number of batteries produced. Thus, the U.S. agreed to provide two kinds of funds, "Grant-Aid," and "Reimbursable Assistance."

The effect of the American and Dutch decisions was to offset (almost completely) the reduction in the French share. These changes are summarized in the following table:

Changes in Financial Shares of Procurement & Production in the NATO Hawk Program

| | Original Shares* of Procurement & Production | Shares* since June 1959 | |
		Procurement	Production
Belgium	10.7 percent	11.5 percent	11.5 percent
France	35.7　　"	11.5　　"	19.3　　"
Germany	32.1　　"	34.7　　"	26.9　　"
Italy	14.3　　"	15.4　　"	15.4　　"
Holland	7.2　　"	11.5 ,　"	11.5　　"
U.S.	0.0　　"	15.4　　"	15.4　　"
	100.0 percent	100.0 percent	100.0 percent

*Based on the number of Hawk batteries to be produced in Europe.

The "shares since June 1959" were adopted by the NATO Council. France would produce about 8 percent more than she could procure. In addition, France would gain financially from the fact that the governments had already agreed to establish SETEL, the Mandate, and the NHMO in France. Expenditures (amounting to about $33 million by July 1964) for these three overall program management organizations were *not* included in the percentage figures shown in the table. (See Exhibits 26–6, 26–11, and 26–16.) Thus, the principle of "proportionate share of financial participation" was not strictly applied. These changes meant the application of a fourth principle of "national economic development," in addition to the three principles discussed earlier: (1) proportionate financial share of participation; (2) maximum utilization of existing European organizations; (3) military urgency.

The shares of production indicated the relative amounts to be spent in industry of each country, except for the U.S. (See Exhibits 26–17 through 26–19.) When it decided to purchase European Hawk batteries, the U.S. did not insist that all Reimbursable Assistance Funds be spent in the U.S.

They were made available for NHMO and SETEL to manage, according to the principles of maximum utilization of European sources and expedient production.[6]

Even though it became another customer along with Belgium, France, Germany, Holland, and Italy, the U.S. government did not request full-fledged, voting membership on the Board of Directors of the NHMO. There were no significant changes in plans that had been made prior to June 1959 for organizing SETEL, NHMO, and the Mandate, the overall management agencies of the Program. (See Exhibits 26–3 through 26–16.)

When the NATO Council adopted these shares of Hawk Procurement and Production in June 1959, it also decided to agree on binding conditions that would penalize any government desiring to reduce its commitment in the future. Under the agreement on technical arrangements, such a government would have to pay all expenses for changing contract commitments made by industry; and, in addition, it would have to pay governments remaining in the consortium for the higher cost per battery that would result from the reduction or withdrawal of its commitment to the NATO Hawk consortium. These conditions were effective in binding all governments for the duration of the production program.

The Lack of Technical Definition and Control of Technical Documents for the NATO Hawk System

Beginning 1 December 1959, Raytheon and the U.S. Army Missile Command sent technical documents to the Mandate at increasing rates. These documents consisted of assembly and detail drawings, wiring diagrams, materials and parts lists, processing instructions, test specifications, etc. They numbered in the hundreds of thousands. In addition to these documents, sample hardware items were also sent to Europe. Along with technical assistance furnished by Raytheon personnel and a series of planned visits by key European technicians to U.S. manufacturing plants, these technical documents were the primary means of transferring the "technical know-how" from the U.S. to Europe. A "Chinese copy" of the U.S. Hawk System was to be produced.

After about nine months, key personnel began to realize that the technical definition for the NATO Hawk was so badly out of control that serious delays would result unless remedial actions were taken. Indeed, this problem *proved to be so* serious that it caused the NATO Hawk Program to be delayed from 10 to 12 months, according to several officials.

The Problem of Technical Definition and Control of Documents   As pointed out earlier, modern weapon systems are constantly being changed to improve their performance *while* they are being produced. Improve-

---

[6]However, by September 1964, total disbursements to U.S. industry were estimated unofficially to be about $60 million *more* than the financial assistance provided by the U.S. Government. Thus the NATO Hawk Program produced trade credits for U.S. industry.

ments are made by some technicians working directly on the hardware at test centers and by other technicians working in design and development laboratories.

Or, changes are made by technicians from two different firms working simultaneously on different equipment for the same weapon system. These changes must be made within specific limits of design configuration for the weapon system and each of its equipment, or else management would lose control system development and production operations. But often these limits, themselves, are subject to change as the system is developed. Indeed, changes in configuration control limits are a means for system development.

Some form of technical documentation is the only practical means for defining and controlling the configuration of the weapon system. However, some documents are changed *after* the hardware has been changed, while others are changed *before* the hardware has been changed. In simple terms, the problem of technical definition and control of technical documents is to establish and maintain a perfect compatibility, completeness and validity between and among the myriads of technical documents and corresponding hardware components that *together* define the weapon system.

The Hawk System consisted of about 100,000 different component parts. Each part had to be fully documented as to: its material, size, and shape specifications; its functional and spatial relationships with other parts; methods, tools, test equipment for its manufacture, inspection and test of its performance; etc. This gives an idea of the myriads of technical documents necessary to define the Hawk System so that personnel concerned with its manufacture, test, operation, maintenance, and improvement would know what was to be done. It also indicates a necessity for a centralized agency to maintain technical definition and control. Such an agency is usually called the system engineering organization.

Initially, the Mandate was *not* made explicitly responsible for validating all technical documents received in Europe from the U.S. (Recall that "technical responsibilities were clearly allotted to the five NPC's.")

Moreover, neither Raytheon nor the U.S. Army Missile Command (AMC) had a valid, complete, and up-to-date set of technical documents that were internally consistent and externally compatible with the sample Hawk equipment sent over for Europeans to reproduce. And Raytheon and the AMC did not validate the technical documents available before sending them to Europe.

Briefly, three steps were taken to establish configuration control for the NATO Hawk Program:

1. A set of major equipment of latest design and for which Raytheon had "adequate" documentation was selected and designated as "Configuration B," the basic Hawk configuration to be produced in Europe. In

effect, this design was "frozen" for purposes of European industry, so that all future changes could be controlled in Europe from "Configuration B" as the reference configuration.

2. Europeans obtained and validated a complete set of technical documents and sample hardware for this system configuration. This set was known as the European Dossier and it contained the Governments' Articulation List of documents for each major end-item of the Hawk System to be produced in Europe.

3. Europeans devised and adopted a set of rules and procedures to control changes to be made in technical documents used and hardware produced in Europe. This set of rules and procedures was approved by U.S. NATO Hawk Liaison Officer.

Technical changes continued to be made in the U.S., and Europeans were notified as these changes were authorized. But Europeans assumed control of the rate of adoptions in Europe of changes initiated in the U.S. These procedures permitted certain minor deviations from U.S. Hawks to be incorporated in European Hawks. Each proposed deviation was approved by U.S. NATO Hawk Officers.

The result has been that European-produced Hawk Batteries are *not* "Chinese copies" of U.S.-produced Hawk Batteries because the European Hawk design configuration did not include *all* the changes adopted and made in the U.S. Hawk equipment. One official stated in September, 1964 that if no further changes were made in U.S. Hawk design, it would take one year for the European Hawks to be made exactly like U.S. Hawks.

The Mandate developed and refined configuration definition and control procedures of the NATO Hawk System. Briefly, the procedures were based on the following principle categories of interchangeability with U.S. produced Hawk equipment:

1. *Complete conformity*—an exact replica of a U.S.-produced item, produced in Europe by a process identical with the one in the U.S.

2. *Industrial interchangeability*—identical in form and function with a U.S.-produced item, but processed differently from the U.S.

3. *Logistical interchangeability*—similar in form and function with the corresponding U.S.-produced item, but with minor differences authorized to permit the use of European standard components and test equipment for maintaining the Hawk equipment.

4. *Operational and functional interchangeability*—similar in form and function with corresponding U.S.-produced item, but with minor differences authorized to permit the use of European standard mechanical components, (e.g., lights and hitches for trailer vehicles; motor-generator sets).

European Engineering Requests (EER's) for changes in "Configuration B" had to be classified in one of these four categories. The Mandate,

NHMO, and the U.S. NATO Hawk Liaison Office reviewed and approved all EER's before they were authorized. Once these principle categories were approved, the Mandate was primarily responsible for coordinating, storing and disseminating *all* technical documents for the NATO Hawk Program.

In more detail, the Mandate developed the following procedures for controlling the technical definition and documentation:

Establishment of the European Dossier:

Standing procedures (approved January 1962)

Regulations on raw materials and components (approved July 1962)

Rules for format and numbering of documents (approved March 1962)

Procedures and forms for processing European Engineering Revisions (EER's) in technical documents (approved September 1962 for production documents; November 1963 for maintenance and supply documents)

Description of Technical Slices

General Rules (Developed November 1962)

Regulations on the format and nomenclature

Technical Acceptance Procedures

Regulations on final acceptance tests (approved 1963).

Beginning late in 1960, the Mandate was transformed from a mere technical documentation servicing center to a system engineering organization. By December 1961, its staff had increased from 100 to 300, and this growth continued to 510 by 1964. In addition to controlling changes in technical documents, the Mandate was made responsible for: (1) planning and staffing the technical activities at the Hawk System Checkout (HASCO) center (where final tests of Hawk Batteries are made pursuant to acceptance by governments); (2) analyzing and evaluating flight-tests of all European-produced Hawk missiles; (3) planning and staffing industrial activities for maintaining and supplying Hawk Batteries after delivery to NATO forces in the field.

By the end of 1963, nearly 2000 EER's had been authorized; by 31 March 1964, this number had increased to nearly 2800. Thus, the scope and authority of the Mandate as "system engineer" became much more substantial than originally anticipated by key officials who organized the NATO Hawk Program.

American and European officials expressed the opinion that the Mandate has performed its functions very satisfactorily. Indeed, one U.S. Army officer suggested that many aspects of configuration control procedures in the NATO Hawk Program are worthy of adoption in U.S. weapon system programs.

Procurement-Production Delays

As previously described, the plans for expanding European production in five "technical slices" required very close coordination between efforts to develop more and more qualified sources in Europe and procuring fewer and fewer Hawk components from qualified suppliers in the U.S.—while building up European production as rapidly and smoothly as possible. Each of the five technical slices contained a larger variety and quantity of components to be manufactured and tested. According to the principle of maximum use of European sources, the NPC's either produced the components in their own factories or sub-contracted with other European companies. If it was not technically or economically feasible to produce an item in Europe, then it was to be produced in the U.S.

Each NPC attempted to develop suppliers in his own country for the major equipment he was responsible for producing (see Exhibits 26–2, and 26–17 through 26–19). For many items, it was necessary to contract with suppliers in other countries. This was coordinated through SETEL and the other NPC's. In effect, each NPC became responsible for all Hawk Program sub-contractors in his own country, and for the final assembly and testing of certain major equipment. In other words, each NPC performed a dual function: (1) that of a "regional manager" of all industrial efforts in his country to produce components for any or all equipment of the Hawk System; (2) that of a "product manager" of industrial efforts in any or all countries to produce the Hawk equipment for which he was particularly responsible.

Each sub-contractor had to be certified as technically capable, financially responsible, and as having adequate provisions for military security. An agency of the defense ministry of each government certified the qualifications of each sub-contractor, on behalf of its own government and the NHMO. These agencies were called Government Surveillance Services (GSS).

There were essentially two reasons why some components continued to be procured from U.S. suppliers:

1. It would delay the Program to try to develop a qualified supplier in Europe.
2. It was not economically feasible to tool up in Europe for production of relatively small quantities.

Procurements from U.S. suppliers were normally channelled through three organizations known as "Procedure 6": (1) SETEL, which prepared the purchase requisitions; (2) NHMO and the U.S. Liaison Office; (3) the U.S. Army Missile Command, Huntsville, Alabama. The U.S. Government exercised a control over the choice, priority of service, and performance of U.S. suppliers and their products, for several reasons:

1. Since Hawk components were needed for the U.S. as well as for European production programs, the U.S. Government desired to influence U.S. manufacturers on questions of price, quality, and delivery service rendered to the U.S. Army and to Europe.
2. Since, at the European's request, the U.S. Government provided transportation from the U.S. to Europe, it needed to have the information on the European purchase orders.
3. Packaging of material for shipment had to be in accordance with U.S. procurement regulations.

It took from three to nine months for European manufacturers to receive the material, after they placed the order. The U.S. government did not charge the European Consortium for the procurement management services performed.

All manufacturing test equipment was procured from U.S. manufacturers in order to facilitate quality-assurance and control of European production, consistent with U.S. quality standards. An idea of the scope of procurement from U.S. sources can be obtained from the fact that for the "C run" (technical slice C), 17,500 different items of about 100,000 were ordered by SETEL in mid-1962 from U..S. sources.

For each production run, the Mandate furnished technical documents to appropriate NPC's. Raytheon technicians assisted Europeans by classifying components according to their production or procurement lead-time, so that long lead-time items could be procured first, and delays in building up European production could be minimized.

By 1963, nearly 500 different European firms and several hundred U.S. firms were involved in the NATO Hawk Program.

With this as a brief introduction to production planning and control problems, the reader might correctly infer that delays in procurement and production continued to occur throughout the history of the program. The net effect of these delays is difficult to estimate. Completed production of all NATO Hawk Batteries was originally scheduled (in late 1959) for early 1964. By mid-1964 the scheduled completion date had slipped by about 20 months. NATO Hawk officials estimated that delays caused by the lack of technical definition and valid documentation amounted to 10–12 months. Thus, we might deduce that procurement-production delays had caused the program to slip from 6 to 8 months.[7] From late 1959 through mid-1964, the Program Schedule was revised at least five times, each revision with a later completion date.

Naturally, government and industry officials do not agree on the major

---

[7] Of course, these slippages are based on the first scheduled completion date for the NATO Hawk Production Program. It can be argued that this date was too optimistic, and that these measures of slippages are not as significant as they seem to be. However, the fact is that completion of production program has taken nearly 40 percent more time than NATO Hawk managers originally said it would. This indicates room for improvement either in planning or in controlling the deliveries of Hawk material.

causes of these delays. And naturally, there is some validity to the asser-
tions by both. In essence, government officials (in NHMO) have said that
SETEL and the NPC's failed to establish and implement a sufficiently
tight and consistent procedure for planning, measurement, and expediting production progress by European manufacturers. European industrialists have said that governments have interposed too much "red tape" in
the procurement and production practices of industry. Both European government *and* industrial officials said that the U.S. government has been a
major cause of procurement-production delays; U.S. government officials
have rebutted this.

Production Planning and Control in European Industry   After the basic
plan for contract repartitioning had been approved (see Exhibit 26–19),
the NPC's proceeded accordingly with more detailed planning, while
SETEL was being staffed. Each NPC established a Hawk Program Office
and selected the jobs that were to be sub-contracted with other manufacturers or produced in his own plants. As a result, production planning and
control functions were essentially decentralized at each of the five NPC's.
The latter kept SETEL advised rather informally of plans and progress of
production in Europe.

Differences in Contracting Policies of NPC's   The five NPC's faced different market conditions and had different policies for sub-contracting
their portions of Hawk production. As a result, some exerted more effort
than others in developing qualified European sources, before reverting to
original U.S. sources. This probably delayed the program to some extent,
although it was impossible to state how long, or which NPC caused the
delay. These differences were manifested with respect to the following:

1. Manufacturing facilities owned and operated by the NPC.
2. Previous experiences in manufacturing modern defense electronic
   equipment.
3. The existing backlog of commercial, industrial, and defense work
   being done in each of the five countries.
4. The extent to which each government influenced "his" NPC in implementing its policies of regional economic development and full
   employment.
5. Languages.

Philips (Holland), Telefunken (Germany), CFTH (France), and ACEC
(Belgium) owned and operated integrated facilities for manufacture, assembly, and testing electronic equipment. Finmeccanica was actually a
nationalized holding company, a division of I.R.I., with most of its financial shares held by the Italian government. It had no facilities of its own,
but held financial interests in other Italian manufacturing firms manufacturing electrical, electronic and mechanical products.

With respect to previous experience in manufacturing modern defense electronic equipment, probably Philips, Telefunken, and CFTH had had more than ACEC and Finmeccanica. ACEC had had more experience with heavy electrical equipment manufacturing than with defense electronic equipment manufacturing.

Industry in Holland and Germany was operating at a higher level of capacity than industries in Belgium, France and Italy. Consequently, Dutch and German manufacturers had somewhat less need for additional contract-work on NATO Hawk than the manufacturers in France and Italy. This helped to explain why Philips continued to rely more extensively on U.S. sources than the other NPC's. It also explained why Hawk production received a different priority in different contractors' organizations.

Regarding influences of government policies of regional economic development and full employment, it was apparent that these influences were exerted more strongly by the French and Italian governments than by the other three. The amount of contract-work for Hawk done by firms located South of Rome reflected the Italian government's policy on regional economic development. From conversations with officials, it was apparent that the French government influenced sub-contracting decisions made by CFTH, more than the Dutch government influenced Philips, or than the Belgian government influenced ACEC.

Differences in language naturally caused delays in communications. English and French were adopted as the two official languages, but, of course, German, Dutch and Italian were used as well. Language problems probably delayed the negotiation and signing of the "definitized" contract between SETEL and each government, perhaps as much as any other reason. It took nearly two years for the provisional contract to be expanded into detailed and explicit legal terms that were identical and suitable to each government and each NPC. The contract was initially negotiated in English and French and drafted under terms of French law. But these terms had to be translated into Dutch, German and Italian, so that SETEL had an identical contract with all five European governments.

None of these differences adversely affected the technical performance of European industry. Flight tests proved that the performance of NATO Hawk batteries produced in Europe was as capable and reliable as those produced by U.S. firms.

Production Planning and Control Procedures   In March 1963, at the suggestion of the U.S. NATO Hawk Liaison Office, SETEL established a set of line-of-balance charts to be used in planning and controlling production. These charts consisted of a vertical list of major and "critical" hardware items along the left-hand side, with a horizontal time-scale showing planned and actual production quantities for each item, like Gantt Charts. "Critical items" were those for which production delayed the overall program, for any reason. In addition, SETEL began to hold

monthly progress review meetings for NHMO and SETEL officials to exchange views and determine future actions that would reduce further delays in the program. SETEL officials prepared the agenda and led the discussions at these meetings, which usually lasted about six hours.

In using these charts, SETEL solicited progress-data from the five NPC's
each month, and updated the charts accordingly. SETEL took about three
weeks to do this. Then, the monthly progress review meetings were held.
Progress on "critical items" was reported weekly so that latest information was available at the meetings; otherwise, the progress information
reported was about 3 to 4 weeks old, when the meetings were held.

None of the NPC's used more detailed line-of-balance charts (subsidiary to those kept by SETEL) to follow up and measure progress in his sector of the program. Less formal procedures were used to measure and control progress by European contractors:

1. informal, non-classified reports of units produced or shipped each
   week or month.
2. telephone conversations or Telex messages among production control personnel in SETEL, NPC's and sub-contractors' organizations.
3. visits by technicians or contract expeditors at contractors' plants.

The NHMO had to rely mainly on SETEL to monitor and report progress of industry. To verify these reports, personnel in NHMO's Production
Planning Division also received progress reports from GSS (Government
Surveillance Services) personnel, who visited at contractors' plants to
check on quality, costs, or delivery of Hawk material. But NHMO and the
governments were not staffed to check on progress as thoroughly as contractors were.[8] To expedite production, NHMO personnel made occasional visits at contractors' factories. These visits were made always after
informing SETEL, which usually sent a representative to be present when
NHMO personnel visited at contractors' plants.

In general, the most reliable "check points" for governments to measure industrial progress were those at which Hawk material was shipped
from one country to another. Within a country the flow of production was
measured and expedited by the NPC. However, certain actions to expedite production required approval by governments before they could be
taken. For examples: waivers in quality specifications; overtime operation
of plants; providing additional equipment or facilities at governments'
expense.

To expedite shipments between countries, governments had to arrange
for waivers of tariffs, custom-inspections, and certain transportation regulations. Usually, these were "ad hoc" kinds of arrangements, worked out
by officials in the Ministries of Defense, Economic Affairs and States of

---

[8] Unlike the Department of Defense in the U.S., European defense ministers did not post "resident" inspectors, auditors, or
contract expeditors in plants of European firms.

countries receiving and shipping Hawk material. A number of inconsistencies were brought to light in discussions for these legal arrangements. For example, in order for explosives to be transported to test centers, German regulations prohibited transportation by truck and required transport by rail, while Italian regulations stipulated just the opposite. So, an accommodation had to be made.

Control of U.S. Produced Items   European industrialists often complained that the NATO Hawk Program was delayed by the U.S. government's controls over procurement of U.S.-produced items. In addition to those cited earlier, another reason why the U.S. government wanted to control U.S. production of NATO Hawk material was to be able to combine orders for both U.S. and NATO Hawk items wherever possible, and thus achieve greater production economy. Nevertheless, even U.S. officials admitted that U.S. government procurement procedures probably caused certain delays in the NATO Hawk Program, for several reasons, notably:

1. Regulations requiring defense contracts to be awarded to small business whenever possible; this sometimes delayed the selection and development of qualified U.S. sources.
2. The Department of Defense policy requiring MILSTRIP and competitive bidding on follow-on contracts for defense material.[9]
3. The Cuban alert in October 1962 temporarily diverted U.S. support away from NATO production programs in Europe.

European and U.S. governments agreed to permit European manufacturers to deal directly with qualified U.S. manufacturers, instead of going through the U.S. government. This shortcut procedure (known as "Procedure 8") was used with the approval of the NHMO in cases where production in Europe would have been seriously delayed or costs exorbitant.

As another of its services, the U.S. NATO Hawk Liaison office in Paris assisted in procurements from U.S. sources. Most routine items were ordered via Army Procurement District Offices (e.g., in Boston or San Francisco). Items requiring special technical advice for procurement decisions were purchased through U.S. Army Arsenals at Redstone or Pickatinny. Progress of these procurements was reported normally via copies of routine documents (e.g., purchase orders, bills of lading, shipping notices, etc.) sent to the U.S. Liaison Office in Paris and to the appropriate European contractors. Cables, Telex messages, and personal visits were sometimes necessary to expedite production and shipments of U.S.-produced items.

---

[9] In its efforts to achieve further economies in 1962, the U.S. Department of Defense adopted policies of consolidating material requirements of its Army, Navy, and Air Force, and of inviting competitive firms to submit competitive bids on materials procured from U.S. industry. This policy increased procurement lead-times.

Financial Penalties for Delays   In its contract with each of the five European governments, SETEL agreed for NPC's to be penalized for failure to complete deliveries of Hawk batteries in accordance with the contractual delivery schedule. Penalties amounted to the loss of up to 65 percent of contractor's fees. In other words, SETEL and the NPC's were to be reimbursed for "allowed" expenses, but 65 percent of their fees (amounting to as much as 9 percent of reimbursable expenses) were to be withheld if they caused the program to slip beyond the completion date stipulated as Annex 4 of the contract.

The definitized, contractual schedule was agreed upon and signed in April 1963. By November 1963, SETEL and NHMO had negotiated at least three extensions to this schedule. Each revision authorized additional program slippage without financial penalties. For example, in February 1964 SETEL proposed to negotiate for an additional authorized delay of about five months, because it claimed that the contractual delivery schedule (which had been revised in November 1963) was unrealistic. But by mid-1964, the Governments agreed to authorize this extension.

Overall Progress Achieved

Overall progress can perhaps best be measured against time in terms of financial expenditures, and number of batteries delivered. Exhibits 26–23

Exhibit 26–23 Actual Total Disbursements for the NATO Hawk Program (U.S. and European Efforts)

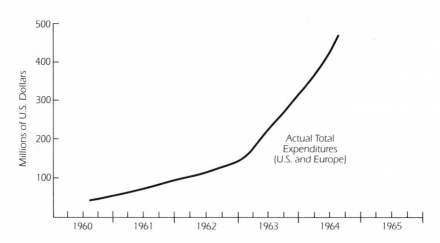

SOURCE: Data from the Financial Division of NHMO.
NOTE: The graph is subject to inaccuracies inherent in the contractor payments procedures.

Exhibit 26—24 Planned & Actual Delivery Rates For the NATO Hawk Program (percent of Planned Max. Batteries per month)

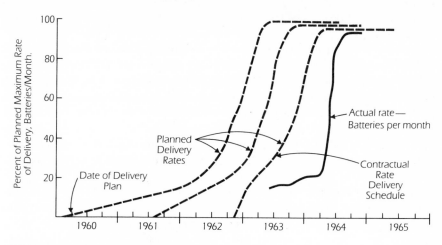

SOURCE: Data from the files of the U.S. NATO Hawk Liaison Office.

NOTE: Planned Maximum rate of delivery remained constant throughout the history of the program.

and 26–24 facilitate comparisons of planned and actual measures of progress in these terms.

The NATO Hawk Program—Epilogue

The NATO Hawk Program proved the effectiveness of multinational governmental-industrial cooperation, for a variety of reasons.

European-produced Hawk batteries were as high in performance quality and reliability and as low in costs as U.S.-produced batteries deployed on the NATO air-defense line across central Europe. U.S. and European industries demonstrated their capabilities to work together on complex systems. Europeans managed technical changes perhaps even more effectively than American counterparts in the NATO Hawk Program.

The program demonstrated that large numbers of managers, staff specialists, military personnel, and trade unionists of different nations with different languages, laws, and customs work effectively together, when jobs, income, and military security are at stake. They overcame their differences and united in taking concrete actions in Hawk production, even while their national leaders took divergent policies and strained the NATO alliance. General de Gaulle forced NATO headquarters to be moved from Paris and withdrew French forces from those integrated under NATO commanders. Europeans increased their conversions of U.S. dollars into gold, thereby exacerbating U.S. problems of deficits in international payments and "gold-flow" from Fort Knox. One U.S. official suggested that operations of the NATO Hawk Program helped substantially to keep NATO "glued together."

NATO Hawk proved the economic, technical feasibility and the military advantages of standardized, complex weapons for NATO.

But, in a larger sense the NATO Hawk Program has not yet proved to be effective. Its momentum was not sufficient to launch a Western policy or process for more and larger NATO cooperative programs, for several reasons.

Information about the methods and effectiveness of NATO Hawk operations remained classified, and therefore, not readily available for assessment and use by Western leaders.

SETEL, the prime contracting agency of industry and NHMO, the managing agency of participating governments, was not permitted to grow strong. Nor was it given resources necessary for developing and executing "follow-on," "next generation" weapon system programs essential to the survival and growth of their market created by the NATO Hawk Program.

Myths remained widespread about differences between U.S. and European abilities and methods for engineering and managing large-scale, complex programs. There were serious allegations about a technological gap and a brain drain from Europe to the U.S. Yet, realities are that U.S., European and Japanese companies organized and expanded their multinational operations concerned with technically complex equipment. For example, the IBM computer System 360 was developed as a result of multinational cooperation by American and European scientists and engineers working at IBM installations in England, France, and the USA.

The U.S. launched its aggressive foreign military sales program to alleviate problems of dollar deficits and gold-flow on international currency exchanges. Even though the NATO Hawk Program provided $100 million in trade credits and currency payments after four years of operation, the Pentagon abandoned its policy favoring defense-industrial cooperation. Since 1962, it has competed for shares in arms export markets with arms ministries of allied governments. Sales of the most modern U.S. weapons to non-aligned governments of Iran and Saudi Arabia are explained by American officials, saying, "If we don't sell U.S. arms, the French or British will." By 1976 U.S. foreign military sales were at the rate of $10 billion a year. Although European governments have launched cooperative programs such as the British-French Concorde supersonic aircraft, Washington has not participated in government-industrial programs comparable with NATO Hawk.

Yet, more multinational governmental-industrial cooperation in programs comparable with NATO Hawk could lead to significant benefits for Western nations.

The military effectiveness of NATO military forces could be increased from 30 to 300 percent for different unit-commands according to General A. Goodposter, former NATO Commander. NATO's expenditures could be reduced by $10 billion annually, if common, standard weapons were deployed (against the standard weapons deployed by Warsaw-Pact forces).

Western governments would be relieved of burdens supporting redundant arms industrial capabilities in North America and Europe. Cooperation would mean that competitive pressures for Western allies to promote arms exports and expand the arms race in non-aligned areas of the Persian Gulf, Latin America or Africa would be reduced, if not eliminated. This would reduce risks of diffusing technological superiority of Western arms, and of armed violence or insurgencies, which have interfered with Western efforts to provide assistance in industrial and economic development in those countries.

Multinational companies would participate under terms of a single contract with cooperating governments. Thus, governments' contracts would channel powers of Western industrial firms to work more effectively in international affairs in the interests of Western governments: to reduce pressures for bribery payments by companies; to make uniform regulations on conditions for employment, trade, energy, currency payments, so as to reduce governments' problems of inflation, unemployment, deficits in trade, or in relations with developing nations.

American firms are expanding their commitments to multinational industrial cooperation. Boeing and McDonnell-Douglas have agreed to cooperate with French and Japanese interests (government and industry) in developing "next generation" medium-range, transport aircraft. Similar commitments have been made by U.S. and German auto firms. The costs of competitive, technological developments are too high and opportunities for common international markets are too great.

How can advantages from experiences in the NATO Hawk Program become precedents for reviving the U.S. Government's policy of the era of its Marshall Plan favoring multinational government-industry cooperative programs?

Necchi S.p.A.

27

The Necchi company, originally a well-known cast-iron foundry, started manufacturing sewing machines in 1919. At that time, Italy imported 120,000 sewing machines, of which about 30% came from Switzerland and 70%, from Germany. At first, production was run on a trial basis and did not exceed four or five units per day. Until 1925, all machines were sold under the brand name I.R.I. (Industrie Riunite Italiane) in order to protect the reputation enjoyed by the company's name from the uncertainties of trial production. In that year, management was confident that they had acquired enough technical and marketing experience to launch on the market a sewing machine under the Necchi name.

In 1938, sales of Necchi sewing machines, whose design had been constantly improved, had increased to 50,000 units per year. A new model with a special head for button-holing and fancy stitching introduced in 1936 had accounted for a large part of this success. This process of expansion, interrupted by the war, continued even more markedly in the postwar years. In 1956, Necchi's production was up to 250,000 units, more than 50% of total Italian production, and their sales were still increasing steadily with no indication of levelling off.

This healthy state of business had been the result of several actions taken by management both in the technical and commercial fields. Necchi's foundry, for instance, which produced the component parts of the sewing machines, was highly rated among similar European shops. A high degree of mechanization in this as well as in other departments had brought about considerable savings in production costs. Moreover, a model of a new design had won world-wide recognition both among the buyers and the experts of industrial design.

The factory, located at Pavia, Italy, spread over an area of 147,881 square meters, 55% of which was under cover. Several types of sewing machine, wooden cabinets, and foundry products such as pipe fittings, engine parts, etc., were turned out at this location. The total work force consisted of 4,500 employees divided as follows: 65% in the sewing machine division, 25% in the foundry and 10% in the cabinet and furniture carpentry.

The head of the industrial engineering department requested Mr. Andreoli, a young engineer trained in motion and time methods by the MTM Association for Standards and Research in the United States, to make a survey of the company's current practices of methods study and time setting. The purpose of this survey was to make an appraisal of the situation and of the problems created by an extensive use of predetermined time standards such as MTM.

Necchi management had introduced the MTM system (see Exhibit 27–1) with a view toward achieving the following goals:

1. To develop and train supervisors to become highly methods conscious.
2. To establish work simplification by improving existing methods and analyzing motions elements.
3. To guide product design, to develop effective tool design, and to select effective equipment through forward planning of work methods.
4. To improve human relations in the plant by reducing the number of grievances on time standards and to overcome workers' resistance to changes in methods. It was recognized that when a man had worked on a given job for a period of time, he came to look at it as *his* job. He developed the feeling that he had vested interest in that job, which became stronger the longer he held it. As a result his inclination was to resist changes. With the MTM approach the manager hoped that it would be possible to carry out any corrections and simplification of methods during the creation and planning stages of a new job.

At that time, the existing methods department was given the responsibility of training people in the new technique. The engineers of the methods study department gathered all the books on the subject they could find and then started applying MTM to some shop operations. The outcome of these first experiments was far from being satisfactory, due to the lack of theoretical knowledge and practical experience of the engineers.

At that time, fóur industrial engineers of Necchi were in the United

---

Exhibit 27–1 Explanation of MTM

Methods-Time Measurement—MTM—is a system originally established by Messrs. Maynard, Stegemerten and Schwab[1] for developing work methods and obtaining work standards. These authors say that MTM is a procedure which analyzes any manual operation and breaks it into the basic motions required to perform it, and which assigns to each basic motion a predetermined time standard which is a function of the nature of the motion and the conditions under which it is made. MTM consists of a concise catalogue of work motions with a table of time values for each. This catalogue divides all work motions into the following basic groups:

1. Reach	6. Disengage
2. Move	7. Release
3. Grasp	8. Apply pressure
4. Turn	9. Body, leg, eye,
5. Position	and foot motions

Each of these basic motions is further divided into a number of classes and cases, and a table of time values furnishes a value for every class and case of each of the basic motions.

The procedure for using MTM can be summarized as consisting of two major steps. First, all motions required to perform the operation must be analyzed, classified, measured, and recorded. Second, the corresponding MTM time values are selected from the tables, applied to the analysis and totaled. A more elaborate outline of the MTM procedure includes the following steps:

□ analyze every motion used in the operations
□ identify then classify each motion used
□ record each motion identified
□ establish distances, adjust for "assisting motions"
□ determine which motions are "limited"
□ select time values from MTM tables
□ total time for all motions in the operation
□ add to total time allowances for fatigue, personnel, etc.

The proponents of MTM claim that the key to successful results with MTM is sound and thorough training, and that a period of guided application will shorten considerably the time required by a trainee to reach an acceptable level of proficiency in analyzing operations. This training is conducted by special consulting firms that are members of the MTM Association for Standards and Research.

[1] See *Methods-Time Measurement*, Maynard, Stegemerten & Schwab, McGraw-Hill Book Company, Inc., 1948.

Exhibit 27–1 (continued)

These firms maintain that MTM has many uses, among which, it offers an improved procedure for handling these four industrial problems:

1. *Selection of Efficient Methods in the Planning Stages*

   The MTM procedure has simplified the investigation of alternative methods for performing an operation before production is started. It provides a very accurate guide for developing and selecting the most practical and efficient method and allows for training of the operators in the prooper procedure at the out-set.

2. *Simplified Methods Training for Operators and Supervisors*

   Detailed MTM motion analyses help operators to learn new operations more rapidly. These analyses go a long way toward preventing operators from developing inefficient habit patterns which later must be corrected. It has been found that when a new operation is explained in terms of MTM motions and times, the operators acquire a better understanding of the nature and requirements of the job.

   Supervisors trained in the use of MTM realize more fully the effect of good methods on costs. Ineffective motion sequences are easily detected by an MTM trained observer; he sees them almost automatically and plans for their elimination.

3. *Establishing Accurate Production Standards*

   MTM makes it possible to establish accurate time standards for manual operations without the use of a stopwatch. This eliminates the pressure imposed on workers who become nervous when being clocked. One of the most significant advantages of MTM is its speed in setting production and wage incentive standards. Often standards can be set with MTM in from 25%–50% of the time required to set standards by conventional time study methods.

4. *Developing Time Standards or Measure of a Fair Day's Work*

   For these purposes, the acceptance of MTM by several labor groups has been an outstanding feature. It is felt that the following factors contribute to this acceptance:

   □ published data which has been independently checked and substantiated by research groups
   □ simplicity of application
   □ elimination or reduction of the use of a stopwatch
   □ elimination of performance rating
   □ an objective approach compared with the relatively subjective approach of stopwatch studies.

Exhibit 27–1 (continued)

METHODS-TIME MEASUREMENT APPLICATION DATA

SIMPLIFIED DATA

(All times on this Simplified Data Table include 15% allowance)

HAND AND ARM MOTIONS	BODY, LEG, AND EYE MOTIONS

HAND AND ARM MOTIONS

REACH or MOVE   TMU
  1″ 2
  2″ 4
  3″ to 12″ 4 + length of motion
  over 12″ 3 + length of motion
  (For TYPE 2 REACHES AND
  MOVES use length of motion
  only)

POSITION
  Fit   Symmetrical   Other
  Loose   10   15
  Close   20   25
  Exact   50   55

TURN—APPLY PRESSURE
  TURN................ 6
  APPLY PRESSURE.. 20

GRASP
  Simple.............. 2
  Regrasp or Transfer... 6
  Complex............. 10

DISENGAGE
  Loose............... 5
  Close............... 10
  Exact............... 30

BODY, LEG, AND EYE MOTIONS

                                    TMU
Simple foot motion....... 10
Foot motion with pressure 20
Leg motion 10

Side step case 1......... 20
Side step case 2......... 40

Turn body case 1....... 20
Turn body case 2........ 45

Eye time............. 10

Bend, stoop or kneel on
  one knee................ 35
Arise................... 35

Kneel on both knees..... 80
Arise................... 90

Sit.................. 40
Stand............... 50

Walk per pace.......... 17

  1 TMU = .00001 hour
        = .0006 minute
        = .036   second

Exhibit 27—1 (continued)

TABLE IV—GRASP—G

Case	Time TMU	DESCRIPTION
1A	2.0	**Pick Up Grasp**—Small, medium or large object by itself, easily grasped.
1B	3.5	Very small object or object lying close against a flat surface.
1C1	7.3	Interference with grasp on bottom and one side of nearly cylindrical object. Diameter larger than ½".
1C2	8.7	Interference with grasp on bottom and one side of nearly cylindrical object. Diameter ¼" to ½".
1C3	10.8	Interference with grasp on bottom and one side of nearly cylindrical object. Diameter less than ¼".
2	5.6	**Regrasp.**
3	5.6	**Transfer Grasp.**
4A	7.3	Object jumbled with other objects so search and select occur. Larger than 1" x 1" x 1".
4B	9.1	Object jumbled with other objects so search and select occur. ¼" x ¼" x ⅛" to 1" x 1" x 1".
4C	12.9	Object jumbled with other objects so search and select occur. Smaller than ¼" x ¼" x ⅛".
5	0	Contact, sliding or hook grasp.

TABLE V—POSITION*—P

CLASS OF FIT		Symmetry	Easy To Handle	Difficult To Handle
1—Loose	No pressure required	S	5.6	11.2
		SS	9.1	14.7
		NS	10.4	16.0
2—Close	Light pressure required	S	16.2	21.8
		SS	19.7	25.3
		NS	21.0	26.6
3—Exact	Heavy pressure required.	S	43.0	48.6
		SS	46.5	52.1
		NS	47.8	53.4

*Distance moved to engage—1" or less.

TABLE VI—RELEASE—RL

Case	Time TMU	DESCRIPTION
1	2.0	Normal release performed by opening fingers as independent motion.
2	0	Contact Release.

TABLE VII—DISENGAGE—D

CLASS OF FIT	Easy to Handle	Difficult to Handle
1—Loose—Very slight effort, blends with subsequent move.	4.0	5.7
2—Close — Normal effort, slight recoil.	7.5	11.8
3—Tight — Considerable effort, hand recoils markedly.	22.9	34.7

TABLE VIII—EYE TRAVEL TIME AND EYE FOCUS—ET AND EF

Eye Travel Time $=15.2 \times \dfrac{T}{D}$ TMU, with a maximum value of 20 TMU.

where T = the distance between points from and to which the eye travels.
D = the perpendicular distance from the eye to the line of travel T.

Eye Focus Time = 7.3 TMU.

Exhibit 27–1 (continued)

TABLE I—REACH—R

Distance Moved Inches	Time TMU A	B	C or D	E	Hand In Motion A	B	CASE AND DESCRIPTION
¾ or less	2.0	2.0	2.0	2.0	1.6	1.6	**A** Reach to object in fixed location, or to object in other hand or on which other hand rests.
1	2.5	2.5	3.6	2.4	2.3	2.3	
2	4.0	4.0	5.9	3.8	3.5	2.7	
3	5.3	5.3	7.3	5.3	4.5	3.6	**B** Reach to single object in location which may vary slightly from cycle to cycle.
4	6.1	6.4	8.4	6.8	4.9	4.3	
5	6.5	7.8	9.4	7.4	5.3	5.0	
6	7.0	8.6	10.1	8.0	5.7	5.7	
7	7.4	9.3	10.8	8.7	6.1	6.5	**C** Reach to object jumbled with other objects in a group so that search and select occur.
8	7.9	10.1	11.5	9.3	6.5	7.2	
9	8.3	10.8	12.2	9.9	6.9	7.9	
10	8.7	11.5	12.9	10.5	7.3	8.6	
12	9.6	12.9	14.2	11.8	8.1	10.1	**D** Reach to a very small object or where accurate grasp is required.
14	10.5	14.4	15.6	13.0	8.9	11.5	
16	11.4	15.8	17.0	14.2	9.7	12.9	
18	12.3	17.2	18.4	15.5	10.5	14.4	
20	13.1	18.6	19.8	16.7	11.3	15.8	
22	14.0	20.1	21.2	18.0	12.1	17.3	**E** Reach to indefinite location to get hand in position for body balance or next motion or out of way.
24	14.9	21.5	22.5	19.2	12.9	18.8	
26	15.8	22.9	23.9	20.4	13.7	20.2	
28	16.7	24.4	25.3	21.7	14.5	21.7	
30	17.5	25.8	26.7	22.9	15.3	23.2	

TABLE II—MOVE—M

Distance Moved Inches	Time TMU A	B	C	Hand In Motion B	Wt. Allowance Wt. (lb.) Up to	Factor	Constant TMU	CASE AND DESCRIPTION
¾ or less	2.0	2.0	2.0	1.7	2.5	1.00	0	
1	2.5	2.9	3.4	2.3				**A** Move object to other hand or against stop.
2	3.6	4.6	5.2	2.9	7.5	1.06	2.2	
3	4.9	5.7	6.7	3.6				
4	6.1	6.9	8.0	4.3	12.5	1.11	3.9	
5	7.3	8.0	9.2	5.0				
6	8.1	8.9	10.3	5.7	17.5	1.17	5.6	
7	8.9	9.7	11.1	6.5				
8	9.7	10.6	11.8	7.2				
9	10.5	11.5	12.7	7.9	22.5	1.22	7.4	**B** Move object to approximate or indefinite location.
10	11.3	12.2	13.5	8.6				
12	12.9	13.4	15.2	10.0	27.5	1.28	9.1	
14	14.4	14.6	16.9	11.4				
16	16.0	15.8	18.7	12.8	32.5	1.33	10.8	
18	17.6	17.0	20.4	14.2				
20	19.2	18.2	22.1	15.6				
22	20.8	19.4	23.8	17.0	37.5	1.39	12.5	
24	22.4	20.6	25.5	18.4				**C** Move object to exact location.
26	24.0	21.8	27.3	19.8	42.5	1.44	14.3	
28	25.5	23.1	29.0	21.2				
30	27.1	24.3	30.7	22.7	47.5	1.50	16.0	

TABLE III—TURN AND APPLY PRESSURE—T AND AP

Weight	Time TMU for Degrees Turned 30°	45°	60°	75°	90°	105°	120°	135°	150°	165°	180°
Small— 0 to 2 Pounds	2.8	3.5	4.1	4.8	5.4	6.1	6.8	7.4	8.1	8.7	9.4
Medium—2.1 to 10 Pounds	4.4	5.5	6.5	7.5	8.5	9.6	10.6	11.6	12.7	13.7	14.8
Large— 10.1 to 35 Pounds	8.4	10.5	12.3	14.4	16.2	18.3	20.4	22.2	24.3	26.1	28.2

APPLY PRESSURE CASE 1—16.2 TMU.   APPLY PRESSURE CASE 2—10.6 TMU

Exhibit 27–1 (continued)

TABLE IX—BODY, LEG AND FOOT MOTIONS

DESCRIPTION	SYMBOL	DISTANCE	TIME TMU
Foot Motion—Hinged at Ankle:	FM	Up to 4″	**8.5**
With heavy pressure.	FMP		**19.1**
Leg or Foreleg Motion.	LM —	Up to 6″	**7.1**
		Each add'l. inch	**1.2**
Sidestep—Case 1—Complete when lead-	SS-C1	Less than 12″	Use REACH or MOVE Time
ing leg contacts floor.		12″	**17.0**
		Each add'l. Inch	**.6**
Case 2—Lagging leg must	SS-C2	12″	**34.1**
contact floor before next motion can be made.		Each add'l. inch	**1.1**
Bend, Stoop, or Kneel on One Knee.	B,S,KOK		**29.0**
Arise.	AB,AS,AKOK		**31.9**
Kneel on Floor—Both Knees.	KBK		**69.4**
Arise.	AKBK		**76.7**
Sit.	SIT		**34.7**
Stand from Sitting Position.	STD		**43.4**
Turn Body 45 to 90 degrees—			
Case 1—Complete when leading leg contacts floor.	TBC1		**18.6**
Case 2—Lagging leg must contact floor before next motion can be made.	TBC2		**37.2**
Walk.	W-FT.	Per Foot	**5.3**
Walk.	W-P	Per Pace	**15.0**

TABLE X—SIMULTANEOUS MOTIONS

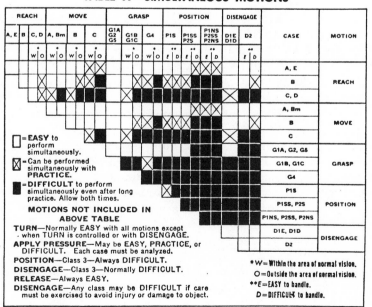

States studying under a M.S.A. scholarship. The Necchi management sent them to Pittsburgh to attend a three weeks' program held by the Methods Engineering Council. When these engineers came back to Italy, they started applying the MTM system anew in an experimental fashion for a few months. Only when it was clear that their engineers were able to master this new technique, Necchi management started planning general training programs. These training programs had the following objectives:

☐   to establish a common language throughout the plant
☐   to sell MTM to the superintendent, foremen and workers
☐   to develop methods men.

It was realized that for the new technique to be successful it would be essential to get production supervisors and foremen to cooperate with the engineers of the methods study department. The training program, therefore, started with a series of two-day courses for foremen and supervisors. The first day was devoted to the explanation of the element motions principles; the second day, the instructors illustrated with practical examples several of the benefits that could be derived from the application of the MTM system.

In accordance with the third objective set for the program, all the time study men took a much longer training course comprising 100 hours spread over a one and a half month period. In this course, the specific MTM technique was presented and discussed in detail. A company's executive remarked that even if MTM would not have resulted in any other gain, the methods consciousness it helped to develop in the time study department justified all the expense and efforts put into this program.

The application of the MTM technique to actual shop operations had purposely a slow start. The subgroup assembly department was deemed to be best fitted, for it offered a wide variety of manual operations which, in the opinion of the engineers, could be greatly improved by an analytical methods study. By this way, the great savings expected could be used as a strong argument to sell MTM to other department superintendents.

The methods engineers established a separate laboratory where a job could be studied and the best method developed, without any outside interference. After the workplace had been studied, the jigs and fixtures were set up, the best sequence of motions was determined, and a "lead-hand" was trained to perform the job according to the established MTM pattern. The "lead-hand" was expected to reach the MTM standard in two weeks. If not, the method was again analyzed and necessary changes made, until the man reached the standard. The time thus established became the basis for production planning, cost estimates and incentive setting.

At this stage all the workers assigned to the operation that had been studied were trained in the laboratory to perform the job in the established time. As soon as they reached the production quota, the new method was introduced in the assembly department and a study of a new job was undertaken.

The results obtained by these first experiments were quite encouraging. In one instance, the number of workers on a sub-assembly line was reduced from twelve to six, and in another, from 110 to 80. To overcome any possible unfavorable reaction from the workers, management made it clear that nobody would be laid off as a result of a method improvement. Since the company was undergoing a sizable expansion, labor released through the application of these methods analyses could be used for increasing production or transferred to another department. It even became possible to create a number of new departments for production of parts, which had been supplied by outside producers.

In spite of these efforts, at the very beginning of its introduction, MTM caused some resistance from the workers. A union newspaper distributed among the workers maintained that MTM and the methods laboratory were new tricks devised by management to arrive at more stringent piece rates.

To offset this reaction, the management made special efforts to stress the methodological aspects of MTM. They, therefore, decided not to use predetermined times for setting incentive rates. Instead, stop watch times were taken on the "lead-hand" at the conclusion of the laboratory training. The only change from the previous stop watch method for incentive rate setting was the adoption of the levelling technique and the elimination of the old rating system.

After a few months it became clear that the engineers of the methods department had won both supervisors' and workers' confidence. The number of grievances about time standards had dropped to practically a nonsignificant value. Being called for training in the methods laboratory was viewed by workers as a distinction and a recognition on part of management. Therefore, management decided to expand the activity of the methods department and to study all the operations in the main assembly lines and in the machine tool division.

To this end the methods and time department was given full responsibility over all the plant to improve existing work methods and to establish production rates. In carrying out this program, a great emphasis continued to be devoted to the educational aspects. The training course was enlarged to include such subjects as scientific management, methods study, time study, MTM, plant lay-out, materials handling, incentive wage plans, job evaluation, merit rating, statistical quality control, production planning and control, and elementary business economics. This educational program, which covered a three months' period, was put under the direct supervision of a special assistant to the general manager.

Participation in this course was no longer limited to methods and time study men. Young foremen, equipment and machine designers, and customers' service engineers were selected to attend the program. The opportunity for attendance was offered also to some suppliers who worked most closely with Necchi. The same assistant to the general manager started publishing a monthly company bulletin where recent problems solved by the methods department were illustrated.

About this time, a change in the management of the engineering department caused the separation of the time study department from the methods department. The former group, because it was primarily concerned with rate setting and incentive payments, became a major department reporting to the cost control department. The methods department remained under the industrial engineering department and continued to be responsible for methods analyses and training through the use of the training laboratory as previously described.

An example which was used to illustrate the MTM technique was the assembly operation of the transmission group. This operation had been studied in the laboratory of the methods department in order to arrive at the best workplace layout. (See Exhibits 27–2 and 27–3.) The methods engineers broke each operation down into elements, which they then further separated into basic MTM motions, which were classified and graded according to MTM tables and the corresponding times were recorded on standard sheets shown in Exhibit 27–2. An allowance was added to the MTM times to get the final time required.

After the job had been introduced into the shop for some time, and the workers had had sufficient training, a time study was taken (see Exhibit 27–4). Time study engineers divided the operation into the same elements as for the MTM study, and they took ten stopwatch readings for each element. The average times were then levelled to the normal worker in terms of skill, working conditions and consistency. The engineers added a rest and fatigue allowance to the levelled times in order to arrive at a standard time, which then became the basis of the incentive system. As a final step, the time study department established the base rate for each job by means of a job evaluation rating.

Mr. Andreoli found out that in the last years the extensive application of MTM and of time study had resulted in some discrepancies. Several operations analyzed with both methods, had shown significant differences between the MTM time and the time arrived at through actual stopwatch observations. The following operations illustrate this point:

Operation	MTM time	Stopwatch time
9660013 A	76	90
9660013 B	103	116
9660013 C	105	112
9660013 D	56	55
9660013 E	44	46
9660013 F	43	69

Exhibit 27–2 Method Study Sheet

<table>
<tr><td colspan="2">NECCHI
U.A.T.</td><td colspan="6" align="center">**METHOD STUDY SHEET**</td><td>SYMBOL</td></tr>
<tr><td colspan="3">OPERATION Transmission Group Assembly</td><td colspan="6">STUDY NO. _____</td></tr>
<tr><td colspan="2">CYCLE _____</td><td colspan="2">DATE ___April 12___</td><td colspan="5">SHEET NO. _____1_____</td></tr>
</table>

LEFT HAND	Wt	LH	TMU	RH	Wt	RIGHT HAND
1) LH picks up shaft d 85508 from container, RH picks up spring 85561 and inserts						
spring on shaft. RH releases spring – RH & LH position shaft on jig – Press pedal						
to close chuck – Release LH & RH – RH picks up connection 85551 from container,						
LH picks up ring 8150 and positions ring on connection – LH releases ring.						
Reach for shaft in container		R40C*	16.8	R30C		Reach for spring in container
Grasp shaft in container		G 4A	7.3			
Move shaft to front		M40B	9.1	G 4B		Grasp spring in container
Hold			11.8	M24B		Move spring to container
Hold			5.6	G 2		Grasp
Hold			1.7	M 2C		Move spring to shaft
Hold			5.6	P1SE		Position spring on shaft
Hold			3.3	M 4B		Thrust spring to shaft butt
Hold			1.7	RL 1		Release spring
Move shaft to jig		M10C	5.0	R 6C		Reach for shaft
		G 2	1.7	G 1A		Grasp shaft
			9.3	M14C		Move shaft to jig
Move shaft to stop		M 2A	1.7	M 2A		Move shaft to stop
Release shaft		RL 1	1.7	RL 1		Release shaft
Reach for ring		R20C	12.0	R22C		Reach for connection
		Release pedal				
			9.1	G 4B		Grasp connection
Grasp ring		G 4C	12.9			
Move ring to front		M30B	13.2	M30B		Move connection to front
Eye focus on ring		EF	7.3			Hold
Grasp ring		G 4C	12.9			Hold
Move ring to connection		M 2C	1.7			Hold
Position ring on connection		P1S	5.6			Hold
Release ring		RL 1	1.7			Hold
	* * * *	* * *	* * *	* *	*	
2) LH picks up cut washer 320070, positions it on groove – Releases – RH & LH move						
connection to stop on fixture to thrust cut washer on groove – Check fitting for						
ease of rotation/						
(As with Element No. 1, the motions for each hand are itemized and timed as						
shown above, but this detail is omitted for the sake of brevity of this Exhibit.)						

NO.	ELEMENT DESCRIPTION	ELEMENT TIME TMU	CONVERTED 1/100 Min	ALLOWANCE %	TIME 1/100 Min	NUMBER PER CYCLE	TOTAL ELEMENT TIME 1/100 Min
1	See above	148.8	8.8	20	10.5	1	10.5
2	See above	128.8	7.8	20	9.3	1	9.3
		Total of operations 3 – 8 (See Sheet 2)					70.2
					TOTAL FOR CYCLE		90.00

*R40C Means "Reach, 40 centimeters, type C"

Exhibit 27—2 (continued)

NECCHI U.A.T.	METHOD STUDY SHEET						SYMBOL

OPERATION ___Transmission Group Assembly___ STUDY NO._____

CYCLE _____ DATE __April 12__ SHEET NO. ___2___

LEFT HAND	Wt.	LH	TMU	RH	Wt.	RIGHT HAND
3) RH positions connection on shaft - LH picks up special blade - LH & RH push						
connection up to reference mark - LH puts down special blade - RH releases						
connection. (Detailed motion tabulation omitted for sake of brevity)						
			* * * * * * * * * * * * * *			
4) RH picks up screwdriver - RH & LH tighten setscrew 85567 on connection 85551						
(Detailed motion tabulation omitted for sake of brevity)						
			* * * * * * * * * * * * * *			
5) LH picks up cut pin 300150 and inserts it on air operated hammer - RH operates						
hammer - LH picks up two-wing casting 85544 - RH releases hammer - Release						
foot pedal. (Detailed motion tabulation omitted for sake of brevity)						
			* * * * * * * * * * * * * *			
6) RH picks up spring 85547 and inserts it into hollow steel cylinder - LH inserts						
hollow steel cylinder into hole on barrel - LH releases - Reaches and picks up						
two-wing casting 85544 and positions it on shaft - Release.						
(Detailed motion tabulation omitted for sake of brevity)						
			* * * * * * * * * * * * * * *			
7) LH picks up special pliers, RH picks up open side washer 084100AT and positions						
it on special pliers - Release - LH, holding pliers, positions open side						
washer on shaft. (Detailed motion tabulation omitted for sake of brevity)						
			* * * * * * * * * * * * * *			
8) RH picks up nut 21339 - LH picks up headless bolt GAB - Screw nut on bolt,						
halfway - RH starts boot in threaded hole on barrel, Releases - LH picks up						
screwdriver, screws, releases - Press foot pedal to open jig - RH picks up						
assembled piece and puts it into tote pan.						
(Detailed motion tabulation omitted for sake of brevity)						
			* * * * * * * * * * * * * *			

NO	ELEMENT DESCRIPTION	ELEMENT TIME TMU	CONVERTED 1/100 Min	ALLOWANCE %	TIME 1/100 Min	NUMBER PER CYCLE	TOTAL ELEMENT TIME 1/100 Min
3	See above	142.0	8.5	15	9.7	1	9.7
4	See above	99.6	6.0	15	6.9	1	6.9
5	See above	154.5	9.3	15	10.7	1	10.7
6	See above	156.0	9.4	20	11.3	1	11.3
7	See above	179.2	10.7	20	12.8	1	12.8
8	See above	260.1	15.7	20	18.8	1	18.8

Exhibit 27–3 Work Place Layout for Method Study

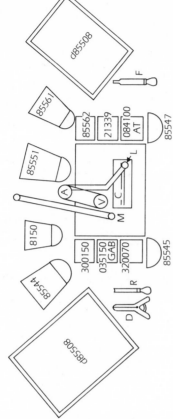

DISTANCES

From container 85561 & 85544 to center—cm 34
From container 85551 & 8150 to center—cm 28
From container d 85508 (left) to center—cm 65
From container d 85508 (right) to center—cm 55

LEGEND

M = Air operated screwdriver for setscrew 035150
D = Special pliers
R = Special blade for connection
C = Jig
F = Screwdriver for setscrew 85562
V = Tool for driving pin 300150

```
JOB DATA SHEET

Part or Group Name
..................................................
Symbol.......... Raw Material........
Operation Description
..................................................
Department.......... Worker........
Machine.......... Required Skill........
Lubrication........
Tools & Equipment
..................................................
..................................................
Work Place Conditions
..................................................
..................................................
Quality Requirements.........
..................................................
Remarks.......................
```

Study Made By:	Approved By:

Exhibit 27—4 Time Study Sheet

NECCHI U.A.T.	TIME STUDY SHEET				DEPARTMENT .... WORK STATION			SYMBOL	

<table>
<tr><td>PART NAME
Transmission Sub-Assembly
....</td><td>Raw Material
d 85508
..............</td><td>MACHINE TOOL .... NUMBER ....</td><td>INDEX</td></tr>
<tr><td>OPERATION
DESCRIPTION ....</td><td>Group Assembly
..............................</td><td>JIGS & FIXTURES ....
TOOLS ....</td><td>1</td></tr>
</table>

DATE 8/25	STUDY NO. 55/1306	SUPERSEDES NO.	WORKER:	STANDING .. SITTING X.	MALE ..... FEMALE ... X	GAGES .... LUBRICATION	OPERATION 10

			WORKING CONDITIONS				LEVELED AVERAGES		
PHASE NO.	DESCRIPTION		Rpm	SPEED	FEED	DEPTH OF CUT	MACHINE IDLE	MACHINE TIME	MACHINE UNATTENDED
	The sub-assembly is made up of the following parts:								
	d 85506 - 85545 - 320070 - 035150GAB - 300150 - 85544 -								
	8150 - 85551 - 85561 - 85562 - 21339 - 084100AT -85547.								
1	RH takes finished piece from jig (completed in previous								
	cycle) and puts it into totepan - RH picks up spring								
	85561. LH picks up shaft d 85508							5.51		
2	Insert spring on shaft - Set group on jig							4.97		
3	RH picks up connection 85551. LH picks up ring 8150 - Mount									
	ring on connection							7.45		
4	LH picks up cut washer 320070 - Thrust cut washer on groove									
	of connection 85551. Check ring-connection fit for ease									
	of rotation.							9.83		
5	LH picks up special blade - Mount connection 85551 on									
	shaft d 85508.							12.74		
6	LH puts down blade - RH picks up screwdriver and tightens									
	set screw 85562 on connection 85551.							11.23		
7	LH picks up cut-pin 300150, inserts it on air operated									
	hammer - At the same time press pedal to move jig under									
	hammer - Operate hammer to insert cut-pin into hole on									
	barrel of d 85508 - Press pedal to move jig back to position.							9.55		
8	LH picks up two-wing casting 85544 - Mount it on ground									
	butt of shaft d 85508, hub facing out.							7.78		
9	RH picks up open side washer 084100AT - LH picks up special									
	pliers - mount washer on groove of shaft d 85508 to hold									
	two-wing casting							17.17		
10	Check for ease of rotation							5.40		
11	RH picks up spring 85547 - LH picks up hollow steel cylinder									
	85545 - Insert spring into hole on cylinder - Assemble									
	cylinder on barrel and fit two-wing casting on cylinder butt.							13.28		
12	LH picks up headless bolt 035150GAB - RH picks up nut 21339 -									
	Screw nut on bolt - Start bolt into threaded hole on barrel.							16.84		
13	RH grasps air operated screwdriver and tightens headless bolt.							3.02		
Ev/1	Unscrew set screw 85562 - pick up another screw and tighten									
	it in connection. (Phase 6) (20% of the times)									
Ev/2	Disassemble open side washer 084100AT if the two wing casting							0.86		
	85544 is not free to rotate - Try another washer.									
	(Phases 8 & 9) (5%of the times)									
								1.35		
								126.88		
	FATIGUE ALLOWANCE .....6%.......							7.61		

APPROVED							Total carried from other sheets					
Time Study man	U.A.T.	Fore-man	Allowed Set-up Time	Job Class	Piece Rate	Wage System	Average Set-up Time	Cycle Time	Average Time	Pieces Per Hour	Workers' Utili-zation	TOTAL	TOTAL	TOTAL
....	......	.....	....	1	336	......	......	1.17	1.46	51	100%	134.49		

Exhibit 27-4 (continued)

TIME STUDY SHEET

SHEET NO. ..1..
OPERATION NO. ..10..

CYCLE NUMBER	Inc	Acc	Inc	Acc	Inc	Acc	Inc	Acc	Inc	Acc	Inc	Acc	Inc	Acc	Inc	Acc	Inc	Acc	Inc	Acc	Inc	Acc	Inc	Acc	Inc	Acc
1	4	4	6	10	6	16	8	24	8	32	13	45	7	52	8	60	16	76	4	80	17	97	30	127	3	130
2	4	4	5	9	7	16	6	22	7	29	5	34	8	42	8	50	12	62	4	66	9	75	12	87	3	90
3	5	5	5	10	6	16	6	22	7	29	5	34	8	42	8	50	12	62	4	66	9	75	12	87	3	90
4	4	4	4	8	6	14	9	23	9	32	13	45	10	55	10	65	18	83	8	88	8	96	14	110	3	113
5	6	6	4	10	7	17	8	25	7	32	10	42	9	51	5	56	15	71	5	76	9	85	15	100	2	102
6	6	6	4	10	10	20	13	33	18	51	10	61	7	68	7	75	10	85	5	90	10	100	10	110	3	113
7	4	4	5	9	7	16	9	25	7	32	10	42	8	50	8	58	20	78	7	85	13	98	11	109	2	111
8	5	5	4	9	8	17	8	25	9	34	10	44	7	51	8	59	18	77	6	83	14	97	12	109	3	112
9	7	7	4	11	11	22	5	27	9	36	11	47	11	58	5	63	19	82	5	87	16	103	20	123	3	126
10	6	6	5	11	6	17	9	26	10	36	11	47	9	56	7	63	17	80	4	84	12	96	21	117	3	120
TOTAL	51		46		69		81		118		104		72		50		159		50		123		155		28	
AVERAGE OBSERVED TIMES	5.1		4.6		6.9		8.1		11.8		10.4		7.2		5.0		15.9		5.0		12.3		15.5		2.8	
LEVEL. SKILL EFFORT	C_2	C_1	C_2	C_1	C_2	C_1	C_2	C_2	C_2	C_1	C_2	C_1	C_2	C_1	C_2	C_1	C_1	C_1	C_1	C_1	C_1	C_1	C_2	C_1
LEVELING FACTOR	1.08		1.08		1.08		1.08		1.08		1.08		1.08		1.08		1.08		1.08		1.08		1.08		1.08	
LEVELED TIME	5.51		4.97		7.45		9.83		12.74		11.23		7.78		5.40		17.17		5.40		13.28		16.74		3.02	
FATIGUE - ALLOWANCE																										
AVERAGE TIMES																										

EV/1 20% EV/2 5%

		Inc	Acc
		15	15
			25
		17	
		32	25
		0.8	1.25
		C_2	C_1
		1.08	1.08
		0.86	1.35

REMARKS

PREPARATION TIME / AVERAGE TIMES

PREPARATION TIME		
Informing the foreman		
Asking for instructions		
Getting tools from toolroom		
Setting up jigs and fixtures		
Getting machine ready		
Cleaning up work place		
Allowance %		
Total		
WORKER'S NAME .....BIANCHI.....		

LEVELING FACTORS

SKILL			EFFORT		
+0.15	A1		+0.13	A1	
+0.13	A2		+0.12	A2	
+0.11	B1		+0.10	B1	
+0.08	B2		+0.08	B2	
+0.06	C1		+0.05	C1	
+0.03	C2		+0.02	C2	
0.00	D		0.00	D	
-0.05	E1		-0.04	E1	
-0.10	E2		-0.08	E2	
-0.16	F1		-0.12	F1	
-0.22	F2		-0.17	F2	

CONDITIONS			CONSISTENCY		
+0.06	A		+0.04	A	
+0.04	B		+0.03	B	
+0.02	C		+0.01	C	
0.00	D		0.00	D	
-0.03	E		-0.02	E	
-0.07	F		-0.04	F	

JOB CLASS

Class 1	Up to 139
Class 2	From 140 to 161
Class 3	From 162 to 183
Class 4	From 184 to 205
Class 5	From 206 to 227

JOB EVALUATION FACTORS

			GRADE	POINTS
1	Education	14	1	14
2	Experience	22	1	22
3	Initiative	14	1	14
4	Physical requirements	10	2	20
5	Mental & visual requirements	5	2	20
6	Responsibility for tools and equipment	5	1	5
7	Responsibility for materials and products	5	1	5
8	Responsibility for safety of others	5	1	5
9	Responsibility for work of others	5	1	5
10	Working conditions	10	2	20
11	Safety	5	2	10
		TOTAL POINTS		130
		JOB CLASS		1
		ALLOWED CLASS		

Exhibit 27–5 Organization Chart

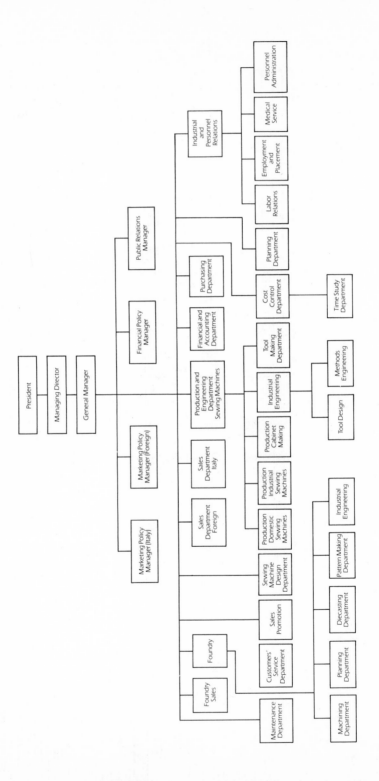

In order to find out the reasons of these discrepancies, Mr. Andreoli met with Mr. Clavello, head of the methods department and with Mr. Lanati, head of the time study department (see Exhibit 27–5).

Mr. Clavello maintained that these differences could be explained by one of two reasons. First, the worker was actually following the method described by the methods department, but the time study man had a concept of normal worker which was different from the normal of the MTM system. When levelling stopwatch readings, they referred to an ideal pace somewhat slower than that of the "MTM worker." Therefore their subjective evaluation of the levelling factor was always higher than it actually should have been. Or, Mr. Clavello said, that the time study man was doing the right evaluation in levelling the worker's performance, but the worker was not following the method established by the methods department. It was very difficult, he added, to discover which was the right cause because for one thing the workers had many subtle ways to "make a job look longer than it actually was."

Mr. Lanati's side of the argument was that the present situation was the result of poor communications between the two departments, namely the methods department and the time study department. He said that the MTM times should have been communicated to his time study men by the people of the methods department. This practice would have eliminated the possibility of setting lenient standards. At present, when it was clear that the workers could largely beat a given standard, the time study man would make a few small changes in the work method. These changes would enable him to make a new time study and set up "a more realistic standard." Oftentimes these changes were decided on by the time study men, and were not communicated to the methods department.

From this discussion Mr. Andreoli got the impression that these problems could be solved by combining both departments into one single unit. He meant to present his proposal to the industrial engineering department manager and to suggest that times standards be set only by applying MTM which, he felt, would eliminate any subjective evaluation of the worker's performance.

Penn Electric Company

28

*(Application of Linear Programming—
Transportation Model in Routing and
Scheduling)*

The Penn Electric Company produced and sold a variety of meters and
instruments used on electric power distribution apparatus. Production
operations were planned and executed on the basis of job-lots of materials
and parts manufactured in three functional, parts fabrication departments
for: (1) primary, heavy machining and stamping operations, (2) secondary
machining, grinding, and polishing operations, (3) metal treatment such
as plating, heat treating, and tumble-deburring operations. These parts
were then delivered via industrial trucks to three assembly departments:
(1) electrical subassembly components, (2) mechanical subassemblies,
and (3) final assembly and product testing. Purchased parts were also delivered directly from the stockroom to the three assembly departments.

As Materials Manager, one of Mr. R. A. Jamison's responsibilities was
to keep the assembly departments supplied with materials. In the Meri-
dith factory the three assembly departments were considered as "users"
and the three parts manufacturing departments plus the stockroom as
"contributors." The departmental layout in Exhibit 28–1 shows the relative locations of the contributor and user departments.

Departmental foremen were responsible for materials handling between any two contributor departments and between any two user departments. This meant that some industrial trucks were used by Mr.

Revised version of an earlier case written by Professor R. E. McGarrah. Copyright © by the President and Fellows of Harvard University.

Exhibit 28—1 Penn Electric Company

Departmental Layout

Stock Room III	Parts Fabrication II	Parts Fabrication I	Final Assembly
Parts Fabrication IV	Sub-assembly B	Sub-assembly A	C

From Contributor Department	To User Department			
	A	B	C	Total
I	15		10	25
II		5		5
III		10	20	30
IV	5			5
Total	20	15	30	65

From Department	To Department		
	A	B	C
I	1000	1000	1500
II	2000	1500	1000
III	3000	2500	1500
IV	3000	2250	1000

NOTE: These distances are measured (in feet) along trucking aisles connecting the contributor and user departments.

Jamison's personnel, and others by materials handlers who served the department foremen. In the past, there had been conflicting opinions about the adequacy of the total number of trucks available.

Discussions at several weekly assembly-parts shortage meetings indicated that Mr. Jamison's handlers probably were a significant cause of parts shortages and work delays in the three assembly departments. This led to a study of the procedures for handling materials between contributor and user departments. Mr. Jamison asked Mr. Bemis, Supervisor of Production Control, to prepare a daily schedule of the number of truck-loads required by the assembly departments, from the contributor departments. Table I in Exhibit 28–1 summarizes the schedule remitted by Mr. Bemis, who said:

I had the production floor dispatchers check on when jobs are ready to be moved to assembly areas. I asked them to take observations of the loading points in the contributor areas at random times to see how often there was one or more lots waiting to be trucked to an assembly department. From the data they came up with, I'd say that any time during the day, there's an 85 percent chance that a lot will be waiting at the contributor area to be moved to a user area, according to this schedule.

Table II in Exhibit 28–1 summarizes the trucking distances between any pair of contributor-user departments in Penn's factory. These distances were fixed by the layout of trucking aisles in the factory.

In studying the problem further, Mr. Jamison reasoned that the total distance traveled while the trucks were loaded was fixed by the schedule Mr. Bemis had given him. However, he could minimize the distance traveled while the trucks were empty, by setting up and solving a linear program for routing the empty trucks from the assembly departments back to the contributor departments. The solution to this linear program would serve as the basis for routing and scheduling his materials handlers. Then, by imputing estimates of average truck speeds and turnaround (unloading and loading) times, he could prove whether or not he had the right (most economical) number of trucks for the materials handling work he was responsible for doing. This would help to settle some squabbles about the adequacy of the firm's total investment in industrial trucks.

REQUIRED:
1. Set up and solve the linear programming problem referred to in the case.
2. State the assumptions affecting the validity of applying linear programming in the situation faced by Mr. Jamison. Also, outline briefly the reasons why each assumption is either justifiable or unjustifiable.

Pharma
Company

The Company

The Pharma Company was a subsidiary of a large, diversified corporation. The company specialized in pharmaceutical and drug products with two manufacturing plants, located in the New York metropolitan area. Research facilities were maintained at one of the two manufacturing plants and also in Argentina. Branch warehouses were maintained throughout the United States and Canada and branch packaging facilities were maintained in various foreign countries. The foreign branches received products in bulk form and then performed their own filling, packaging and distribution of the products.

A wide assortment of drug items were produced by the Pharma Company, some of which were toothpaste, vitamins (liquid, tablet and capsules), radio-isotopes, medicinal lotions, mineral oil, antibiotics (liquid, powder, tablets and capsules), veterinary items, and Bio-Parenterals (injectables).

The City Orders

Periodically the Pharma Company filled orders for the seven insulin products for the City of New York (see Exhibit 29–1). Although the packaging

This case was prepared by Professor Gordon Chen, with the assistance of George W. Haupin, for class discussions only. All rights reserved to the author.

components were the same as for the standard insulin packages, all orders had to have *"Property of the City of New York"* printed on the bottle label, individual carton, carrier label and shipper label. These orders were handled in the past by using finished stock, soaking off the bottle label and then relabeling and repacking with components printed especially for City of New York orders. This involved a high material cost, since the original bottle label, individual carton, carrier and shipper were dis-

Exhibit 29—1 City of New York Order Quantities and Order Dates for Items A through G (1971 and 1972)

Item	Order Date	Order Quantity
A	1/16/71	4,000
A	2/9/71	2,500
A	4/11/71	4,000
A	8/24/72	1,500
B	1/24/72	250
B	2/11/72	250
B	4/11/72	2,000
C	8/11/71	200
C	10/7/71	200
C	1/11/72	400
C	2/11/72	400
D	2/16/71	10,000
D	8/15/72	2,000
E	2/23/71	1,500
F	1/23/71	12,000
F	8/15/72	10,000
G	1/31/71	5,000
G	4/12/71	15,000

Exhibit 29—2 Standard Factory Cost Breakdown for Manufacturing, Filling, and Packaging of Regular Orders for Items A through G

Item	Material	Labor	Prime	Factory
A	$ .260	$ .028	$ .288	$ .383
B	.468	.032	.500	.614
C	.478	.062	.540	.829
D	.251	.024	.275	.362
E	.467	.031	.498	.621
F	.251	.029	.280	.379
G	.454	.033	.487	.606

Exhibit 29—3 Additional Costs to Package City of New York Orders for Items A through G (to be added to costs in Exhibit 29–2)

	Material	Labor	Prime	Factory
Present (Repack & Relabel)	$ .024	$ .038	$ .063	$ .161
Alt. #I (Unpack w/sticker label)	.005	.031	.036	.016
Alt. #II (From stock of filled vials)	—	.005	.005	.016
Alt. #III (Imprint w/o sticker label)*	.001	.031	.032	.112

*This method would necessitate the purchase of a markem imprinting machine (Model PLBR) at an expenditure of $1,500.00.

Exhibit 29—4 Actual Annual Production, Direct Labor Hours Used, and the Direct Labor Hours per Unit Produced for Filling and Packaging all Orders of Items A through G (1970 and 1971)

	Units	1970 Direct Labor Hrs.	Labor Hrs./ Unit Produced	Units	1971 Direct Labor Hrs.	Labor Hrs./ Units Produced
Item A	121,094	1503.1	.0124	181,318	1774.1	.0098
Item B	52,862	786.5	.0149	96,986	1145.6	.0118
Item C	8,631	156.3	.0181	26,569	517.9	.0195
Item D	183,575	1778.2	.0097	174,534	1193.6	.0068
Item E	68,771	656.9	.0096	131,147	1032.4	.0079
Item F	353,754	3990.6	.0113	502,165	3918.8	.0078
Item G	387,832	4609.2	.0119	612,536	5195.0	.0085

carded. Labor costs were also high due to the relabeling and repacking required. Exhibits 29–2 and 29–3 reflect the additional costs involved in relabeling and repacking as compared to the costs for the standard package for items A through G.

The City of New York stipulated a two-week delivery from the date their orders were placed. Due to the special operations required, the company experienced difficulty in meeting these delivery dates. This would have resulted in loss of orders if the method of operation had been continued.

If it had been possible to anticipate when these special orders would be received, it would facilitate a simple solution to the problem; however, Exhibit 29–1 illustrates how unpredictable the frequency and size of these orders were for items A through G.

A comparison of Exhibits 29–4 and 29–1 reflects that City of New York orders were only a small portion of the total annual volume for items A through G (Exhibit 29–5).

Exhibit 29—5 Forecasted Annual Production for Filling and Packaging all Orders of Items A through G and the Number of Production Runs per year (1970 through 1973)

	1970		1971		1972		1973	
	Units	Runs/ Year	Units	Runs/ Year	Units	Runs/ Year	Units	Runs/ Year
Item A	144,000	5	183,000	7	150,000	5	140,000	5
Item B	78,000	3	112,000	4	100,000	4	84,000	4
Item C	24,000	2	28,000	2	20,000	2	21,600	2
Item D	228,000	5	175,000	3	200,000	4	208,000	4
Item E	108,000	4	130,000	4	120,000	5	104,000	5
Item F	480,000	10	532,000	9	450,000	12	432,000	12
Item G	440,000	10	642,000	10	540,000	13	486,000	13

Some technical consideration for the products involved were as follows:

1. Items A, B, D and E had (24) month expiration dates from the time the bottles were filled.
2. Items C, F and G had (18) month expiration dates from the time the bottles were filled.
3. Six months were required to manufacture master Insulin solutions—from which batches of a particular potency were made.
4. Prior to bottle filling, all Insulin bulk required (10) days to test for sterility.
5. After the vials were filled and packaged, (4) to (5) weeks were required to test and secure a release from the government (FDA).

The Industrial Engineering Department was asked to develop alternate methods for handling these City of New York orders and to determine which alternate would be the most economical. Three alternate methods that were developed are as follows:

Alternate I — Unpack filled stock, apply sticker label over original bottle label and hand stamp individual carton, carrier label and shipper label. This method would save the labor cost of soaking off bottle labels and the material cost of the extra carton, carrier and shipper.

Alternate II — Maintain a stock of "Filled Only" bottles for each of the (7) products. When City of New York Orders are received, the filled bottles could be toted onto the packaging line and labeled and packed with City of New York labels and package components. No additional material costs and only slightly higher direct labor costs would be incurred.

Alternate III— Unpack finished stock and imprint the bottle label, individual carton, carrier label and shipper label with *"Property of the City of New York."* This method would save on material costs, but labor costs would remain high. In addition, a special imprinting machine costing $1,500.00 would have to be purchased to imprint bottle labels.

Exhibits 29–2 and 29–3 present cost data for comparing the three alternate methods with the method and also reflect how these costs compare with those for standard orders for items A through G (Exhibits 29–6 through 29–8).

From the information presented, Alternate II appears to be the most satisfactory solution to handling City of New York orders. The Pharma Company must now develop answers to three important questions which are as follows:

1. How will filled stock inventories for these (7) City of New York items be established?

Exhibit 29–6 Operational Data for Filling and Packaging Regular Orders for Items A through G

Item	Operation	No. of Operators	100% Std. Production per Shift	Production per Shift @ 75% of Std. Performance
A	Fill, inspect & pack	23.5	34,080	25,560
B	" " "	24.5	34,080	25,560
C	" " "	23.5	34,080	25,560
D	" " "	13.0	29,824	22,368
E	" " "	17.5	29,824	22,368
F	" " "	18.5	38,344	28,758
G	" " "	18.5	38,344	28,758

Exhibit 29–7 Standard Direct Labor Cost for Filling and Packaging Regular Orders for Items A through G

Item	1971	1972
A	$ .022	$ .023
B	.022	.026
C	.021	.026
D	.016	.015
E	.016	.020
F	.021	.016
G	.021	.016

Exhibit 29—8 Price Data for City of New York Orders for Items A through G

Item	Regular Price/Unit	Minimum Resale Price/Unit	Price/Unit to Retailer
A	$1.40	$1.26	$ .84
B	2.75	2.47	1.65
C	3.17	2.85	1.90
D	1.65	1.48	.99
E	3.15	2.83	1.89
F	1.65	1.48	.99
G	3.15	2.83	1.89

NOTE: Wholesalers receive a 40% discount on the price to retailer.

2. What quantity of filled stock should be kept in inventory for each of these (7) items?
3. How long should filled stock be kept in inventory before using for other regular orders?

United Food Products Company (A)

30

Mr. H. van Roehm, Managing Director of United Food Products (Benelux), S.A., said to the casewriter,

If members of your Institute can tell us how to improve our distribution system this would be more than recompense for the cooperation we're giving you in describing our situation. Distribution problems are among our most difficult ones to solve. With about 56,000 retail grocery outlets to serve about 8 million people in Belgium and Luxembourg, we can't realize the efficiencies of mass distribution like they can in the U.S. where there are only 1½ retail grocery outlets per 1000 persons. I'm reasonably satisfied with our performance in buying, production, sales, and advertising, but I think we've got to improve our effectiveness in distribution.

Company Background

Organization

United Food Products, U.S.A. produced and sold a growing variety of consumer food products: breakfast cereals, dehydrated soups, instant coffee, and various flours and cake mixes. Unlike some of its large U.S. competitors which had competed in European markets for over 50 years, United

This case was prepared by Professor Robert E. McGarrah as a basis for class discussion. It is not designed to present an illustration of either effective or ineffective handling of an administrative problem. Copyright © 1964 by l'Institut pour l'Etude des Méthodes de Direction de l'Entreprise (IMEDE), Lausanne, Switzerland.

had not marketed its products in continental Europe until 1953. However, since 1931 when it purchased the Henry Morehead Company, Ltd., which operated a factory at Hull in England, the parent company was actively developing markets for its breakfast cereals, dry soups, and instant coffee in the United Kingdom. In 1953, United Food Products Co. (Geneva), S.A. was established as a continental headquarters for directing the development of new markets. The Geneva company did not operate factories; its function was confined to market development. As one of its first actions the Geneva organization moved into the marketing region of the European Economic Community (EEC). In 1953 it contracted with Mr. van Roehm of Brussels, Belgium, to act as General Sales Agent in the Belgium and Luxembourg markets, and with Mr. P. van der Woeld as General Sales Agent for Holland. Products were imported from the factory in England. By 1955, sales of the "Potage-Minute" dry soups had increased so that an arrangement was made for the Moulins Generaux, S.A., a diversified Belgian food processor, to produce "Potage-Minute" for the Benelux markets. Sales continued to more than double each year. In 1955, the general agency arrangement for Benelux was terminated and a new company, United Food Products Co. (Benelux), S.A. was established with Mr. van Roehm as General Manager. Main offices were shifted from Brussels to Antwerp and construction of a new $4,000,000 factory was started in Louvain. Mr. van der Woeld was continued as General Sales Agent for Holland, but his contract was administered by the new Benelux Company, instead of by the Geneva company. Imports from England were discontinued shortly after the new factory went on stream in the fall of 1956. Exhibit 30–1 is an abbreviated organization chart of United Food Products Co. (Benelux), S.A.

Production

Most breakfast cereals were made by either rolling out, as in the case of flake cereals, or steam-exploding, as in the case of "puffed" or "popped" cereals, the individual cereal grains. The flakes or pops were then mixed with various flavoring ingredients such as salt, malt, sugar, barley, and corn syrup, and sent to ovens where they were carefully baked to the desired crispness. Some breakfast cereals—those of the formed type— were made by grinding the cereal grains together with the flavoring ingredients to form a paste. The paste was then extruded into the desired shape and sent to the baking operation. The cereal was then packaged in branded cartons and sent to the factory warehouse for shipment to customers. Shelf-life for breakfast cereals was limited because after 8 months the flakes might become stale or spotty. Except for rolling and exploding, the same processing and packaging equipment was used for all flake and exploded products. Alteration of the final recipe and package size to suit the particular needs of a market presented no major manufacturing problem. In 1963, the Louvain factory produced 200 different combinations of

Exhibit 30—1 United Food Products Company Benelux Company Organization

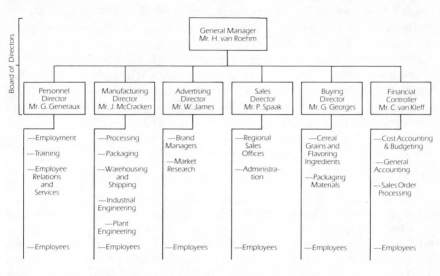

SOURCE: Mr. H. van Roehm, General Manager.

recipe and package sizes of 8 different brands for the Benelux-Holland market.

Intensive market research into housewives' menu planning and taste peculiarities in different regions led to the necessity for specific recipes and package-sizes sold in each region. This was in accord with a long established United Foods policy on marketing and product quality.

The packaging equipment installed at Louvain was of European design; it operated at lower speeds than the equipment used in the U.S., but it could be changed for different package-sizes in 8 hours. Comparable change-overs required as much as 24 hours in the U.S.

From 1953 to 1963 shipments to the Benelux-Holland markets had doubled every two years, and management believed this rate of growth would continue.

Distribution

From 1953 to 1956, while he was the General Sales Agent exclusively for United Foods, Mr. van Roehm engaged a contract trucking firm, Coerts S.A., that owned and operated a warehouse in Brussels to store all the shipments from England and to deliver most of the shipments made to Belgian wholesalers. Some of the wholesaler-customers picked up their own orders from the Brussels warehouse, under an arrangement known as *laissez-suivre*, to be described in detail later. Deliveries to the Holland market were also made from the "outside warehouse" in Brussels via a Dutch trucking firm.

Since 1956 two additional Belgian trucking firms, de Steeg and Knokkaert, made deliveries to Belgium and Luxembourg customers respectively from the factory warehouse in Louvain, while the Brussels and Dutch truckers made deliveries from the outside warehouse in Brussels. Railroad rates and delivery times were so unfavorable within the Benelux area that United Foods management felt rail transport to be out of the question for at least the next five years.

In 1960, the factory warehouse in Louvain was expanded to twice its original size; still the Brussels warehouse had to be rented. Commenting on the continued necessity for outside warehouse space, Mr. J. McCracken, Director of Manufacturing, said,

We've had such an increase in the number of brands and package sizes while we've boosted our overall volume of shipments that, in order to store factory output and load shipments 48 hours after receiving orders from our customers, we've had to utilize the Brussels warehouse. This outside space was needed even though sometimes it meant trucking cases of breakfast cereal from Louvain to Brussels and back again before shipping them to customers in Belgium and Luxembourg. In addition to being a depot for loading shipments to customers, the Brussels warehouse is used to store our safety stocks while the Louvain warehouse is used to store what we call "planning" stocks. Actually, we carry two distinct kinds of planning stocks. One kind provides us with standby inventory so that we can use the same equipment for processing different brand-sizes. This type of planning stock allows us to schedule production runs in Economic Lot Sizes. The other type of planning stocks allows us to build inventory in anticipation of scheduled promotional efforts. Our safety stocks don't move as fast as our planning stocks; safety stock is an amount we maintain to cushion the effects of surges in the difference between production and shipping rates for each brand-size of product. These safety stocks have to be physically turned over once every 13 weeks, so we are certain to send good quality products to our customers.

After several months of study by industrial engineers, Mr. van Roehm endorsed a proposal to again double the size of the factory warehouse. The study showed that significant savings could be realized, mainly by eliminating the need for the outside warehouse space in Brussels. The proposal was finally approved by executives at continental headquarters in Geneva, and a construction project was planned.

Six months after expanding the factory warehouse the company completed negotiations to purchase Mr. van der Woeld's business in Holland. This meant a transfer of the administration of Mr. van der Woeld's marketing and accounting functions to the United Foods Benelux organization in Antwerp.

It was against this background that Mr. van Roehm expressed his concern for strengthening the organization and procedures for distributing products to customers in Belgium, Holland, and Luxembourg. As he put it,

How much more profit we actually realize by eliminating the outside warehouse and by taking over marketing management in Holland will depend as much upon controlling the costs of giving our customers an efficient delivery service as it will upon more efficient marketing that we expect to be able to do in Holland.

Detailed Description of the Present Distribution System

The load and performance of any distribution system are affected by marketing and production activities, as well as the organization and facilities chosen to deliver products from the factory to customers. Hence this discussion will highlight relevant details of advertising, sales, and factory warehousing activities as well as the methods and procedures for distribution.

Marketing Considerations

The company marketed eight different brands of breakfast cereal, each in three standard package sizes. To promote the sales of each brand-size each of four brand managers, working in conjunction with Mr. James, the Advertising Director, would plan a variety of special sales promotions during a year. All divisions of United Foods operated on a basis of a year comprised of 13 four-week periods, called sales canvass periods. Sales promotions were planned for twelve canvass periods in a coming year; these plans were updated four times a year. Sales promotions usually consisted of "special packs" containing offers of lower prices, premium coupons, or premiums inserted in the package. Mr. James said,

We budget promotions expenses according to several key factors: (1) the goals we set for the market share for each brand, (2) the availability of new, attractive promotion schemes, (3) the marginal income we have to work with for each brand-size. We usually plan to promote each brand four times a year. But during the year we actually stage some promotions during canvass periods and at frequencies different from our plans. We have to do this mainly for two reasons: (1) to counteract promotional efforts of our competitors, and (2) to take advantage of "hot" promotional schemes that may become available during the year. As you know, United Foods has a reputation for its emphasis on advertising and sales promotion activities. Of course, before we stage a promotion, we consult with the Sales, Buying, and Manufacturing Departments to be sure they can support each scheme, because each scheme means a fast filling and emptying of pipelines with special packages that have to be on the shelves of all our retailers at the same time. To be effective, a special promotion stock should be exhausted by the end of a four-week canvass period. I know these special promotion schemes create problems for the boys in sales, manufacturing, and buying, but they boost our volume and market share. As Advertising Director, I have to concentrate mainly on boosting sales volume, even though I realize my promotional budget for each scheme doesn't precisely account for all the expenses incurred by the buying, manufacturing, and distribution departments that have to shift from standard packs to special packs for each promotion. It's their problem to live within their budget.

Mr. Spaak, Director of Sales, highlighted procedures of his organization:

We have analyzed and classified our wholesale and retail customers and our selling efforts (see Exhibit 30–2). The first 3 to 5 days of each canvass period are spent concentrating on our wholesaler-customers; the next 8 to 10 days on retailer-customers. The remaining 5 to 10 days are for repeat-calls at our top wholesaler-customers. In this way our salesmen are able to give our customers the best service. In fact our emphasis is on helping

---

Exhibit 30–2 United Food Products Company Analysis and Classification of Customer Sales Efforts

Market Served	No. of Wholesalers	No. of Retailers	Population
Belgium and Luxembourg	860	58,400	9,300,000
Holland	635	23,500	11,000,000

Sales-Manpower Allocation (Belgium and Luxembourg only)

Wholesaler	Average Call Frequency	No. in Class
Class 1	14 days	563
Class 2	35 days	257

Retailer		
Class 1	35 days	18,600
Class 2	70 days	13,100
Class 3		26,500

Each salesman is expected to make a weighted average of 16 calls per working day; a call at a wholesaler-customer is weighted 1.5 times a call at a retailer-customer.

Customer classifications are established by such criteria as customer's estimated annual turnover, his purchases of United Foods brands and package-sizes, his affiliation (or independence from) a retail buying group (or volunteer retail chain stores).

SOURCE: Mr. P. Spaak, Director of Sales.

our customers to plan to boost their sales. Each salesman makes an analysis of a customer's future needs for restocking each brand and size, and submits his analysis to the wholesaler or retailer. He also advises the customer about plans and schedules for special advertising product-displays, and special pack-promotions during the canvass period. The customer then adjusts the proposed order quantities up or down, signs the order and the salesman mails it back to our Sales Office in Antwerp at the end of the day. From a variety of market research sources we've found that on the average, wholesalers carry approximately a one month stock and retailers between a two and three month stock. Nevertheless we have good reason to believe that at any one point in time an average of 6% of our Belgian retailers are out of stock in Flakes-O-Corn. For FLOCODAV and Oat Pops the figures are 7% and 8% respectively, and for Sparkies and Rice Puffies 1% and 11%.

Office and Clerical Considerations

The "Sales Office" received customers' orders, checked the status of customers' credit, and prepared 5 copies of the invoice (one copy being the waybill or shipping instructions) for each order. These tasks were completed by the end of the day after a salesman mailed the customer's order. The Sales Office was managed by Mr. van Kleff, Financial Controller, who said,

It may seem unusual that these activities are part of my organization instead of Mr. Spaak's, but we've found that they function best this way, because they are closely related to our accounting activities. As you would expect, our Sales Office activities are much heavier during the first half than during the last half of a sales canvass period. During the first half we've processed as many as 425 orders per day, and during the last half we've processed as few as 15 orders per day. Orders received on peak days may not be processed until the day after receipt.

Waybills were then transmitted by messenger to the office of the trucking company designated to deliver the order.

Deliveries to customers were performed either by trucking companies under contract with United Food Products Co. (Benelux) S.A., or by the customers themselves, under terms known as *laissez-suivre*. This meant that a customer received a price allowance because he used his own trucks to pick up his orders. The amount of the allowance was determined more by negotiations with the customer than by a rationalized formula. About 17 percent of the total shipments to Belgium and Luxembourg markets were under the *laissez-suivre* arrangement. The customer could pick up his order any time at his convenience up to seven days after he placed his order with the United salesman. Commenting on this arrangement, Mr. McCracken said,

The seven day limit for the customer to pick up his order has proved to be meaningless. Frequently customers will pick up only part of their order because there's no space on their truck. Most of the time, our *laissez-suivre* customers have several orders at our warehouse, waiting to be picked up. It is very difficult for us to schedule the work of preparing shipments (stock picking, assembling cases in the order on the shipping platform, counting and verifying cases with quantities ordered, etc.). This is because *laissez-suivre* customers don't give us advance notice of when their truck will pick up their orders. And of course, when they do arrive, we have to give a customer's truck priority over our contractors' trucks that may have to be loaded at the same time. You can see the disruptions that occur when our planned work has to be stopped while our warehouse and shipping crews work to load a customer's truck.

Shipments to Benelux Markets

As mentioned earlier, by 16:30 each day, the Sales Office transmitted waybills to each of three contract trucking firms responsible for delivering 83 percent of total shipments to customers in Belgium and Luxembourg. The largest of the three trucking firms, Coerts, operated the outside warehouse in Brussels and handled deliveries between his warehouse in Brussels and the factory warehouse in Louvain (23 kilometers), as well as deliveries from his warehouse to customers.

Each contract-hauler had a dispatcher who decided (1) which of his available trucks would be used to haul customers' orders, (2) the route of travel to be taken by each truck (hence, the sequence in which customers' orders were to be loaded and unloaded).

Frequently, in making these decisions, the dispatcher was not able to load all cases ordered by all customers located along a route to be travelled during the day by one truck. This meant that he would either have to send another partially loaded truck if available, or plan to deliver portions of customers' orders the next day his truck would travel this route. This meant that the warehouse had to keep an accounting record of quantities ordered and quantities actually shipped to customers. A map showing the geographical districts served by each trucker is given in Exhibit 30–3. The distribution of shipments to the various districts is given in Exhibit 30–4.

Warehousing and Shipping

In the early afternoon of each day, at about 2:00 p.m., the truckers sent a summary of the delivery plans to the Shipping Department in Louvain. These delivery plans enabled the foreman of the Shipping Department to schedule the activities of warehouse and shipping personnel who prepared the shipments to be loaded each day. This schedule was completed by 4:00 p.m. each day and usually planned the activities through the morning and early afternoon of the following day.

The factory warehouse was operated daily between the hours of 06:00

Exhibit 30—3 United Food Products Benelux S.A. District Map of Belgium and Luxembourg

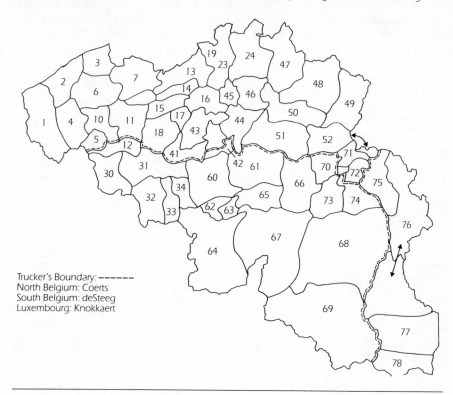

Trucker's Boundary: ------
North Belgium: Coerts
South Belgium: deSteeg
Luxembourg: Knokkaert

and 23:00, five days a week. For each order, the required number of cases of each brand-size was picked from designated factory stocks. If a truck was at the shipping platform waiting to be loaded, the cases were moved directly to the truck; otherwise they were assembled by truckloads in the shipping area and then loaded on a highway truck.

Stock picking and loading were done by means of an industrial clamp-truck. The clamps enabled the truck to grasp the cases quickly, without using pallets or skids. If a highway truck was to be loaded with cases of only one brand-size, then a single clamp truck could pick the stock and load at the rate of 1,500 cases per hour; this rate was reduced to 500 cases per hour for truckloads of mixed brand-sizes. Since a single brand-size was usually stored in several warehouse locations in order to maximize the utilization of total factory warehouse space, the shipping foreman had to designate to the clamp truck operator the particular stock-location of cases to be picked for each customer's order. The foreman also tried to move out the oldest stocks first. He could, however, if stocks were not

Exhibit 30—4 United Food Products Company Shipments

Area	Number of Customers	% of Total Shipments	Area	Number of Customers	% of Total Shipments
1	23	1.114	45	28	.981
2	25	1.451	46	23	1.231
3	25	1.335	47	23	1.024
4	19	1.841	48	10	.940
5	32	.520	49	10	.324
6	25	.738	50	9	1.584
7	23	1.342	51	15	1.254
8/9	45	2.328	52	9	1.135
10	21	.702	60	19	1.688
11	40	.891	61	11	.765
12	24	2.054	62	27	2.992
13	25	.563	63	23	1.597
14	32	2.089	64	11	.639
15	21	.709	65	17	1.726
16	19	1.336	66	20	1.218
17	22	1.198	67	10	.854
18	19	.523	68	19	1.702
19/23	115	14.320	69	18	1.314
24	27	1.659	70	18	1.205
30	25	2.202	71	25	.449
31	24	.689	72	27	1.150
32	18	.638	73	11	.449
33	23	1.295	74	22	.781
34	24	1.406	75	28	1.333
35/40	137	14.026	Liege	4	2.702
41	12	.811	Grand-Duche de		
42	15	.366	Luxembourg 76/78		7.020
43	18	1.583	Rounding		.350
44	25	1.864			100.000

near the maximum point, ship more recent stocks in an effort to cut handling costs.

Industrial engineers had developed a rationalized routine to help the warehouse and shipping foremen in their work of storing cases coming in via the packaging line conveyors and loading delivery trucks at the shipping dock. This routine required the maintenance of a master stock location and warehouse space availability file and a detailed checklist of steps in planning for efficient utilization of warehouse space, manpower, and materials handling equipment as well as for efficient materials handling methods.

Shipments to Holland

Shipments to Holland customers were presently being dispatched from the Brussels (outside) warehouse via the Dutch trucking company. This company operated three intermediate, storage and dispatch depots. Daily, Mr. van der Woeld's office in Rotterdam sent via telex to the trucking company a list of customers' orders to be delivered. The trucking dispatcher then prepared the daily schedule of pickups and routings to customers. Shipments destined for northern Holland were delivered directly from Brussels to retailers. Shipments to the remaining sections of Holland were routed to customers (wholesalers and retailers) via one of the three intermediate depots, otherwise called "shuttle points," where they were reloaded and routed further to final destinations.

Mr. McCracken said,

We are not satisfied with this Dutch shuttle-point system. We've had too many damaged cases returned by our Holland customers. When we checked into the cause of this we found that storage facilities were not

---

Exhibit 30—5 United Food Products Company Sales Canvass Period 30/9–25/10

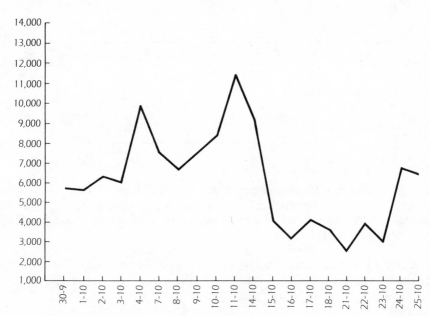

SOURCE: Industrial Engineering Department.

Graph Showing Number of Cases Shipped Each Day of Sales Canvass Period 30 Sept.–25 Oct.

NOTE: A "case" at United Food Products Company was actually a weighted average of all case sizes for all products and brands. Each case weighs approximately 12 kg.

Exhibit 30—6 United Food Products Company Sales Canvass Period 28/10–22/11

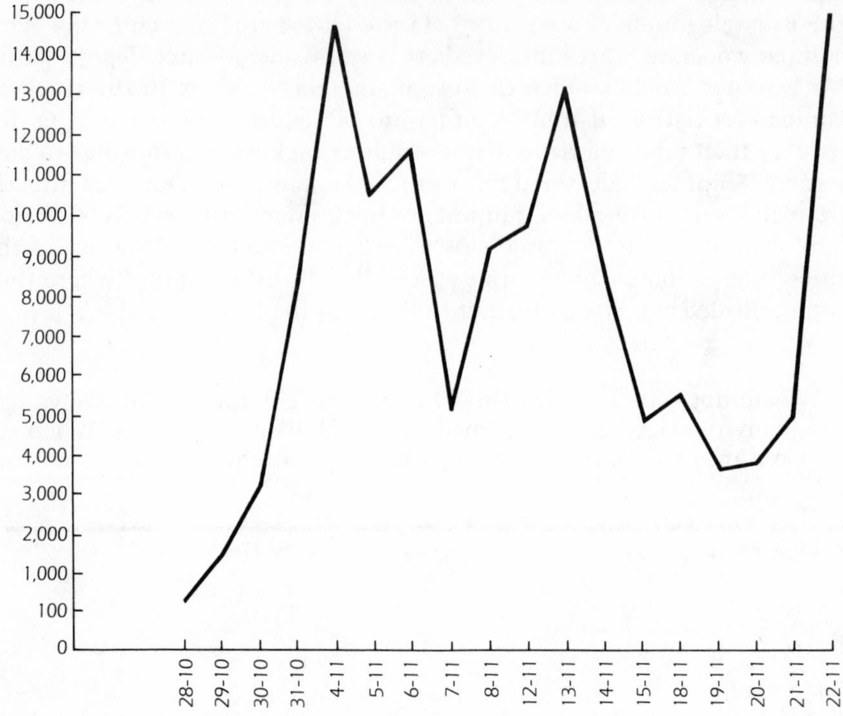

SOURCE: Industrial Engineering Department.

Graph Showing Number of Cases Shipped Each Day of Sales Canvass Period 28 Oct.–22 Nov.

NOTE: A "case" at United Food Products Company was actually a weighted average of all case sizes for all products and brands. Each case weighs approximately 12 kg.

adequate and handling was careless. Once we learned that cases were stored temporarily on the deck of a ship in Rotterdam, under a tarpaulin. Another time we saw depot crews using a greased wooden ramp to slide our cases down to the truck dock.

United Foods managers all agreed that distribution procedures for the Holland market would have to be changed, but they were not certain about what changes should be made.

Variations in Shipping Activities

Pursuant to plans for expanding and improving the Louvain warehousing activities, the industrial engineers made some studies to measure the variations in shipments. They determined that 4% of shipments in Belgium were in lots of 10 to 24 cases, 17% of shipments were in lots of 25 to 99 cases, and the remaining 79% was in lots of over 100 cases each. They also derived a graph showing the number of cases shipped each day for three different sales canvass periods given in Exhibits 30–5 through 30–7 and a table summarizing numbers of truck arrivals and truck departures per hour from the Louvain warehouse each day for 3 consecutive operating days given by Exhibit 30–8.

Mr. McCracken made the following comments about these variations:

Our analysis of these variations shows that about 70 percent of our total shipments are made during the first half of a canvass period. The number of cases shipped on the peak shipping days is about five times the number shipped on the low shipping days. If we're going to stick rigidly to our policy of shipping 48 hours after a customer gives us his order, then we're going to have to tolerate overtime and idle time of our warehouse personnel and equipment.

Exhibit 30—7 United Food Products Company Sales Canvass Period 25/11–20/12

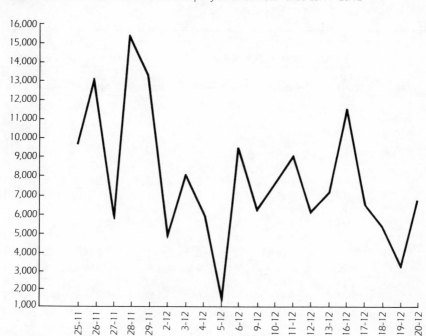

SOURCE: Industrial Engineering Department.

Graph Showing Number of Cases Shipped Each Day of Sales Canvass Period 25 Nov.–20 Dec.

NOTE: A "case" at United Food Products Company was actually a weighted average of all case sizes for all products and brands. Each case weighs approximately 12 kg.

Exhibit 30—8 United Food Products Company Summary of Truck Arrival and Service Times for Canvass Period January 3–February 14 (31 working days)

TRUCK ARRIVAL PER HOUR
Hour of Day

	6	7	8	9	10	11	12	13	14	15	16	17	18	19	20
Total—31 days	35	40	60	44	24	27	24	42	44	39	21	28	6	6	1
Average	1,13	1,29	1,94	1,42	0,77	0,87	0,77	1,35	1,42	1,26	0,68	0,90	0,19	0,19	0,03
Maximum	4	6	4	7	3	3	4	5	4	3	3	4	2	2	1
Minimum	0	0	0	0	0	0	0	0	0	0	0	0	0	0	0

TRUCK DEPARTURE PER HOUR
Hour of Day

	6	7	8	9	10	11	12	13	14	15	16	17	18	19	20
Total—31 days	1	11	34	33	45	34	18	47	42	47	50	27	20	20	12
Average	0,03	0,35	1,10	1,06	1,45	1,10	0,58	1,52	1,35	1,52	1,61	0,87	0,65	0,65	0,39
Maximum	1	2	3	5	6	6	4	4	5	4	3	4	2	3	2
Minimum	0	0	0	0	0	0	0	0	0	0	0	0	0	0	0

No arrivals or departures after 20:00

		TRUCK ARRIVAL PER HOUR				TRUCK DEPARTURE PER HOUR			
Date		Total Each Day	Average	Max.	Min.	Total Each Day	Average	Max.	Min.
Jan.	3	10	0,59	3	0	10	0,59	3	0
"	6	22	1,29	7	0	22	1,29	3	0
"	7	18	1,06	4	0	18	1,06	6	0
"	8	17	1	4	0	17	1	3	0
"	9	13	0,76	3	0	13	0,76	3	0
"	10	11	0,65	3	0	11	0,65	2	0
"	13	16	0,94	4	0	16	0,94	3	0
"	14	20	1,18	5	0	20	1,18	4	0
"	15	21	1,24	4	0	21	1,24	4	0
"	16	20	1,18	4	0	20	1,18	4	0
"	17	5	0,29	2	0	5	0,29	2	0
"	20	10	0,59	2	0	10	0,59	3	0
"	21	11	0,65	2	0	11	0,65	2	0
"	22	7	0,41	2	0	7	0,41	2	0
"	23	10	0,59	2	0	10	0,59	2	0
"	24	11	0,65	3	0	11	0,65	2	0
"	27	21	1,24	6	0	21	1,24	5	0
"	28	26	1,53	4	0	26	1,53	5	0
"	29	8	0,47	2	0	8	0,47	3	0

Exhibit 30–8 (continued)

		TRUCK ARRIVAL PER HOUR				TRUCK DEPARTURE PER HOUR		
Date	Total Each Day	Average	Max.	Min.	Total Each Day	Average	Max.	Min.
" 30	7	0,41	2	0	7	0,41	1	0
" 31	11	0,65	4	0	11	0,65	2	0
Feb. 3	15	0,88	4	0	15	0,88	4	0
" 4	13	0,76	4	0	13	0,76	3	0
" 5	17	1	4	0	17	1	6	0
" 6	19	1,12	4	0	19	1,12	4	0
" 7	21	1,24	4	0	21	1,24	4	0
" 10	18	1,06	4	0	18	1,06	3	0
" 11	10	0,59	3	0	10	0,59	2	0
" 12	6	0,35	2	0	6	0,35	2	0
" 13	12	0,71	4	0	12	0,71	3	0

SOURCE: Industrial Engineering Files.

Warehousing and shipping expenses are part of our Manufacturing departmental budget, not of the Sales Department. Yet it is the deliberate concentration of sales and advertising efforts early in each canvass period that causes our performance to look poor as far as budget measures are concerned. I agree that sales promotions have boosted our market share and sales volume but they also make it more expensive for us to give prompt delivery service to customers.

Arrangements with the three contract trucking firms delivering to the Belgium and Luxembourg markets have been negotiated by the Sales Department. Reimbursements to these contractors were based on Belgian Francs per ton and amounted to 460 francs per ton for Coerts S.A., 580 francs per ton for deSteeg, and an average of 700 francs per ton for Knokkaert.[1] In addition, Coerts also received 85 francs per ton for performing the loading operation at their Brussels warehouse. Mr. McCracken thought that these reimbursements might preferably be based on the number of cases delivered instead of tonnage, and that the number of pickups and deliveries should also be accounted for in reimbursing the trucking firms. The Dutch trucking firm operated under similar arrangements and negotiated with Mr. van der Woeld in Rotterdam.

[1] One Belgian Franc was approximately equal to 2 U.S. cents.

Mr. Van Roehm said,

I realize that our contract trucking firms make their own truck-routing and dispatching decisions daily, and that these decisions have significant effects on our distribution costs and services to customers. If our organization were to make these decisions would they become the responsibility of the Sales Department or the Manufacturing Department? Even if we did manage the traffic problems of distribution, how could I be certain that we should solve them any more economically than they're being solved now by the contract trucking firm?

United Food Products Company (B)

31

Introduction

Mr. Henry F. Russo, Vice-President for European Operations of the United Food Products (UFP) Company, was concerned with the proposal by the management of UFP (France) to include a production facility for French FLOCODAV in the new plant now under construction, at St. Quentin, France. At present, FLOCODAV, cooked cereal much like ordinary porridge, was being produced for the French market at the UFP (Benelux) factory in Louvain, Belgium. The Benelux company, as a result, was opposed to the French proposal. Mr. Russo, in describing the problem said:

This one is going to be a tough nut to crack. It's the first problem of interdivisional rivalry that we've had here in Europe. Our French and Benelux managers seem to have good arguments in their favor but they're deadlocked. Something has got to be done, though, and done quickly. If we don't take some action by the end of this week, the decision will have been made by default. Construction activities are already well underway at St. Quentin.

This case was prepared by Mr. Donald L. Wallace under the direction of Professor Robert E. McGarrah as a basis for class discussion. It is not designed to present an illustration of either effective or ineffective handling of an administrative problem.
Copyright © 1964 by l'Institut pour l'Etude des Méthodes de Direction de l'Entreprise (IMEDE), Lausanne, Switzerland.

Company Background

The United Food Products Company produced and sold a growing variety of "convenience foods" including breakfast cereals, dehydrated soups and vegetables, instant coffee, and various flours and cake mixes. The company had been started in the latter half of the 19th century as a minor flour-milling operation but by the 1920s it had grown to become a major company in the U.S. food products industry. After weathering the Great Depression, the company went on to even further prosperity and by the 1960s it had become one of the 500 largest industrial corporations in the U.S.

United Foods first began expanding its operations into Europe in 1931, when it purchased Henry Morehead, Ltd., to form its first overseas subsidiary: United Food Products Co. (U.K.), Ltd. From 1931 onward the U.K. company was actively engaged in developing and servicing markets, throughout the British Isles, for its breakfast cereals, dry soups, and instant coffee.

It was not until 1953, however, that the company began to exploit the continental European market. In 1953 United Food Products Co. (Geneva), S.A. was formed as a continental headquarters for directing the development of new markets. UFP Geneva did not, however, operate any factories. Products were imported into Continental Europe from the U.K. company across the channel. As one of the first actions, the Geneva company moved into the marketing region of the European Economic Community (EEC) by contracting with a Mr. H. van Roehm of Brussels, Belgium to act as General Sales Agent for the Belgian and Luxembourg markets. A similar contract, for the Dutch market, was negotiated at the same time with a Mr. P. van der Woeld, in Amsterdam.

During the mid-1950s, total sales in these markets more than doubled each year and, in 1955, the General Agency Agreement with Mr. van Roehm was terminated so that a new company, United Food Products Co. (Benelux) S.A. with Mr. van Roehm as General Manager, could be formed. Mr. van der Woeld was continued in his role as General Sales Agent for the Dutch market but his contract was now administered by the new Benelux Company. This allowed the Geneva Company to concentrate all of its efforts on other areas of continental Europe. The Geneva Company was already laying the ground work for a major effort in the Italian market. (See Exhibits 31–1 through 31–4 for United Foods organization and product line).

In the same year, 1955, two other events occurred which greatly affected United Foods' manufacturing capacity in the EEC. Sales of the "Potage-Minute" brand of dehydrated soups alone had, as a direct result of the efforts of the two sales agents, increased to the point where the factory in England was experiencing difficulty in keeping up with orders. To ease this situation a contract-manufacturing arrangement was negotiated with

Exhibit 31—1 United Food Products Company Corporate Organization and Products

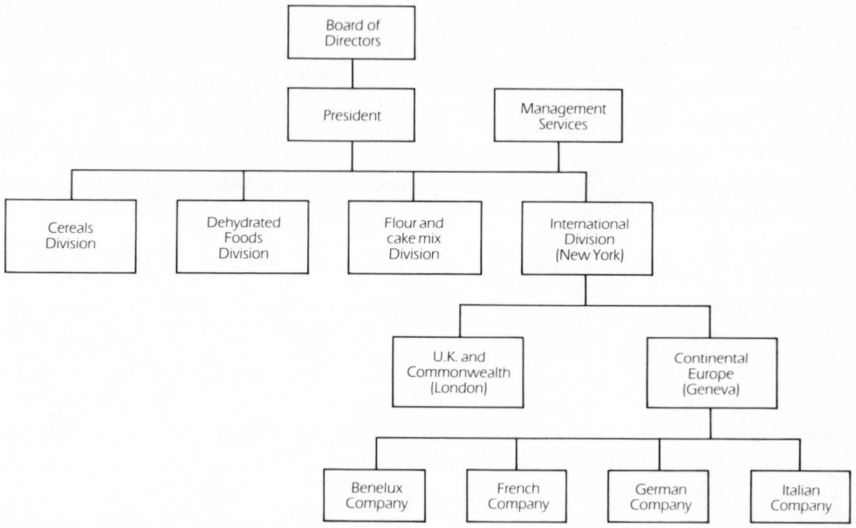

SOURCE: Annual Report.

Moulins Généraux, S.A., a diversified Belgian food processor, to produce "Potage-Minute" for the entire Benelux market. In addition, construction of a new $4,000,000 dry cereals factory was begun at Louvain, Belgium to give the Benelux Company an independent manufacturing capability. When the new plant went on stream, in the fall of 1956, imports from England were discontinued. The new plant, together with the contract-manufacturing agreement with Moulins-Généraux, thus put the Benelux Company on a self-sustaining basis within its own marketing area.

The French Subsidiary

Having achieved such a notable success in the Benelux market, United Food Products Co. (Geneva) S.A., decided to begin more active operations in the French marketing area. In 1955, United Foods purchased a modern food processing plant at Montpellier, in southern France. This plant had been operated by a French firm that had gone into receivership. When United Food Products took over the Montpellier operation and formed United Food Products Co. (France) S.A. the plant was producing less than 1,000,000 cases of ready-to-eat cereal a year. This was a result of labor militancy in the Montpellier area and a history of poor management within the company, both of which kept production perennially snarled. By assigning its own management and technical staff at Montpellier, UFP

Exhibit 31—2 United Food Products Company Corporate Organization and Products

U.S.	U.K.	Benelux	France
Cereals, Ready-to-Eat:			
Sparkies .... (1922)[1]	Sparkies .... (1931)	Sparkies .... (1953)	(1955)
Rice Puffies ...... (1924)	Rice Puffies ...... (1934)	Rice Puffies ...... (1954)	(1956)
Flakes-O-Corn ... (1925)	Flakes-O-Corn ... (1931)	Flakes-O-Corn ... (1953)	(1955)
Oat Pops .... (1927)	Oat Pops .... (1935)	Oat Pops .... (1954)	(1956)
Bowl-O-Bran .... (1932)	Bowl-O-Bran .... (1936)	Bowl-O-Bran .... (1955)	(1957)
Cereals, Cooked:			
Bowl-O-Cream Oatmeal .... (1924)	Bowl-O-Cream Porridge .... (1931)	Flocodav .... (1955)	(1956)
Dehydrated Products:			
Minit-Reddy Soups .... (1951)	Minit Reddy Soups .... (1953)	Potage-Minute ... (1953)	(1958)
Quik-Cup Coffee . (1953)	Quik-Cup tea and coffee .... (1955)	Quikcafé .... (1955)	(1958)
Cream-Whipt Potatoes .... (1954)	Cream-Whipt Potatoes .... (1955)	Insta-Purée ...... (1955)	(1958)
Flour and Cake Mix:			
Abby Lincoln Cake Mixes .... (1948)	Jennifer .... (1950)	Yvonne .... (1956)	(1959)
First Prize Flour ... (1912)	First Prize .... (1932)	Premier Choix .... (1953)	(1955)
Featherlite Cake Flour .... (1948)	Featherlite .... (1950)	Petit-Patissier ..... (1954)	(1956)

SOURCE: Annual Report.

[1] Numbers in parentheses represent year of introduction.

Exhibit 31—3 United Food Products Company Benelux Company Organization

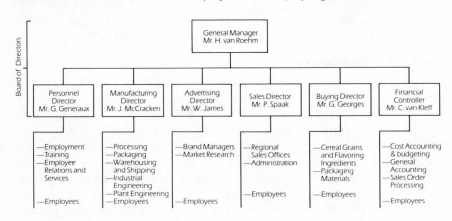

SOURCE: Mr. H. van Roehm, General Manager.

Exhibit 31—4 United Food Products Company French Company Organization

Board of Directors			General Manager Mr. V. Sandhurst			

Personnel Director Mr. P. Maillet	Manufacturing Director Mr. J. P. Broussard	Advertising Director Mr. R. Flint	Sales Director Mr. K. Williams	Buying Director Mr. F. Gautier	Financial Controller Mr. H. Sandoz
—Employment —Training —Employee Relations and Services	—Processing —Packaging —Warehousing and Shipping —Industrial Engineering —Plant Engineering	—Brand Managers —Market Research	—Regional Sales Offices —Administration	—Cereal Grains & Flavoring Ingredients —Packaging Materials	—Cost Accounting & Budgeting —General Accounting —Sales Order Processing
—Employees	—Employees	—Employees	—Employees	—Employees	—Employees

SOURCE: Mr. V. Sandhurst, General Manager.

(France) was able to increase this output tenfold and in 1963 the plant was producing over 10,000,000 cases per year.[1]

Sales in the French marketing area, which were initially handled by the sales arm of the recently acquired Montpellier company, expanded even more rapidly than in the Benelux area. This situation was compounded as the French Company began hiring additional salesmen and imposing a more consistent and aggressive marketing strategy on its selling activities. By 1961, the "Sparkies" brand of dry cereal had shot to number two position in the French market, commanding a 15% market share.

Faced with the rapid expansion of the entire French dry cereal market, United Food Products Co. (France) S.A. decided in late 1962 to begin construction the following spring on a $3 million plant at Saint Quentin in Northern France. The choice of this plant site rested largely on three factors: the desire to keep shipping costs, within the French market, at a minimum; the availability of a reasonably sized labor market; and the French government's incentive policy which was to provide housing for much of the labor force, an enormously important factor in getting and keeping plant workers. The plant was to be designed in the United States by the engineering staff of the parent company. The French subsidiary did, however, send its own representatives to the U.S. to provide data on European prices for materials, equipment, and construction and to participate actively in the design of the plant. The Saint Quentin plant was to be completed and on stream by January 1, 1965.

[1] A "case" at United Food Products Company was actually a weighted average of all case sizes for all products and brands.

It was against this background that the question of building a new manufacturing facility for French FLOCODAV arose. United Food Products
(France) was anxious to include a FLOCODAV facility in the new St.
Quentin plant thus bringing responsibility for both manufacture and sale
of French FLOCODAV under their authority. The Benelux company,
which was at present manufacturing the FLOCODAV product on a contract basis for the French company, was opposed to this scheme and
sought to maintain production of FLOCODAV for the French market at
the Louvain plant.

The FLOCODAV Product

The FLOCODAV product itself was what is commonly known as porridge, being basically an oat cereal requiring further cooking and being
served hot. FLOCODAV and, in fact, hot cooked cereals generally, did not
hold a major position in United Food Products cereal line—representing
in 1963, slightly less than 10% of the total breakfast cereal unit volume
in both the French and Benelux markets. The product was, however,
firmly established in both markets and, since its introduction in 1955,
had grown to a volume of over 1,000,000 cases a year. (See Exhibit 31–5.)

The manufacturing process for FLOCODAV consisted first of taking
the cleaned oat grains and dicing them into small bits. This was accomplished in order to facilitate rapid cooking of the product and, since the
quick cooking variety was the only type being offered to the European
market, the entire FLOCODAV output went through this process. The
finely diced oat grains were next processed through a stream treatment to
prepare them for the rolling equipment. The steam-treated grains were
then rolled out into tiny flakes and mixed with various seasonings and
preservatives to form the finished product. Unlike the ready-to-eat cereals, which had to be mixed with some care to prevent crumbling of the
individual flakes, the FLOCODAV product was not at all subject to damage and could be mixed in what amounted to little more than a large bowl
equipped with an automatic stirring device. Packaging was done on the
same high-speed equipment that was used for the higher volume ready-to-
eat cereals. This equipment could be used for both FLOCODAV package
sizes and each packaging machine was capable of putting out 1000–4000
cases per shift according to the package size being run.

Although the recipe for the FLOCODAV product sold in the French
market differed slightly from that sold in the Benelux market to cater to
existing taste differences, this difference was minor and had little or no
effect on the manufacture of the product. Packaging too was altered according to the needs of the market being served. The printed material on
the box had, in each case, to conform to the cultural wishes and labeling
laws of the market. An obvious example of the former was the desirability

Exhibit 31—5 United Food Products Company FLOCODAV European Sales: 1955–1970 (in 000's of cases)[1]

	Benelux	France	Germany
1955	4.8	—	—
1956	103.2	8.4	—
1957	181.5	124.8[2]	—
1958	201.6	69.6	—
1959	160.8	339.6	—
1960	164.4	351.6	—
1961	146.4[3]	522.0	142.8
1962	162.0	580.8	600.0
1963	174.0	903.6	630.0
1964	186.0 (est.)	966.0 (est.)	660.0 (est.)
1965 (proj.)	205.0	780.0	690.0
1966 (")	225.0	900.0	—
1967 (")	250.0	990.0	—
1968 (")	275.0	1100.0	—
1969 (")	300.0	1150.0	—
1970 (")	330.0	1200.0	—

SOURCE: Mr. Russo's Office.

[1] A "case" at United Food Products Company was actually a weighted average of all case sizes for all products and brands.

[2] Production shifted to Louvain

[3] Recipe Change

of having "Made in France" plainly marked on the packages being distributed to the French market.

The European Odyssey of the FLOCODAV Product

United Foods first introduced FLOCODAV into continental Europe through the Benelux market in 1955. Until late 1956, product for the Benelux market was imported from the U.K. company. After 1956, however, FLOCODAV for the entire Benelux market was supplied by the new Louvain plant.

The rapid success that the product enjoyed in the Benelux market encouraged the French company, in 1956, to introduce a similar product into their own marketing area. The French product was manufactured at a temporary facility in the Montpellier plant and was packaged on the same equipment that was serving the dry cereal line. Procurement of all raw and packaging material for the French product was, of course, done in France. By late 1957, however, the French FLOCODAV volume had expanded to the point where the original temporary facility could no longer meet requirements. At the same time, French dry cereal sales were put-

Exhibit 31–6 United Food Products Company Monthly Material Requirements

From: J. McCracken, Mfg. Director (Benelux)
To: F. Gautier, Buying Director (France)
Subj: Raw and Pkg. Material Requirements for French FLOCODAV—June, 1965

May 11, 1965
Schedule: 42,000 cases 20's
12,000 cases 12's
Total: 54,000 cases

Item	Per Case	Required for 54,000 cases	To be delivered for June, 1965 Production	For delivery to Louvain Plant on:								
				June 1	2	3	4	5	6	15	16	17
Raw Materials												
No. 4 Oats	3506 gms.	169,324 kgs.	170 ton	25	25	25	25	25	25	—	20	—
No. 6 Oats	2606	140,724	140 ton	20	20	20	20	20	20	—	20	—
No. 12 Oats	2606	140,724	140 ton	20	20	20	20	20	20	—	20	—
Malt	238	12,852	13 ton	7	—	—	—	6	—	—	—	—
Salt	10.03	542	500 kg.	500	—	—	—	—	—	—	—	—
F 1232 KT	8.92	484	500 kg.	500	—	—	—	—	—	—	—	—
Pkg. Materials												
Glue	45	2,430 kgs.	600 kg.	—	—	—	—	600	—	—	—	—
CS 20 (cases)	1.005 ea.	42,210	42,000	42M	—	—	—	—	—	—	—	—
CN 20 (cartons)	20,400	856,800	850,000	850M	—	—	—	—	—	—	—	—
CS 12 (case)	1.005	12,060	12,000	—	—	—	—	—	—	12M	—	—
CN 12 (cartons)	12,240	146,880	150,000	—	—	—	—	—	—	150M	—	—

SOURCE: Mr. McCracken's Office.

ting pressure on overall packing machine capacity. The decision was made, therefore, to shift manufacture of French FLOCODAV to the Louvain plant which was closer to the major market centers and where there was excess capacity for both processing and packaging. Since the actual manufacture of FLOCODAV was relatively simple and did not require any additional equipment at Louvain, the shift in location presented no serious manufacturing problems. French law, however, required that at least 50% of the product's final value must have its origin in France if the product was to be labelled "Made in France." Since the marketing department felt that it was imperative to have this label on the French product, all raw and packaging materials continued to be procured in France. Although management at United Foods (Benelux) thought that Belgian suppliers for both raw and packaging materials could have been found without much difficulty, they recognized the need for the French label and were content to continue the established relations with the French suppliers.

Raw and packaging materials continued, therefore, to be procured in France, after which they were shipped via railway to the Louvain plant where they were held in inventory until they were ready for processing into finished goods. Finished product was then shipped back into France to the various United Foods warehouses scattered throughout the country where it was again held in inventory pending eventual distribution to retail and wholesale outlets.

The Current Situation

FLOCODAV situation had not changed much from what it had been in 1957. Materials were still being procured in France, exported to Belgium where they were processed into finished product and then reimported into the French marketing region. Mr. Broussard, Manufacturing Director of the French company, collected each month from the 14 warehouse locations, an estimate of their product needs for the coming month. He then totalled these needs and forwarded them on to the Louvain plant. At Louvain this total was integrated by the manufacturing staff into the overall plant production schedule, and a detailed plan of raw material requirements for the FLOCODAV product was determined. This detailed plan (see Exhibits 31–6 and 31–7) was then sent to Mr. Gautier, Buying Director of the French company, and from it and the Louvain inventory data two procurement schedules were worked out—the "A" schedule (see Exhibit 31–8) being for materials shipped direct from the suppliers to Louvain and the "B" schedule (see Exhibit 31–9) for materials shipped to Louvain from an outside warehouse located in Brussels. The major objectives of the two schedules were to assure: (1) that the materials would be on hand when required, (2) that stocks at Brussels would be completely turned every three months to prevent spoilage of the cereals, and (3) that inventories would be kept as low as possible within the first two con-

Exhibit 31—7 United Food Products Company Schedule A

From: F. Gautier, Buying Director (France)
To: Maillet Frères,* Jeumont, J. McCracken, Mfg. Director (Benelux)
Subj: Schedule A—June
For delivery to Louvain on the dates indicated.

Order No.	Item	Total	May 25	May 26	May 27	May 29	June 5
64—821	No. 4						
	Oats	200 T	—	—	25	25	25
64—823	No. 6						
	Oats	150 T	20	20	20	20	20
64—824	No. 12						
	Oats	140 T	20	20	20	20	20

No. 4 Oats: Remainder of Order No. 64—821:125 T   For delivery to Brussels
No. 6 Oats: "   "   "   " 64—823: 50 T   as soon after June 5 as
No. 12 Oats: "   "   "   " 64—824: 40 T   possible; Rail carrier.

F 1232 KT : Order No. 64—822:350 kg.   For Delivery to Jeumont
Salt   : Order No. 64—825:650 kg.   May 16, 1965.

* Maillet Frères was a freight forwarding establishment at Jeumont that handled UFP's account with the French customs authorities.
SOURCE: Mr. Gautier's Office.

Exhibit 31—8 United Food Products Company Schedule B

From: F. Gautier, Buying Director (France)
To: J. McCracken, Mfg. Director (Benelux)
Subj: Schedule B—June
For delivery to Brussels warehouse on the dates indicated:

Item	Total	June 1	June 2	June 3	June 4	June 5	June 6	June 15	June 16
No. 4 Oats	95 T	25	25	25	20	—	—	—	—
No. 6 Oats	40 T	20	20	—	—	—	—	—	—
No. 12 Oats	40 T	20	20	—	—	—	—	—	—
Malt	13 T	7	—	—	—	6	—	—	—
Salt	500 kg	500	—	—	—	—	—	—	—
F 1232 KT	500 kg	500	—	—	—	—	—	—	—
Glue	600 kg	—	—	—	—	600	—	—	—
CS 20 (cases)	42,000	42,000	—	—	—	—	—	—	—
CN 20 (cartons)	850,000	850,000	—	—	—	—	—	—	—
CS 12 (cases)	12,000	—	—	—	—	—	—	10,000	—
CN 12 (cartons)	150,000	—	—	—	—	—	—	150,000	—

SOURCE: Mr. Gautier's Office.

Exhibit 31—9 United Food Products Company Sample Order

Gaillard, Simon et Cie, S.A.
24 Rue de Maubeuge
Paris, 10ᵉ

Gentlemen:

No 4 Oats, Order No. 64 — 821 / 200 T.

Ship to Maillet Frères, Jeumont as per our Standing Order No. 64 — 800 the following:

25 T	27 May, 1965
25 T	29 May, 1965
25 T	5 June, 1965

The remaining 125 T to be forwarded as quickly as possible following 5 June, 1965.
All shipments to be made via rail carrier.

F. Gautier

SOURCE: Mr. Gautier's Office.

straints. With the two schedules in hand, Mr. Cautier placed orders with the various suppliers (see Exhibit 31–9) sufficiently in advance to have the materials arrive on schedule at Louvain. In practice, however, Mr. Gautier found that the variability in delivery time was so great that he had to continually increase the lead time to insure on-time delivery at Louvain. The lead times from the various suppliers to the Louvain plant averaged 9 to 10 working days but occasionally went as high as 15 working days.

The suppliers, when they had filled the orders, shipped them by rail to a customs location, Jeumont, on the Franco-Belgian border. Delivery time from the suppliers to Jeumont averaged 3 or 4 days. At Jeumont the French customs authorities made a record of all materials entering Belgium so that these materials, less a small yield allowance, could be credited to United Foods on the return trip when the finished product was brought back into France. In this way United Foods paid duty only on that part of the product's value which was added in Belgium. This special Re-import Permit, which was renewable every six months, made it necessary, of course, for United Foods to disclose the recipe for FLOCODAV to the French customs authorities. United Foods management felt, however, that this was not critical because the French customs authorities kept the recipe confidential and because the formulas of the ingredients themselves, some of which were prepared by secret United Foods processes, did not have to be disclosed.

After passing through the border point at Jeumont the shipments continued on their way, still by rail, to Louvain and Brussels. Delivery time from Jeumont to Louvain and Brussels including the layover time during customs inspection, averaged 6 days. At Louvain materials were held in inventory for 2 or 3 days until they were required for processing. At Brussels, materials were accumulated into what was called the "Bogey Stock." The function of this Brussels Bogey Stock, which could be delivered to the Louvain plant in one working day, was to protect the factory against fluctuations in delivery time from the suppliers, against the receipt of poor quality materials from the suppliers, and against any unforeseen delays which the suppliers might encounter in meeting a specific order.

When the FLOCODAV was completely processed, packaged, and put in cases, it was again put on railroad cars and returned to the border point at Jeumont. Here it was checked by French customs against the incoming shipments to insure that no more material was being brought into France than had originally been expected and that no excesses of material were being permanently exported to Belgium. The Reimport Agreement did, however, provide for a 1.0% processing loss of raw materials, a .5% loss of cases, and a 2% loss of cartons.

The French then levied a 7.2% tariff on that portion of the product's value which had originated in Belgium. This was determined by deducting the cost of materials from the export price of the FLOCODAV. The cost of materials was well documented by suppliers invoices and the like and could be readily determined. The export price, on the other hand, was determined unilaterally by UFP (Benelux) and was, by long-standing policy, equal to the transfer price paid by the French company. This export price was registered with the French customs authorities for inclusion in the Reimport Agreement. Theoretically, the French government was at liberty to challenge this export price at the close of any six month period. In practice, however, the customs officials tended to let the old figures carry over from agreement to agreement.

United Foods (France) also paid a $2 per $1000 customs tax on all goods crossing the border as well as a 2% stamp tax on the customs duty paid. Both these taxes, however, were later deductible from the French Tax on Value Added (Taxe sur la Valeur Ajoutée or "TVA") and they did not, therefore, add anything to the cost of operations. TVA itself amounted to 25% of the total value added but, since it was very similar to a sales tax,

Exhibit 31–10 United Food Products Company Distribution Program for French FLOCODAV
May.

		Size 20	Size 12
1. Lyon	1 car: 2300 cases	2300	
2. Le Mans	1 car: 2300 cases	2300	
3. Rouen	1 car: 1600 cases	1600	
4. Reims	1 car: 2300 cases	2300	
5. Nantes	1 car: 1800 cases	1800	
6. Metz	1 car: 2250 cases	2250	
7. Montpellier	1 car: 2300 cases	2300	
8. Le Mans	1 car: 2300 cases	2300	
9. Reims	1 car: 2300 cases	2300	
10. Lyon	1 car: 2300 cases	2300	
11. Reims	1 car: 2300 cases	2300	
12. Lyon	1 car: 2300 cases	2300	
13. Reims	1 car: 2300 cases	2300	
14. Nevers	1 car: 2300 cases	2200	100
15. Strasbourg	1 car: 1700 cases	1600	100
16. Toulouse	1 car: 2200 cases	1800	400
17. Limoges	1 car: 1700 cases	1200	500
18. Bordeaux	1 car: 2300 cases	1800	500
19. Metz	1 car: 2250 cases	1650	600
20. Rouen	1 car: 1300 cases	800	500
21. Reims	1 car: 2000 cases		2000
22. Lyon	1 car: 1800 cases		1800
23. Le Mans	1 car: 750 cases		750
24. Reims	1 car: 2000 cases		2000
25. Montpellier	1 car: 750 cases		750
26. Reims	1 car: 2000 cases		2000
27. Lille (Deliver via truck)	2300 cases	2300	
		42000	12000

SOURCE: Mr. McCracken's Office.

was passed on to the consumer in its entirety. From Jeumont, shipments
of FLOCODAV were sent on to the 14 United Foods warehouses scattered
throughout France in accordance with the orders these warehouses had
placed with Mr. Broussard in Paris. A sample delivery schedule for finished FLOCODAV is given in Exhibit 31–10. There was no transhipping
between warehouses so that all replenishment was done exclusively by
the Louvain plant. The location of these warehouses with the delivery
times and transport costs to them is given in Exhibit 31–11. Inventories at

Exhibit 31–11 United Food Products Company French Warehouse Location

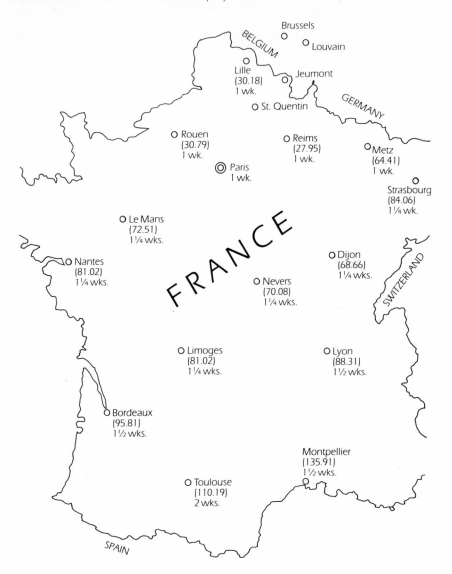

Brussels
o

o Louvain

o
Lille
(30.18)
1 wk.

o Jeumont

o St. Quentin

o Rouen
(30.79)
1 wk.

o Reims
(27.95)
1 wk.

o Metz
(64.41)
1 wk.

◎ Paris
1 wk.

o
Strasbourg
(84.06)
1¼ wk.

o Le Mans
(72.51)
1¼ wks.

o Nantes
(81.02)
1¼ wks.

o Nevers
(70.08)
1¼ wks.

o Dijon
(68.66)
1¼ wks.

FRANCE

BELGIUM

GERMANY

SWITZERLAND

o Limoges
(81.02)
1¼ wks.

o Lyon
(88.31)
1½ wks.

o Bordeaux
(95.81)
1½ wks.

Montpellier
(135.91)
1½ wks.
o

o Toulouse
(110.19)
2 wks.

SPAIN

Numbers in parentheses represent shipping cost from St. Quentin in $ / 1000 cases. Time in weeks represents average lead time to each warehouse. (Lead times were within 20% of the average roughly ⅔ of the time and within 40% of the average 90% of the time.)
SOURCE: Mr. Sandhurst's Office.

each location were controlled from Paris by Mr. Williams' office in the Sales Department.

Shifting FLOCODAV Production to St. Quentin: The Benelux Company's Viewpoint

The decision being faced by United Foods management was whether to build a facility for producing French FLOCODAV at the new St. Quentin plant or to continue producing it at Louvain. Mr. van Roehm, General Manager of the Benelux Company, claimed that continuing the present arrangement was the better alternative. When questioned on the proposal to move FLOCODAV production to St. Quentin he argued:

I know that according to the way Geneva has set up the analysis, the customs duties and the extra shipping costs we have to pay make our cost structure here at Louvain look higher (see Exhibit 31–12), but that's only part of the story. Some of those costs aren't really relevant to the FLOCODAV situation. More than ⅔ of the processing and packaging costs associated with FLOCODAV would go on whether we were making it here or not and it isn't right to include them in the analysis. These costs include things like depreciation, supervision, and the fixed portion of heat and power. Moving FLOCODAV to the new plant won't change them one bit. Our packing equipment is running below capacity as it is and it just seems like bad business to put us even further below capacity. Then, too, the fee that the French company pays us for making FLOCODAV shouldn't be included either. The fee is computed according to a well established UFP formula for transfers between operating companies. It represents a charge of 7.5% of the total cost of FLOCODAV, F.O.B. the Louvain factory. This money stays inside the company, however, and doesn't represent any net drain on United Foods as a whole.

Another thing to be considered is our favorable tax situation here in Belgium. Our tax rate is only 36% compared to the 50% tax the French Company is paying. When this is taken into consideration, the dollar advantage at St. Quentin completely disappears. (See Exhibit 31–13.)

Those figures surely don't justify the construction of a $385,000 facility. (See Exhibit 31–14.) Don't forget, also, that these figures represent the relatively short term future. Three years hence all internal tariffs in the EEC will be removed. When tariffs are eliminated another chunk of the cost differential between Louvain and St. Quentin will disappear.

Another short term aspect of these figures that I don't like is that they reflect the situation exactly as it is today, not the way it should be. Only 50% of the product value *must* originate in France but right now over ⅔ of it does. We could locate at least a few Belgian suppliers and significantly reduce our transportation costs. Furthermore, we might be able to reduce manufacturing and inventory costs as well. With Paris handling all scheduling and inventory control for the FLOCODAV product, we can't make a lot of the improvements that I know are possible. For example, to offset the high variability in delivery times, Paris just keeps setting higher and higher inventory limits—and materials still arrive behind schedule more than half the time.

To sum it up, I think that the figures are in our favor, we already have an operating FLOCODAV facility and we're in a good position to make improvements in delivery and inventory control. I really don't see any advantage to moving FLOCODAV production to the new plant.

Exhibit 31—12 United Food Products Company Annual Cost of FLOCODAV to the French Company[1]

	(a) if manufactured at Louvain			(b) if manufactured at St. Quentin		
	Total Cost	Out-of Pocket Cost	Allocated Cost	Total Cost	Out-of Pocket Cost	Allocated Cost
Raw Materials	$629,856	$629,856	—	$586,976	$586,976	—
Packaging Materials	328,320	328,320	—	323,957	323,957	—
Yield Losses	11,318	11,318	—	10,454	10,454	—
Processing & Packaging Expense	102,125	43,177	$58,948	81,216	77,760	3,456
Warehousing & Shipping Expense	12,096	12,096	—	17,280	17,280	—
General Plan Overhead	69,120	10,368	58,752	41,184	50,688	(9,504)
Benelux Company's "Fee"[2]	86,463	—	86,463			
Benelux Company's "Fee"				—	—	—
Freight Out[3]	102,816	102,816	—			
Freight Out				53,568	53,568	—
Total	1,342,114	1,137,951	204,163	1,114,635	1,120,683	(6,048)
After Tax (36.5%)	852,242	722,600	129,644			
After Tax (50%)				557,317	560,341	(3,034)

[1] Based on 1965–1968 average production of 1,080,000 cases.

[2] Paid by United Food Products Co. (France) S.A.

[3] Freight cost from weighted average shipping cost to the 14 warehouses. This figure includes the customs duty levied at the Franco-Belgian Border.

NOTE: The figures in Exhibit 31–12 were extracted from a cost-study made by Mr. Russo'a staff. Raw and packaging material costs were based on current prices and current freight rates. Since these were relatively stable, the current cost was projected ahead and used as a 3 year average. Yield losses, processing and packaging expense, warehouse and shipping expense, and general plant overhead were based on engineering estimates prepared by Mr. Russo's staff. For the Louvain plant, the estimates were based on historical data which was submitted weekly to Geneva by the Benelux Company. For the St. Quentin plant, the estimates were based on the engineering data used to design the plant. The fee was, as explained previously by Mr. van Roehm, the standard one used throughout the United Foods organization. Freight out, which included the customs duty paid on the product, was again based on current rates except for the duty which was reduced by half to take into account the scheduled EEC tariff reductions. All of the data in Exhibits 31–1 through 31–13 were available to Mr. van Roehm and Mr. Sandhurst as well as to Mr. Russo.

Exhibit 31—13 United Food Products Company Cash Flows of French and Benelux Companies Under Present and Proposed Conditions

		France	Benelux	Net Cost
At Present:	Revenue	—	1342	
	Expense	(1342)	(1138)	
	Net	—	204	
	After tax	(671)	129	(542)
Proposed:	Revenue	—	—	
	Expense	(1121)	—	
	Net	—	—·	
	After tax	(563)*	—	(563)

*After adding lost tax shield of $3,024 at French Company.

SOURCE: Mr. van Roehm's Office.

NOTE: The above figures were derived from the data in Exhibit 31–12 by Mr. van Roehm's staff in support of the Benelux argument.

Exhibit 31—14 United Food Products Company Capital Requirements for FLOCODAV Facility at St. Quentin

	Cost	Annual Depreciation
Processing Equipment	$100,000	$ 5,000
Packaging Equipment	125,000	6,250
Warehousing	75,000	2,250
Building and Grounds	85,000	2,550
Total	$385,000	$ 16,050

SOURCE: Mr. Sandhurst's Office.

The French Company's Viewpoint

Mr. Sandhurst, General Manager of the French Company, was equally insistent that the shift of FLOCODAV production to the new St. Quentin plant should be effected. In answer to Mr. van Roehm's argument he stated:

I know van Roehm doesn't want to lose the FLOCODAV production and I don't blame him. He lost 600,000 cases a year in FLOCODAV production when the new German dry cereal plant went on stream two years ago. That shift was made without even putting the figures together and he claims it should never have been made. Maybe he's right on that one, I don't know, but this time I think it's pretty clear that the shift should be made.

In the first place our costs are going to be lower at St. Quentin and it doesn't make sense to me to pay for all that extra shipping and to pay for customs duties when it isn't really necessary. On an after tax basis, considering only the relevant costs, the company would save over $160,000 a year by manufacturing FLOCODAV at St. Quentin. This represents a little less than a two year payback on $385,000 which puts it well above the company cut off point for this type of investment.

As for the tax break that the Benelux Company is getting, you've got to be very careful when you take that into consideration. Moving company profits into low tax areas can open a very nasty Pandora's box. United Foods has always had a good relationship with the income tax authorities primarily because we don't move money around like that and I for one wouldn't want to jeopardize that relationship. And that's only one drawback to the system. Shifting profits around like that also tends to confuse the local situation. In some companies local managers don't even know their true profit figure and they're less efficient managers because of it. United Foods has never operated this way, of course, and what I'm saying is that I don't think we should start now.

I can't get too excited about the undercapacity situation at Louvain either. Obviously it costs less out-of-pocket to fill orders when you're under capacity but, for this decision, we're talking about a long term commitment. Louvain isn't going to be under capacity forever and when they start needing FLOCODAV packing capacity for their ready-to-eat cereals, they'll be glad they shifted it to St. Quentin. Besides, operating a little under capacity puts pressure on the marketing people. If everything is operating full tilt, the marketing people are the fair-haired boys, but when there's idle plant and equipment around management starts looking very sternly towards the sales and advertising departments and this, of course, tends to keep them moving a little faster.

Mr. Sandhurst also had this to say about the elimination of internal tariffs in the EEC:

Sure, I realize that the EEC internal tariffs will be eliminated in the next two or three years, but I also realize that tax differentials may be eliminated too. Elimination of tax differentials is mentioned in the Rome Treaty and, with the way things have been going in the tariff area, this may be pushed through much earlier than people have been expecting. That would certainly change any figures based on tax considerations.

I do agree with van Roehm on one thing though. We're not really looking at the right figures in the first place. The costs at St. Quentin reflect what it would cost to make FLOCODAV at St. Quentin if we used the same procurement and scheduling system they're using now and that, I can assure you, we would not do. There is a lot of slack in the present system and I'm certain that we could bring those costs down. Furthermore, inventory costs, which don't appear at all in the figures, could also be reduced by shifting FLOCODAV production to St. Quentin. All that extra lead time required to go through customs and across Belgium means extra inventory—inventory that would not be required if FLOCODAV were being made at St. Quentin.

Finally, I think we should get out of that Reimport Agreement. I don't like the idea of disclosing recipes to the French government and I like even less the idea that French customs could step in after any six month period and either cut us off altogether or radically change the conditions of the contract. This might not seem very critical right now but, *après* de Gaulle, who knows?

In summary, I believe that the present situation is an unusual one that grew out of temporary expediency. The thing to do now is to put FLOCO-DAV production for the French market on a more rational basis. This will be the only way to get the real long term gains in efficiency and total cost reduction and it can only be done by bringing FLOCODAV production back into France.

The Dilemma at European Headquarters in Geneva

The final decision on the location of FLOCODAV production was to be made at European Headquarters in Geneva. Mr. Russo, Vice-President for European Operations and General Manager of the Geneva Office, was troubled, first of all, by the precedent-setting nature of this decision. In this regard he stated:

This will be the first time that Geneva has acted as an arbiter for two of the operating companies. Up to this time expansion has been so rapid that our major task has been to approve individual company requests for new facilities. Except for the German FLOCODAV situation, which seemed to have an obvious solution at the time, we haven't had to resolve any major intra-company squabbles. The action we take now can have far-reaching effects.

Mr. Russo's major problem was to balance conflicting company policies against each other and to arrive at some final decision. There was, for example, an explicit United Foods policy for maximizing profits to the company as a whole. This policy had often been used to resolve similar problems in the United States. However, it was also company policy, in international operations at least, to take profits at the local subsidiary and not to shift them, by resale agreements, to low tax areas. These two policies were obviously in direct conflict.

Mr. Russo was also concerned about the motivation of local managers and the company's relation with local governments. He felt that unless local management had real control over profit and loss, they would begin to direct their attention towards other more arbitrary goals, to the detriment of United Food Products Company as a whole. Furthermore, United

Foods now had a big stake in Europe and Mr. Russo was averse to damaging existing relations with any of the various Common Market governments. Naturally, Belgium and France both wanted to have FLOCODAV production on their own soil.

Finally, it was Mr. Russo's task to make his own analysis of the figures and to decide how they should be weighted. For example, the timing of tariff reduction and tax equalization in the EEC was critical. When, Mr. Russo wondered, will these events actually take place? Projected sales volume was also subject to error and it, too, could importantly affect the entire analysis.

Mr. Russo, in grappling with the problem, summed the situation up this way:

We have all the facts that we're going to get and we've heard both the arguments. What we need now is a decision. The St. Quentin plant is well under way and we can't waste any more time thinking. By the end of this week we'll have to decide whether to add a FLOCODAV facility or not.

University Book Store

32

The University Book Store was one of the operating units of the Campus stores providing exclusive textbook services to students and faculty of the Northern State University (NSU). The store was currently located about a quarter of a mile away from its main store, housed in the Campus Center. The main store sold only trade books and other supplies.

NSU had experienced a phenomenal growth. In 1973, its total enrollment was about 22,000 undergraduate and graduate students, nearly triple its size of ten years before. The rapid growth in enrollment and accompanying increase in course offerings resulted in a great increase in the number and variety of textbooks handled at the textbook department and placed a strain on the operations of the Campus Store. To alleviate the situation, the textbook operation was moved to a separate building known as the "Textbook Annex," containing 10,000 square feet of space for office, storage, and loading facilities (see floor plan, Exhibit 32–1).

The Book Store Problems

In spite of the many improvements in its physical facilities, the book store was plagued with the problem of having the right number of books

This case was prepared by Professors Gordon K. C. Chen and Sidney J. Claunch of the University of Massachusetts/ Amherst as a basis for class discussion rather than to illustrate either effective or ineffective handling of an administrative situation. Presented at the Case Workshop of Dartmouth College and Intercollegiate Case Clearing House, October 1974. All rights reserved to the authors.

Exhibit 32–1 Floor Plan

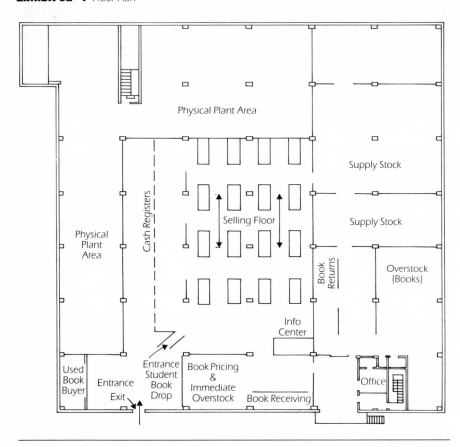

at the right time. Because the book store was the only official supplier of textbooks on campus, it was expected to have all the texts ready on time for classes each term. Failure to do so invariably drew severe complaints and criticisms from students, faculty members, and sometimes the university administration. A survey conducted by the university faculty senate service committee indicated that professors had experienced various text book problems for their courses. (See Exhibit 32–2.) Most of the complaints stemmed from the book store's failure to order a sufficient quantity of the books needed or from receiving the books too late in the term.

In an attempt to elicit students' views about book store services, an opinion poll was conducted by a student for a class project. Of the one hundred students who responded to his questionnaires, some 27 percent thought that books were generally understocked, 77 percent said they had trouble finding books in the store, partially (about 45 percent of the time)

Exhibit 32—2 Summary of Complaints

Professor	Dept.	Course	Book Title	Type of Problem	No. of Copies
Oswald	Botany	101-3C	?	Took weeks to get balance of books (1st term last year). Did not order 1 out of 3 required books.	430
Mann	Zoology	101	?	Textbook publishers sending books (promised) late.	?
Carlson	Botany	201	?	Last year when Ogden Book Store in neighboring town cooperated because campus book store would not.	?
Carlson	Botany	100	Scien. Amer. Offpr. recommended	Only 25 were ordered for each of 11 reprints; needed 100.	100
Carlson	Botany	311	?	Only 8 ordered	12
Bryant	Zoology	101	?	No information to	?
		135	?	instructor about no. of books, availability, etc. ½ class have no books for 1st 6–10 weeks.	?
George	Geology	121&231	?	No books for 1st week or two.	?
Hart	Psychol.	325	?	Underordered by 100 copies, not available until Oct.	100
Peters	Chem.	716	Basic Gas Chroma.	Bookstore added 20% markup, could be less if ordered independently. Ditto.	?
			"Liquid" Chem. Sep. Methods	Not received after 2 months of reassurance.	?
Roberts	Music	217/517	Piano Music Nine Songs Quiet City	Music Scores—suspect of underordering policy of bookstore.	?
Michael	French	162	Conversation	18 students without books	18
		123	Langue et Langue	200 extra copies ordered,	200
		171	Fr. Poetry & Novel	Too small quantities ordered, so late books, order for 32, but only 25 ordered by b.s.	? / 32
Lock	Theatre	385A	Richard III and the Princess In The To.	Ordered 75 copies for 75 students (68 actually in crs) ordered short from England, not enough.	75

Exhibit 32—2 (Continued)

Professor	Dept.	Course	Book Title	Type of Problem	No. of Copies
German	History	390D	They Gath. at Riv.	No news of shipment until Nov. (Out of stock)	?
Williams	P&S Sci.	s-1	Intro. pl. scien. Dev. Struc. Plan.	Not enough books ordered by book store.	?
Zenon	Italian	340	Teatro	Told order was O.K., but book was out of print.	?
Hogan	Rhetoric	100B	The Oedipus Cycle	Insufficient copies received until too late.	?
Allan	Physics	190C	?	1 of 2 texts not available from publisher, not 'til too late.	?
Joseph	Biology	262/565	Wildlife Mgt. Tech.	Delay of Bus. Office in processing pre-payment orders.	?
Vernon	English	125	Divine Comedy	Random House late in notifying book store (out of stock).	?
Johnson	Acctg.	370&371	Intro. to Taxation	Continually lowering ordered amount, after reassurance.	?

because they were sold out, 17 percent said books were not easy to find, 22 percent felt that the book store was too far away, 18 percent experienced slow check-out lines and services, 20 percent were not satisfied with the used book policy, and 77 percent thought the books were too expensive. When asked what they liked about the book store, 24 percent liked the fact that all books were under one roof, 17 percent liked the convenience of its being on campus, 15 percent felt the books were easy to find, 3 percent found that the check-out lines and the used book policy were quite satisfactory.

The book store purchased used books from students at about 50 percent and resold them at about 75 percent of the list price.

In response to the criticism and complaints, the book store manager conceded that although he had tried to execute all book orders as accurately and expeditiously as possible, it was not always possible to get all needed books in on time and in the right quantity because of such problems as publisher's delay, stock outs, out of prints, and human errors. Furthermore, the book manager claimed that it is virtually impossible to predict in advance the exact number of copies that would be sold. This was attributable to several causes. First, the quantities requested by the instructors were generally rough estimates and sometimes grossly inaccurate and exaggerated. He cited one case in which he bought 2,000 copies of a computer science book ordered by an instructor but sold only 50 copies, because the instructor left soon after the order. The book store ended up with over 1,900 surplus books which were neither returnable because they were printed to special order, nor resalable to other dealers, because the text had become obsolete as a result of fast changing computer technology.

Another reason the demand for textbooks was highly unpredictable was that students did not always buy books for their courses. The number of students who actually acquired books depended upon whether the book was required or recommended, upon the extent to which the instructor made specific assignments or tests on the materials therein, and upon the price of the book. For those courses which required infrequent readings, students often shared books with others. Many students also tried to get used books if the text had been used before. There were several student-operated used-book exchanges on campus. The book store also had a separate department selling used books repurchased from students and from outside sources.

Forecasts for demand were further complicated by the fact that preliminary estimates based on preregistration figures or given by instructors were often distorted by the numerous students' change of mind at registration time: adding, dropping, and changes of courses. In addition, shortages occurred when students from neighboring small colleges shopped for their books at the University book store to take advantage of its policy of allowing a five percent discount for all text books to all students. There were some ten private and community colleges in the surrounding area, with a total enrollment of over 10,000 students. The book store manager had no idea how many of them shopped at the University Book Store.

The inability to estimate demand accurately would not have been much of a problem if it had been possible for the book store to return all of its unsold books to the publisher, as it did some years ago and still did to some publishers. The store could always order more than enough to cover the maximum possible demand and return the left-overs. However, according to current policies, only 15 percent of the publishers allowed unlimited returns on textbooks and about 75 percent allowed only limited returns, usually up to 20 percent of purchases. All returns were subject to a certain time limit, say within a year of purchase. Nearly 10 percent allowed no returns at all. These included imported books, government documents, and journal article reprints, etc.

The book store manager contended that while he strived to meet the demands of students and faculty, he was also concerned with over-stocking and excess inventory, which can be very costly. For example, it was estimated that at the end of the fall term in 1973, approximately $35,000 worth of textbooks valued at retail prices were unreturnable. In addition to the above mentioned overstocks, approximately $20,000 worth of inventory was tied up in the various manuals, monographs and books published by the University Press for different courses. These include such manuals as Computer Science, Introductory History, Chemistry, Education, etc. which were overruns and had become obsolete with the introduction of new manuals. These overstocks were included in the store's total inventory, valued at nearly $500,000.

To illustrate the overstocking problem, the book store cited some examples of the excess inventory resulting from the wide differences between the order quantities requested by instructors and the actual number of copies sold. For instance, from the physical inventory taken on October 30, 1973, of the 47 titles purchased from Wadsworth Publishing Company, Belmont, California, the following unsold quantities far exceeded the 20 percent returns allowed by the publisher:

Title	Quantity Ordered	Quantity Unsold
Beliefs Attitudes & Human Affairs	145	97
The Black Family	57	29
The Plant Kingdom	24	12
Great Awakening at Yale	25	19
Cognitive Psychology	80	62
Logic & Rhetoric	185	78
Of Children	500	300
The Plant Cell	60	50
Plants & Civilization	290	180
Poverty American Style	22	18
Reason and Responsibility	70	57
Roles Women Play	25	20
Self-Directed Behavior	64	35
Television Production	25	10

The overstocks that could neither be returned nor salvaged were a direct loss to the book store. Although the University Book Store was a non-profit business supported by student activity fees, any loss incurred in its operations necessitated an increase of such fees and aroused student complaints. It was therefore incumbent upon the store management to remain solvent and self-supporting. During the second half of 1973 the book store yielded a net income of over $80,000 on total textbook sales of $870,000, and contributed more than 51 percent of the net income produced by the total University Store operations. The manager said he would be better satisfied if both the number of complaints and the amount of overstocks could be reduced.

The Textbook Operations

As indicated earlier, the book store (annex) was one of the three major operating units of the University Store headed by the store manager, Mr. Wells, who reported to the Director of Campus Center, Mr. Corcoran. The Campus Center was a student oriented facility supported in part by student fees and controlled by a board of governors composed of students, faculty, and administration. Although it was an autonomous body, the Vice President of Student Affairs of the University had a voice in the choice of its directors and policy matters.

The text book operations were headed by the book store manager, Mr. Peters, and his assistant manager, Mr. Lewis. There were eight full-time employees, including the two managers, and three part-time helpers handling the normal work loads throughout the year. During the peak periods at the beginning of each term, some twenty additional temporary helpers were usually needed to man the check-out cash registers and to take care of the "text book rush." Mr. Peters had been promoted to his present position about two years ago. Prior to this, he was the assistant to the previous store manager, Mr. Wells, who had since been promoted to the position of University Store Manager. (The relationship between the book store staff and the Campus Center office is shown in the partial organization chart, Exhibit 32–3 below.)

Exhibit 32–3 Relation of Book Store to Campus Center

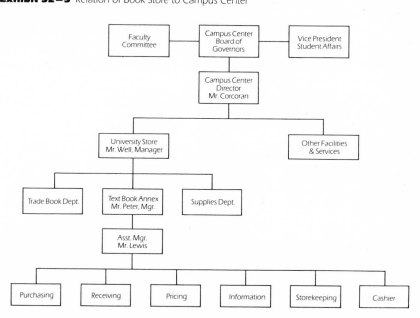

The Text Book Ordering Process

The book store processed nearly 1,700 book orders from professors each semester, involving some 5,000 different titles and as many as 100,000 copies of books. The work load for handling these orders and books was spread very unevenly throughout the years forming a pattern of extreme peaks and valleys at least twice a year with the lead time between the placing of an order and the receipt of the shipment as long as four months.

The book store had been processing these orders manually, following a system developed and revised over the years by different managers. During the past four years, the book store had three different managers and each had some different ideas about how best to handle the book orders.

The process began about six weeks before the end of each semester when each instructor was sent a set of yellow textbook order cards (Exhibit 32–4), usually accompanied by a memorandum from the manager (Exhibit 32–5). The instructors were requested to complete and return the order cards within about three weeks. Experience had shown that only about 60 percent of all book orders were received by the book store on or before its requested deadline. Approximately 15 percent were received within the last month before classes began and 10 percent after classes began. The rest of the orders arrived between the deadline and the last month before classes. The book store personnel complained that not only were a large number of orders not received on time but also that many of those received contained incomplete information (missing publisher's name, course number, or professor's signature, etc.), thus causing delays. The book store claimed it required about 11 to 12 weeks lead time

---

Exhibit 32–4 (Yellow) Textbook Order Card

Dept. & Course No.			Professor	
Book(s) ordered below are to be used during			semester.	Date
Estimated Enrollment	Quantity Desired	Author Title (Edition. hardcover, paper, etc.) (recommended/required)		Published

Faculty Signature _____ Book Dept. use only Carded _____ Checked _____

Exhibit 32—5 Memo to Faculty

To: All Department Heads and Faculty Members
Subject: Spring Semester Book Orders
Date: October 21, 1971

It is requested that spring semester book orders be submitted to this office no later than November 12, 1971. Any orders received after this date may experience the following difficulties:
1. This is a peak season for trucking concerns and mail; HOLIDAY SHIPPING WILL INCREASE DELIVERY TIME BY AT LEAST TWO WEEKS.
2. Publishers will be at a peak period; orders will be processed slower and confusion often reigns in their shipping departments.
3. Other schools could deplete a publisher's inventory and faculty would be faced with an "out of stock" situation.
4. If a book is received from the publisher that is the wrong title, edition, quantity or cover, the mistake could not be corrected in time for the beginning of classes.

Departmental secretaries have the textbook order cards. Please read the instructions and fill them out completely; include department, course number, using faculty member, author, title, publisher, volume or edition, estimated enrollment and the appropriate signature. INCOMPLETE ORDER FORMS WILL BE RETURNED TO THE RESPECTIVE DEPARTMENTS. No book will be placed on sale without a current order. Even if you know we have a particular book in stock and you have used it every semester for the past five years, it will not be on sale unless it has been ordered. Your secretaries also have desk copy order forms.

We realize that enrollments are often nothing more than an educated guess, especially at this early date. If it is later discovered that enrollments are larger than anticipated, let us know as soon as possible. IN ANY CASE, PLEASE DO NOT HOLD ORDERS BECAUSE ENROLLMENT FIGURES ARE UNCERTAIN.

You may be wondering why we need so much time to order books. The following is a schedule of how long it takes to receive a book once we get an order:
1. From publisher or importer whose warehouses are in the North East   3–4 weeks
   "   "   "   "   Mid-Atlantic   4–5 weeks
   "   "   "   "   South   5–6 weeks
   "   "   "   "   Mid-West   4–5 weeks
   "   "   "   "   West Coast   6–8 weeks
2. Foreign books that must be imported or books from a foreign country   12–18 weeks
3. Anything from Superintendent of Documents—Washington, D.C.   16–20 weeks

These times are an average and are under ideal shipping conditions. Any problem with an order will delay shipping times considerably and this factor is always considered when we establish a deadline date. Another important factor is that we need time to compile a booklist so that we may be able to purchase used books and schedule our used book buying trips. Used books offer a substantial saving to the student and is an area in which we must make a concerted effort to help our students.

May we express our thanks for your co-operation in the past and if myself or my staff can be of any assistance, please do not hesitate to call us at 545-2619.
                    Sincerely yours,

                    B. F. Wells, Manager

between the time it received the order card and the time the book was ready for sale.

Upon receipt of the yellow order card, the book store clerk transferred the information to a Master Title card (Exhibit 32–6). The card served as a permanent record for inventory as well as a guide for determining order quantity. All transactions pertaining to ordering, receiving, and inventory were recorded manually. There were about 5,000 active plus a couple thousand inactive cards in the file, arranged by publisher's names in alphabetic order.

After the information on the yellow order cards was transferred to the green Master Title Cards, the book manager checked those books that had been used previously to see if any were in stock. If so, he subtracted the amount from the quantity requested by instructors and sent an inquiry to the used book dealers via "Telex" (a direct teletype network system) inviting bids and quotations for the balance of the needed books. There were several major used book dealers from whom the book store bought a large quantity of used books and to whom it also sold surplus books. If necessary, it would also deal with some smaller dealers across the country. The responses from the dealers were very fast, usually within 24 hours.

While the information about the used books was being gathered, the book manager proceeded with the preliminary process of ordering directly from publishers those new books which had no available used copies he should order for a particular title. He used no single formula but applied a number of rules of thumb to arrive at an ordering quantity. For example, he would take into consideration such factors as whether the book was required or recommended, whether it had been used in any courses before or was a new adoption, whether or not it had a used book market for resale, the publisher's return policies, and the previous history or record of sales, if any. He began with the quantity requested by the instructor and subtracted a certain percentage if it was only recommended. His experience indicated that no more than 50 percent of the students would purchase the text if it was not required. He would subtract a certain percentage if the text had been used the previous term and a larger percentage if used in the two or three previous years. Also, he was more cautious in ordering more than the absolute minimum necessary if the publisher allowed no returns. And if the record showed poor sales relative to the amount purchased, it was likely that the order quantity would be further reduced.

The process of assigning order quantity was one of the most time-consuming tasks faced by the book manager. He usually reviewed personally the entire 4,000 titles that require ordering each term and assigned order quantities individually, one by one. The whole process could take him as long as four or five weeks to complete.

The final order decided by the manager represented, in a large measure,

Exhibit 32—6 Master Title Card

									Textbook Annex	
AUTHOR				TITLE				PUBLISHER		
SEM.	INV.	PROFESSOR	DEPT. & COURSE NO.	ENROLL	ORDERED		RECEIVED			
					Qty	Date	Qty	Date	Price	
					P.O. #		Inv. #		Inv. Date	
					Qty	Date	Qty	Date	Price	
					P.O. #		Inv. #		Inv. Date	
					Qty	Date	Qty	Date	Price	
					P.O. #		Inv. #		Inv. Date	
					Qty	Date	Qty	Date	Price	
					P.O. #		Inv. #		Inv. Date	
					Qty	Date	Qty	Date	Price	
					P.O. #		Inv. #		Inv. Date	
					Qty	Date	Qty	Date	Price	
					P.O. #		Inv. #		Inv. Date	
					Qty	Date	Qty	Date	Price	
					P.O. #		Inv. #		Inv. Date	
					Qty	Date	Qty	Date	Price	
					P.O. #		Inv. #		Inv. Date	
					Qty	Date	Qty	Date	Price	
					P.O. #		Inv. #		Inv. Date	
					Qty	Date	Qty	Date	Price	
					P.O. #		Inv. #		Inv. Date	
					Qty	Date	Qty	Date	Price	
					P.O. #		Inv. #		Inv. Date	
					Qty	Date	Qty	Date	Price	
					P.O. #		Inv. #		Inv. Date	

his personal estimates of what the actual demand was likely to be, based primarily upon his own perception, judgment, experience, and intuition. Not only was he constrained by the uncertainties of the various factors mentioned earlier, but he was also handicapped by the lack of preliminary enrollment figures from pre-registration. Although the book store usually wanted to have instructors' book orders turned in about six weeks before the end of the term, the students' pre-registration for courses did not customarily take place until four or five weeks before the term ended. If pre-registration could have taken place a week or two earlier or the book store could wait until after pre-registration to ask instructors for orders, the preliminary enrollment could have been used in estimating quantities. According to a study conducted by some industrial engineering students, the actual enrollments correlated closely with the pre-registration figures, at least for the engineering courses in the sample.

Once the manager had decided on the order quantities, he marked them on the green cards. A purchase order was then typed by the clerks and mailed to the publisher or book dealer. The delivery of books took anywhere from 3 to 4 weeks to 16 to 20 weeks, depending upon sources of supply and distance (see Exhibit 32–5). Suppliers with warehouses nearby took the shortest time, while foreign suppliers and government printing offices took the longest. Many things could happen even after the purchase orders had reached the publisher or supplier. The books might have been out of stock, out of print, not yet in print, or have been published in a new edition, etc. In such cases the publishers often notified the book store, but after a long delay. By the time the book store received new instructions from the instructor, the books often arrived too late for classes in spite of expediting the orders through Telex, telephone, or special handling. The book store used these means for placing last minute rush orders or reorders also.

If everything went well, the shipments usually started arriving by truck before classes began. The book store desired to receive the last shipment no later than two weeks before the first day of classes because it took two weeks for unpacking, pricing, record keeping, shelving each incoming shipment. The book store customarily notified instructors about the arrival and the availability of books. It placed the text books on sale a few days before the start of classes to enable early-arriving students to obtain books in advance of the usual textbook rush in the first week.

The "Text Book Rush"

The "text book rush" occurred twice a year with a minor one during the summer session. During the first week of each semester, the store had to handle over 22,000 customers who made a total purchase of some 100,000 books and paid more than $800,000 for them. With such a massive onslaught of humanity during the first few days of each semester, it was little wonder that confusion and frustration often reigned. Numerous complaints and questions were raised and had to be answered. To alleviate the situation, the book store set up an "information center" for this purpose. Statistics showed that in the fall term of 1973, there were 1900 requests and questions for information per day during the first week. The number fell to around 700 a day in the second week and to about 400 a day in the third week. The types of questions and complaints most frequently raised are summarized below in descending order of frequency:

1. Where is the book located? None on shelf.
2. Where is the course located?
3. Is the book used elsewhere?
4. Are there any course books out back?
5. What are the store hours?
6. Is the book that was used last semester still on hand this semester?
7. Has the reorder for book come in yet? When is the reorder due?
8. What are the used book buyer's hours?
9. How many books were ordered?
10. Can individual copies be ordered from publisher?

As indicated in the list above and in the student survey mentioned earlier, the most frequent and persistent question asked at the store had been "where is the book located?" Either the shelf was not properly marked, was not located conveniently, or the books were not properly shelved. The books were shelved by major fields, such as political science, sociology, marketing, etc., in alphabetic order. A title card indicating the field was hung above the shelf from the ceiling. Although the store had about 10,000 square feet of space, a large proportion was used for storage, administrative, and handling areas. The shelves occupied a little over half of the total space and appeared inadequate during the peak-selling periods. Books were stacked on the floor around the shelves and contributed to congestion and confusion when large crowds were milling among the shelves. There were about ten check-out cash registers occupying a space for check-out activities.

As the text book rush got into full swing, some casualty losses took place. For instance, in spite of various security measures taken by the store, loss of books through theft and shoplifting occurred. The unofficial estimates were that the losses were as high as one percent of gross sales. To make certain that the students did not mix their own books with the purchased books, the store installed a series of lockers near the entrance in which they could deposit their own books while shopping. They were allowed to carry out only the books they purchased. Prior to the installation of the lockers, students complained of their personal books and articles being stolen while they were left unsecured at the entrance. However, since the students used the same door for entrance and exit, it was possible for shoplifters to steal a book and leave the premises through the entrance without checking out at the cashiers.

The store employed about 20 part-time temporary cashiers. Cash shortages were experienced occasionally. In one six month period, approximately $400 was lost. The Faculty Senate Service Committee and the University administration agreed that something had to be done to improve the book store services.

University Physical Plant

33

In August, 1977, Mr. Ted Quigley, Comptroller of the University Physical Plant (UPP), was discussing the systems and procedures currently in operation at his plant for controlling work, inventory, and costs. While satisfied with the relative smoothness of the operations, Mr. Quigley was still interested in finding ways for further improvement.

Organization

The UPP was the central support and supply unit of a large state university with a total enrollment of some 23,000 students in 1977. The campus was situated on a rural setting 90 miles from a major metropolitan center. The UPP was charged with the responsibility of providing maintenance, repair, engineering, utility and custodial services and supplies to all buildings and grounds on campus, ranging from janitorial or snow removal services to building repairs and renovations. Exhibit 33–1 shows a summary of trouble calls received at its Work Control Center during the night for the month of September, 1976. There were 365 building structures, 8,900,000 square feet of floor space, 18 miles of roadways, 23 miles of

This case is prepared by Professors Gordon Chen and Robert McGarrah of the University of Massachusetts, Amherst, as a basis for class discussion rather than to illustrate either effective or ineffective handling of an administrative situation. Copyright © 1977 by Gordon Chen and Robert McGarrah. Presented at the Case Workshop held at the Temple University, Philadelphia, Nov. 1977 and distributed by Intercollegiate Case Clearing House, Soldiers Field, Boston, MA 02163. All rights reserved to the contributors. Printed in the U.S.A.

Exhibit 33—1 Work Control Center Trouble Calls for Month of September, 1976

WORK CENTER TROUBLE DESK

The following is a breakdown of trouble calls received by the Work Desk.
(Monday through Friday 4:00 PM—8:00 AM)
(Saturdays, Sundays and Holidays 8:00 AM—8:00 AM)

661	Calls were received. Out of the 661 calls:
29	dorm maintenance calls required overtime.
6	calls required others to be called in for overtime.
49	elevator calls requiring overtime.
33	dorm elevator calls requiring overtime.
16	"other" elevator calls requiring overtime.
435	calls were taken care of by shift workers.
82	calls were temporarily resolved by shift workers, but required parent shop completion follow-up during regular working hours.
60	calls did not require immediate attention and were deferred to regular day time shop performance.
56	dorm maintenance calls cited as student damage.
3	"other" maintenance calls cited as student damage.

The following is a breakdown by days of the week:

84	occurred on Sunday
87	occurred on Monday
91	occurred on Tuesday
115	occurred on Wednesday
93	occurred on Thursday
90	occurred on Friday
101	occurred on Saturday

A further breakdown on types of services:

17	due to heat control—heating and ventilation.
1	due to refrigeration.
0	due to air conditioning.
7	pumps and compressors.
100	due to electrical trouble.
84	elevators.
188	due to locks, windows, or doors.
147	due to water closet.
8	steam pipe leaks.
13	due to water piping.
2	due to water leaking through ceilings from other causes than plumbing, such as showers and bath tubs running over or leaking roof.
50	due to waste line stoppages in buildings.
0	due to sewers backing up from outside of building or ground water entering building.
44	other.

Exhibit 33—1 (continued)

A further breakdown on time occurrences:

86	occurred between MDT & 8:00 AM Mon.–Fri.
372	occurred between 4:00 PM & 12 MDT Mon.–Fri.
20	occurred between MDT & 8:00 AM Sat.
44	occurred between 8:00 AM & 4:00 PM Sat.
37	occurred between 4:00 PM & 12:00 MDT Sat.
14	occurred between MDT & 8:00 AM Sun.
35	occurred between 8:00 AM & 4:00 PM Sun.
35	occurred between 4:00 PM & 12 MDT Sun.
2	occurred between MDT & 8:00 AM Holidays.
8	occurred between 8:00 AM & 4:00 PM Holidays.
8	occurred between 4:00 PM & 12 MDT Holidays.

A further breakdown by sections:

144	Academic Buildings	9	Food Services
52	Male Dorms	22	College Stores
40	Female Dorms	5	Utilities
304	Coed Dorms	0	Farm
37	Married Student Apartments	48	Other

Date of Issue: October 1, 1976

James R. Knightly, Work Control Section

sidewalks, 90 acres of parking lots, 450 acres of lawn and 250 motor vehicles maintained by the UPP.

In the Spring of 1977, the UPP had on its payroll 785 employees, of which 300 were assigned to custodial and 375 to maintenance work, the rest were on administrative, engineering, and heating plant staff. The numbers of employees represented less than eighty percent of its authorized total work force of nearly a thousand due to the recent drastic cut of state budgets. The full work force, which was considered necessary to maintain adequate and prompt services as determined by work measurements, was seldom achieved, however, even before the cutback. The total employment on the campus numbered about 3,700, including faculty and staff.

The UPP was divided into four major divisions reporting to its director, Mr. Gordon Nelson. These were the divisions of Administration, Utility, Design and Construction, and Maintenance. By far the largest was the Maintenance Division, which had 675 employees. While the Maintenance Division was responsible for all the work, the bulk of paper work and record keeping was handled of the Comptroller's office in the Admin-

Exhibit 33—2 Partial Organization Chart

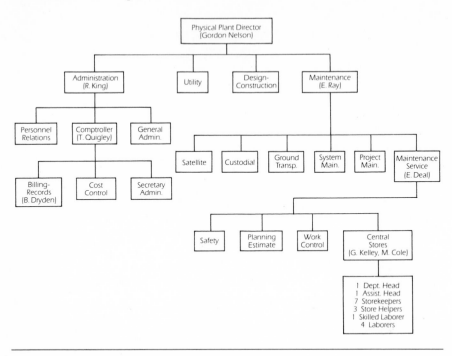

istrative Division. A partial organization chart and its administrative structure is shown in Exhibit 33–2.

The Work Control System

According to its report issued in 1976, the UPP executed nearly 50,000 Routine Maintenance Orders (RMO) annually. In addition an average of 2,100 labor hours of work a week was done on non-routine projects. The system by which these work orders were processed and controlled is described in the report, a portion of which is reproduced in Exhibit 33–3.

While the procedures for RMO flows were well documented in the report, only general guidelines were provided for its priority system. The actual assigning of priority to a given RMO is primarily a matter of judgment and discretion on the part of the Work Controller and the shop foremen. The Work Controller not only assigned the priority status of a job, he also set a deadline by which the job had to be completed. By arranging the work orders by the expected completion dates, each shop foreman was able to prepare an informal schedule that he regarded as best to complete the jobs by his crew.

Exhibit 33—3 Work Order Procedures

Physical Plant's Work Order System Consists of Two Viable Work Paths
    1. RMO's (Routine Maintenance Orders)
              &
    2. PROJECTS

RMO Means: ROUTINE MAINTENANCE ORDER
         and
. . . it requests that Physical Plant repair or replace an existing part or component which is broken or otherwise defective.

Routine Maintenance Order

Form No. PP-79
Work Order No. _____
Cost Account No: _____

Building: _____
Location: _____
Requestor: _____
Priority: _____ Attnt: ☐

Date: _____ Time: _____
Issued By: _____
Complete Before: _____
Date Completed: _____

Labor _____
Material _____
Equipment _____
Cont. _____
      Total: _____

JOB DESCRIPTION

A	Prev. Maint.		R	Refrig. Shop	
B	Plumb/Sh. Mtl		O	Elevator	
C	Carp/Roof		P	Pump Repair	
D	Mason		Q		
E	Painter		R	Other	
F	Electrician		S	Typewriter	
G	Communicat.		T	Locksmith	
H	Mtr. Gen. Rep.		U	Pneumatics	
I	Custodial		V		
J	Grounds		W	Upholstery	
K	Weld Shop		X	Rugs	
L	Motor Pool		Y	Auto. Contrl	
M	Machine Shop				

Person Notified: _____ Time: _____
Materials Used & Description of Work:

Service Man: _____ Total Hours: _____

RMO PATH

1. Requestor communicates by telephone or in person to the Work Desk in Physical Plant, his complaint or problem. (During normal working hours, requests from dormitories are transmitted directly to the satellite Physical Plant operation in the dormitories.)
2. The Work Desk issues a Routine Maintenance Order (below) citing location of problem and specifics. There are three copies made of the RMO . . . green, yellow and pink.
3. The Work Desk retains the yellow copy for cost accounting purposes and transmits the green and pink copies to the appropriate trade foreman. The foreman places the pink in his "tickler" file and gives the green to a tradesman for execution of the assignment.
4. After the tradesman completes the assignment, he indicates completion on the green copy and returns it to his foreman. The latter matches the returned green to his filed pink tickler. The foreman files the pink in his "completed" file and sends the green back to the Work Desk.
5. The Work Desk mates the returned green to their yellow; sends the green to Cost Accounting and discards the yellow.

NOTE: Where the assigned work is in the dormitories, the yellow is returned to the requestor, indicating job completion. (Logistics preclude this policy for non-dormitory work.)

PATH OF A WORK REQUEST

1. The Work Request is prepared by the requestor in the using department or agency. Four copies are prepared . . . white, yellow, pink and blue.
2. The requestor's department head approves the request before it is sent to Physical Plant.
3. The requestor retains the blue copy for his file. Physical Plant's Work Control Center receives the others.
4. Physical Plant logs in the request; assigns a work Order Number for identification and date stamps it.
5. A "Work Request Acknowledgment/Status Report," plus the yellow copy is sent back to the requestor . . . notifying him of receipt of the request by Plant.
6. Two copies are now in Physical Plant . . . the white and the pink.
7. The pink and the white copies are sent to the Chief Estimator in Planning and Estimating . . . who determines if . . .
   a. the job can be estimated by the estimators or if . . .
   b. the job needs the attention of Engineers with a subsequent design estimate.
8. When the estimate is prepared, the pink copy is retained by the P & E; the white copy is sent back to the appropriate funding authority for the requestor's department. The white copy has the dollar estimate. Another Acknowledgment/Status Report is sent to the requestor notifying him of this action.
9. When Physical Plant receives funding approval from the appropriate funding authority, Physical Plant again notifies the requestor of the action; informs him that Physical Plant will start preparing the job. The requestor is also informed who the Project Manager will be for the project.
10. The Work Request is now developed into a project . . . engineering/design/specifications . . . man-hour estimates and work sequencing are all cranked into the package.
11. The Project is forwarded to Scheduling for posting. Involved trade shops are given copies for review. Central Stores is notified so that they can start ordering material.
12. When the required material is received by Central Stores, the job is placed on the "Awaiting Scheduling Board," in a position dependent upon the priority attached to the project.
13. As soon as the project is scheduled, the requestor is again notified of the action.
14. When the project is completed, it is held "Open." The requestor is notified by the project's Project Manager. Both the requestor and the Project Manager inspect and review the job.
15. If the job meets the satisfaction of the requestor and the Project Manager, the job is "Closed Out."

PHYSICAL PLANT HAS AN RMO PRIORITY SYSTEM

GROUP I . . . Immediate to 2 or 5 days
The RMO is placed in Group I if there's a possibility of loss or damage to State property . . .
If it requires the restoration of disrupted essential service . . .
If it will eliminate or prevent potential health/safety situations . . .

Work Request	Send or deliver to: WORK CONTROL CENTER Physical Plant Department, Campus Center Way	For Physical Plant Use Work Order Number

Instructions—Insert carbon paper.
Use separate Work Request form for each job. Complete all items in Box 1 in quadruplicate—carbon copies required. Retain blue copy and send all others to above address. Provide complete information including sketches and attachments as necessary to expedite work. Complete all items in Box 4 after receipt of estimate.

1

Attachments: ☐ Yes ☐ No

Requestor's Name   Department   Telephone

Requestor's Mailing Address   Building and Room(s) Requiring Work

Describe Work:

Authorized Approval Signature   Date

2 For Physical Plant Use
Work to Be Done By: Project Estimate:

Contract ☐   Labor $ _____   Estimator   Date

University Labor ☐   Material $ _____   Estimate Approval   Date
Equipment $ _____

Total $ _____   Project Manager   Date

3 Total Amount to Be Funded by Approving Authority: $ _____

4

Specific Account Number   Funding   Authorization Signature*   Date

*Note: No work shall be undertaken without a proper authorized signature and in an adequately funded account.

5 Status Notification Dates:

1 _____ 2 _____ 3 _____ 4 _____ 5 _____ 6 _____

Comments:

Shop Copy

Exhibit 33—3 (continued)

GROUP II . . . 5 to 10 days

The RMO is placed in Group II if execution will preclude class interruptions or conferences . . . to meet activity or target deadlines . . . prevent breakdown of services, equipment or property . . . or to avert extreme inconvenience to personnel . . .

GROUP III . . . 10 to 15 days

The RMO is placed in Group III if there is not applicable circumstance for placing it in the other two groups . . . if it involves work that can be performed within established time limits and with the best utilization of manpower.

NOTE: Emergencies are reacted to immediately—day or night, every day. If permanent repairs can't be made on first-call, safe, temporary repairs are made.

Here are some RMO statistics . . .

1. MAIN Physical Plant personnel respond to about 37,000 RMO's/year. Of these, approximately 10,000 are for residence halls.
2. MAIN Physical Plant personnel respond to 7500 After-Hour-Emergency RMO's/year. (Included in the 37,000 above.)
3. About 5000 of these After-Hour-Emergencies are in the dormitories.
4. Dormitory Area Physical Plant personnel respond to an additional 12,000 RMO's/year, in behalf of dorms.

The arithmetic looks like this for RMO's . . .

10,000 + 12,000 = 22,000 RMO's / year / dormitories

37,000 + 12,000 = 49,000 RMO's / year / all-campus

WHAT'S A WORK REQUEST?

Normally, a Work Request is a request for a CHANGE or an IMPROVEMENT to an EXISTING facility OR for NEW CONSTRUCTION.

(A Work Request may also include LARGE-SCOPE MAINTENANCE.)

A Work Request differs from a RMO because it isn't "Routine."

NOTE: Physical Plant maintains on-going written and oral liaison with the Project requestor through each important phase of development, to conclusion.

PROJECT MANPOWER

How much do we have? Where do we use it?

Physical Plant has approximately 2100 hours/week for assignable project work. On the average . . .

Dorm projects consume 41% or 861 hours/week

Provost projects consume 27% or 567 hours/week

Maintenance projects consume 27% or 567 hours/week

Campus Center projects consume 2% or 42 hours/week

Dining Commons projects consume 2% or 42 hours/week

Infirmary projects consume 1% or 21 hours/week

100% = 2100 hours/week

Physical Plant receives about 339 Project Requests/year—or 28.3/month

Physical Plant completes 286 Projects/year—or 23.8/month

Number of projects on scheduling board for one year, average 250

Average time to complete project from date posted to actual completion is 6 months.*

*This time is attributable to lengthy waiting time for parts and material plus large scope of some projects such as complete dormitory renovations.

Exhibit 33—4 Routine Maintenance Order. Group Priority Change Report

From: _____ Shop

To: WORK CONTROL CENTER

It is requested that Work Order Number _____ be

changed from priority _____ to priority _____.

Reason for change is: _____

_____

_____

_____

_____

_____

_____

_____

_____

_____

_____

_____

_____

_____

_____

_____

_____

_____

Date Issued _____ Signature _____
                                       Supervisor or Shop Foreman

The determination of priority status was by no means rigid. In certain instances, an RMO appeared urgent and was given the highest priority but later was found less so, or the problem was solved by a temporary measure, and thus was no longer considered as a top priority item. In this case the shop foreman had to file a Group Priority Change Report (Exhibit 33–4) to that effect. With hundreds of work orders a week flowing through the Work Control Center and various shops, and as a result of numerous priority changes, rearrangements of job assignments and schedules often

Exhibit 33—5 Request for Material Information

From: Work Control

To: Central Stores

Date: _____

The following RMO's are being held in the _____ Shop
and can not be completed due to awaiting materials. Please indicate date materials can be
expected, so that same can be entered on RMO copy for up to date status.

W/O#	Building	Job	Issued Shop On	Group Prior	Delivery Expected

Exhibit 33—6 Routine Maintenance Order. Performance Delay Report

From: _____ Shop

To: WORK CONTROL CENTER

      Work Order Number _____ under Group

priority _____ will be delayed for performance within the

group priority time limitation for the following reasons: _____

_____

_____

_____

_____

_____

_____

_____

_____

_____

_____

_____

_____

_____

_____

_____

_____

_____

_____

Approximate date above mentioned job can be performed _____

Date Issued _____ Signature _____

                                         Supervisor or Shop Foreman

were necessary. In addition, jobs also were held up due to other reasons. For example, in frequent occasions a job was behind schedule due to material or tool shortages. To monitor such delays and deviations, the Work Control Center addressed periodic inquiries (Exhibits 33–5, 33–6, and 3–7) to the parties concerned to elicit reasons for the delay. Because of the large turnovers of RMO's, no detailed statistics were compiled for the job

Exhibit 33—7 Routine Maintenance Order. Purification Form

From: Work Control

To: _____ Shop

Date: _____

Our records show that the RMO's listed below have been forwarded to your shop for performance and now exceed the group priority time limit. Please complete and return forms PP 74 or PP 100, whichever applies to job status, together with this form to Work Control by the end of the second full working day from date this form is issued.

W/O#	BUILDING	JOB	DATE ISSUED	GROUP PRIOR.	REMARKS

delays. However, the Work Control Center was fully aware and informed of the job status at all times by simply referring to the copies of work orders that were still pending on the control board orders. Based on a rough estimate, the backlogs during the school year ranged from a couple of weeks in the mason shop to one year in the painting shop.

While the status of RMO's was reviewed informally, the control of non-routine projects had received close attention at the Work Control Center. This was due to the relatively longer duration and higher costs of the projects. Exhibit 33–8 is a sample of a monthly status report for project backlogs.

To monitor the status and progress of jobs and to assign the job costs, the UPP relied on three work control reports prepared by computers. One report known as the Work Control Section Job Status Report (Exhibit 33–9) was prepared weekly listing labor and material inputs and costs for the period and accumulated totals to date by job numbers. This report was designed to keep track of all jobs regardless of whether or not any work had been performed on the job.

Once a month, a Monthly Job Report—By Account (Exhibit 33–10) and a Status of Job Cost Accounts (Exhibit 33–11) were supplied by computer summarizing total job activities and their costs. These reports included not only data on RMO jobs but also those of routine activities performed regularly by UPP employees, including such services as custodial or ground maintenance for which standing work orders instead of separate RMO's were issued only once in a given period.

The reports were prepared by the University Central Computer Center. Input data were provided by the UPP in the form of punched cards. The normal routine was that when a RMO was issued for a particular job, a card was punched based on the information from a copy of the RMO. Additional cards were punched as soon as the data on labor and material inputs used on the job were reported back to the Work Control Section. With these input cards, the computer center registered, updated, and produced reports as shown in Exhibits 33–9, 33–10, and 33–11.

According to Ms. Bea Dryden, Assistant to the Comptroller for billings and records, the system had worked quite well so far. The only complaint she had was when the reports were not ready on time because the delay would create a backlog for her billing process which was based on the cost figures from the reports. Although this did not occur too frequently, it had set back her billing routine for as long as a month when it did. Ms. Dryden believed that the delay was caused primarily by human errors such as loading the wrong computer tape during processing.

Stock Control System

Most of the maintenance, repair, or construction jobs required the use of materials, supplies, or equipment. The UPP maintained a large Central

Exhibit 33-8 Physical Plant Department Work Control Section Project Backlog Status Report Month Ending June 30, 1977 P. & E. SECTION

MONTH ENDING June 30 77
P. & E. SECTION

	6-2	6-9	6-16	6-23	6-30
1. Work Requests on hand beginning of week	522	513	444	444	522
2. Work Requests received during week	7	34	0	92	31
3. Projects issued during week	0	25	0	9	8
4. M.W.A.'s issued during week	13	51	0	5	13
5. Work Requests cancelled during week	2	26	0	0	4
6. Work Requests issued as contracts during week	1	1	0	0	2
7. Work Requests on hand end of week (items 1 & 2) - (3 & 4 & 5 & 6)	513	444	444	522	526

Project Scheduling Section

	6-2	6-9	6-16	6-23	6-30
1. Projects received during week	1	14	8	0	15
2. Projects completed during week	0	4	3	7	5

Project Backlog Status
Estimated Manhours

	No. of Proj.	Plum	Carp	Masn	Paint	Elect	Grnds	Mach	Comm	Weld	Refrg	Lock	Uphol	Rugs	Pneu	Contrs
Awaiting Materials																
Awaiting Scheduling	66	1088	2084	541	6726	1869	1273	278								
Master Schedule	138	3459	2229	1640	15364	1197	3828	418								
(in Process)	36	300	976	297	3124	307	901	:26								
Total	240	4847	5289	2478	25214	3373	6002	822								
Manpower Availability/Week/Shop		160	480	100	380	160	160	160								
No. of Weeks Backlog by Shop		30.3	11.0	24.8	66.4	21.1	37.5	5.1								

Exhibit 33-9 Work Control Section—Job Status Report

```
MC2096h 07/27/77          WORK CONTROL SECTION — JOB STATUS REPORT          WEEK ENDING 07/23/77                              PAGE 510

                                                                                                                                    - 18 -

M5232E  PAINT LINES & DIRECTIONAL ARROWS    SHOP:PAINTER       R-16-3  OPEN:100474  CLOSE:                      START:            END:
        REG LABOR   307.5 HRS   $2,186.45    REG LABOR   307.5 HRS   $2,186.45   EST LAB HRS                                        360
        OT LABOR      0.0 HRS       $0.00    OT LABOR      0.0 HRS       $0.00   EST LABOR                                       $2,322
        TOT LABOR   307.5 HRS   $2,186.45    TOT LABOR   307.5 HRS   $2,186.45   EST MAT                                          $162
        MATERIALS               $232.74      MATERIALS               $232.74    EST TOTAL                                       $2,484
        MONTH-TO-DATE TOTAL   $2,419.19      JOB-TO-DATE TOTAL     $2,419.19

M5232F  PAINT LINES & DIRECTIONAL ARROWS    SHOP:ELECTRICAL    R-16-3  OPEN:100474  CLOSE:                      START:            END:
        REG LABOR    16.0 HRS    $102.18     REG LABOR    16.0 HRS    $102.18    EST LAB HRS                                          0
        OT LABOR      0.0 HRS      $0.00     OT LABOR      0.0 HRS      $0.00    EST LABOR                                          $0
        TOT LABOR    16.0 HRS    $102.18     TOT LABOR    16.0 HRS    $102.18    EST MAT                                            $0
        MATERIALS                 $7.49      MATERIALS                 $7.49     EST TOTAL                                          $0
        MONTH-TO-DATE TOTAL     $109.67      JOB-TO-DATE TOTAL       $109.67

M5232J  PAINT LINES & DIRECTIONAL ARROWS    SHOP:GROUNDS       R-16-3  OPEN:100474  CLOSE:                      START:            END:
        REG LABOR     8.0 HRS     $37.02     REG LABOR     8.0 HRS     $37.02    EST LAB HRS                                        120
        OT LABOR      0.0 HRS      $0.00     OT LABOR      0.0 HRS      $0.00    EST LABOR                                         $612
        TOT LABOR     8.0 HRS     $37.02     TOT LABOR     8.0 HRS     $37.02    EST MAT                                            $7
        MATERIALS                 $0.00      MATERIALS                 $0.00     EST TOTAL                                         $619
        MONTH-TO-DATE TOTAL      $37.02      JOB-TO-DATE TOTAL        $37.02

M5232   PAINT LINES & DIRECTIONAL ARROWS    SHOP:MACHINE SHOP  R-16-3  OPEN:100474  CLOSE:                      START:            END:
        REG LABOR     0.0 HRS      $0.00     REG LABOR     0.0 HRS      $0.00    EST LAB HRS                                          0
        OT LABOR      0.0 HRS      $0.00     OT LABOR      0.0 HRS      $0.00    EST LABOR                                          $0
        TOT LABOR     0.0 HRS      $0.00     TOT LABOR     0.0 HRS      $0.00    EST MAT                                            $0
        MATERIALS                 $0.00      MATERIALS                 $0.00     EST TOTAL                                          $0
        MONTH-TO-DATE TOTAL       $0.00      YEAR-TO-DATE TOTAL        $0.00

M5232   PAINT LINES & DIRECTIONAL ARROWS    PROJECT TOTALS     R-16-3                                           START:            END:
        REG LABOR   335.5 HRS   $2,354.23    REG LABOR   367.5 HRS   $2,571.79   EST LAB HRS                                        524
        OT LABOR      0.0 HRS      $0.00     OT LABOR      0.0 HRS      $0.00     EST LABOR                                      $3,241
        TOT LABOR   335.5 HRS   $2,354.23    TOT LABOR   367.5 HRS   $2,571.79   EST MAT                                          $260
        MATERIALS               $242.57      MATERIALS               $339.67     EST TOTAL                                      $3,501
        MONTH-TO-DATE TOTAL   $2,596.80      JOB-TO-DATE TOTAL     $2,911.46

M5244B  INSTALL NEW CEILING FLOOR TILE LAB  SHOP:PLUMBER       T-35-3  OPEN:012475  CLOSE:                      START:            END:
        REG LABOR     0.0 HRS      $0.00     REG LABOR     0.0 HRS     $53.40    EST LAB HRS                                          0
        OT LABOR      0.0 HRS      $0.00     OT LABOR      0.0 HRS      $0.00    EST LABOR                                          $0
        TOT LABOR     0.0 HRS      $0.00     TOT LABOR     0.0 HRS     $53.40    EST MAT                                            $0
        MATERIALS                 $0.00      MATERIALS                 $7.38     EST TOTAL                                          $0
        MONTH-TO-DATE TOTAL       $0.00      JOB-TO-DATE TOTAL        $60.78

M5244C  INSTALL NEW CEILING FLOOR TILE LAB  SHOP:CARPENTER     T-35-3  OPEN:012475  CLOSE:  402.5 HRS          START:            END:
        REG LABOR     0.0 HRS      $0.00     REG LABOR   402.5 HRS   $2,639.88   EST LAB HRS                                        468
        OT LABOR      0.0 HRS      $0.00     OT LABOR      0.0 HRS      $0.00     EST LABOR                                      $2,966
        TOT LABOR     0.0 HRS      $0.00     TOT LABOR   402.5 HRS   $2,639.88   EST MAT                                        $1,985
        MATERIALS                 $0.00      MATERIALS               $849.46     EST TOTAL                                      $4,951
        MONTH-TO-DATE TOTAL       $0.00      JOB-TO-DATE TOTAL     $3,489.34

M5244D  INSTALL NEW CEILING FLOOR TILE LAB  SHOP:MASON         T-35-3  OPEN:012475  CLOSE:                      START:            END:
        REG LABOR     0.0 HRS      $0.00     REG LABOR     0.0 HRS      $0.00    EST LAB HRS                                          0
        OT LABOR      0.0 HRS      $0.00     OT LABOR      0.0 HRS      $0.00    EST LABOR                                          $0
        TOT LABOR     0.0 HRS      $0.00     TOT LABOR     0.0 HRS      $0.00    EST MAT                                            $0
        MATERIALS                 $0.00      MATERIALS                 $0.00     EST TOTAL                                          $0
        MONTH-TO-DATE TOTAL       $0.00      JOB-TO-DATE TOTAL         $0.00
```

Exhibit 33-10 Monthly Job Report—By Account

ACCOUNT 8-02-6 -- GORMAN-PROJECT I   MAJOR PROJ. - ENV. (IN FORCE)

```
510046  PAINT VARIOUS AREAS  GORMAN HOUSE      SHOP:PAINTER       8-02-6  OPEN:020377  CLOSE:          START:                        END:
        REG LABOR    0.0 HRS    $0.00 REG LABOR    0.0 HRS    $0.00 REG LABOR    0.0 HRS    $0.00          EST LAB HRS         1,110
        OT LABOR     0.0 HRS    $0.00 OT LABOR     0.0 HRS    $0.00 OT LABOR     0.0 HRS    $0.00          EST LABOR          $7,604
        TOT LABOR    0.0 HRS    $0.00 TOT LABOR    0.0 HRS    $0.00 TOT LABOR    0.0 HRS    $0.00          EST MAT             $967
        MATERIALS            $0.00 MATERIALS            $0.00 MATERIALS            $0.00                    EST TOTAL         $8,571
        MONTH-TO-DATE TOTAL  $0.00 YEAR-TO-DATE TOTAL  $0.00 JOB-TO-DATE TOTAL   $0.00

U2111C  INSTALL MISCO GLASS                     SHOP:CARPENTER     8-02-6  OPEN:070677  CLOSE:          START:                        END:
        REG LABOR    8.0 HRS  $58.90 REG LABOR    8.0 HRS  $58.90 REG LABOR    8.0 HRS  $58.90          EST LAB HRS            8
        OT LABOR     0.0 HRS   $0.00 OT LABOR     0.0 HRS   $0.00 OT LABOR     0.0 HRS   $0.00          EST LABOR             $54
        TOT LABOR    8.0 HRS  $58.90 TOT LABOR    8.0 HRS  $58.90 TOT LABOR    8.0 HRS  $58.90          EST MAT               $15
        MATERIALS           $14.00 MATERIALS           $14.00 MATERIALS           $14.00                EST TOTAL             $69
        MONTH-TO-DATE TOTAL $72.90 YEAR-TO-DATE TOTAL $72.90 JOB-TO-DATE TOTAL  $72.90

MATERIALS USED THIS MONTH ON JOB U2111C  ITEM NO ITEM DESCRIPTION                        UNIT  UNIT COST  USED  COST
                                         EF44915  LUMBER BIRCH KILN DRY 1 IN              BDFT   0.875     16    $14.00
                                                                                              TOTAL             $14.00

U2111E  INSTALL MISCO GLASS                      SHOP:PAINTER       8-02-6  OPEN:070677  CLOSE:          START:                        END:
        REG LABOR   26.0 HRS $194.21 REG LABOR   26.0 HRS $194.21 REG LABOR   26.0 HRS $194.21          EST LAB HRS           95
        OT LABOR     0.0 HRS   $0.00 OT LABOR     0.0 HRS   $0.00 OT LABOR     0.0 HRS   $0.00          EST LABOR            $651
        TOT LABOR   26.0 HRS $194.21 TOT LABOR   26.0 HRS $194.21 TOT LABOR   26.0 HRS $194.21          EST MAT               $55
        MATERIALS           $14.39 MATERIALS           $14.39 MATERIALS           $0.39                EST TOTAL            $716
        MONTH-TO-DATE TOTAL $194.60 YEAR-TO-DATE TOTAL $194.60 JOB-TO-DATE TOTAL $194.60

MATERIALS USED THIS MONTH ON JOB U2111E  ITEM NO ITEM DESCRIPTION                        UNIT  UNIT COST  USED  COST
                                         EF11570  BRAD BRIGHT STEEL WIRE 3/4IN X 17 GUAGE  PKG   0.309      1    $0.39
                                                                                              TOTAL             $0.39

U2111I  INSTALL MISCO GLASS                      PROJECT TOTALS     8-02-6
        REG LABOR   34.0 HRS $253.11 REG LABOR   34.0 HRS $253.11 REG LABOR   34.0 HRS $253.11          EST LAB HRS          103
        OT LABOR     0.0 HRS   $0.00 OT LABOR     0.0 HRS   $0.00 OT LABOR     0.0 HRS   $0.00          EST LABOR            $705
        TOT LABOR   34.0 HRS $253.11 TOT LABOR   34.0 HRS $253.11 TOT LABOR   34.0 HRS $253.11          EST MAT               $80
        MATERIALS           $14.39 MATERIALS           $14.39 MATERIALS           $14.39                EST TOTAL            $785
        MONTH-TO-DATE TOTAL $267.50 YEAR-TO-DATE TOTAL $267.50 JOB-TO-DATE TOTAL $267.50

TOTALS FOR ACCOUNT 8-02-6 -- GORMAN-PROJECT I                      MAJOR PROJ. - ENV. (IN FORCE)
        REG LABOR   34.0 HRS $253.11 REG LABOR   34.0 HRS $253.11 REG LABOR   34.0 HRS $253.11
        OT LABOR     0.0 HRS   $0.00 OT LABOR     0.0 HRS   $0.00 OT LABOR     0.0 HRS   $0.00
        TOT LABOR   34.0 HRS $253.11 TOT LABOR   34.0 HRS $253.11 TOT LABOR   34.0 HRS $253.11
        MATERIALS           $14.39 MATERIALS           $14.39 MATERIALS            $8.40
        MONTH-TO-DATE TOTAL $267.50 YEAR-TO-DATE TOTAL $267.50 JOB-TO-DATE TOTAL $1,094.71

JOBS COMPLETED THIS MONTH      YTD LABOR    YTD MATERIALS     $0.00 YTD MATERIALS     $0.00 YTD TOTAL    $0.00 ESTIMATED TOTAL
JOBS COMPLETED THIS FISCAL YEAR  YTD LABOR                   $0.00 YTD MATERIALS     $0.00 YTD TOTAL    $0.00
```

Exhibit 33–11 Status of Job Cost Accounts

		LABOR				MATERIALS		
	BUDGET	MOS. EXPEND	YRS. EXPEND	BALANCE	BUDGET	MOS. EXPEND	YRS. EXPEND	BALANCE
BAKER STATE								
A01A MAJ PROJ ENVIRONMENTAL CONT	2,757	0.00	0.00	0.00	0	0.00	0.00	0.00
A01B DAMAGES	31,929	96.02	1,774.65	982.35	178	9.06	54.42	123.58
A010 CUSTODIAL MAINTENANCE	22,938	2,179.60	30,124.83	1,804.17	2,816	173.92	2,038.63	777.37
A011 ROUTINE MAINTENANCE	0	1,102.22	12,573.56	9,964.44	3,441	88.01	2,946.68	492.32
A012 CONTRACT MAINTENANCE (OUTSIDE)	0	0.00	0.00	0.00	0	0.00	0.00	0.00
A013 MAJOR PROJ. MAINT. (IN FORCE)	0	0.00	1,782.99	1,782.99-	0	0.00	375.04	375.04-
A014 MAJOR BLDG. RENOV. (IN FORCE)	0	0.00	0.00	0.00	0	0.00	0.00	0.00
A015 MAJOR BLDG. RENOV. (CONTRACT)	0	0.00	0.00	0.00	0	0.00	0.00	0.00
A016 MAJOR PROJ. - ENV. (IN FORCE)	0	0.00	182.87	182.87-	35	164.80	178.06	178.06-
A017 MINOR WORK - ENV. (IN FORCE)	321	0.00	47.69	273.31	0	0.00	9.60	25.40
T O T A L	57,945	3,377.84	46,886.59	11,058.41	6,470	435.79	5,604.43	865.57
BROOKS STATE								
A02A MAJ PROJ ENVIRONMENTAL CONT	0	0.00	0.00	0.00	0	0.00	0.00	0.00
A02H DAMAGES	904	0.00	719.15	184.85	134	6.90	6.90	127.10
A020 CUSTODIAL MAINTENANCE	11,118	802.33	9,205.22	1,912.78	980	59.79	1,069.51	89.51-
A021 ROUTINE MAINTENANCE	10,982	424.06	8,748.86	2,233.14	1,249	152.69	1,296.48	47.48-
A022 CONTRACT MAINTENANCE (OUTSIDE)	0	0.00	0.00	0.00	466	0.00	300.08	155.92
A023 MAJOR PROJ. MAINT. (IN FORCE)	8,000	0.00	1,859.07	6,141.93	0	0.00	0.00	0.00
A024 MAJOR BLDG. RENOV. (IN FORCE)	0	0.00	0.00	0.00	0	0.00	0.00	0.00
A025 MAJOR BLDG. RENOV. (CONTRACT)	0	0.00	0.00	0.00	0	0.00	0.00	0.00
A026 MAJOR PROJ. - ENV. (IN FORCE)	1,457	0.00	1,614.64	157.64-	735	0.00	103.69	631.31
A027 MINOR WORK - ENV. (IN FORCE)	321	0.00	321.00	321.00	35	0.00	0.00	35.00
T O T A L	32,782	1,226.39	22,145.94	10,636.06	3,597	212.48	2,784.66	812.34
BUTTERFIELD STATE								
A03A MAJ PROJ ENVIRONMENTAL CONT	0	0.00	0.00	0.00	0	0.00	0.00	0.00
A03R DAMAGES	581	114.83	618.55	37.55-	143	0.00	31.06	111.94
A030 CUSTODIAL MAINTENANCE	10,243	1,004.61	11,997.90	1,754.90-	963	35.83	1,195.99	232.99-
A031 ROUTINE MAINTENANCE	14,695	304.12	14,229.26	465.74	1,652	0.00	586.30	1,065.70
A032 CONTRACT MAINTENANCE (OUTSIDE)	0	0.00	0.00	0.00	0	0.00	0.00	0.00
A033 MAJOR PROJ. MAINT. (IN FORCE)	6,485	0.00	5,270.81	1,275.59	93	0.00	1,509.48	1,602.48-
A034 MAJOR BLDG. RENOV. (IN FORCE)	117,000	0.00	116,358.16	641.84	29,000	0.00	41,300.81	12,300.81-
A035 MAJOR BLDG. RENOV. (CONTRACT)	0	0.00	0.00	0.00	0	0.00	0.00	0.00
A036 MAJOR PROJ. - ENV. (IN FORCE)	974	0.00	1,390.24	416.24-	443	0.00	670.26	272.74
A037 MINOR WORK - ENV. (IN FORCE)	321	0.00	198.14	122.86	35	0.00	18.32	16.68
T O T A L	150,299	1,423.56	150,002.06	296.94	32,829	35.83	42,293.26	9,464.24-
CHADBOURNE STATE								
A04A MAJ PROJ ENVIRONMENTAL CONT	0	0.00	0.00	0.00	0	0.00	0.00	0.00
A04H DAMAGES	854	22.41	667.69	186.31	217	77.48	22.35	194.65
A040 CUSTODIAL MAINTENANCE	12,773	937.94	12,232.69	540.31	1,154	56.12	1,047.54	106.46
A041 ROUTINE MAINTENANCE	7,116	170.11	5,751.00	1,365.00	1,692	0.00	807.02	884.98
A042 CONTRACT MAINTENANCE (OUTSIDE)	0	0.00	0.00	0.00	0	0.00	0.00	0.00
A043 MAJOR PROJ. MAINT. (IN FORCE)	0	0.00	0.00	0.00	0	0.00	0.00	0.00
A044 MAJOR BLDG. RENOV. (IN FORCE)	0	0.00	0.00	0.00	0	0.00	0.00	0.00
A045 MAJOR BLDG. RENOV. (CONTRACT)	0	0.00	0.00	0.00	0	0.00	0.00	0.00
A046 MAJOR PROJ. - ENV. (IN FORCE)	418	0.00	475.69	57.69-	90	0.00	116.23	26.23-
A047 MINOR WORK - ENV. (IN FORCE)	321	0.00	321.00	321.00	35	0.00	0.00	35.00
T O T A L	21,482	1,130.46	19,127.07	2,354.93	3,188	133.60	1,993.14	1,194.86
CRABTREE STATE								
A05A MAJ PROJ ENVIRONMENTAL CONT	0	0.00	0.00	0.00	0	0.00	0.00	0.00
A05H DAMAGES	956	43.44	595.04	360.96	188	0.00	21.09	166.91
A050 CUSTODIAL MAINTENANCE	11,158	939.52	9,566.96	1,591.04	1,022	108.47	1,237.02	215.02-

Store (CS) carrying an average of 14,000 items in stock at the cost of around $500,000. In fiscal year 1976–1977, CS handled some 150,000 transactions. (A transaction is any movement of stocks in or out of the CS.) During the same period, 1.3 million dollars worth of materials were issued and a slightly less amount was received at the CS.

The job of maintaining and controlling inventory was the responsibility of Gilbert Kelley and his assistant, Matt Cole, aided by a staff of 15 (see Exhibit 33–2 for details). Inventories at the CS were classified into ten major categories, each assigned to a specific location and personnel. Each stock item was identified by a two-digit alphabetic code followed by a five-digit numeric code. The detailed alphabetic classifications are shown in Exhibit 33–12. The codes carry no special meaning other than identifying a particular stock item.

The CS had established a standard routine for issuing and receiving stocks. When a work order called for materials or supplies for a certain job, the assigned worker filled out a Stock Transaction Slip (Exhibit 33–13), had it approved by his foreman or supervisor, and presented it to the store room clerk for the item. If the item was in stock, the clerk issued it and, at the same time, withdrew a stock card which was placed in front of the bin with the item's identification code prepunched on it. After issuing the stock, the clerk had to write the job number, the quantity issued, and his initial on the card, which was keypunched and later forwarded to the computer center for batch processing.

If the item was not in stock or the stock level was sufficiently low to necessitate reordering, the clerk was required to follow a prescribed reordering procedure to replenish the stock. While the mechanics as to how to order materials had been routinized, the decision concerning what, when, and how much to order remained a matter of the store keeper's discretion and judgment, guided only by some informal rules of thumb. Mr. Kelley explained that this was so for a number of reasons. One was that except for routine housekeeping supplies, the demand for repair and maintenance materials was highly irregular and unpredictable. Another problem affecting order quantity was that the lead time for purchases varied widely between different types of orders, sources of funding, and amounts of purchase.

As the University was a state supported institution, the law required that all purchases costing $250 or more be subject to competitive bidding. This was known as the Commission Order and was an expensive process that would take from one to two months. If the cost of purchase was less than $250, a direct order was permitted. This took anywhere between three to six weeks. By far the simplest way of ordering was through the use of contracted suppliers. If an item had a high turnover and had to be reordered frequently, it was more convenient and economical to sign contract with a supplier who provided reliable and on time delivery. The

Exhibit 33—12 Physical Plant. Code Letters for Stores

A—Electrical

AB   Electric
AC   Communications & Electronics
AD   Refrigeration
AE   Air Conditioning
AF   Elevator
AG   Electric Controls
AH   Utilities
AJ   Electric Motor Repair

C—Plumbing

CB   Plumbing
CD   Heating
CE   Pneumatic Controls
CF   Machine Shop
CG   Welding
CH   Circulator & Pump Repairs
CK   Underground Facilities

E—Carpentry

EF   Carpenter
EG   Mason
EH   Locksmith
EJ   Roofing
EK   Door Closer
EL   Window Shades & Venetian Blinds

G—Paint

GB   Paint
GC   Glass

GD   Sign Making
GE   Sand Blasting

J—Custodial

JA   Custodial
JB   Rug Cleaning & Repair
JC   Vacuum Cleaning Repair

L—Automotive

LA   Automotive
LB   Grounds
LD   Construction Material
LF   Gas-Oil
LH   Tires & Tubes

N—Office Supplies

NA   Office Supply
NB   Typewriter

P—Chemical Stock

PA   Chemical Stock

R—Upholstry

RB   Upholstery

T—Handtools & Salvage

TB   Handtools

choice of a contracted supplier required the usual process of competitive bidding first. The contract once concluded generally guaranteed a minimum amount of purchases a year. As long as the annual purchases stayed within the committed sum, no dollar limit was set for each individual purchase. The lead time for this type of order ranged between immediate delivery to a couple of weeks.

Another factor that affected order quantity was related to the nature of the job itself. If the material was used frequently for routine maintenance,

Exhibit 33—13 Physical Plant Stock Transaction Slip

Stock Transaction Slip

CENTRAL STORES
PHYSICAL PLANT DEPARTMENT

Work Order No. _____ Transaction Date _____

Building _____ ☐ Stock Issued ☐ Stock Returned

Type Work Order: ☐ RMO ☐ Project ☐ Other

Quantity	Unit Measure	Item(s)	Stock Number

_____   _____
Signature of Requestor   Representing Shop/Sect./Dept.
Issued By: _____   Comments: _____

the storekeeper usually referred to the Stock Status Report (Exhibit 33–14) for the past history. The report provided only a rough guide, as evidenced in the sample output that the use rate could fluctuate widely from year to year. Included in the report also were those items which were stocked for some special orders. These items usually were ordered for some particular repair or project jobs that were unlikely to be repeated

Exhibit 33-14 Stock Status Report All Items Week Ending 04/01/77

S T O C K   S T A T U S   R E P O R T
STOCK STATUS ALL ITEMS
WEEK ENDING 04/01/77

ITEM NO	ITEM DESCRIPTION	UNIT	UNIT COST	ON HAND (qty)	ON HAND ($)	QTY ON ORDER	MTD RECEIVED (qty)	MTD RECEIVED ($)	MTD ISSUED (qty)	MTD ISSUED ($)	YTD RECEIVED (qty)	YTD RECEIVED ($)	YTD ISSUED (qty)	YTD ISSUED ($)	ISSUED PREV YR
A896880	WIRE PLASTIC STRANDED 18-5	FEET	$.046	1270	$58.42	0	0	$.00	0	$.00	0	$.00	625	$28.75	355
A896960	WIRE THW-2 STRANDED	FEET	$.648	0	$.00	0	0	$.00	0	$.00	150	$95.26	150	$95.26	1000
A897040	WIRE THW-3 STRANDED	EACH	$.344	1247	$428.97	0	0	$.00	0	$.00	0	$.00	335	$115.24	545
A897120	WIRE THWN-2 STRANDED	FEET	$.498	0	$.00	0	0	$.00	0	$.00	0	$.00	90	$44.82	40
A897200	WIRE THWN 4 STRANDED	FEET	$.195	0	$.00	0	0	$.00	0	$.00	0	$.00	0	$.00	0
A897220	WIRE THWN-6 STRANDED	FEET	$.141	799	$112.66	500	0	$.00	80	$11.28	1500	$211.18	1365	$204.51	1831
A897280	WIRE THWN-8 STRANDED	FEET	$.093	0	$.00	0	0	$.00	0	$.00	0	$.00	1750	$162.75	1430
A897360	WIRE THWN-10 STRANDED	FEET	$.047	3490	$164.03	2000	0	$.00	480	$22.56	4000	$168.92	3942	$213.18	14853
A897440	WIRE THWN 12 STRANDED	FEET	$.030	22545	$676.35	0	0	$.00	565	$16.95	34500	$1101.25	41058	$1377.76	93771
A897520	WIRE TW-1 STRANDED	FEET	$.664	240	$159.36	0	0	$.00	0	$.00	5500	$1724.38	5500	$1732.00	0
A897600	WIRE TW-2 STRANDFD	FEET	$.250	0	$.00	0	0	$.00	0	$.00	0	$.00	50	$12.50	770
A897680	WIRE TW-4 STRANDED	FT	$.264	1841	$486.02	0	0	$.00	0	$.00	0	$.00	1624	$428.74	225
A897760	WIRE TW-6 STRANDED	FT	$.174	143	$24.88	400	0	$.00	0	$.00	0	$.00	665	$115.71	207
A897840	WIRE TW-8 STRANDFD	FT	$.064	1497	$95.81	0	0	$.00	480	$30.72	0	$.00	533	$34.11	0
A897920	WIRE TW-10 STRANDED	FT	$.062	7398	$458.68	0	0	$.00	0	$.00	0	$.00	723	$44.83	2071
A898000	WIRE TW-12 SOLID	FT	$.033	35542	$1172.89	0	0	$.00	0	$.00	0	$.00	8673	$286.22	12828
A898080	WIRE TW-14 SOLID	FT	$.018	24455	$440.19	0	0	$.00	525	$9.45	6000	$118.52	7760	$139.68	22395
A898160	WIRE UF 10-3	FEET	$.258	695	$179.31	0	0	$.00	0	$.00	0	$.00	0	$.00	10
A898240	WIRE UF 12-2	FT	$.137	0	$.00	0	0	$.00	0	$.00	45	$5.36	160	$21.93	280
A898320	WIRE UF 14-2	FEET	$.054	0	$.00	0	0	$.00	0	$.00	0	$.00	0	$.00	0
A898400	WIREWAY RACEWAY 6X6X36 IN	EACH	$77.000	0	$.00	0	0	$.00	0	$.00	0	$.00	0	$.00	6

Exhibit 33—15 Supply Order Request

Supply Order Request

Type (Check which)   Classification (Specify)   Recommended Vendor
                                                                        and Complete Address
Commission Order   Stock:
D Order   Building Charge (include work order no.)
Contract Item   Equipment List (include Proj. Name no.
Monthly Number   and Contract no.)
Other (Specify)   Other:

If Confirming Order, List Order Number:

Quant.	Unit Meas.	Stock Number	Item Description (If for Building Equipment List include item number)	Estimated Cost

Request Submitted by _____ Approved by _____
                                                               Department Head
Date: _____
                                                               _____
                                                               Supt. of Physical Plant

---

again. The demand for such items accounted to about 20 to 25 percent of the work orders and was totally unpredictable.

Having decided on what, when, how much and from whom to order, the storekeeper proceeded with the ordering process. The first step he took was to fill out a Supply Order Request (Exhibit 33–15) and to have it approved by the CS head before forwarding it to the Comptroller for approval. After the request was approved, a purchase requisition form was

Exhibit 33—16 Fiscal Year 1978 Physical Plant Budgets

		State	General Service Trust Fund	Facilities Planning & Operation Personnel Trust Fund	Total
01	Payroll Positions	6,364,200		2,289,400	8,653,600
02	Overtime & Other	120,000			120,000
03	Services & Students	79,800			79,800
05	Clothing	2,000			2,000
06	Housekeeping	75,000	93,600		168,600
09	Farm & Grounds	24,000			24,000
10	Travel & Auto	105,000	65,000		170,000
11	Adv. & Printing	5,000			5,000
12	Maint.—Repairs	872,000	307,800		1,179,800
13	Special Supplies & Insurance Overhead	15,000	95,000	2,500	112,500
14	Adm. & Telephone	23,000			23,000
15	Equipment	50,000			50,000
16	Rental	25,000			25,000
	Contingency			127,000*	127,000*
Sub-Total		7,760,000	561,400	2,418,900	10,740,300
08	Utilities	5,863,000	1,278,300		7,141,300**
Total		13,623,000	1,839,700	2,418,900	17,881,600

*Contingency funds towards FY '78 payroll cost of living increase.

**Coal	3,174,000
#6 Oil	468,000
Electricity	2,667,700
Water/Sewer	591,600
All Other	240,000
Total	7,141,300

then prepared. This form became the official purchase order. However, before the form could be sent to the vendor, funds had to be appropriated for the purchase. This was done by sending three copies of this form to the University Accounting Office, which in turn would allocate the amount from the account if sufficient amount has been budgeted for it. A sample annual budget for various accounts under several funding sources is shown in Exhibit 33–16. After the funds were provided for the purchase, the form was then forwarded to the vendor via the University Procurement Office.

Any time the status of a stock item was affected by a transaction, a Transaction For Stock Status form (Exhibit 33–17) had to be filled out. The form was used for preparing the weekly Transaction Report (Exhibit 33–18) and the Stock Status Report mentioned earlier. These reports provided information about the activities and status of each stock item and helped storekeepers monitor and control inventory and make reordering

Exhibit 33—17 Physical Plant. Transactions for Stock Status

VENDOR: _____

ACCOUNT: _____

PURCHASE

ORDER NO. _____

(28-33)

Check the type of transaction:

_____ AA — Adjustment up

_____ AM — Miscellaneous receipt

_____ AR — Receipt

_____ AT — Return to stock

_____ SI — Issue

_____ OR — Order

_____ OX — Cancel order

_____ SA — Adjustment down

_____ SV — Return to vendor

JOB NO. _____

(23-27)

DATE: _____

(17-22)

Item no. (3-9)	Quantity (11-16)	Amount (34-40)

Exhibit 33–18 Transaction Report Week Ending 11/21/76

T R A N S A C T I O N   R E P O R T

W E E K   E N D I N G   11/21/76

ITEM NO	ITEM DESCRIPTION	CODE	QUANTITY	UNIT	UNIT COST	TOTAL COST	JOB #	ORDER #	
JC03701	AGITATOR LESS BRUSH 46854 HOOVER VAC 913	AR	1	EACH	$11.876	$7.90		017899	
JC03701	AGITATOR LESS BRUSH 46854 HOOVER VAC 913	SI	1	EACH	$11.876	$11.88	A1417		
JC16123	BEARING ASSEMBLY UPPER MOT OR 32676 HOOVER VAC 913	AR	1	EACH	$2.070	$10.75		017899	
JC16123	BEARING ASSEMBLY UPPER MOT OR 32676 HOOVER VAC 913	SI	1	EACH	$2.070	$2.07	A1417		
JC26638	BLADE REPLACEMENT SQUEEZE 24 IN WET VAC	AR	3	EACH	$6.270	$18.00		017899	
JC26638	BLADE REPLACEMENT SQUEEZE 24 IN WET VAC	SI	3	EACH	$6.270	$18.81	A2600		
JC28040	BRUSH AGITATOR LONG 47159 HOOVER VAC 913	AR	6	EACH	$.949	$3.66		017899	
JC28040	BRUSH AGITATOR LONG 47159 HOOVER VAC 913	SI	6	EACH	$.949	$5.69	A1417		
JC28741	BRUSH AGITATOR SHORT 47160 HOOVER VAC 913	AR	6	EACH,	$.938	$3.66		017899	
JC28741	BRUSH AGITATOR SHORT 47161 HOOVER VAC 913	SI	6	EACH	$.938	$5.63	A1417		
JC54679 JC62266	HANDLE ADAPTOR ASSEMBLY GR 828532 HYGIENE VAC 880	SI	1	EACH	$3.855	$3.86	T3251		ITEM NUMBER INVALID
JC61688	HOSE ELECTROLUX VAC 41686	AR	1	EACH	$15.000	$15.00		017899	
JC61688	HOSE ELECTROLUX VAC 41686	CR	1	EACH	$15.000	$15.00		017899	
JC61688	HOSE ELECTROLUX VAC 41686	SI	1	EACH	$15.000	$15.00	A3196		
JC62389	HOSE WET/DRY VAC KENT 101	AR	2	EACH	$8.500	$17.00		017899	
JC96429	SWITCH MOVING 4662 ELECTRO LUX VAC MOST MODELS	SI	1	EACH	$3.750	$3.75	T2452		

Exhibit 33—19 Physical Plant. Inventory Book

TB—Hand Tools

1975	Orders	On Hand	Issues	Receipts
January	39	681	214	57
February	73	524	184	75
March	44	415	138	44
April	181	321	79	165
May	64	407	87	64
June	124	384	124	140
July	100	400	100	100
August	80	400	60	40
September	55	380	75	95
October	40	400	67	40
November	85	373	62	75
December	120	386	83	70
Totals	1005	373	1273	965

decisions. In addition to these reports, Mr. Kelley also kept a hand posted inventory book summarizing the movement and status of stock each month. A sample summary of the inventory book is shown in Exhibit 33–19.

Mr. Kelley was satisfied with the stock control system at CS, but felt that the current inventory was a little too low due to the cutback in budget allocation. Although he did not have recorded statistics about the frequency of stockouts, he was not surprised if it had occurred more than 10% of the time. He added, however, because of the nature of his operations, a stockout would ordinarily mean a slight delay of work schedule, perhaps with some complaints from the requesting parties, but would not involve the loss of customers like in ordinary businesses.

Index